CW01064715

A History of Infanticide in Britain *c.* 1600 to the Present

*Also by Anne-Marie Kilday (*published by Palgrave Macmillan)*
WOMEN AND CRIME IN ENLIGHTENMENT SCOTLAND

HISTORIES OF CRIME: Britain 1600–2000 (*co-edited with David Nash*)*

CULTURES OF SHAME: Exploring Crime and Morality in Britain 1700–1900 (*with David Nash*)*

A History of Infanticide in Britain c. 1600 to the Present

Anne-Marie Kilday
Professor of Criminal History and Pro Vice-Chancellor & Dean,
Oxford Brookes University

First published 2013 by
PALGRAVE MACMILLAN

Palgrave Macmillan in the UK is an imprint of Macmillan Publishers Limited, registered in England, company number 785998, of Houndmills, Basingstoke, Hampshire RG21 6XS.

Palgrave Macmillan in the US is a division of St Martin's Press LLC, 175 Fifth Avenue, New York, NY 10010.

Palgrave Macmillan is the global academic imprint of the above companies and has companies and representatives throughout the world.

Palgrave® and Macmillan® are registered trademarks in the United States, the United Kingdom, Europe and other countries.

ISBN 978–0–230–54707–0

This book is printed on paper suitable for recycling and made from fully managed and sustained forest sources. Logging, pulping and manufacturing processes are expected to conform to the environmental regulations of the country of origin.

A catalogue record for this book is available from the British Library.

A catalog record for this book is available from the Library of Congress.

Typeset by MPS Limited, Chennai, India.

To my brother, John-Paul, the baby doctor!

Contents

List of Figures   viii

Acknowledgements   x

1 Investigating Infanticide – An Enduring Phenomenon   1

2 The Archetype of Infanticide in the Early Modern Period   23

3 Murderous Mothers and the Extended Network of Shame   51

4 Monsters of Inhumanity? Methods of Infant Disposal   77

5 The Pendulum of Opinion: Changing Attitudes to Infanticide   111

6 Explaining Infanticide: Motives for Murder?   151

7 The Modern Debate: Getting Away With Murder?   183

Notes   218

Bibliography   299

Index   329

List of Figures

1.1 Examples of early pamphlet literature regarding infanticide   20

2.1 Gender and infanticide indictments: Britain, 1700–1799   26

2.2 Trends in infanticide prosecutions: London, 1700–1799   28

2.3 Trends in infanticide prosecutions: Wales, 1730–1799   29

2.4 Trends in infanticide prosecutions: Scotland, 1700–1799   30

2.5 Relationship between indictments and convictions for infanticide in Scotland, 1700–1799   46

2.6 Sentencing practices for infanticide in Britain, 1700–1799   47

2.7 Trends in capital punishment sentences for infanticide in Britain, 1701–1799   48

2.8 Trends in sentencing practices for infanticide in Scotland, 1700–1799   49

3.1 Frontispiece illustration from *The Bloudy Mother, or The Most Inhumane Murthers, Commited by Iane Hattersley* (1610)   67

4.1 Methods in known cases of infanticide in Britain, 1700–1830   97

5.1 Trends in infanticide and concealment of pregnancy in England and Wales, 1805–1899   122

5.2 Trends in infanticide and concealment of pregnancy in Scotland, 1800–1899   123

5.3 Trends in sentencing practices for concealment of pregnancy in England and Wales, 1805–1899   132

5.4 Trends in sentencing practices for concealment of pregnancy in Scotland, 1830–1899   133

5.5 Sentencing practices for concealment in England and Wales and Scotland, 1800–1899   134

5.6 Gender differences in indictments for infanticide and concealment of pregnancy in Britain, 1800–1899   135

6.1 Minnie Wells appearing at the Old Bailey   177

7.1 Trends in concealment in England and Wales, 1900–1999   196

7.2 Trends in concealment in Scotland, 1900–1979   197

7.3 Trends in infanticide in England and Wales, 1900–1999   197

7.4 Gender differences in indictments for infanticide and
     concealment of pregnancy in Britain, 1900–1999   201

7.5 Trends in punishment for infanticide in England and Wales,
     1920–1999   208

7.6 Trends in punishment for concealment of pregnancy in
     England and Wales, 1900–1999   209

7.7 Trends in punishment for concealment of pregnancy in
     Scotland, 1900–1999   209

Acknowledgements

Numerous people have helped in the writing of this book. Firstly, I would like to express my thanks to staff at the Bodleian Library, the British Library, Hereford Record Office, the National Archives, the National Archives of Scotland, the National Library of Scotland, the National Library of Wales, Powys County Archive and the University of Glasgow Library for their patience and helpful advice. Secondly I would like to acknowledge the help and support of colleagues at Oxford Brookes University, especially Katherine Watson and, in particular, David Nash. Their comments, criticism and unflagging support were essential in the completion of this work. I would also like to acknowledge the help of the following individuals: Adrian Ager, Joanne Bailey, Janet Beer, Katherine Bradley, Hannah Chandler, Alistair Fitt, Daniel Grey, Rhian James, Alysa Levene, Melanie Reynolds, Laura Taylor, Daniel Vicars and Clifford Williamson. Without their patience, encouragement and detailed advice, this book would simply not have been possible.

I would also like to thank Palgrave Macmillan and those directly involved in the production of this book. Thanks go to my commissioning editors Michael Strang and Jenny McCall and to my editorial contact Holly Tyler. I would also like to thank two anonymous reviewers for their insightful, positive and important contributions.

Finally, as ever, I would like to thank my parents and my brother John-Paul for all their love and constant support.

1
Investigating Infanticide – An Enduring Phenomenon

To die by other hands more merciless than mine.
No; I who gave them life will give them death.
Oh, now no cowardice, no thought how young they are,
How dear they are, how when they first were born –
Not that – I will forget they are my sons.
One moment, one short moment – then forever sorrow.[1]

Infanticide is an intensely emotional and emotive subject – one that has been a central part of human experience from the outset. It leaves strong feelings in its wake, which has led to sorrow, anger and a desire (in modern times) for whole societies to hide this phenomenon from their population. Thus, both the taboo and the hidden nature of infanticide have made this subject area incredibly difficult for historians to approach. This work provides, for the first time, a detailed history of new-born child murder in mainland Britain from 1600 to the modern era. It examines continuity and change in the nature and characteristics of infanticide in Scotland, England and Wales over a chronology of more than four centuries. As well as offering a comparative analysis of the types of individuals suspected of the offence, and a detailed appreciation of the different ways in which the crime was carried out, the work also exposes the broad nexus of causal factors which underpinned its enactment. In addition, the work investigates the evolving attitude in social, medical and legal contexts to the killing of young infants in Britain, over a substantial time period. Thus, the work as a whole is both compelling and innovative, as it provides the reader with much more than a mere history of infanticide. The book also contributes much to our understanding of criminal history, gender history, legal history, medical history and social history in its analyses of the different contexts allied to the offence. It does this also through its exploration of the complex characteristics of accusers, commentators and perpetrators across cultures, borders and time.

This introductory chapter begins by making the case for a study of infanticide as a crime in its own right. It starts by looking at the enduring and persistent nature of the killing of new-borns throughout history, as well as the extent and significance of the offence across cultures and civilisations. The chapter then examines the existing historiography of infanticide to uncover the key areas of scholarship on the subject and to determine the lacunae that exist, especially in the context of the British experience of this phenomenon. The parameters of the book's analysis and its key research questions are then presented alongside an overview of sources used and a brief outline of the structure of the remaining chapters. Finally, the chapter ends by explaining how the murder of new-born children came to be criminalised in Britain over the course of the seventeenth century. This explanation creates the necessary initial contextual framework for the analysis which begins in Chapter 2.

Infanticide as an enduring phenomenon

Present day episodes of new-born child murder indicate that infanticide is an offence which still occurs with comparative frequency.[2] The enduring and persistent nature of infanticide is made more evident by Peter Hoffer and Natalie Hull's statement that the crime of infanticide (or the murder of a child by his or her own parent) '...is as old as human society'.[3] Certainly, infanticide can be traced back to prehistoric epochs and the very beginnings of recorded history, as archaeologists and anthropologists have offered strong evidence to suggest that Palaeolithic parents practised new-born child murder on a fairly regular basis.[4] Similar evidence of the commonplace nature of infanticide can be found in the ancient civilisations of Mesopotamia, Greece and Rome, as well as among early peoples such as the Vikings, Irish Celts, Gauls and Phoenicians.[5]

Infanticide is an international phenomenon which has been encountered in nearly every civilisation, culture and continent across the globe, so assumptions made about its exceptional nature are something of a comparatively modern invention.[6] As Laila Williamson points out:

> Infanticide is a practice present-day westerners regard as a cruel and inhuman custom, resorted to by only a few desperate and primitive people living in harsh environments. We tend to think of it as an exceptional practice, to be found only among such peoples... who are far removed in both culture and geographical distance from us and our civilized ancestors. The truth is quite different. Infanticide has been practiced on every continent and by people on every level of cultural complexity, from hunters and gatherers to high civilizations, including our own ancestors. Rather than being an exception, then, it has been the rule.[7]

Although the coming of Christianity brought a change in attitudes towards the killing of infants, the practice persisted nonetheless, because in many societies it was regarded as a conventional and accepted part of everyday life.[8] From ancient civilisations to modern ones, albeit to varying degrees, infanticide has been considered a permissible enterprise for some parents to engage in. Indeed, in some ancient cultures and jurisdictions (such as Roman law) children were regarded as a species of property which belonged to the patriarch of the family. Fathers thus had the right as head of the household (*patria potens*) to commit infanticide if they thought it was prudent to do so.[9]

As Michelle Oberman explains, '…infanticide was common among early people, particularly insofar as it enabled them to control population growth and to minimise the strain placed on society by sickly newborns.'[10] In the main, therefore, there have been two contexts for child murder throughout history: first, the killing of what were considered to be 'defective' offspring, and, second, the killing of 'normal' but unwanted children.[11] The exposure and/or infanticide of sickly or disabled infants was an accepted feature of ancient Greco-Roman cultures, as is evident from various contemporary literary sources such as Plato, Aristotle, Seneca and Pliny. In the city-state of Sparta, for instance, only children expected to make good soldiers or healthy citizens were allowed to survive past infancy. In Ancient Egypt, in China, India and throughout the Orient, a similar approach was adopted toward 'defective' infants.[12]

More widely, other motives dominated the practice of infanticide and prolonged its acceptability amongst early cultures and civilisations. The killing of normal but unwanted infants typically involved economic pressures, and was often tied to the social stigma of illegitimacy or the difficulties which stemmed from prolificacy. Population control, therefore, was probably the key causal factor for new-born child murder throughout antiquity. Likewise this was true in former societies where knowledge concerning the prevention of conception was limited and where the availability of abortion was virtually non-existent. Child murder was often regarded as an acceptable means to an end, whereby such poverty could be prevented and shame and destitution avoided.[13] Thus for many people, infanticide appears to have functioned as a late form of family planning, especially, it seems, when the offspring concerned was female.

Infanticide against female children was commonplace in a variety of societies and cultures (both early and modern) due to the perceived weakness and relative unimportance of female progeny in comparison with male. For instance, girls had little or no hope of inheritance, they were unlikely to be able to support their parents in old age, they were unable to continue the family line, and they were not permitted to legally own their possessions or belongings. Indeed, the birth of a daughter was often seen as a shameful and disappointing event and certainly not a cause for celebration. Consequently, a stark gender imbalance is evident in the victimology of infanticide in more conservative traditions, where girls were killed far more commonly than boys.[14] In addition, the birth of a daughter was also deemed problematic in those cultures where it necessitated the pressure of saving for a suitable dowry.[15]

The other key factor which made infanticide a quasi-acceptable practice, particularly in relation to ancient and early civilisations, was the influence that superstition had on people's daily lives. The Bible, for instance, contains some significant allusions to the link between new-born child murder and ominous portents. In the book of Exodus, Pharaoh commissioned midwives to destroy all the male Hebrew offspring as he feared they would become a future military threat; and likewise Matthew's gospel describes the order made by King Herod for all new-born infants to be slaughtered at the time of Christ's birth.[16] In other cultures, additional superstitions and social prejudices came to the fore and could result in ritual infant sacrifice. For instance, in some cultures children were killed as an offering to the gods in order to secure an abundant harvest, or some other good fortune, as it was believed that their bodies could transfer growth and fertility. Other infants were slain for medicinal purposes as it was held that the blood and flesh of neonates could confer health, wellbeing and even youthfulness to the recipient. In various primitive societies twins were considered evil and condemned to be destroyed immediately after parturition. And elsewhere, children with deformities of any kind were often rejected and exterminated in the belief that their physical handicap was evidence that they were the soulless outcome of a liaison between a woman and the Devil.[17]

Although new-born child murder was tolerated by some societies, it was also outlawed by others. We have already seen how pantheistic cultures prescribed infanticide as a form of population control. However, the practice came to be rejected by those monotheistic civilisations, characterised as the 'Peoples of the Book', who followed the Judeo-Christian-Islamic tradition. In these faiths, over time, infanticide came to be regarded as a grave sin as it all too flagrantly broke the precious bond of normal maternal instinct where a mother is supposed to act as the ultimate protector of her child.[18]

In addition, from the late medieval period onwards, there was a growing desire to restrict the perpetration of behaviours which had come to be regarded with particular horror. Infanticide, blasphemy, heresy, witchcraft, parricide, incest, sodomy, arson and homicide were activities thought to threaten the existing moral and socio-political order amongst many early European societies, and so they became increasingly 'criminalised' and subject to serious disciplinary sanction by the authorities of the day.[19] This sharpened, punitive attitude towards infanticide in particular is evidenced by the specific and exacting punishments that were advocated for those individuals convicted of killing their new-born children in many countries during the Middle Ages and beyond. Torture (such as being flogged, blinded and then clawed at the breast with red-hot pincers) typically preceded execution via decapitation (sometimes with quartering) or live burial after impalement. Alternatively, those convicted might likewise be sewn into sacks along with dogs, cats, roosters and/or vipers and be thrown into a local river and left to drown amidst the frenetic and fatal struggle which must have ensued.[20] Savage and inhumane punishments such as these are illustrative of a wider historical truism related to infanticide, namely that the crime has always been treated, and indeed regarded, as somewhat 'different' from other mainstream criminal offences brought before the authoritative and public gaze.[21] New-born child murder, as this volume will clearly demonstrate, has always been an emotive, debated and highly controversial practice, which seems to occasion response and reaction of an arbitrary and unpredictable nature.

The scholarship of infanticide

In the early 1960s, the discovery of 'battered child syndrome' by the American physician Henry Kempe stimulated early works on the history of infanticide which defined the phenomenon as a form of child abuse and thus took for granted the inclusion of all children up to the age of eight (or even older) as falling within the remit of the term 'infanticide'.[22] Maria Piers, for example, clearly inspired by her realisation that children in the past had commonly been victims of abuse and deprivation, used evidence from a range of periods and cultures to demonstrate the prevalence of child murder and child abuse, and sought to understand why parents and indeed the state had allowed this to happen. In the process, Piers identified factors that have since become a regular aspect of studies of child murder in the British Isles and elsewhere: unrelieved poverty, the shame of unmarried motherhood, and the lack of emotional engagement between mothers and their infants.[23]

Other early works, several of which appeared in the first issues of the psycho-historical-oriented journal *History of Childhood Quarterly*, focused largely on the medieval period.[24] Like Piers, the authors of these articles adopted a survey approach, and from a legal perspective concluded that the killing of infants was not considered as serious a crime as the killing of an older child or an adult.[25] Some years later, Zefira Rokeah queried these findings. She conducted a closer investigation of thirteenth-century English sources that addressed cases of child murder (of individuals under the age of twelve and not just infants). She offered a tally of unnatural deaths of young victims and briefly concluded that where death was caused deliberately, the accused were dealt with harshly.[26] Most recently, Sara Butler has revisited the question of whether child murder was treated with indifference during the medieval period. She has concluded that it was not, although few defendants stood trial: flight, outlawry and abjuration were by far the most common outcomes of the cases uncovered.[27]

Whilst early work on the history of infanticide was carried out by a mixed group of doctors, psychologists and historians who sought to explain why the authorities were seemingly uninterested in child murder, the eighteenth century was identified as a key turning point in the softening of attitudes both to children and to unmarried mothers who killed their newborn infants. This finding was strengthened by the work of a new group of scholars in the 1970s and 1980s. They approached the subject from the perspective of social history and, increasingly, the history of crime (now very much a discipline in its own right), drawing on sources generated by the criminal justice system such as the records of the Old Bailey, assize indictments and depositions, and coroner's records. This led to an allied concentration on perpetrators and legal definitions.[28]

Two important conclusions emerged from this pioneering research. Firstly, it became clear that infanticide was a more nuanced crime than was at first assumed by those who thought it a crude form of population control or the reaction of a deranged new mother. Rather, as historians like Keith Wrightson, John Beattie and Ann Higginbotham showed, infanticide was largely confined to the illegitimate, for clearly defined reasons rooted in social norms and practices. Secondly, the conclusions of early work tended to diverge when it came to the ages of the children under discussion, from new-born to several years old. Increasingly, however, and following the legal definitions adopted in Britain and elsewhere, the word 'infanticide' came more and more to refer to the murder of the newly born. This distinction was fixed in the historiography largely as a result of the work of Mark Jackson, which formed a watershed in the British scholarship on infanticide.[29] Although legal records prior to the nineteenth century often used the word 'infant' to refer to an older child, and the legal definition of infanticide in present day Britain embraces babies up to the age of one year, most historians have followed Jackson in adopting the term 'new-born child murder'. Consequently, when the word 'infanticide' is used, it is generally understood to mean 'new-born child murder'.

The late 1980s witnessed the beginning of a steady production of publications on the history of infanticide, primarily regional studies that focused on female perpetrators in various parts of the world.[30] The British historiography was particularly strong in its concerted effort to unravel the motivations of, and socio-cultural pressures on, the women accused of the crime, and thus investigated everything from economics to shame, rage and insanity.[31] Work on the medical understanding of infanticide has been particularly innovative, and in fact, infanticide continues to be a regular feature of the fairly small literature on the history of forensic medicine in the British Isles.[32] The focus of interest here is two-fold. A larger literature has considered the mental health of the accused mother,[33] but there has been some detailed work on the medical difficulty of proving the cause of death in new-borns.[34] In this volume, the author maintains all of these strands in the exploration of the socio-economic, medical and emotional aspects of new-born child murder in Great Britain since 1600.

By the mid-1990s, then, the history of infanticide had become an established facet of research on the history of crime (particularly female offending), discipline and morality, childbirth, illegitimacy and insanity. It was at this point that a rather different approach to the subject developed, one which adopted a more explicitly literary methodology. Whilst making use of historical documents such as trial accounts, this literature adopted a more cultural focus by examining contemporary writings such as novels, poems and ballads in order to draw links between the crime of infanticide and the wider societal anxieties about motherhood, feminine virtue, gender and civilisation that they highlighted.[35] The most sophisticated exemplars of this new form of writing on the history of infanticide are Josephine McDonagh and Jennifer Thorne, who published their volumes in the same year.[36] Both scholars show how important the subject of new-born child murder was as a point of reference for journalists, doctors, lawyers, writers and novelists. They sought to create authority amongst audiences during a time when the expansion of print media transformed society's ways of thinking. This impacted upon both popular and professional attitudes to individuals who were charged with the most barbaric of crimes, yet treated with the greatest leniency.

The 1990s also marked the beginning of a distinctly national appreciation of infanticide within the British Isles. Previously, the historiography had focused on England, but there is now a separate, though small, historiography of infanticide in Ireland, Scotland and Wales.[37] Key continuities with other areas have emerged, such as the fact that young single women were the main culprits; that there was a high proportion of domestic servants charged with concealing their pregnancy, giving birth in secret and killing the infant almost immediately after delivery; and that there was clear evidence of a growing degree of leniency around the offence after the mid-eighteenth century.

More recent scholarship, which largely falls outside the British context of new-born child murder, has extended this analysis still further. By looking more specifically at the causal factors for infanticide, studies have analysed the variable reactions to the crime and have tried to better understand those individuals who perpetrate it.[38] Perhaps more importantly, the current literature is far more interested in discussing means of detection and methods of prevention than was previously the case. Nevertheless, modern research still places great emphasis on the need for a more consolidated historical and medico-legal appreciation of the offence.[39] This volume is indebted to the work which precedes it, and makes a significant contribution to the increasingly refined national, European and indeed global picture of the crime of new-born child murder. The work also adds to our understanding of the men and women who committed this offence in the past and offers some suggestions as to why this offence persists in the present.

Research objectives, sources used and methodology

In her study of legal attitudes towards child murder, Catherine Damme described infanticide as '...always being unique in history in its incidence, commission, pleading, defence and penalty'.[40] It is clear from present day instances of the offence that not only does infanticide still persist as part of the repertoire of British criminals, but that the offence has retained its distinctiveness and remains highly controversial and intensely problematic. This is particularly the case since there continues to be no consistent judicial or popular attitude to its perpetration and no agreement on the most appropriate way to deal with its aftermath. For instance, it remains unclear to this day whether women who murder their children should be regarded as the primary agent or the primary victim in this kind of domestic tragedy. Although we now understand much more than ever about baby-killing and the individuals who perpetrate it, there seems still as much confusion, incoherence and uncertainty surrounding new-born child murder today, as there was in the early modern period when the offence was first recognised.[41]

This work is a substantive and detailed history of new-born child murder in Britain since 1600. It is the first work on any aspect of British criminal history to provide a truly integrated British picture of a given offence over a long period, as it offers a detailed analysis of infanticide in Scotland, England and Wales over a time spanning more than four centuries. In this respect, the work makes a significant contribution to the historiography of British crime and it also broadens our understanding of new-born child murder in a European and indeed global context. In addition, as the volume largely concentrates on a specific form of gendered criminality, it adds much to the burgeoning scholarship on the history of female illegality and more particularly to our understanding of women's perpetration of violence.

Traditionally, research has tended to describe the relative unimportance of female crime in British history, not only owing to its apparently static or declining incidence after 1800, but more significantly because of the consistent absence of women brought before the courts in comparison to men – a trend clearly in evidence since medieval times.[42] The apparent lack of deviant women, of course, fits in conveniently with traditionally gendered notions (and a surprising amount of subsequent historiography) of how women, especially in the pre-modern period, were supposed to behave.[43] If a woman did breach accepted gender norms through criminality at this time, she was 'doubly damned' and was more likely to be viewed as a deviant rather than as a criminal: she was not only simply breaking the law, she was also betraying the 'notional' qualities of her sex.[44] As David Taylor explains:

> Discussions of female criminality were profoundly influenced by the dominant gender ideologies of the day. Although the male criminal was a deviant figure, much of his behaviour was consistent with accepted,

if not wholly acceptable, male characteristics. Men were expected to be physically strong and brave... A female criminal was more likely to be seen as a deviant, breaching strongly held beliefs about the nature of femininity, than her male counterpart. Women were seen to have peculiar moral qualities and responsibilities that did not fall on men.[45]

Women's crimes, though rare, regularly came to be regarded as 'unnatural' rather than 'criminal', and as a result much of the research carried out on felonious women focused on offences which were considered 'abnormal' or 'deviant' and, therefore, more stereotypically female: witchcraft, scolding, prostitution and indeed infanticide, for example.[46] Popular literature that was widely available in the pre-modern period distinguished between criminal and deviant behaviour. Criminal activity was conventional lawbreaking. Deviant behaviour, according to early modern pamphlets, was also unlawful, but it was additionally associated with sin and immorality. As women were not thought to have the characteristics necessary for criminal behaviour, such as assertiveness and bravado, their acts of illegality had to have an alternative explanation. Men, as Taylor points out, came to be associated with crime as it emphasised the traits of masculinity. Women, on the other hand, were said to be deviant rather than criminal, as deviancy reflected characteristics such as irrationality and impressionability, thought to be key elements of the female psyche.[47]

The belief in women's potential for innate deviance was propounded vociferously in the early modern period, especially in popular literature.[48] Social commentators regarded deviant women as threatening, but, at the same time, the notion that women were subordinate, timid creatures created something of ambivalence in contemporary ideological thinking.[49] By restraining the discussion of female criminality to more deviant or 'sinful' offences, contemporaries made women more morally responsible than men, but less criminally culpable. This insinuated that for women to perpetrate crimes other than 'unnatural' offences, they must have been influenced by male superiors when doing so.[50] The subordinate position of women meant that it was believed that they could not be criminal in their own right and by their own ends, but rather only at the coercion of men.

The assumption of women's limited criminality has meant that historians have paid scant attention to violent female behaviour. As Martin Wiener explains:

A mass of scientific study has established that from birth, males on average tend to be more aggressive, restless and risk-taking than females, and in general less amenable to socialization... with greater physical strength combined with greater aggressiveness, men are and always have been far more seriously violent than women... It is in fact a cliché of criminology that violent criminals are far more likely to be male than female.[51]

Certainly, it is clear from the assorted evidence that, statistically at least, women were less often indicted for violent offences than men.[52] Nonetheless, this scarcely renders the study of female violence anomalous and insignificant, as some claim. Even so, for this reason, women have been largely rejected from the analysis of more mainstream, regular or stereotypically 'masculine' offences such as homicide, assault or violent theft. As these crimes involved the use of overt aggression (which was not an accepted characteristic of the 'gentler' sex) they were assumed to be irrelevant to women's experiences of unlawful behaviour in the pre-modern period. The crime of infanticide too was said to exemplify women's inherently passive role in acts of illegality, as it was a crime thought to be committed via neglect rather than direct intervention. Indeed, more broadly, perceptions of women's involvement in criminal activity have been dominated by their role as victim rather than perpetrator.

Yet, recent work by scholars such as Vanessa McMahon, Jennine Hurl-Eamon, Garthine Walker, Shani D'Cruze and others has illustrated convincingly that since 1600, women in Britain were not merely passive participants in criminal activity, nor did they function solely as victims.[53] Just as women have failed to conform to 'gendered roles' in other aspects of their 'public' lives over the centuries since the early modern era, so they have been prepared to step outside the confines of femininity and behave in a violent, aggressive and unpredictable manner when it came to lawbreaking.[54] In many instances women's violence was an act of self-defence for the protection of family interests. In other instances, women were quite capable of being arbitrarily bad and violent in just the same way as men. Although much of the analysis of women's violence is in its infancy and has largely been confined to episodes within the domestic sphere, it is clear that the nature and effect of female violence (and attitudes to behaviour of that type) have many new things to tell us about the experiences of women in former times. A detailed analysis of those women who were accused of killing their new-born infants can certainly add to this growing body of literature which now offers a serious challenge to traditional assumptions about British criminal women and the level of their involvement in enterprises of a felonious nature.

In common with other recent historiographical accounts of women and crime, this work will argue that although infanticide did differ from other offences in many respects, it was not necessarily so anomalous or so elusive as to be unworthy of inclusion in the wider pantheon of violent crime. New-born child murder should no longer be simply dismissed as an example of unconventional female deviancy. Rather, it should be considered as a central and persistent example of active criminal behaviour which was largely dominated by women. Moreover, a study of infanticide also offers some challenges to more familiar models of female criminality since 1600. Most importantly, it argues that while women generally might have been less likely than men to commit crime, especially violent crime, infanticidal women, in particular, were not averse to using extreme violence in certain situations. Infanticidal women, then, were instead typically *active* agents in criminal activity, rather than passive participants or individuals who merely acted as accessories or decoys. An investigation of their actions will therefore contribute much to the burgeoning historical appreciation of direct female agency in matters of criminality.

The largely gendered focus of this study means that it can also enhance our broad understanding of women's history in Britain across the centuries after 1600. It expands our range of knowledge about the place of women in British society and expectations regarding female behaviour (especially in the context of maternity). However, it also illuminates reactions to deviancy and criminal behaviour on the part of women and the extent to which all of these aspects changed over the course of history. Moreover, it reveals much about the history of British women's relationship with the law and judiciary, with religion and society, with public opinion, with science and medicine (and indeed their own bodies), with paramours and spouses, with their families, with communities and of course, with each other.

There are a variety of objectives and research questions that this volume addresses. In the first instance, it ascertains the key characteristics of infanticide and whether these have changed over time. How common was infanticide in Britain? What type of individual killed their new-born offspring? Which individuals were more likely to be indicted for this offence and why? How was new-born child murder typically carried out? Were there favoured locations for this type of murderous activity? Was there an evident pattern in relation to victimology? Why did some individuals resort to killing their babies while others did not? Can any common motives be discerned in those individuals accused of committing infanticide? How was the crime of new-born child murder regarded by legal authorities, by medical men, by social commentators and by the general British populace, and to what extent did these opinions influence conviction rates and sentencing policy? Answering these questions will help us to understand not only the nature of infanticidal behaviour throughout British history, but they will also help us to move to a closer appreciation of why the crime persists to this day and how reactions to the offence have dramatically evolved over time.

As well as establishing the British history of infanticide over a long chronology, this work also addresses several significant historiographical lacunae in our understanding of the offence. For example, this volume is the first to analyse and examine male defendants accused of killing their new-born offspring, as well as other non-maternal co-accused. Previous studies have ignored these types of assailants, preferring to concentrate on more obvious mainstream offenders. In the same vein, the work also addresses the understudied area of married women's involvement in new-born child murder, in order to reveal the often hidden complexities of the crime which was not merely perpetrated by unmarried domestic servants, as previous scholarship would seem to imply. Another ground-breaking aspect to the work is its inclusion and analysis of the various forms of infant disposal used by British individuals since the early modern period (such as induced abortion, exposure, abandonment, wet-nursing and baby-farming). To date, no other study has brought these different methodologies together and examined the changing nature of their usage in comparison with the practice of new-born child murder over time. The evolving medical and legal interpretations of the offence are also further key themes evident in the analysis presented in this volume, as the fluctuating nature of both of these contexts (in terms of their understanding and appreciation of infanticide) has not yet been fully explored over the entirety of British history since 1600. Moreover, the conflict generated when the opinions of different disciplinary professionals collide is also under-researched. To that end, this volume charts the argument between medical and legal professionals over the possession and right to pronounce over the infanticidal mother – a long-standing dialogue between discourses of criminality and discourses of victimology.

A large number of diverse sources have been used in the construction of this volume. These include prison files and court records (typically assorted indictment or appeal evidence) relating to jurisdictions which spread right across Scotland, England and Wales; personal papers, contemporary writings, poetry, correspondence, pamphlet literature and broadside material; newspaper and magazine articles as well as other media sources including televised news reports; medical texts and medical journals; legal papers and published statutory decrees; other official sources such as parliamentary and state records; judicial statistics; local and government commissioned consultations and reports from committees and commissions; and debates and papers emanating from the House of Lords and other significant organisations.

The multi- and inter-disciplinary nature of the primary material consulted in this study has facilitated an analysis of infanticide over a long period. It also enabled the analysis to straddle the boundaries of the cultural and jurisdictional map of Great Britain. Moreover, this eclectic approach enabled the volume to assimilate and appreciate a range of different perspectives and contexts for new-born child murder which are rarely analysed concurrently. Although the volume contains a comprehensive analysis of a significant amount of primary source material, it has, in the main, adopted a case-study approach in each chapter. These particular examples were chosen as they illuminate and emphasise the various themes and analysis present in the content and discussions of individual chapters.

The caveats and pitfalls that need to be borne in mind with specific types of sources are likewise discussed where they appear in the volume.

For now, however, there are three general issues that need to be borne in mind when reading this work. The first of these relates to interpretation and comprehension. The killing of new-born infants is obviously a very emotive issue and one which can elicit extremes of opinion and controversy whenever it is discussed. This volume has tried to remain as dispassionate as possible in describing episodes of infanticide in Great Britain since 1600, but recognises that the source material used to underpin this analysis is not routinely objective, and thus any prevailing prejudice or partiality needs to be acknowledged.[55] The second qualification to be made concerns the comparative material included in subsequent chapters. Information and data on new-born child murder from other countries outside of Great Britain is included for illustrative purposes only. Such material is not intended as a direct comparison with the information uncovered for Scotland, England and Wales after 1600, as recognised differences in cultural norms and expectations, religion, law and judicial practices, would render such an analysis almost meaningless.

Finally, we must concede that there is a significant potential for inaccuracy in relation to recorded instances of infanticide, not only in the early modern period, as one might expect, but also in the present day. The very nature of new-born child murder and its evidential close ties with concealment, make the offence difficult to uncover and hard to investigate thoroughly. Consequently, infanticide may contribute much to the so-called 'dark figure' of unknown or unreported crime.[56] Often, for this very reason, historians have dismissed the killing of new-borns as being rare and insignificant in terms of the repertoire of British criminals across time, but as we will see in due course, the offence was not uncommon and it has certainly endured.[57]

Structure of the book

After this initial overview of the objectives, parameters and context for a study of infanticide in mainland Britain subsequent to 1600, Chapter 2 investigates the preponderance and accuracy of the traditional conceptualisation of the infanticidal culprit from the early modern period, namely an unmarried woman, typically working as a domestic servant, and accused of the murder of her newly-born illegitimate infant on the basis of (at times) highly dubious or inconclusive evidence. As well as offering an analysis of the incidence of new-born child murder in the early modern period, the section considers how attitudes to new-born child murder developed during that era and examines the extent to which these opinions became manifest in judicial responses to reported instances of the offence.

Chapter 3 examines the experience of pregnancy and maternity for women in the pre-hospitalisation era, with a view to understanding the variable contexts within which infanticide took place. The chapter addresses the extent to which non-maternal suspects, accomplices and married women were involved in this crime, contrasting with the more orthodox image of the infanticidal mother presented in the previous chapter. In addition, this section also looks at how accusations of new-born child murder were made and how investigations were conducted and evidence gathered in preparation for the initiation of formal legal proceedings.

Chapter 4 discusses the alternatives open to women who experienced an unwanted pregnancy during the period before 1900. The choices ranged from abortion, abandonment and exposure, to wet-nursing and baby-farming. The chapter will also explore evidence relating to the methodological evidence relating to new-born child murder itself in the pre-modern era in order to determine whether women (and mothers in particular) were active or passive agents in the killing of young children. Finally, the chapter will explicate the problems associated with determining the cause of death amongst neonates and the ramifications these may have had in determining the fate of the individuals accused of this crime.

The fifth chapter looks at how attitudes to the crime of new-born child murder have changed in Britain since 1800. Although at first glance, the original statutory provision for infanticide seemed severe, this chapter will demonstrate that, in practice, the general judicial approach appears to have been one of leniency peppered by a few instances of serious and exemplary punishments used for deterrent effect. The reason for this latitude is explored in detail in this section, alongside more inconsistent changes evident amongst wider societal opinion. The chapter also looks at the nature and incidence of infanticide in the Victorian era and introduces new ways of thinking about the offence during a period of intense moral panic over the protection of infant life. This period witnessed assiduous and relentless calls for judicial change with respect to child murder.

Chapter 6, deals with the regularly elusive and typically complex task of trying to determine which motives or causal factors lay behind the perpetration of new-born child murder during the pre-modern era. Particular attention in this section will be given to the most commonly proffered explanations for infanticidal activity in Britain in the period before 1900 which include shame and isolation, prevailing economic conditions, deliberate child destruction as a form of family limitation, and the more multifarious medical and psychosocial explanations for the offence. Additional (and seemingly more controversial) explanations will also be considered at this juncture, in an attempt to discern why some women were able to embrace maternity in pre-modern Britain and others could not or would not bring themselves to do so.

Chapter 7, the final chapter, investigates the phenomenon of new-born child murder in modern Britain – a hitherto under-researched area of scholarship. It begins by tracing various judicial changes related to new-born child murder which occurred over the course of the twentieth century.

It also examines trends in the nature and incidence of infanticide since 1900 and offers an insight into modern explanations for the crime and attitudes towards the offence to determine whether causal factors and opinions have changed substantively over time. Specifically, it focuses on trying to adopt a more appropriate, informed and nuanced understanding of infanticide in the twentieth century by utilising an approach which integrates the historical aspects of the offence with burgeoning developments in the fields of medicine and science to better inform our understanding of this crime and the individuals who perpetrate it.

Definition and legal context

Although scholars and commentators have interpreted the boundaries of the term infanticide differently throughout history, in this volume infanticide is defined according to its most commonly recognised status in both law and the popular consciousness. As the Oxford English Dictionary defines, infanticide is '...the crime of murdering an infant after its birth, perpetrated by or with the consent of its parents, especially the mother'.[58] Consequently, this work will be concerned with the killing of newly born infants: those determined to be less than one year old.[59] The terms 'infanticide' and 'new-born child murder' will be used interchangeably throughout this volume and are taken to mean the same thing.

It is clear from the material already included in this chapter that infanticide was not always regarded as a criminal offence. Indeed, in the early history of parts of England, and especially it seems in rural areas, infanticide was a measure that was often regarded with tacit acceptance as a relatively crude form of population control.[60] Medieval legal records, for instance, reveal few cases of this kind of crime.[61] Part of the reason for the initial paucity of indictments lies in the toleration of infant killing (albeit to a limited degree) and the aforementioned difficulty of uncovering and then prosecuting assaults, particularly instances of overlaying. In addition, as Barbara Kellum has pointed out, the fact that infanticide was regarded as a crime which was of comparably less importance than homicide rendered it insignificant in the early annals of British criminality.[62]

Over time, however, attitudes towards new-born child murder, and indeed those who perpetrated it, began to change. The initiation of pan-European moral and legislative opposition to child murder evolved as a result of the confluence of three contemporary concerns amongst the authorities of the day. The first was a determination to protect infant life. Across Europe, from as early as the seventeenth century, there was a growing concern that little was being done to eradicate violence against foetal or new-born life. Legal and religious institutions were thus encouraged to be more proscriptive in their defence of 'innocent blood' at this time, by becoming more overtly opposed to interference with the natural course of human generation.[63]

The move to foetal protection was mirrored by a nascent desire to improve the life experience for children and adolescents, although this was a very gradual process which was initially confined to the upper classes. Even by the Victorian era, although attitudes to children and child care had improved, the process of change was far from complete.[64]

The second crucial concern with the nature of child murder voiced in the pre-modern period was the crime's obvious link with maternal deviance. The killing of a new-born child by its mother was wholly inconsistent with normally understood and expected maternal feelings and was generally regarded as a wholly unnatural offence. As we have already seen, infanticide was clearly seen as a crime against womanhood, and more importantly a crime against perceptions of how women, and mothers in particular, were expected to behave. Women who transgressed this norm and killed their new-born infants had turned their backs on humanity, civil society and, of course, their gender. Clearly, in order to protect notions of maternity and gendered normality, infanticide could not be tolerated in a more 'enlightened' society.[65]

The final aspect of contemporary thinking was the apparent need to control the sexual morality of the general populace. A growth in the number of the itinerant poor across Europe from the seventeenth century onwards resulted in the authorities becoming increasingly anxious about how sexual immorality and criminal behaviour could be effectively managed.[66] Over time, however, this distaste and concern over sexual non-conformity was transferred from the actual act of fornication itself to the frequent end product of such activity: illegitimacy. This issue will be discussed in more detail in Chapter 2, but it remains pertinent to explain here that in the very early modern period, there was a growing preoccupation with moral discipline across Europe from which England, Scotland and Wales were not immune.[67]

The real concern at the forefront of this newly formed, inquisitive moral regime was in fact more pecuniary in nature than didactic. It hinged on a belief in the community's right to know about any illegitimate offspring which would prove to be a future financial burden on a given parish.[68] Consequently, the burgeoning of the more affectionate attitude towards children which developed alongside more intrusive approaches to pregnancy and maternity in the early modern period meant that attitudes to deliberate infant killing needed to be placed on a much more formal footing than had hitherto been the case.[69] By the beginning of the seventeenth century, infanticide came to be more regularly regarded as a species of homicide rather than something less than this, as it all too flagrantly functioned in direct contrast to accepted constructions of good motherhood.[70] Moreover, and as Ulinka Rublack describes, '...the murder of kin weighed heavy; the destruction of a family from the inside was a highly threatening image in a society dependent on strong kinship ties.'[71]

In England and Wales, legislation against bastardy was passed in relation to secular court jurisdictions for the first time in 1576 and then revised in 1610.[72] This move not only signalled official displeasure at illegitimacy itself (which had already been evident in church courts for some time) but it also emphasised despondency with the financial burdens placed on parishes through their obligations to care for the poor. Consequently, unmarried mothers in particular were targeted for punishment by this early legislation, as both they and their illegitimate offspring came to be regarded as '...unwelcome and undeserving burdens on this system of parochial poor relief.'[73] As a result of this harshening of attitudes, and in order to avoid the punishment and opprobrium associated with unmarried motherhood, the authorities believed that single women were concealing their pregnancies, giving birth in secret and then causing the death of the infant either by direct or indirect means.[74]

Prior to the third decade of the seventeenth century, individuals suspected of new-born child murder were tried by common law rules of evidence, which decreed that the prosecution had to prove that the victim had been born alive, before proceeding in their attempts to prove murder. Achieving a conviction was therefore inherently problematic owing to the standards of evidence required in an age when medical understanding of parturition and the causes of infant death was rudimentary at best and when forensic science was in its infancy.[75] These prosecutorial difficulties, coupled with the aforementioned hostility towards women who burdened parishes with illegitimate progeny resulted in the passing of a statute in 1624 which afforded special evidential rules to facilitate the prosecution of infanticide. 'An Act to Prevent the Destroying and Murthering of Bastard Children' stated that:

> Whereas many lewd Women that have been delivered of Bastard Children, to avoid their shame and to escape Punishment, doe secretlie bury, or conceale the Death, of their Childre, and after if the Child be found dead the said Women doe alleadge that the said Childe was borne dead; whereas it falleth out sometymes (although hardlie it is to be proved) that the said Child or Children were murthered by the said Woman their lewd Mothers, or by their assent or procurement: For the preventing therefore of this great Mischeife, be it enacted by the Authoritie of this present Parliament, That if any Woman after one Moneth next ensuing the end of this Session of Parliament, be delivered of any Issue of her Body Male or Female, which being born alive, should by the Lawes of this Realme be a Bastard, and that she endeavour privatelie either by drowning or secrett burying thereof, or any other way, either by herselfe or the procuring of others, soe to conceale the Death thereof, as that it may not come to light, whether it were borne alive or not, but be concealed, in every such Case the Mother soe offending shall suffer Death as in case of Murther,

except such Mother can make proof by one Witness at the least, that the Child (whose Death was by her soe intended to be concealed) was borne dead.[76]

The statute established the legal presumption that if a mother had concealed the *death* of her illegitimate child, she had presumably murdered it, unless she could provide material evidence to the contrary. Thus, whilst concealment of pregnancy and hiding parturition evidence may have been grounds for suspicion of foul play, and indeed these suspicions were often referred to in the proceedings of criminal trials, they were not grounds by which the statute could be applied.[77]

This aspect of the legislative provision for new-born child murder in England and Wales stands in stark contrast to its Scottish equivalent passed some sixty-six years later in 1690. The 'Act Anent Murdering of Children' read:

Our Soveraigne Lord and Lady the King and Queens Majesties Considering the frequent Murthers that have or may be committed upon innocent infants, whose mothers doe conceale their being with childe and doe not call for necessary assistance in the birth whereby the new borne childe may be easily stifled or being left exposed in the condition it comes to the world it must quicklie perish, For preventing whereof Their Majesties with advice and consent of the Estates of Parliament, doe statute enact and declare that if any woman shall conceale her being with child during the whole space and shall not call for and make use of help and assistance in the birth, the child being found dead or amissing the mother shall be holden and repute the murderer of her own childe, And ordaines all criminall Judges to sustaine such processes, and the lybell being remitted to the knowledge of ane inqueist, it shall be sufficient ground for them to returne their verdict finding the Lybell proven and the mother guiltie of murder tho there be no appearance of wound or bruise upon the body of the Childe, And ordaines this act to be printed and published at the mercat Cross of the head burghs of the severall shyres and to be read in all the paroch Churches be the Reader of the parish.[78]

Here we can see that the Scottish judiciary placed much more emphasis on there being a direct link between concealment and intent to commit murder. North of the Tweed, concealment of pregnancy and failure to engage help at parturition (*as well as* concealment of the actual death of the infant itself) were sufficient grounds for an indictment. This was true in instances where deliberate killing was not clearly evident and even when murder was suspected but a corpse had not actually been found.

The reasons for the broader reach and significance of the Scottish infanticide statute are not entirely clear, but it may have something to do with the association of concealment with female deviancy most blatantly exemplified by the burning of witches throughout Scotland since the 1500s and indeed in the earlier part of the century in which the legislation against new-born child murder was passed.[79] In any event, single women were the evident targets of the new legislation enacted and enforced across Britain by the last decade of the seventeenth century. Not only did the new statutory provision punish unmarried mothers for the seemingly cruel disposal of their unwanted offspring, but, more importantly, the legislation was intended as a deterrent to those women likely to produce burdensome illegitimate infants in times of economic uncertainty.[80]

According to historians such as Mark Jackson, Peter Hoffer and Nathalie Hull, the immediate impact of the new statutes brought something close to a four-fold increase in prosecutions for infanticide against unmarried women.[81] Certainly, and even before the legislation was enacted in England and Wales, it seems to have been the case that child murder had come to be regarded as a very serious crime, akin to homicide, and was regarded by many as abhorrent and abominable example of anti-motherhood. Indeed, popular literature from the first half of the seventeenth century depicted infanticidal mothers as monstrous and inhuman, both in visual and narrative form as suggested by the pamphlet literature covers shown in Figure 1.1.[82]

Despite a sterner approach to new-born child murder in some quarters of British society, problems and dissatisfaction with the legislation quickly arose elsewhere. First of all, social commentators and even members of the judicial authorities criticised the provision for being too harsh.[83] This resulted in various attempts to make the legislation more malleable through the permissibility of certain defences which could work to strongly undermine the initial charge laid. These will be discussed in more detail in Chapter 2, but in effect, they rendered the prosecution of infanticide something of a lottery in terms of outcome predictability and significantly impacted upon conviction rates, factors which led to further criticisms emerging.[84] In addition, the intended targets of the legislation, lewd women, were rarely indicted for the offence. Rather, it was far more common for women of a good character to be charged with new-born child murder, as they were more likely to have solid reputations to maintain. Thus the avoidance of opprobrium to maintain decency was (as we will see) a strong contributory factor in episodes of infanticide, and the authorities became uncertain about the extent to which this kind of behaviour should be punished. Moreover, it was claimed that the nature of the legislation actually incentivised the concealed killing of bastard children whilst at the same time it soundly ignored the killing of legitimate new-borns.[85]

The mounting disquiet surrounding the legislation linked to infanticide culminated in an attempt to repeal the English and Welsh version of the act in 1772.[86] Led by individuals such as Edmund Burke and Charles James

A pittilesse Mother.

That most vnnaturally at one time, murt[hered]
two of her owne Children at Acton within sixe miles t[?]

London vppon holy thursday last 1 6 1 6. The ninth of May.
Being a Gentlewoman named Margret Vincent, wife of
Mr. Iarnes Vincent, of the same Towne.

With her Examination, Confession and true discovery of a[ll]
proceeding in the said bloody accident.

Whereunto is added Andersons Repentance. [?]
was executed at Tiburne the 18. of May being Whitson-Eue. [?]
Written in the time of his prisonment in Newgate.

Bloody News from Dover.

BEING
A True
RELATION
OF

The great and bloudy Murder, committed by Mary Champion (an Anabaptist) who cut off her Childs head, being 7.
weekes old, and held it to her husband to baptize. Also a-
nother great murder committed in the North, by a Scottish Commander, for which Fact he was executed.

Presbyterian   Anabaptist

Printed in the Yeare of Discovery, Feb, 13: 1647, 1646

Figure 1.1 Examples of early pamphlet literature regarding infanticide. *A Pittilesse Mother That most Vnnaturally at one time, Murthered two of her owne Children at Acton within sixe miles from London vppon Holy Thursday last 1616. The ninth of May.* (London: J. Trundle); and *Bloody Newes from Dover. Being a True Relation of the Great and Bloudy Murder, Committed by Mary Champion (an Anabaptist) who Cut off her Childs Head, being 7. weekes old, and Held it to her Husband to Baptize. Printed in the Yeare of Discovery, Feb. 13. 1647* (London: S.N). [Both accessed from Early English Books On-line via: http://www.jischistoricbooks.ac.uk/Search.aspx.]

Fox, the proponents of reform articulated the concerns outlined above by arguing that:

> ...nothing could be more unjust, or inconsistent with the principles of all law, than first to force a woman through modesty to concealment, and then to hang her for that concealment; that it was infinitely better that ten guilty persons should escape, than one innocent person should suffer; that this law, on the contrary, asserted it to be better, that ten innocent persons should be hanged, than one guilty person should escape... that the concealment of the birth of a bastard might proceed from the best causes, from real modesty and virtue... that nothing could more strongly prove the absurdity and inexpediency of the law, than the impossibility of putting it in execution, under which the judges found themselves; that laws were to be executed, not dispensed with...[and] that the parliament which made this law was not infallible; that while all due praise was allowed to legitimate children, it was not just to give a squeeze in the neck to bastards; and that humanity and justice pleaded strongly for the alteration contended for.[87]

Despite gaining some momentum, this bill was quickly defeated, largely due to the conservative mindset of the opponents of reform who were more concerned with national crime trends and political stability in the wake of burgeoning unrest in the American colonies. Subsequent reform attempts in later decades of the eighteenth century also failed due, in no small measure, to the widespread and persistent support for what Mark Jackson describes as 'the doctrine of maximum severity' or the retention of capital punishment for serious offences. Lessening the punishment for infanticide would diminish the seriousness of a crime now regarded as a species of homicide and the authorities of early modern Britain were not ready or indeed willing to let that happen.[88]

The legislation passed against infanticide in 1624 and 1690 provides the initial foundations for the study that follows this introduction. Although the statutory provision remained steadfast in 1772, it was not long before dissatisfaction with legislation was renewed. Indeed, over the four centuries since 1624 there has rarely been a time when authoritative, legislative and popular opinion towards the crime of new-born child murder has remained either unequivocal or uncontroversial. As Keith Wrightson describes 'the history of infanticide has been punctuated by periods of augmented public concern with the crime, each of which bred legal responses appropriate to its time and helped to shape future developments'.[89] From the bastardy and concealment-focused legislation of the sixteenth and seventeenth centuries, through the legislative reforms and attempts to protect infant life in the eighteenth and nineteenth centuries, to the preoccupation with understanding the psycho-social causes of infanticide in the present day, new-born child murder has endured as a tragic but fascinating component of criminal history. It has also been a battleground between law and medicine for possession over the reproductive life and rights of women. This work captures the British experience of the journey from 1624 to the present and offers a detailed analysis of a complex crime which persistently mirrors the ethical and moral preoccupations of society, regardless of time or place.

2
The Archetype of Infanticide in the Early Modern Period

> People of substance may sin without being exposed for their stolen pleasure; but servants and the poorer sort of women have seldom the opportunity of concealing a big belly, or at least the consequences of it.[1]

On 13 April 1681 a servant woman called Ann Price was arraigned and then tried at the Old Bailey 'for felloniously Murthering her Bastard Male-Infant in the Parish of St Margaret's, Westminster'.[2] The court heard Ann confess that she 'was got with Child' after having a relationship with a manservant. Ann might have been thought to be generous with the term 'man' as a newspaper report alleged that the father of the child was a boy of no more than 16 years of age.[3] In any case, upon the discovery of her condition, Ann decided to conceal her pregnancy. It seems she did this 'so cunningly' that she managed to successfully deceive everyone in the household until after the child had been delivered.[4] Ann then explained how, after the birth – which had been unaided, by her own admission – she wrapped the child in an apron and locked it up in her box before returning to her bed to recover.[5]

When Ann rose before the expected time in the morning, lit a fire and then returned to her bed, the mistress of the house was confused over Ann's condition, owing to the fact that her servant had been so desperately ill overnight.[6] Upon investigation, the mistress was astonished at Ann's 'sudden amendment'[7] but nevertheless she found her 'out of order' and 'began to examine the cause'.[8] The mistress soon suspected what had happened and so she asked for a midwife to come and examine her servant. The midwife, after her inquiry, declared that Ann Price had recently been delivered of a child. Initially, Ann 'stoutly denied' the accusation against her, but eventually confessed that it was true, but that as the child had been still-born, she had locked it away in her box. The child's remains were duly recovered and the authorities called.[9] Whether the child had been born dead or alive was not contested in court and no associated medical testimony was provided. As one newspaper report put it 'no body but her self knew'.[10]

After all of the evidence for the prosecution had been heard, Ann alleged in her defence that she had tried to call for assistance during her delivery. She described how, after 'finding her self sick of the Gripping of the Guts'[11] and 'her pains come fast upon her [she] knocked with her shoo, as loud as possible, but could make none hear her, by reason she lay up three pair of stairs'.[12] The court decided to dismiss Ann's pleas in defence, and instead reiterated its opinion that 'the concealing of the child [was]... a material point of evidence against her'. Subsequently, and after the 1624 statute was recited before all persons present, Ann was 'found guilty of Murther' and was sentenced to death by hanging.[13]

The case against Ann Price includes elements which mean that it can be regarded – at first sight – as a typical example of an indictment for infanticide in the early modern period. Indeed, these elements appear to be so common amongst new-born child murder episodes from this era that they could be said to embody an archetype of infanticide, accepted by contemporary authorities, social commentators and historians alike. The first common trait of indictments for new-born child murder in the early modern period is that women protagonists predominated. Although men could, on occasion, be involved in episodes of infanticide, on the whole women accused of this crime significantly outnumbered men. This has resulted in infanticide being labelled as an example of a gender-specific crime, where men were seldom involved.[14]

The second typical characteristic of indictments for infanticide in the early modern period was that the vast majority of defendants were unmarried. The strong association between illegitimacy and infanticide, perhaps best evidenced through the statutory provision for the offence first applied in England in the early seventeenth century (and briefly discussed in Chapter 1), has meant that married women's involvement in new-born child murder has come to be regarded as rare, or more undetected, by comparison.[15] Moreover, the preponderance of unmarried mothers amongst those accused of new-born child murder is said to have mirrored a contemporary anxiety in early modern society related to the need to control sexual non-conformity amongst the populace.[16] This led some contemporary commentators to suggest that unwed mothers accused of infanticide should be specifically and regularly targeted by the authorities for severe punishment.[17] This was because the women concerned had not only engaged in what was perceived to be illicit sexual activity, but had also committed a crime regarded as irreconcilable with expected feminine behaviour.

In addition to a common marital status, the women accused of new-born child murder during the early modern period appear to have shared common ground in their employment standing. When occupational descriptions are given in indictment evidence relating to new-born child murder, the majority of the women accused are found to be employed in domestic service of one kind or another.[18] This has led some historians to portray infanticide suspects as women whose lives had been immersed in exploitation – of both an economic and sexual nature.[19]

The final common characteristic amongst indictments for new-born child murder in the early modern period relates to the standard of proof provided in court. In many instances, the evidence presented by both the prosecution and the defence lawyers was deficient, dubious and uncorroborated. As a result, early modern judicial attitudes to infanticide seem to have been unpredictable in terms of whether the defendant was found guilty or otherwise, as we will see in due course.[20] Even when a conviction did result, remission of sentence or pardon for this offence could regularly be obtained by the women concerned.[21] In sum, there was seemingly a disjuncture between contemporary disquiet about the frequency and nature of the crime of infanticide on the one hand and the judicial reality of how accused women might be treated on the other.

All of these four elements were certainly evident in the indictment brought against Ann Price in 1681. Yet, only upon closer inspection of the evidence will we find how typical were these traits across Britain and Europe during the seventeenth and eighteenth centuries. How accurate are the acknowledged characteristics of infanticide and how applicable are the historiographical arguments which have stemmed hitherto from their acceptance? Can the notion of an archetype of infanticide be confirmed, or have historians been too quick to establish the parameters and characteristics of this offence and the individuals who perpetrated it, basing their conclusions upon flimsy or cursory readings of the evidence? This chapter will look at the four putative attributes associated with new-born child murder in the early modern period to see how conventional these characteristics really were, especially within the early modern 'British' context. By doing this, we will be able to determine the extent to which the fundamental historiographical foundations for a study of new-born child murder since 1600 have, thus far, been effectively and accurately laid.

Women and the incidence of infanticide

The first commonly accepted characteristic of infanticide to be examined in this chapter is that women predominate in indictments for this type of offence. During the early modern period, some contemporary commentators expressed an anxiety that the killing of new-born infants had become an occurrence of epidemic proportion. Daniel Defoe, for instance, famously claimed in 1728 that 'not a session passes, but we see one or more merciless Mothers try'd for the Murder of their Bastard-Children; and to the shame of good Government, generally escape the Vengeance due to shedders of Innocent Blood'.[22] It is clear from Defoe's statement that he blamed women and, in particular, the mothers of illegitimate children, for the fact that infanticide had seemingly become commonplace in the early eighteenth century.

Although men were actively and indirectly involved in the perpetration of new-born child murder in the early modern period, as both assailants and accomplices, this offence was dominated by women. This is shown most clearly in Figure 2.1.[23] Moreover, as Chapter 4 illustrates, collaborators or accessories in cases of new-born child murder tended to be female rather than male, largely mirroring the gendered nature of the network of child-birth and maternity during the pre-modern era. Women also predominate amongst those indicted as the principal suspects in episodes of infanticide across both Europe and North America at this time. As James Kelly succinctly describes: 'Most infanticides were committed by women.'[24]

Most of the women accused of new-born child murder were, quite reasonably, suspected to have been the mothers of their victims. Their dominance of the indictment data is not only due to the nature and context of the offence itself, but is also linked to the constitution of the statutory provision under which they stood accused. Mothers, especially those carrying illegitimate offspring, had arguably more means, motive and opportunity than other women for committing this crime. Moreover, the specific components of the seventeenth-century legislation relating to new-born child murder meant that it was very difficult for anyone *other* than an unmarried mother to be accused of the offence in the first place. The courts found it

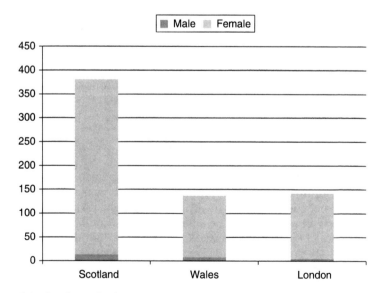

Figure 2.1   Gender and infanticide indictments, 1700–1799

very difficult to indict married women, accomplices or male protagonists for new-born child murder as, in effect, the law did not make explicit provisions for their involvement in the crime.[25] Consequently, although indictment evidence makes it seem incontrovertible that infanticide was a crime dominated by women, the reality of the offence was far more nuanced and complicated than has previously been assumed.

In a similar vein, we also need to qualify, or at least scrutinise, Daniel Defoe's insistence that new-born child murder was a regular and common occurrence during the early modern period. This particular undertaking is fraught with a range of difficulties. As we saw in the previous chapter, the so-called 'dark figure' of enigmatic statistics is considered by historians and criminologists alike to be a particular problem for the crime of new-born child murder.[26] Clearly, the highly covert nature of this offence, coupled with the lack of testimony from the victim, make infanticide 'one of the most secretive of all crimes'.[27] Indeed, as we have already seen, the very statute charged against those accused of infanticide explicitly emphasised the act of 'concealment'. Consequently, the number of women who were successful in hiding their pregnancy, the actual act of infanticide itself and the related incriminating evidence can never fully be known.[28]

The potential invisibility of new-born child murder is especially acknowledged for the early modern period, when the birthing process was carried out in private and when methods of criminal detection were primitive and haphazard. Therefore, as Peter Hoffer and N.E.C. Hull maintain, 'It seems reasonable to assume that more infanticide occurred than was prosecuted.'[29] Even when cases were brought to court, it was often very difficult to determine whether a deliberate act of criminality had taken place, whether a fatal accident had occurred or whether the child had tragically died under non-suspicious circumstances, such as still-birth. In the main, this was owing to the inadequacies of the evidence presented to court; a subject to which we will return later in this chapter. Another factor to consider when contemplating numerical data on infanticide in the early modern period is poor or inconsistent record survival. This makes calculations such as infanticidal death rates, trend analyses and statistical comparisons with other offences or locations especially problematic.[30]

Whilst, for the reasons stated above, it is virtually impossible to glean any notion of the 'real' incidence of infanticide in the early modern period from indictment statistics, these sources can, at least, provide an indicator of how often this crime was discovered and revealed to the authorities in a given location at a given time. Generally, however, historians conclude that far from being rampant and endemic, as Defoe suggested, infanticide was a relatively rare occurrence during the pre-modern period.[31]

Peter Hoffer and N.E.C. Hull, for instance, uncovered 76 indictments for infanticide in Massachusetts between 1630 and 1780 and G.S. Rowe established that there had been 92 such cases in Pennsylvania between 1682 and

1800.[32] A similarly low incidence of recorded infanticide was evident across mainland Europe during the pre-modern era. Marcin Kamler could find only 21 cases of infanticide in Polish towns between 1554 and 1646.[33] Sjoerd Faber's work on Amsterdam between 1680 and 1811 revealed less than 30 reported cases of new-born child murder, and René Leboutte's extended study of infanticide in Belgium from the fifteenth to the early twentieth century revealed only around 100 pertinent cases.[34] In France, too, a similar pattern emerges, with the Parlements of Paris and Toulouse rarely deliberating over an infanticidal charge.[35] A simple calculation reveals that, on average, less than one case of new-born child murder a year was brought to the courts' attention in these North American and European jurisdictions. The only evidence from mainland Europe which contrasts with the general picture of minimal infanticide accusations relates to Otto Ulbricht's work on eighteenth-century Germany. He uncovered 340 cases of infanticide there between 1700 and 1810 which equates to no more than three prosecutions being brought per year, which is still hardly evidence of an epidemic.[36]

Figures 2.2, 2.3 and 2.4 show that prosecutions for infanticide and concealment of pregnancy persisted in Britain over the course of the eighteenth century.[37] Although the number of indictments was never high (especially

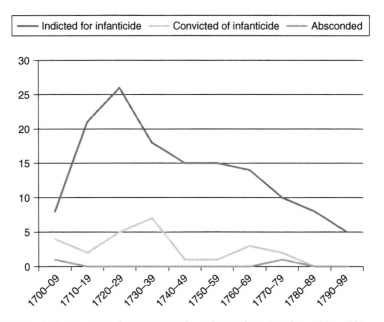

Figure 2.2   Indictments and convictions for infanticide in London, 1700–1799
Notes: All female, except for five individual male indictments in 1727, 1745, 1752, 1766, and 1788. There were no indictments for concealment at the Old Bailey 1700–1799.

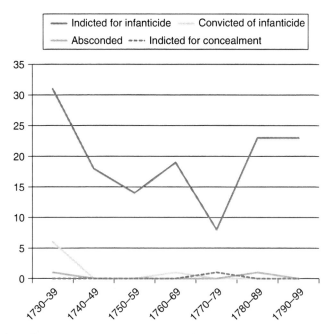

Figure 2.3 Indictments and convictions for infanticide and concealment in Wales, 1730–1799

Note: No petitions for banishment or confessions or convictions for concealment.

in relation to concealment), the Scottish data shows a greater propensity for prosecuting these crimes than the evidence for London or Wales.[38] Figure 2.2 shows an obvious decline over time in the number of indictments for infanticide in London, whereas the corresponding Welsh and Scottish data (Figures 2.3 and 2.4 respectively) appear to fluctuate with greater intensity over the course of the eighteenth century, so that no real pattern regarding indictment trends can be discerned. Prosecutions for infanticide appear to have been more vigorous immediately after the infanticide statutes were passed in each constituent part of the British Isles. The evident oscillations thereafter, in both the Welsh and Scottish data series, may be explained by a heightened sensitivity to fears over rising illegitimacy levels or a simple reaction to perceived increases in instances of infanticide amongst authority figures and/or the general populace in a given place at a given time.[39]

The evidence seems to show a degree of regional disparity between infanticide indictment levels in the British Isles during the early modern period. In parts of England, for instance, the average indictment rate for new-born child murder was slightly higher than the general trend in mainland Europe. However, it was still only a little more than one prosecution per year. James

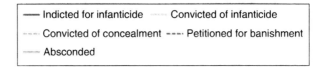

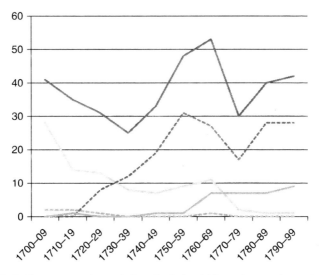

Figure 2.4   Indictments and convictions for infanticide and concealment in Scotland, 1700–1799

Note: All female except for 13 individual male indictments in 1702, 1706, 1720, 1747, 1751, 1754, 1757, 1758, 1765, 1770, 1791, 1797, and 1798.

Sharpe, for instance, calculated that between 1620 and 1680 83 women were accused of child murder at the Essex assizes.[40] Laura Gowing uncovered 70 cases of neonatal infanticide in the assizes of the Northern Circuit (Northumberland, Cumberland and Westmoreland) between 1642 and 1680, and 123 indictments for the offence were laid in Cheshire between 1650 and 1800.[41] Robert Malcolmson illustrates that 61 cases of infanticide were tried at the Old Bailey between 1730 and 1774, and from a 95-year sampling survey of the Surrey assizes between 1660 and 1800 John Beattie could reveal that only 62 women were indicted for the murder of their new-born children during that entire period.[42]

A detailed, but incomplete, survey of Scottish infanticide prosecutions over the period 1700 to 1820 has uncovered 480 cases brought before the High Court of Justiciary and its North and South Circuits.[43] This means that on average more than four cases of new-born child murder a year were brought before these Scottish courts. Whilst this figure seems to imply a higher incidence of recorded infanticide than that encountered elsewhere (perhaps on account of the effectiveness of surveillance and vigilance within the northern parish context), it is, of course, a national rather than a regional statistic, and needs to be considered in this light. Specific proportional data based on evidence from the circuit courts (which is in many ways more directly comparable with English assize evidence) also displays a far higher rate of infanticide prosecutions in Scottish counties compared to her southern counterparts. However, if we consider that this only amounts to around two cases a year on average, the volume of business was not seemingly onerous for the court officials involved. In eighteenth-century Wales, a similar average of around two indictments a year is evident from the 190 suspected cases of infanticide which were prosecuted between 1730 and 1830 and in Dublin at that time Irish newspapers recorded 235 suspected instances for new-born child murder, although it is unclear how many of these reports became formal indictments within the remit of court procedure.[44]

The indictment evidence we have, however imperfect, suggests that infanticide was not a common 'problem' for the judicial authorities in the early modern period. Although it is likely that indictment figures under-estimate the true incidence of new-born child murder to a fairly substantial degree, the evidence suggests, nonetheless, that this crime was not as habitual or proliferated as Daniel Defoe and many of his contemporaries implied, although it was certainly dominated by accusations levelled against women.

Unmarried mothers and infanticide

Despite the relative infrequency of indictments for infanticide, perceptions of its inexorable rise, along with the very nature and context of the offence itself, meant that it became a real cause for concern in early modern Europe. In many ways, contemporaries' understanding of the nature and incidence of infanticide in the seventeenth and eighteenth centuries represented one of the first moral panics to occur across most of the northern hemisphere. The main reason for this anxiety was the way in which new-born child murder became inextricably linked to sexual non-conformity and illegitimacy. The relationship between infanticide and illegitimacy was symbiotic in the minds of many: if one was on the increase, so was the other.[45]

As Keith Wrightson explains: 'In Germany, France, England, Scotland, Sweden, Russia and the Netherlands, women tried for murdering their children between the fifteenth and nineteenth centuries were overwhelmingly either single women or widows, and their children illegitimate.'[46] As we have already seen, the predominance of unmarried women in indictments for new-born child murder was largely a product of the statutory provision under which they were prosecuted. In essence, the laws against infanticide could only be levelled at 'bastard-bearers' or unwed mothers with any effectiveness, and thus indictment statistics merely reflect this legislative bias.

This chapter has already dispelled the notion that new-born child murder was a frequently indicted offence during the early modern period. Although 'common enough'[47] to intrigue historians and commentators through the centuries, as far as we can tell infanticide was not an endemic feature of society in the sixteenth, seventeenth, and eighteenth centuries. Was this also true of illegitimacy? A great deal of scholarship has been carried out on the incidence of illegitimacy, particularly in the pre-modern British context. In relation to England, for instance, Richard Adair and Peter Laslett have provided detailed evidence from ecclesiastical courts records and other sources of an increase in illegitimacy from the 1560s to the 1600s, a marked decline to 1650 and then a steady increase thereafter to 1760.[48] This increase in illegitimacy from the mid-seventeenth century was not mirrored in Scotland, despite the north experiencing higher illegitimacy levels compared to its southern counterpart.[49] Moreover, even when increases in illegitimacy are evident from trend analyses, it is important to remember that illegitimate births only constituted a minority of the overall births recorded in the early modern period.[50] Legitimate births were the norm and were far more prevalent.

Historians agree that regional trends in illegitimacy are far more revealing and potentially more accurate than national statistics.[51] This is because in the early modern period significant variations occurred in the incidence and configuration of illegitimate births, both between communities and even in the same place over time.[52] To give an example, the data for the Lothians, Fife and the Central Lowlands of Scotland in the eighteenth century reflects a downwards trend in illegitimacy. At the same time in Ayrshire and the south-west of the country the pattern of illegitimacy is upward and markedly so.[53] Significant regional variations in the incidence of illegitimacy are evidenced across Britain during the early modern period and reflect not only the highly complex phenomenon of unwed motherhood but also serious and fundamental methodological problems with the sources used to calculate the rates in the first place.[54]

Despite these drawbacks, increases in illegitimacy do seem to have occurred across Britain at various points during the pre-modern era, giving some credence to contemporary fears of a rise in sexual non-conformity and associated 'deviant' behaviour. Explanations for the growth that occurred have been the subject of extensive historiographical debate. Yet, as so many of the women accused of new-born child murder at this time were unmarried mothers, it is important for our understanding of this offence to explore the potential causes of their 'unfortunate' circumstances.

One of the earliest explanations for increased illegitimacy levels during the early modern period was the notion that a sexual revolution had occurred, as a result of which people placed much more emphasis on pleasure and sexual enjoyment than on conforming to the moral strictures of the Church.[55] Socio-economic and cultural changes over the seventeenth and eighteenth centuries in particular were said to have encouraged 'the high mobility of adolescents and young adults [and] their assimilation to a popular culture centred on the alehouse rather than the church, which permitted a considerably larger area of flexibility in social and sexual behaviour than was strictly allowed by either church or magistrate...'. This resulted in a situation 'relatively free of either the constraints or safeguards of parental control'.[56] Yet, the suggestion of a more liberated attitude to sexual activity at this time is strongly refuted by the work of Nicholas Rogers. Rogers' evidence from ecclesiastical court testimonies convincingly argues that the sexual encounters men and women enjoyed during the early modern period were not of a casual nature, as the sexual revolution theory implies. Rather, he maintains, they were more likely to be long-term unions which simply occurred outside the boundaries of formal marriage vows.[57] Moreover, if early modern society had become more promiscuous at that time, given the absence of effective contraceptive methods and devices, surely the illegitimacy rates would have been far higher than they appear.

Another reason given for the growth in illegitimacy, especially over the course of the eighteenth century, was an increase in the sexual exploitation of women at a time when fertility levels rose across the Western world and when the options available for the restriction or termination of pregnancies were limited and ineffective.[58] The concept of 'sexual exploitation' in this particular context is a vast and varied one. For some historians it relates to the sexual assault and rape of single women.[59] To others it relates to the power imbalance that some women had to endure in the workplace, where men could use their status to dominate the women they worked alongside or supervised.[60] Clearly there is evidence to support the hypothesis that women could, on occasion, be exploited by men during the early modern period. However, we should not exaggerate the role that this played. As Richard Adair argues, exploitation of this sort 'is one causal factor for illegitimacy, but we should not think of it as the only factor or even the predominant one'.[61] The evidence relating to Ann Price's indictment cited at the outset of this chapter, for instance, suggests that she was more likely to have exploited her fellow servant than the other way round.

Most historians agree that it was fractured courtships which were one of the key causes of increased illegitimacy in the early modern period, rather than widespread sexual exploitation.[62] As Alysa Levene *et al.* explain, 'many cases of illegitimacy were those where sexual activity had been entered into by women under the expectation or promise of marriage, but that obstacles (economic or otherwise) may have prevented such a union'.[63] Some women may have simply been abandoned by their suitors after the sexual act had been consummated. Other couples, however, seem to have made a conscious decision to delay marriage due to their personal circumstances. Evidence to support this contention can be derived from the significant and increasing number of pre-marital pregnancies in evidence in England between 1550 and 1849.[64] 'Courtship intensity' appears to have decreased in times of hardship and increased in times of economic stability or growth. Marriage was only entered into when the economic conditions were appropriate and not before.[65]

The fractured courtship hypothesis appears convincing in relation to England, based on the evidence to date. What it also reflects, however, is the importance of the local and regional context in understanding why illegitimacy increased in a given place at a given time. Socio-economic change and/or cultural dislocation could have a significant impact upon courtship practices and, in turn, upon illegitimacy levels.[66] As Richard Adair maintains: 'illegitimacy… lies at a nexus at which economic, legal, social and cultural issues interact, and all these dimensions need to be fully considered' in order for us to understand 'the kaleidoscopic and multifaceted nature of the topic'.[67]

One final explanation for increases in the illegitimacy rate during the early modern period relates to the records of the births themselves. Certainly, it is hard to discern the accuracy of birth registration in the sixteenth, seventeenth and eighteenth centuries. As Peter Laslett explains, historians of bastardy face a problem when 'deciding how far the changes observed were changes in the habit of registering illegitimate births rather than changes in their frequency'.[68] This difficulty is exacerbated by the fact that different definitions of what constituted a marriage or what was meant by an illegitimate birth prevailed across Britain during the early modern period, making comparisons between different areas unreliable.[69] Such definitional inconsistencies were especially prevalent after Lord Hardwicke's Clandestine Marriage Act came into force in England in 1754. This legislation outlawed previously 'accepted' versions of marriage which had been conducted outwith an officially sanctioned church ceremony. Such relationships were labelled as clandestine 'no-marriages' and the children from these 'illicit' unions were characterised as illegitimate, which must have resulted in an increase in the number of 'bastard' births registered at that time.[70] In some instances, then, increases in recorded illegitimacy were not directly related to increases in sexual non-conformity and, as such, we have to approach illegitimacy sources with extreme caution.[71]

Clearly David Levine and Keith Wrightson were not exaggerating when they described illegitimacy in early modern England as 'a compound phenomenon' and one which is not easily explained.[72] Although questions remain about the rate and extent of illegitimacy during this era, the prevailing attitudes towards unmarried pregnancy seem to be uniform and unambiguous. Illegitimacy was clearly regarded by many as a social evil and an explicit example of deviant behaviour. As Peter Laslett explains, 'bastardy was taken as a prime example of something which interrupted the proper functioning of social processes, and revealed a failure of social control: the control of individual behaviour by family and kin, by political and educational authority, by all the influences which persuade most people to obey established norms'.[73] An illegitimate child thus came to represent the living embodiment of social and moral irregularity and the mother of a bastard child, in particular, was exposed to shame and opprobrium. She was 'reviled and shunned' by family, friends and the local community for an indefinite period of time.[74] For many women, as we will see, an illegitimate pregnancy meant dismissal from employment and the potential of destitution, whilst for others such circumstances could adversely affect their marriage prospects, at least in the short to medium term.[75] Given this, it is somewhat surprising that the recorded incidence of infanticide is so low across early modern Britain. Our evidence suggests that either British women were not perturbed by the implications of an illegitimate pregnancy and thus rarely resorted to infanticide at that time, or, they were relatively successful in committing new-born child murder and were simply not caught or not prosecuted for doing so.

However, we should not exaggerate or generalise about the implications of illegitimacy in early modern Britain. Some studies have indicated that the stigma of illegitimacy was subject to regional variation, and that unwed mothers had little trouble finding marital partners as their fecundity had been unequivocally proven.[76] Nevertheless, as Patricia Crawford contends, the prevailing attitudes which associated illegitimacy with deviancy meant that: 'Unlike a married mother, an unmarried one was always suspected of criminal intentions.'[77] As a consequence of this, local communities tended to operate a network of scrupulous surveillance over the sexuality and general behaviour of young, single women in local communities – a subject to which we will return in Chapter 3.[78]

As we saw briefly in the previous chapter, there were two main types of societal concern about illegitimacy in the early modern period: moral and economic. A growth in vagrancy across Europe at that time resulted in the authorities everywhere becoming increasingly anxious about how sexual immorality and criminal behaviour could and should be effectively managed.[79] Since the sixteenth century, young, single women who were sexually active were viewed with 'increasing abhorrence' by the contemporary authorities, and the Church in particular.[80] Alison Rowlands describes how pre-marital sex was increasingly regarded as 'ungodly and a threat to social order' during this era.[81] This was because such activities were believed to be carried out in defiance of God's laws and in an attempt to tarnish the sanctity of marriage.[82] Illegitimacy, as the regular end product of this kind of illicit activity, was consequently regarded as a moral transgression in its own right. Mark Jackson suggests that 'the persistent prosecution of single women for the murder of their new-born children stemmed from concerns about the appropriate behaviour of unmarried women [and] about the concealment of what was regarded as illicit sexual relationships....'[83] Certainly, illegitimacy was regarded as shameful: it not only brought shame upon the child, its father and its mother, in particular, but it could also bring disgrace on the wider family and kin of the individuals involved.[84]

It is evident that not all communities condoned sexual non-conformity and illegitimacy,[85] ecclesiastical attitudes towards these issues were fairly clear and consistent, and in various parts of Britain religious authorities drew up particular sanctions in an attempt to curb moral lapses of this kind. In pre-modern England mothers and alleged fathers could suffer physical punishment and endure public shaming, although it is as yet uncertain how widespread such practices were and how commonly they were inflicted.[86] In pre-modern Scotland, however, such sanctions seem to have been more rigorously applied and more opprobrious to the individual or individuals concerned. It was also the case that in Scotland the mother of the illegitimate child was more often punished than the reputed father, unless she was prepared to name him in front of the assembled ecclesiastical court, known as the Kirk Session.[87]

As Rosalind Mitchison and Leah Leneman argue: 'The Scottish Church in the pre-modern period displayed extreme distaste for physical intimacy between the sexes: it usually labelled any such demonstration "scandalous carriage" and penalized it.'[88] Instances of admitted illegitimacy brought before the Kirk Session had particularly onerous consequences for the woman concerned. The penalty was typically an order to make repeated 'shaming' appearances before the congregation dressed in sackcloth. These episodes were meant to enable the woman to repent her sins before the parish community. As many as 26 'appearances' could be sanctioned for a given case, although regional variations were evident in practice.[89] Yet, despite these moral strictures, Scotland experienced a higher rate of illegitimate births than England during the seventeenth and eighteenth centuries.[90] This evidence seems somewhat at odds with the omnipotent doctrine and disciplinary provision that the Scottish Church enjoyed, and suggests that the reach and significance of the Church was not as extensive as we might have imagined. Of course, the fact that more Scottish cases of illegitimacy came to light might also be because a more sophisticated surveillance system operated in some northern communities, or because there was a better activation of the individual conscience in certain areas, which encouraged individuals to confess their condition. Alternatively, this evidence might also indicate that some Scottish communities condoned extra-marital pregnancies to some degree rather than castigating those involved.[91]

It is likely, however, that the toleration of illegitimacy only went so far amongst early modern communities. This is primarily due to the expense involved in caring for a child (especially one which had been conceived in sinful fornication) during a period where the economic conditions were unpredictable and precarious. Mark Jackson maintains that the threatened financial burden which illegitimacy could bring on any given parish (particularly in the English context) largely explains why unmarried women were targeted in prosecutions for new-born child murder and concealment during the early modern period.[92] As Alison Rowlands perceptively maintains, 'a single woman who refused to admit that she had had sex and was pregnant was also refusing to take any steps to organize material support for her child'.[93]

In addition to causing potential problems with legitimacy, lineage and inheritance, increased illegitimacy levels could also threaten the economic stability of a community. As Peter Laslett describes: 'For only if the family system is maintained, marriage carefully protected, and procreation socially controlled, can the population be kept within the means of subsistence known and seen to be available.'[94] Parishes in the early modern period were very reluctant to support illegitimate children due to the long-term cost involved.[95]

Evidence to support this argument comes in the form of gendered legislation passed in England at the beginning of the seventeenth century and briefly mentioned in Chapter 1. Under the provision of the Bastardy Act of 1610, the mother of an illegitimate child could be imprisoned for up to one year by order of the Justices of the Peace if she burdened a parish with a chargeable bastard.[96] The aim of this enactment was 'to prevent the economic, rather than simply the moral burden of bastardy'.[97] Towards the later part of the early modern period, and before the implementation of more regulated forms of welfare, a further kind of punishment for illegitimacy began to be enacted across Europe and North America: communities actively withheld relief to unwed mothers to reprimand them for their lewd condition and circumstances.[98] This must have rendered many women impoverished, especially if support from family or kin was in short supply.

During the early modern period, legal authorities and social commentators alike often believed that in order to avoid both the social stigma from the moral lapse associated with illegitimacy and the economic misfortune that could result from such circumstances, women like Ann Price, whose case was cited at the outset of this chapter, resorted to infanticide. In this way, in the minds of contemporaries at least, illegitimacy and new-born child murder were inextricably linked. Moreover, it was upon a particular subset of unwed mothers that the focus of concern seemed to fall.

Domestic servants and infanticide

Like so many other women accused of new-born child murder in the early modern period, Ann Price earned her living as a domestic servant. James Sharpe contends that the servant-girl was 'very vulnerable to unmarried motherhood, from which it might be inferred that she was correspondingly prone to infanticide'.[99] Servants did make up a significant proportion of the women registered with illegitimate offspring during this era.[100] Moreover, across Europe and North America from the sixteenth century to the 1800s, wherever the occupation of the accused can be discerned, servant women predominated in indictments for new-born child murder. Of the 480 cases of infanticide indicted at the Scottish Justiciary Courts between 1700 and 1820, for instance, 93 per cent of those accused were employed in domestic service. This trend was also clearly in evidence in Massachusetts, Poland, Germany, Belgium, France, Amsterdam, England, Wales and across other parts of the northern hemisphere during the pre-modern period.[101] The high incidence of domestic servants as leading protagonists in recorded episodes of infanticide is the third typical characteristic of this offence which will be examined in this chapter.

One reason why so many domestic servants were indicted for new-born child murder relates to the broad definition of their occupational status. During the early modern period a servant could undertake a multitude of tasks in a given household, including cooking, catering, sewing, mending, cleaning, attending, nursing, childminding, washing laundry, ploughing, planting, animal husbandry, and harvesting, and any or all of these duties could be part of a servant's daily experience. This wide range of employment activities meant that the classification of 'servant' applied to a large proportion of working women.[102]

Domestic service was certainly a very common occupation in early modern England, for women especially. For instance, Paula Humfrey estimates that '58% of all London households had at least one servant' in the mid-1690s.[103] By the eighteenth century, servitude of this kind seems to have become even more common: D.A. Kent calculates that at least 10 per cent of the entire London population in the period after 1750 were servants of one sort or another, equating to around 67,500 people.[104] Not all of these individuals would have been women of course, but, in the main, women were drawn to this particular type of occupation in larger numbers than men.[105] In essence, there were two key reasons for this. The first relates to the potential wage earnings available from this type of employment.

In a survey of female servants working in London during the mid-eighteenth century, D.A. Kent shows that the earnings of young, single servant girls were better than many other female occupations at that time. In addition to guaranteed food and lodging, a woman would typically earn between £4 and £5 10s a year from urban domestic service in London.[106] These wages could also increase over time, once servants had mastered the duties and responsibilities given to them and for as long as they had the capacity to perform the tasks required.[107] These working conditions were considered highly favourable by early modern women. At a basic level, they offered more than mere protection against poverty: the value of the cash wages paid was comparatively substantial, especially when we take into account the subsistence costs of board and lodging, which women in most other occupations would have to pay for.[108] As Kent argues: 'Domestic service was an occupation which allowed women a measure of choice and relative economic independence.'[109] Indeed, there is evidence to suggest that for many serving women 'the prospect of regular employment, a cash income and basic security seemed preferable to the position of a supplementary wage-earner in a labourer's or craftsman's household'.[110] As a result, female domestic servants often either delayed marriage for as long as possible, or took the conscious decision to choose service instead of marriage and made it their lifelong career.[111]

The provision of a cash wage for domestic servants gave women a degree of independence in the early modern period, and therein lies the other key attraction of this type of employment. The very nature of domestic service enabled young women to act and think independently about a range of different issues. For instance, when entering service, a woman was removed from her parental household and became exempt from its associated rules and restrictions. Whether this resulted in her being more promiscuous and sexually independent in comparison with other early modern working women is the subject of some conjecture. Certainly, however, she was more autonomous economically. She had full and unrestricted use of her earnings and could even opt to save a proportion of her income if she chose to do so.[112]

In order to maintain this 'independent' and seemingly privileged position, a female domestic servant had to behave respectfully and respectably at all times and, usually, she had to remain single and childless. In the early modern period, servants had to abide by a strict code of conduct during their employment, and any deviation from these rules was considered dishonourable and grounds for dismissal. Mistresses and masters were particularly exercised with maintaining the discipline and respectability of their domestic servants during this era, and supervised their behaviour accordingly.[113] In addition, as a servant was valued for her flexibility and an underpinning devotion or dedication to the household of her employment, marriage and/or child-rearing were considered distractions from duty and were thus life choices which undermined, rather than complemented, domestic service. Within this relatively rigid context, sexual impropriety, and especially any resultant illegitimacy, was necessarily condemned and would often, but not always, result in dismissal.[114] Domestic servants were meant to be chaste and childless, as these characteristics were best suited to the needs of their employers.

Yet, in reality, the experience of domestic service in the early modern period made it very difficult for young women to remain sexually innocent and virtuous. For one thing, they worked in proximity to men on a daily basis, without any form of chaperoning or parental control.[115] Relationships with fellow servants, and with masters and their sons, must have occurred with some frequency, although it is difficult to determine the extent to which these associations were exploitative or consensual. Historian Marcin Kamler, for instance, maintains that it was more likely for female domestic servants to voluntarily engage in long-term sexual relationships with male colleagues and masters in the early modern period. These affairs only came to an end when the woman discovered that she was pregnant.[116] Bridget Hill, Cissie Fairchilds and others, however, emphasise the vulnerability of young women in domestic service at this time and have demonstrated how exposed these women were to sexual harassment, both from male co-workers and from the 'predatory' behaviour of their employers and their employers' kin.[117]

In any event, in the early modern period female domestic servants were regularly regarded as a sexual threat, especially by the other women of the household.[118] Single women and widows were particularly suspect, and this meant that their actions were more likely to be scrutinised and dissected by those around them.[119] If we also consider the lack of privacy that domestic servants had to endure in the seventeenth and eighteenth centuries (especially in urban locations), then it is clear that one of the main reasons for the significant number of female domestic servants indicted for new-born child murder is the continued close surveillance that they worked under, which meant that they were more likely to be suspected and then accused of perpetrating this type of offence.[120] As Bernard Mandeville stated in 1723, quoted at the outset of this chapter, 'servants... have seldom an opportunity of concealing a big belly, or at least the consequences of it'.[121]

If we consider this context, where economic independence and sexual freedom, of sorts, was combined with close scrutiny and supervision, and place this alongside the fact that these women were typically of child-bearing age, it is scarcely surprising that domestic servants were so prevalent in recorded instances of infanticide.[122] This is not to suggest that domestic servants were 'prone' to new-born child murder, but rather to acknowledge that they were more exposed to circumstances where an illegitimate pregnancy could result. In addition, female domestic servants had much to lose from dismissal: the prospect of rearing an infant on their own, in the absence of the privileges that their employment had afforded them, was a grim one.[123]

Unreliable evidence and attitudes to early modern infanticide

The final common characteristic associated with cases of new-born child murder in the early modern period relates to the inadequate nature of the evidence presented in court. As we saw from the Ann Price case, the very fact that the 1624 statute had to be reiterated towards the end of the trial proceedings suggests that there may have been questions raised over the testimony presented and some potential sympathy with Ann's claims that she had called for assistance during her labour and that her child had been still-born. Indictment material from the courts of England, Wales and Scotland in the period 1600 to 1800 suggest that whilst the standard of proof to bring an infanticide case to court was often flimsy and insubstantial, the standard of proof necessary to bring about a conviction was much more robust and comprehensive. However, it is also clear that where a case came to light in the aftermath of the initial application of the statute, the evidence required to indict and convict did not have to be as strong. In other words, the evidence used in these cases became more critical to judicial verdicts as time went on. If a woman was indicted for new-born child murder in seventeenth-century England and Wales (where the statute was passed in 1624) or early eighteenth-century Scotland (where the statute was passed in 1690), she was more likely to be convicted than in the subsequent periods, and the strength of the evidence brought against her was largely irrelevant.[124] Statutes were more rigorously enforced in the initial decades following their ratification. You might argue, then, as a result, that Ann Price was comparatively unlucky in terms of when she was indicted. If her case had come to trial just a few decades later, it is unlikely that she would have suffered the same fate.

In Britain, Europe and North America, by the seventeenth and early eighteenth centuries, 'popular' attitudes to infanticide were clear, consistent and unremitting. Women who committed new-born child murder were routinely condemned with abhorrence and regarded as despicable, malevolent and monstrous.[125] Indeed, in 1743, for instance, one Scottish commentator referred to infanticide as 'an occult crime committed by the grotesque handmaidens of Satan'.[126] We saw previously that prosecutions for infanticide persisted over the early modern period within this broad context of denunciation, but, as Chapter 6 will show, attitudes towards this offence, and the individuals who perpetrated it, began to change over the course of the eighteenth century. As a growing sense of medico-legal humanitarianism pervaded the minds of social commentators and judicial authorities alike, a more nuanced understanding of why individuals resorted to committing this crime evolved and impacted upon the way that infanticidal women were regarded over time.

One common feature of Figures 2.2, 2.3 and 2.4 is the low number of convictions for infanticide throughout the eighteenth century. As the data shows, there is a substantial gap between indictment levels and conviction rates, especially in relation to the evidence for London and Wales. This pattern, which rather qualifies the condemnatory 'popular' attitude to new-born child murder outlined above, was nevertheless a common feature of judicial reactions to the offence during the early modern period: actual prosecutions were infrequent and convictions a rarity.[127]

The reasons for this seeming lack of judicial interest in new-born child murder are multifarious, complex and partly based on supposition. One reason for the lack of prosecutions for this type of offence might be that, owing to the secretive nature of the offence, few infanticides were reported in the first instance.[128] As noted above, the true contribution of new-born child murder to the so-called 'dark figure' of criminal statistics can never be fully known, but is thought by scholars to be significant, especially in relation to the early modern period. Alternatively, it might have been the case that when a suspected episode of infanticide *was* recounted to the authorities, it did not result in an indictment being laid because of lack of pertinent evidence for the prosecution regarding the suspect or the cause of the victim's death. Moreover, if a community felt particular sympathy for a given suspect, they might conceal evidence and information in the belief that the statutory punishment potentially available upon conviction was not warranted, justified or appropriate.[129] Finally, of course, a suspect could abscond from justice, although it is clear from Figures 2.2, 2.3 and 2.4 that this was not a frequent course of action in eighteenth-century Britain.[130]

One aspect of the early modern legal system not usually considered a contributory factor in the low conviction rates for new-born child murder was the increase in numbers of defence lawyers who offered support and advice to indicted individuals and applied their expertise to arguments relating to the technicalities of infanticide prosecutions.[131] Their involvement, which increased over the course of the eighteenth century, was likely to have played a significant part in the number of trials dispensed with and the number of acquittals achieved – although this theory needs to be more fully investigated by legal scholars. Historians, on the other hand, when striving for an explanation as to why indictments for new-born child murder generated so few convictions, have typically placed far more weight on what they perceived to be a burgeoning sympathy towards infanticidal women. This growing sympathy is thought to be evident from the mid-eighteenth century onwards amongst the populace in general, but is particularly evident in the courtroom.[132]

There were three key manifestations of this more humanitarian or legally efficient approach towards infanticide defendants which directly impacted upon conviction rates in the early modern period. First, from the second decade of the eighteenth century onwards, accused individuals were for the first time allowed to submit defences of various types. This mechanism gave them the chance to reaffirm their femininity and re-establish their credibility as women with 'normal' maternal instincts. Claims of still-birth, prematurity or surprise delivery, for instance, were commonly invoked to rebut the accusation that an infanticidal act had been deliberate or premeditated.[133] The use of this kind of defence resulted in the acquittal of many British infanticide suspects in the early modern period, such as Christian Oliphant (1701), Eleanor Scrogham (1743), Sarah Church (1762), Rebecca Cowley (1781) and Martha Miller (1790).[134] In a similar vein, the production of linen for the baby, as evidence of preparation for the birth, often undermined prosecution attempts to paint a defendant as a cold and heartless killer who had harboured murderous intentions since first realising her condition.[135] Sarah Dickenson (1728), Hannah Spires (1751) and Diana

Parker (1794) all successfully deployed this defence in prosecutions brought against them for new-born child murder in Britain during the eighteenth century.[136]

The second way in which a growing sympathy towards infanticide suspects became evident in prosecutions was the increased use and acceptance of mitigating circumstances, which were brought to the court's attention via exculpatory evidence from the early 1700s onwards. Defence witnesses increasingly came to court to testify to the accused's formerly good character, to prove that revelation of pregnancy had occurred, or to affirm that a suspect was married and thus unindictable under the seventeenth century statutory provision for infanticide.[137] This kind of testimony resulted in the acquittal of female defendants across Britain, such as Anna Nairn (1711), Mary Bristow (1718), Pleasant Roberts (1721), Elizabeth Kempt (1742) and Elizabeth Warner (1770).[138] However, mitigation of this type was only successful if the accused woman was docile, meek and utterly remorseful when she appeared before the court. Any woman who challenged the charges against her, or who came across to judicial officials as either indifferent to her plight or displaying an aggressive disposition, would find little sympathy in the courtroom or amongst her peers.[139]

Other witnesses provided explanations for infanticidal behaviour, describing how horrendous impoverishment had influenced the actions of a given suspect, or providing instances when an accused had formerly displayed signs of mental instability, or recounting the way that a defendant had been seduced and abandoned by a former suitor and had acted out of desperation within a context of isolation.[140] Through these last means, in particular, female infanticide defendants were increasingly portrayed as victims rather than criminals in need of prosecution and punishment, and this may well have tended to reduce conviction rates. This can be seen in the testimony produced in cases such as that of Elizabeth Johnstoun (1715), Mary Doe (1733) and Margaret McLean (1791).[141] Admitting and listening to this evidence was not only humanitarian, it also demonstrated the adoption of a more professional legal approach in judicial proceedings relating to infanticide.

The reliability of the medical evidence presented to courts in England and Wales during the early modern period was questionable at best.[142] As we will see in Chapter 6, medical testimony has always been important in infanticide indictments, but in the period before 1800 such evidence was more typically used in the defence of individuals accused of infanticide.[143] Even when surgeons, midwives and medical men had provided quite compelling or incontrovertible evidence of wrongdoing on the part of an accused suspect, in many instances this did not override the more merciful outlook of the courts toward defendants. As John Beattie describes, 'The legal and human doubts seem clearly to have preceded the medical doubts' in England and Wales at this time.[144] However, there were limits to the marginalisation of medical testimony. For instance, if marks of violence were clearly evident on the infant victim's body, then medical evidence was heard far more closely and considered far more carefully by the legal authorities and jury.[145]

In the main, two crucial facts had to be established for a successful prosecution. First, it had to be proved that the child had been born alive but had been subsequently murdered. Second, it had to be shown that the individual accused had committed this crime with wilful intent.[146] In the absence of eye-witnesses to the offence, establishing and substantiating both of these facts was very difficult to achieve.[147] Within the limits of early modern medical knowledge, proving whether or not a child had been born alive was a difficult task, especially if the victim's remains had become putrefied after exposure to the elements, as was the case in the trials against Barbara Troup (1709), Mary Wilson (1737) and Ann Foster (1781).[148] Indeed, various medical men who were called to provide evidence in infanticide prosecutions regularly attested to the difficulties they faced. For instance, at the trial of Elizabeth Curtis in 1784, London surgeon William Holt was examined by counsel regarding the dead body of a new-born female child suspected to have been murdered. He was asked: 'Could you, from any observation you made upon it, be able to say whether it was born alive or dead?' Holt answered 'No man can ever swear to that.'[149] Moreover, tests performed upon cadavers to establish live births (such as the hydrostatic test discussed in Chapter 4) were increasingly regarded as rudimentary and problematic.[150]

Establishing the intent of the accused at the time the alleged crime was committed was similarly challenging.[151] Cause of death was notoriously tricky to prove beyond doubt and this enabled many women to claim a defence of still-birth or death by natural causes.[152] In addition, given that so many of the indicted women had self-delivered, it was difficult to establish whether marks of violence on the body of the victim had been occasioned by deliberate malice or by the effects of parturition, as was evident in the cases brought against Jean Cowan (1734), Sarah Russell (1782) and Mary Lewis (1793).[153] Determining wilful purpose was almost impossible, particularly in the early modern period. In 1798, one judge at the Old Bailey summed up the dilemma that jurors faced: he said that infanticide was 'the greatest offence that can be committed by a human being, under the aggravated circumstances of the object of it being a poor unprotected child, the fruit of her own body, which had no power to struggle for the preservation of its own existence'. Nevertheless, he advised the assize of the 'arduous task' before them, and predicted that because of the nature of the evidence presented they 'will hardly, perhaps, be prepared to decide, with satisfaction to their own minds, to what the death of this child was owing, whether the mother intentionally killed her child and to whom guilt attaches'.[154]

The increasing rejection of circumstantial evidence by the courts in England and Wales over the course of the pre-modern period meant that proving concealment of pregnancy became increasingly problematic, especially if evidence relating to cause of death was being questioned.[155] Consequently, many infanticide trials were abandoned owing to a lack of evidence or because a defendant had managed to establish doubt that they were in any way linked to the victim in question. Some typical examples from eighteenth-century Britain include the indictments deserted against Agnes McGuffock (1738), Elizabeth Fletcher (1747) and Margaret Minna (1753).[156] Moreover, the nature of the statutory provision was such that the courts were effectively faced with a decision to capitally convict or utterly acquit in cases of new-born child murder, in the absence of any lesser charge such as a form of manslaughter or culpable homicide.[157] Many individuals who dealt with the application of the law in practice saw the statutory provision for infanticide as being unnecessarily cruel.[158] As a result, over the course of the seventeenth and eighteenth centuries, the courts in England and Wales tried their best to avoid applying the full force of statutory law against women accused of killing their new-born children. However, as this resulted in many more acquittals than convictions, it must have meant that some guilty women were released and exonerated.

As we can see from Figures 2.2–2.4, prosecution evidence in British trials for new-born child murder was regularly contested successfully. Even when the evidence in a case seemed strong or irrefutable, if the court or community had a particular sympathy with a given suspect, or they thought the legal provision under which the case was tried was outmoded or inappropriate, they could adopt certain tactics to undermine the prosecution's case. For instance, the prosecution could fail to bring an indictment to trial by the necessary date, thus nullifying proceedings entirely (such as in the trial against Janet Philp in 1715[159]). Alternatively, witnesses could absent themselves from the courtroom on the day they were supposed to testify, resulting in the trial being abandoned indefinitely (such as in the case brought against Mary Angus in 1752[160]).

It is evident that successful prosecutions for new-born child murder were difficult to achieve during the early modern period. Yet, the Scottish data for infanticide in the eighteenth century suggests that judicial attitudes to this offence north of the Tweed were somewhat different. Figure 2.4, for instance, shows the existence of a closer relationship between prosecutions and convictions in Scotland than was the case elsewhere in Britain during the same period. The staunch religious context evident in early modern Scotland meant that infanticide was regarded as much more than a simple statutory offence. Illicit sexual activity coupled with child murder and thus the spilling of innocent blood resulted in this offence being seen as an explicit example of a composite crime against God, with two compounded elements that obviously brought forth evidence of sin. Consequently in cases of infanticide, the Scottish Church had a key part to play in the proceedings at every turn, as has already been indicated. The Kirk's high level of involvement in these types of cases demonstrated its moral superiority to the outside world, and supposedly acted as a disincentive to any would-be infanticidal women. In addition, the level of evidence and testimony gleaned by the Kirk elders from the local community meant that infanticide cases were intrusive, detailed, precise and damning. The intensive scrutiny that unmarried women appeared to be under in early modern Scotland through the actions of the Church and its community must go some way to explain the higher incidence of infanticide indictments and convictions north of the border.[161]

However, an aspect of judicial proceedings introduced in the early 1700s provides a further reason why the legal authorities in Scotland were able to convict more infanticidal women. In Scotland, women indicted for new-born child murder could petition the court for banishment instead of entering a plea. Most of these petitions were granted, and, although it meant a lengthy or permanent ban from the homeland, it also meant avoiding the ignominy of a trial and the potential threat of the hangman's noose. The provision of this extra non-capital option made it easier for the authorities to convict individuals indicted for new-born murder in eighteenth-century Scotland. Indeed, as Figure 2.5 shows, when petitions for banishment are

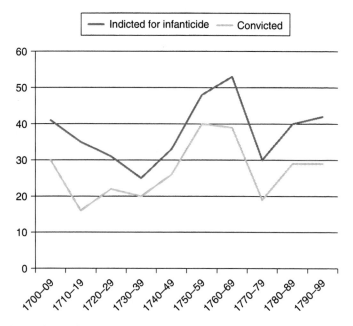

Figure 2.5 Relationship between indictments and convictions for infanticide in Scotland, 1700–1799

added to basic conviction figures, the Scottish data reflects a judicial system that was highly effective in maintaining a strong conviction rate.

In some parts of Europe, during the early modern period, individuals convicted of new-born child murder could expect to receive a capital sentence for their crime.[162] In Britain, in the main, the sympathetic attitude towards defendants was maintained when it came to sentencing. In sum, while convictions were rare, executions were rarer.

Although Figure 2.6 shows an over-reliance on capital punishment for those convicted of infanticide in London and Wales, this was only in relation to a very small number of convicts. In eighteenth century Wales, for instance, only eight women were sentenced to execution for killing their new-born offspring and, of these, only four were actually hanged. Remissions and pardons from capital sentences were more commonly generated in relation to female criminality in early modern Europe and North America.[163] In addition, women were able to 'plead the belly' upon or after sentencing if their pregnancy was verified by medical experts.[164]

Figure 2.7 reflects the limited use of capital punishment in Britain for infanticide convicts over time and indicates that after 1776, no women were executed for the offence in the remainder of the century. Although

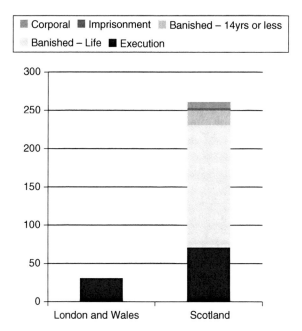

Figure 2.6 Sentencing practices for infanticide, 1700–1799
Note: These are the main punishments recorded.

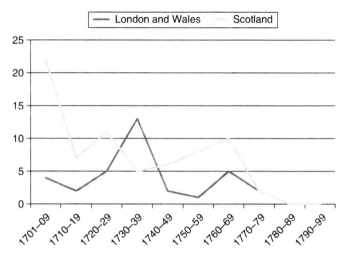

Figure 2.7 Capital punishment sentences for child murderers, 1701–1799
Note: Four reprieves recorded, all in Wales, in 1731, 1733, 1735, and 1762.

the Scots executed more infanticidal women compared to their English and Welsh counterparts, this was largely because, in numerical terms, they had more convicts to deal with. Moreover, the Scottish judicial authorities were also more likely to use a broader range of penal strategies when sentencing offenders (as Figures 2.5 and 2.8 show).

Not only does Figure 2.8 show the predominance of banishment in the sentencing of those convicted of new-born child murder in eighteenth-century Scotland, but it also shows that, over time, the Scots were disinclined to employ physical punishment (both capital and corporal) to deal with this offence. This trait was reflected throughout Britain at this time. There was a definite reluctance to execute women or punish them in an official public setting.[165] Whether this hesitation was on account of a disposition to leniency towards women, a recognition of the limitation of the evidence presented in infanticide trials, a greater willingness to appreciate the context in which new-born child murder took place, a more fundamental dissatisfaction with the statutory provision for the crime, or a growing perception of the need for decorous treatment to mediate against bad behaviour – especially in relation to female offenders – is not entirely clear.[166]

Rather than adopt a consistent policy towards infanticidal women in the early modern period, it seems that the British courts decided that the selection of a few offenders as examples of the potential reach and significance of the law was a sufficient deterrent to curb this kind of criminal activity. Although some contemporaries regarded infanticide with abhorrence, in general a more lenient, humanitarian and sympathetic attitude to infanticidal

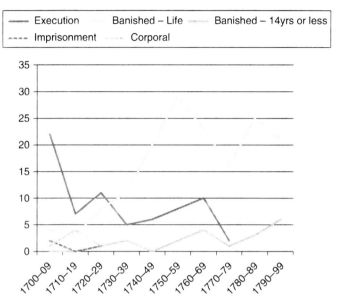

Figure 2.8 Sentencing practices for infanticide in Scotland, 1700–1799
Notes: These are the main punishments recorded. No instances of imprisonment are recorded after 1727, no corporal punishment after 1738, and no executions after 1776.

women prevailed in the courtroom, where the legal provision for the offence was increasingly regarded with disdain. Predicting the kind of defendant that would be selected for 'exemplary' treatment at this time is fraught with difficulty. For instance, it would seem entirely sensible to suggest that episodes of infanticide which were proven to be particularly violent, or women who appeared diffident or without remorse for their crimes, would be likely targets for the wrath of the authorities. However, this was not the case. Even in the face of compelling and irrefutable evidence of brutality, or when confronted with an especially aggressive or unrepentant defendant (such as in the trials of Sarah Hunter (1769), Elizabeth Parkins (1771) and Anne Taylor (1778)[167]), the courts could still be lenient. Consequently, the only thing a woman on trial for infanticide in eighteenth-century Britain could be sure of was that the process she was about to undergo was something of a lottery in terms of predicting the end result.[168] Over time, however, infanticidal British women came to be seen as individuals in need of protection rather than prosecution.[169] Unfortunately for Ann Price, however, such sentiment was not in evidence at the Old Bailey in 1681.

This chapter has shown that there is indeed an archetype of new-born child murder in the early modern period in terms of what the recorded indictment evidence reflects, but suggests that the reality of this offence was more subtlety nuanced. Women were more likely than men to be indicted for infanticide, but this did not mean that male protagonists were entirely absent from the criminal record. On the whole, the women accused of infanticide in early modern Europe and North America were the mothers of the victims concerned, although accomplices and non-maternal suspects were not unknown, as we will see in due course. The strictures of the laws applying to this crime also made it more common for single women or widows to be indicted for the offence, but married women also killed their new-born infants on occasion, as we will see in the next chapter. Another reason for the predominance of unmarried women amongst infanticide suspects lies with contemporary concerns regarding sexual non-conformity and illegitimacy. Scholarship does suggest that illegitimacy levels increased substantially over the eighteenth century in various parts of the British Isles. As infanticide and illegitimacy were held to be closely linked, worries over the increase in 'bastardy' may well have resulted in the authorities being more determined to prosecute suspected infanticides by unwed mothers, in an attempt to curb the slide into immorality which was perceived to be in evidence. Similarly, the community at large was more likely to inform upon an 'unfortunate' woman.

Another common feature of recorded instances of new-born child murder is that many of the defendants were domestic servants. In part, however, this prevalence can be explained by the popularity of this type of employment for women in the early modern period, and the fact that young domestic servants were more likely to find themselves in situations which could result in an illegitimate pregnancy and a subsequent suspected infanticide. Finally, we have seen how attitudes to the standard of evidence in cases of new-born child murder changed over the course of the pre-modern period. The evolution of a more lenient attitude towards those women suspected of the crime in Britain reflects a reticence amongst the judicial authorities to enforce fully the statutory provisions available to them.

As we will discover in the course of this book, infanticide is a complex crime with a long history. The rest of this volume is dedicated to providing a nuanced picture of the offence which acknowledges the archetypes of infanticide, but seeks to look beyond the themes which have ruled the study of this subject for so long.

3
Murderous Mothers and the Extended Network of Shame

> Going with child is as it were a rough sea, on which a big-belly'd woman and her infant floats the space of nine months: and labour, which is the only port, is so full of dangerous rocks, that very often both the one and the other, after they are arriv'd and disembark'd, have yet need of much help to defend them against divers inconveniences which usually follow the pains and travail they have undergone in it.[1]

In the previous chapter, we examined the perceived archetypal characteristics of new-born child murder in the early modern period. We also identified the circumstances that could result in the conception of illegitimate infants in the British Isles and further afield. In this chapter, we need to move past this initial context to understand the circumstances associated with pregnancy and birth of infants during this era, before hospitals became the standard provider of maternal and neonatal care from the late nineteenth century onwards.[2]

Central to our understanding of the nature of infanticide throughout history is the concept of concealment. As we saw in the opening chapters of this work, concealment of pregnancy and the delivery of an illegitimate infant were central to the initiation of prosecutions for new-born child murder. Moreover, in instances of premeditated infanticide, successful concealment was clearly regarded by some as the key to self-preservation. Consequently, facilitating successful concealment lay at the heart of the strategies, behaviour and actions that certain women employed during the course of their pregnancies and in the immediate aftermath of childbirth. Yet, the 'maternal' experience of unmarried women, in particular, remains relatively unexplored by scholars, especially their involvement in the death of new-born infants.[3]

Clearly, prior to the rapid advancements in medicine in the twentieth century, reproduction was a process fraught with difficulty. As the quotation at the outset of this chapter illustrates, the journey of pregnancy and childbirth was a dangerous one for women to undertake in the seventeenth, eighteenth and nineteenth centuries. The journey must have been all the more problematic and precarious if it was carried out alone and in secret. Yet, to what extent were pregnant single women truly isolated and set adrift from communities in this era? Was new-born child murder the crime of a sole protagonist, or could other individuals be involved in its perpetration, or at least be complicit with its committal? Were married women culpable in instances of infanticide or did the network of shame associated with this crime revolve solely around the spinster and the widow? To what lengths did these women go in order to conceal their condition? How were suspicions of illegitimate pregnancy initiated and communicated and what was done to verify the accusations made? How accurate was medical and common knowledge about pregnancy and delivery in the pre-modern period? What strategies did women adopt in attempting to hide childbirth? Conversely, in what situations were labour and delivery detected and how did investigations proceed after such a discovery had been made?

This chapter will address each of these questions by engaging with the experiences of women accused of infanticide in the period before the introduction of widespread professional healthcare. In doing so, it will refine the notion that new-born child murder was a crime of isolation, committed solely by maternal protagonists. In addition, it will offer a more nuanced understanding of the attitude, state of mind, resolution and conduct of those women accused of killing their new-born infants, which is central to our understanding of this crime across times, places and cultures.

Concealment of pregnancy – suspicions and denials

For most women in the seventeenth and eighteenth centuries, and even during the nineteenth century, pregnancy was a very private experience. As Laura Gowing argues: 'Only in exceptional, usually negative circumstances were women likely to be recorded talking about their bodies, about sex, pregnancy and childbirth. All the force of conduct literature, ideologies of shame and social ritual seemed to insist that the female body was private and secret.'[4] Even married and openly pregnant women commonly concealed their condition, as they were embarrassed by their shape and the fact that their condition was so explicitly related to sexual activity.[5]

Yet, as we saw in Chapter 2, for some women, privacy was hard to come by during the pre-modern period owing to the nature of their living arrangements, the type of employment they were involved in and, most significantly, their marital status. Single women and widows of child-bearing age were regularly seen as a threat to the stability of families and communities, especially if there was concern amongst contemporaries about a perceived rise in illegitimacy levels. Consequently, their conduct and the nature of their appearance were subject to much closer scrutiny than that of their married counterparts.[6] Indeed, Lynn Abrams has gone as far as to suggest that, during this era, 'Attempts were made to claim single women's bodies as public property, especially when they were suspected of being pregnant or having given birth.'[7]

In many communities, and especially in rural locations, where neighbourhood ties endured for longer, the closer surveillance of unmarried women and the generation of suspicion relating to potential pregnancies was something that was not only encouraged but was also legitimised and sanctioned by the wider populace. Parishes, for instance, did everything they could to protect themselves from the moral and financial burden of an illegitimate pregnancy. The investigations and scrutiny practised could often enable a parish to move a woman whose offspring would be burdensome to another district, thus becoming a drain on another parish's resources. Many individuals saw concealment of pregnancy as:

> an offence against the 'right to know' that the village demanded of a pregnant woman not just because she wanted to live as a member of the locality or the community. If she removed herself from their control, she abandoned the fundamental, common notions of order. Putting these into question, she threatened the established economic structure, which had to be maintained.

Thus, in many communities in pre-modern Europe, 'Children of unknown fathers' were regarded as 'unwanted parasites'.[8]

As well as the desire to avoid the financial burden of illegitimacy, another key reason for the generation of suspicions about concealment of pregnancy was the need for other members of the community to avoid charges of complicity should their concerns prove accurate and the death of a newborn child ensue at a later date.[9] For this reason, as well as those outlined above, a tremendous amount of hearsay and accusation was generated in pre-modern communities around the issue of illegitimate pregnancy.[10] Court indictments and witness depositions for new-born child murder from across Europe during the seventeenth, eighteenth and nineteenth centuries, for instance, 'reveal a world of gossip and rumour, in which the moral conduct and physical appearance of women were made a matter of comment among other women in the community'.[11] In Scotland, in the eighteenth and nineteenth centuries, informal reports of this kind were encouraged, collected and collated by Kirk Session ministers intent on uncovering sexual non-conformity and the potential repercussions of this illicit activity.[12] Elsewhere, at the same time, the scrutiny and surveillance of unmarried women was typically the sole preserve of other women from the community in which the suspect worked or resided.[13]

Pregnancy (and indeed its detection) in the pre-hospitalisation era was predominantly a woman's world, in which men did not participate.[14] In part, this was due to the ritualistic association between maternity and femininity, but it was also because women were thought to be appropriately familiar with the bodily changes and transgressions related to their own sex.[15] This knowledge and 'natural' experience rendered women best placed to recognise and detect the signs of conception and pregnancy in others, although usually it was only the accusations from women of a certain age and social position that would be taken seriously.[16] As Mark Jackson explains in relation to early modern England, 'The day-to-day identification, investigation and accusation of specific women... depended upon a neighbourhood's ability to recognise the signs of pregnancy and signs of labour and recent delivery, and to discover and examine the body of the dead child.'[17] As, in the main, this responsibility was given to local women, they were almost exclusively 'the driving force' behind accusations and prosecutions related to new-born child murder in the pre-modern period.[18]

In effect, these women were charged by their communities with preventing concealment of pregnancy and, by implication, new-born child murder.[19] They rigorously, strenuously and repeatedly questioned unmarried women, particularly those in domestic service, about their physical condition and were quick to challenge any complaints of ill-health or changes to bodily appearance that took place. For example, in 1704, on six or seven separate occasions, Jane Lyne was asked by her landlady: 'By what reason do you look so big? Are you with child?' Jane continually answered 'No', but was later indicted at the Old Bailey for new-born child murder when the dead body of a male infant was discovered in an outhouse.[20] Londoner Mary Ashtol was similarly questioned by her fellow servant Elizabeth Arthur in 1717 after suspicions were raised that Mary had been recently delivered of an illegitimate child. When Elizabeth confronted her co-worker she asked 'What ails you Mary? Why did you call in the night? Why are your sheets in an odd pickle? How did they come to be so? Why do you look so pale? Have you been delivered of a child?' Elizabeth initially refused to answer the barrage of questions put to her, but eventually she confessed to the murder of her baby son.[21] In Leith, near Edinburgh, in 1720, Anna Brown was approached by two women she was acquainted with: Kathrine Moodie and Jannet Sutherland. The two women continually questioned Anna over the fact that she 'was much swamper [bigger] than she had been some time before' and demanded to know why her appearance had changed so dramatically in such a short space of time. Anna replied to the women that she 'had been very bad but blessed be God she was much better'. Anna Brown's new-born baby was found the same day, battered and bruised in a ditch.[22]

In addition to the role of inquisitor, local women also routinely encouraged single women and widows to move to a different parish to avoid the shame of their condition in the midst of their own kin and the wider neighbourhood, and sought to warn women about the possible punishments that would ensue if they murdered their new-born offspring.[23] These women regarded the delivery of warnings and advice such as this to be part of the 'natural duty' that their community had bestowed upon them. In addition, and in order to avoid any charges of complicity, the women also advised those individuals they suspected to be pregnant that they would enjoy a better birth if they revealed their condition to those around them. Not only would the pregnant woman concerned be 'emotionally open' to the labour that she would eventually endure, but she would also be 'socially open' to accepting help when the time of delivery came, which was more likely to result in a successful outcome for all concerned.[24]

However, the constant and intense surveillance undertaken by local women to reduce the prospect of new-born child murder, which is evident throughout communities in pre-modern Europe, may not have had the desired effect. The sense of growing isolation that unmarried pregnant women felt upon recognising their condition must have increased significantly when they were confronted with the pressure of regular taunts and accusations at their workplace or in the neighbourhood in which they lived. Such circumstances, which forced single women to deny their condition vehemently and repeatedly, may well have limited the options available to them at the end of their pregnancies. As René Leboutte illustrates: 'Rumor played the role of public prosecutor in such a way that sometimes the rumor itself was the actual instigator of the crime – to silence the talk the accused tried to eliminate the child.'[25] For many pregnant single women and widows, privacy must have become an absolute necessity that had to be vigorously defended for the purposes of self-preservation in the face of attempts to make their maternity a shared experience and their condition public.

The accurate determination of pregnancy in the seventeenth, eighteenth and nineteenth centuries was inherently problematic.[26] During this era, the 'Signs of pregnancy might sometimes be so ambiguous or hard to interpret that a woman was wrongly believed to be pregnant when she was not, while an actual pregnancy was not discovered until quite well advanced.'[27] As Laura Gowing argues, the symptoms and signs of conception were so unreliable and subjective prior to the professionalisation of medical provision, that the lack of conclusive proof must have been a definite aid to those women intent on concealing their condition from others.[28]

The extent of the ambiguity surrounding pregnancy is best evidenced by the nature of the crude, and rather bizarre, pregnancy tests which were in existence across Europe, especially in the early modern period. These included: changes to bird-song in the vicinity of a pregnant woman; water-divining (which could also determine the sex of the infant); uroscopy or examinations of the colour and consistency of the woman's urine; and the garlic test.[29] The garlic test was seemingly employed on a regular basis to determine conception. As Jacques Gèlis describes:

> The woman's body was thought of as a sort of sheath, open to the outside at top and bottom. Before going to bed, a woman who thought she might be pregnant would slip a clove of garlic into her genital organ. In the morning, if she breathed out the characteristic odour, she was assuredly not pregnant. An embryo, if present, would certainly get in the way of this diffusion: sweet breath proved conception.[30]

The popularity and trust afforded to this test amongst the early modern populace was seemingly strengthened by the similarity in shape of a curled-up foetus to that of a clove of garlic.

Aside from these more popular and 'customary' forms of detection, the French royal surgeon Cosme Viardel identified four signs of conception in the seventeenth century: the shiver during intercourse; the closure of the neck of the womb; the cessation of menstruation; and the swelling of the breasts.[31] Added to these over time were symptoms such as loss of appetite, nausea, irritability, changes to the colour and form of the breasts and/or abdomen and indigestion.[32] However, local women tended to look for the three most obvious signs of pregnancy in those unmarried women suspected to be with child: the development of an extended abdomen; the presence of breast milk (after the fourth month since conception in particular); and the cessation of the menses.

A marked change in a single woman's body shape was one of the most obvious signs of pregnancy and, although a suspect could claim that her swollen belly was a result of natural weight-gain or a medical complaint such as dropsy or colic, she could still expect to be questioned directly and challenged about any explanation she had provided for the alteration in her appearance.[33] In 1728, for instance, Katharine Toshiak from Fife was questioned by her neighbour Isobell Adam about the cause of her big belly. Katherine replied that 'water was not for her, as she had been swelled with it for four years'. Isobell strongly encouraged Katharine to go and see a physician about her condition but Katharine resolutely refused. On hearing this, Isobell went to her local minister and told him of her suspicion that Katharine Toshiak was pregnant with an illegitimate child. The body of a dead infant was subsequently found floating in a local waterway and Katharine was quickly arrested.[34] In 1732, at St Giles in London, Hannah Bradford refuted accusations that she was suffering labour pains by saying that she merely 'complain'd of a Twitching in her Stomach with the Cholick'. Her co-workers did not believe her explanation and sent for help to investigate the matter further. Hannah Bradford's new-born baby was later found dead in an outside toilet and she was subsequently prosecuted for infanticide.[35] Finally, in 1761, the High Court of Justiciary in Edinburgh heard about a case of infanticide involving a woman called Jannet Heatly. Jannet's mistress had repeatedly questioned her servant about why she 'appeared to her bulky' and why she seemed 'lusty and fat' when she ate so little? The accused had replied that 'she was so big because she had not for some time been so regular as other women are and that she had not been in the custom of women but once since she came to her service'. The mistress did not believe this story, especially when afterbirth from a recent parturition was found stuffed into a hole in a nearby dyke and a dead baby's body was also found.[36]

As well as undergoing verbal interrogations, unmarried women could also be physically examined by a network of midwives and neighbours if they were suspected of pregnancy. Typically, this involved an inspection of the suspect's breasts to see if milk was present. However, some women claimed that the presence of milk related to a previous pregnancy, to the process of weaning or to an alternative medical condition, such as dropsy. However, on the whole, evidence of lactation was taken as a fairly definitive indication of pregnancy by female examiners in the pre-modern period.[37]

According to Gèlis, the cessation of menstruation was the 'essential sign' of pregnancy for women across Europe in the seventeenth, eighteenth and nineteenth centuries.[38] As with the other two most obvious symptoms of pregnancy, women tried to explain away the absence of monthly bleeding by blaming other medical conditions and claiming they were suffering from wind, colic or a 'blockage' of one kind or another.[39] Although menstruation was regarded as fairly mysterious, and certainly a very private matter for individuals, during this era, this privacy did not extend to unmarried women, who, as we have already seen, were always under close scrutiny from other women in their community. In any case, amenorrhoea (an abnormal absence of menstruation) was seen as a serious condition for women of child-bearing age, regardless of their marital status. This is because it was widely believed that 'only when the menses flowed were women's bodies preserved from the most terrible diseases' because menstruation purified women's blood and purged them of abnormalities, which might subsequently result in abnormal growths. Moreover, a cessation of the menses in a given woman 'would allow excess blood to run to her brain, which would become overheated' and result in her prolonged mental incapacity and instability.[40] In consequence, if a woman was suffering from an absence of menstruation, she would be offered various solutions and remedies for her condition, including pessaries, fumigations and purgatives.[41]

When challenged with an accusation of concealment of pregnancy, many unmarried women in the British Isles and beyond vehemently denied that they were with child.[42] Some claimed that, as they had no knowledge of what it was like to be pregnant, they could not recognise the signs. Others claimed that because they did not suffer from any of the recognised symptoms, they could not tell whether conception had been achieved or not.[43]

Many women must surely have been aware of their pregnancy, but chose to conceal it for reasons which we will explore in more depth in Chapter 6. Women used the uncertainty and ambiguities associated with proving conception in the pre-modern period, along with the advantages afforded them by the contemporary fashion for loose fitting hoop skirts, to hide the advancement of their condition from those around them.[44]

As the signs of pregnancy could not be proven conclusively, it is easy to imagine single women and widows successfully concealing their pregnancies, despite the context of heightened surveillance that existed across Europe during the pre-modern period.[45] Unmarried women were able to develop personal strategies to hide their pregnancies from those around them. Sometimes this involved moving from place to place so as to conceal the advancement of their condition and sometimes it was simply down to a basic determination to control their fate.[46] From court testimonies and indictment evidence it seems clear that many of the unmarried women accused of infanticide and concealment during the pre-modern period used prolonged subterfuge of one kind or another to maximise their chances of self-preservation at a later date, after childbirth had occurred.

Childbirth

Knowledge about the progress of pregnancy, the process of childbirth and the aftermath of delivery was available in the pre-hospitalisation era, but commonly this information was only accessible to women of the propertied classes across Europe and to their literate advisers and assistants.[47] Even then, medical historians have been quick to point out that the pre-modern literature on parturition was rudimentary at best and dangerously inaccurate at worst.[48] Nevertheless, openly pregnant women usually had experienced and well-informed support networks at their disposal when their labour pains came upon them. This was because childbirth was regarded as a community-based 'ceremony', in which there were multiple participants. In the main, these participants were women. They were typically close female relatives of the woman about to give birth, or local women deemed to be mature enough and to possess sufficient expertise as to be able to lend a hand with the delivery process.[49]

As Patricia Crawford describes, 'Childbirth was the female rite of passage *par excellence.*'[50] In the pre-modern period it was almost exclusively a woman's business.[51] Traditional births were female-only occasions, attended by relatives, friends and neighbours (known as 'gossips') and also midwives, unless some sort of emergency or complication developed, in which case a male medical practitioner would be called. Usually this latter course of action was only resorted to in the most desperate of situations, for instance when a child had become obstructed in the birth canal for an inordinate length of time and consequently the mother's survival became in doubt.

As Adrian Wilson explains: 'The task of the midwife was to deliver a *living* child, the task of the male practitioner was to deliver a *dead* one'; thus, the presence of a man at a birth was 'regarded with fear and dread'.[52]

It was far more conventional for a midwife to take the lead in the birthing process and to be supported in this by other women from the local community. An ideal midwife was an older woman who had experience of childbirth herself, or at least experience of making the necessary provisions for delivery. It was best if she had no other commitments to detain her from her duties as she had to be available at short notice. For this reason, widows tended to be preferred for this role, and if they had children they needed to be fully-grown and not burdensome. In addition, a midwife had to be physically strong and sturdy because of the demands that labour could involve. She also had to be strong in principle as she was commonly charged by the community and/or the Church with ensuring that foul play was avoided and that moral strictures were upheld.[53] Although learned society and members of the medical elite regarded midwifery as 'the most filthy and lowly part of surgery', 'a discredited profession' and 'the vilest of trades', many midwives were both feared and revered by communities, who saw their expertise as invaluable and their moral scrupulousness commendable. This entrusted midwives with a power and authority within communities that was rarely afforded to other women in the pre-modern period.[54] Midwives were usually paid in kind by the particular family being assisted, although this ad-hoc arrangement was transformed with the introduction of *accouchers* or man-midwives across Europe from the second half of the eighteenth century onwards.[55]

The supportive network of childbirth provision described above was not available to all pregnant women in the pre-modern era. As Laura Gowing explains, 'For legitimate mothers labour was a period to be planned for and managed in the semi-public female world of neighbourly support. For illegitimate mothers it was exactly the opposite: a time to hide and afterwards deny.'[56] Those women who had successfully managed to conceal their pregnancy, or had fended off accusations related to their condition, now had to maintain their secret when it came to the moment of delivery. In order to achieve this, they had to give birth in private, in silence and without assistance. This was not only difficult to achieve, as we will see in due course, but it was also dangerous, especially in the pre-modern period.

The relatively rudimentary understanding of childbirth alluded to above, which generally prevailed in the pre-hospitalisation era, meant that women who engaged with the reproductive process lived in the 'shadow of maternity'.[57] Advice on antenatal care was limited and the birth itself was certainly a hazardous experience for both the mother and the child, in a time before anaesthetics, anticoagulants and prescribed pain relief.[58] Although the material conditions of birth did improve substantially over the course of the eighteenth and nineteenth centuries, with the introduction of instruments to aid the birthing process, the establishment of 'lying-in' facilities and the availability of drugs of various forms based on natural remedies, childbirth was still routinely painful and dangerous.[59] Not all deliveries were straightforward and fatalities could occur, although maternal deaths were in fact relatively rare in pre-modern Europe.[60] The maternal death rate in Tudor and Stuart England has been estimated at around five deaths per 200.[61] By the nineteenth century this figure had been reduced: in England and Wales only one pregnancy in 200 led to the death of the mother concerned. This figure still applied until the 1930s.[62]

In many respects, the new-born infant was more vulnerable than its mother in pre-modern times, especially in the initial hours and days of its life.[63] After delivery, resuscitation of the neonate was sometimes required and the umbilical cord had to be tied off properly to avoid a fatal haemorrhage.[64] A mother had to be sufficiently knowledgeable about postnatal (and postpartum) care to tend to her infant appropriately and to prevent infection from occurring.[65] Within the context of a community-based network of childbirth support, a midwife was on hand to provide timely medical assistance immediately after the birth, and advice on nursing and puerperal care was in abundance from other women present at the delivery.[66] However, for those women who had concealed their pregnancies and their subsequent labours, no such provision was available.

Judith Leavitt insists that there were four classifications of childbirth in the pre-hospital era: 'institutional', where women went to charity organisations for support; 'traditional', where women accessed the assistance of midwives and female networks; 'integrationist', where wealthy or propertied women sought a mix of midwives' and physicians' expertise; and 'privileged', which related to high-end medical services provided exclusively to the female elite.[67] At no point does Leavitt mention the potential for self-delivery. This oversight is repeated by Tina Cassidy in her work *Birth: A History*, where she states that: 'Around the world, solitary human births are unheard of.'[68] Yet, some contemporary commentators actually encouraged unassisted births during the pre-modern period. For instance, during the seventeenth century, the man-midwife Percivall Willoughby and the scientist William Harvey both independently suggested that unassisted births were more natural and more effective than assisted ones, as they avoided the unnecessary intrusions and ill-judged intervention of midwives.[69]

Moreover, we know from indictment evidence and court depositions for new-born child murder that women in the pre-modern period did give birth alone, unaided and in secret. It was, after all, part of the statutory legislative provision that, for a woman to be indicted for infanticide, she had to have concealed her pregnancy *and* concealed the birth, by not calling for assistance during her labour or at the time of her delivery. The reason for the inclusion of the concealment of birth clause in the statute was because it was often during the delivery process that midwives asked those unmarried mothers who had revealed their pregnancy to name the father of their unborn child. By withholding assistance in the birth until paternity was resolved, midwives helped to ensure that the burden of illegitimacy was borne by the appropriate parties.[70] If the opportunity to make such an intervention could not occur, because the birth had been carried out in secret, it added weight to the belief that new-born child murder was regularly a premeditated and deeply deviant crime. It was these 'qualities' which rendered infanticide a capital offence in the seventeenth and eighteenth centuries.

Concealing the birth of a new-born child was very difficult for a whole host of reasons. For one thing, the inherent lack of privacy for many of the women involved meant that they had to give birth in the same room or even the same bed as others and not arouse suspicion.[71] As Mark Jackson states, in relation to eighteenth-century England, 'concealing the signs of labour and child-birth presented even greater problems than concealing pregnancy'.[72] Many of the women suspected of concealing birth were already under surveillance for concealing the pregnancy which preceded it. Unmarried women, therefore, ran a high risk of detection in relation to childbirth. They were regularly forced to manipulate circumstances so that they could be alone at the time of delivery, even though this meant that they would be liable to charges of not calling for assistance in the birth. The most common way for them to do this was to feign illness so that they could retire to their bed or the privy or, alternatively, they fabricated a story about the need to go on an errand so that they could leave the household in which they worked or resided for a short period of time.[73]

For example, in 1726, when Isobell Stirling from Haddington realised that she was in labour, she became increasingly worried that her mistress and a fellow servant with whom she shared a room would discover her predicament. Consequently, she told them she was suffering from a stomach complaint and wanted to be left alone. When they offered to stay the night with her, she said she 'needed it not but preferred to lock the door and take the key inside with her for ease and quiet's sake'. The next morning Isobell's co-worker made the grim discovery of a dead baby amongst the bed sheets lying next to its mother. It had been strangled with a piece of blue ribbon.[74]

Margaret Stewart was indicted at the High Court of Justiciary in 1743, accused of infanticide. The court heard from a witness called Anne Brown, who testified to hearing a new-born baby's cries in the middle of the night. When she asked the accused about the noise and whether she knew where it had emanated from, Margaret initially told Anne that it had not been the sound of a new-born but the cry of an older child from the local neighbourhood. Dissatisfied with her response, Anne asked the question again. This time Margaret changed her story and said that Anne Brown was dreaming. Anne refuted this and pressed Margaret Stewart once more for a proper answer. Margaret eventually replied that the noise the witness heard was 'the cry of a cat'. Despite her denials and protestations, Margaret Stewart was arrested on suspicion of new-born child murder after an infant's remains were uncovered near to her residence.[75] In 1755, Isabella Buckham had the atypical experience of being a patient at a lying-in ward at St Bartholomew's Hospital. In the midst of her labour, she asked her nurse (Ann Smith) to go away and wash some linen for her and to get her a fresh bed pan. In the interim, Isabella delivered her child and quickly suffocated it with one of her petticoats.[76] In this instance, even the rare provision of maternal and neonate support was not enough to prevent an episode of infanticide. Time and again, we can see evidence from indictment material which emphasises the determination of unmarried mothers to manipulate their circumstances in order to ensure privacy at the moment of parturition. Clearly, they recognised that this was an essential component in their attempts at undetected infant disposal.

In addition to creating the necessary context for delivery, these women had to endure childbirth itself under exceedingly difficult and strained circumstances. The women were cognisant of the fact that their time for delivery was limited before suspicions were aroused. They knew that silence had to be maintained at all times, despite the pangs of labour, and they recognised that soiled linen and blood stains, in particular, had to be disposed of or explained away.[77]

Some historians have tried to suggest that, in a number of pre-modern cultures, and especially for women from the lower orders, childbirth was a relatively easy experience, as the individuals concerned were comfortable with the harsh realities of life. As Audrey Eccles argues: 'Sometimes the hardy Scots or the wild Irish were said to have almost painless labours: sometimes working countrywomen, sometimes whores and doxies, who being accustomed to brutality and harshness, set light the pain and peril of childbirth.'[78] Evidence from the confessions of women indicted for new-born child murder in the pre-modern period also suggests that some of the accused women enjoyed quick, painless and unexpected deliveries.[79] However, it is likely that these particular narratives were constructed in an attempt to negate the conditions of the early statutory provision for infanticide, by implying that labour had come upon the women concerned too quickly to allow them to call for timely assistance in the birth. In reality, unassisted birth must have been a terrifying experience and a painfully exhausting ordeal.

In addition to the silent endurance of labour pains and the actual physical strength and psychological determination required to self-deliver, an unmarried woman who had concealed her parturition also had to bring out her own afterbirth with care, she had to tie off the umbilical cord, she had to clean up the delivery area and dispose of all evidence relating to the birth and she then had to return to work as if nothing had happened.[80] This might be possible if the delivery had been straightforward. Adrian Wilson's work on difficult births in the pre-modern period indicates that varieties of childbirth obstruction (for instance presentations other than head-first) could cause serious problems during the delivery process.[81] In addition to this, minor complications, such as fainting, vomiting and tearing of the perineum, and major complications, such as 'flooding' (or haemorrhaging) and convulsions (known now as eclampsia), were all potential hazards that had to be overcome during delivery and were seen as critical to whether fatality occurred even when the birth was assisted.[82]

As Laura Gowing argues, the disposal of evidence from childbirth, in particular the disposal of the infant's body, 'posed a cultural and emotional problem as well as a practical one for the woman concerned'.[83] For many women who had concealed their pregnancies in the pre-modern period, the actual physical evidence of pregnancy must have made their circumstances, their plight and their desperation real for probably the first time since knowledge of conception had dawned upon them. The selection of the method and site of disposal was dictated by the specific circumstances in which the particular woman found herself, although often actions were improvised and thoroughness gave way to haste.[84]

Evidence of recent childbirth was discovered in a range of different locations during the pre-modern period, as is clear from witness testimony presented to courts across Europe at this time.[85] Sometimes women kept the dead bodies of their infants with them: either locked in a trunk in their room (as Anne Mackie from Tranent in East Lothian did in 1776), in the bed alongside them or hidden on their person whilst they returned to work.[86] More commonly, during the seventeenth, eighteenth and nineteenth centuries, however, bodies were disposed of in the privy or water closet. This was the case in the trials of Christian Russel at the Old Bailey in 1702 and Wenllian David at the Court of Great Sessions in 1752.[87] In part, women must have used this site because it was one of the few places where they could be afforded some privacy without creating too much suspicion.[88] Moreover, some women who had never mentally acknowledged or accepted that they were with child may have regarded the privy as an appropriate place for the disposal of something that had been a burden to them over a number of months: something that they regarded to be essentially non-human and merely waste-matter.[89]

Across Britain and Europe, luck was a significant factor in determining whether or not the evidence of a purported infanticide was discovered, as animals frequently dug up shallow graves (as happened in the case brought against Pembrokeshire woman Catherine Lloyd in 1798[90]) and bodies were often washed ashore, resulting in the initiation of formal investigations. Successful disposal was possible, but timing was the critical factor.[91] As Nella Lonza explains: 'The body should have remained undetected until all reliable clues based on its appearance (maturity, live birth, violence) disappeared and the woman's body bore no more signs of carrying a child.'[92] It was also crucial for the woman's self-preservation, as we have seen, that she returned to work or to any household duties as if nothing had occurred and nothing had changed in relation to her demeanour or appearance.[93]

If a woman was challenged to explain evidence relating to a suspected childbirth or the discovery of an infant's body or remains she usually denied it, often reciting and recycling the explanations proffered when she had been initially challenged with concealment of pregnancy. Thus, many women claimed that their colic had eased, that their menses had returned in abundance or that the obstruction that they had previously suffered from had been relieved.[94] Alternatively, some women claimed they had suffered an early abortion or miscarriage and that they had not known that they had been with child.[95] Usually, however, explanations such as these were mistrusted and regarded as a delaying tactic by the authorities concerned. The suspicions of the local community were not usually satisfied until a physical examination of some sort was carried out as the prelude to more formal investigative procedures, as we will see in due course.

Married women, accomplices and non-maternal suspects

So far in this chapter, we have examined the experience of unmarried mothers in relation to the concealment of pregnancy and childbirth. As part of this analysis, we have also seen how the network of surveillance associated with new-born child murder tried to break down the barriers of isolation associated with hidden conception and delivery. However, by attempting this in an aggressive and explicitly shameful manner, in practice these efforts often had the opposite effect. The solitary nature of infanticide was reinforced by the perceived necessity of self-preservation during the pre-hospitalisation era. Yet, we know from court testimony and indictment evidence in England, Scotland and Wales in the sixteenth, seventeenth and eighteenth centuries, that new-born child murder was a crime not solely committed by unmarried women nor indeed by women acting alone. Consequently, in the next section of this chapter, we will look at the wider participation in instances of infanticide during this era.

We saw in Chapter 2 that the specific nature of the legal directives within the original new-born child murder statutes made it very difficult for the authorities to accuse married women of this crime. The courts believed that married women could have no possible motive for concealing their pregnancies or killing their new-borns, so there was no need to include them in the statutes relating to infanticide or to make separate and distinctive provision for their actions.[96] It was assumed that married women would have no need to give birth in secret and, instead, would typically employ medical assistance of one sort or another when labour began and parturition was imminent. In turn, this would limit any propensity they had to infanticide and would lessen the chances of infant mortality due to self-delivery.

These assumptions explain why so few married women were charged with infanticide across Europe during the pre-modern period. For instance, in eighteenth-century Wales, 6 per cent of the 190 women indicted for new-born child murder were married and in Scotland between 1700 and 1820 the figure was less than 3 per cent of the 480 women accused.[97]

Married women were rarely suspected of infanticide and, indeed, it could be argued that, as a result, many women used their marital status as an alibi when foul play was suspected in relation to the death of a new-born child.[98] Certainly, infanticide by a married woman was hard to uncover and even harder to prove convincingly. Largely this was because the methods married women used to commit infanticide were more ambiguous than those regularly employed by spinsters and widows, as we will see in Chapter 4. As Katherine Watson explains, 'Married women... allowed their infants to die from neglect and passive cruelty... such cases were by their very nature difficult to detect.'[99] It is likely, then, that there were many more cases of new-born child murder committed by married women in the pre-modern period than is suggested by the available indictment evidence.

According to Dana Rabin, in relation to judicial opinion in eighteenth-century England, 'Infanticide by married women was considered so shocking and so unlikely that the only motive assigned to it was insanity.'[100] Other historians have suggested that the desire to limit family size was the key reason behind married women's infanticide in the pre-modern period. We saw in Chapter 1 that early civilisations and cultures practised infanticide in order to control the size and constituency of family structures, so perhaps it is not implausible to think that some pre-modern communities retained elements of these more 'primitive' attitudes towards birth control in the centuries before contraceptive aids were widely understood or readily available.[101] More commonly, however, historians have blamed the spectre of poverty, and its associated shame, for causing married women to dispose of their new-born infants in this era. Katherine Watson, in particular, has argued convincingly that families with lots of young children in the seventeenth and eighteenth centuries were at risk from chronic 'life-cycle' poverty owing to the need to feed, clothe and care for their offspring. Their situation would only be resolved when the children were old enough to make a contribution to the household economy or if charitable support was available to provide some means of assistance.[102] Some married women must have wanted to avoid the hardship that would inevitably result from the introduction of a new-born infant into a family that was already hard pressed to make ends meet.

One regular characteristic recorded amongst infanticide cases perpetrated by married women across Europe in the seventeenth, eighteenth and nineteenth centuries is that the offence was commonly committed by an accomplice.[103] Moreover, it is evident from various forms of evidence presented in court that even mothers who were solely accused of committing new-born child murder, were often helped by the support and actions of others. However, scholars have to look very carefully for examples of complicity of this kind. Judicial authorities were reluctant to expose the existence of accomplices as it very obviously negated charges of concealment, which were so central to indictments, and thus convictions, for new-born child murder during the pre-modern period. Once again, the limitations and prescriptive nature of the statutory provision for infanticide provided the courts with few options when faced with an accused who was anything other than the unmarried mother of the victim. Indeed, it was not until the second half of the nineteenth century that English courts recognised that infanticide could be committed by 'any person' and revised and consolidated its legislation accordingly.[104]

Prior to this change, the courts in Britain and across Europe struggled to find suitable charges on which to indict accomplices to infanticide. Some individuals were accused of 'harbouring an unmarried pregnant woman', others were charged with 'procuring an abortion' or 'accessory to murder', whilst in a few cases the accomplice was charged separately with 'wilful murder' or 'parricide'.[105] It seems that in the majority of instances, however, the accomplice was ignored, and only the mother herself was indicted under the provisions of the statute. This often occurred despite strong witness testimony and even hard physical evidence that the women had not acted alone. Accomplices rarely appeared in court to fully account for their involvement in instances of new-born child murder during the pre-modern period.[106]

Although formal indictments for complicity were uncommon, we can still glean information from the testimony of judicial witnesses regarding the characteristics, activities and behaviours of those individuals who aided women in the disposal of their new-born infants. Several historians have argued that men, particularly fathers of the infant victims, did not take a prominent role as accomplices in this sort of crime, as they had regularly fled from their responsibilities by the time of delivery so as to avoid the cost and the opprobrium associated with illegitimate parenthood.[107] However, fathers did get involved in infanticidal practices from time to time. In 1737, John Thomas was implicated as the father of the victim in an infanticide case which was heard at the Court of Great Sessions in. In 1752, William Nun was accused of aiding and abetting the infanticide of his child at the Old Bailey, along with his lover Grace Gates. In 1801, James Thomson was tried alongside his unmarried servant Margaret Whiggham for his part in the murder of her new-born son.[108] As accomplices, they were often involved in attempts to prevent the discovery of any wrong-doing, rather than being directly involved in the actual killing itself. Amongst other things, fathers helped to deny pregnancy in the first instance, they provided weapons to facilitate an infanticide, they covered for the woman at the time of labour and, perhaps most commonly, they assisted with the disposal of the body after delivery had occurred.[109] Witness evidence does indeed testify to this type of involvement, although collusion of this sort was largely ignored by the authorities and contemporary commentators, as the courts were unsure about how to deal with accomplices to the crime of infanticide. Instead they reserved their indignation for the mother of the victim alone.

A good example of the gendered attitude towards episodes of infanticide comes with the early seventeenth-century work *The Bloudy Mother*.[110] This famous piece recounts a series of 'inhuman murders' committed by an unmarried domestic servant called Jane Hattersley, which were carried out on numerous infants said to be 'the issue of her owne bodie'. The text itself solely concentrates on the actions and character of Jane. Yet, the frontispiece of the work (below) clearly depicts a man called Adam Adamson – Jane's master and erstwhile lover – helping her to bury one of the infants' bodies in the garden of his home. However, the piece gives no description of Adam's involvement in the crimes that occurred, or the attempts he made to hide the evidence after the fact. Clearly, his contribution to events and the degree of his culpability were considered largely unimportant and incidental by the contemporary author. We might not have known about Adam's

Figure 3.1 Frontispiece illustration from *The Bloudy Mother, or The Most Inhumane Murthers, Committed by Iane Hattersley* (1610). [Accessed from Early English Books On-line via: http://www.jischistoricbooks.ac.uk/Search.aspx.]

connection to the murders if it had not been for the wood-carved image which implicates him directly.

In other instances of complicity in the pre-modern period, accomplices to infanticide were family members directly related to the principal woman involved. Sometimes a father or grandfather of the woman helped to kill the infant or dispose of its body. For instance, at the Court of Great Sessions in Wales, a case was brought against Joseph Emerson who had tried to help his desperate daughter dispose of the body of her new-born baby.[111] More commonly, however, it was female relatives that came to the assistance of their kin, although they pointedly refused to admit so publicly or in court for fear of reprisals by association.[112] Mothers, grandmothers, sisters and aunts were often referred to where collusion was reported in witness testimony or in the few specific indictments laid against individuals for aiding and abetting new-born child murder. In 1754, for instance, Elizabeth Maddox was indicted for infanticide along with her mother Sarah Jenkins at the Old Bailey. In 1782, Margaret McDonald and her sister Florence McIntyre were jointly accused of the murder of Margaret's baby at a court in Inverness. And, in 1817, Eliza Cornwall was indicted alongside Diana Thompson for 'the wilful murder of a bastard child'.[113] Many of the women alleged to be accessories to infanticide were active participants, but the extent of their involvement and the degree of their complicity is difficult to glean from the piecemeal evidence available.

Midwives, too, on occasion could be implicated in the death of a new-born infant.[114] Usually, though, their involvement was more indirect in nature. It tended to transpire in instances where concealment of pregnancy had long been suspected and where at the moment of delivery a midwife had burst in on a woman trying to give birth in secret. In order to avoid a charge of complicity, the midwife might then have aided the woman in the latter stages of her delivery and then subsequently testified for the prosecution that assistance had not been called for prior to parturition if the child had not survived.[115]

From the limited evidence available, it is clear that, just like the women directly accused of infanticide in Britain and Europe in the seventeenth, eighteenth and nineteenth centuries, not all those suspected of complicity in this crime had deviant intentions in mind. Many of the men and women who attempted to help in instances of new-born child murder were desperately concerned about the future health and welfare of their young, typically unmarried, pregnant relatives. The hazardous nature of childbirth in the pre-modern period must have been recognised by contemporaries and may have resulted in individuals being inclined to assist their loved ones when labour pains took hold.[116] For other individuals, the menace of poverty, the threat of shame or a combination of these as repercussions of an illicit birth may well have been critical factors which motivated their collusion.[117]

In addition to accomplices, court evidence from the pre-modern period in Europe and the British Isles also provides us with examples of non-maternal suspects who challenge the orthodoxy that infanticide was a crime solely committed by young, unmarried women. In Scotland between 1700 and 1820, 23 non-maternal individuals were indicted for infanticide, and Nick Woodward notes a handful of similar cases which came to light in eighteenth-century Wales.[118] Although not substantial in number, from time to time individuals who had killed a new-born infant in direct opposition to requests of its mother came before the judicial authorities. Moreover, such an action had often taken place when an illicit pregnancy had been admitted or revealed by the woman concerned, thus exonerating her from accusations of concealment and enabling her to act as a witness for the prosecution.

Unlike the other non-traditional forms of infanticide that we have examined in this chapter, the courts were more certain of the charges which could be laid against those suspected of non-maternal infanticide. The individuals were accused of 'offering abortifacients to a pregnant woman', they were indicted for the 'murder' of the new-born infant, or they were charged with the 'assault with intent to murder' of the mother of the neonate.[119] Usually, the individuals who perpetrated this form of infanticide were the illegitimate fathers of their eventual victims.[120] Many of them desperately wanted to avoid the long-term financial burden of a child born out of wedlock or as a result of an adulterous liaison. Men committed infanticide in an attempt to conceal their illicit sexual activity from their wives and to preserve their reputation in the community in which they worked and resided.[121] These incentives appear to be particularly evident in a sensational and well-publicised case from the early eighteenth century, relating to a man called George Dewing, who was charged with the murder of his bastard child.

Dewing was keeper of the House of Correction at Halstead, in Essex. On 20 March 1728, he was indicted before Chelmsford Assizes for the murder of a bastard child begotten by him upon the body of one of his prisoners, a single woman called Susan Baldwin.[122] The court heard how Susan Baldwin was committed to the House of Correction in Halstead in May 1725 to serve a 12-month sentence for having had a bastard child, which the parish had taken from her and provided for. About 12 weeks into the sentence, George Dewing started to visit Susan on a regular basis, bringing her meat and other victuals which she described as 'better than ordinary'.[123] Dewing made it clear to Susan Baldwin at this time that he wanted to lie with her, but she resisted him, despite her growing fears of abuse and 'ill-usage'.[124] George Dewing grew impatient, however, and as Susan was the only prisoner in the House of Correction at this time, he knew he had ultimate control of the situation. Eventually, he threw Susan Baldwin to the ground and 'had carnal knowledge of her body'.[125] There was no-one around to hear Susan cry for help, nor anyone who could come to her rescue. In full knowledge of these circumstances, Dewing repeated his assaults upon Susan on numerous occasions over the ensuing months, until it became obvious to both parties that she was with child. Realising the potentially perilous nature of her condition, Susan Baldwin said to Dewing: 'You have done what you ought not to have done; I was committed here for Sin, and you have sinned with me, and ruined me. What you have done must be known.'[126] After this declaration by Susan Baldwin, Dewing abruptly 'fell out' with her, and he 'damned and cursed her in a very barbarous manner, whipping her very cruelly, several times, in order – as she believed – to make her miscarry'.[127] Yet, these abuses did not work and Susan felt herself quick with child.

About six weeks before the end of her sentence, George Dewing ordered her down to the whip-post in the gaol to be punished by Thomas Diss, the whip-man, in the presence of Dewing and Thomas Diss's daughter Judith. Both Thomas Diss and his daughter served as witnesses for the prosecution in Dewing's subsequent trial. Thomas Diss testified to giving Susan seven or eight lashes in punishment for a minor act of insubordination at the insistence of George Dewing. This happened despite Susan pleading with Dewing 'I am with child by you, and you know how long I have to go, pray do not whip me!'[128] This plea was entirely disregarded, however, and immediately after the punishment was concluded, Thomas Diss heard Susan Baldwin say that she was very unwell and in need of assistance. He then saw the body of a child fall from her on to the ground.[129] Judith Diss, Thomas's daughter, testified that she saw George Dewing 'take the child up in his hands'. 'That she saw the child alive and stir in his hands.' 'But that nonetheless he squeezed it very hard until its bones were crushed.'[130] After squashing the child's remains into a chamber pot, Dewing ordered Thomas Diss to throw it into the 'House of Office' (or privy), which he duly did. At this sight, Susan Baldwin cried out 'Murder' and then promptly collapsed at the whipping-post in front of her abusers.[131]

This case highlights various characteristics common amongst recorded instances of men having a direct and active involvement in new-born child murder in Britain during the pre-modern period. Broadly, these characteristics can be summarised as follows: First, the male protagonists were usually married (as, indeed, George Dewing was) and had engaged in an extra-marital relationship, which had resulted in an illegitimate pregnancy and which they had then desperately tried to cover-up.[132] Second, most of the infants killed by men were strangled. It is quite rare to come across bloodshed in an infanticide perpetrated by a male. This contrasts with infanticide undertaken by women, as we will see in Chapter 4. Thirdly, all of the male participants had a position of some social standing in their local community and committed murder to protect their status and to avoid the shame and embarrassment associated with fathering illegitimate offspring.[133] In this respect, men's motives for the committal of infanticide appear not wholly dissimilar to women's. Avoidance of the shame of illegitimacy was the critical factor involved, as will be discussed more fully in Chapter 6. The final common characteristic apparent from the evidence is one already alluded to in this chapter, the seeming reluctance to convict non-maternal suspects on charges of new-born child murder.[134] Although formal charges were more easily laid in these instances compared to episodes of complicity, the judicial authorities were still undecided about what verdict to give. Even in trials where men had confessed to the actual killing of a new-born, a not guilty verdict could still result. The difference with the case of George Dewing, of course, was that there were independent witnesses to the crime committed.

Perhaps for this reason, and arguably in the context of his role in the community as gaoler, public opinion against George Dewing was uniformly damning when news of his misdeeds came to light. The court proceedings, for instance, make clear the authorities' feelings towards Dewing, describing him as an 'unhappy and wicked wretch' whose 'ignominious name' should be 'drop'd into the lowest oblivion, and a detestable Triumvirate in wickedness would be made up of a Coke, a Wild and a Dewing'.[135] The local community also signalled their contempt for Dewing when he went on the run after his initial arrest warrant was laid. Groups of locals armed with pitchforks (described in the contemporary press as 'enraged mobs') went round all of the houses in Halstead to flush out Dewing, in an attempt to 'muzzle this wild Bear broke loose among them'.[136] Eventually, they cornered him in a public house whilst he was in the middle of a very dramatic, emotional and impassioned speech declaring his innocence to his wife (of whom Dewing seemed to be much more fearful than of any 'enraged mob').[137] This plea before his wife, as well as the one he was to make in court in his defence a few days later, fell on deaf ears. The weight of the multiple testimonies levelled against him served to convict George Dewing of murder and he was sentenced to death by hanging.[138]

So, what does this case tell us about non-maternal infanticide in the pre-modern period? Firstly, the case emphasises how important gender was in criminal proceedings. It could be argued that if George Dewing had been a woman convicted of this new-born child murder in 1728, he probably would not have lived to enjoy a pardon seven months later. At this particular point in history, capital convictions were fully realised and remissions were rare, as we saw in the previous chapter. The courts' confusion over how to deal with men who committed new-born child murder served to protect them from the full wrath of judicial authority in ways that women were not afforded. Secondly, this case, and others like it, highlights that childbirth and pregnancy were not solely the preserve of women. By looking at witness testimony in more depth, it is evident that men were concerned with pregnancy, birth and maternity in the seventeenth, eighteenth and nineteenth centuries. We need to know more about men's role in these matters and the criminal behaviour potentially associated with their involvement. Thirdly, the case also underlines the fact that in the pre-modern period shame and reputation were key imperatives for social survival and social advancement and, thus, averting opprobrium was potentially worth killing for. This avoidance of shame was a frequent motive in infanticide cases in the pre-modern period, and it seems that this was as true for men as it was for women. It is interesting that shame in this case (and arguably the ultimate destruction of George Dewing) was seen to be a product of illegitimacy and infanticide. Why did Thomas Diss not simply claim that Dewing whipped someone who did not deserve it? Or, that he mistreated his prisoners or was careless in his supervision of them?[139] The use of illegitimacy and child murder in an attempt to totally destroy an individual's reputation reflects the contemporary connection between shame and unmarried parenthood, and clearly emphasises the torment of many men and women who found themselves in this unenviable position in the pre-modern period.

Investigations, accusations and evidence gathering

When the remains of a new-born child were discovered, the find required detailed investigation regardless of the gender, character or status of the likely suspect, and whether or not accomplices were involved. These investigations were carried out by a range of different individuals, most typically co-workers, neighbours or relatives, and could not simply be passed over.[140] As Laura Gowing describes, 'The burial or disposal of a dead child's body usually took place secretly; the search that might follow was very often a collective drama.'[141]

There is some debate in existing historiography as to whether this 'drama' was played out more commonly in rural or in urban areas. Keith Wrightson and Ann Higginbotham, for instance, argue that the anonymity that a bustling city afforded unmarried women in the seventeenth, eighteenth and nineteenth centuries made it easier for them to hide the births and deaths of unwanted infants. They suggest that new-born child murder was more difficult to conceal in the countryside, as rural communities were more close-knit and, therefore, surveillance was more effective in detecting suspicious behaviour.[142] Conversely, Sjoerd Faber and Robert Malcolmson claim that the opposite scenario prevailed across pre-modern Europe. They maintain that it was the rural community which offered more favourable conditions for secret pregnancies, concealed births and undetected disposal of the evidence.[143]

In Scotland and the Republic of Dubrovnik, detected infanticide during the pre-modern period seems to fall somewhere in between these two arguments. Although there was no striking difference between the numbers of new-born child murders recorded in urban areas as compared to rural locations, there was a difference in the *way* in which the crime was discovered. It seems that in Scotland and the Republic of Dubrovnik, from 1600 to 1800, the nature of working and living arrangements, as well as the prevailing natural environment, meant that concealment of pregnancy was more likely to be detected in the countryside, whilst human remains were more likely to be discovered in the town or city. Consequently, most investigations in the countryside during this period were predicated on suspicions of concealment of pregnancy. In urban areas, on the other hand, an infanticide investigation typically began when an infant's remains were discovered.[144]

The discovery of physical evidence relating to a suspected new-born child murder gave credence to community suspicions over the physical condition of an unmarried woman.[145] A dead body transformed rumours into reality, and many of those individuals who accused a suspect of being pregnant were subsequently called upon to testify to the denials and excuses that they had formerly been given. These initial investigations into a suspected concealment and associated infanticide were typically carried out by officials at a local level, at least in the first instance. Community leaders and state authorities interviewed relatives, co-workers, midwives and neighbours in order to derive a short-list of suspected individuals.[146] The Church was often involved in the evidence-gathering process and in Scotland especially, as we have already seen, ministers were regularly at the vanguard of the rigorous enquiries that took place.[147]

Investigations into new-born child murder during the pre-modern period could involve multiple suspects and were certainly a collective endeavour. As Laura Gowing describes:

> In a way that the actual birth could never be... [the investigation] was a public event, uniting neighbours in a fraught and frightening enterprise. Secret pregnancies when they were discovered, ended in a drama that was the precise opposite of, and the substitute for, the public, acknowledged births of legitimate mothers. In cases like these, midwives and women worked not to help to separate mother and child through labour, but to reunite them after the child's death. The project of reuniting the mother and child, officially and eventually the law's responsibility, was a neighbourhood enterprise.[148]

It was also a highly invasive process for the suspect or suspects concerned.

In order to ascertain the likely guilt of a given suspect, the authorities in the pre-modern period sanctioned two forms of examination. The first of these was more psychological in nature, where the woman concerned was asked a series of robust and deeply personal questions regarding her physical appearance, her sexual experience and her recent whereabouts and activities. This was done in an attempt to procure a confession, which would speed up any subsequent judicial proceedings. Regularly, the authorities tried to pressure suspects to admit that they had hidden their pregnancies, given birth unaided, killed their offspring and subsequently disposed of the evidence. Sometimes these interrogations were carried out using threats, abuse and emotional torture, such as placing the dead body or remains of the infant directly in front of the suspect, in order to test her reaction.[149] In 1721, for example, the body of an unidentified dead child was found floating in a waterfall near Prestonpans in the south east of Scotland. A large number of local people gathered to witness the unfolding scene and the local minister proposed 'that the breasts of the unmarried women among the gathered crowd should be inspected and searched'. When a woman called Janet Hutchie was observed attempting to sneak off unnoticed, she was wrestled to the ground and her breasts were exposed, pressed and examined in front of everyone. Janet soon confessed that the dead child was her own.[150]

Regardless of whether or not a confession was forthcoming, a subsequent examination was carried out on those women suspected of new-born child murder in Britain and Europe during the pre-modern period. This second examination was more physical in nature and until the nineteenth century, when the process became routinely carried out by medical professionals, it was normally undertaken by midwives or local women with experience of childbirth.[151] The midwives were looking for the symptoms of a 'green woman', or to put it another way, they were looking for evidence that the woman concerned had recently given birth.[152] Through touch, and by force if necessary, women examined the genitals and the breasts of suspected individuals.[153] They looked at the size and colour of nipples, evidence of stretch marks on the abdomen and traces of postpartum bleeding.[154] The breasts were the particular focus of these investigations (as was evident in Janet Hutchie's case cited above) as it was believed that they were the key to establishing recent parturition. As Mark Jackson explains, 'the demonstration of milk in a suspect's breasts was taken to indicate that the woman had given birth to a full-term child'. As a result, midwives drew the breasts of suspects by squeezing them or sucking them in order to stimulate lactation in what must have been a terrifying, opprobrious and painful procedure.[155] Although the actions of midwives in this context were sanctioned by the multifarious authority given to them via the state, the Church and their local community,[156] arguably this kind of invasion could border on the prurient. For instance, in the eighteenth century, a German physician suggested that all unmarried women between the ages of 14 and 48 should be examined monthly at public baths in order to determine whether or not their bodies showed any signs of pregnancy.[157]

In addition to the examination of the suspect or suspects, the new-born victim was also inspected as part of the investigations. In the main, this scrutiny took place in order to determine the cause of death; a subject that will form the basis of the next chapter. The remains of the infant were also examined, however, in order to establish the viability of the birth and the maturity of the child upon delivery, to refute defence claims of miscarriage.[158] More specifically, with the limited medical knowledge which prevailed in the pre-modern era, the absence or presence of hair and nails as well as the size of the infant's body were seen as being particularly significant in determining whether or not the child had been born at full term.[159]

Across Britain and Europe in the pre-modern period, the evidence gathered from witness statements and from the examinations carried out on both the accused individual and the supposed victim were the basis upon which indictments for infanticide were laid. However, it is important to acknowledge that, even if the physical evidence gathered in relation to a given case was slight and inconclusive, if concealment of pregnancy and not calling for assistance in the birth were substantiated, the indictment would persist and a court case and trial procedure would ensue. Concealment of pregnancy was, without doubt, the dominant consideration in infanticide indictments and convictions could result in the absence of any other forms of proof, or in the face of evidence which pointed to the innocence of the accused in relation to murderous intent. Guilty verdicts could even result without the discovery of the dead body of a new-born child.

This chapter has shown that during the seventeenth, eighteenth and nineteenth centuries, new-born child murder was a crime which could involve a wider sphere of individuals than just unwed mothers. Nevertheless, as far as the judicial authorities were concerned, only single women and widows could have a motivation for committing this crime and so, in the main, they were the protagonists typically indicted. We have also recognised that infanticide was a crime that did not necessarily occur in isolation. Yet, in order to meet the conditions of the statutory provision for the offence, and especially the clauses relating to concealment, new-born child murder had to be presented and portrayed as a deviant crime perpetrated by individuals on their own, without the assistance, complicity or knowledge of others.

Concealment of pregnancy, and of the birth of a new-born child, was difficult to achieve in the pre-modern period without suspicion being aroused, but it was possible given the constraints of knowledge about conception and maternity at this time. Once a woman had decided to hide her condition from others, it was difficult for her to subsequently reveal her true status and instead, if it was to be 'successful', the concealment had to be maintained for the entire duration of the pregnancy, throughout her labour and after the child had been born and disposed of. However, the contemporary disdain for illegitimate pregnancies, which we considered in Chapter 2, meant that there was a high degree of supervision and surveillance of young single women. As a result, suspicion and gossip were rife in certain close-knit communities. This prevailing context of insinuation and intrusion may have added to the sense of isolation and desperation that some women felt in the face of unwanted pregnancies and may have limited the options they felt were open to them when the moment of delivery came.

Childbirth itself, whether assisted or otherwise, was certainly a 'dangerous journey' and a precarious process in the pre-hospitalisation era and it is surprising that the maternal mortality rate was not higher than is presently recorded for that period. Moreover, it is not difficult for us to imagine the pain and anguish of those women who delivered their new-born infants alone, in seclusion and in silence for fear of discovery. For some women, however, this task was too great and they called for the intervention and assistance of others to aid them in infanticidal practices, usually their close female relatives. Accomplices, by their actions, became accessories to the crime of new-born child murder, but it was relatively rare for state authorities to formally investigate the actions of anyone other than the mother of the neonate concerned. The exception to this was when non-maternal suspects were indicted for the murder of a new-born child. In the main, these protagonists tended to be the fathers of the eventual victims. As the case of George Dewing illustrated, the reasons for their involvement were not noticeably distinct from those of their female counterparts – they wanted to avoid the embarrassment and opprobrium caused by an illegitimate child, and they wanted to protect their character and status within the community where they worked and resided.

Local suspicions of deviancy and illicit behaviour were made reality when physical evidence relating to a new-born child murder was uncovered. This might be evidence relating to parturition or the discovery of the baby's remains. As the blame for new-born child murder was routinely and entirely laid at the feet of the suspected mother, it was she who had to endure the invasive and regularly brutal examinations which were conducted by midwives and local officials in an attempt to establish a relationship between the suspect and the dead child. Crucially, however, in instances where concealment of pregnancy could be substantiated, the accumulation of physical evidence was deemed only of secondary importance in determining whether an indictment should be laid.

Many unmarried women who gave birth during the pre-modern period might have felt that they had gone through their pregnancy and labour in isolation, but the reality was far more complex than this. The intricate surveillance networks present in communities across Europe during the seventeenth, eighteenth and nineteenth centuries were such that a woman in this position was rarely truly alone. Whether the presence of these networks affected attitudes to new-born child murder when it was discovered, or whether that was more connected with the way in which the crime was committed, will be the focus of the next chapter.

4
Monsters of Inhumanity?
Methods of Infant Disposal

> [It] is of a most shocking Nature... to destroy the Fruit
> of the Womb carries something in it so contrary to the
> natural Tenderness of the Female Sex, that I am amazed
> how ever any Woman should arrive at such a degree of
> Impiety and Cruelty, as to attempt it in any manner... it
> has really something so shocking in it, that I cannot well
> display the Nature of the Crime to you, but must leave it to
> the Evidence: It is cruel and barbarous to the last Degree.[1]

In this chapter we will investigate the different options open to women in
the pre-modern period who experienced an unwanted pregnancy. Although
new-born child murder constituted a significant proportion of recorded
female criminality, as we established in previous chapters, the offence was
not perpetrated on a wide-scale or on a regular basis.[2] Consequently, it
would seem safe to assume that the majority of women, who recognised
their condition, simply accepted their fate, bore their child – legitimate
or otherwise – and embraced motherhood and child-rearing, to whatever
extent their circumstances would allow. However, for some women maternity was not an option; we will explore the reasons for this in Chapter 6.

Before 1900, there was a variety of mechanisms by which women could
dispose of their unwanted offspring. These choices included interventions
during pregnancy, specific action employed during parturition or in the
immediate aftermath of childbirth, and postnatal strategies, adopted to
displace childcare on to a third party. I begin this chapter by looking at
the practices associated with the first and last of these categories, looking
at women's recourse to abortion, exposure, abandonment, wet-nursing and
baby-farming during the pre-modern period. I will then move on to look
more specifically at the methodologies specifically associated with new-
born child murder. In particular, this chapter will investigate whether the
women indicted for this offence were passive or active participants in the
crime of which they stood accused. Were the offspring of infanticidal women

typically killed by accident, deliberate agency or wilful neglect? Were weapons commonly employed? Was there a significant victim typology in new-born child murders at this time?

The final section of this chapter will address the complex problem of determining the cause of death in new-born infants in a pre-hospitalisation era. In suspected infanticide cases, medical experts were frequently asked to provide testimony on a range of issues: whether the victim was a viable or mature infant; whether the child had been still-born (that is, dead-born) or live-born; determining the means by which the victim had met its death; and reflecting on any evidence that could be gleaned from the infant's corpse with regard to 'marks' or 'signs' of violence. Over the course of the eighteenth century, in response to developments in medical knowledge, the infant cadaver gradually became more important than the body of the suspected mother in determining whether an indictment for new-born child murder should be laid. Moreover, the medical evidence associated with the methodology of new-born child murder was crucial in determining the fate of the accused, through its influence upon the verdict and sentence of the judicial authorities. The methodology of infanticide is, thus, of central importance to our understanding of this crime and how it was perceived by society in pre-modern Britain, Europe and beyond.

Strategies for avoiding maternity

Abortion

According to Rosalind Petchesky, 'throughout history and to the present day, even when effective methods of contraception are known, women have continued to rely on abortion. Among all fertility control methods, abortion has been the most persistent and the most prevalent'.[3] Anthropological studies have shown that knowledge about how to terminate conception is evident in most societies and, for Britain more specifically, the use of abortifacients is documented as early as the sixteenth century.[4] Despite this evidence, the practice of abortion was a hidden activity, largely due to the fact that the procedure and the repercussions from it were difficult to detect if conducted in the early stages of pregnancy.[5] For the early modern period, for instance, it is estimated that one in every two conceptions did not go to term. Miscarriages were common and, as a result, it remained exceedingly difficult for medical professionals, even as late as the nineteenth century, to distinguish been a natural and an induced abortion.[6] Many pregnancy terminations may well have occurred safely and without detection in the pre-modern period as, typically, abortions only came to light when disaster befell the proceedings (for instance, if the woman became ill or died) or when evidence of a mother's attempts to end her pregnancy was used against her to establish intent during infanticide trials. However, both of these scenarios were relatively rare occurrences.[7]

Perhaps because of the hidden nature of abortive practices, there is a fierce debate in the prevailing historiography over how common pregnancy terminations were before 1900. Lawrence Stone, for instance, has argued that no family planning of any kind existed before the eighteenth century, as people lacked both the means and the desire to control their fertility.[8] Christopher Wilson, in a similar vein, has suggested that the low level of English fertility in the early modern period was caused by long birth intervals via maternal breastfeeding, rather than recourse to contraception and abortion, and Nick Woodward has said that before the middle of the nineteenth century, abortion was 'unusual' in Britain.[9] John Keown, on the other hand, contends that abortion was in fact a common practice in England during the pre-industrial period and Linda Gordon maintains that abortion was employed far more regularly than infanticide as a means to end an unwanted pregnancy.[10]

Certainly, it is agreed that by the nineteenth century abortion had become more prevalent, at least in terms of it being brought to the public's attention. Patricia Knight, Angus McLaren and Francis Smith all describe abortion as becoming increasingly 'widespread' amongst the populace of Victorian Britain and it was a practice especially attributed to the working-classes and their 'flight from maternity'. This trend was seemingly apparent in other countries at that time too.[11] Whether this opinion was based on evidence of an actual increase in induced terminations or whether it was merely the by-product of contemporary concerns about a perceived upsurge in unlicensed abortionists is difficult to discern. Rather, it is more appropriate to contend that before 1967, when the state began regulating abortion and more consistent medical records were kept, it is almost impossible to comment on the frequency of abortion with any degree of precision.[12]

Yet, evidence to support the idea of abortion being more prevalent prior to 1900 than is commonly assumed comes from examining attitudes to its existence in the pre-modern period. According to Cyril C. Means Jr: 'During the late seventeenth, the whole of the eighteenth, and early nineteenth centuries, English and American women were totally free from all restraints, ecclesiastical as well as secular, in regard to the termination of unwanted pregnancies, at any time during gestation.'[13] It is clear from court records and judicial writings that abortion was never considered a serious legal offence.[14] Moreover, from before 1500, it was widely believed that an unborn infant did not possess a soul before the quickening (the moment when the mother first detects the foetus moving; typically 18–20 weeks into the gestational period).[15] Therefore, the termination of a pregnancy before 'ensoulment' was not considered sinful until the second half of the nineteenth century, when certain ecclesiastical figures declared that ensoulment began at the precise moment of conception.[16]

Abortion or 'abortment', as it was sometimes referred to, could either be artificially or naturally induced. From a more medical perspective, abortion was defined as: 'either the issuing of an imperfect infant or his extinction or death in the womb'.[17] Although, as we have seen, a deliberate abortion before the quickening was not considered a sin, it was commonly regarded by religious commentators as an 'evil' undertaken by 'bad women' and seen as something that was 'displeasing to God'.[18] More widely, however, abortion was regarded as an alternative or back-up form of contraception, especially when adopted in the early stages of pregnancy, and it was considered just one of many fertility control options available to women in the seventeenth, eighteenth and nineteenth centuries.[19]

In Britain more specifically, attitudes to abortion were similarly relaxed and tolerant for the most part of the pre-modern era. In Scotland, prior to the twentieth century, abortion 'was a common law offence with no strictly defined limits', which meant in practice that unless criminal intent could be proven there was no case to answer. Indeed, as long as the practitioner concerned could testify that he or she was acting in good faith in the interests of the health and welfare of the patient, the abortion was not illegal.[20] Similarly, in England, prior to the nineteenth century, the practice of abortion was a rarely prosecuted common law crime until Lord Ellenborough's Act of 1803.[21] This legislation made it a capital offence to:

> unlawfully administer to, or cause to be administered to or taken by any of His Majesty's Subjects, any deadly Poison, or other noxious and destructive Substance or Thing, with Intent such His Majesty's Subject or Subjects thereby to murder, or thereby to cause and procure the Miscarriage of any Woman then being quick with Child.

The legislation further enacted that, even if it was not proven that the quickening had taken place, it was a felony to cause or procure a miscarriage. In these instances, if found guilty, a culprit was:

> liable to be fined, imprisoned, set in and upon the Pillory, publicly or privately whipped, or to suffer One or more of the said Punishments, or to be transported beyond the Seas for any Term not exceeding Fourteen Years, at the Discretion of the Court.[22]

The reason for the introduction of this legislation at the beginning of the nineteenth century is unclear, though this was a period when modernisation of the law occurred. According to John Keown, there were three prevailing factors which explain the timing of the Act. The first was Lord Ellenborough's intention to clarify the legal position on infanticide, which had consequent implications for the judicial stance on abortion and wilful miscarriage.[23] In addition, there was a perception at the turn of the century that abortion was becoming a growing social problem in need of control, and that the existing common law provision was insufficient to suppress it.[24]

Finally, Keown points to the increased influence of medical practitioners on legislative concerns. Some doctors criticised the moral significance attached to the quickening, arguing that foetal life should be protected by the law at all stages of gestation. They also attacked illicit practitioners of abortions, who were untrained, unqualified and 'irregular competitors', during a period when medicine was becoming increasingly professionalised.[25]

The legal position on abortion established by Lord Ellenborough's Act was quickly seen as being too severe and, in addition, the wording of the Act was criticised for being vague and inadequate. Consequently, the law was refined in 1828 with the passing of Lord Lansdowne's Act, although these changes were in the main not substantive but rather semantic clarifications.[26] It was not until 1837, in the Offences Against the Person Act, that capital punishment for post-quickening abortion was abrogated.[27] The 1837 Act was also significant as it abolished the distinction between pre- and post-quickening interference through the clause:

> whosoever, with intent to procure the miscarriage of any woman, shall unlawfully administer to her or cause to be taken by her any poison or other noxious thing, or shall unlawfully use any instrument or other means whatsoever, with the like intent, shall be guilty of Felony, and, being convicted thereof, shall be liable, at the discretion of the Court, to be transported beyond the Seas for the term of his or her Natural Life of such person, or for any term not less than Fifteen Years, or to be imprisoned for any term not exceeding Three years.[28]

Although the 1837 Act made the administration of abortion a non-capital offence, the punishment provision was still fairly harsh. This remained the case in the last pre-modern legislation to affect the practice – the Offences Against the Person Act of 1861. In this set of revisions, both procuring an abortion and self-abortion became punishable by life imprisonment. Likewise, providing an individual with the means to commit an abortion was liable, upon conviction, to five years imprisonment.[29]

On the whole, the legislative changes relating to abortion prior to the twentieth century were largely concerned with controlling the burgeoning number of unlicensed abortionists thought to be prevalent in the conurbations of Britain, rather than controlling, or even condemning, those women who sought abortion.[30] The medical profession was increasingly aware of, and uneasy about, the encroachment and persistence of untrained midwives, lay practitioners and quack doctors, who were willing to perform illicit, secret abortions.[31] 'Barbarous' and 'unnatural' cases, such as that of the Derbyshire abortionist Eleanor Beare, who used an iron skewer to perform deadly terminations, were regularly reported in the *Gentleman's Magazine* in the eighteenth century, and investigative campaigns organised by the *British Medical Journal* into the practices of so-called 'professional abortionists' in the second half of the nineteenth century, seemed to support the contention that abortion had become a particularly dangerous enterprise.[32] As well as the obvious physical dangers associated with abortion, the practice was also problematic for unmarried women who were intent on concealing their pregnancies. In order to procure a termination, the woman concerned had to reveal not only her 'unfortunate' condition, but also her abortive intentions to at least a second party.[33] Despite these concerns, it is clear that women did resort to abortion in the period before surgical operations of this nature became routine and before anaesthetics, antibiotics and effective pain relief were available.

Women had a variety of reasons for choosing abortion over other methods of family limitation in the pre-modern period. Angus McLaren, for instance, has argued that psychologically it was preferable for a mother to use contraception or to terminate a pregnancy than to carry the baby to term and dispose of it afterwards, through active infanticide, abandonment or wilful neglect.[34] For unmarried women, abortion was seen as the most effective way to conceal a pregnancy as it removed all 'the irrefutable evidence that bastardy was in the process of occurring'.[35] Terminations were also used to protect clandestine relationships of one kind or another: in this respect, as well as others, abortion appealed to a broader spectrum of women over the eighteenth and nineteenth centuries, as married women adopted the practice.[36] As Angus McLaren explains, economic anxieties were of particular concern. He argues that abortion 'would be a solution for the married woman for whom the advantages of having an additional child were far outweighed by the disadvantages of loss of income, added expenditure, injury to health. The working woman's goal was still the traditional one of maintaining and protecting her family; abortion was merely one means towards that end'.[37]

Aside from income considerations amongst working women, women more widely adopted abortion as a recognised and acceptable tool by which they could limit the size of their families, or at least space out the intervals between births.[38] Abortion enabled women to have a degree of control over their fertility, and was regarded as advantageous since it could be conducted with or without the knowledge of a partner or spouse. Terminations were regularly employed as a back-up to other contraceptive methods, which in the period before 1900 were often odious, unreliable or simply ineffective.[39] Some women considered abortion to be a far cheaper and simpler alternative to the contraceptive measures available (for instance, the sheath was regarded as being too expensive and the douche was deemed overly-complicated), whilst other women engaged in terminations as a last resort in the midst of desperate or uncertain personal circumstances.[40]

Women in the pre-modern period were certainly knowledgeable about abortive techniques and procedures and were cognisant of the effects of abortifacients, through their discussions with other women.[41] Moreover, women at this time were aware of where they could access whichever means they had decided would work best to alleviate their 'situation'.[42] Women who had decided to terminate their pregnancies had a range of options. In earlier centuries, they undertook one or more of a range of peculiar practices including: magic spells; superstitious adornments, such as wearing a girdle made of snake-skin; bleeding of the feet and thighs; undertaking strenuous exercise, such as excessive dancing or the lifting of heavy objects; slamming stomachs into walls; tight lacing; and even deliberate provocations to incite domestic violence.[43] It was more common, however, for women to have recourse to herbal abortifacients, which were either consumed as a potion or inserted as a pessary or suppository.[44]

A vast array of herbal abortifacients was available in the early modern period, and their 'qualities' were widely known: indeed, such information was regularly published in contemporary recipe books.[45] The three most effective (due to their anti-oestrogenic properties) were known to be savin, ergot of rye and pennyroyal.[46] The effect of ingesting these herbal preparations was to act as an emmenagogue, restoring the menses by causing either 'violent bowel movements or violent vomiting. The idea seems to have been that the violence would loosen the foetus or weaken it so that abortion would occur'.[47]

Herbal abortifacients were the early precursors of the more modern pills and drugs which came to be widely advertised in the popular press from the eighteenth century onwards, when, according to Angus McLaren, abortion became commercialised.[48] These pseudo-medical 'treatments', as well as other widely recommended folk-based remedies such as alcohol and hot baths, stood alongside arguably more dangerous and invasive procedures, which used crude, rudimentary instruments, becoming the principal options for women seeking a termination in the period preceding the advent of modern medicine.[49]

The extent to which abortive measures were effective in the pre-modern period is unclear and is vigorously debated in the pertinent historiography. Generally, historians agree that abortion in the eighteenth and nineteenth centuries was a dangerous enterprise and something of a gamble in terms of the potential implications for the mother's health.[50] Certainly, there is plenty of evidence of unsuccessful abortions, where the patient either became ill as a result of a botched termination or went on to abandon the child or kill it during or after parturition.[51] There must also have been many other unrecorded instances where an abortion failed but the woman decided to keep the child and reared it normally. Yet, there is also testimony which supports the notion that abortion was far more successful in earlier centuries than has typically been assumed.[52] The true success or failure rate of attempted terminations in the pre-modern period can never be known because of the hidden nature of the practice, because disclosure was closely related to its failure, and because medical records of women's health experiences were rarely kept.[53]

Attitudes towards abortion in the pre-modern period are also difficult to discern from the evidence at hand, but seem to be diverse, ranging from both tacit and overt acceptance or regret that the provision was not more widely available, to vehement repugnance and objection.[54] We have already seen that, although abortion was not officially outlawed by the Church or considered to be sinful until the second half of the nineteenth century, the practice was nonetheless condemned by many contemporary moralists and medical practitioners, who were also critical of other forms of birth control.[55] Generally, however, attitudes to abortion seem to have been more tolerant in the pre-modern period than we might have expected, given the prohibitions of subsequent eras.[56] Prosecutions were rare and when they occurred, condemnation was reserved for the unscrupulous abortionist rather than the patient. Perhaps this partly explains why the number of women adopting this version of fertility control seems to have increased over the course of the nineteenth century.[57] Angus McLaren sums up many women's view of abortion prior to the twentieth century, when he says: 'The evidence all seems to support the notion that, though they appreciated the dangers of the practice, many regarded it as their right – should the situation demand – to have recourse to abortion.'[58]

Abandonment and Exposure

Another option open to women seeking to rid themselves of an unwanted child, for whom they would not, or could not, provide, was to abandon the infant, thereby exposing it to an indeterminable fate. The practice of infant abandonment can be traced back to ancient civilisations.[59] In the Classical era, however, abandonment was used very specifically as a means of population control by which children of complex or irregular parentage, supernumerary offspring and infants with physical or psychological impediments were deserted on a seemingly significant scale.[60] During the pre-modern period, although abandonment was applied to a far wider range of children in terms of their backgrounds and capabilities, it was more common amongst younger infants and new-borns and thus was regularly 'chosen as an alternative to outright infanticide'.[61]

For this reason, moralists and social reformers across Europe during the eighteenth and nineteenth centuries regarded infant abandonment as a serious problem, it was 'a barometer of the morality and health of working-class society' and 'was both a rural and urban dilemma [*sic*] that transcended geographical and national boundaries'.[62] However, abandonment (or exposure as it was more commonly referred to in that context) was not an offence regularly prosecuted at common law. Strenuous efforts to track a suspect down were only made if the child had not survived its desertion, and these investigations were inherently problematic owing to the anonymous nature of the practice and the associated difficulties of conclusively linking a particular woman to a discovered infant.[63] Exposure was very much regarded as a hidden crime during the pre-modern period and it may well have made a significant contribution to the so-called 'dark figure' of unrecorded criminality at that time. Certainly, indictments for exposure were never very numerous, especially in Britain. For instance, Leah Leneman and Rosalind Mitchison only record 78 cases of infant abandonment amongst the 8,429 instances of illegitimacy that came to light in their records of seventeenth and eighteenth century Scotland, and Nick Woodward uncovered just two cases of infant abandonment in his survey of Welsh infanticide between 1730 and 1830.[64]

Despite the low levels of prosecution for infant exposure, we know that the practice was still condemned, tracked and recorded by contemporaries concerned about the cost that abandoned infants imposed on communities.[65] Although, on occasion, moral concerns were voiced about the practice (for instance William Gouge described women who abandoned their offspring as 'unnatural and lewd' in the early seventeenth century[66]), it seems clear that economic anxieties overshadowed all other fears concerning this practice during the pre-modern era. Indeed, it could even be argued that an abandoned infant found dead or dying was in some instances more 'welcomed' by certain authorities than an infant which had survived, owing to the immediate and on-going financial burden that would ensue from the care and upkeep of the orphan concerned.[67] Perhaps this attitude, along with the anonymous nature of the offence, explains why more individuals were not prosecuted in fatal episodes of infant exposure. Nevertheless, although exposure may have been under-reported in the courtroom, the evidence we have from contemporary commentators has enabled historians to point to the 'staggering dimensions of infant abandonment in European history',[68] and to conclude that the practice occurred on a substantial scale, in the eighteenth and nineteenth centuries in particular.[69]

The reach and scope of infant abandonment seems to have been significant in the pre-modern period and some historians have convincingly argued 'that more newborn children were abandoned than were victims of infanticide'.[70] By the middle of the nineteenth century there was concern across Europe that infant abandonment had reached epidemic proportions.[71] In Britain, this concern was most obviously manifested in clause 27 of the 1861 Offences Against the Person Act, which clarified the legal position on exposure for the first time. This section, entitled 'Exposing Children whereby Life Endangered', states:

> Whosoever shall unlawfully abandon or expose any Child, being under the Age of Two Years, whereby the Life of such Child shall be endangered, or the Health of such Child shall have been or shall be likely to be permanently injured, shall be guilty of a Misdemeanor, and being convicted thereof shall be liable, at the Discretion of the Court, to be kept in Penal Servitude for the Term of Three Years, or to be imprisoned for any Term not exceeding Two Years, with or without Hard Labour.[72]

The timing of this legislation was probably not a reaction to a significant increase in infant abandonment in nineteenth-century England *per se*. It was rather a reflection of wider European and local concerns about the spiralling costs of caring for orphans and foundlings, as well as the first phase of a burgeoning contemporary preoccupation with the protection of infant life. This resulted in more specific legislation in the ensuing decades, as we will see in due course.[73]

The methods of infant abandonment and exposure in the pre-modern period were fairly straightforward. The most common practice was simply to leave the child in a place where it was likely to be discovered, such as the steps of a church or the porch of a well-to-do household.[74] On other occasions, it might be argued that the place where the child was dropped was more indicative of an intention that it should not survive, but rather it should die from exposure to the elements or be eaten by wild animals, in a form of 'delayed infanticide'.[75] Consequently, the motivation of mothers who deserted babies on hillsides, in woods and at the side of the road seems less certain than that of those who left their children in locations where they were more likely to be found.[76] Clearly, however, in either scenario, the fate of the infant was, at best, unpredictable and precarious.

Although the act of infant abandonment seems to have been relatively simple, the practice was still hazardous for the mother concerned and, on occasion, she would have to elicit assistance.[77] Certain conditions had to be in place in order for an infant abandonment to succeed undetected. As Robert Malcolmson explains:

> To abandon a baby a mother had to be able to carry the infant some distance from her residence, and she had to be prepared to keep the baby alive until she was ready to move from her place of delivery. And these were two important conditions which many women – particularly servant maids – could not have accepted: they could not risk the baby's cries, which would quickly attract attention, and their circumstances of service would usually not have allowed them the time or the excuse to leave the house at their own pleasure and safely abandon a living baby.[78]

The inherent problems associated with infant abandonment during the pre-hospitalisation period, in particular, were recognised by contemporaries across Europe, and resulted in a belief that individuals would resort to active infanticide in increasingly greater numbers, as no dedicated provision was available to support those women carrying unwanted pregnancies.[79]

The common answer to this moral dilemma was to protect infant life by making abandonment easier to commit, through the introduction of foundling hospitals. Foundling hospitals were established in some cities as early as the Middle Ages, the first being built in Milan in 787.[80] More generally across Europe, however, the foundations of this provision were laid in Italy from the sixteenth century onwards,[81] in France from the seventeenth century[82] and in England, Ireland and Russia from the early to mid-eighteenth century.[83] Many foundling hospitals were equipped with a *'tours d'exposition'*: a revolving door or turntable where children could be left anonymously to be cared for by the municipal authorities. As René Leboutte describes, 'the mother... could place the child on one side, ring a bell, and have a nurse take the child by turning the table, the mother remaining unseen and unquestioned'.[84] Moral, social and religious campaigners believed that the setting up of these homes, and the provision of the turntable system, would result in unwanted children increasingly being deposited in safety, rather than being killed immediately after birth by direct infanticide or prolonged exposure.

Certainly, foundling hospitals were established in many principal cities during the pre-modern period, and their more sustained introduction in the eighteenth century accounts for much of the rise in recorded abandonments from that time until the early 1900s. In the Dublin Foundling Hospital, for instance, annual admissions increased on average from 546 in the 1730s to 2,152 by 1780.[85] In the equivalent institution in London, 2,523 children were admitted between 1750 and 1755 rising to a substantial 16,326 between 1756 and 1760.[86] More widely across Europe, Alysa Levene estimates that by the mid-nineteenth century, 'around 120,000 infants were being abandoned annually in Europe, with nearly 35,000 of these in Italy, more than 30,000 in France, 15,000 in Spain and 15,000 in Portugal'.[87]

The plight of foundlings in England was first highlighted by Joseph Addison, writing in *The Guardian* newspaper on 11 July 1713:

I shall mention a Piece of Charity which has not yet been exerted among us, and which deserves our attention the more, because it is practiced by most of the Nations about us. I mean a Provision for Foundlings, or for those Children who for want of such a Provision are exposed to the Barbarity of cruel and unnatural parents. One does not know how to speak of such a subject without horror: but what multitudes of infants have been made away with by those who brought them into the world and were afterwards ashamed or unable to provide for them! There is scarce an assize where some unhappy wretch is not executed for the murder of a child... It is certain that which generally betrays these profligate women... is the fear of shame, or their inability to support those whom they give life to... This is a subject that deserves our most serious consideration.[88]

However, it was not until the well-respected retired sea-captain Thomas Coram took up this initiative, and engaged in twenty years of persuasion and negotiation with the government and society notables, that the foundation of London's Foundling Hospital was agreed in 1739. The key tactic that

Coram employed to sway public opinion was to send a petition outlining his case to the elite and titled women who resided in and around London. In this document Coram explained that:

> Whereas among the many excellent designs and institutions of charity, which this nation and especially the city of London has hitherto encouraged and established, no expedient has yet been found out for the preventing the frequent murders of poor miserable infants at their birth; or for suppressing the inhuman custom of exposing new born infants to perish in the street; or putting out such unhappy foundlings to wicked and barbarous nurses, who undertake to bring them up for a small and trifling sum of money, too often suffer them to starve for the want of due sustenance or care; or if permitted to live, either turn them into the streets to beg or steal, or lure them out to loose persons... For a beginning to redress so deplorable a grievance, and to prevent as well the effusion of so much innocent blood... and to enable them, by an early and effectual care of their education to become useful members of the commonwealth, we whose names are underwritten, being deeply touched with compassion for the sufferings and lamentable conditions of such poor abandoned helpless infants,... and for the better producing of good and faithful servants from amongst the poor and miserable cast off children or foundlings... are desirous to encourage and willing to contribute towards erecting an hospital for infants.[89]

The London Foundling Hospital finally opened in 1741 and catered for the abandoned children of the metropolis, as well as infants from further afield whose mothers had travelled to the capital to relieve themselves of their 'unfortunate burden'. The hospital did not employ a turntable or a revolving door, but instead invited individuals to bring children to the hospital with no questions asked, as long as the infant concerned was less than two months old and was free from disease.[90] In 1756, a few years after the hospital had moved into new surroundings, a more open-house policy was introduced, and children were no longer screened for sickness or infection. This period of 'general reception' saw the numbers of foundlings abandoned increase markedly, and in the first week of this new policy some 229 children were left in the hospital's care.[91]

We have already noted that the victims of infant abandonment in the eighteenth and nineteenth centuries tended to be new-borns, and it was rare to find an exposed child who was more than a year old.[92] We can also say, with a fair degree of certainty, that there was no marked preference of one gender over another in the victims discovered at this time.[93] This contrasts with infant abandonment in earlier periods, where evidence suggests that girls were more commonly exposed than boys, for a variety of economic and cultural reasons.[94] In addition, it is clear from the evidence of foundling home records that it was not only illegitimate infants that were abandoned to these. For instance, approximately 30 per cent of infants abandoned at the London Foundling Hospital in the second half of the eighteenth century were legitimate children, a figure which is not only reflective of the scale of the number of children abandoned but also emphasises the diverse and multifaceted nature of the motives behind resorting to this kind of infant disposal.[95]

The large numbers of infants put into the care of foundling hospitals was the prime cause of the nineteenth-century concern about the costs of caring for abandoned children.[96] This factor alone was enough to convince society that foundling hospitals were inherently problematic, and they largely fell into disuse over the course of the later decades of the nineteenth century.[97] In addition to economic anxieties, however, concerns were voiced in the mid-Victorian era that, whilst these homes might have reduced the incidence of infanticide, conversely, they were a potential encouragement to illicit sexual relations and illegitimate pregnancies, as women across Europe had access to the foundling home provision and thus an easy remedy to their shame.[98] Finally, and more importantly, commentators were alarmed at the significant mortality rates evident in foundling institutions, arguing that, in effect, foundling homes were merely delaying the act of infanticide and deputising for the murderous actions of the infanticidal mother.[99]

In the London hospital, the period of 'general reception' caused a significant rise in the institution's infant mortality rate, from 45 per cent beforehand to 81 per cent during the initial post-1756 period, although the situation was recovered via tighter controls in the decades after 1760.[100] Although between 1741 and 1799 'almost two thirds of entrants did not survive their time at the hospital',[101] in general terms, the London institution's mortality rate was far better than other institutions on the continent, owing to the fact that before and after 'general reception' the hospital had stringent health screening practices in operation.[102] The quality of care and standard of cleanliness in other European foundling hospitals was abysmal, to the extent that abandoning a child to one of these institutions was increasingly seen as being 'tantamount to a death sentence'.[103] For instance, of the 3,558 infants abandoned at Rouen's Foundling Hospital between 1782 and 1789, only 482 survived infancy.[104] As Keith Wrightson demonstrates, 'Institutional neglect by well-intentioned but overburdened and under-financed charitable institutions made what was probably the largest single contribution to infanticide in pre-modern [*sic*] Europe....'[105] For many Europeans in the eighteenth and nineteenth centuries, abandonment and infanticide were indistinguishable and interchangeable.

How do these facts relate to the intentions behind infant abandonment and exposure? Why did women resort to this form of indirect infanticide? Certainly, some of the women who risked the hazards associated with infant abandonment must have had murderous motives in mind when they exposed their babies naked, without shelter and in a location where they were unlikely to be discovered.[106] On the whole, the women who undertook this type of deliberate exposure were the most desperate. Typically, they were unmarried mothers who were anxious to keep their pregnancy and parturition a secret, and they risked much in their attempts to avoid all association with their new-born offspring.[107]

Infant abandonment amongst married women was probably more closely related to pressing economic concerns, rather than any consideration of shame. The overwhelming majority of women who left their infants at the London Foundling Hospital in the eighteenth century, for instance, used 'a rhetoric of need' in the petitions they submitted in the hopes of getting their child admitted to the institution. Married and single women alike offered up explanations such as 'low circumstances', 'great distress', 'poor state of health', 'incapacity to work', an 'inability to get the bread', and emphasised their general struggle for survival in their attempts to garner support.[108] Through their actions, many of the women involved in exposure were simply attempting to shift the responsibility for their maternity, the upkeep of the child and the circumstances of its ultimate fate on to others.[109] As Brian Pullan points out in relation to early modern Europe: 'by abandoning a child to a hospital you could kill it with a good conscience' whilst at the same time avoiding an allegation of infanticide.[110]

It is likely that many of the women who chose infant abandonment over either abortion or new-born child murder had a complex range of reasons, very particular and commonly private to the individual woman concerned, for selecting this option.[111] Nevertheless, historians agree that on the whole, the women who gave over their children to 'the kindness of strangers' probably had good, humane intentions for the future of their offspring. They probably acted in good faith, believing that their infant would be better off taking its chances with public welfare, rather than enduring the impoverished, miserable and regularly ignominious childhood that would be its fate if it remained in maternal care.[112] On the whole, mothers were probably unaware of the fact that the very high mortality rates in foundling institutions across Europe meant that the death of their infant was only slightly delayed, rather than prevented altogether, by their decision to opt for abandonment. The fact that some women expressed a desire to reclaim their child when their personal and economic situation improved is further evidence of a lack of murderous intent within the specific context of institutional abandonment.[113]

Wet-Nursing and Baby-Farming

Wet-nursing can be defined as the 'breastfeeding of another woman's child either in charity or for payment'.[114] The practice has a very long history and can be found in all civilisations since antiquity.[115] Wet-nurses were employed in three contexts in the pre-modern period. The first was their use by wealthy women. As early as the medieval period it was noted that mothers often preferred not to breastfeed because they were too delicate, too haughty, too vain, or did not want to suffer the inconvenience. For this reason, it became fashionable amongst elite women to employ live-in wet-nurses, whereas poorer women were more likely to suckle their own children.[116] Another reason for the employment of wet-nurses by women of means was the widespread belief that breastfeeding had a contraceptive effect. Although still debated today, the use of prolonged lactation as an ovulation-inhibiting tool, by which a woman can lengthen her intergenesic intervals, was routinely cited as medical fact across Europe from the sixteenth century onwards.[117] Consequently, in elite families, the husband did not want his wife to breastfeed as he was anxious for her to become pregnant again and add to the lineage of the family.[118]

The second, and most significant, context in which wet-nurses were used links to the previous section of this chapter: significant numbers of nurses were employed by foundling hospitals, especially in the eighteenth and nineteenth centuries. When a healthy new-born infant was admitted to the hospital, he or she would only stay there for a few days before being taken to a wet-nurse (usually in the countryside), with whom they would live until they were at least four years old. At that point, or perhaps when they were older, they would return to the foundling institution to be raised and to receive a basic education. The foundling hospitals paid these women for their services, and, as a result, thousands of women offered themselves as surrogate mothers.[119] There is evidence to suggest that, on occasion, women abandoned their new-born infants at foundling hospitals with the deliberate intention of reclaiming their baby as its wet-nurse. This meant that the hospital paid these women to look after their own child.[120] Certainly, the financial benefits of this employment were great, to the extent that many wet-nurses turned over their own children to be weaned by others, so that they could increase their earnings by taking on more than one foundling. Wet-nurses employed cheaper counterparts to provide them with childcare and wet-nursing for their own children.[121] This third context in which wet-nurses were employed illustrates the complex matrix of pseudo-maternal support and out-nursing that developed and extended across pre-modern Europe.[122]

The financial rewards of wet-nursing were substantial in comparison to most other available employment for women in the pre-modern period, especially for those women taken on privately by wealthy families.[123] Women who worked for foundling institutions benefitted from a regular, monthly cash wage which was higher when weaning was taking place and lower thereafter, but which could last over several months.[124] Valerie Fildes describes wet-nursing as 'the second oldest profession', after prostitution: it was one key way in which women could make ends meet in the pre-modern period.[125]

The selection criteria for wet-nurses were more stringent for private, live-in nurses than for out-nurses. For instance, in the eighteenth century, wealthier families tended to want younger nurses who possessed 'sweetness of breath, good general "appearance" and strong teeth that indicated blooming health'.[126] The women also had to have good personal hygiene habits. Nurses with freckles, moles and red-hair (said to be the sign of a fierce temper) were to be avoided, and the quality of the available milk (which was examined for viscosity, taste, colour and quantity), as well as the size of the nurse's breasts were seen as essential elements that influenced the selection process. 'Overly large breasts were regarded suspiciously' and, in general, medium sized but prominent breasts were preferred over 'long', 'sagging' ones.[127] By comparison, foundling hospitals varied in how rigorously they vetted the nurses in their employment. Some countries (such as Italy) required a letter confirming the good moral standing of the woman from a parish priest, alongside evidence of their lactational status, which was attained through a physical examination. In the main, however, the only real criteria the majority of foundling nurses had to meet was that they could prove rural residency, away from the corruption and disease of the city.[128]

The lack of scrutiny of foundling nurses meant that the practice grew in scale across Europe in the pre-modern period, with some organised systems of wet-nursing in place as early as the fourteenth century.[129] Despite the popularity of the occupation, the demand for nurses exceeded supply, especially during the eighteenth and nineteenth centuries, when 'it was practiced on such a scale that it can be classed as a cottage industry' at that time.[130] However, as time wore on, wet-nurses and the foundling homes which employed them came under close scrutiny as a consequence of the relationship between the nature of care provided and the mortality rates of new-born infants.

We have seen in this chapter that, in the nineteenth century in particular, foundling institutions came under attack due to their poor standards of care and hygiene. Wet-nurses were also heavily criticised for their substantial contribution to an infant mortality rate which, according to some historians, was as high as 75 per cent of all infants nursed in some European countries. In the main, this high death rate was said to be directly related to incapability, neglect and malpractice on the part of the nurses concerned.[131] Some overly ambitious wet-nurses, for instance, took on too many new-born infants (as many as seven per nurse have been recorded) and ran out of their own milk, which meant that they had to turn to other options, such as animal milk or rudimentary artificial (or dry) feeding products, often with disastrous consequences.[132] Other nurses simply neglected their responsibilities and the infant died from a lack of care, sustenance and attention.[133] Increasingly, wet-nurses were seen as a source of ghastly contamination, as it came to be understood that not only could nurses infect their charges with diseases (especially syphilis), but it was believed that they could also transfer unwanted physical and temperamental traits to the infant via their breast milk.[134] As a consequence of this contemporary opinion, it was increasingly argued that mother's milk was best and that wet-nurses should only be resorted to if a mother could not sufficiently provide for her child.[135]

Further criticism of wet-nursing suggested that (as with foundling institutions) the profession condoned immorality and illicit sexual behaviour, as it provided a relatively simple alternative to maternity for unmarried women who found themselves pregnant. Moreover, for some commentators, wet-nursing acted as an incentive to irregular pregnancy and even infant disposal. For instance, there is anecdotal evidence which indicates that some unmarried women were deliberately getting pregnant in order to ensure that they possessed the physical qualities necessary to be a fully-paid wet-nurse – principally the ability to lactate over prolonged periods.[136] These women then neglected the care of their own infant, passed it on to a cheaper nurse to be weaned or abandoned the child. In this way, and due to its growing association with the spread of disease, wet-nursing was increasingly seen as a catalyst for infant mortality and a prop to infant abandonment.

By the middle of the nineteenth century, particularly in England, attitudes to wet-nursing had become antagonistic and hostile, and the practice came to be described as 'heartless', 'inexcusable', and a 'Great Social Evil'.[137] As one English nineteenth-century tract put it: 'What with laudanum, gin, bad air, dirt and neglect, the wonder is, not that the lamb of the poor man's household flock often dies, but that it ever lives... the act of engaging a wet-nurse seems almost the same as signing a death warrant....'[138] Yet, there is some evidence that historical and contemporary portrayals of the wet-nurse are largely inaccurate and have been exaggerated.[139] For instance, if we consider that some foundling hospitals (such as the London institution) routinely inspected the standard of care provided by wet-nurses and offered them financial bonuses if the nursing was of a particularly high standard, then it would seem illogical to simply assume that the vast majority of wet-nurses were unscrupulous characters who would neglect their responsibilities. Rather, it was in their interests to do a good job.[140] As Alysa Levene points out, 'There is relatively little evidence for nurses neglecting or mistreating foundlings' during the eighteenth and nineteenth centuries.[141] Of course, this is not to say that malpractice did not occur, but rather to suggest that a range of different factors were likely to have contributed to the high mortality rate of foundlings in the pre-modern period, and the standard of nursing was just one possible cause of infant death.[142] Moreover, it is impossible to generalise about the nature of new-born childcare in the eighteenth and nineteenth century, as experiences were many and diverse.

The extent to which wet-nurses were involved in deliberate infanticide in the pre-modern era has been debated by historians, and opinion remains divided. However, the intentions of a variant of these nurses, commonly known as baby-farmers, are consistently condemned in modern historiography. Baby-farmers, or infanticidal nurses, were women who were paid by parents or guardians to take on babies (both legitimate and otherwise) to nurse on the understanding that once the child was delivered to the nurse's care, it would not be seen again.[143] As Keith Wrightson explains, baby-farmers 'at best provided poor nourishment and at worst tacitly guaranteed a child's early death'[144] through direct infanticide or wilful neglect.

Baby-farming was a practice which involved the boarding and care of infants in return for money. Some baby-farmers 'adopted' children for lump-sum payments on a permanent basis. Others cared for infants in return for periodic financial contributions. The practice was said to be widespread and, during the nineteenth century in particular, it became established in Britain's main cities, ports and manufacturing districts.[145] The true extent of the practice is difficult to gauge, as it was arranged through a clandestine system of newspaper adverts, anonymous cash payments, fake identities and covert child transfers.[146] Moreover, the associated practice of 'baby-sweating' where a nurse 'looked after' a series of infants in quick succession (when one died they took in another and earned a fee for doing so each time) also complicated matters, as the high turnover of 'patients' meant that it was exceedingly difficult to trace the eventual fate of these children.[147]

Keith Wrightson describes baby-farming as 'a system of veiled infanticide': by its very surreptitious nature, a hidden practice. As a result, the total number of infant victims of the practice is difficult to assess, although one study has estimated that the figure for mid-Victorian England may have been in excess of one thousand infant deaths per annum, and that the mortality rate in some baby-farms was as high as 90 per cent, with fatalities being markedly higher amongst illegitimate babies.[148]

Although baby-farming no doubt existed for generations, it was only brought to the British public's attention during the second half of the nineteenth century, when it was variously described as 'organised villainy', 'the darkest, most ghastly shame in the land', 'cold-blooded cruelty', and a 'vile trade'. One baby-farmer was denounced as 'the undertaker for the unwanted baby's death'.[149] Indeed, at that time, baby-farming was regarded as far worse than infanticide, because the perpetrator was not the mother of the victim, and thus had only callous economic motives for the murder.[150] There were several reasons why the practice of baby-farming became such a *cause célèbre* in mid-Victorian Britain: the importance of family life became a central theme of contemporary writings, with associated calls for a return to the centrality of motherhood and the need to protect infant life; linked to this preoccupation were concerns over the maternal practices of working-class women, in particular, and the necessity of providing them with better education and support in their childcare experiences; in addition, there were arguments from medical men who became increasingly anxious to introduce measures to reduce infant mortality in an era when their profession was becoming increasingly formalised and regulated;[151] and finally, evidence came to light that baby-farming was not only widespread in Britain, but that demand for the 'service' was on the rise.[152]

Several well-publicised baby-farming cases came to light from the 1860s onwards, which, in the era of new journalism and heightened press sensationalism, resulted in a sustained moral panic about its prevalence. The principal court cases in question were those brought against Charlotte Windsor (1865), Margaret Waters and Sarah Ellis (1870), Sophie Todd (1877), Jessie King (1888), and Amelia Dyer (1896).[153] As a consequence of this burgeoning interest, a series of investigations were conducted and reported in the *British Medical Journal* and other publications in the late 1860s. Their findings pointed to a 'fatal trade' which was 'doing a brisk business' and implied that all paid nursing of infants seemingly pointed to infanticide, by neglect and by more direct means, on a significant scale.[154] Although there was a great deal of hyperbole and generalisation in these publications, their impact on contemporary perceptions was significant.[155] Take, for instance, the desperate description of a baby-farm given by one English investigator at this time:

> It was the back room of a tumble-down labourer's cottage, scarcely fit for a coal place, about twelve feet square. Crouching and sprawling on the floor, in their own excrement was two of them. Two were tied to rickety chairs, one lay in a rotten bassinet. The stench of the room was so abominable that a grown man vomited on opening the door of it... In bitter March, there was no fire. Two children had a band of flannel round their loins; one had a small shawl on; the rest had only thin, filthy, cotton frocks. All were yellow, fevered skin and bone. None of them cried, they were too weak... There was not a scrap of children's food in the house. In a bedroom above was a mattress, soaked and sodden with filth, to which they were carried at night, with two old coats for covering. All the children's clothes in the place were the handful of rags they wore. And a man and his wife sat watching them die of filth and famine, so making their living. It was their trade... These five weary creatures were all removed into restorative care: all injured for years; some for life. Two never recovered and died in hospital.[156]

Popular contemporary concerns about baby-farming resulted in attempts to regulate how childcare was administered, chiefly through legislative change and the introduction of the Infant Life Protection Act in 1872. Initially stringent proposals for a rigorous system of registration and inspection of childcare facilities were rejected, and instead the Act proposed a more diluted system of essentially *voluntary* registration, without inspection, alongside stipulations that all births and deaths in lying-in institutions were to be recorded, as were the names of individuals who accepted payment to care for infants for longer than one day.[157] The Act was criticised by contemporaries for being weak, ineffective and 'a pompous introduction to next to nothing'[158] because it did not apply to baby-farmers who routinely rid themselves of their charges in less than twenty-four hours and because it was too costly and difficult to enforce in practice.[159] Thus, high profile baby-farming cases were still being prosecuted over twenty years after the Act was passed. Early feminists also denounced the Act's blanket approach to short-term childcare, arguing that it would cause chaos for married working women who depended on this type of provision. They also pointed to the Act's negligence in not doing more to extract financial assistance for unwed mothers from their erstwhile partners, which would enable them to care for their children properly and not resort to illicit practices, such as baby-farming, wet-nursing, abandonment or worse.[160]

Critics maintained that the Act did little to curb deliberate infanticide of this nature and called for tougher legislation so that crucial intercessions could be made. As Benjamin Waugh complained: 'We have just raised a baby in England to the rank of a dog, we now need to raise it to the rank of a sixpence. To obtain money under false pretences, that is felony; to obtain a baby under false pretences, that must be felony too.'[161] Yet, further change was slow in coming and when it occurred, was more related to the prevailing socio-economic and cultural conditions of the times, rather than direct state intervention, as we will see in Chapter 7. In the interim, baby-farming and wet-nursing seem to have continued relatively unchecked in Victorian Britain.

The methods of new-born child murder

The methods associated with the more 'direct' forms of new-born child murder in the pre-modern period were certainly varied. It is important to note that historians maintain that there is little evidence of the kind of gender-targeted infanticide that existed in earlier civilisations. Rather, in the seventeenth, eighteenth and nineteenth centuries, male and female new-borns were the victims of infanticide in equal measure.[162] Where dissent between historians does arise, is in regard to the general way in which this crime was committed: was infanticide a passive or active crime? As Marilyn Francus asks: were infanticidal mothers docile or rebellious?[163]

On the whole, historians agree with Laura Gowing, who observes that, during the pre-modern period, infanticide was 'understood to be a crime not of violent activity but of passivity and neglect'.[164] Rather than adopting more overt forms of violence, it seems that child murder, in England at this time, was carried out through more 'peaceable' or 'docile' means, such as overlaying or forms of asphyxia such as suffocation.[165] Certainly, married women intent on committing infanticide were more likely to resort to neglect of care as a *modus operandi*, as it was essentially undetectable.[166] In addition, the seemingly more temperate methods said to prevail fit well with the traditional notion that female offenders south of the Tweed (and indeed elsewhere in Europe) were largely passive actors in criminal activity; a consideration which has recently been challenged.[167]

Figure 4.1 shows the mix of approaches adopted by the individuals accused of new-born child murder in Britain during the eighteenth century.[168] Although many historians point to the prevalence of 'passive' methods amongst instances of infanticide, the evidence in this figure does not substantiate that contention. This is for two reasons. Firstly, when historians have seen suffocation listed as a cause of death, they have rarely investigated further to see what type of suffocation took place.[169] For instance, did the baby die from accidental suffocation or was there evidence in the indictment, such as linen, soil or straw having been found stuffed deep into the oral cavity of the infant (as was the case in the indictment brought against Lucy Drake at the Old Bailey in 1750, for instance[170]), which would suggest a more deliberate act of child murder?[171] This kind of detailed investigation makes it possible to distinguish accidental suffocations from deliberate ones, although as we will see in the next section of this chapter, determining the cause of death in instances of new-born child murder was fraught with difficulty during the pre-modern period, and thus, only conclusive evidence of deliberate suffocation was admissible. The second reason why passive methods are not as well represented as we might expect is that practices such as neglect, overlaying and accidental suffocation were the hardest for the authorities to detect and, therefore, may well be under-represented in recorded instances of new-born child murder – although it is clear, from the

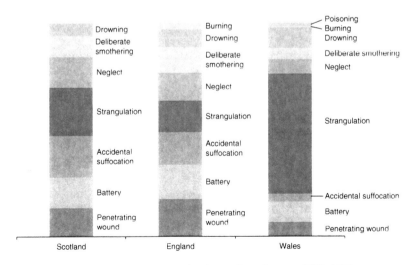

Figure 4.1   Methods in known cases of infanticide in Britain, 1700–1830

Scottish evidence at least, that prosecutions for this kind of 'passive' practice could still be undertaken in the face of ambiguous evidence.[172]

The most common method employed in the recorded instances of infanticide in all three countries shown in Figure 4.1 was strangulation. However, this *modus operandi* is probably the most problematic. The evidence to substantiate an indictment of suspected strangulation was typically the discovery of marks of violence around the infant's neck. However, such marks can be explained by either the umbilical cord being wrapped around the child's neck or by the difficulties associated with self-parturition. As we will see, it was almost impossible for medical experts to determine whether an apparent instance of strangulation had been carried out with deliberate intent or not, and, as a result, the suggested prevalence of this kind of new-born child murder should be considered and interpreted with a great deal of care.

If we exclude strangulation charges from our data series, it is evident that 'active' methods (battery, burning, deliberate smothering, drowning and receiving a penetrating wound) outnumber the more 'passive' approaches (accidental suffocation and neglect) in all three geographical areas. In Scotland 66.8 per cent of cases involved 'active' methods and 33.2 per cent were 'passive'. In Wales, the figures were 76.3 per cent and 23.7 per cent respectively. In the English series the results were closer, with 56.3 per cent of known cases involving 'active' methods and 43.7 per cent 'passive'. The apparent prevalence of more actively interventionist types of infanticide is perhaps not surprising, given that the evidence in these instances was more certain, more likely to lead to discovery, and thus prosecutions were easier to effect. However, we should not pass over these findings too readily, given that they not only challenge the historiographical perceptions of the methods of new-born child murder, but they also challenge the notion that women were not active agents in criminal activity in the pre-modern period.

The criminologist Carol Smart explains that, in general, 'Violent offences... do not appear to be reconciled with the traditional conceptualisation of feminine behaviour. Murder and other violent acts against the person appear to be the complete antithesis of the gentle, retiring role of the female sex.'[173] Yet, in relation to indicted infanticide, women did engage in forms of overt violence. Drownings and burnings only made up a small proportion of this type of recorded activity, battery (or assault) and attacks with sharp instruments of one kind or another were far more common.[174] Nonetheless, once again we need to remember that some of the injuries sustained could have occurred as a result of the difficulties associated with self-delivery or due to negligence in the aftermath of parturition.

The individuals who more obviously violent assaulted new-born babies in pre-modern Britain regularly used weapons. These included implements such as knives, razors, axes, pitchforks, rakes, lances, cudgels or clubs, scissors, nails and needles (typically used to pierce the brain, genitals and/or eyes). Babies were also thrown from windows, flung over cliffs and hit off inanimate objects such as trees and the side of buildings. Sometimes common household goods or items of clothing were used in attacks, such as candlesticks, irons, pokers, buckles, shoes and clogs.[175] To give some more specific examples: in pre-modern Scotland, for instance, Marion Dalgleish stabbed her new-born son to death with a pair of shears near Edinburgh in 1703; Highland-woman Jean Black battered her baby to death with a spade in 1747; Helen Munro dismembered a neonate with an axe in 1763; and, in 1818, Margaret McLaren from Perth slit her infant's throat with an open razor.[176] In England, during the long eighteenth century, Ann Armor was indicted for infanticide for having fractured her new-born baby's skull after throwing it into a 'house of office' or latrine where it received a mortal bruise on the side of its head; in 1737, Mary Shrewsbury was accused of killing her child through attempted decapitation using a knife; in 1774, Jane Cornforth used a nail to rip open the stomach of her new-born child, thus exposing its bowels and intestines, resulting in its immediate death; and in 1809, Elizabeth Tomlin admitted to having squeezed and forced her alive new-born baby's body into a pipe within a water closet.[177] In Wales during this era, Mary Robert from Pembrokeshire forcefully dashed her baby off the ground several times, which occasioned its death, in 1766; in 1793, a woman called Margaret Evans from Montgomeryshire battered her new-born infant to death with a brick; in Carmarthenshire in 1802 Gwenllian Richard stabbed her child repeatedly in the throat with a knife; and in 1818, Ann Jones from Breconshire placed her baby in a pot of water which was boiling on the fire.[178]

The selection of a weapon in these instances tended to be opportunistic rather than pre-determined and depended on what was available when parturition occurred. In this respect, the weapons used in new-born child murder in the pre-modern period may simply be a reflection of the social setting within which the crime took place or may be related to the occupation of the accused. For instance, women involved in food preparation may well have been more likely to use a cutting instrument that they used on a daily basis, rather than something unfamiliar and alien to them.[179] In those instances where overt violence was the undisputed cause of a new-born child's murder, the wounds inflicted were regularly numerous, severe, extreme and seemingly unremitting. This seems to have been especially the case amongst Scottish women indicted for violent infanticide, who were far more likely than their erstwhile Welsh and English sisters to shed blood when killing neonates.[180] A typical example of this would be the case of Anne Morrieson, which was brought before the High Court of Justiciary in Edinburgh on 4 December 1758. Anne was an unmarried servant who worked for an Edinburgh lawyer called James Stewart. She had not been in Mr Stewart's service long when suspicions were aroused that she was with child. Upon being questioned about her condition, however, Anne denied her pregnancy, claiming that she had merely put on weight after the unexpected cessation of her menses. A few months after she had issued these denials, Anne appeared to have returned to her former lean size and shape and when questioned about this by the local authorities, Anne eventually directed a search party to the body of a new-born infant, which was found in a cornfield near her master's house, wrapped in a linen cloth. According to bystanders who witnessed the grim discovery, the infant had been murdered 'in a most wicked, inhumane and unnatural' manner.[181]

Upon a more detailed examination by surgeons Thomas Young and James Hay, and based on multiple witness testimonies that were provided in court, it was established that the child 'was wounded and hurt in several parts of the Body... after having been battered and then attacked with a pair of scissors'. The court heard the catalogue of injuries that the child had received: 'the nose was cut off... the throat was much bruised... the skull and spine crushed to oblivion... the arms, legs and thighs stabbed in several places... and... the right eye was pierced through to the back of the head.' In all, it was estimated that the baby had sustained at least sixteen wounds to its body. The wound through the eye socket was most likely to have been the fatal blow.

One question that remains unanswered in relation to the methods used in new-born child murder is why did some women resort to violent methods when arguably more covert, non-violent techniques may well have been easier to achieve, more difficult to detect and less likely to result in a conviction owing to the ambivalence of the evidence? The tentative answer to this relates to the conditions and environment in which the crime took place. Almost all of the women indicted for 'active' forms of infanticide were young and unmarried: they had concealed their pregnancies and were attempting to give birth in secret. For this reason, many of the women may have been caught unawares by their labour, being inexperienced in such matters. When parturition was over, a woman might have thought, in her panicked-state of mind, that violent methods were the quickest way by which to terminate the life of the child and to stifle the new-born infant's cries, which, after all, were probably the most significant threat to her actions being discovered. Moreover, as has already been indicated, some women may have used methods which were familiar to them from their occupations. For instance, many women in the pre-modern period were scarcely unused to using knives and other implements to kill chickens, rabbits and other forms of livestock in the course of food preparation. Indeed, one Radnorshire woman, Ann Price, who was indicted for new-born child murder at the Court of Great Sessions in Wales in 1809, had allegedly dislocated the neck of her new-born infant by mimicking the way she slaughtered poultry prior to defeathering.[182] Perhaps some women seamlessly transferred occupational skills they had acquired to the context of infant disposal, and even believed that they would remain undiscovered nonetheless, because the corpse and its associated evidence could be readily concealed after the fact if they acted quickly.[183]

Anne Morrieson confessed to having murdered her child and was sentenced to death by hanging, followed by public anatomisation and dissection on 7 March 1759 at Edinburgh's Grassmarket. In Anne's case the extreme levels of violence that she seemingly employed were probably enough (alongside a detailed confession) to seal her fate, although the prosecution's evidence that she had previously given birth to another illegitimate child which also did not survive infancy, probably did not help her cause.[184]

Anne Morrieson's indictment was widely publicised amongst eighteenth-century Scottish society. The case was reported twice in *The Caledonian Mercury* newspaper during the course of the trial proceedings in January 1759 and details of her execution were reproduced in other national publications later that year.[185] In addition, her penitent confession on the scaffold was reproduced as a broadside 'as a warning to all young Women, and others', whereby Anne repented by saying 'the Devil taking all Opportunities to deceive the Ignorant engaged me early into his Services... I acknowledge myself a great Sinner, and much given to that of Uncleanliness, which has brought me to this shameful and untimely end'.[186]

The public's reaction to an episode of infanticide, just like that of the judicial authorities, was regularly determined by three factors: how the crime had been carried out, the extent to which premeditation could be established and, crucially, whether the cause of death was obvious or certain. The last of these three criteria was probably the most difficult to establish, especially in an era where medical appreciation and understanding of obstetrics, gynaecology, neonatology and paediatrics was in its infancy, and it is to that subject that the final section of this chapter is dedicated.

Determining the cause of death in neonates

From the seventeenth century onwards, one of the key factors in trials for new-born child murder was the evidence given by medical experts. We saw in the last chapter how testimony relating to the physical signs of parturition was regularly provided in court. From the eighteenth century onwards, however, the focus of judicial attention shifted from interest in the medical condition of the accused, to interest in the forensic pathology of the victim. Normally, in the pre-modern period, a conviction for new-born child murder could only result if the cause of the infant's death was certain and obvious.[187]

New-born infants were particularly vulnerable during the pre-hospitalisation era, and this was especially the case if they were illegitimate.[188] Historian Ann Higginbotham has claimed that medical experts may have exaggerated the extent of infant mortality in the pre-modern period, as 'this was one area in which they could demonstrate the social benefits of their technical expertise at a time when medical practitioners were seeking wider recognition and professional status'.[189] However, in relation to Britain in the eighteenth and nineteenth centuries, there is enough evidence to support the claim that the infant mortality rate, amongst new-borns at least, was considerable. Moreover, it is evident that the high level and wide scope of the mortality rate for neonates persisted for a long period, at least until the 1930s.[190]

A wide range of factors could cause the death of a new-born child in the pre-hospitalisation era; 'wasting diseases' such as atrophy, want of breast milk, debility, marasmus (severe protein–energy malnutrition), injury at birth, congenital defects and prematurity were the most commonly listed causes of fatality during this time. These were followed by 'diarrhoeal diseases', including enteritis and gastritis, and then 'respiratory disorders', like pneumonia and bronchitis. Seizures and convulsions also killed a fair number of new-borns, but this kind of description was regularly used as a blanket term to cover a range of underlying causes, such as acute indigestion, teething and gastritis. The more common infectious diseases, such as measles, smallpox, diphtheria, scarlet fever and whooping cough, were more common amongst older infants than neonates during the pre-modern period.[191] In instances of infanticide, it was up to medical experts to determine whether one of these factors was the cause of the baby's death or whether foul play was involved.

Medical opinion was not routinely asked for in legal trials during the early modern period, with the exception of infanticide trials, where, due to the wording of the early statutory provision, medical opinion was necessary in order for an indictment to be laid and subsequently proven.[192] In England and Wales, this necessity was normally provided by a Coroner's inquest, which grew in prominence over the course of the eighteenth century. In Scotland, this type of pre-trial inquiry was not employed; instead, medical experts were called as witnesses during criminal trials brought against infanticide suspects.[193] However, the growth in importance of medical opinion in the courtroom from the 1700s onwards was not necessarily helpful in expediting judicial process. This was because the medical evidence presented, especially in relation to episodes of new-born child murder, was frequently inconclusive and often perceived to be unreliable.[194] As Kristin Ruggiero explains, 'Infanticide was the crime par excellence for the difficulties it presented to forensic medical experts.'[195] Part of the reason for the ambiguous nature of the testimony provided related to the individuals providing it. As the eighteenth-century Scottish anatomist and physician William Hunter explained in 1783:

> Many of our profession are not so conversant with science as the world may think; and some of us are a little disposed to grasp at authority in a public examination, by giving a quick and decided opinion... To form

a solid judgment about the birth of a new-born child, from the examination of its body, a professional man should have seen many new-born children, both stillborn, and such as had outlived their birth a short time only; and he should have dissected, or attended the dissections of, a number of bodies in the different stages of advanced putrefaction.[196]

Hunter's opinions were echoed by other medical men from the pre-modern period, such as the English surgeon Christopher Johnson writing some thirty years later:

medical practitioners frequently fail in the performance of their duty when examined in criminal cases, not from professional ignorance, or want of zeal, but solely from the novelty of their situation, and never having considered the subject in that particular point of view which is necessary to elucidate the doubts of a court of law... [thus] Child-murder... is particularly interesting, on account of the great difficulties in which it is involved, and on account of the erroneous opinions in regard to it.[197]

The medical men called as experts in infanticide cases in the eighteenth and early nineteenth centuries clearly had varied experience of forensic pathology. The post-mortem techniques they employed also varied, as until 1788 there was no comprehensive guide on how autopsies should be performed.[198] This meant that forensic testimony was often problematic, and some infanticide trials, such as that of Jane Lyall who was indicted at the Old Bailey in 1800, were dismissed owing to the medical evidence being deemed unsatisfactory and inconclusive.[199] Even today, determining the cause of death in neonates is often difficult to ascertain and may remain obscure.[200]

Testimony from medical practitioners may not have been certain or accurate in the pre-modern period, as suggested earlier in this volume. Nonetheless, the courtroom accepted that, as their medical knowledge was superior to the average person, they should be given an acknowledged status as experts. This prominence was not afforded to other witnesses.[201] Moreover, in many instances, the uncertainties raised by the testimony of medical experts were in fact welcomed by the courts of Britain in the pre-modern period. As Mark Jackson outlines:

First, they served to undermine the strength of neighbours' accounts of maternal negligence and murder. Secondly, they provided a legitimating rationale for acquitting women accused of this crime. In this way, the courts could mitigate the severity of the law by steering a middle course not only between the conflicting accounts of events offered by suspects and their accusers, but also between the rigours of the law and emerging humanitarian concerns.[202]

This attitude must go some way to explaining the low conviction levels for infanticide and concealment trials in early modern Britain which we saw in Chapter 2. We will return to these issues in relation to developments in the Victorian era in Chapter 5.

Over the course of the eighteenth century, the corpse of the new-born infant became the key piece of evidence in trials for new-born child murder.[203] In the main, as we will see, the pathology of the cadaver itself was the main evidence presented to the courts. However, the infant corpse could contribute to court testimony in another way too, through a practice called cruentation (sometimes referred to as the 'bier test'). This was when a corpse was presented to the individual accused of its murder to see what kind of reaction would be forthcoming. As Katherine Watson explains, 'Standard procedure called for the suspected murderer to approach the dead body, call it by name, walk around it two or three times, and stroke its wounds. Evidence of guilt was revealed if during the process fresh bleeding occurred, the body twitched or foam appeared at the mouth.'[204] In reality, however, the reaction of the suspect was far more important to observers than the reaction of the corpse, and cruentation was typically employed in order to extract confessions from suspects in eighteenth-century Britain and beyond.

The value and significance of the evidence an infant cadaver could provide to court proceedings depended on how soon it had been discovered and where the body had been located. In cases of new-born child murder, if there had been a lapse in time between birth and discovery to the extent that decomposition had begun or if the body had been placed in a location which would speed up that process or affect the state of the cadaver's presentation (such as a privy, latrine, sewer, field or animal pen), then, in those instances, medical deliberation was meaningless, as determining the time and cause of death was almost impossible.[205] These locations were the most popular sites for the disposal of dead infants in pre-modern Britain, and this may well have made a significant contribution to the difficulties medical experts encountered when examining infant corpses. Take, for example, an English infanticide case from 1762, where an unmarried woman called Ann Haywood was eventually acquitted of murdering a male neonate whose body was discovered in an outside privy belonging to a lying-in hospital. Due to the conditions prevailing where the corpse had lain, 'fermentation' had occurred over a very short period of time to the extent that the surgeon called to court could not provide any conclusive testimony as to how and when the baby had died.[206]

Essentially, medical experts of the pre-modern period had to answer five questions in their deliberations over the forensic pathology of new-born infants alleged to have been murdered: Had the child been born alive? Had the child had a separate existence from its mother when it died? Had the child been viable and mature at birth? What had caused the child to die?

And, if marks of violence were detected on the infant's corpse, what was their precise cause? Evidence relating to all of these points (either independently or collectively) was often presented by defence lawyers and by women accused of new-born child murder in Britain during the eighteenth and nineteenth centuries. Women did this in an attempt to prove their innocence, to elicit sympathy from the authorities, to avoid charges of premeditation or to get indictments reduced from an initial allegation of infanticide, parricide or child murder to one of concealment of pregnancy alone, which would result in a more minor penalty being inflicted upon conviction.[207]

The most common defence strategy employed in trials for new-born child murder was to claim that a foetus had been born dead. The number of still-births which occurred in Britain during the pre-modern period is difficult to calculate, since they were not registered in England and Wales until 1927 and in Scotland until 1939.[208] Nonetheless, from the evidence we do have, it seems that still-births were not as common as we might expect, accounting for less than 4 per cent of all births in studies of neonate mortality from 1750 to 1870.[209] A variety of signs were acknowledged by medical experts as being indicative of a live birth. These included the baby's cries, the apparent warmth of the child's body and the distinctiveness of its first bowel movement, where meconium was typically ejected.[210] In other instances, where the infant was clearly non-responsive or deceased, medical experts could also examine the hands of the child concerned. As explained by a midwife in an infanticide case against a Hertfordshire woman called Ann Mabe in 1718, 'a Child that is new born, if alive, came into the world with its hands expanded, but if dead, with its hands clenched'. In Ann Mabe's case her female child had been born with clenched fists and she was accordingly acquitted.[211]

The most commonly used test for still-birth in the pre-modern period was also the most controversial – the lung test or hydrostatic test. This test had its origins in the seventeenth century and was first put to practical use in an infanticide case in Silesia (part of the Habsburg Empire) in 1682, although it was not until the eighteenth century that it became a regular feature in trials for new-born child murder in Britain.[212] Essentially, as Mark Jackson describes, 'The test involved removing the lungs of a new-born child to see if they floated in water. In theory, if the lungs floated, it was assumed that the child had breathed and had, therefore, been born alive; if they sank, it was supposed the child had been stillborn.'[213]

Although the lung test was widely used by the British courts, particularly in the eighteenth century, it was not without its critics. Contemporary medical men increasingly argued that the test was flawed and that the scholarship behind the procedure was nothing more than 'scientific humbug'.[214] In particular, it was established that the lungs could be adversely affected by the gases of decomposition, by attempts at resuscitation or even brief respiration. Since there was no standard procedure for the implementation of the test, the results gleaned from this experiment clearly should be regarded with caution, if not outright scepticism.[215] As one correspondent to *The Gentleman's Magazine* put it in October 1774, in reference to the lung test, 'although it may sometimes prove true, upon the whole it should be regarded no other ways than as a very uncertain and precarious proof on the fact in question'.[216] This was certainly how the courts began to see the test from the second half of the eighteenth century onwards, where allegations of infanticide, such as that brought against Sarah Russell in 1782 and Joanna M'Carthy in 1802 at the Old Bailey, were dismissed after prolonged legal debate regarding the validity of the test's findings, which one surgeon condemned as 'worthless' and 'inconclusive'.[217] The unreliability of the lung test resulted in alternative experiments being introduced during the nineteenth century, such as the weighing of the lungs and the examination of other internal organs to check for independent functioning, but all of these were equally discounted, so that determining whether or not a child had been born alive remained problematic in trials for new-born child murder right through to the modern era.[218] Even in the present-day, without more conclusive alternatives, the lung test is still employed in neonate autopsies, albeit with due caution and consideration of its limitations.[219]

Establishing that a new-born child had existed separately from its mother before it had died was an important consideration in both English and Scottish law during the pre-modern period. Technically, unless a child had been completely expelled from its mother (excluding the umbilical cord and placenta) it had not been born and therefore could not be the victim of a murderous act.[220] Therefore, if an infant had been killed during the process of parturition and before complete expulsion had been achieved, then its mother could not be guilty of infanticide. In addition, if a child breathed or cried during parturition but had died before being completely expelled then, legally at least, it was born dead. The hydrostatic test would be unhelpful in the latter instance, as because the child had breathed, however temporarily, the lungs were likely to float even though a still-birth had occurred. Consequently, proving separate existence in the pre-modern period was just as problematic as proving whether or not the child had been born alive.[221]

Establishing whether or not the child was delivered prematurely was probably slightly easier for medical experts to ascertain than some of the other deliberations they had to make in the seventeenth, eighteenth and nineteenth centuries. Many women at this time used miscarriage and preterm parturition as a defence in trials of new-born child murder, claiming that they had been delivered unexpectedly (without aid) and that their offspring did not constitute a fully developed infant.[222] The maturity and viability of the child was established by medical experts who examined the size and bulk of the neonate, as well as whether it had hair, fingernails and toenails.[223] If a discovered corpse was small and had none of these characteristics it would be deemed still-born and the indictment would be dismissed.

Trying to establish the precise cause of death in a discovered neonate corpse was very challenging in the pre-hospitalisation era. Crucially, it was difficult to determine whether death had been caused by active infanticide or passive neglect. Although the former was certainly regarded as more culpable than the latter, prosecutions could still result if an individual simply took no action to save the life of a new-born that they knew to be in jeopardy, regardless of the reason for this.[224] In the absence of marks of violence on the corpse of the child concerned, medical experts tried to determine the extent to which a suspect could be culpable for the death of a new-born in relation to the evidence that the child's corpse presented to them. However, as each infant and each case was different, this was a lot to ask, even of professional men.[225]

One aspect of potential postpartum neglect that was often noted in the courtroom was whether or not the umbilical cord of the infant had been ligated properly, so as not to cause a mortal haemorrhage. For instance, in the trial of Sarah Hopkins for new-born child murder in 1767, the court heard how the navel-string of the victim had been broken off too close to the navel rendering it impossible to tie-off securely and as a result the baby would only have lived for a minute or two before it bled out.[226] It would seem that many new-born infants died during the pre-modern era because their mothers (exhausted from the process of self-delivery) were unable to tie the umbilical cord off properly, or were unaware that such a procedure was even necessary in order for the infant to survive.[227] The fate of the suspect involved often depended on whether or not the medical and judicial authorities regarded ligating the cord as a natural and instinctive thing for a mother to do, or whether they believed it was something that had to be taught. For this reason, there was often a very fine line between culpability and innocence in instances of new-born child murder where umbilical haemorrhage was cited as the cause of death.

Although medical experts, judicial authorities and public officials often placed a lot of weight on the presence of marks of violence on the body of an infant corpse, such evidence could also be misleading and inconclusive. Certainly, there were instances where no other explanation than murderous intent could be advanced for the cause of death, for example in episodes of burning or in some brutal and repeated assaults where the infant was battered to death. On these occasions, evidence of marks of violence undermined all other evidence presented in defence and would usually result in the conviction of the accused.[228] More commonly, however, there was ambiguity around the precise nature of marks of violence uncovered on the body of a new-born child, and medical experts had to be careful to ensure 'that they distinguished between unintentional and intentional damage during and just after birth'.[229]

Take, for example, the case brought against Elizabeth Jarvis for infanticide at the Old Bailey in 1800, where extensive legal debate ensued after the initial presentation of medical expert testimony relating to marks of violence discovered in the mouth and around the throat of the victim. Specifically, as the court could not determine whether the injuries sustained by the child were inflicted deliberately by the suspect or were occasioned by the process of self-delivery, the case was dismissed and the defendant was found not guilty.[230] Secondary injuries maintained from self-delivery, or owing to the way in which the infant's body was disposed, needed to be extricated from the actual cause of death and often this was exceedingly difficult to achieve.[231] For instance, was bruising found around the child's neck evidence of strangulation by a suspect or unintentional asphyxiation by the umbilical cord? Was bruising about the child's head due to the infliction of an assault or due to the child falling from its mother unexpectedly during the course of delivery? Were cuts to the child's throat evidence of barbaric intent or a sign of a suspect's panic when trying to free a child from the umbilical cord wrapped tightly around its neck? Evidence of marks of violence was, often ambiguous, problematic and subject to degrees of doubt, just like all of the other medical evidence presented in court in Britain during the pre-modern period in relation to new-born child murder. In consequence, the outcome of infanticide trials at this time often depended greatly on the character of the accused, on circumstantial evidence presented in the courtroom and on the opinions and mind-set of a judge and jury in a given place at a given time.

There was a variety of options open to women who wanted to dispose of unwanted new-born infants during the pre-modern period. The extent to which women engaged in abortion at this time is uncertain, for a variety of reasons, but attitudes towards the practice were perhaps more relaxed than we would have anticipated, particularly in relation to the legal context where unlicensed abortionists rather than their patients were targeted for concern. Women seem to have used abortion as an alternative contraceptive measure in the seventeenth, eighteenth and nineteenth centuries, especially when other forms of fertility control had failed. Many women may well have chosen to dispose of their unwanted offspring during pregnancy rather than deal with their 'problem' and its associated circumstances after the birth had occurred. Indeed, several of the women indicted for new-born child murder in Britain prior to 1900 had admitted attempting terminations at various stages of their pregnancy. Although these attempts had very obviously failed, this evidence shows, at the very least, that women knew of the practice and the mechanisms by which it might be achieved.

As with abortion, it is extremely difficult to gauge how common infant abandonment was as a method of child disposal in the pre-modern era. This is because, unless an infant died as a result of being 'exposed' or abandoned, no criminal investigations ensued. Where contemporaries *were* concerned, however, was in relation to the financial burden of infant abandonment at this time, and in this respect, they regarded the practice as a serious and significant problem. An act of undetected infant abandonment was quite difficult to achieve in the early modern period, but was facilitated in many major urban areas with the introduction of foundling institutions, which came to particular prominence during the eighteenth century. As well as being an escalating expense, these institutions were strongly criticised because of the excessively high mortality rates therein, particularly amongst new-borns. For this reason, foundling hospitals came to be seen as a mechanism which merely served to delay the practice of infanticide, rather than prevent it, as had been the original intention.

Aside from abandoning a child in a foundling institution, women during the pre-modern period also chose to delegate childcare to other individuals, such as wet-nurses (who were regularly employed by foundling hospitals) and baby-farmers. The extent to which this kind of maternal devolution was in effect infanticide by proxy is difficult to ascertain. Certainly, there is evidence of both wet-nurses and baby-farmers acting unscrupulously, and infant deaths undoubtedly did result on occasion, but the negative portrayal of aspects of paid childcare, especially in the second half of the nineteenth century, should not be regarded uncritically. Infant mortality was caused by a variety of factors in the pre-hospitalisation era, and inadequate nursing was only one of many explanations. It is also important here to state an enduring truism – that successful and uneventful childcare scarcely leaves an imprint upon the historical record.

Despite the alternative options illustrated above, some women still resorted to new-born child murder in the period between 1600 and 1900. Conceivably the physical complications and risks associated with abortion may have been unpalatable to many of these women, or perhaps previous attempts at termination had proved unsuccessful. Infant abandonment may have been regarded as too dangerous to carry out undetected and other devolved forms of childcare had to be paid for, either immediately or on a regular basis, which may well have been problematic for many women – married and unmarried alike. Historians tend to agree that infanticide in the pre-modern period was typically a passive crime, largely committed through neglect or by accident. Yet this chapter has shown that such a conclusion may well be too simplistic. Closer scrutiny of the evidence, whilst bearing in mind key deficiencies in determining the cause of neonate, suggest that active and more violent methods of infanticide prevailed in known instances of the offence in the eighteenth century in particular. Of course, it could be argued that this skew in the evidence is due to the fact that more serious instances of infanticide were more likely to be reported and brought to trial. Many more instances of passive infanticide may well have been success-fully hidden or were not prosecuted owing to a lack of evidence. Certainly, however, we should not merely assume that new-born child murder was car-ried out without blood being shed or injury being inflicted simply because the perpetrators were female and were typically the mothers of the infants concerned. Our evidence illustrates that British women were evidently capable of criminal violence in the pre-modern period, and that new-born babies were the victims of this hostility on occasion. Understanding why women resorted to this type of infant disposal prior to the twentieth century, and why some chose to employ overtly violent methods of neonate murder, is the subject of the next chapter.

5
The Pendulum of Opinion: Changing Attitudes to Infanticide

> Infanticide is as horrible and hellish a crime as can be committed by a human being... It is not a pleasant subject for reflection that in the reign of Queen Victoria the murder of infant children should have grown into a regular profession. The most self-satisfied Englishman will have some difficulty in extracting food for his pride from the fact that, in the matter of child murder, England is at the head of the civilized world.[1]

> The fearful increase in the crime of Infanticide has been a long and familiar fact, and year by year the country has been made painfully sensible of the annual increase of this crime, both as respects certain localities and the kingdom at large... The Slaughter of the Innocents by Herod, and the wholesale butcheries committed by the ancients, sink into insignificance beside this secret, ceaseless, and unnatural murder that day and night, in all directions, in every street, and almost every house, is perpetually going on around us. Smiles on the face and murder in the heart, and this is the state of society to which a high degree of civilisation and a morbid philanthropy have reduced the people of England.[2]

These forthright and visceral comments contain two key themes that will be examined in this chapter. First, it builds on the analysis carried out in Chapter 2, examining how infanticide was regarded by contemporaries during the nineteenth century. The chapter will also investigate the extent to which 'popular' opinion was consolidated or challenged in the courtroom during this era. Second, the chapter focuses on the nature and incidence of reported new-born child murder in nineteenth-century Britain. During this period, as the opening quotations suggest, contemporaries were fearful of an exorbitant rise in infanticidal behaviour and, by mid-century, a moral panic over this issue was clearly evident, as numerous individuals came forward to suggest remedies to curb the perceived growth in murderous depravity. Why was there such a focus on neonate murder in the nineteenth century? Were Victorian comments about the reach and significance of new-born child murder mere hyperbole or was there a genuine increase in this criminal activity during the period? How did infanticide in nineteenth-century Britain differ from, or compare with, that uncovered in previous centuries? Were different types of individuals involved? Was the crime committed using more modern methods? Were there changes in how the crime was investigated or dealt with by the courts? How did the Victorian judicial authorities react when faced with an infanticide suspect, and how did this compare with earlier conviction rates and sentencing regimes? Were the motives behind new-born child murder different in the nineteenth century to the early modern era?

This chapter is divided into three sections. The first of these outlines key changes to the legal context for new-born child murder which were introduced at the beginning of the nineteenth century and had a significant impact on prosecutions for the offence. This new legislation (although considered by contemporaries to be demonstrably imperfect for dealing with a crime as complex and multifaceted as infanticide) was largely to remain in place for over a hundred years. An understanding of the reasons for its emergence and an analysis of the significant extent of its effect is essential for a comprehensive history of new-born child murder.

The second section investigates prosecutions for infanticide and concealment of pregnancy during the nineteenth century in order to ascertain judicial attitudes towards new-born child murder during that period. The case study of a young Welsh woman who was indicted, convicted and subsequently executed for the murder of her new-born child in 1805 is used to show the generally unpredictable and wholly unsatisfactory nature of British infanticide trials at this time. Dissatisfaction with these trials resulted in repeated calls for legislative reform from the 1860s onwards. The chapter then looks more specifically at the nature of recorded instances of new-born child murder in Victorian Britain. As well as considering whether the moral panic over infanticide in the mid-Victorian era was justified, this section will also compare defendant characteristics, methods and motives for the offence in the nineteenth century with those of the early modern period. This illuminates continuities and changes in relation to the offence and its perpetrators over time.

Finally, and before offering some general conclusions, the chapter discusses the various solutions that contemporaries offered to the infanticide 'problem', which was perceived to be spreading like a contagion across Victorian Britain. However, despite intense social scrutiny, and although numerous remedies were offered, no viable solution to new-born child murder achieved consensus or was adopted during the nineteenth century. The reasons for this failure will be addressed as part of the discussion, but the inevitable consequence of this inertia was that the issue of infanticide continued to loom large in the public consciousness well into the twentieth century (as we will see in Chapter 7), despite the best intentions of Victorians to find a workable solution.

The legal context for infanticide in nineteenth-century Britain

Dissatisfaction with the seventeenth-century statutory legislation relating to new-born child murder grew over the course of the eighteenth century. As Mark Jackson describes: 'In the light of changing attitudes to the character of accused women, and to the nature of the evidence and the standard of proof required to secure a conviction, extensive discussions of the statutory presumption served only to limit the statute's scope and application in the courts.'[3] For many individuals (including lawyers and other judicial authorities) this constrained legislative context was unsatisfactory and highly problematic, resulting in four attempts to repeal the statute in the 1770s. These initial efforts at dismantling infanticide law (led by Sir William Meredith, Sir Charles Bunbury and Thomas Lockhart) need to be seen as part of a growing tide of humanitarianism with regard to penal policy, where statutory provision in general faced criticism from various quarters.[4]

The main argument put forward at this time was that statutes were not enforceable because the punishment prescribed was too severe and was routinely disproportionate to the crime committed. This criticism was particularly levelled at the laws against new-born child murder; a crime which was regarded by some commentators as less serious than homicide.[5] In 1772, one of the proponents of repeal, Thomas Lockhart, suggested that transportation to the colonies of North America be substituted for hanging as a more appropriate punishment for individuals convicted of killing their new-born offspring.[6] Difficulties relating to the standard of proof required to secure a conviction in infanticide cases also formed a key part of the debate over the repeal of the statute, as discontent over the persistent inability to successfully prosecute the offence intensified.[7]

Despite these misgivings, and an apparent clamour for legal change, all four attempts at repeal failed. In a practical sense this was a consequence of parliamentary prorogation and objections to statutory change in the (typically) conservative House of Lords.[8] In the wider context, however, there were other important contributory factors. A general increase in crime rates at the end of the eighteenth century made both parliamentary and judicial authorities nervous about reducing the number of statutory offences punishable by death. In addition, the American Wars of Independence (1775–1783) increased political instability and hampered the more widespread adoption of alternative penal strategies, such as transportation, at least in the short-term.

It was also significant that the proponents of legal change were isolated political players with limited influence over their parliamentary colleagues. Of course, we should not underestimate the fact that, for many, what was being suggested was regarded as too radical during a period of intense political and socio-economic unrest, both at home and abroad.[9]

In relation to infanticide more specifically, although some regarded the offence as being less serious than homicide, others were unhappy at the proposed move toward a more humanitarian approach to the crime and the individuals who perpetrated it. They argued that to reflect society's distaste for the practice of infant destruction, the authorities needed to be able to employ the 'ultimate sanction' in instances where the murder of a new-born child had been proven. Consequently, a continuation of the principle of maximum severity, mitigated through judicial leniency, was regarded as the best strategy.[10] Moreover, it was argued that the unpredictable nature of infanticide prosecutions was actually expedient in the judicial context, not a hindrance or a problem to be resolved. For many, the arbitrary application of the seventeenth-century legislation, where the conviction of a few random individuals served to exemplify the potential force of the law, was regarded as the chief element in the armoury used to deter infanticide.[11]

There are various reasons why attitudes toward infanticide legislation did change, some thirty years after these initial attempts failed. To some extent, the humanitarian arguments of the eighteenth century resurfaced in the early 1800s, and the existing statutory provision for the offence was once again criticised for its severity, as the context and motivations for new-born child murder were beginning to be more readily understood.[12] However, it is important not to exaggerate the role that this new climate of opinion played in the legislative change that occurred. Far more important in the minds of reformers was the need to make convictions for the offence more straightforward and secure. In other words, demands for remedial action on the legislation, which was considered unfit for purpose (a view voiced since the early modern period, as we have seen), significantly intensified at the beginning of the nineteenth century.

In the face of increasing crime rates and pressures on poor relief, the authorities deemed it necessary to curb the perceived moral laxity of the populace and reduce the burden that immorality placed on the parish. Dissolute women, in particular, were the intended targets of this crusade, and one practical consequence of this was a desire to improve the conviction rates in trials for new-born child murder by making the standards of proof easier to achieve.[13] In reality then, a toughening of attitudes and a desire to shore up loopholes in the law, rather than a burgeoning sympathy or greater toleration towards infanticidal mothers, lay at the heart of the bill Lord Ellenborough (Lord Chief Justice of the King's Bench) introduced to parliament on 28 March 1803. The bill received royal assent some three months later.[14]

The rationale for the repeal of the 1624 statute is made plain in the body of the new legislation. The 1803 Act stated that:

doubts have been entertained respecting the true sense and meaning of a certain act of parliament, made in England in the twenty-first year of the reign of his late majesty King James the First, intituled, An act to prevent the destroying and murthering of bastard children, and also of a certain other act of parliament, made in Ireland in the sixth year of the reign of her late Majesty Queen Anne, also intituled An act to prevent the destroying and murthering of bastard children; and the same have been found in sundry cases difficult and inconvenient to be put in practice.[15]

To remedy these problems the earlier legislation was repealed and instead:

from and after the said first day of July in the said year of our Lord one thousand eight hundred and three, the trials in England and Ireland respectively of women charged with the murder of any issue of their bodies, male or female, which being born alive would by law be bastard, shall proceed and be governed by such and the like rules of evidence and of presumption as are by law used and allowed to take place in respect to other trials for murder, and as if the said two several acts had never been made.[16]

This part of the new legislation is particularly important in three respects. First, it makes clear that infanticide was now to be tried in the same way as homicide and that evidence of concealment no longer constituted evidence of murder.[17] Secondly, proving live birth was retained as a key component of the evidence required for proving an indictment[18] and thirdly, the law was still restricted to single mothers and their illegitimate offspring.[19]

Further legislative change and clarification was provided in the remainder of the Act, which stated:

Provided always, and be it enacted, That it shall and may be lawful for the jury by whole verdict any prisoner charged with such murder as aforesaid shall be acquitted, to find, in case it shall so appear in evidence that the prisoner was delivered of issue of her body, male or female, which, if born alive, would have been bastard, and that she did, by secret burying, or otherwise, endeavour to conceal the birth thereof, and thereupon it shall be lawful for the court before which such prisoner shall have been tried to adjudge that such prisoner shall be committed to the common gaol or house of correction for any time not exceeding two years.[20]

This concluding section has two key aspects. First, and perhaps most significantly, if an indictment for new-born child murder failed in England,

Ireland or Wales, and an individual was acquitted of that charge, it was now possible to still convict them via an alternative verdict of concealment. In other words, defendants could now be sentenced for a crime which they had never been accused of at any stage in the trial process.[21] David Seaborne Davies explains that, as concealment 'did not involve the same difficulties in proving live-birth as homicide did', it was commonly used in the judicial context as 'a convenient stop-gap'.[22] The second key aspect of the concluding section of the 1803 legislation on infanticide is that the Act made the clear provision of a maximum penalty of two years imprisonment for any individual convicted of concealment.[23]

There are some obvious criticisms which can be levelled at the 1803 law on infanticide and its related offences. While the Act did bring the law into line with evidential standards developed during the eighteenth century, it failed to endorse any reassessment of the culpability or character of accused women and neglected to acknowledge the socio-economic pressures faced by single women in particular. In reality, then, the bill effectively amended, rather than repealed, the statute of 1624 and preoccupations with the legal and moral significance of concealment were sustained.[24] There were also practical problems with the application of the new law in the immediate aftermath of its royal assent. For instance, although the 1803 Act only referred to concealment of birth, the courts still occupied themselves with evidence relating to concealment of death. In addition, lawyers and defendants alike were confused by the notion that a woman could be charged with one offence but be convicted and punished for an entirely different one. This resulted in some courts trying to work around the new legal provision by charging individuals with the crime of concealment alone, even though strictly no such offence existed at that time.[25]

The Scots passed an equivalent statute on infanticide and concealment on 20 March 1809, which repealed the former legislation established in 1690. The new law enacted that:

> if, from and after the passing of this Act, any Woman in that Part of Great Britain called Scotland, shall conceal her being with Child during the whole Period of her Pregnancy, and shall not call for and make use of Help or Assistance in the Birth, and if the Child be found dead or be amissing, the Mother being lawfully convicted thereof, shall be imprisoned for a Period not exceeding Two Years, in such Common Gaol or Prison as the Court before which she is tried shall direct and appoint.[26]

We can see from this new Act that the Scottish judiciary's approach to dealing with new-born child murder and its associated offences was quite different from that south of the Tweed. In the first instance, the Scots acknowledged concealment to be a separate and distinct offence in its own right. As one Scottish judge put it, establishing the charge of concealment was simply a mechanism which enabled the authorities to bring 'within the reach of the criminal law a few women who have improperly escaped the graver charge of intentionally killing the child'.[27] After 1809, indictments for infanticide 'proper' in Scotland were subsumed into those for homicide and not indicted separately. Thus, an individual suspected of killing their new-born infant was either indicted for homicide or indicted for concealment. The Scots wanted to ensure that a clear provision was made for all aspects of this offence.

In addition, we can see from the wording of the statute that what constituted an act of concealment was much broader in Scotland than in England, Wales or Ireland, although there was a similar maximum penalty upon conviction.[28] More significantly perhaps, whilst the new legislation was gendered, it was not restricted to single mothers and illegitimate victims but could be applied to any woman suspected of concealment. In many respects the Scottish legislation is arguably more progressive and forward-thinking than its southern equivalent, and the flexibility of its application has profound implications for nineteenth-century prosecution and conviction rates, as we will see in the next section of this chapter.

The English and Welsh statutory provision for infanticide and concealment was amended twice during the course of the nineteenth century: in 1828 and in 1861. In June 1828, an Act was passed which consolidated and amended various statutes related to offences against the person. As well as repealing the legislation from 1803 and criminalising attempts at deliberate miscarriage, the Act stated:

> That if any Woman shall be delivered of a Child, and shall, by secret burying or otherwise disposing of the dead Body of the said Child, endeavour to conceal the Birth thereof, every such Offender shall be guilty of a Misdemeanor, and being convicted thereof, shall be liable to be imprisoned, with or without hard Labour, in the Common Gaol or House of Correction, for any Term not exceeding Two Years; and it shall not be necessary to prove whether the child died before, at, or after its Birth: Provided always, that if any Woman be tried for the Murder of her Child shall be acquitted thereof, it shall be lawful for the Jury, by whose Verdict she shall be acquitted, to find, in case it shall so appear in Evidence, that she was delivered of a Child, and that she did, by secret burying or otherwise disposing of the dead Body of such Child, endeavour to conceal the Birth thereof, and thereupon the Court may pass such Sentence as if she had been convicted upon an Indictment for the Concealment of the Birth.[29]

The significant elements of this legislative change are threefold. First, under this new provision concealment became an offence in its own right. In part, this brought English law more into line with its Scottish equivalent. However, the retention of the uniquely English alternative verdict, whereby an individual could be convicted for concealment when they had been not been originally indicted for that offence, still drew stinging criticism from many contemporaries.[30] Secondly, in evidential terms it is clear from this Act that it was no longer crucial for the prosecution (or indeed the defence) to prove whether the child had died before birth or afterwards. This is because proof of concealing the birth and the child's body (regardless of the outcome of parturition) was now regarded as the most crucial element in determining the outcome of the judicial process.[31] Finally, in 1828, the English law on new-born child murder and concealment became applicable to all women and was no longer restricted to single mothers.[32]

Thirty-three years later, in August 1861, abandoning or exposing a child under the age of two was criminalised for the first time and the legislation around deliberate attempts to procure an abortion or miscarriage was extended to include consumers as well as suppliers. In addition, the law relating to infanticide and concealment was amended once more, to operate as a more inclusive deterrent. The Act stated that:

> If any Woman shall be delivered of a Child, every Person who shall, by any secret Disposition of the dead Body of the said Child, whether such Child died before, at, or after its Birth, endeavour to conceal the Birth thereof, shall be guilty of a Misdemeanor, and being convicted thereof shall be liable, at the Discretion of the Court, to be imprisoned for any Term not exceeding Two Years, with or without Hard Labour: Provided that is any Person tried for the Murder of any Child shall be acquitted thereof, it shall be lawful for the Jury by whose Verdict such Person shall be acquitted to find, in case it shall so appear in Evidence, that the Child had recently been born, and that such Person did, by some secret Disposition of the dead Body of such Child, endeavour to conceal the Birth thereof, and thereupon the Court may pass such Sentence as if such Person had been convicted upon an Indictment for the Concealment of the Birth.[33]

Under this Act, a charge of concealment could be applied to any individual – male or female – and it no longer mattered whether the victim had been born dead or alive.[34] The potential for concealment as an alternative verdict for individuals acquitted of the murder of their new-borns was retained, and punishment for concealment was still fixed at a maximum of two years imprisonment, with or without hard labour.[35] The legislative amendments made in 1861 were the last significant changes made to the laws relating to new-born child murder and its associated offences in the nineteenth century. Substantial judicial reform was enacted in relation to infanticide in 1922: this will be discussed more fully in Chapter 7.

Prosecuting infanticide in nineteenth-century Britain

The quotations which opened this chapter are evidence of a moral panic about new-born child murder that gripped England during the second half of the nineteenth century. The printed press, whose circulation and reach was increasing rapidly at this time, was the chief medium through which proliferating fears about the seeming escalation in the rate of infanticide were expressed.[36] For instance, in 1857, the weekly British newspaper *The Era* reported that: 'Infanticide, unfortunately, has become so stereotyped a fact in the annals of crime that our sensibilities have grown deadened by its frequency, and we look on it with less horror and detestation than under other circumstances we should do.'[37] Similarly, *The Morning Post* commented in 1863 that there was an 'alarming increase of infanticide, which was now almost committed in the open day with impunity, and to the entire absence of any adequate means to grapple with the evil'.[38]

Scaremongering also occurred in a range of other publications and contexts, with professional medical men leading the way in the commentaries provided. For example, lectures and presentations on the perceived incidence of new-born child murder in the mid-nineteenth century were reproduced in publications such as the *British Medical Journal* and *The Lancet* and generated great interest amongst readers. Commentary from coroners and surgeons elicited the most attention. Individuals such as Dr Edwin Lankester and J. Brendon Curgenven provided alarming raw statistical information on infant deaths. One, for instance, testified in 1867 that 'upwards of 50,000 infants under one year of age were annually sacrificed in England to the ignorance, neglect and prejudices of the mothers and nurses, including "direct infanticide" and "infanticide by wilful neglect"'.[39] Evidence such as this led correspondents to report that, by the mid-Victorian era, infanticide was 'a thing of daily occurrence... so common was it, that the police seemed to think no more of finding a dead child than they did of finding a dead cat or a dead dog'.[40]

In a famous 1862 publication, William Burke Ryan stridently contributed his voice to the growing moral panic over infanticide. In probably the most extreme and powerful description of the perceived prevalence of infanticide in Britain, Burke Ryan noted that:

> the feeble wail of murdered childhood in its agony assails our ears at every turn, and is borne on every breeze. The sight is horrified as, day after day, the melancholy catalogue of murders meets the view, and we try to turn away the gaze in the hope of some momentary relief. But turn where we may, still are we met by the evidence of a wide spread crime. In the quiet of the bedroom we raise the boxlid, and the skeletons are there. In the calm evening walk we see in the distance the suspicious-looking bundle, and the mangled infant is within. By the canal side, or in the

water, we find the dead child. In the solitude of the wood we are horrified by the ghastly sight; and if we betake ourselves to the rapid rail in order to escape pollution, we find at our journey's end that the mouldering remains of a murdered innocent have been our travelling companion; and that the odour from that unsuspected parcel too truly indicates what may be found within.[41]

The reach and significance of the moral panic over new-born child murder should not be underestimated by historians; its effects were such that infanticide was widely regarded by many to be the greatest social evil of the Victorian era.[42] The issue was even debated in Parliament, with the surgeon and MP for Finsbury, Thomas Wakley, ominously concluding that 'child-murder was going on to a frightful extent, to an enormous, a perfectly incredible extent: and the means of destruction in a number of cases was such as to make detection impossible. There were no means of detecting it.'[43]

The reasons behind this increasing concern with new-born child murder in the Victorian era are complex and difficult to discern. Certainly, as the previous chapter showed, regular newspaper reports regarding the practices of unscrupulous wet-nurses and infamous cases of baby-farming kept the issue of infanticide in the minds of authorities and the general populace for a significant part of the nineteenth century.[44] Yet, there were other key causal factors.

In the first instance, new-born child murder was seen as a moral crime, which needed to be curbed before it escalated out of control, because its incidence had profound implications for the structure of modern society. The discovery of a murdered infant came to be regarded as evidence of moral degradation, which had the potential to penetrate many aspects of daily life.[45] At this historical juncture, the fears over infanticide seem to be less to do with the value of infant life and more to do with the actions and behaviour of mothers. For instance, concerns were voiced during the nineteenth century that economic considerations were encroaching on the domestic sphere and eroding the values of motherhood: women were neglecting their child-care responsibilities in favour of earning a regular wage. For many, infanticide was an extreme variant of this problem; it was believed that women were killing their new-borns in increasing numbers, either to avoid the cost of rearing a child or to facilitate their move into the world of work with minimal responsibilities at home. Infanticidal women were regularly labelled 'anti-mothers' at this time, not only on account of their actions, but also owing to the perceived motive behind their crimes.[46]

Another reason for such intense interest in infanticide during the nineteenth century was the link that social commentators drew between the perceived increase in new-born child murder and the implementation of the New Poor Law. As we will see in more detail in the next chapter, under legislation passed in 1834, mothers (rather than fathers) were expected to bear the full moral and financial burden of any illegitimate offspring they produced. The pressure that the New Poor Law placed on single mothers was thought to actively encourage new-born child murder, as it rendered many women desperate to avoid long-term penury. The new legislation was routinely criticised, and whenever fears about infanticide rates were voiced, it was common for the 1834 Act to be stipulated as a causal factor.[47]

Two other contextual issues are worth considering when explaining the reasons for the Victorian moral panic over infanticide. The first relates to worries voiced by some nineteenth-century commentators that imperial ventures (particularly in the Indian sub-continent) had led to illicit practices that were culturally acceptable in the colonies being introduced and assimilated into British society. In the case of infanticide, this assimilation had occurred to such an extent that it had become conventional and commonplace.[48] It is difficult to support this contention when it is evident that infanticide was practised in Britain long before the nation even considered extending its territorial advantage across the seas.

Far more compelling is the argument that the introduction of the office of coroner had a significant impact upon Victorian perceptions of infanticide and its incidence. In order to justify their existence, and the cost of their services, many coroners believed that they had to show their value and worth to society on a regular basis. However, some did this by overstating the size of their workload, by providing flawed and inflated statistics regarding local, regional and national fatalities and by instigating zealous crusades about issues which related to their official concerns. Consequently, by routinely raising their disquiet about the increasing incidence of infanticide in the press, citing inaccurate data, and employing colourful, hyperbolic language, coroners made a significant contribution to the moral panic.[49]

We now need to consider how justified this moral panic was in the light of evidence of recorded instances of new-born child murder and its associated offences in Britain during the nineteenth century. It is important to recognise from the outset that, in the main, the analysis provided in this section will relate to prosecutions for concealment, rather than infanticide proper, as after the passing of the early nineteenth-century legislation on the subject, indictments for concealment came to dominate the courtroom in prosecutions for new-born child murder.[50]

Trends in the prosecution of infanticide and concealment of pregnancy in nineteenth-century Britain are shown in Figures 5.1 and 5.2.[51] Both figures show a greater inclination toward the prosecution of infanticide-related offences after the new legislative provision was enacted in the early decades of the century, and both reflect an increase in prosecutions for concealment, which peak in the 1860s, before declining thereafter. This pattern of prosecutions is fairly typical in many jurisdictions the nineteenth century.[52]

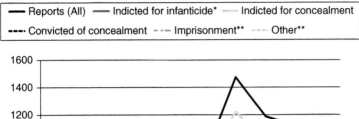

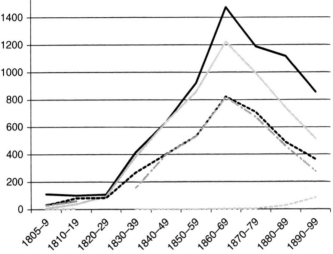

Figure 5.1 Trends in infanticide and concealment of pregnancy in England and Wales, 1805–1899

Notes: One execution recorded (in 1805).
*No records after 1817.
** No records between 1818 and 1833.

The steep rise in indictments in Britain occurred against a backdrop of falling illegitimacy rates.[53] However, the mid-century moral panic surrounding new-born child murder seemingly nullified the effect of that trend and instead encouraged individuals to report the offence to the authorities more regularly. This, in turn, resulted in more prosecutions, whilst panic spread and intensified. Another significant feature evident from Figures 5.1 and 5.2 is that there is a close correlation between reports of concealment and indictments for the offence in Great Britain throughout the nineteenth century. Clearly, the modern legal provision facilitated prosecutions more readily than the seventeenth-century legislation had.

Nevertheless, it is also clear from contemporary evidence, and from recently examined archival material, that although there were more prosecutions for offences related to new-born child murder in the Victorian era compared with the century before, it is likely that we are still dealing with only a fraction of the actual crimes that were committed. For one thing, and

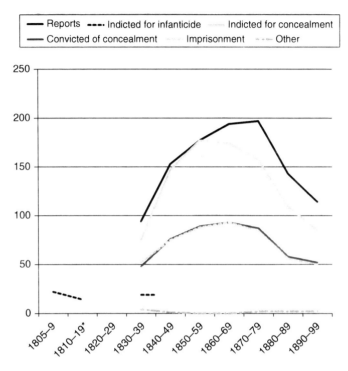

Figure 5.2 Trends in infanticide and concealment of pregnancy in Scotland, 1805–1899
Note: *No records between 1815 and 1831.

in the context of a very high infant mortality rate, any statistical information based on infanticide prior to 1874 must be treated with caution, as it was not until then that the registration of births became mandatory.[54] In addition, and perhaps more importantly, infanticide and concealment were still notoriously difficult crimes to detect.

Concealment, by its very nature, is a hidden crime and, as a result, infanticide and its allied offences must have made a significant contribution to the 'dark figure' of unknown illegality. If a woman successfully concealed her pregnancy, gave birth in secret and then subsequently killed her offspring, there was still a strong possibility – even in the nineteenth century – that this episode would go undetected by the authorities. As Jolie Ermers states, 'The crime of neonaticide was dramatically enveloped in darkness; presumably the majority of cases went unrecorded.'[55] Moreover, in order for a prosecution to be deemed appropriate and warranted, proof of intent had to be evident right from the start. Even as early as the coroners' inquest, when it was determined whether or not a case should be investigated, sufficient proof was often hard to come by. As Kenneth Wheeler remarks, with respect to the nineteenth century, 'firm conclusions [were] often elusive in the study of infanticide'.[56]

Greater social mobility and a persistent willingness on the part of friends, relatives and neighbours to cover up episodes of infanticidal behaviour are also suggested as reasons why detection was hampered during the Victorian era.[57] Certainly, there are numerous newspaper reports from the period which suggest that the bodies of new-born infants were regularly found in nineteenth-century Britain. But what these reports also testify to is the fact that it was often impossible to tie a cadaver to a suspect, despite the best intentions of the newly formed police force. For instance, the *Nottinghamshire Guardian* reported that the body of a newly-born female child was found under the goods table at the Midland Railway Station in 1863. According to the surgeon's description, the child had been destroyed after being deliberately buried alive under a pile of coal.[58] In the Taff Valley, in 1875, a labourer found the battered remains of a new-born baby at the side of a river.[59] At York, in 1877, the body of a newly-born female child was found in a field by a schoolboy.[60] The child had been strangled. And in Dundee, in 1890, some workmen found the body of a child floating in a hot water pond at a textile factory. The child had been put into an old cement bag with some pieces of lime to hasten decomposition and to make the remains sink. However, the weight of the lime was insufficient for this purpose and quicklime (or calcium oxide) generates vast amounts of heat when it comes into contact with water. Both of these factors contributed to the package remaining afloat and being recovered.[61] All of these cases reached a similar conclusion: that a wilful murder had been perpetrated by some person or persons unknown and that prosecution was highly unlikely.

In terms of successfully prosecuting an indictment for concealment or infanticide that *did* come to trial, Figures 5.1 and 5.2 show that a fairly close correlation existed between indictments and convictions, for concealment at least, across Britain during the nineteenth century. This was especially true in Scotland, reflecting a trend which had persisted in the northern jurisdictions since 1700. The charts also show a relatively high conviction rate for concealment and the total disappearance of convictions for infanticide proper after 1818.[62]

Andrew Payne has described how, 'During the nineteenth century, English courts took an increasingly lenient view of mothers who killed their own children.'[63] We have already seen that a sympathetic attitude to infanticidal women was prevalent in the courtrooms of Britain during the eighteenth century: this leniency became even more explicit by the Victorian era. The new legislation on concealment enabled juries to evade the convicting of mothers for infanticide proper; instead they could and did convict on the alternative charge of concealment. In addition, even on the odd occasion in the nineteenth century when a capital sentence was ordered by the courts, it was rarely enforced. Remissions and reprieves were common, as judges and juries did their best to mitigate the capital provision that still existed for new-born child murder, but which was increasingly seen as inappropriate and outdated.[64]

Determining which defendants would receive a capital sentence for their crimes remained as unpredictable in the early decades of the nineteenth century as it had been during the previous century. In the decades prior to Victoria's reign, the sentencing of infanticide defendants continued to be something of a lottery, as some women were made examples of and others were acquitted, with no clear trends or patterns emerging to explain the judicial decisions made. A good example of the prevailing haphazard sentencing policy in nineteenth-century Britain comes with the case of Mary Morgan.

Mary Morgan was baptised not long after her birth, on 30 January 1788, in Llowes Parish, Radnorshire by her parents, Rees and Elisabeth Morgan.[65] At the age of fifteen or sixteen she entered into service for the Wilkins family at Maesllwch Castle, near Glasbury, and took up the position of under-cook. However, not long into her service, Mary became pregnant with an illegitimate child. On Sunday 23 September 1804, Mary was found in bed by her fellow servants with the dead body of a female child hidden in the bed-clothes next to her. Mary denied that the child was hers and rebutted claims that she had killed her baby. She was arrested and taken to Presteigne, the county town of Radnorshire, where she was imprisoned awaiting trial.[66] According to one nineteenth-century commentator, what unfolded there-after was 'the scene of such a pitiful tragedy as cannot easily be surpassed in the annals of suffering humanity'.[67]

Mary Morgan was tried for infanticide on 9 April 1805 as part of the spring circuit of the Court of Great Sessions, held at Presteigne.[68] It was alleged by the prosecution that Mary had concealed her condition, and her subsequent parturition, and eventually gave birth to a female bastard child. Moreover, 'not having the fear of God before her Eyes but being moved by the Instigation of the Devil, she afterwards... then and there... feloniously, wilfully and with malice aforethought did make an assault' upon the body of her child, which resulted in its death.[69] More specifically, in evidence from the coroner's inquest it was charged that:

> with a certain Penknife made of Iron and Steel to the value of 6d which she the said Mary Morgan had and held in her right hand... she did strike and cutt... the Throat of the Female Child... and did then and there give to her the said Female Child one Wound of the length of three Inches and the depth of one. Of the said Mortal Wound... the Female Child there instantly died.[70]

Three witnesses appeared in court for the prosecution: Margaret Haverd, Elizabeth Eveylyn and Mary Meredith. All three of these women worked in service alongside Mary Morgan at Maesllwch Castle. Margaret and Elizabeth's testimonies were particularly crucial. Both women testified that, on the afternoon of 23 September 1804, they encountered Mary Morgan, who at that time appeared very ill. Suspecting that she was in labour, they quizzed her about her condition, but she strongly denied that she was pregnant and 'was very angry at being asked the question'. Mary asked the women not to disturb her for a while as she thought a restful sleep would make her feel better. However, when Mary Meredith went to the room she shared with Mary Morgan to change her clothes, she found the door to the room fastened from the inside and Mary Morgan refused to let her in. When Margaret and Elizabeth heard about the locked room, they forced their way in and charged Mary Morgan that she had been recently delivered of a child. According to them, Mary 'strongly denied it with bitter oaths for some time'. However, eventually, Mary did admit to the women that she had bore a child and that it could be found in the under bed. Upon looking there, the women discovered a baby 'cutt open, deep sunk in the Feathers with the Child's head nearly divided from the Body supposed by a Penknife which was found... bloody under the pillow of the same bed the next morning'.[71]

The weight of the evidence against Mary Morgan was seemingly conclusive and, on 11 April 1805, she was 'capitally convicted of Felony and the Murder of her female Bastard Child'. It was ordered by the judge that she be hanged at Presteigne just two days after his verdict was pronounced. He further ordained that after her death, her body was to be 'delivered to the Surgeons to be dissected and anatomised', although, in the end, this form of post-mortem punishment (reserved for individuals convicted of particularly violent crimes) was not carried out.[72] Despite rumours that a petition for clemency was sought, there is no evidence to suggest that any pardon was requested on Mary Morgan's behalf.[73] Seventeen-year-old Mary Morgan was hung on 13 April 1805 and was subsequently buried in Presteigne churchyard.[74]

The outcome of Mary Morgan's trial was surprising for a variety of reasons. First, there was the defendant's age. Not only was it unusual for women to receive a capital sentence in the nineteenth century, it was even rarer for a teenage girl to go to the gallows at this time.[75] Moreover, there was an evident lenient attitude towards women indicted for new-born child murder at the Court of Great Sessions in Wales in the century between 1730 and 1830, which makes Mary Morgan's conviction and sentence all the more anomalous and irregular. For instance, between 1730 and 1804 149 women were indicted for infanticide at the Court of Great Sessions. Only seven of these women were convicted and only two executed: Jane Humphries in 1734 and Elinor Hadley in 1739.[76] In other words, no woman had been executed for infanticide in Wales for 66 years prior to Mary Morgan's capital conviction.

After the Morgan case, and up until 1830, a further 46 women were indicted for infanticide at the Court of Great Sessions but not one was convicted.[77]

In trying to explain why Mary Morgan was executed for infanticide when so many women, before and after, avoided that fate, we need to consider three factors. First of all, contemporaries made much reference to Mary's character and demeanour in the courtroom and, more particularly, her seeming lack of remorse and indifference to the accusations levelled against her. For instance, one newspaper described how Mary Morgan 'exhibited no impression of guilt or apprehension of her fate' in court.[78] The presiding judge in the case, George Hardinge, also commented on Mary's behaviour, saying she 'had scarcely ever heard the Saviour's name... She had no religious abhorrence of her crime, till a few short hours before she terminated her existence'.[79] Elsewhere, in a letter he wrote to the Right Reverend Dr Horsley, Lord Bishop of St Asaph, Hardinge described how Mary 'took it for granted that she would be acquitted... [and] had ordered gay apparel to attest the event of her deliverance'.[80] The apparently nonchalant attitude that Mary Morgan exhibited, despite the seriousness of her circumstances, may have played a significant part in sealing her fate.

Another factor which may go some way to explain the rationale behind Mary Morgan's conviction and execution relates to the suggested identity of the father of her illegitimate child. Whilst it is most likely that a relationship with a fellow servant resulted in Mary's pregnancy (as she herself was purported to confess to the presiding judge in his chambers),[81] two other men were considered suspects both by contemporaries and by historians and commentators interested in the case. The first was Judge George Hardinge, the presiding judge in the case, who was apparently a frequent visitor to Maesllwch Castle and a distant relative of the Wilkins family. The theory supposes that he ordered Mary Morgan's conviction and execution to cover up his indiscretion.[82] However, there is no evidence to support this contention.

The second potential father of the new-born victim was a man called Walter Wilkins junior, the son of the proprietor of Maesllwch Castle. He was said to be particularly fond of Mary and there is evidence to suggest that he gave her money to pay for her defence counsel during her trial.[83] However, Wilkins came from a very well-to-do background. His father (also called Walter Wilkins) was one time governor of the Indian Province of Chittagong and became a member of the Supreme Council of Bengal in the second half of the eighteenth century. Walter Wilkins senior amassed a fortune in the subcontinent, and on his return to Britain in 1771, he bought land and estates in various parts of Wales and southern England. Eventually Wilkins senior became a Justice of the Peace and subsequently MP for Radnor.[84]

Clearly then, Walter Wilkins junior had solid prospects for social advancement, given the high standing of his father. If he had indeed fathered Mary Morgan's illegitimate child, the scandal would have damaged his status within the local community and might well have ruined his credibility and his plans for the future. In this supposed context, where his circumstances were under threat, we can understand that he might have felt the need to keep an eye on the proceedings to ensure his best interests were served. This may go some way to explain why he agreed to act as one of the 21 members of the grand jury who served on the trial of Mary Morgan. It may also explain why, despite any personal attachment he might have felt, he found Mary guilty of new-born child murder after only limited deliberation amongst his peers.[85] If he was the father of the child, he may have put his own interests above that of a modest servant-girl. His prospects had to be protected at all costs.

The suggestion that Walter Wilkins junior was the father of Mary Morgan's child is unsubstantiated. Indeed, it should be noted that in the supposed private confession that Mary Morgan gave to Judge George Hardinge, she categorically denied that Wilkins was her lover. Rather, Mary stated, Wilkins had offered to maintain both her and her bastard child, even though he was *not* the baby's father.[86] Regardless of the true extent of Wilkins' involvement in this affair, it is plain that he should not have been considered an impartial and objective member of the jury; he should never have been permitted to act in that capacity. Why he did so, and why he was able to do so, is the subject of speculation and conjecture.

The third, and most plausible, explanation for Mary Morgan's treatment by the judicial authorities relates to the influence and opinion of the presiding judge in the case, George Hardinge. When Hardinge delivered his sentence upon Mary Morgan he addressed the jury, giving what one newspaper described as, 'one of the most pathetic speeches that was ever heard'; the Judge was in floods of tears during the entirety of his oration.[87] In effect, Hardinge explained to Mary Morgan that she needed to be convicted and sentenced to death because her crime was explicitly violent and premeditated. Moreover, he made it plain that Mary was going to be used as an example to other potentially like-minded single mothers. He said:

> Guilt is always a coward; guilt like yours prompts the offender to accuse herself and prove the crime by evidence of the fact in the moment of despair, fear, or surprise. Madness like this comes too late; it is the effect, and the doom of guilt; it is no shelter for it. You have no plea of sudden impulse to this act (not that any such plea could avail you if in fact it existed) yours was a deliberate murder – the implement of the death's wound obtained, and set apart for its destined office and victim. Had you escaped, many other girls (thoughtless and light as you have been) would have been encouraged by your escape to commit your crime, with hopes of impunity; the merciful turn of your example will save them.[88]

Judge Hardinge's attitude to women accused of new-born child murder could be perceived as erratic and unpredictable. On 2 April 1805, for instance, just seven days before he heard the Mary Morgan case, Judge Hardinge presided over another Welsh infanticide case, against a single woman by the name of Mary Morris. Morris was accused of the murder of her illegitimate daughter at Hay in Breconshire. The court heard that:

> with a certain scissors of the value of sixpence... she did strike and cut... upon the neck and throat of the said female bastard child... giving one mortal wound of the breadth of four inches, of depth of two inches and of the length of six inches of which mortal wound the said child there and then instantly died.[89]

Despite the obvious similarities between this case and that of Mary Morgan, Mary Morris was found not guilty of infanticide, but guilty of the lesser charge of concealment. Hardinge's actions in this case, when set alongside the outcome of the Morgan trial, suggest that he was capricious in his use of authority.

However, closer scrutiny of the infanticide indictments dealt with by Judge Hardinge reveals that, rather than adopting an inconsistent approach to these cases, where certain women were given exemplary punishment on random occasions, he was remarkably predictable in his management of the judicial process. More importantly, he was routinely sympathetic to the women concerned. For instance, 22 women were indicted at the Court of Great Sessions for infanticide and concealment of pregnancy in the time between Mary Morgan's case and the death of Hardinge in 1816. Six of these women were found guilty of concealment alone; ten indictments resulted in no bill being found; and the remaining six women were acquitted.[90] Mary Morgan's case defied the general trend towards leniency in infanticide cases, not only in relation to criminal trials presided over by Hardinge, but also with respect to indictments throughout nineteenth-century Britain. Mary's fate could be described as unlucky or unfortunate, to say the least.

Judge Hardinge made no pretence about his dissatisfaction with the new infanticide legislation passed in England and Wales in 1803. When providing further explanation for his treatment of Mary Morgan in works published just after his death, he explained his exasperation that the new law neglected consideration of the infant victims in instances of new-born child murder. In his view, like so many of his contemporaries, concealment as a substitute verdict for infanticide proper minimised the seriousness of the crime.[91] To that end, he proposed that judge's should be 'equivocal' about the potential verdict in a given case of infanticide and 'must not overlook the danger of impunity'.[92] For Hardinge, making infanticide cases something of a judicial lottery in terms of outcome predictability was the best deterrent that the authorities could deploy. The *potential* judicial threat of a capital conviction was what mattered most for preventing infanticide.

Sentencing the odd defendant to 'the ultimate fate' in order to show that this threat was serious was all that was required.

It is fair to say that Judge George Hardinge was deeply affected by his decision in the Mary Morgan case, as his copious explicatory writings on the subject testify.[93] He apparently paid several visits to Presteigne churchyard to see Mary's grave.[94] He seemed obsessed with justifying his decision in the Mary Morgan case; indeed, he penned a poem on the subject, entitled 'On Seeing the Tomb of Mary Morgan', which read as follows:

> Flow the tear that Pity loves,
> Upon Mary's hapless fate:
> It's a tear that God approves;
> He can strike, but cannot hate.
> Read in time, oh beauteous Maid!
> Shun the Lover's poisoning art!
> Mary was by Love betray'd,
> And a viper stung the heart.
> Love the constant and the good!
> Wed the Husband of your choice,
> Blest is then your Children's food,
> Sweet the little Cherub's voice.
> Had Religion glanc'd its beam
> On the Mourner's frantic bed,
> Mute had been the tablet's theme,
> Nor would Mary's child have bled.
> She for an example fell,
> But is Man from censure free?
> Thine, Seducer, is the knell,
> It's a Messenger to thee.[95]

The trial of Mary Morgan is much more than a case study in this volume. Rather, it is an event that highlights the range of responses that nineteenth-century individuals had towards the crime of infanticide and the women who perpetrated it. More generally, for many people, Mary Morgan came to be regarded as something of a martyr, who represented the harshness of a pre-modern judicial system which had the power to execute a 17-year-old girl for a crime conceived in isolation and committed in fear and desperation. The public at large seem to have been wholly sympathetic to Mary Morgan's plight, especially given the fact that her seducer was able to remain anonymous and go unpunished: a fact Hardinge himself points to in his poem.

Contemporary commentators were quick to publish their opinions in print and prose. The most famous of these works is undoubtedly 'An Elegy

Written in the Churchyard of Presteigne', written by T. Horton, in 1818. Considering the justification of Mary's capital sentence, the verse reads:

> The tempter – Satan – enemy to joy,
> Bade thee, the fruits thy folly made, destroy;
> Bade thee forbid the vital spark to glow,
> Forbid the crimson blood of life to flow.
> Taught thy poor heart another crime to know,
> And whisper'd Murder to complete thy woe.
> No longer under virtue's strict controul,
> And horror seizing on thy trembling soul,
> The deed was done – the tempter's conquest gain'd
> Whilst thou to sad despair a prey remain'd.
> But nature anxious in her children's cause,
> Sought satisfaction from the injur'd laws,
> And justice, strict impartial Justice came,
> To prove her right, and to enforce her claim;
> Tho' by her side, sweet mercy trembling stood,
> Blood! She exclaim'd, must be repaid by blood!

He continues:

> Poor child of error, this we trust's thy lot,
> Peace to thy soul, and be thy faults forgot…
> Be not afraid to visit Mary's tomb,
> Or drop a pitying tear upon her doom;
> And ever as you do her stone survey,
> Hope that her suff'rings wash'd her sins away.[96]

Overall, the Mary Morgan case emphasises the typical despair and desolation that young single women must have faced on discovering themselves to be pregnant. It also highlights more prominently that reactions and attitudes to infanticidal women were not always predictable. Rather, the outcome of a trial depended on the circumstances of an individual case, the historic moment at which the offence occurred and the particular mind-set of the witnesses and judicial authorities concerned. On occasion, this mix of prevailing influences could result in a seemingly arbitrary outcome, which defied the general trend towards sympathy and leniency in cases of new-born child murder throughout the nineteenth century.

Figures 5.3–5.5 show the sentencing patterns for offences associated with new-born child murder in Britain during the nineteenth century. It is evident from the data that, although judgments could be unpredictable at times (as we have just seen), imprisonment eventually came to be the most commonly employed punishment for individuals convicted of infanticide and concealment in modern Britain. For Scotland, this marked a significant departure from the use of transportation as the principal penal strategy against new-born child murder and its allied crimes. In England and Wales, most individuals convicted of concealment could expect to receive a short prison sentence, typically of six months or less. Moreover, sentencing data mirrors trends in prosecutions and convictions (see Figure 5.3), and increased leniency is evident over time.[97] Scottish individuals could expect a longer stint in prison for concealment: usually around 18 months. Sentencing over time was more stable in Scotland and, unlike in England and Wales, did not follow prosecution/conviction trends (see Figure 5.4).[98] In both contexts it could be argued that the punishment for concealment was relatively mild, even at the height of the mid-century moral panic, given that the maximum sentence prescribed was two years' imprisonment.[99] In any case, for the Victorian judiciary, the criminal trial in itself increasingly came to be seen as the best shaming tool to deter other would-be criminals. Capital or corporal punishment became increasingly redundant and imprisonment was adopted as a more reformative approach to justice was encouraged.[100]

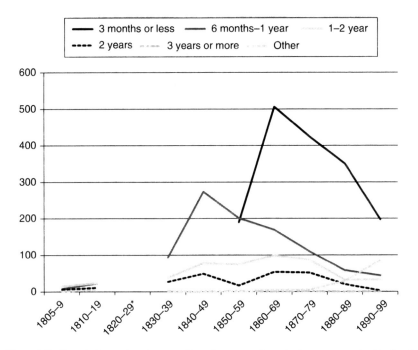

Figure 5.3   Trends in sentencing practices for concealment of pregnancy in England and Wales, 1805–1899
Note: *No records between 1818 and 1833.

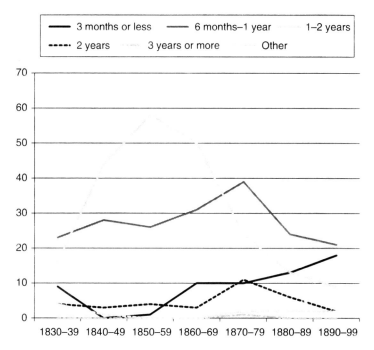

Figure 5.4 Trends in sentencing practices for concealment of pregnancy in Scotland, 1830–1899

The relative leniency shown towards individuals convicted of conceal-ment in nineteenth-century Britain did not go unnoticed by contemporaries. Indeed, some commentators held that the increase in infanticidal behaviour around the 1860s was due to weak judicial authority.[101] William Burke Ryan, for instance, said that the courts no longer considered infanticide and its associated offences to be as serious as other forms of murder. He believed this to be 'little more than a mockery of justice. There is no crime that meets with so much sympathy, often of the most ill-judged kind; and an almost partisan feeling has been evinced, not only by the legal, but even by the medical pro-fession.'[102] According to Burke Ryan, the overly-sympathetic attitude to those accused and convicted of infanticide after the first third of the nineteenth century gave 'a silent sanction to the detestable practice, and indirectly encourages a system which brings indelible disgrace upon a nation'.[103]

The reasons for the more lenient approach to infanticide and conceal-ment evident in nineteenth-century Britain are not dissimilar to those outlined in relation to the early modern period. For one thing, the majority

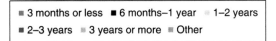

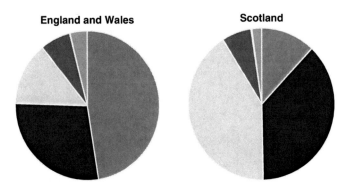

Figure 5.5 Sentencing practices for concealment in England and Wales (3505 cases) and Scotland (509 cases), 1800–1899

of defendants were female, as Figure 5.6 illustrates. Judicial sympathy for female offenders was maintained and extended over the Victorian era, and it is clear that the courts increasingly preferred to give indicted women the benefit of the doubt, even when evidence of guilt was emphatic.[104] In 1842, for example, Mary Milnes was indicted at Nottingham Assizes for the murder of her new-born son. The child was found in bed with the defendant and its throat had been cut so severely that the 'head was only retained on the body by the skin and muscles of the back'. Despite Mary admitting to her doctor that she had inflicted this horrific injury, her remorseful appearance in court resulted in her being convicted of the lesser charge of concealment.[105]

The reasons for the adoption of judicial leniency in the sentencing of Victorian infanticidal women were two-fold. First, there was a determination to better understand *why* women committed infanticide, and, second, there was a growing disbelief that women could be innately violent. Nineteenth-century commentators started to suggest that there must be alternative explanations for why women concealed their pregnancies and killed their new-born offspring after parturition, other than mere vindictiveness in an attempt to avoid opprobrium. As we will see in more detail in the next chapter, two explanations came to dominate motivational theories relating to new-born child murder at this time: poverty and insanity.[106] The latter explanation, in particular, was well received, as it suggested that not only were these women acting unconsciously when they murdered their new-borns, but also that episodes of this kind were a mere aberration, and

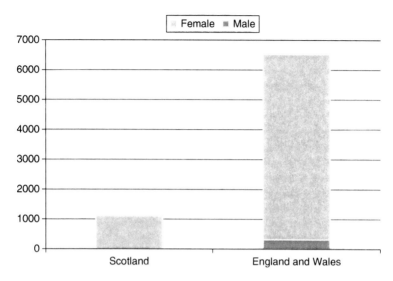

Figure 5.6 Gender differences in indictments for infanticide and concealment of pregnancy in Britain, 1800–1899

not related to a fundamental flaw in the expression of natural maternal sentiment or the characteristics of femininity.

There were other factors too, which militated against the harsh treatment of infanticide suspects. Firstly, the employment of defence lawyers in these cases (a trend which originated in the second half of the eighteenth century) meant that, by the Victorian era, fewer women confessed to killing their new-borns. Instead, a range of defence strategies were adopted in attempts to attain acquittal or persuade the court to accept mitigating circumstances, which would justify lenient treatment when it came to sentencing. Women increasingly claimed that they had experienced a still-birth, that they had fainted upon parturition and the baby had died accidently owing to want of care or that they were suffering from some sort of mental irregularity.

The standard of evidence required to convict individuals – especially in instances of infanticide proper – was still vexing and problematic in the nineteenth century, and contributed to judicial leniency in these cases.[107] As one Scottish doctor, John Barclay, detailed in a letter to the *British Medical Journal* in 1866:

Cases of infanticide are unfortunately of too-frequent occurrence all over Great Britain; but their frequency, and the experience that ought to be derived therefrom, has not rendered the examination of the murdered infants very much easier, nor smoothed away the difficulties attendant on the giving of evidence when the mothers are brought to trial.[108]

Determining the cause of death, estimating the time at which injuries were inflicted, proving that parturition had been completed before fatality had occurred, as well as establishing the degree of intent the accused harboured, were all routinely challenging to medical professionals in the Victorian era.[109] Yet, the provision of this kind of evidence was crucial for conviction and vital in determining the sentence incurred.

For instance, at an inquest heard at Appleton Roebuck in North Yorkshire in 1871, a woman called Eliza Proctor was suspected of killing her new-born child. The baby's body had been rescued from a dog that was devouring the corpse after pulling it out from under a hedge in the Proctor family's garden. Upon her arrest, Eliza said to her arresting officer, 'Don't take my father and mother; they know nothing about it; they were out at the time and I buried it before they came home.' Yet, because of the wounds inflicted by the ravages of the dog, the surgeon to the case could not determine whether the child had been born alive, and so the jury found that there was no case to answer due to the uncertainty of the medical evidence provided.[110]

Problematic judicial cases, such as the one cited above, only served to emphasise the fundamental mismatch between the prevailing moral panic over new-born child murder in the mid-Victorian era and the blatant clemency practised by the criminal courts at this time.[111] This dichotomy led to renewed and repeated calls for legal reform in relation to infanticide and its allied offences over the second half of the nineteenth century. Contemporary commentators were perturbed by judicial obliviousness, where, as Roger Smith describes:

> The cumulative effect was a legally exculpatory attitude towards infanticidal women. A blind eye was turned in the first place, a charge of concealment of birth was brought in the second, the criminal law have women the benefit of doubt about moment of birth in the third, and the Home Secretary ensured finally that women were not hanged... This filtering process left few women to face a capital sentence for murdering their children.[112]

Contemporaries largely agreed that the legislation relating to new-born child murder and concealment in nineteenth-century Britain was too extreme. The laws concerning infanticide were regarded as too harsh and the laws concerning concealment were considered too lenient.[113] There was a need for something in between. Consequently, and as part of a review of capital punishments in 1866, it was suggested that a new offence of grievous bodily harm upon an infant be introduced, in order to make the law more malleable and readily applicable.[114] This suggestion was ultimately rejected, but it did not stop other politicians, social commentators and interest groups, such as the Harveian Society and the Infant Life Protection Society, campaigning for similar sorts of legal change in 1872, 1874, 1878 and 1879.[115]

The objective of these attempted legislative amendments was to reinstate judicial discretion, in order to enable a charge of murder to be reduced to manslaughter, and to facilitate the introduction of an insanity defence.[116]

These various attempts at reform failed, and the law concerning infanticide and its allied offences was not changed further during the nineteenth century. This was largely because infanticide was eclipsed in its political importance by other related issues, such as baby-farming, wet-nursing, abortion, child cruelty and parental neglect, as we will see in Chapters 6 and 7.[117] For now, we must turn to look at the actual nature of infanticide in Victorian Britain and the characteristics of those individuals who were indicted for its perpetration at that time.

The nature of infanticide in nineteenth-century Britain

As we saw in Figure 5.6, the vast majority of defendants for new-born child murder and concealment in nineteenth-century Britain were female. This was a typical characteristic of the offence at this time.[118] As in previous centuries, most of the women indicted for infanticide and its allied offences during the Victorian era were single. However, married women's involvement in recorded instances of infanticide did increase over the course of the nineteenth century, especially when the use of insanity defences became both popular and successful, but the numbers were not substantial. On the whole, the offence was still regarded as the domain of spinsters, as the notion that married women would have no cause to commit infanticide persisted. In the cases involving married women that did come to light in the Victorian era, two motivational factors were typically cited: the desire to limit family size and the need to conceal an extra-marital affair.[119]

Typically, nineteenth-century infanticide defendants were young (under 25 years of age) and either still lived at home or resided in work-related accommodation.[120] As in the case of Mary Morgan seen above, some of the defendants were mere juveniles. For instance, in 1845, an inquest was held on the body of a female child discovered in the garden of a cottage in Malvern, Worcestershire. Suspicion fell on a sixteen-year-old girl (who was fifteen at the time of the offence) called Jane Kings. The inquest heard that, although Kings was 'a single woman and had only just turned sixteen years of age... it seems she has one son now two years and a half old'. Kings claimed that she had been surprised by parturition when she had gone to fetch some water and that the baby had been still-born. Despite evidence of live-birth being provided by a surgeon, the inquest jury believed Jane Kings' explanation of events and it was decided that she had no case to answer.[121]

One interesting aspect of Jane Kings' case is that her mother evidently assisted her with the burial of her dead child. Most women were prosecuted for carrying out the offence on their own, since suggesting the presence of an accomplice undermined any charge of concealment. Nevertheless, it is clear from nineteenth-century evidence that non-maternal individuals were also accused of both infanticide proper and aiding and abetting new-born child murderers. Often, infanticidal mothers were aided by family members to cover up the evidence of parturition and neonatal death.[122] Increasingly in the Victorian era, however, the father of the victim had more of an explicit role to play in new-born child murder, or at least the courts were more willing to prosecute such individuals for their involvement. Indeed, according to Hermann Rebel, 'Men were the driving force behind some acts of infanticide' during the nineteenth century.'[123] Men typically participated in infanticide during this period for two reasons: first, if the new-born child was likely to prove a financial burden in the future; and, second, if the child was perceived as some sort of obstruction to the man's life and future advancement.[124]

For instance, in 1824, *The Morning Post* reported on an infanticide that had occurred in north-west Dorset, where a new-born female child had been found strangled. The case came to light when a Mr Samson was seen by a young boy burying a small box near a footpath. With his curiosity piqued, the boy went to see what was in the box and discovered a baby's body with petticoat strings tightly wrapped around its neck. The court discovered that Samson had been engaged in an illicit relationship with the unmarried daughter of his landlord. The girl had subsequently become pregnant and, fearing he would lose his job as a wagoner on account of the scandal, he aided the girl and her mother in killing the child and disposing of its remains.[125]

In 1848, *The Newcastle Courant* led with the headline 'HORRID CASE OF INFANTICIDE'. The piece continued to describe 'a most unnatural and revolting deed', which was committed by local man and so-called 'inhuman monster' Thomas Mitchell. Mitchell murdered his nine-month-old illegitimate child by:

> dashing its innocent head with considerable violence against the brick floor. This brutal act he rapidly followed by two others – first by taking up the child by the feet and striking its grandmother violently with it over her head; and secondly, by throwing it into the cradle; and, finally, leaving the house, uttering a fearful sentence of satisfaction at the horrible deed.[126]

Despite the child being quickly taken to hospital, it died soon afterwards from its considerable injuries. Mitchell apparently committed this act after being unhappy about a court order which had directed him to pay two shillings a week for the maintenance of the child.

The vast majority of Victorian infanticide defendants were domestic servants and, as we have already seen, this was a common trait amongst suspects in earlier periods too.[127] The widespread association between infanticide and servitude was such that in the 1890 edition of the *Encyclopaedia*

Britannica it stated: 'The modern crime of infanticide shows no symptom of diminution in the leading nations of Europe. In all of them it is closely connected with illegitimacy in the class of farm and domestic servants.'[128] Dr Edwin Lankester similarly reported, in the *British Medical Journal* in 1866, that 'In the great majority of cases the perpetrator of the crime is the mother, who is usually employed in domestic service. In fact, it seems almost impossible that any other class of women can be implicated.'[120]

There were several reasons for the persistent dominance of domestic servants as defendants in infanticide cases. First of all, as domestic service was the biggest employer of women in nineteenth-century Britain, it was far more likely for an infanticide suspect to be employed in this type of occupation.[130] Domestic servants were also more vulnerable than other women in relation to the environment in which they worked. Indictment evidence shows that young servant girls were often impregnated by their masters, by members of their employers' family and by co-workers (sometimes against their will), and this regularly resulted in unwanted pregnancies.[131] *The Times* newspaper highlighted the problem of the working conditions for domestic servants in 1865, with one of its correspondents lamenting: 'I regret to say, in domestic service, the heads of families are far too negligent in much they could do to help their female servants to preserve that self-respect and religious principle in which their safety lies.'[132]

One case of suspected infanticide, from 1843, demonstrates the kind of ill-fated relationship that could exist between master and servant in Britain during the nineteenth century. Described in the press as a man of independent means, a Mr Alven from Somerset repeatedly seduced his young servant-girl, Martha Clarke, and she subsequently became pregnant. After revealing her condition to her employer, Martha described how 'he had behaved kinder to his dog than to her'. Alven aided his servant through her parturition and, by her testimony, after the child was born, he took the infant away, killed it by strangling it with a hayband and buried it amongst some reeds in the garden, where it was later discovered. Apparently he did this on both of their behalves, so that they could avoid the shame of an illegitimate child.[133]

Another reason for the significant number of domestic servants in infanticide cases in nineteenth-century Britain relates to the contemporary socio-economic context in which women lived and worked. As we saw in Chapter 2 and will see in the next chapter, many of the women who worked as domestic servants were utterly reliant on their earnings and knew that if their employer discovered that they were pregnant it would result in their immediate dismissal without a reference.[134] Nevertheless, many of the women who worked in this profession were utterly reliant on these earnings and knew that if their employer discovered that they were pregnant they could expect immediate dismissal without a reference. This is because the working hours and duties of a domestic servant were not conducive to child-rearing and because the shame associated with illegitimacy would not be tolerated in respectable households.[135] This may well have meant that there was a greater temptation to commit infanticide amongst those unwed servant girls who found themselves pregnant. When threats of opprobrium and privation are placed alongside the greater scrutiny of servants' behaviour in nineteenth-century households,[136] a context of desperation and isolation begins to emerge around the unmarried servant population, which helps explain their predominance in instances of new-born child murder and its allied offences during the Victorian period.

Aside from gender, marital status, age and occupation, other defendant characteristics associated with new-born child murder in nineteenth-century Britain are harder to discern.[137] For instance, although some European studies have suggested that rural infanticides were far more prevalent than urban ones, there does not appear to be a clearly favoured *locus operandi* in the British practice of the offence.[138] Infanticides occurred in both rural and urban environments, usually near to the woman's workplace or close to her home.[139] There is also no evident trend in relation to the gender of victims in Victorian Britain. Male infants and female infants were killed in almost equal numbers.[140] Finally, recidivism (which was a clearly articulated concern of nineteenth-century authorities and social commentators) was, in reality, a rare occurrence in England, Scotland and Wales at that time.[141] Most women indicted for infanticide and its allied offences were accused of killing their first-born child.

The methods that nineteenth-century infanticide suspects employed when killing their infants were addressed in the previous chapter. As we have seen, Victorian commentators were especially preoccupied with the rise of wet-nursing, baby-farming and burial clubs, which, in their minds at least, all expedited the rise in neonatal mortality evident by the 1880s and 1890s.[142] The moral panic associated with these practices occurred within broader concerns about new-born child murder at a time when alternatives to pregnancy and parturition, such as contraception, were still rudimentary and unavailable to many. This was also a time when abortion was a highly dangerous procedure and was outlawed by the Offences Against the Person Act of 1861.[143]

In her study of new-born child murder cases from Victorian England, Cathy Monholland describes how new methods, such as 'decapitation, poisoning, hanging, starvation, stabbing and garrotting', were introduced to the infanticidal woman's repertoire at that time. Yet, we saw in the previous chapter, that, with the exception of poisoning, all of these methods had been practised long before the nineteenth century. It is more appropriate to argue that there was more of a *status quo* in infanticide methods across British history, than any significant change. A wide variety of practices were evident. One thing that nineteenth-century commentators *did* become much more interested in was how they could best categorise the different methods associated with the offence. In his thesis on infanticide, produced in 1817, John Beck divided the methods of new-born child murder into two categories: infanticide by omission and infanticide by commission.[144] Later writers used the terms 'passive' and 'active' infanticide.[145]

According to Beck, infanticide by omission took four forms. The first of these was neglecting to aid the baby upon or immediately after the birth, resulting in it drowning in the discharges associated with parturition. Failure to provide warmth or nourishment for the new-born child was also considered a passive version of infanticide, as was failure to tie the umbilical cord properly at the appropriate time. These approaches to infanticide were just as deadly as more active methods, and were arguably crueller, as it generally took longer for the infant to expire than in instances where direct violence was employed.[146] Neglect of care of one sort or another was thought to be a significant factor in many nineteenth-century infanticides, but, as Beck himself pointed out, it was notoriously difficult to prove.[147] It was difficult to discern whether a woman had deliberately refused to care for her child, whether she was simply incapacitated by the effects of parturition or whether the child had been still-born. Indeed, some contemporary commentators bemoaned the fact that women could be indicted for new-born child murder for simply being caught in the act of disposing of their child's remains after an intrauterine foetal death. If they had concealed their pregnancy and parturition, they were liable to prosecution, even if they had not actually harmed their offspring in any way.[148]

Other variants of passive infanticide which were thought to be particularly prevalent in the Victorian era included infant abandonment or exposure and overlaying. Once again, however, indictments for this type of new-born child murder were relatively rare in Britain at this time owing to difficulties with the standard of evidence required to establish proof of foul play or intent.[149] A Pembrokeshire case from 1895 clearly illustrates the contemporary problems in prosecuting infanticides by omission. After the body of a new-born male child was discovered in a gap in a hedge, at Narbeth, naked and frozen, suspicion fell upon two gypsy women (Catherine Jones and her mother Elizabeth) who had been seen camping nearby. Catherine Jones had admitted to police-sergeant Phillips and his colleague, police-constable Wheeler, that she had been pregnant with an illegitimate child, but did not know what had become of it. When the inquest took place, the coroner made two conclusions. First, he said that the cause of death was '*probably* through the neglect of those responsible in not properly tying the umbilical cord'. He then went on to add, 'But under what circumstances or who are the parties connected with the death of the child there is no evidence to show'. Consequently, the prosecution was abandoned.[150]

Cases of active infanticide were much more commonly brought before the courts of Britain, as the evidence associated with this kind of practice was more difficult to rebut, although marks of violence could still be explained away by attempts to extract the infant during a difficult and protracted self-delivery. John Beck identified seven categories of infanticide by commission. These were: the deliberate ripping of the umbilical cord; the infliction of wounds and contusions; the active prevention of respiration; drowning; strangulation; breaking of the neck; and poisoning.[151] He described this kind of infanticide as 'a crime of the deepest dye'.[152] Most methods employed in active infanticide were pragmatic in nature, where an individual sought to kill the child as quickly as possible before its cries were heard and they were discovered. Asphyxiation via strangulation or drowning was common in alleged infanticide cases during the Victorian era, and could be carried out with a fair degree of violence.[153] For instance, *Reynolds' Newspaper* reported on an infanticide which occurred on the outskirts of London in 1859, where the body of a three-month-old baby was discovered in a field by a young boy. The remains of the infant had been wrapped up in a parcel of old rags, but the legs of the child were protruding from the bundle, so he ran to find a policeman. When the parcel was opened and the body of the child exposed, 'There seemed to be a piece of cord around the deceased's neck, tied in two or three knots at the front of the throat.' In the inquest that followed the discovery, the coroner determined that the infant had indeed died from manual strangulation completed with 'significant force'. He also reported that, from the state of the skin of the child, 'the body had been hung up for a considerable time... and had since death, been placed in an exposed state'. Despite the best investigative intentions of the newly established local police force, the murderer of the infant remained at large.[154]

It is difficult to discern just how common the use of weapons was in episodes of infanticide in Britain during the nineteenth century. Certainly, press reports and indictment material from the time seem skewed towards the suggestion that these active methods were more regularly employed than their passive equivalents. However, it is likely that, as ultra-violent episodes of new-born child murder were far more likely to be prosecuted in the first instance owing to the uncontroversial and explicit nature of the presenting evidence, they were more likely to feature in the judicial context and would, thus, be more commonly reported in the press.[155] The weapons selected for violent infanticides were typically those close at hand when parturition occurred, although, on occasion, greater thought was put into the method of despatch.[156]

The acknowledgement that 'bloody' infanticides are likely over-represented in the official and popular evidence associated with this crime in the nineteenth century should not detract from the fact that this kind of method could be brutal and vicious when employed. In his work on child murder in New England during the Victorian era, Randolph Roth suggests that the aggressive nature of infanticides there intensified over the course of the period to such an extent that, by the final decades of the century, 'neonaticides looked like abortions in their physical violence'.[157] Although there is no evidence to support a similar escalation of violence in Britain at that time, cases which were committed in a ferocious manner still came to light.

For instance, in 1829, a thirty-eight-year-old woman called Barrett was accused of the murder of her new-born child in Stepney Parish. In order to protect her livelihood as a domestic servant, and to conceal the birth of an illegitimate child, she cut the head off her new-born baby not long after its birth. She hid the infant's skull under a flower pot which stood on the window-sill in the room in which she lodged and then proceeded to cut up the rest of the body into small pieces with a large knife (which was subsequently recovered behind a door) and burned the infant's remains in the fire.[158]

At Everton, near Bawtry, in South Yorkshire, in 1842, a servant girl called Mary Milnes was suspected of the murder of her new-born son. When the surgeon, Dr Hall, was summoned to investigate, he discovered 'a most appalling sight, for not only had the throat been dreadfully cut even through the spine, but the mouth of the child had been cut on each side, as if to stop its cries'. A bloody dessert knife was found in the sink in the back kitchen of the house in which the suspect resided.[159]

In 1863, *The York Herald* reported on a 'Shocking Case of Infanticide at Hartlepool', charged against an eighteen-year-old woman called Sarah Ann Smith. Smith was taken unwell and her brother Thomas went off to glean some medical assistance on her behalf, although he was unaware of her true condition. The doctor who arrived on the scene, Dr Mackechnie, proceeded to discover a bloody bundle at the foot of Smith's bed. He opened it and discovered the body of a newly-born male child with ' a number of wounds on its throat and abdomen'. Despite the severity of the wounds inflicted, the child was miraculously still alive and so Mackechnie vainly attempted respiration three times, but to no avail. The doctor demanded that Sarah Ann Smith show him the weapon she had used to kill her child and after she 'made some movement about her dress... [she] handed out to him a two-bladed pen-knife'. According to the doctor's testimony at the subsequent inquest into the child's death, the boy had received 'fifteen distinct wounds' on its neck and a further 'seven distinct and separate wounds on the abdomen'. Clearly Sarah Ann had panicked and had killed her baby in frenzy, as she desperately tried to dispatch her child before her brother returned.[160]

A more detailed examination of the motives for deliberate acts of new-born child murder in British history will be dealt with in the next chapter of this volume. However, as it was in the nineteenth century, in particular, that the courts became much more interested in having an explanation for the offence, we will analyse the most common motivations described by British infanticide defendants in the Victorian era here.[161] Aside from a few cases involving married men and women, most of the episodes of new-born child murder reported in England, Scotland and Wales during the nineteenth century occurred within the context of illegitimacy, which contemporaries feared was spiralling out of control.[162] Bearing this in mind, there are five explanations that can be discerned from the testimony provided by infanticidal women to account for their actions: poverty; shame; isolation and desperation; insanity; and pragmatism.

Extreme hardship seems to have been one explanation behind episodes of new-born child murder in Britain (and indeed further afield) during the Victorian era.[163] For instance, in Wales in 1828, Catherine Welch was indicted for the murder of her new-born child after her husband abandoned her soon after the baby was born and she realised that she could not provide for it on her own. She strangled her child by 'pressing her hand on its throat. The eyes of the innocent were by this application violently strained and she finished her infernal act by pressing them close into the skull. By these means the eye balls were nearly crushed' and, unsurprisingly, the infant soon died.[164] In 1851, an episode of infanticide was discovered at Suffolk involving a woman called Maria Stewart who killed her new-born daughter by putting her hand over its mouth and nipping it in the throat with her fingers. When this course of action did not have the desired effect, Maria took her garter and tied it tightly round the baby's neck, 'so that it might die easy'. As Maria explained to a local minister, 'I killed it because I thought I should not have a father for my child and because I had not the money for milk. I pray to God and tell him if he forgives me, I would not do so again.'[165]

As we have already seen, the introduction of the New Poor Law denied outdoor relief to young, single women and, thus, if they found themselves pregnant, they were largely reliant on their families or employers for support.[166] It was incredibly difficult for unmarried women to support themselves independently during this period, owing to the depressed nature of the female wage, and if they had an additional mouth to feed they would not only struggle to make ends meet, their options for work would also diminish significantly because of the demands and cost of childcare.[167] Unmarried pregnant women faced a precarious future, unless they could rely on help or charitable assistance. A lack of this kind of aid might result in some women adopting an altruistic approach to their new-born child; believing that the termination of a life that would only experience misfortune and deprivation was in the child's best interests.[168]

The shame of an illegitimate pregnancy was probably the most commonly stated motive amongst women charged with infanticide.[169] To give a typical example of the causality described, Sarah Ellen Thompson, an eighteen-year-old domestic servant, was accused of the murder of her illegitimate son at Thirsk, in 1891. The prisoner had repeatedly denied her condition to her mother, her father and her co-workers. On 22 April 1891, Sarah Ellen's mother found a chemise saturated with blood in her daughter's bedroom and sent the girl's father to investigate further. The father of the defendant found a bundle in a tin trunk at the foot of her bed. Inside the bundle were the remains of a child cut up into small pieces. When her father asked Sarah Ellen why she had committed this 'shocking and despicable act' she answered, 'because I did not want you to deny me as your daughter on account of my shame'.[170]

It is interesting to note that, even by the end of the nineteenth century, illegitimacy could still carry an intense social stigma for women across Great Britain, as it very flagrantly provided proof of immoral behaviour and sin.[171] For married women too, concealing the shame of an illicit extra-marital affair was often given as a rationale for new-born child murder and its allied offences, as is alluded to above. Women accused of new-born child murder had to be careful if they chose to articulate opprobrium as the root cause of their criminality. On the one hand, the rationale of shame did enable defendants to show remorse for the original act of illicit conception, but on the other hand, such an explanation also demonstrated a long-standing intention to conceal pregnancy, hide parturition and kill the child in secret.[172] Such a blatant display of intent and pre-meditation was not always easily mitigated by the leniency of judicial authority in these cases.

The shame associated with illegitimate pregnancy during the pre-modern period must have resulted in many unmarried pregnant women feeling utterly isolated and alone. In order to avoid opprobrium and alienation, either they had to become solitary figures, who bore the burden of their condition in silence, or they had to move away from established and existing systems of support, to places where less suspicion would be aroused by the changing nature of their appearance. For many individuals, the stress of isolation must have been intense.[173] Indeed, we can only ever speculate about the degree of fear and desperation which must have overtaken many women when the time of parturition occurred. These feelings may have encouraged some women to behave irrationally and to terminate the source of their misery. The kind of stress unmarried women were under in attempting to self-deliver what was usually their first-born child, is likely to have been overwhelming and some may well have suffered from a temporary mental aberration (such as psychological dislocation or denial), of the kind that increasingly interested nineteenth-century medical men, as we will see in Chapter 6.[174]

For example, in 1823, Worcester Assizes heard a case of infanticide brought against a woman called Lucy Dancer for killing her new-born son. The testimony of surgeon Mr Downing explained that: 'The cause of its death was an extensive wound in its throat; the head was nearly severed from the body. The knives by which it was done were very dull, and it must have been very difficult to inflict such a wound and must have taken some time.' When Lucy was asked to explain why she had attacked her own child in this way, she declared that 'a thought suddenly came into her head that she would kill her child'. The surgeon expressed his belief that the defendant was insane at the time the infanticide was committed, and also noted that she had attempted to take her own life four times whilst in prison, which was deemed to be further evidence that 'she was of unsound mind'.[175]

Similarly, in Lincoln in 1857, a married woman called Mrs Woolfitt was indicted for the murder of her youngest infant son. The baby was found on the hearthstone by his father, with 'its head completely severed from its body, and beside it [he found] a cork hatchet covered with blood'. According to newspaper reports, 'The mother sat on a chair close by, calmly gazing on her horrid work. In reply to questions, the woman said she had killed the baby, but she loved it and all her children, and had she not been interrupted it was her intention to have destroyed all her children.' The report continued: 'We understand that the wretched mother has been in a low, desponding way for some time past.'[176]

Finally, we must also consider that, for some women, infanticide was a deliberate and intentional act, regarded as a practical solution to a potential problem.[177] Many Victorian women may well have regarded infanticide as a sure form of late birth control, when there were few other viable options whereby a pregnancy could be prevented or terminated.[178] Infanticide may, therefore, have been seen as a pragmatic and necessary activity, resorted to when no other solution was possible and when control over social and economic destiny was tantamount.

Solutions considered and remedies offered

The moral panic over infanticide and its related offences in nineteenth-century Britain, whether justified or otherwise, increased awareness of the crime amongst the populace and, as we have seen, encouraged attempts to better understand why individuals committed new-born child murder. As a result of this interest, various learned and popular societies (such as the Harveian Medical Society) considered the infanticide problem and, indeed, some organisations were even created for this very purpose, such as the National Society for the Prevention of Infanticide and the Infant Life Protection Society.[179] This concentration of effort resulted in contemporary commentators offering a wide range of solutions designed to eradicate the problem of infanticide. For the purposes of this chapter, we will only address the most commonly offered remedies.

Reform of the legislation regarding new-born child murder and its allied offences was often suggested by contemporaries as one of the best means to curb the crime. As indicated above, many thought that the introduction of concealment as an alternative verdict in infanticide cases had made the law overly lenient, to such an extent that it was no longer efficacious as a deterrent to crime. As John Beck declared, in 1817, 'the dread of severe punishment is the most effectual preventative'.[180] Other commentators added to these concerns, arguing that the laws on infanticide proper were too severe, and suggested that the offence no longer warranted its status as a capital crime. Instead, advocates of legal change craved the creation of a new offence (with a non-capital provision), which would sit somewhere in between concealment and infanticide.[181] The quest to resolve these issues formed the basis of the attempts at legal reform which were to dominate discussions of the offence from the mid-Victorian era until the first third of the twentieth century, as we will see in Chapter 7.

Probably the most common solution to the infanticide problem suggested by nineteenth-century commentators was a revision of the poor laws to make the fathers of illegitimate children more responsible for the maintenance and upkeep of their offspring. As W. Tyler Smith wrote, in 1867, the introduction of the New Poor Law in 1834 meant that 'The great burden of maintaining her illegitimate child up to the age of 16 is thrown upon the mother... the father is practically allowed to escape... and the results are most disastrous as regards the child.'[182] It was suggested that, in order to counteract this, fathers' names should formally appear on birth certificates. In this way they could be compelled to pay maintenance. William Burke Ryan, writing as a member of 'The National Society and Asylum for the Prevention of Infanticide' in 1863, went as far as to suggest what the maintenance amount should be. He said: 'the putative father of a child should, according to his means, be called upon to pay for its support a sum varying from 2s. 6d. to 7s. 6d., which should be the maximum'.[183]

As well as legislative change, contemporaries also called for the formal cataloguing of still-births, the official registration and close supervision of child minders and the criminalisation of baby-farming and wet-nursing. In addition, individuals wanted to see greater powers of surveillance and arrest being granted to the police, to better facilitate the apprehension of offenders.[184] Remedies to the social problems which were believed to underpin new-born child murder in the Victorian period were also suggested. For instance, one commentator sanctioned improved living conditions for the lower classes as a means of eradicating new-born child murder. In a letter to the *Aberdeen Weekly Journal*, in 1877, he stated:

All those who are in positions of authority whether in town or country, and all owners of house property, are all more or less able to aid in the repression of infanticide. The rescue of boys and girls from the streets, from the beginning of leading dissolute and abandoned lives, the pulling down of houses unfit for human habitation, the substitution of houses where overcrowding in rooms is strictly guarded against and a proper division of the sexes rigorously maintained, these will be found efficacious in the social repression of infanticide.[185]

More commonly, improving the morality of the populace was seen by many as a key means by which the 'Hydra-headed evil'[186] of illegitimacy could be eradicated, and it was believed that this, in turn, would lead to a diminution of infanticidal activity.[187] As one nineteenth-century writer put it: 'With regard to infanticide, it is impossible to suggest any method of arresting it completely, unless there be a total reformation of that corruption of manners which lies at the root of the evil.'[188] Consequently, it was the clergy, in particular, who were reminded of the duties of their office 'in warning the people committed to their charge, in instructing them in the path of virtue and religion, and in ministering to the fallen'. It came to be widely believed that the crime of infanticide could be oppressed by religion and religious observance.[189]

The final remedy to the problem of new-born child murder and its allied offences that was commonly suggested by nineteenth-century commentators was more practical in nature than those mentioned above. It was widely proposed that, in order for single mothers to feel less ashamed of their condition, more state-sanctioned support should be offered. This could be enacted through the establishment of more open-access Foundling Hospitals throughout the country or by the development of improved maternal care and childminding facilities as part of the workhouse regime.[190] The available assistance would not only help the women concerned through their parturition, but it would also aid them in the initial weeks after lying-in. As a writer to *The Times* articulated in 1865:

> When so much is done to provoke a crime which, once committed, is so lightly punished, there could be little national disgrace if at some cost we provided these sinning mothers with other homes than the grave for their offspring.[191]

Although some of the solutions suggested above were implemented (for example, via the Infant Life Preservation Act of 1867), in the main, these proposals were not wholly adopted, consistently applied, effectively enforced or routinely evaluated and, indeed, several were simply ignored by the Victorian authorities. This meant that the 'infanticide problem' was one that persisted, festering above and below the surface of British society through to the twentieth century, as we will see in due course. The inability of British society to deal with the issues surrounding new-born child murder dismayed nineteenth-century commentators, who were quick to suggest that this stasis merely added to the crisis. As one writer to *The Morning Post* put it in 1863:

> What inducement is offered to the unfortunate mother to protect her offspring beyond natural affection? None. What, on the other hand, are the inducements to child murder? Protection from open shame; ability to seek her usual employment, instead of the uncertainty of the union or the prison; or the alternative of seeing her child miserably starve, she

herself an outcast and wanderer, or maintaining herself and it by a life of more awful misery and still deeper degradation.[192]

It is clear that there was a growing reluctance to convict women of killing their new-born children under the existing statutory provision. This reluctance became problematic in the early years of the nineteenth century, when fears of increasing crime rates surfaced. Rather than evidence of a rising tide of humanitarianism, the legislative change enacted within the first years of the new century was a response to criticisms of over-leniency within the judicial context and a burgeoning dissatisfaction with the original seventeenth-century legislation. Although distinct legal approaches to the crime of infanticide were adopted by the various constituent parts of Great Britain at different points over the course of the nineteenth century, in the main we can conclude that it was during this century that concealment came to be recognised as a separate crime in its own right, for which a fixed penalty of imprisonment was warranted.

The moral panic over infanticide, and its allied offences, was especially evident in press reports and other writings from the 1860s onwards. In part, this preoccupation with new-born child murder was fuelled by a growth in prosecutions for the lesser offence of concealment, which had been facilitated by the legal changes made in previous decades and by a more systematic investigation of suspected cases, through the introduction of a professional police force. Although we can only ever analyse rates of reported crime, indictments and convictions for concealment did increase over the course of the nineteenth century until the last two decades, where a discernible downturn is evident. Although sentencing policy associated with new-born child murder and concealment could still be unpredictable on occasion during this era (as evidenced by the Mary Morgan case), on the whole, the courts increasingly adopted imprisonment as their chosen punishment for convicted offenders. Although a few capital convictions still persisted, to showcase the potential severity of the law, by the second half of the Victorian period the courts were generally more inclined to give suspected individuals the benefit of the doubt. Judicial authorities became more interested in why individuals committed the offence and tried to find explanations for maternal violence, such as temporary insanity.

The nature of new-born child murder and the characteristics of the defendants accused of the offence during the nineteenth century did not differ substantially from that of the early modern period. Unmarried female domestic servants still made up the majority of suspects, although a growing number of accomplices were accused, and more married women were indicted once concealment was affirmed as a separate offence and insanity defences were permitted on a regular basis. The methods used in infanticide were as varied in the Victorian era as they had been for centuries, although there was more of a determination to categorise the type of killing that took place, along the lines of whether it was done with or without intent. Certainly, the press were more interested in reporting episodes of violent infanticide, which sat well within the advent of new journalism and the growing forms of mass media, which used sensationalism as a tactic to increase the salience of the case for moral reform against perceived social evils. The motives behind new-born child murder and concealment were of more interest to nineteenth-century contemporaries, although, once again, they were not dissimilar from those experienced in the early modern period. Poverty, shame, isolation, desperation, temporary insanity and basic pragmatism were all evident causal or contributory factors in the nineteenth-century infanticide indictments examined for this study.

A variety of solutions and remedies were suggested by nineteenth-century commentators to eradicate the infanticide problem from British society. Most of these centred on the perceived need for legal change of one kind or another. For instance, calls were made to revise the legislation covering infanticide and concealment to make it fit better with contemporary understandings of the crime. Likewise, it was suggested that fathers should bear more of the financial burden and moral responsibility of rearing an illegitimate child, through the formal recognition of their status on birth certificates. Further suggested remedies included the criminalisation of baby-farming and wet-nursing and the introduction of a clear registration process and supervisory regime, to better monitor childcare arrangements across the country. In addition to these suggestions, solutions to social problems thought to relate to instances of new-born child murder, such as illegitimacy, lack of morality and poverty, were also considered, as were more practical remedies, such as improved postnatal care for mothers and the provision of charitable accommodation for mother and baby once the child was born. Despite the good intentions of these suggestions, little was effectively done to implement or enforce legislative or societal change in relation to the incidence of new-born child murder during the nineteenth century. Even though historic crime data shows that a moral panic over infanticide was unwarranted at this time, fear was still rife that the problem of infanticide was a significant threat to the moral fabric of British society and that the situation was worsening, with no evident solution to be found. As one commentator put it, when writing to a London newspaper, in 1863: 'I fear the day is far distant when the tide of infant blood, which is swelling around us, will be stayed.'[193] Fears like this were set to persist for decades to come, as subsequent chapters will show.

6
Explaining Infanticide: Motives for Murder?

> women who are pregnant, without daring to avow their
> situation, are commonly objects of the greatest *compassion*;
> and generally are less criminal than the world imagine.[1]

As we saw in Chapter 4, the options for infant disposal that were open to pregnant women in Britain before the twentieth century were limited. Abortion, infant abandonment, wet-nursing and baby-farming were all problematic because of their potential fallibility, the expense they necessitated and the threat they posed to both physical health (in the case of pre-modern terminations) and future security, given that these mechanisms were commonly predicated on the need for the woman concerned to reveal her condition to another party. For many women, when faced with few alternatives, infanticide must have seemed like their only reliable course of action or was their last resort, when other options had failed.[2]

We must remember, however, that not all instances of new-born child murder were carried out with deliberate intent and, of course, not all women in precarious or problematic circumstances resorted to committing new-born child murder.[3] We need to try to understand why some women chose to kill their offspring during the pre-modern period and others did not. What motivational factors and underlying causes were involved in this type of 'criminality'? Were some factors more prevalent or more important than others? Did motives for infanticide change over the course of the pre-modern period? How did society, and the judicial authorities in particular, react to the explanations given for this offence?

Historians have been quick to point out the complex and individual nature of motivations for new-born child murder. Keith Wrightson, for instance, describes this area of research as a 'morass of complexity', where explanations for the offence are largely dependent on the personal circumstances and particular mind-set of a given individual on a given day.[4] Whilst Wrightson's argument is true to an extent, he neglects to address the causal explanations for infanticide and its allied offences regularly offered in court by defendants and witnesses, as well as the motives which can be gleaned from a closer reading of press reports. Consequently, although it might indeed be difficult to discern one profound motive for this type of behaviour, it is possible – and indeed more appropriate – to think of a nexus of prevailing factors, which culminate in a decision to commit infanticide.[5]

From the evidence we have relating to new-born child murder in Britain between 1600 and 1900, it is not possible to collect accurate quantitative data on motives for infanticide. Indeed, specific motives are very difficult to discern from the material available.[6] In the main, this is for two reasons: first, in relation to the seventeenth and eighteenth centuries at least, the courts were usually only interested in whether a case could be proven, so explanations for the perpetration of a given offence were seen as being of secondary importance to the judicial process and were rarely admitted as evidence.[7] Although the preoccupation with securing a conviction waned to some extent in the second half of the eighteenth century, it was still rare for motives to be given, largely because so much of the court's time was taken up with determining whether the new-born child was viable, had enjoyed a separate existence from its mother or had been born alive. By the Victorian era, motives for infanticide were still being concealed from the British public, albeit for different reasons. As we will see in due course, the growing reliance upon insanity defences in trials for new-born child murder from the 1830s to the turn of the century resulted in psychological explanations coming to dominate society's understanding of infanticide. This brought the issue of motive to the forefront of debate. Moreover, as insanity pleas for infanticide proper were typically successful, and resulted in either the acquittal or minimal punishment of indicted individuals (as shown in the low conviction rate after 1830, evident from Figures 5.1 and 5.2), there was no need to elaborate on the details of specific crimes and no desire to offer any other explanations for the events that had transpired. Insanity became the only explanation for new-born child murder.

As a consequence of the relative weakness of quantitative evidence regarding motives for infanticide, this chapter will be an analysis of the testimony of a range of witnesses, experts and lay-observers who presented their opinions during criminal trials in courts across England, Scotland and Wales between 1600 and 1900. Commentary gleaned from press reports over that period will also be scrutinised. On occasion, women suspected of new-born child murder did offer their own explanations. However, these instances were very rare and typically only occurred if the woman had confessed to her crime.[8] Given that so many British prosecutions for infanticide failed to result in a conviction from the mid-eighteenth century onwards, confessing to the offence was unusual, so that this type of insight is seldom available.

In general, we can identify four categories of motive for new-born child murder during the seventeenth, eighteenth and nineteenth centuries: shame and isolation; economic factors; deliberate or malicious intent; and medical and psychosocial explanations. This chapter will investigate each of these categories in turn.

Shame and isolation

Shame (and the fear associated with it) was seen as a significant causal factor for infanticide throughout the early modern period. Indeed, the issue was specifically highlighted in the first infanticide legislation passed in Britain, in 1624, as we saw in Chapter 1.[9] In the 'Acte to Prevent the Destroying and Murthering of Bastard Children' it was stated that: 'many lewd Women that have been delivered of Bastard Children, to avoyd their shame and to escape Punishment, doe secretlie bury or conceale the Death of their Children'.[10] By the eighteenth century, the concept of shame had come to dominate contemporary commentators' explanations for new-born child murder. Bernard Mandeville, for instance, writing in 1723, described the plight of a single woman debauched by a suitor:

> If she proves with child, her sorrows are unspeakable, and she cannot be reconciled with the wretchedness of her condition; the fear of shame attacks her so lively, that every thought distracts her. All the family she lives in have a great opinion of her virtue, and her last mistress took her for a saint. How will her enemies, that envied her character, rejoice! How will her relations detest her! The more modest she is now, and the more violently the dread of coming to shame hurries her away, the more wicked and more cruel her resolutions will be, either against herself or what she bears.[11]

Similarly, writing a little later, the English physician Erasmus Darwin also highlighted the importance of shame as a motive for infanticide, when he wrote a letter to a magistrate friend in 1767:

> The Women that have committed this most unnatural Crime, are real Objects of our greatest Pity: their Education has produced in them so much Modesty, or Sense of Shame, that this artificial Passion overturns the very Instincts of Nature! What struggles must there be in their Minds, what agonies! And at a Time when, after the Pains of Parturition, Nature has designed them the sweet Consolation of giving Suck to a little helpless Babe, that depends upon them for its hourly Existance! Hence the Cause of this most horrid Crime is an excess of what is really a Virtue, of the Sense of Shame, or Modesty. Such is the Condition of human Nature![12]

In 1784, the Scottish anatomist and physician William Hunter added his voice to those individuals who saw opprobrium as the principal explanation for women's recourse to new-born child murder in the eighteenth century. As Hunter described:

> In some (it is to be hoped *rare*) instances, it is a crime of the very deepest dye: it is a premeditated contrivance for taking away the life of the most inoffensive and most helpless of all human creatures... But, as well as I can judge, the greatest number of what are called murders of bastard children are of a very different kind. The mother has an unconquerable sense of shame, and pants after the preservation of character: so far she is virtuous and amiable. She has not the resolution to meet and avow infamy.[13]

On the one hand, writings such as these signalled a growing humanitarian attitude towards women accused of new-born child murder, an attitude which became more prevalent as the eighteenth century wore on.[14] However, this sympathetic attitude only stretched so far. Firstly, as both Bernard Mandeville and William Hunter explain, it was commonly believed at the time that only worthy women could feel shame. 'Dishonourable' or 'disreputable' women could not fully engage with this emotion, as they had 'lost their modesty to greater degree, and the fear of shame... [made] hardly any impression upon them',[15] therefore, fear of opprobrium could not function as an appropriate rationalisation for their actions in instances of new-born child murder. Secondly, some eighteenth-century writers negated the profound power of humiliation as an explanation for infanticide by emphasising that a sense of shame had not been a pressing concern for the women concerned when they had originally lost their virtue and engaged in illicit sex (sometimes on numerous occasions), which resulted in them becoming pregnant outside of wedlock. For these commentators, the women accused of infanticide were merely using shame as a bespoke defence, which had been fashioned for their needs at a given time but was not reflective or representative of their true feelings.[16] Finally, paradoxically, some contemporaries regarded shame as an utterly despicable motive for new-born child murder, which was borne out of selfishness and the desire for self-preservation. As Christopher Hodgson, a magistrate from Castor, near Peterborough, put it in 1800:

> The poor unhappy Innocent was doomed to die; its life was determined to be made a sacrifice to the preservation of its mother's character and reputation in the world – a character wilfully intended to have been stained with infant blood, and preserved by secret murder. The horrid intention contracts the guilt, and the inhuman act confirms it.[17]

Despite not being universally accepted as a plausible or appropriate explanation for new-born child murder in the pre-modern period, shame and opprobrium were prevalent in the explanations given for this crime during that era, and in the eighteenth century in particular. By the nineteenth century, shame did not dominate recorded motives for infanticide as it had done in previous centuries, but it played an important role in court proceedings nonetheless. There were two particular contexts within which shame was used as an explanation for new-born child murder between 1600 and 1900: the first related to personal feelings of opprobrium in the context of an illicit pregnancy; the second to attempts to avoid family or community-based dishonour in the hope of preserving reputation.

Most women accused of new-born child murder in the pre-modern period had engaged in illicit sexual relations of one sort or another and, upon discovery of conception, had been abandoned by their erstwhile suitors and left to deal with the consequences of their former relationship alone.[18] As we have seen in previous chapters, the majority of those indicted for infanticide were single women who had tried to conceal illegitimate pregnancies, although, of course, the targeted nature of the statutory provision, which singled-out 'bastard-bearers' for particular judicial attention, had a lot to do with the prevalence of this category of accused.

According to Alison Rowlands, one of the typical reasons why a mother committed infanticide was 'to conceal her own lewdness – the fact that she had conceived a child in a non-marital context'.[19] Not only were women ashamed of being pregnant out of wedlock, they were also embarrassed by the fact that they had been seduced and abandoned by their paramours. By piecing together indictment evidence, alongside other accounts, it is clear that many of the women accused of new-born child murder had engaged in sexual activity with a partner on either the promise or the presumption of marriage, which turned out to be illusory.[20] As Regina Schulte explains, 'Disgrace meant having visibly sold oneself for the wrong price and having become a laughing-stock.'[21]

The shame of an illegitimate pregnancy, and the associated sense of abandonment, was one of the most common explanations given for the committal of new-born child murder in Britain in the eighteenth and early nineteenth centuries. Elizabeth Arthur, for instance, was indicted at the Old Bailey in September 1717 charged with the murder of her male bastard child, whom she had drowned in a privy after she had been suddenly abandoned mid-pregnancy by her lover. A constable who investigated the case recounted that, when he asked the accused why she had perpetrated this act, she told him 'that now she was alone she did it to conceal her shame, and that by doing so she had brought herself to more, and was now heartily sorry for it'.[22] Another woman, Janet Stuart, was indicted at the North Circuit in Scotland in 1734 for an infanticide she committed on her child in the Shire of Elgin and Forres. Janet had killed the child by flattening it with a spade until it was nothing but 'bloody clouts and bones' because she was 'ashamed to bring a child into the world alone', after her relationship with a soldier had ended unexpectedly when he was posted elsewhere.[23] In a similar vein, in 1804, Middlesex woman named Ann Smith was indicted for the murder of her new-born daughter, whom she had choked and smothered to death in order to 'hide her shame' at having become pregnant and being unsure as to who the father was, as she had 'enjoyed the lusts of many a man'.[24]

Although the shame of an illegitimate pregnancy did not prevail to the same extent in all communities across Europe in the pre-modern period, in some areas the opprobrium of an illicit pregnancy had a deeper significance.[25] This was most evident in areas where religiously based opprobrium compounded the general societal displeasure. As we saw in Chapter 2, women across Europe in the seventeenth and eighteenth centuries could be publicly shamed and punished for enjoying evident sexual relations outside marriage, since the Christian churches took a particularly severe moral stance on matters of this kind.[26] As a result, some women accused of new-born child murder may have been pushed to this crime in order to avoid the religious stigma that would follow from an illicit pregnancy.

In British mainland indictments for infanticide between 1600 and 1900, religiously based opprobrium was revealed as a potential or evident causal factor only in Scottish instances of this offence. For example, in 1712, Christian Strachan, a widow from Berwickshire, was indicted for new-born child murder after she killed her son by filling his mouth with sand and then burying him in a field, where he was later found dead. During her pregnancy Christian had been brought before the Scottish Church Court (or Kirk Session) on three different occasions, accused of carrying an illegitimate child. Despite being under considerable pressure, she denied her pregnancy at each of these 'appearances'. Although she later confessed to being fully aware of her condition and impending circumstances, she nevertheless felt compelled to maintain her lies to the church elders and to her friends and family. As she herself explained to the Justiciary Court, 'I didnae want to hurt the child in my belly... but I widnae [would not] face the Elders and their Terror once more for onything [sic].'[27]

Marjory McCanday, from Inverness, was accused of infanticide in 1749, after she battered her new-born child to death with a gravestone. She told the local 'Minister of the Gospel', Mr Alexander McBean, who interrogated her after the infant's body was found, that he was the person who was ultimately responsible for what she had done to her child. McBean had brought Marjory before the Kirk Session during her pregnancy to confess her sins before the parish, but she had refused and had vehemently denied her condition. Upon her arrest, she snapped at McBean shouting 'You gard [made] me do this! You and your questions and your talk of Hell!'[28] In 1762, Agnes Walker was indicted at Dumfries for the murder of her new-born child, which had been suffocated and subsequently buried in a field, where it had been uncovered by dogs that proceeded to ravage the corpse. Agnes had appeared twice before the Kirk Session during her pregnancy, but had persistently denied being with child. In her eventual confession before Mr Nathaniel McKie, a local 'Minister of the Gospel', Agnes explained that she had killed her baby in order 'to avoyde [avoid] going before the Session a time... she being alone with no one in the world'.[29] Clearly, these women fervently wanted to avoid being further exposed to scrupulous interrogation about their personal lives in a public socio-religious forum.

It is important to recognise that infanticide during the pre-modern period was not only resorted to because of an illegitimate pregnancy. For instance, some accused individuals committed new-born child murder in an attempt to conceal an extra-marital affair.[30] This motive seems to have been particularly common amongst men indicted for the offence. Adam Wilson, from Kinross, for instance, was indicted for new-born child murder in 1747. He stood accused of murdering his new-born child, which had been conceived after a prolonged period of fornication with his servant, Margaret Arnot, while his wife was recovering from parturition herself. Adam had desperately tried to persuade Margaret to have an abortion and had visited surgeons and apothecaries pretending that his servant 'had been wronged and hurt by a man' and that he now sought medicines on her behalf which would result in 'her ultimate salvation'. These remedies were not forthcoming, however, and when all other means failed, Adam took the new-born from his lover and drowned it in a bucket of water, in order, by his own words, 'to hide or conceal his shame'.[31] Similarly, Welshman Rees Jones, from Llansanffraid-yn-Elfael, Radnorshire, was indicted for the murder of a bastard child born to his servant in 1771. He strangled the child with its own umbilical cord in order 'to conceal his shameful affair from his wife and her mother who was large and most fearsome'.[32]

Some women accused of new-born child murder may well have committed the crime because of shameful feelings associated with being the victim of a sexual assault, as was reported to have been the cause of conception on a few occasions.[33] Some women committed this offence in response to the opprobrium associated with the kind of sexual activity they had engaged in: a few of the infanticide indictments brought before British courts refer to incest and the shame associated with abusive and clandestine relationships as being motivating factors. Elizabeth Peacock from Stirling, for instance, was indicted for new-born child murder in 1709. Although Peacock was a married woman, her brother was the father of her child and she suffocated the baby in an attempt to conceal their relationship.[34] In 1782, Mary Lloyd, from Llangathen, Carmarthenshire, was indicted for strangling her new-born child, which had been 'conceived in union with her father John'. Upon further investigation, the corpses of two more neonates were found in the garden of the family home and were also acknowledged to be the children of the accused and her father. Mary explained that she had killed her offspring to 'conceal her shame and the shame of her fall from her mother'.[35]

Many of the indictments for infanticide in pre-modern Britain associated with an illicit pregnancy could be described as 'crimes of outrage', carried out by women who felt deeply ashamed by their 'illegitimate' condition.[36] These women may have felt so humiliated that they believed they had little option but to conceal their pregnancies and subsequently dispose of the cause of their opprobrium. Many of these women, by their own admission, felt utterly isolated and alone in the latter stages of their pregnancies. To them, the unmarried mother had a perilous future; one which ought to be avoided at all costs. As one nineteenth-century pamphleteer explained, for many women 'the infant at her breast was her stigma, her burden, her curse'.[37]

As well as trying to avoid personal feelings of opprobrium, many women committed the crime in order to avoid being shamed and shunned by others or because they feared they would be isolated from their families and ostracised from supportive kin networks.[38] An illegitimate pregnancy often brought dishonour to a family, and, in the seventeenth and eighteenth centuries in particular, the head of the household could be publicly derided for his inability to control the sexual behaviour of family members.[39] Many young, unwed mothers must have feared their parents' reaction to news of an unwanted and unexpected addition to the family. Magdalen Bowman, for instance, was indicted for drowning her illegitimate son at Defynnog, Breconshire, in 1790. When she was asked by the Court of Great Sessions in Wales why she had done this 'grievous deed', Magdalen replied that she had concealed her pregnancy and then killed her new-born child 'being afraid of her father and mother'.[40]

As well as tarnishing the immediate standing or status of the family, an illegitimate pregnancy could also harm future prospects for a pre-modern household. The open admittance or revelation of an illegitimate pregnancy could destroy the honest character and good reputation of a woman, thereby seriously inhibiting her marriage prospects.[41] As a consequence, it was not only the new-born infant which threatened to become an unwanted burden on the family, but also the mother of the child. The pressure to avoid isolation from familial support may have been a significant causal factor in instances of new-born child murder, especially in the seventeenth and eighteenth centuries, particularly in instances where a woman had already 'shamefully' borne one illegitimate child and was now pregnant with another.[42]

Family-based opprobrium was not the only type of shame that women indicted for new-born child murder between 1600 and 1900 sought to avoid. Sanctions and derision from employers and the community in which the woman lived could be equally damning, especially if the woman concerned was a migrant who had moved from her family to find work and was now isolated and exiled, without any means of support.[43] Communities were not only perturbed by the moral disgrace and loss of honour associated with illegitimate pregnancies in their midst, they also felt threatened by the financial burden that a bastard child would inflict on them in times of economic uncertainty.[44] As a consequence of this, community members and employers often shunned and ridiculed unmarried mothers. Women living in these communities must have been aware of prevailing attitudes, and may have desperately wanted to avoid censure. On occasion, this desperation may have encouraged unwed pregnant women to become peripatetic, moving around from parish to parish trying to find a more sympathetic milieu, but sometimes it must have resulted in the concealment of pregnancy and an ensuing new-born child murder.

Ann Terry, for instance, was indicted at the Old Bailey in 1744 for delivering her new-born daughter and then afterwards 'flinging it out of a certain window in a lodging room... three stories high', whereupon it fell upon a paved yard below and was mortally wounded. Ann explained to her landlady immediately after she was discovered that she had committed the crime 'to hide my shame and for fear you should see it and think ill of me'.[45] In 1775, a London woman called Sarah Reynolds was indicted for 'the wilful murder of her male bastard child', which had been strangled with the use of a large blue and white linen handkerchief. When Sarah was examined by the court, she explained that she committed the murder so as 'not to bring shame upon my master and distress upon myself'.[46]

For Ann Terry, Sarah Reynolds and many women like them, the seclusion and loneliness felt as a result of their circumstances must have been a significant causal factor for the murderous activity they subsequently carried out.[47] As Cesare Beccaria explained in 1764:

> infanticide results from the unavoidable conflict in which a woman is placed if she is given in to weakness or violence. How could one who finds herself caught between disgrace and the death of a being unable to feel what harms it, not prefer the latter to the certain misery to which she and her unhappy fruit would be exposed?[48]

Many of the women who committed new-born child murder in Britain and Europe during the pre-modern period endured a deep isolation. For some, desperation and a decision made on the spur of the moment probably determined their action. However, many must have felt that once they had concealed their 'shameful' pregnancies they were on an inescapable and inevitable journey to infanticide.[49] For these women, the only conceivable means by which they could control their fate and resolve their situation was to terminate the life of the object that threatened to make their existence opprobrious and distressing.[50] Of course, this does not explain precisely why some women resorted to infanticide to conceal their shame and avoid being dishonoured and others chose to endure such misery, but it is clear that a wish to reassert control in the face of shame was certainly a causal factor for many women who resorted to killing their new-born offspring in the three centuries before 1900.

Economic factors

According to Joel Harrington, 'for single women, issues of reputation and economic solvency were so closely interwoven as to be indistinguishable from one another'.[51] Consequently, we must examine the extent to which economic factors were behind women's recourse to infanticide in the pre-modern period. Did women seek to seize control of their fate in terms of their own financial security through instances of new-born child murder? For the early modern period it is difficult to answer this question directly from the evidence at hand. As Marcin Kamler insists, in relation to the European experience of infanticide at this time:

> There are almost no attempts to explain the crime by the living conditions and the fear of not being able to earn one's living with an illegitimate child to support; one can assume that such motives would have been mentioned in the statements if these factors had played a significant role in the subsequent fate of the unmarried mothers.[52]

One reason for the paucity of material explanations for infanticide in the sixteenth, seventeenth and early eighteenth centuries is provided by Otto Ulbricht. He argues that economic causal factors were only rarely provided in trials for new-born child murder during this period because they would be considered 'base motives' by the judicial authorities, and might result in more serious sanctions when it came to verdict and sentencing.[53]

Whilst it is true that economic want was not a commonly voiced explanation for infanticide in trials in the pre-modern period, it can be found on occasion if we look at the evidence more closely. Indeed, many historians believe that economic want was as important as shame as a motive for deliberate infanticide at this time.[54] Moreover, after 1800, the notion of financial hardship as a motive for infanticide grew in significance and became the routine explanation given by women accused of this crime, alongside claims of temporary insanity.[55] For these reasons, economic motives for infanticide are worthy of further investigation.

Falling pregnant during employment (especially as a domestic servant) meant dismissal without a reference and a loss of livelihood and means of support.[56] We saw in Chapter 2 that a single woman could enjoy a relatively comfortable living as a domestic servant. If pregnancy was discovered, however, her ability to earn an independent wage was immediately terminated, and she would find it difficult to attain subsequent employment elsewhere. This forfeiture of income was compounded by the spectre of financial hardship caused by the additional mouth to feed, clothe and care for. As Martin

Daly and Margo Wilson comment, 'If the history of infanticide reveals anything... it is surely that acts of desperation are principally the products of desperate circumstances.'[57]

For many women, faced with a lack of options to resolve their precarious situation and contemplating penury in the longer-term, infanticide may well have been regarded as a means of survival. As Michelle Oberman explains, 'The prospect of single motherhood in this era was overwhelmingly grim.'[58] Women could not hope to support themselves and their children if they were without a working wage. In addition, in some cases, the working wage women received was insufficient to support them. Consequently, survival was clearly at issue if the expense of a child had to be factored into the cost of living.[59] One solution to this problem might have been to combine childcare with gainful employment, but few women earned enough in the pre-modern period to procure this sort of support. Moreover, women workers (as well as their male counterparts) were subject to the vagaries of economic fluctuations and personal misfortune, such as ill health, which could limit the extent of their earning capabilities over sustained periods of time. To put it simply, for many women, the economics of single motherhood between 1600 and 1900 did not add up.[60]

This is evident from many of the cases of new-born child murder indicted in Britain during the pre-modern era. For instance, extreme poverty and destitution were cited by defence lawyers (appointed by the Crown) in the case of Jean Stourie, who was indicted at Jedburgh in 1725 for the murder of her baby daughter. The court heard how, although Jean had concealed her pregnancy, she was not tempted to destroy the infant upon parturition. Instead, she carried the infant about her for nearly a month, until, 'owing to her extreme poverty... and in order to shun the trouble of carrying and begging with it up and down the country', she choked the infant with her bare hands and left it in a shallow grave.[61] In 1768, spinster Jane Evan, from Cerrigydrudion, Denbighshire, was indicted for strangling her female bastard child 'on account of her poverty' and because she already had a six-year-old daughter to bring up by herself with no-one to support her.[62] In 1841, Harriet Longley, from Islington, was indicted for the murder of her three-week-old daughter Eliza. Harriet had confessed to a policeman that she had thrown her child into the river because 'she had no food for herself, and no milk to give the child... that she had not a farthing of money to support it'.[63]

Many impoverished single mothers were forced to rely on support from their parish community in order to get by, and in some areas of Britain this provision could be fairly generous.[64] However, increasingly over the late eighteenth and early nineteenth centuries, this kind of support diminished as parishes 'preferred to place children in the institutional care of the workhouse while mothers earned a living outside'.[65] Prior to 1834, Poor Law legislation made the fathers of illegitimate children liable for routine maintenance payments. However, it is difficult to determine with any accuracy just how common it was for women to apply for this kind of support, which entailed naming the individual responsible for their misfortune. Moreover, it is unclear how frequently these men were tracked down and whether full or partial payment was obtained from them on a regular basis.[66]

At any rate, in 1834, revised bastardy legislation was introduced through the New Poor Laws, which required the mother, rather than the father, to bear the financial burden of illegitimacy.[67] These changes were said by many contemporaries to have actively encouraged mothers to commit new-born child murder, and did little to suppress the rise in illegitimacy which was perceived to exist at that time. One publication which was highly critical of the new legislation noted in 1871 that the changes to maintenance had made 'poverty the immediate, often the sole, motive prompting to the crimes of child murder and desertion'[68] in the second half of the nineteenth century. This was because under the new legislation, although a father was liable to contribute as much as five shillings per week to the mother of his illegitimate child, these payments diminished after the baby reached six weeks old, and were reduced to a maximum of half-a-crown per week. Such payments were only to continue until the child reached its teenage years and were to terminate entirely if the mother married at any point before this.[69] Amendments to the New Poor Laws in 1844 dictated that it was up to the woman concerned to obtain a maintenance order (which was organised at a cost) and to see that it was enforced. Unless a maintenance agreement was signed within twelve months of the infant's birth, the father was thereafter absolved from all legal and financial responsibility for his child's wellbeing and upkeep.[70] Furthermore, by previous legislation, 'every woman neglecting to maintain her bastard child, being able wholly or in part to do so, whereby such child becomes chargeable by any parish or union, shall be punishable as an idle and disorderly person'.[71]

In addition to the end of 'outdoor relief', which many impoverished women relied upon, these arguably misogynistic legislative changes were criticised for impoverishing women, single mothers in particular. This may have further increased the likelihood of their being tempted to commit new-born child murder, as reflected in indictment evidence.[72] Nevertheless, when challenged, the Poor Law Commissioners did not believe that economic misfortune could ever be a motive for infanticide: 'We believe that in no civilized country, and scarcely in any barbarous country, has such a thing ever been heard of as a mother's killing her child in order to save the expense of feeding it.'[73] From the evidence provided in this chapter we know this statement to be grossly inaccurate, and the individuals acting on this committee to be considerably misinformed.

For example, in 1752, single woman Elizabeth Coupar was brought before the North Circuit in Aberdeen charged with killing her new-born child by battering it repeatedly with a wooden shoe. When a midwife examined her for symptoms of her recent delivery, Elizabeth told the woman that she had killed her son 'so that she would not beg her bread with it over the world... for she was in such misery'.[74] In 1856, eighteen-year-old Emma Riley was indicted at the Old Bailey 'for feloniously killing and slaying a certain male child, born of her body, and called Richard James'. Richard was around three or four months old at the time of his death. The mother of the accused, a woman called Margaret Riley, outlined the impoverished and destitute circumstances in which she and her daughter were trying to survive, even before the baby came along. When asked to describe the attempts that had been made to care for the child, she explained: 'We did for it as far as laid in our power, but I had not money enough to get food for it – I had just come out of the infirmary with typhus fever, and was very badly off and I depended only on charity for my living – the child always threw up what it took – I gave it arrowroot, but what I gave did not appear to nourish it.' In frustration at her impoverished circumstances, Emma Riley abused and subsequently killed her child by repeatedly beating, slapping and shaking him vigorously to avoid 'dragging it about the streets any longer' and because she 'could not give it the nourishment it ought to have'.[75]

The spectre of poverty or financial hardship also seems to have been a motive for married women who were accused of infanticide in pre-modern Europe. Some of these women seem to have practised new-born child murder as a form of family limitation, when the burden of an extra mouth to feed would stretch the family purse too far, and where other forms of fertility control had failed or were unavailable.[76] However, this kind of infanticide was regularly under-reported, as discussed in previous chapters. This is because an unexpected fatality could be more readily explained away as a death by natural causes if it was non-violent and occurred within the context of a stable and formalised relationship.

Another possible economic motive for women committing infanticide related to the profit that could ensue from registering an infant with a burial club. This tended to be associated with married women. Burial insurance became popular in Britain from the mid-nineteenth century onwards. A pregnant woman would pay a few pennies a week into a fund set up in case anything happened to her child during labour and delivery, in order to enable her to pay for its funeral. Lionel Rose contends that women were deliberately killing their infants after birth but making the deaths appear accidental. They were then claiming the money (plus interest accrued) from the burial insurers, giving the child an inexpensive funeral and reaping the profits made.[77] Rose suggests that such practices were common across nineteenth-century Britain, and he calculates that by 1858 there were over 20,000 burial societies in England and Wales alone, with more than two million registered members.[78] Amongst contemporaries in the Victorian era, burial clubs came to be equated with a burgeoning and 'nefarious trade in infant life'.[79] However, both Aeron Hunt and Robert Sauer remind us that most burial clubs did not make full payment upon the death of an infant unless it had reached its first birthday.[80] Their evidence suggests that profit-making from burial clubs was less of a motive for new-born child murder than it was for the killing of older children.

It is clear from the evidence we have in relation to infanticide in Britain during the period 1600 to 1900 that many of the individuals concerned were desperate to avoid economic hardship. New-born child murder may have been seen by many men and women, both married and unmarried, as necessary in order to ensure their survival in the longer term.[81] Moreover, this desperation did not necessarily mean that infanticide was resorted to out of selfishness or malevolence. Some women clearly had more altruistic intentions in mind when they killed their babies, and believed that they were killing 'out of love', so as to protect their child from the unremitting grind of hunger, want and desperate need.[82] More complex calculations might be involved if the individual or couple concerned already had one child and recognised the implications and pressures of having another. In some instances, the health and material wellbeing of the older child may have been prioritised over the survival of any new addition to the 'family unit'.

Deliberate or malicious intent

As we have already seen, and as William Hunter's comment at the outset of this chapter testifies, some infanticides were carried out for seemingly 'well-intentioned' reasons. Likewise, there were accidental infanticides, which were borne out of the fear, ignorance, pain and confusion associated with self-delivery and isolated parturition. However, it is also apparent that some infanticides were carried out deliberately and with malicious intent. William Hunter himself argues that, on occasion, infanticide

> is a crime of the very deepest dye... a premeditated contrivance for taking away the life of the most inoffensive and most helpless of all human creatures, in opposition not only to the most universal dictates of humanity, but of that powerful instinctive passion which, for a wise and important purpose, the Author of our nature has planted in the breast of every female creature, a wonderful eagerness about the preservation of its young.[83]

We saw in Chapter 1 how traditional historical investigations and historiographical conclusions depicted female criminality as anomalous, trivial, and unworthy of detailed analysis. Women were regularly perceived as passive actors in the commission of crime. Recent work by scholars has utterly demolished this perception.[84] Women were criminal: they participated in a wide range of offences in just the same way as their male counterparts. They could perpetrate crime just as violently and aggressively as men could. In addition, rather than committing crime solely at the behest of men, as was often believed to be the case, women regularly behaved independently in their 'criminal' endeavours throughout the pre-modern period.

Women's autonomy actors in criminal activity was as true of infanticide as of any other illegality perpetrated between 1600 and 1900. Women could commit infanticide in a malicious, calculated and, indeed, violent way, as is evidenced by some of the testimonies already explored in this volume.[85] As Donna Cooper Graves points out, to see infanticidal women

> only as victims of poverty, ignorance and the male-dominated social order is to deny them human agency. Infanticide can be seen, as the nineteenth-century reformers saw it, as a desperate, self-destructive reaction to experiences of material and moral poverty. But it can also be viewed in its positive aspect, as an act of autonomy, self-assertion, and self-definition... Choosing infanticide deliberately could not only save women from economic ruin, it could release her from being held a lifelong hostage to the constraints imposed by motherhood – something men simply could not understand.[86]

Thus, some of the women indicted for new-born child murder in Britain during the pre-modern era committed the crime with deliberation, as a pragmatic means to an end. For these women, infanticide was a simple, quick and practical solution, which enabled them to avoid the responsibilities of motherhood. They concealed their pregnancies in an attempt to evade arrest after the fact, rather than on account of feeling shamed by an illegitimate pregnancy, and they were not facing particularly acute economic hardship either. Rather, and in the face of few alternatives, killing the baby after its birth was regarded as an effective means to terminate both current problems (as it stopped the baby from crying and minimised their chance of discovery) and other long-term socio-economic problems.[87] Some women were convinced that what they were doing was unproblematic, as, for them, infanticide was just an alternative means of fertility control, in the form of a late abortion, and they planned this outcome from the realisation of conception.[88]

Christian Munro, for instance, was indicted at Inverness for a crime of child murder committed in 1761. She was a domestic servant working for a man called Robert Leslie, who lived in Rothes, in the Highlands of Scotland. She was charged with concealing her pregnancy, giving birth to a fully mature male child and subsequently killing the baby by slitting its throat with an open razor. She then buried the child in a nearby field, where it had been picked upon by wild animals so that only one hand of the infant was recovered and taken into evidence.[89] Christian latterly confessed to the infanticide of her child and explained to the court: 'I did what I had to do... I did not want the bairn... I did not want to be undone... or hear its crys [*sic*.]'.[90]

Other women saw their unborn child as an inconvenience, and were more maliciously inclined to kill it. Many of these women had been abandoned by their suitors during the course of their pregnancies, and chose to take out their anger on the new-born child, perhaps explaining the ultra-violent tendencies in evidence amongst some of the women accused of this crime.[91] To give an example, Isobel Tait, from Salton, Haddington, was indicted at the High Court of Justiciary in Edinburgh charged with new-born child murder in 1788. Isobel had been seduced and then abandoned by her erstwhile lover after his wife found out about the affair and forced the family to move elsewhere. The court heard that after having been delivered of a fully-grown male bastard child, Isobel had 'wilfully and maliciously' attacked the infant with a clasp knife, repeatedly stabbing it about the face and chest until it had received upwards of thirty different penetrative wounds upon its body. When Isobel Tait appeared in court she confessed to killing her child, explaining that she wanted the child to 'feel the pain of her brok'd [broken] heart, seeing as it was the cause of her misery'.[92]

In any event, it was unusual for the British courts to be presented with evidence of deliberate intent and malevolence in infanticide cases between 1600 and 1900. This obviously masks the intention of these women and further influences the stereotypes created around women and their criminality. This was because such testimony stood in stark contrast to the accepted stereotypes of feminine behaviour. Women were meant to be passive and lacking in responsibility, especially in relation to matters of reproduction and maternity.[93] Consequently, when evidence of autonomous criminality and violent tendencies was presented in trials for new-born child murder during the pre-modern era, it was more reasonable to consider them within the context of a temporary frenzy or insane impulse which could account for the aberrance from 'normal' behaviour.[94] These explanations were thought to be especially fitting and appropriate when so many of the cases of new-born child murder suggested some sort of mental disassociation between the mother and her child. It is to these types of 'psychological' mitigation for infanticide that we now turn.

Medical and psychosocial explanations

Toward the end of the eighteenth century, judicial attitudes to accused women changed, as the courts became increasingly interested in explanations for female criminality, particularly that of a violent nature.[95] This change manifested itself in two ways in relation to trials for new-born child murder in Britain at that time. First, there was an increase in the use of character testimony in prosecutions, encouraged by the court and the judiciary. This was especially prevalent in relation to the use of defence witnesses, who regularly referred to the former good character and sound moral conduct of the suspect and tentatively suggested that the infanticidal act under investigation was a temporary aberration on the part of the woman concerned, caused by 'emotional' stress of one sort or another.[96] The second change (which clearly related to the first) was the development of a far more sympathetic attitude towards infanticidal women, which significantly diminished the conviction rate for the offence from the second third of the eighteenth century onwards.[97]

Even before these judicial changes occurred, rudimentary forms of medical and psychosocial explanations for women's involvement in new-born child murder were beginning to be heard by British courts. Perhaps surprisingly, being under the influence of alcohol seems an explanation never offered in British infanticide indictments during the pre-modern period. This was probably because such an excuse would not be regarded as valid and because confessing to inebriation during or immediately after parturition would stain the character of the accused in the mind of the judge and the assize, who were about to determine her fate. Rather, it became more common for defence teams in infanticide trials during the seventeenth and eighteenth centuries to assert the ignorance of the accused. Many of the women indicted for infanticide were on trial for killing the infant from their first pregnancy. Their inexperience in matters of parturition and maternity enabled some of them to claim that they did not know they were pregnant, that they did not know they were giving birth or that they had been out of their mind with fear, panic and confusion at the moment of delivery. Thus, the killing of their child had resulted from a temporary frenzy caused by unexpected, excruciating pain.[98] Such was the explanation given to the Court of Great Sessions in Wales in 1818, for instance, when Ann Jones, from Merthyr Cynog, in Breconshire, was indicted for placing her baby in a pot of hot water on the fire.[99] As Dana Rabin elaborates, with reference to infanticide indictments from the second half of the eighteenth century, in some cases:

> the defendant made a narrow claim about the state of her mind during the crime itself. Each argued that the actual fact of childbirth produced a mental state similar to a 'blackout' during which she had no control over her behaviour. The women's descriptions gave the impression that they did not remember this time and that they could take no responsibility for their actions. They did not deny that a murder took place, but they argued that their behaviour was not criminal because they lacked intent. They established the temporary nature of their insanity by introducing evidence about the preparations they had made for the birth of their child before the onset of labour.[100]

Psychological distress relating to childbirth was not a new phenomenon in the second half of the eighteenth century, when the judicial authorities started to become interested in it. From the sixteenth century, and arguably before then, it was widely held that women's proclivity to feeble-mindedness and irrationality was entirely related to their capacity for reproduction. As Joel Eigen identifies, throughout history 'the secret to women's psychological frailty was sought in their particular constitution... female biology... predisposed women to insanity, particularly emotional instability owing to the ordeal of carrying a foetus and ultimately to the delivery itself'.[101] William Hunter agreed that there was a psychological link between parturition and temporary insanity when he wrote about the potential causes of infanticide in the 1780s. He maintained that many pregnant women suffered under a 'phrensy from despair' at the moment of delivery and that 'their distress of body and mind deprives them of all judgment and rational conduct'.[102]

Temporary insanity and diminished responsibility were, nevertheless, defences that were used relatively sparingly, and with a great deal of care, in infanticide trials in the centuries before 1800. For instance, a woman claiming that she had killed her child after being tempted by the Devil had to judge the mood of the court with precision, as presenting testimony such as this could have unpredictable consequences with regard to sentencing and punishment. Women claiming to have committed murder under satanic influences were not necessarily guaranteed pity at this time. The case against Aberdeenshire woman Janet Boag, in 1820, illustrates this point. Janet was indicted for the murder of her new-born son after she had been found feeding his dismembered remains through a laundry mangle. When she was asked why she had committed this 'barbarous' act against her child, Janet replied that she had been tempted by the Devil to kill both herself and her child, but that she had been too readily discovered and was unable to complete his wishes. Despite evidence presented to the court that Janet had been suffering from delusions since parturition and was evidently 'deprived of her reason' at the moment she had killed her child, she was, nevertheless, regarded by the judicial authorities as 'evil', 'in league with the Devil' and described by the circuit judge as 'the handmaiden of darkness'. She was convicted and executed, with subsequent public anatomisation.[103]

Unmarried female suspects also rarely deployed the defence of temporary insanity in the seventeenth and eighteenth centuries, as they feared that this kind of explanation would necessitate an admission of guilt and would not adequately explain recourse to concealment of pregnancy.[104] Perhaps more importantly, some of the eighteenth-century judicial authorities became perturbed that, by introducing temporary insanity as an explanation for crime, they had also introduced an excuse for it. As Dana Rabin explains, 'Courtroom observers worried that if applied more broadly, this language could lead to the equivalence of all crime with insanity and open the possibility that no one would be held responsible for any criminal behaviour.'[105]

Despite these initial reservations, and largely because insanity provided such an apt explanation for the actions of violent women in particular, in the second half of the eighteenth and early decades of the nineteenth centuries, the mind of the defendant, rather than the body of the infant, grew in importance and became the key determinant in trial outcomes for new-born child murder.[106] As Scottish legal authority Archibald Alison explained in 1832:

> Their distress of mind and body deprives them of all judgment and they are delivered by themselves... and sometimes destroying their offspring without being conscious of what they are doing. Accordingly, it is a principle of law, that mere appearances of violence on the child's body are not *per se* sufficient, unless some circumstances of evidence exist to indicate that violence was knowingly and intentionally committed; or they are of such a kind as themselves to indicate intentional murder.[107]

In part, medical and psychosocial explanations for infanticide became more important because of the judicial authorities' move to a more compassionate attitude. Courts became increasingly inclined to give female suspects in infanticide trials the benefit of the doubt owing to the fact that, as the nature of their behaviour was so nakedly unfeminine and non-maternal, it could only be explained by mental incapacity of one sort or another.[108] However, this transformation of judicial attitudes also took place as a result of the development and professionalisation of psychiatry (or alienism), which was increasingly referred to in judicial proceedings for new-born child murder from the end of the eighteenth century onwards.[109] Lucia Zedner illustrates that the development of this particular aspect of medico-legal practice occurred with astonishing speed, and points to the medical professionals' 'remarkable achievement... in persuading lawyers of the validity of this psychiatric exculpation, effectively replacing traditional legal discourse with that of psychiatry'.[110]

By the 1820s and 1830s, 'Both alienists, the emerging psychiatric profession, and obstetric practitioners added significantly to the brief remarks and observations of men-midwives, midwives and other medical observers on the depression, disorientation, occasional craziness and violent tendencies of women post-partum described in previous centuries.'[111] This growing expertise tended to concentrate on trying to reach an understanding of the dissociative aspects of new-born child murder, where some of the women accused of infanticide were mentally unable to acknowledge that they were pregnant or that they had given birth. In effect, these women refused to give the child an identity or admit its existence.[112] Over a relatively short period of time, however, this medical research and scientific investigation progressed, grew more expansive and came to be associated with a more specific type of postpartum illness, which was said to be directly related to instances of infanticide: puerperal insanity.

Puerperal insanity became a defined medical term in the early nineteenth century, although its existence as a recognised illness can be traced back to antiquity.[113] It was often regarded as an ambiguous condition because it lay between the boundaries of two different medical specialisms – obstetrics and psychiatry – and, as a result, a variety of different terms have been used to describe it, including 'puerperal psychosis', 'puerperal mania', 'lactational insanity', 'mania lactea', 'mania in childbirth' and 'mania furibunda'.[114] Robert Gooch was the first British physician to write about this type of insanity, in his influential work *Observations on Puerperal Insanity*, published in 1820, but it was the French physician–alienist Louis Victor Marcé who became the accepted medical authority on the 'insanities of reproduction' by the mid-nineteenth century. He was the first medical professional to suggest, in a textbook produced in 1858, that there was an interplay between the process of reproduction and mental disorder.[115]

Puerperal insanity, as a defined medical condition, allowed nineteenth-century psychiatrists to develop their own medical specialism.[116] Two types of puerperal insanity were said to exist: mania and melancholy. Mania was said to occur sooner after parturition and, although more severe in its intensity, was thought to be more easily and rapidly cured than melancholy. Mania was characterised by overt aggressiveness and unpredictable tendencies towards violence. Melancholy, on the other hand, was typically evidenced by general despondency and lethargy.[117] Puerperal insanity could come on in the immediate aftermath of parturition or several months after, when the body was still sustaining nourishment of the infant through nursing.[118]

The characteristic symptoms of the condition are described by Hilary Marland as including:

> sleeplessness, rapid pulse, pallor or flushed skin, vivid eyes, furred tongue and constipation and delirium... great excitability, expressed through constant chattering, delusions, singing, swearing, tearing clothes and lewd sexual displays. In the worst-case scenario the mother became 'forgetful of her child', or expressed murderous intent toward the infant, her husband or herself.[119]

Despite this detailed description, it is clear from contemporary medical writing that the symptoms of puerperal insanity were profuse and almost impossible to record with any precision, as they differed so starkly from one individual to another.[120] The relatively flexible parameters and definition of the illness contrast somewhat starkly with the increasing judicial calls for precision with regard to how and when new-born babies had died and whether they had been born alive. Nevertheless, puerperal insanity was universally regarded in the nineteenth century as a sudden, serious, but temporary, condition, which could be cured either at home or in an institutional setting with 'regular purging, tonics, calming medicines, nutritious diet, careful observation, nursing and rest, combined with moral therapy'.[121] Moreover, although it is difficult to tell how prevalent or extensive diagnoses of puerperal insanity were in the nineteenth century (estimates of asylum admissions vary nationally between 5 and 20 per cent),[122] medical men were assured of the significance of the condition and its undoubted relationship to instances of new-born child murder. Indeed, by the first few decades of the Victorian era, infanticide came to be regarded as a symptom of puerperal insanity, albeit an extreme manifestation.[123]

By the 1830s, the relationship between puerperal insanity and infanticide was widely accepted by medical men, and it was soon acknowledged by the courtroom too. Temporary insanity became a successful plea for women to adopt after the first quarter of the nineteenth century, as evidenced by the few convictions for new-born child murder from that time until 1900, which we saw in Chapter 5.[124] The high acquittal rate defied the concerns voiced about a perceived increase in infanticide in the 1860s and 1870s, as previously discussed. As a result, some contemporary commentators (such as Thomas Wakely, Edwin Lankester and especially William Burke Ryan) tried to reorientate thinking about new-born child murder to concentrate on the seriousness of the offence, as they were convinced that deliberate intent, rather than a temporary mental aberration, was required. They criticised what they saw as a misplaced public leniency towards infanticidal mothers and emphasised the scale of the public health problem that they perceived.[125]

Despite these criticisms, puerperal insanity came to dominate defence tactics employed in British courtrooms during the nineteenth century and eclipsed all other explanations for new-born child murder.[126] From 1843 onwards, judicial authorities usually referred to the M'Naghten Rules when faced with insanity claims from defendants. The key criterion to establish an acquittal on the grounds of insanity was to establish whether the accused knew right from wrong at the time of the offence.[127] In cases of puerperal insanity, however, the M'Naghten Rules were replaced by a more refined understanding of the mental status of the accused. In these instances, women could be conscious of their actions at some level, but owing to their temporary or partial insanity at any given moment they 'failed to understand their moral wrongfulness' or were 'incapable of self-restraint'.[128] The key aspect in establishing the validity of a defence of puerperal insanity was to emphasise the temporary nature of the frenzy or impulse to kill, as this meant that the scale and severity of the episode was immeasurable, incalculable and difficult for the courts to interpret with any accuracy, resulting in judicial decisions which erred on the side of caution and leniency.[129] As the English lawyer, judge and writer James Fitzjames Stephen described to a commission debating capital punishment in 1865:

> the operation of the criminal law presupposes in the mind of the person who is acted upon a normal state of strength, reflective power, and so on, but a woman just after childbirth is so upset, and is in such a hysterical

state altogether, that it seems to me that you cannot deal with her in the same manner as if she was in a regular and proper state of health. I believe also (though that is more a medical than a legal question) that women in that condition do get the strongest symptoms of what amounts almost to temporary madness, and that they often hardly know what they are about, and will do things which they have no settled or deliberate intention whatever of doing.[130]

Judicial authorities, medical professionals and the public largely embraced and accepted the notion that women could suffer from puerperal insanity in the immediate aftermath of parturition or during the subsequent months of lactation, not least because this explanation fitted multiple scenarios. Puerperal insanity applied to young unmarried women who had concealed their pregnancies and gone on to commit infanticide as well as those who had tried to care for their infants but discovered they could not quite cope with the responsibility of unwed motherhood. It also applied to older women and those who were married, and it affected the fate of infants up to one year old as well as new-borns.[131]

There were other reasons why puerperal insanity was seen as an acceptable explanation for new-born child murder during the nineteenth century. First, by rooting the explanation in a medical condition, infanticide was rendered a personal problem, rather than a social concern, much to the dismay of contemporary commentators such as William Burke Ryan.[132] In addition, the very nature of puerperal insanity rendered it a temporary problem that was ultimately recoverable in time and was thus presented as something society should not be overly concerned about managing or controlling.[133] Most importantly of all, puerperal insanity reinforced contemporary perceptions regarding the intrinsic weakness of women and provided an explanation for female criminality that stepped outside the boundaries of 'acceptable' behaviour.

Contemporaries agreed that as no 'normal' woman would desire to kill their own child, an act of infanticide could *only* be explained by the presence of temporary, 'abnormal' emotions.[134] Instances of acute infanticidal violence could also be accounted for by this type of explanation. By propounding such an argument, judicial authorities and medical professionals enabled women accused of infanticide to be treated with a great deal of compassion and sympathy during most of the Victorian period. However, this groundswell of opinion also facilitated the retention of the stereotypical labels of femininity, which were regarded as key to contemporary notions of domesticity and patriarchy.[135] Moreover, the acceptance of puerperal insanity as an explanation for infanticide marginalised and patronised women still further, as they were once again considered non-autonomous beings, who were dominated, controlled and ultimately defined by the unpredictable nature of their emotions and sensibilities.[136]

The broad applicability of puerperal insanity in relation to new-born child murder, as well as the symptoms associated with the illness and the attitudes towards this explanation, are best evidenced by three case studies, which span the nineteenth century.

A coroner's inquest held in London on 4 January 1838 heard how 21-year old Elizabeth Hodges, a married woman who already had one child, had murdered her four-week-old baby by smothering it and then placing it in a copper filled with water. Witnesses, including the accused's husband and father, testified that Elizabeth had been in very ill health after her confinement, describing how she had been 'accompanied by a great depression of spirits and absence of mind'. One individual recounted how they had found an open razor on Elizabeth's dressing-table, which they believed she had intended to use for the purposes of 'self-destruction'.[137] A surgeon, Mr James Hay, had examined the accused after her arrest and 'was decidedly of opinion that she was totally unconscious of what she was doing. She was now in a most dangerous state, and was not likely to recover'.[138] The coroner summed up the case by saying that he 'thought there could be little doubt that at the time she committed the rash act she was labouring under an aberration of intellect', but, as the question of the accused's sanity had to be tried elsewhere, he bound the case over to the determination of the Central Criminal Court after the jury passed a verdict of 'wilful murder'.[139]

When the criminal trial was brought before the Old Bailey, later in January 1838, the court heard testimony from a neighbour and friend of Elizabeth Hodges, a woman called Leah Mills. The witness recounted two dreams that Elizabeth had told her about, which had occurred just a few days before the murder of the child had been committed. Elizabeth had said to Leah that in her dreams 'the devil came to me and told me to kill my child'. Further testimony was then presented by Mary Ann Harvey, who had been Elizabeth's midwife during her confinement. She testified that she was the one who found the body of the dead child and asked Mrs Hodges how she could have carried out such a deed? Elizabeth had not replied to that question, 'but looked in a most wild, distracted state' and latterly said that 'the devil had tempted her very frequently' and that she thought she 'should make away with herself'.[140]

Despite the original testimony at the coroner's inquest of Elizabeth's derangement, by the time of the trial her condition had improved dramatically and the same medical professional, Dr James Hay, now deemed Elizabeth to be 'in a state of perfect consciousness and fit to stand trial'. He also added that 'it is not unfrequented for women during parturition, and shortly after, to be affected with a mania peculiar to that state – it is called puerperal mania – deficiency of milk, and the milk flowing upwards, would very probably cause such circumstances'. In other words, Hay claimed that a lactational blockage had caused an excess of milk to flow to Elizabeth Hodges' brain, causing her to be temporarily frenzied. Elizabeth was found not guilty of her crimes, as the court and jury believed 'her to be insane at the time of committing the offence'.[141]

When Adelaide Freedman was indicted for infanticide at the Old Bailey, some 31 years after Elizabeth Hodges, her case attracted more public interest (being reported in at least 16 national newspapers). The trial offers the historian fresh insight into contemporary attitudes towards culpability, theories regarding the symptoms of puerperal insanity, and the ways in which the illness came about. Adelaide Freedman was a married 30-year-old Jewish woman who lived at 71 Rutland Street, Whitechapel. Her husband was a sailor and, for the five years prior to her arrest, he had been in Peru. In the autumn of 1869, Adelaide had given birth to a female child and, upon receiving a letter from her husband that he was about to return from his travels, she bought some salts of lemons (commonly used to remove ink stains), poisoned her child with them and consumed some herself.[142]

Soon afterwards, Adelaide's four-week-old child was found dead and she was removed to the London Hospital to recuperate.[143] At the inquest into the child's death, a Dr Henry Letheby reported his observations on seeing the body of the child, saying that 'the tongue showed the presence of a corrosive or caustic agent' and upon analysing the stomach contents he 'found in it a quantity of oxalic acid and potash'. He also added that there had been a history of insanity in the woman's family.[144] The inquest jury returned a verdict of 'wilful murder' against Adelaide Freedman, but expressed the opinion that she was insane at the time she committed the crime and that she had done so 'that her husband might not know the immoral life she had been leading during his absence at sea'.[145]

The case was then delivered to the Old Bailey, where proceedings began on 22 November 1869. The court heard testimony from the accused's sister, Rebecca Marks, who testified that soon after her confinement, Adelaide 'looked vacant and strange... she was always with melancholy, and used to complain dreadfully of her head'. Rebecca also testified to the fact that her mother and two of her aunts were afflicted with mental illness and said that when 'her mother was carrying her, she attempted to hang herself and her father had to cut her down'.[146]

Another woman, Elizabeth Markham, described in court how Adelaide Freedman had confessed to her that she had poisoned her child. Elizabeth rushed over to Adelaide's lodgings and found her baby foaming at the mouth. She picked the child up, but it died in her arms shortly after. Adelaide was standing behind Elizabeth when the child finally succumbed and said 'My head is so bad I shall go mad, my troubles are so great... Let me die! Let me die!' When saying this, Adelaide was described as being 'very excited; her eyes were rolling in her head, and there was something very strange about them'. She was also described as subsequently being 'in a low, melancholy state' and was frequently seen 'wringing her hands and putting them to her head and crying... there was a restlessness about her eyes'.[147]

A Dr Morrison had cared for Adelaide Freedman during and after her confinement, and he was asked to provide the court with his medical opinion as to her state of mind. Morrison explained that:

> she had a wild and vacant look; not so much to warrant interference to have her confined in a lunatic asylum, but sufficient to attract notice, and make me suspicious of her sanity – she had the peculiar look of puerperal mania, which is a well-recognised form of insanity with women about the period of their confinement – it affects them when they are not able to give milk to a child, and is the consequence of it – this form of puerperal mania develops itself sometimes by acts of violence to the nearest and dearest, and to the offspring of the woman – there is no fixed period at which it arrives at intensity, sometimes one and sometimes two weeks after confinement – there are two forms, the acute, wild raving, and the other is the melancholy sort, with which there are no delusions.[148]

Dr Morrison was asked two further questions on cross-examination. The first was whether puerperal insanity was hereditary? Morrison replied in the affirmative, but provided no evidence to substantiate his answer. He was then asked whether a woman suffering from puerperal mania was conscious that what she was doing would cause death. Morrison answered 'I believe that in this form of mania they would be conscious that they were doing wrong, and still not be able to prevent themselves from doing it.' The prosecution were seemingly unsatisfied with this particular response, and so the court called a further medical professional to answer the same question. He replied:

> I think the depression, the melancholy, may be so great that, though she knew the result, still it would be an uncontrollable impulse – the mind may not be so disordered as to render the individual incapable of judging between right and wrong, yet the melancholy may be so great that she might commit the act, and try to poison herself as well – I think she would know that what she was doing was wrong; but if carried to its greatest extent, it might prevent her knowing that it was wrong.[149]

After hearing all the evidence, the jury decided that at the time of the crime the defendant was 'in such a mental condition as to be incapable of distinguishing right from wrong'. Adelaide Freedman was found not guilty on the ground of insanity and was ordered to be detained at Her Majesty's Pleasure.

The final case study relates to the indictment of a 22-year-old unmarried servant and laundress called Minnie Wells. Minnie was indicted at the Old Bailey in October 1894, accused of killing her month-old twin daughters, Minnie and Lilly, who had been born at Lambeth Workhouse.[150] This case was widely publicised across Britain, and appeared in more than 24 local and national newspapers. The details of the trial are interesting because the court proceedings makes clear that there was real debate and uncertainty as to whether the accused had suffered from puerperal insanity or whether she had deliberately killed her children on account of her impoverished circumstances. In this respect, the trial against Minnie Wells mirrors the various criticisms that were being levelled at puerperal insanity defences in infanticide trials across Britain towards the end of the nineteenth and the beginning of the twentieth centuries, discussed in more detail below.

Minnie confessed to drowning both infants separately, in two different ponds in Reigate. The criminal court heard that she was already the mother of a young toddler, and that up until her confinement she had been living with her father – Thomas Frederick Wells. Not long after she had been delivered of the twins, however, Minnie's father had been evicted from his home. Upon realising that she had no place of residence to go to after her confinement in the workhouse, and would most likely have to sleep in an unused woodshed, Minnie resolved to give up all three of her children for adoption and told her friends of her plans. A few days later, Harriet Creasy and Laura Ritchie, both former neighbours of Minnie Wells, found Minnie by the side of the road looking dishevelled. As they described, 'her stockings... were wet up to her knees, and her boots were sopping wet and smothered in wet sand'. When asked why she was in this condition, Minnie Wells said "Good gracious, talk about London mud!" and went indoors and dried herself.[151]

Various witnesses, such as Hannah Whitren, testified to seeing Minnie Wells on the day that she had allegedly killed her twins, describing her variously as 'all right and quiet', 'quite pleasant' and 'a very affectionate mother'. When the infants' bodies had been recovered and identified, Minnie was arrested and confessed (under caution) before police sergeant George Jeffrey, saying: 'On Monday, June 18th, I put the child in the moat some time before I saw Mrs Whitren. The other child was in the pond by Waterloo Park; I drowned that the same night. I can't give the time, but it was before I drowned the one in the moat. The one you found in the moat was Minnie May, and the other one in Waterloo Park was Lilly Mary.'[152]

The medical officer for the district, Joseph Loarne was examined in court and testified that, in his experience:

> in the period immediately after confinement, extending over some weeks, a woman is peculiarly liable to excessive emotional disturbance, which is liable to take the form of revulsion of feeling towards the children and an attempt to murder – I should call that an instance of puerperal mania; that may come on suddenly without any apparent cause, and it may as suddenly cease.... The delivery of twins would, I think, cause a greater strain on the mother then when there was only one child; it would seriously impair the nervous energy and the vitality – in the case of such a

Figure 6.1 Minnie Wells appearing at the Old Bailey, 1894 (*The Penny Illustrated Paper and Illustrated Times*, 3 November 1894, No. 1745.)

woman as the prisoner two or three weeks after her confinement sudden disappointment would be a probable cause – a woman who was the victim of such an attack of mania would certainly not be a free agent during the existence of the attack.[153]

On cross-examination, however, it was revealed that Dr Loarne had actually vaccinated both of the twins on the day of their death, in Minnie's presence. When asked how she appeared at that time, the doctor replied that the accused exhibited no signs of puerperal mania whatsoever. After due debate and deliberation, Dr Loarne further emphasised to the court that 'There are no symptoms by which we can Ascertain the approach of puerperal mania; very frequently, it is impossible to observe Any except from what afterwards takes place – there are no symptoms recognisable by medical skill, either before or after.'[154]

The imprecision of the symptoms and diagnosis associated with puerperal insanity, and its relevance to this particular trial, necessitated the courts to call two further medical witnesses to testify. Local man Dr Charles Spencer Palmer recounted that, in his opinion, if the actions of an individual were rational before and immediately after a criminal act occurred, then puerperal mania could not act as a valid explanation for that criminality.

Moreover, when he was asked 'Supposing you found that a person who had killed her children had remembered that she had done it, and remembered where she had drowned the two children in different places, would not that be evidence that she was sane at the time?' Dr Palmer answered 'It would, certainly.'[155]

George Edward Walker, medical officer of Holloway Prison, also added his expertise to the proceedings. He testified that, although the symptoms of puerperal mania are difficult to perceive in the initial stages of the illness, they would not simply cease with immediate effect, but would persist for some time after an attack had occurred. Moreover, in relation to infanticide cases more generally, it was Dr Walker's opinion that insanity only prevailed in instances where 'no other explanation for the act could be found'. As he explained, 'if a woman with legitimate children, and in ample and comfortable circumstances, suddenly murders them, I should certainly have a very strong suspicion of insanity... the absence of motive is a strong evidence of insanity'.[156] In other words, if poverty and shame were contextual circumstances in a given instance of new-born child murder, it was more likely that they were the true motives for the crime that had taken place, rather than any mental malady or disorder. This proposition serves, of course, whether wittingly or not, to target the crime towards women in marginal situations and circumstances.

Thus, the destitute nature of Minnie Wells' personal circumstances came to count against her and this, as well as her behaviour upon her arrest, ultimately undermined the possibility of a successful defence of puerperal insanity. Instead, Minnie was found guilty of the murder of her daughters and was sentenced to death. Upon hearing the sentence passed against her, Minnie Wells 'broke down completely' and was 'removed from the court sobbing violently'.[157] Minnie was reprieved from her death sentence, after an appeal was granted by the Home Secretary, Herbert Asquith, in November 1894. Eventually, Minnie's sentence was commuted to penal servitude for life.[158]

Despite the acceptance of puerperal insanity as a defence plea in indictments and trials for new-born child murder from 1830 onwards, by the turn of the century, as Minnie Wells' case testifies, this medical and psychosocial explanation for infanticide had diminished in significance, and was largely eliminated from consideration in the judicial context after 1900. This sea-change in opinion came about for a variety of reasons. First, medical professionals came to scrutinise and question the validity of the link between parturition and insanity and, in the absence of a distinct diagnosis, postpartum insanity eventually became an unidentifiable condition. As Hilary Marland explains:

Aside from agreement on the broad categories, for the rest puerperal insanity was an untidy, elusive disorder. Despite being pursued by many 'experts' in the fields of psychiatry and obstetrics, no firm conclusions could be reached, regarding its onset, preconditions, causes, prevalence, precise timing or duration, where it should be treated (at home or in the asylum), how it should be treated, if it was more likely to affect first-time mothers or women who had borne many children, the chances of re-occurrence, and whether it would prevail most amongst undernourished, mistreated and deserted poor women or amongst well-to-do, feebly-constituted ladies for whom childbirth was considered a massive physical and mental shock.[159]

In particular, of course, medical professionals were concerned about the blanket application of puerperal insanity as a defence tactic, when it was clear that not all women succumbed to the illness.[160] In other words, over time, psychiatrists and other medical men ultimately undermined the very explanation which had given their specialism so much credibility and authority in the early years of the nineteenth century. The elasticity and flexibility of the definition, symptoms and duration of puerperal insanity – which was once its most appealing characteristic – was now responsible for its undoing.

Contemporaries of the late Victorian era also began to renew their interest in the value of infant life, and tended to concentrate on this rather than on the health of the woman concerned.[161] The underlying causes of infanticide – such as shame and poverty – returned once more into the spotlight, and infanticide came to be regarded as a social problem again, rather than merely a personal one.[162] In addition, there was a growing call for men to be more liable in matters of maternity and childcare and to be more regularly called to account if they had abandoned the responsibilities of fatherhood.[163] For instance, one Welsh newspaper reported in October 1894 that:

> In the assizes in London last week, the death sentence was announced for a lady by the name of Minnie Wells, for killing her child. It is on her cheater – the one who left her after bringing her down – that this sentence should be passed. Not knowing where to turn, she went mad, and in her madness, she committed the awful deed. You can be sure she won't hang. But, should the true criminal (in a moral meaning) get to escape?[164]

The collision of all of these factors served to negate the power of puerperal insanity as the dominant explanation for new-born child murder by the last decades of the nineteenth century. This change paved the way for the gradual introduction of more nuanced explanations for infanticide, as we will see in the next, final, chapter.

This chapter has made it clear that the motives for new-born child murder in Britain and elsewhere during the period 1600–1900 were complex, changeable, and intangible, involving a cocktail of different factors, which were experienced to different degrees depending on the specific nature of the individual and their personal circumstances. We are still unable to explain why some mothers committed infanticide and some not, but we do have more of a sense of the most likely issues involved.

In the early modern period, escaping feelings of opprobrium was regarded as the most obvious reason why some unmarried mothers concealed their pregnancies, gave birth in secret and then went on to kill their new-borns. Women (and indeed men) committed the crime owing to personal feelings of shame associated with illicit pregnancy of one sort or another. They also did this to avoid religiously based opprobrium and family or community sanctions, which would do much to destroy future prospects in relation to both employment and marriage. In a context of desperation and isolation, many women sought to avoid the shame and uncertainty of unmarried motherhood.

Economic explanations for infanticide within the judicial context were not as common as we might have expected between 1600 and 1900. This was because penury was regarded as a petty and inappropriate excuse for murder. Nevertheless, both married and unmarried women indicted for the offence did refer to the misery of their impoverished circumstances as a causal factor for the crime. Working women feared dismissal, they contemplated the expense of another mouth to feed, clothe and care for and they fretted about meeting the cost of childcare. Parish-based financial support for unmarried mothers dwindled over the course of the first part of the nineteenth century and, increasingly, women became solely responsible for the maintenance and livelihood of their children, especially if the child was illegitimate and the father had abandoned his responsibilities. Some women clearly perpetrated infanticide in order to avoid a miserable future, both for themselves and for their children.

Shame and economic distress were undoubtedly involved in the committal of new-born child murder, but so-called 'human motives' existed too.[165] In some instances, new-born infants died accidentally or owing to want of care and attention at the moment of parturition, because the woman was inexperienced at self-delivery, confused by her circumstances or in shock from the pain of childbirth. On other occasions, however, it is clear that women were capable of being pragmatic and autonomous actors in episodes of infanticide. They killed their child because they did not want it. They used the most effective means possible for a quick and undetected 'termination'. They saw the child as a burden to get rid of, and they considered the use of infanticide to be akin to a late method of fertility control.

The dissociative tendencies involved in deliberate infanticide, which were evident in indictments for the offence during the pre-modern period, did not sit well with contemporary notions of femininity and maternity. In order to understand why some women conducted themselves in this way – stepping outside the boundaries of 'acceptable' behaviour – the judicial authorities adopted a more sympathetic and humanitarian attitude after 1760, where evidence which testified to the temporary or fleeting nature of infanticidal inclination was permitted. This paved the way for the introduction of more medical and psychosocial explanations for new-born child murder during the nineteenth century. After 1830, puerperal mania, or puerperal insanity, quickly came to dominate motives for infanticide. The fact that the condition was temporary, unpredictable and indeterminate meant that it could be applied to various scenarios, and could account for the application of violence in certain infanticidal episodes. Women suffering from puerperal insanity were considered criminally conscious but not criminally responsible, and as a result, infanticide came to be regarded as a personal medical problem related to women's inherent emotional weaknesses, which were tied to their capacity for reproduction. This neatly reintroduced and reinforced gender stereotypes into considerations of female criminality, and categorised the crime of new-born child murder (alongside others such as witchcraft and poisoning) as an irregular and deviant offence, rather than a mainstream form of criminal activity. Despite the seeming advantages of this particular explanation, the significance of puerperal insanity diminished in indictments for infanticide in British courts after 1900, as medical professionals became dissatisfied with the lack of clarity surrounding the symptoms and diagnosis of the condition. Instead, motives and explanations for infanticide travelled full circle, and the spotlight once again fell on the more 'traditional' explanations for infanticidal behaviour – shame and poverty – which had largely been ignored for the best part of a century.

Motives for infanticide in Britain between 1600 and 1900 were clearly multifarious and complicated, and no single common or simple explanation is discernible from the evidence. As Peter Hoffer and Natalie Hull conclude:

Motivation for the crime of infanticide was as varied as the personalities of the men and women who attempted it and the situations in which they found themselves. External pressures like social ostracism, shame, loss of employment and reputation, and forcible intercourse, were certainly motives for the crimes, but before any individual would undertake it, these circumstances had to pass through a filter of individual character and perception. Outside forces created stress, but response to stress was not uniform. When fear and anger were overwhelming enough to cause the perpetrator to view the child as a thing, a cancer or a foreign object, or to make the perpetrator believe that such injustices as led to the conception and would follow from successful birth were unsupportable, the crime might follow... [Infanticidal mothers] frustrated at their own lives and unable to reach back into their own childhoods for resources to nurture the growth of the new lives entrusted to them... struck out at the immediate cause of their misery.[166]

Sometimes, all four categories of motive examined in this chapter were jointly responsible for the decision to commit infanticide, sometimes just one or two applied; occasionally none of these factors were involved. In many instances we will never know why a particular woman resorted to killing her new-born child, because her motives were intensely private and personal to her and because hiding her feelings was a crucial part of the concealment of her condition. Thus, the chances of her evading censure or arrest after the fact depended on her silence. After all, offering an explanation for an instance of infanticide was tantamount to admitting guilt and responsibility. This was probably not recommended as a course of action, especially in the sixteenth, seventeenth and eighteenth centuries, when judicial reaction tended to be unpredictable.

7
The Modern Debate: Getting Away With Murder?

> Scores of women who have really wilfully killed their offspring at birth every year are acquitted... The crime of infanticide still goes on, and receives little or no check by punishment... I don't think that the law as it stands can be said to act much as a deterrent to women, who, of course, will continue to have illegitimate children and get rid of them somehow.[1]

In this final chapter, we will trace the history of infanticide since 1900. This was an era of both continuity and change in relation to new-born child murder. Even in the present day, various 'historical' aspects of infanticide have endured. Instances of child murder still persist in modern Britain and across the world,[2] and it remains a crime strongly associated with mothers. It is still notoriously difficult to provide proof of an act of infanticide, despite advances in modern forensic science and pathology. Likewise, public reactions to new-born child murder continue to be unpredictable, as attitudes towards perpetrators flit between sympathy and condemnation.[3]

Despite these enduring traits, changes have occurred. For instance, the definitions of specific types of infanticide have become clearer and more thoroughly delineated. Writing in the late 1960s and early 1970s, Phillip J. Resnick was the first to properly disaggregate infanticide from filicide, and to introduce the term neonaticide to the lexicon of criminality. He explained that infanticide should be applied as a general term to describe child murder. Filicide should be used in instances where the perpetrator is the parent of the victim and the victim is more than twenty-four hours old. Neonaticide he defined as a form of filicide restricted to the killing of a son or daughter less than 24 hours old.[4] For the purposes of our discussion, and to ensure parity of analysis, the terms new-born child murder and infanticide will be retained, according to the definition set out in the introductory chapter.

There have also been substantial changes in the legal context for child murder during the twentieth century. Modifications to the judicial approach to infanticide which were made in the 1920s and 1930s are still debated, and have resulted in courts in England and Wales operating an entirely different approach to the offence from their Scottish counterparts. The nature and incidence of new-born child murder has also altered over the last century, and our understanding both of the individuals who perpetrate the offence and the factors which made them resort to it, have become clearer and more nuanced.

This chapter investigates all of these issues amidst the rapidly changing socio-economic milieu of modern Britain. In this way, it breaks new ground in the study of infanticide, as no scholar has previously attempted to analyse the topic over the entirety of the twentieth century, or indeed beyond 1940. We will begin by examining the altered legislative context for infanticide at the start of the twentieth century and go on to investigate how these changes have affected and shaped the way the offence is regarded in the present day. The chapter then moves on to study trends in the incidence of infanticide and considers the common characteristics of those accused of new-born child murder in the twentieth century. It analyses the methods employed in infanticidal episodes at this time and establishes the extent to which this is a significant factor in determining the outcome of trials. Causes and explanations for new-born child murder are then surveyed in order to see whether a better understanding of the motives for this crime has impacted upon reactions to its perpetration from the judiciary, the media and the general public. The concluding section of the chapter summarises the findings made and critiques various suggestions which have been offered in attempts to limit the offence and confine it – once and for all – to the annals of history.

The modern legislative context

The significant legislative changes relating to infanticide in the first third of the twentieth century in England, Wales and various other countries throughout the world occurred at the confluence of three key social and legal concerns. The first of these was a growing interest in child welfare and a consequential closer scrutiny of motherhood. After the Boer War, in 1903, a campaign began to improve both the quantity and quality of the British population, as part of a drive to enhance physical efficiency in the face of potential future threats to national security and imperial interests.[5] This cause intensified in the aftermath of World War One, when infant mortality levels were perceived to be so high as to inhibit the recovery of the population and the recuperation and resurgence of the nation.[6] These largely eugenic concerns about the stamina of the population resulted in legislation which brought creeping improvements to maternal and child-welfare services, so that by 1939 antenatal care had been enhanced and skilled childbirth attendants, infant welfare clinics and health visitors had been introduced.[7]

Good motherhood, or 'mothercraft', was seen as being central to the development of future generations and, as a result, maternal practices were debated and dissected in the public arena. In particular, infant mortality came to be regarded as an explicit failure of motherhood. It needed to be understood, contained and reduced. Crucially, however, the determination to inculcate more moral responsibility on to mothers was done through notions of self-help, rather than any form of state intervention. This meant that no birth control advice or direct material assistance was given to mothers, which would have ameliorated issues that were regularly the cause of infant death at this time, such as poverty, poor nutrition, unsanitary living conditions and overwork. Instead, studies into the causes of maternal and child death were instigated and mothers were educated in personal hygiene, as it was believed that maternal ignorance was one of the chief failings of early twentieth-century motherhood.[8]

At the very time that the campaign to promote good motherhood was getting under way, three well-publicised instances of baby-farming came to light in England and Wales. All three indictments resulted in capital convictions. The cases against Ada Chard Williams in 1900, Amelia Sach in 1903 and Rhoda Willis (alias Leslie James) in 1907 led to contemporaries questioning whether the prevailing legislative provision for the protection of infant life was robust enough.[9] In addition, these trials reignited the 'moral panic' over unscrupulous mothers and childcare practices which had dominated nineteenth-century discourse on women's criminality, as we saw in Chapter 5.[10]

The second concern voiced at the turn of the twentieth century in relation to infanticide (and one which is still mooted, as we will see in due course) was the persistent and 'historic' difficulty with the quality of the evidence provided when cases came to trial. Some medical and legal professionals complained that the imperative of having to prove *both* separate existence and live birth in infanticide cases made successful prosecutions of the offence exceedingly difficult to achieve.[11] They argued that too much weight was given in judicial proceedings to issues which were routinely the subject of scientific debate and uncertainty.[12] Furthermore, the complexity of establishing an accurate explanation for the cause of death of a new-born infant was also inherently problematic. As Fiona Brookman and Jane Nolan have argued, the 'blurred boundaries' between maltreatment, abuse, neglect and accidental death have meant that, even by the twentieth century, infanticide was still able to make a significant contribution to the 'dark figure' of unrecorded or unknown criminality in the British Isles and beyond.[13] Added to these issues were concerns from health specialists, who argued that the effects of parturition – both mental and physical – were not being properly taken into account in trials for new-born child murder, and that the law needed to reflect modern medical opinion, where that opinion was essential to determining the outcome of events. The tussle between medical men and lawyers over who should possess professional ownership of this crime, which dated back in the seventeenth century, not only continued, but intensified in the twentieth century.[14]

The final key issue debated in the early years of the twentieth century was, at least in part, linked to the evidence problem outlined above. Many scholars, medical professionals, lawyers and social commentators believed that women indicted for killing their infants were being treated too leniently by the criminal courts, and, as a result, women were effectively getting away with murder. The comments by F.G. Frayling provided in a speech given before the Medico-Legal Society in 1908 (and cited at the outset of this chapter) clearly illustrate the prevailing disquiet. Contemporaries were concerned about the alarming regularity with which sympathy was shown to women accused of new-born child murder and the elaborate tactics employed in the courtroom to facilitate clemency.

As historian and politician David Seaborne Davies explains: 'The wide-spread dislike of the application of the law of murder in all its severity to cases of infanticides by mothers led to such a divorce between law and public opinion that prisoners, witnesses, counsel, juries and even many of H.M. judges, conspired to defeat the law.'[15] In practice, although judges regularly passed the death sentence against women found guilty of infanticide, they left the Home Secretary to make the decision as to whether or not a reprieve was appropriate. In this way judges were able to portray themselves as upholders of the law, whilst at the same time avoiding both personal criticism and individual moral responsibility for the course of action that they had endorsed. To this end, it was believed that sentencing in infanticide cases was becoming farcical and was proving a mockery of both the law and the judicial process.[16]

This issue, coupled with deficiencies in medical knowledge, meant that the full and proper legal provision for the offence was rarely enforced or, indeed, enforceable. Moreover, when these anxieties are considered alongside contemporary fears regarding infant mortality and the prevailing quality of motherhood, it is evident that there was a desire to criminalise infant death in a more consistent and coherent way. As Frayling emphasised in 1908, 'the law with regard to infanticide was bad and unsatisfactory, and required alteration'.[17]

Formal attempts to reform the legislation on infanticide were initiated in 1908 by the Liberal Lord Chancellor, Lord Loreburn, who attempted to add an amendment to the Children's Bill of 1908 which would enable judges to impose a non-capital sentence of penal servitude on mothers who had murdered an infant of less than one year of age.[18] Opposition to this suggestion came from the Lord Chief Justice, Lord Alverstone, who roused a significant minority in the House of Commons and the House of Lords to argue that the removal of the death sentence for child murder would result in a significant increase in the occurrence of the offence.[19] Instead, Alverstone proposed that judges be allowed to record, rather than pronounce, capital punishment in proven cases of infanticide where a mother had not recovered from the effects of giving birth. Alverstone's attempt to retain the death penalty for new-born child murder, whilst facilitating a route by which judges were able to publicly recommend clemency in specific cases, did not satisfy either side of the debate. His bill fell owing to insufficient parliamentary time.[20]

The outbreak of World War One put paid to any further attempts at reform in the short-term, but the trial of 21-year-old Edith Roberts in Leicester in 1921 for the murder of her new-born baby daughter brought the socio-legal debates concerning infanticide sharply back into focus. Roberts, who had concealed her pregnancy from friends and family, was accused of the murder of her infant after it was discovered stuffed into a wooden chest with a camisole tied tightly around its mouth. The medical examiner testified that it was likely, but not absolutely certain, that the child had achieved a separate existence from its mother and that it had breathed of its own accord after birth. He also suggested that it was possible that Edith Roberts had not been conscious of her actions owing to the agonies of childbirth.[21] Despite the relatively dubious nature of the evidence levelled against her, the all-male jury (chosen by the defence counsel who believed men to be fairer than women when considering this kind of indictment) took only fifteen minutes to convict Edith Roberts of the murder of her child, although they made strong recommendations for mercy. The judge then sentenced Roberts to death. A mere six days after this sentence was handed down it was commuted to penal servitude for life.[22]

The case of Edith Roberts highlighted many of the contemporary concerns with the prevailing legislation relating to new-born child murder, and despite several additional prevarications along the way, reform finally came a year after the Roberts trial, when the 1922 Infanticide Act was passed.[23] The Act created a separate offence of infanticide for the first time in England and Wales and attempted to make the punishment more suitable for the crime. It stated, with echoes of Lord Alverstone's former bill, that:

> Where a woman by any wilful act or omission causes the death of her newly-born child, but at the time of the act or omission she had not fully recovered from the effect of giving birth to such child, and by reason thereof the balance of her mind was then disturbed, she shall, not withstanding that the circumstances were such that but for this Act the offence would have amounted to murder, be guilty of felony, to wit of infanticide, and may for such offence be dealt with and punished as if she had been guilty of the offence of manslaughter of such child.[24]

As well as reducing infanticide from murder to manslaughter in certain circumstances, the Act also made clear that verdicts of manslaughter, murder where guilty but insane and concealment were permissible as alternative verdicts in instances of new-born child murder, if the jury thought it appropriate.[25]

Although the 1922 Act was welcomed as a significant step-forward in dealing with infanticide, it was not long before it was strongly criticised with respect to two clauses in its provision. Firstly, medical professionals were at pains to point out that the 1922 Act did not give enough protection to parturient and, more specifically, *nursing* women.[26] Secondly, the phrase 'newly-born', which was used in the Act, was not deemed precise enough. Indeed, as the act provided no definition of a time limit for what constituted a new-born child, courts were regularly reluctant to deploy indictments on the specific charge of infanticide and operated their own judgement in the area. This resulted in the continuation of the less than ideal practice where death sentences were pronounced in the courtroom only for the Home Secretary to issue a reprieve at a later date.[27]

The case of Mary O'Donoghue, at the Old Bailey in 1927, proved pivotal in demonstrating the need for further legislative reform. O'Donoghue was indicted for the murder of her thirty-five day old son, who had been strangled with a napkin and whose body kept in a cardboard box under her bed. O'Donoghue admitted to killing her child, saying she did it because she had no-one to help her care for him and she was in dire poverty. Although the judge in the case, Mr Justice Talbot, accepted that there was justification for considering insanity on the grounds of *both* childbirth *and* lactation, he could not proceed on a charge of infanticide, because he believed that the child concerned was too old. O'Donoghue was subsequently convicted, sentenced to death and then reprieved, her sentence being commuted to penal servitude for life.[28] A similar fate almost befell a married Hertfordshire woman named Brenda Hale, in 1936. She had cut the throat of her 3-week-old child and had subsequently attempted suicide. Once again the judge, this time Mr Justice Humphreys, deemed her child not to be 'newly-born', but in this instance he took into account the severe depression of the defendant brought on by parturition and lactational exhaustion. Mrs Hale was found guilty but insane on the charge of child murder. She was ordered to be detained at His Majesty's pleasure.[29]

The ramifications of these two cases were such that, not long after the Hale case had concluded, calls were made for a reconsideration of the legislation relating to infanticide and new-born child murder. This time, calls were made for more specificity in relation to the term 'newly-born', for the time limit on puerperal insanity to be extended, and for the effect of lactation on the mother's state of mind to be considered as a factor in mitigation. Progress was stalled by the Abdication Crisis of 1936, but new legislation was eventually passed in 1938.[30] The new Infanticide Act stated that:

> Where a woman by any wilful act or omission causes the death of her child being a child under the age of twelve months, but at the time of

the act or omission the balance of her mind was disturbed by reason of her not having fully recovered from the effect of giving birth to the child or by reason of the effect of lactation consequent upon the birth of the child, then not withstanding that the circumstances were such that but for this Act the offence would have amounted to murder, she shall be guilty of felony, to wit of infanticide, and may for such offence be dealt with and punished as if she had been guilty of the offence of manslaughter of the child.[31]

Once again (as had happened in 1922) provision was made for alternative verdicts, as per Section 60 of the Offences against the Person Act, 1861.[32]

The new Infanticide Act made it clear that infanticide related to children under the age of twelve months. Moreover, and in order to make this time limit plausible, the mental imbalance of the mother concerned could now be attributed to *either* the birth of the child or the more prolonged consequences of lactation. This was as long as such causal factors could be proven to have existed at the time the crime was committed.[33] This new legislation came to be regarded as a compromise whereby the law was able 'to maintain a generally punitive stance to a social problem, laced with an unthreatening show of compassion'.[34]

Despite general contentment with the 1938 statutory provision, and its enduring persistence today in England and Wales, strong attempts at repeal and reform were nevertheless attempted in the twentieth century. The first came in the wake of the passing of the Homicide Act of 1957,[35] which allowed for a verdict of diminished responsibility for the first time. As the 1938 Act already acknowledged the causal link between mental health abnormalities and infanticide, contemporaries asked whether the offence should be subsumed into the general legal provision relating to diminished responsibility in murder cases. In this way, the defendant would be declared insane, charged with manslaughter and her puerperal mania would be considered alongside other factors which had a contributory effect on the committal of the crime.

In addition to this suggestion, three main criticisms were levelled at the 1938 Infanticide Act. The first of these related to the fact that the legislation affirmed notions concerning the inherent physical and emotional weaknesses of women on account of parturition and its aftermath. This male-chauvinist sentiment, which had been influential since the seventeenth century, was now enshrined in law.[36] Discrimination of a different kind provided the foundations for a further attack on the 1938 Act. Some suggested that the provision discriminated against men. As men could not bear children and were thus incapable of suffering from postnatal stress and trauma, so they were unable to enjoy the more sympathetic judicial attitude afforded to women accused of infanticide. Indeed, the punishment policy associated with infanticide was typically lenient in comparison with that for murder or manslaughter: the only charges applicable to men who killed young children.[37]

The final, and probably most robust, criticism levelled at the 1938 Infanticide Act relates to a series of caveats regarding its practical application. First, it has been argued that the Act cannot be applied consistently. For example, if a mother kills an older child, or someone else's child, it cannot be treated as infanticide.[38] Moreover, the provision of a distinctive offence based on mental aberration creates a 'slippery slope' when establishing culpability, as, in theory, a whole range of other conditions could be considered as factors in mitigation, such as pre-menstrual syndrome, physical illness, general depression or post-traumatic stress disorder. In addition, accepting the notion that criminal responsibility might be impaired by the effects of childbirth and its aftermath suggests that such a defence could also be applied to the committal of other offences. For instance, a woman who had robbed a bank could reasonably claim that she had done so on account of postpartum stress.[39]

The psychological model prevalent in the 1938 Infanticide Act is the one aspect of the legislative provision that has been routinely attacked, even in recent years. The medical concepts of puerperal and lactational insanity, although not utterly discounted by medical professionals, are certainly regarded as outdated. In addition, it has been argued that, in relation to infanticide, 'Mental illness is rarely a factor and social and psychological stresses are more relevant.'[40] Indeed, medical and scientific research has identified that mental disease is far more likely to be a causal factor in the killing of older children rather than new-borns.[41] We will return to these issues later on in this chapter.

The aggregation of all these criticisms is best evidenced in three reports, which were produced and widely circulated in the last third of the twentieth century. All three strongly recommended changes to the content and tenor of the 1938 Infanticide Act. The Butler Report on Mentally Abnormal Defenders, produced in October 1975, argued that the mandatory life sentence for murder be abolished in order to facilitate proportional sentencing suitable to each individual case. This would render the retention of a separate offence of infanticide superfluous.[42] If this suggestion could not be adopted, the report suggested that 'in order to rationalise and simplify the law... the special provision for the offence of infanticide should be abolished... [as] the Act is unsatisfactory in a number of respects. Its purposes are now sufficiently covered by the more recent provision for diminished responsibility'.[43] By charging manslaughter by reason of diminished responsibility in appropriate cases, via the provisions made by the Homicide Act of 1957, 'the stigma of a charge of murder will be removed, and the mental element will be accepted from the outset'.[44] The Report also largely rejected the medical principles upon which the existing legislation was based, saying that they were no longer relevant, and that 'puerperal psychoses are now regarded as no different from others, childbirth being only a precipitating factor'.[45]

The Royal College of Psychiatrists' Working Party on Infanticide (1978)[46] and the Criminal Law Revision Committee (1980) both rejected the Butler Report's calls for infanticide to be absorbed into the 1957 Homicide Act, on the grounds that it would exclude cases currently dealt with as infanticide and would be too restrictive.[47] Again, we see medical and legal professionals struggling for control in contemporary debates on infanticide and its allied offences. Despite the Royal College of Psychiatrists arguing against the medical basis for the present Infanticide Act (especially the references made to lactational insanity), the Criminal Law Revision Committee sought an amendment to the existing legislation, which would extend the definition of the offence to include socio-economic and environmental stresses as factors which might precede an infanticidal act.[48] Crucially, however, the Committee went to great lengths to link these additional causal factors to 'the fact of the birth and the hormonal and bodily changes produced by it'.[49] However, the inclusion of this clause rather undermined their argument, as it could be said that their suggestions were already effectively covered by the provisions set out in the 1938 Act.

The Committee's other recommendations were that women accused of murder and manslaughter should be able to plead, or be convicted of, infanticide and that the maximum penalty for the offence should be restricted to five years' imprisonment.[50] The Working Party agreed with this penal limitation and also suggested that infanticide should be extended to include the killing of any child under the age of five.[51] Ultimately, none of these recommendations were adhered to, as preference was given to the flexibility of the current provision, which was thought to be more appropriate. However, one suggestion made by both parties, that it should be possible to charge a woman with attempted infanticide, was incorporated in the 1981 Criminal Attempts Act.[52]

Additional attempts at legislative reform were made in 2005 and 2008. The Law Commission's Consultation Paper entitled 'A New Homicide Act for England and Wales?' reiterated all of the criticisms previously discussed, which had been levelled almost three decades before.[53] Once again, uncertainty over the link between childbirth and mental illness was reiterated, with one contributor describing the medical underpinnings of the 1938 Act as 'myth-making by legislation'.[54] The paper also decried the privileges enjoyed by women accused of infanticide, which were 'bought at the expense of making legal invalids of women, of excluding them from their full status as legal subjects and of perpetuating their social and legal subordination'.[55]

The Consultation Paper provided three reform alternatives: minimal, moderate and radical. The minimal option proposed that reference to lactational insanity be removed from the current legislation, as it was deemed an 'unfounded' medical theory.[56] In addition to removing this terminology, the moderate model extended the definition of a newly born child to include infants up to the age of two.[57] Moreover, the existing Act would be reworded so that the phrase 'disturbance of the mind' was linked to the actual act committed, rather than to parturition and its aftermath. This suggestion came in the wake of a child-murder case involving a Birmingham woman called Chaha'Oh-Niyol Kai-Whitewind in 2005. Kai-Whitewind (who changed her name after adopting American Indian cultural practices) had asphyxiated her twelve week old son (allegedly conceived as the result of a rape and sexual assault) in frustration when he refused to breastfeed. As the suspect had provided a clear reason for killing her child, and because no evidence could be brought to suggest that her mind was disturbed at the time of the killing, she was indicted for murder and sentenced to life imprisonment. Although the Court of Appeal found the conviction to be safe, the judge in the case, Mr Justice Judge, called for a judicial review into the problems arising from and connected to the offence of infanticide, with particular reference to the consideration of causal factors other than those related to the effects of parturition and lactation.[58]

The more radical set of reform proposals would have removed all references to lactational insanity and reworded the existing Act, as described above, but it would also remove any age restriction for victims of infanticide and make the offence chargeable to a much wider range of perpetrators – mothers, fathers and carers.[59] The Law Commission gave its final report on these recommendations in November of 2006.[60] At the very outset of the paper, the Commission stated that the subject matter of infanticide 'belongs to a territory where law and medicine meet, and to some extent carries with it difficulties which attach to both'.[61] Indeed, the Report was at pains to point out that, because so many professionals and different disciplinary bodies had to be consulted over the suggested plans for reform, little consensus was reached over whether the Infanticide Act should be retained or how it should be amended. Almost inevitably, the Commission concluded that no change to the law should occur.[62]

In 2007, the case of R v. Gore, at the Court of Appeal, contributed to yet another debate on proposed changes to the law on infanticide in England and Wales. Lisa Gore had pleaded guilty to the infanticide of her new-born son in 1996. The boy had died owing to the absence of medical provision at his birth. Gore was sentenced to probation for three years on condition that she attended psychiatric treatment. Sadly, the defendant died from cancer in 2003, so it was left to her parents, Mr and Mrs Thomas Gore to bring an appeal against their daughter's conviction on the grounds that Lisa did not fully appreciate the nature of the charge levelled against her and because the prosecution had failed to prove that the defendant had *intended* to kill her baby son. After fierce legal debate, Lisa Gore's conviction was eventually upheld by Lady Justice Hallet.[63] A subsequent 2008 Home Office consultation paper on proposals to change the laws relating to murder, manslaughter and infanticide referred to the implications of the Gore verdict in relation to the question of proving intent in infanticide cases. It made it clear that 'it is unnecessary to show the intention for murder in order for a charge or defence of infanticide to succeed; it is sufficient that a wilful act or omission on the part of the mother caused the death'.[64] Once again, the 1938 Infanticide Act held firm.

The existing legislation for new-born child murder remains fiercely divisive. Adrian Grounds, for instance, states that the current law 'remains useful because it enables women with relatively little or no psychiatric abnormality (who would not qualify for the diminished responsibility defence) to avoid a murder conviction, and to be dealt with in a humane and flexible way'.[65] Taking a slightly different tact, Josephine McDonagh argues that the law has 'relieved women of criminal agency in infanticide cases, but it also tended, less specifically, to pathologise maternity, institutionalising an expectation of female insanity'.[66] Susan Edwards, on the other hand, criticises the 'gross limitations' of the 1938 Infanticide Act and maintains that it is 'at best an act of misguided toleration, at worst retrogressive and inconsistent'.[67] The lawyer Katherine O'Donovan summarises the existing position astutely and skilfully when she explains the judiciary's reluctance to deal with mothers who kill their children. As she insists, 'To admit that social and economic circumstances, or motherhood, may cause crime is to open a hitherto tightly closed box. To deny recognition of infanticide as a separate, lesser crime is to invite juries to refuse to convict for murder. So the solution has been to fudge the issue by retaining discredited medical theory.'[68]

Although there are obvious problems with the infanticide legislation in England and Wales, this model has nonetheless been adopted by 22 other nations in the twentieth century.[69] There are, however, some notable exceptions. Scotland, for instance, does not have a separate legislative provision for infanticide. Instead, a mother who kills her infant north of the Tweed is charged with either murder or common law culpable homicide. As with any other type of homicide, mitigating factors concerning fitness to plead and mental status at the time the act was committed are taken into account. Indeed, it is interesting to note that the Scots were very quick to adopt the concept of diminished responsibility in serious criminal cases. Trials incorporating this kind of verdict can be found in Scottish courtrooms as early as 1844, more than a century before the model was adopted in England.[70] Perhaps for this very reason, the Scots chose not to follow the example of their southern neighbours and embody the perceived causal links between parturition, lactation, mental illness and infanticide in legislation. They had already discovered that the use of diminished responsibility was more appropriate to their needs in instances of new-born child murder and were used to employing that provision.[71]

In North America, too, there is no specific legal provision for infanticide, despite repeated calls for reform along these lines owing to the remarkably inconsistent and random application of the law governing infanticide in Canada and the United States of America.[72] The contrast between the English and American legal approaches to infanticide was most clearly realised in the midst of the Caroline Beale case of 1994. Caroline Beale was an English woman who was arrested at a New York airport after it was discovered that the dead body of her new-born daughter was stuffed inside the waistband of her trousers. It was alleged that the infant had died owing to suffocation. After a long wait for trial, which included being held in the notorious Riker's Island penitentiary for 8 months, Caroline plea bargained and admitted to the manslaughter of her child. She was sentenced to 8 months in prison (time served), five years' probation and was subsequently extradited to Britain to undertake twelve months of psychiatric treatment.[73] In the immediate aftermath of the trial, Caroline's father, Peter Beale, told reporters outside the court that he thought the US system of justice was 'cruel and medieval', 'barbaric and uncivilised' and said that the US courts had fallen on his daughter like 'a pack of hyenas'.[74] Calling Mr Beale 'a big mouth', the judge in the case, Justice Hanophy, retorted, saying, in relation to the prevailing English legislation:

> I believe that any law that grants a blanket exemption from prosecu-
> tion or punishment to those people who kill their children when their
> children are under the age of one is a law that is primitive and uncivi-
> lised. Granting parents a law to kill their children harkens to uncivilised
> times... We aim to protect the children rather than excuse the killer...
> I say to our friends in Britain, God Bless America.[75]

Despite these notable differences in practice, there remain some significant similarities in the overall legal context for new-born child murder.
For instance, most countries have retained concealment of pregnancy as a
separate indictable crime and, in Britain at least, this offence has enjoyed
a long legal history, largely remaining untouched since the first decade of
the nineteenth century.[76] What is clear, then, is that despite variations in
practice, a determination to criminalise acts of new-born child murder has
persisted across the globe throughout the modern era, with some nations
going to fairly inordinate lengths to establish firm but flexible legal provision against individuals who kill young children. Whether or not this
resolve is warranted, or indeed justified, by the nature and/or incidence of
instances of this kind of offence, specifically in Britain since 1900, is the
subject of the next section.

Nature, trends and incidence

Infanticide is a crime which has 'lingered on' in the twentieth century
and persists to this day in many countries.[77] In Britain today, new-born

child murder occurs with perhaps more regularity than we might expect, with an estimated thirty to forty potential incidents occurring every year.[78] Providing an accurate calculation is of course notoriously problematic. Infanticide, as we have already seen, makes a substantial contribution to the 'dark figure' of unrecorded or unknown crime. It is difficult to determine whether an infant death was accidental or intentional, as so many of the victims (by the twentieth century at least) either suffocated or drowned.[79] This inevitably made court proceedings difficult to conclude. For example, in 1940, the case against Florence Mabel Howard of Whittlesey was heard at Cambridge Assizes. Medical testimony pointed to the fact that the child was mature and viable; it had 'probably' attained a separate existence from its mother and had 'likely' breathed of its own accord. The cause of death was 'believed' to be asphyxiation by indeterminate means. The judge summing up the case, Mr Justice Singleton, reminded jurors that there needed to be 'conclusive proof' of separate existence and live birth in order for an infanticide conviction to be considered. The jury took the hint and acquitted Howard of the charge.[80]

In addition to these problems, some infant deaths remain undiscovered. Moreover, medical and scientific developments in the modern era have complicated matters further, as established explanations for infant fatality – which give the benefit of the doubt to those suspected of infanticide – have now been called into question. For example, in the 1980s and 1990s there was a growing belief that ruling an infant death as an instance of Sudden Infant Death Syndrome (a common conclusion since the 1970s) ought now to be considered unsound and unsafe, as the statements of medical professionals to this effect had at times been undermined by individuals subsequently confessing to homicide.[81] On the back of this contention, somewhat controversially, Professor Roy Meadow asserted that 'between 2 and 10 per cent of babies currently labelled as dying from Sudden Infant Death Syndrome have probably been smothered by their mothers'.[82] This hypothesis caused heated reaction from grieving parents, and led to an intensification of the long-standing debate amongst lawyers and medical professionals, which has never fully abated. The result of this confusion is that the phrase 'undetermined' is now typically used in statements that relate to the cause of infant death where uncertainties linger. Inevitably, this heightens the difficulty of establishing whether or not foul play has occurred.[83]

We need to bear in mind all of these issues when considering the statistical evidence used in this chapter relating to instances of infanticide and concealment of pregnancy recorded and labelled as such by the criminal courts of Great Britain. What follows then, is not presented as an accurate reflection of the incidence of new-born child murder or its associated offences over the twentieth century, it is merely a best guess based on the most accurate data available. Moreover, the different legal approach taken to new-born child murder in Scotland means that data on infanticide north of the Tweed cannot be collated, as they are not disaggregated from statistics on homicide.[84] This means that the only comparable data available relates to that of concealment of pregnancy, although we must remember that the nature of the offence underlying allegations of this nature varied considerably from case to case. Figures 7.1 and 7.2 show the incidence of reports, indictments and convictions for concealment of pregnancy in Britain during the twentieth century.[85] Both graphs reveal that concealment was still being brought before courtrooms during the twentieth century, where it was typically used as an alternative charge (or verdict) to infanticide or homicide.[86] The persistence of charges of concealment can be explained by the fact that accusations of this nature require less conclusive proof compared with infanticide, where the issues of establishing live birth and separate existence are routinely problematic. In addition, as convictions for concealment result in a relatively minor punishment, it is thought to be a more appropriate charge for the complex, emotive and ambiguous circumstances associated with the death of a young child.[87]

It is interesting to note the distant relationship on both graphs between the number of reports and indictments and the corresponding close relationship between the number of indictments and convictions. Clearly, as the twentieth century progressed, criminal cases of this kind were only brought to court if they were likely to be proven. This observation may provide one explanation for the significant diminution in reported instances of concealment of pregnancy after the 1950s.

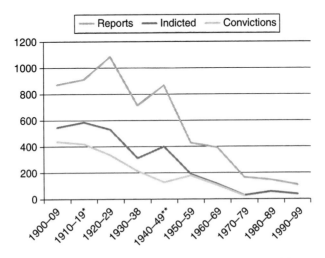

Figure 7.1   Trends in concealment in England and Wales, 1900–1999

Notes: *No records of convictions are available for 1915 and 1916.
**No records of any kind are available for 1939, nor of convictions for 1940–1945.

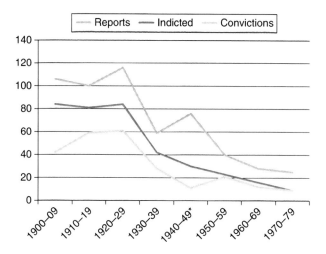

Figure 7.2 Trends in concealment in Scotland, 1900–1979
Notes: Infanticide was not recorded as a separate offence.
*No records of convictions are available for 1939–1945.

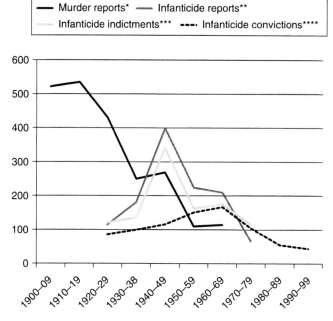

Figure 7.3 Trends in Infanticide in England and Wales, 1900–1999
Notes: *No murder reports after 1968.
**No infanticide reports before 1924 or after 1972.
***No infanticide indictments before 1923 or after 1979.
****No infanticide convictions before 1923; no convictions recorded for 1939–45.

Figure 7.3 shows the incidence of reports, indictments and convictions for infanticide in England and Wales during the twentieth century. Reports of homicide where the victim was less than one year of age have also been charted, in order to include all instances of new-born child murder reported to the police between 1900 and 1999 and to reflect the impact of legislative change in 1922 and 1938. Unfortunately, information on indictments and convictions with regard to infant homicides was not discernible from the judicial evidence recorded. Unlike the graphs showing trends in conceal-ment of pregnancy, there is a small gap between reports, indictments and convictions in cases of infanticide or child murder. This suggests that it was more likely for a reported case of this kind to be prosecuted to the full extent of the law.

At first glance, the pattern of recorded infanticide and child murder in England and Wales seems to be on a steeply downward trajectory during the course of the twentieth century, save for a spike in activity in the mid-1940s (something that can also be clearly seen in the data relating to concealment of pregnancy).[88] Certainly, the pattern of convictions shows the most marked downward trend in all three graphs, so that by the close of the century, per annum convictions for concealment of pregnancy and infanticide never rose above ten after 1972.[89] The apparent decrease in women's involvement in recorded instances of new-born child murder does not mirror trends in their participation in other types of criminal activity during the twentieth century. Indeed, after 1960, there has been a discernible increase in female offending, including acts of violence, although it should be pointed out that this is part of a general growth in illegality, which is also evident in relation to male offenders and is not a gender-specific trend.[90]

Yet, if we take into account certain socio-economic factors which infl-uenced women's lives during the twentieth century, we can see these statistical trends in a different light. As women's lives became more public and economically driven in the second half of the twentieth century, the hitherto faltering family limitation campaigns, led by individuals such as Margaret Sanger and Marie Stopes, finally gathered some pace and impe-tus.[91] In 1910, for instance, only 15 per cent of married women had ever used birth control, but, by the end of the 1940s, this figure had dramatically increased to 80 per cent.[92] Married working-class women began to follow the example of their middle-class counterparts in the employment of traditional and more modern methods of birth control, although progress was sluggish, inconsistent and unpredictable until the introduction of the pill in the early 1960s.

Eventually, the safety, effectiveness and accessibility of biochemical and hormonal contraception opened up the possibilities of birth control to married and single women alike, giving them potential control over their fertility – although many women still preferred to devolve responsibility in these matters to men.[93] Nevertheless, a sexual revolution of sorts did take place in Great Britain in the second half of the twentieth century. For instance, 19 per cent of the women born in the early years of the century said that they engaged in sexual activity prior to marriage. When women born in the 1950s were asked the same question, the proportion was 94.7 per cent.[94] Despite an evident increase in sexual activity, the advent of effective and accessible birth control caused fertility rates to continually decline in the twentieth century.[95]

So, if we take into account the fact that fertility rates declined after 1960, we would expect to see an even more marked decline in instances of infanticide and new-born child murder since that period, as there were fewer potential victims available. However, this is an illusory judgement as over the last forty years of the twentieth century the figures of reported incidents remained remarkably consistent. It could be argued, therefore, that the actual or true rate of recorded concealments and infanticides in Great Britain was in fact fairly static over the century, especially in the last quarter.[96]

One of the main reasons for the persistence of new-born child murder in the twentieth century is the lack of viable alternatives open to women who find themselves unexpectedly pregnant.[97] This is a trend which has endured since the early modern period. During World War Two, and in its immediate aftermath, for instance, the statistical evidence suggests that an increased number of women resorted to infanticide and concealment in order to cover up extra-marital affairs undertaken whilst their husbands or sweethearts were serving overseas.[98] This probably accounts for the temporary acceleration in recorded instances of these offences. Even beyond the 1950s, many desperate women still regarded child murder as a 'preferable' option, employed as a last resort when other mechanisms failed.[99]

We have already noted that the adoption of birth control measures was slow and piecemeal in Britain until the latter part of the twentieth century. In addition, although there is evidence to suggest that abortions were undertaken more readily by women in the twentieth century, the act of procurement and performing the operation itself remained criminalised until 1967; this means that arriving at an accurate estimation of the number of terminations since 1900 is difficult.[100] Certainly, newspaper adverts for abortifacients were common in the twentieth century, and some women regarded self-medication of this kind, as well as mechanical terminations, as 'a necessary survival strategy'.[101] However, growing medical concerns over the safety of abortions after the 1920s, alongside widespread press reports of various botched operations, may have dissuaded many women from this course of action.[102] Indeed, many historians argue that the legalisation of the procedure had less to do with feminist demands that women should control their own fertility and more to do with medical professionals wanting to control the decision to terminate and the way in which the procedure was carried out. This represents yet another example of professional interlopers acting in the realms associated with infant disposal.[103]

The only other option open to women wanting to rid themselves of unwanted offspring in the twentieth century was to abandon their infant soon after birth or at such a time as it could no longer be properly cared for. Infant abandonment persisted in the twentieth century, but it was not as common as it had been in earlier centuries.[104] The main reason for this was that, in the wake of the baby-farming scandals in the latter part of the nineteenth and the first decade of the twentieth centuries, calls were made for the regulation of adoption. The introduction of the 1926 Adoption Act in England and Wales (with a similar act passed in Scotland four years later) brought an end to unscrupulous childcare practices by 'surrogate' parents and wet-nurses, as it initiated a regionally based system of supervision and inspection.[105]

By the twentieth century, the options open to women facing the repercussions of an unwanted pregnancy were especially limited. Coupled to this, attitudes to illegitimacy were still relatively antiquated in Britain, at least until the 1970s.[106] After that time, the stigma attached to having a child out of wedlock diminished, and between 1975 and 1995 the percentage of families with a lone mother increased from 9 to 20 per cent.[107] Nevertheless, as Christine Alder and Ken Polk describe, 'Despite modern day social conventions and attitudes, the stigma of bearing an illegitimate child remains a key motivation for new-born child murder in the twentieth century and beyond.'[108] The persistence of opprobrium, coupled to the fact that unmarried women were the last to access modern forms of contraception, meant that some single women undoubtedly experienced an unwanted pregnancy and sought a remedy for their condition, but they were faced with few viable options. This factor alone goes a long way to explain why a small, but consistent, number of British women still resorted to new-born child murder, despite the introduction of modern mechanisms for the limitation of family size.

In some respects, we can be more precise with our identification of defendant characteristics in instances of child murder in twentieth-century Britain. The establishment of new sub-categories of this offence has enabled scholars and medical professionals to distinguish character traits belonging to individuals who commit neonaticide (the murder of a child within twenty-four hours of its birth) from those who commit infanticide (the murder of an infant under the age of one). Neonaticides tend to be committed by young women (often late teenagers), who are inexperienced in matters of sexuality or maternity and who are typically unmarried.[109] Perpetrators of infanticides are more difficult to determine as they do not form any sort of homogenous group. The context, rationale and method for infanticide are wholly dependent on individual, and, therefore, entirely variable, circumstances.[110] In the main, however, they tend to be young (although not as young as those who commit neonaticide), are often lacking in educational attainment and financial resources and are usually engaged in an ongoing relationship of sorts.[111]

The contraction of domestic service in Britain after World War One, and the expansion of employment opportunities for women from the 1950s, meant that the close bond between infanticide and servitude was eventually broken in the twentieth century.[112] Defendants accused of new-born child murder in the twentieth century had a range of occupations, and a significant number were unemployed. The background and character of the accused remained crucial to court proceedings, however, and attitudes to prostitutes and substance abusers were markedly different from those towards individuals able to sustain respectable employment or a stable relationship.[113]

Another constant feature of the crime of infanticide into the twentieth century is the persistent dominance of women. As Figure 7.4 shows, in all categories of the offence reported in Britain between 1900 and 1999, there were many more females accused than males.[114] Nevertheless, men's

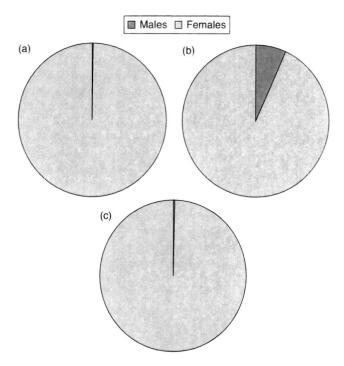

Figure 7.4 Gender differences in indictments for infanticide and concealment of pregnancy in Britain, 1900–1999. a) Infanticide in England and Wales (921 female: 2 male); b) Concealment in England and Wales (2921: 207); c) Concealment in Scotland (315: 1)

involvement in instances of child murder was formally recognised on a more regular basis than was the case in previous centuries, largely on account of modern societal pressures which called for men to take some share of the blame for the women's condition, even if they had little to do with the actual termination of life itself.[115] Men were also much more directly involved in child murder. However, this tended be in relation to the killing of older children, and it was very rare for a man to be implicated in an instance of neonaticide.[116] If men were involved in infanticide, it was typically either in relation to the killing of an illegitimate baby that they did not want, or it was linked to child abuse, most commonly conducted when in the role of surrogate parent or step-father.[117]

In terms of identifying common characteristics amongst the victims of infanticide, it is clear that the younger the infant, the greater the risk of them being killed.[118] In their analysis of infanticide in England and Wales between 1975 and 1987, Maureen Marks and Ramesh Kumar state that, 'An infant under one year is four times more likely to become the victim of homicide than either a child aged from 1 to 4, or someone over 4 years old.'[119] Moreover, 'Children aged between 1 day and 3 months are about four times more likely to be killed than children aged between 9 months and 1 year, when the risk of homicide approaches that of the total population.'[120] There are no indications that the gender of the victim is a specific causal factor in new-born child murder in Britain since 1900.[121]

The difficulties in determining cause of death in young children (despite modern scientific and medical advancements) has made identification of the methods by which a child has been murdered problematic.[122] However, the significant increase in the hospitalisation of childbirth since 1946 has meant that live birth is now effectively assumed and thus the death of any new-born infant is treated with suspicion. This means that more rigorous efforts are made in establishing whether a child died naturally, by accident or as a result of criminal intent.[123]

The methods of infanticide employed during the twentieth century are exceedingly varied, just as they have been since 1600. Killings are rarely planned, but do sometimes show evidence of premeditation.[124] Blatantly violent methods of killing, such as strangulation, stabbing and battery, occur almost as frequently as 'non-wounding' techniques, such as suffocation, drowning or poisoning.[125] Interestingly, scholars have pointed out that in modern neonaticides, as the victim cannot put up much resistance to an attack, the methods used tend to involve less violence than in the murder of older babies and typically entail neglect of some kind.[126] In addition, women who kill their new-borns are much more likely to have concealed their pregnancies in the first place and will thereafter attempt to hide their crime, and indeed the corpse of their baby, whereas children murdered in the days, weeks or months after parturition are more easily and readily discovered.[127]

Take, for instance, the case of 24-year-old waitress Doreen Featherstone, who was indicted at Manchester County Magistrates Court in 1955 charged with the murder of her son immediately after his birth. With the aid of an accomplice (Margaret Williams), who had been unaware of her room-mate's condition until after parturition occurred, she killed the baby by stuffing its mouth with cotton wool and tying a bandage tightly round its neck. Featherstone then kept the infant's remains in a suitcase beside her for three weeks before eventually leaving the body on waste-ground near Old Trafford.[128] Featherstone's defence counsel described her as 'a pathetic, loose sort of figure, with no mental balance', and she was subsequently found guilty of infanticide and imprisoned for three years.[129]

By contrast, in the same decade, a 29-year-old married woman called Edith Butler, described by the police as 'a devoted wife and mother', was indicted at South Western Magistrates Court (London) for the murder of her 3-week-old son, who was christened *post-mortem* Stephen John. Edith openly admitted that whilst out on a shopping errand to the local chemists, and in front of various people, she tried to strangle her child in his pram. When this attempt failed, Edith quickly picked up the baby and threw him over a bridge into the river below, where he subsequently drowned. Numerous eye-witnesses confirmed Edith's story. A medical professional who acted as a witness for the defence in the case, Dr Gustav Canaval, told the court that he believed that 'the balance of Mrs Butler's mind was disturbed because of the effect of lactation'.[130] This explanation was accepted by the court, and Edith Butler was granted a conditional discharge.[131]

The cases of Doreen Featherstone and Edith Butler reflect the varied range of methods employed by women who killed their children during the twentieth century. They also reflect prevailing divergent attitudes towards the crime and the individuals who perpetrated it. In addition, the indictment evidence heard against Featherstone and Butler shows the heterogeneous nature of motives and explanations for the offence in the modern era: it is to this subject that we will now turn.

Explanations and attitudes

The growth of interdisciplinary scholarship on infanticide and child murder since the 1970s has resulted in sub-categories of the offence being defined which directly relate to motives and explanations of the offence. For example, altruistic or 'mercy killings' and retaliatory or 'spousal-revenge murders' are now labels that medical and legal professionals apply to episodes of infant murder, especially in the US.[132] In Britain, on the other hand, more traditional motives for infanticide seem to have persisted.

As Philip J. Resnick makes clear, in the twentieth century as before, most infanticides and neonaticides occur 'simply because the child is not wanted'.[133] Typically, in instances of new-born child murder, the woman concerned had become pregnant with an illegitimate child which was been conceived out of wedlock or was the result of an extra-marital affair. As we have already seen in this chapter, the shame and opprobrium associated with illegitimacy did not wane in Great Britain until the later decades of the twentieth century. In the face of few alternatives, many women accused of child murder seem to have concealed their pregnancies and committed the crime in order to avoid discovery of their condition and the ensuing embarrassment for themselves and their families.[134] In 1986, for instance, Sharon Evans, a 16-year-old girl from Plymouth, was indicted for an infanticide carried out on her new-born son. Sharon had killed her baby in order to stop her father discovering she was pregnant.[135]

Often committed amidst the pain and confusion of self-delivery, and commonly when the woman concerned felt herself to be socially isolated and desolate, infanticide and neonaticide are carried out by manifestly desperate individuals.[136] Indeed, as we have seen elsewhere in this volume, many of the women accused of killing their offspring were in a state of denial about their situation. In their despair and anguish they convinced themselves that they were not pregnant and that their problems would somehow magically disappear. Accordingly, they made no preparation for parturition and were often very much surprised by the onset of labour. Under extreme forms of emotional stress, these women then panicked when they realised what was happening to them and killed their infant quickly in the process of delivery or immediately afterwards, either by accident or by wilful intent, in order to prevent the baby's cries and their subsequent detection.[137] Sharon Evans, for instance, managed to hide her pregnancy, give birth in secret and in silence, and choke her son to death in the bathroom of her family home, whilst her parents were in another room watching television. She was convicted of infanticide and sentenced to three years' probation.[138]

The debate over the extent to which psychiatric illness was a key causal factor in instances of infanticide, which began during the nineteenth century, was still going strong in the twentieth century, although the arguments involved became more sophisticated as advancements in psychiatric medicine were made. Some scientists and medical professionals (including members of the Butler Committee of 1975) argued that there were no proven links between parturition, mental illness and infanticide.[139] Other commentators, including correspondents to academic journals and popular magazines, argued that puerperal insanity was an appropriate medical condition, which had a direct bearing on instances of infanticide. In particular, they emphasised the convenient way in which mental health issues related to childbirth explained women's irrational and at times violent behaviour towards their own offspring.[140]

To that end, in 1960, the *British Medical Journal* reviewed an infanticide case heard at the Somerset assizes against a married woman called Mary Spraggs. Mrs Spraggs had given birth to a child but had tremendous difficulties breast-feeding her baby. The court heard how the child became ill and Mrs Spraggs 'had no proper sleep for six weeks'. Approximately two months after the child's birth, Mr Spraggs found his wife lying on the floor of their kitchen fully dressed. The baby was then discovered lying face down having been strangled with the aid of a silk scarf found wrapped around its neck. Medical testimony was provided at the trial which described Mary Spraggs as being 'profoundly distressed and suffering from agitated melancholia' upon her arrest and the journal concluded that this was exactly the kind of case which supported the contention that there was an explicit link between childbirth, lactation, mental illness (in this case via exhaustion and frustration) and incidents of new-born child murder.[141]

Some scholars suggest that there are national and regional differences in the prevalence of puerperal illness as a causal factor for infanticide in the twentieth century. Maureen Marks and Ramesh Kumar, for instance, insist that mental illness was more often given as an explanation for infanticide amongst Scottish women than their English and Welsh counterparts.[142] A far more common assertion, and one that has enjoyed wide acceptance in recent years, is that psychiatric causes for child murder are more relevant in instances of infanticide than in episodes of neonaticide, which are much more to do with maintaining concealment and remaining undiscovered.[143]

In general terms, a lack of consensus remains over the validity of conditions and diagnoses such as puerperal insanity or lactational insanity, and doubt still exists over whether childbirth can cause mental instability to the extent of child murder.[144] However, as Ian Brockington explains:

> Childbirth is a complex event, packed with somatic and psychological incident. It is a period of rapid biological, social and emotional transition. It is a social and psychological crisis, requiring intrapsychic adaption and interpersonal reorganisation, especially after the first child. There is physical discomfort, and there may be loss of employment, financial pressures, changes in the social network, decreased recreation, confinement to the house and boredom. Marriage and other relationships may come under strain. It would not be surprising if such a challenge provoked a wide variety of different psychiatric disorders. Although there are examples of extreme stress, such as bereavement, imprisonment and battle, the psychiatry of childbirth if probably more complex than any other human situation.[145]

Moreover, it is clear from the evidence we have that mental illness can cause individuals to kill their children, although a definitive explanation for what triggers that sort of mental abnormality remains an elusive element in our understanding of this kind of crime. Acute mental illness has, and indeed does, cause infanticides to occur, largely because its onset is difficult to predict, especially in sufferers with no prior symptoms or episodes of instability. Moreover, the actions of someone suffering from a manic or psychotic episode are typically unstable and highly erratic, so it is immensely difficult to diagnose or treat them appropriately in advance of a serious psychiatric disturbance.[146]

Take, for instance, the case of Sandra Riley from Chester, who admitted the infanticide of two of her sons in 1983. Her first son, Anthony, died a few weeks after birth, the victim of an unexplained 'cot-death', in 1974. Another son, called Christopher, was born in 1981 but only lived for a few weeks, as did Philip, who was born two years later. Clearly, Mrs Riley had not received sufficient counselling or appropriate medical intervention in between the deaths of these infants, despite strong evidence to suggest that she had underlying mental health issues. Sandra Riley admitted to asphyxiating both Christopher and Phillip, and she was put on probation for two years.

In the second year of her probation, Mrs Riley killed her remaining son, Andrew, aged eight, after a prolonged sequence of physical abuse. Andrew was drowned in the bath by his mother who, in struggling to hold him under the water, repeatedly battered his head off the bath taps. In the aftermath of her crime, Sandra Riley could provide no explanation for her actions. She was sentenced to be detained indefinitely in a maximum security hospital. In summing up the case, the director of social services in Cheshire, said 'with hindsight, the psychiatric reports of the earlier case may have underestimated Riley's condition, but the decision of the court to release her back to the family home effectively tied the hands of his department'.[147]

The one significant development in our understanding of infanticide and new-born child murder in the twentieth century is our appreciation of causal factors unrelated to child-bearing. As Andrew Payne explains:

> To attribute these killings to a disturbance of the balance of mind due to the effects of birth or lactation conceals more useful explanations such as the presence of social and economic stressors, a lack of knowledge about contraception and childcare, and a lack of support. These factors, if confirmed, might lead to appropriate changes in education and social policy rather than the current concentration on individual psychopathology, important though this might be in the few cases where there is evidence of serious mental illness.[148]

It is clear that, whilst some women accused of infanticide during the twentieth century certainly did display signs of mental causation for their offences, others did not.[149] Consequently, socio-economic stresses, rather than morbid personality traits, became the focus for scholars interested in understanding why individuals killed their children.[150] Economic hardship as a lone parent, often combined with chemical substance abuse, can result in both men and women committing new-born child murder, sometimes with underlying altruistic intensions.[151]

Revenge killings in response to an extra-marital affair, ill-treatment or the demise of an established relationship are also encountered, as are homicides committed through jealousy and frustration with the alteration of personal circumstances attendant upon childbirth.[152] In 1986, for instance, Christine Annesley was indicted for infanticide at Birmingham Crown Court. Annesley had strangled her new-born son on the floor of a hospital lavatory 'to spite her executive husband because she did not believe that he was giving her the support that she needed'.[153] Clearly, after 1900, the motives and explanations for new-born child murder were as complex and varied as they had ever been and were wholly dependent on the personal circumstances of the individuals concerned. As Julie Wheelwright explains, the reality of explanations for infanticide in the modern era 'inevitably lies somewhere between the two poles of criminality and insanity'.[154]

Modern reactions to episodes of new-born child murder and infanticide do, at least at first glance, appear far more measured and consistent than in previous centuries. Some twentieth-century commentators (such as F.G. Frayling) thought this approach too lenient and described it as 'regrettable' and 'lamentable'.[155] Maureen Marks and Ramesh Kumar reinforce the validity of this sentiment in their study of infanticide in England and Wales in the 1980s, where they estimated that 'mothers who killed their newly-delivered child have a greater than 50% chance of not being indicted for the offence'.[156] Yet, the statistical evidence presented in this chapter shows a different picture. As can be seen in Figure 7.3, there is in fact little difference in the number of infanticides reported and indictments laid over the entirety of the twentieth century. A similar close correlation exists in relation to accusations and charges of concealment of pregnancy, although it is more variable (see Figures 7.1 and 7.2).

Moreover, Figures 7.1–7.3 demonstrate that conviction rates for the offences in question remained consistently high over the period, even if the incidence of the crimes more generally was on a downward trajectory, especially after mid-century. This finding is somewhat at odds with the work of scholars such as Fiona Brookman, Jane Nolan and Phillip Resnick, who argue that one of the most evident traits which emphasises the lenient treatment of offenders accused of infanticide and new-born child murder, is the low conviction rate for this crime.[157]

Another finding of scholarship relating to reactions to infanticide and concealment of pregnancy is the relatively lenient approach taken to sentencing and punishment of convicted individuals since 1900. For instance, no woman has been executed for infanticide in Britain since the middle of the nineteenth century.[158] In addition, scholars point out that sentences of imprisonment for infanticide became less frequent over the twentieth

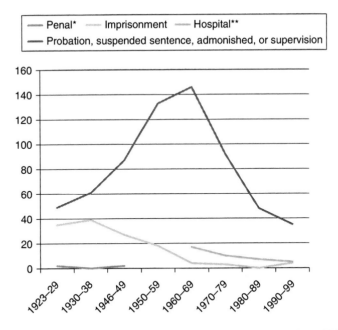

Figure 7.5   Trends in punishment for infanticide in England and Wales, 1920–1999
Notes: No records are available for 1939–1945.
*No penal servitude recorded after 1947.
**Hospital treatment first recorded in 1964.

century in favour of periods of probation with compulsory psychiatric treatment.[159] Of course, sentences of this type are entirely justified given the specific medical rubric contained within the 1938 Infanticide Act.

Figure 7.5 substantiates the contention that probation came to dominate the sentencing of individuals convicted of infanticide during the twentieth century, in England and Wales at least. Figures 7.6 and 7.7, which relate to convictions for concealment of pregnancy, on the other hand, show a more mixed approach to punishment, though this could be down to the fact that the legislative provision for concealment is more prescriptive in relation to sentencing, as we saw in Chapter 5.

The lenient treatment of infanticidal women, which is particularly evident in the criminal statistics, echoes a similar attitude to female offenders more generally in modern Britain. Traditionally, scholars have suggested four reasons for the more indulgent or compassionate judicial approach adopted towards female criminals in the twentieth century. Firstly, as women are more likely to be indicted for a less serious offence in the first instance, their punishments are accordingly more minor in nature. Secondly, it has been suggested that judges regularly act chivalrously towards women appearing

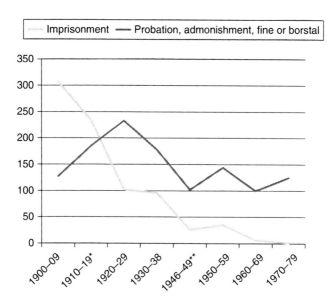

Figure 7.6 Trends in punishment for concealment of pregnancy in England and Wales, 1900–1999

Notes: *No records are available for 1915 and 1916.
**No records are available for 1939–1945.

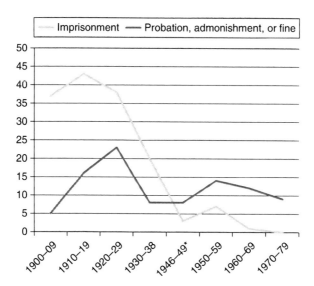

Figure 7.7 Trends in punishment for concealment of pregnancy in Scotland, 1900–1979

Notes: Infanticide was not recorded as a separate offence.
*No records of convictions are available for 1939–1945.

before them and baulk at the prospect of sentencing them to a serious or significant punishment. Thirdly, it is argued that more extraneous factors are taken into account when sentencing female offenders. For instance, if a woman has young children to care for, the chances of her receiving a custodial sentence are reduced; as such a decision might have a deleterious impact on her family. Finally, it has been suggested that women are treated more sympathetically than men in the courtroom because their crimes more regularly exhibit evidence of psychiatric abnormality, and they are, therefore, are more likely to require medical treatment than incarceration.[160]

Although some of these contentions may hold true, it seems that attitudes towards infanticidal women, and indeed criminal women more widely, have recently changed. Rather than punishing women who do not conform to customary gender roles and expectations (such as domesticity and motherhood), legal authorities and society more widely have come to appreciate that 'women in desperate circumstances were forced to make difficult decisions'.[161] Moreover, the inconclusive and problematic nature of the evidence presented in trials for infanticide, concealment and new-born child murder, even by modern day standards, may well have a bearing on the reluctance of judges to inflict serious or significant sentences on women convicted of these crimes.[162]

However, leniency did not prevail in *every* instance of new-born child murder in twentieth-century Britain. Individuals found guilty of the wilful death of their infants but falling outside the boundaries of the prevailing legislation relating to infanticide or concealment could expect to be treated very differently, and a lengthy prison sentence could result on occasion. Cases of child homicide where the victim concerned was less than one year of age but where the death could clearly not be attributed to the effects of parturition or lactation were not common in modern Britain, but the judicial and public attitude towards the individuals involved varied significantly depending on the circumstances of each case. In these instances it seems that men were punished more harshly than women. Men were typically indicted on a homicide charge and, if convicted, received longer prison sentences. Women involved in the same kind of offence were typically accused of manslaughter and, although often sentenced to long-term imprisonment, they were commonly reprieved on medical or psychiatric grounds, rarely serving their full sentence.[163]

Sally Clark's case, in 1999, exemplifies an instance where a woman *was* given a substantial punishment for new-born child murder, but also clearly demonstrates the deficiencies of judicial evidence in the modern era. Sally was indicted for the murder of two of her infant sons.[164] She was a happily-married solicitor who lived in Wilmslow, Cheshire. Her first son, Christopher, was born in September 1996 but died two months later, initially it was thought, from an infection. Her next son, Harry, was born the following year, in November 1997, but died just eight weeks after birth and his death was originally attributed to a respiratory problem. Subsequent routine pathology tests on Harry Clark suggested the possibility of foul play, on account of the discovery of unusual bruises on his body and an injury to his mouth. An investigation was launched into the deaths of both boys, and evidence was collated from witnesses who reported that Mrs Clark's reaction to the death of her first son was 'superficial' and 'untypical', to the extent that suspicion over her conduct intensified. Sally Clark was eventually arrested for the murder of her two sons and her trial was fixed for early November 1999.[165]

Robin Spencer QC, the chief prosecution lawyer in the Sally Clark case, stated at the outset of her trial: 'The idea that a mother could deliberately kill her own baby is almost too horrific to contemplate, but... you can be sure that the unthinkable is the truth.'[166] The media portrayed Sally as a spoilt, rich lawyer who had a serious drink problem which was exacerbated by loneliness owing to her husband being absent for long periods because of the demands of his career. Sally was variously described as 'the reluctant mother', 'the lonely drunk', and 'the depressed alcoholic' who was 'prone to bouts of severe binge drinking'. Effectively, she was described as someone unfit for motherhood, and especially the care of young infants.[167]

The evidence presented in Sally Clark's trial was regularly conflicting and did not appear to fully substantiate a charge of murder against her. Medical professionals, for instance, disagreed on the cause of death in both cases and could not claim with confidence that either child had been deliberately killed. Nevertheless, the entire case arguably hinged on the testimony of Professor Roy Meadow who, at the time of the trial, was the country's most eminent paediatrician and leading expert on the causes of infant death. Meadow had previously stated, in his *ABC of Child Abuse* published in 1997: 'There is no evidence that cot deaths runs in families... but there is plenty of evidence that child abuse does.' His rule of thumb was that, 'unless proven otherwise, one cot death is tragic, two is suspicious and three is murder.' Although it is now believed that this pronouncement did not originate from Meadow's own lips, it has become almost universally known as 'Meadow's law'.[168]

In Sally Clark's trial, Meadow testified that the chance of two cot-deaths happening in one family was 73 million to one, or a double cot-death happening once every century. He somewhat crassly likened the potential for this to happen as being equivalent to someone successfully backing an 80-1 winner of the Grand National each year for four years running.[169] Sally Clark was convicted of the double murder of her sons. The court heard that at the time she supposedly killed her children she was not drunk, nor had she been suffering from a mental disorder of any kind. Consequently, she was given two life sentences for her crimes.[170]

Not long after her conviction, Sally Clark launched an appeal for her release on the grounds that the prosecution's evidence against her was deeply flawed and 'just plain wrong'. In particular, Sally's legal team pointed to the suggestion that the wounds and bruises found on the bodies of Christopher and Harry may have been caused by vigorous attempts to revive them. They also argued that Roy Meadow's testimony was 'dangerous', as it had been wrongly calculated.[171] Support for this latter contention was found amongst mathematicians and statisticians, who were quick to point out that Sir Roy Meadow's calculation using probability theory was fundamentally incorrect and that the true figure was likely closer to a double cot-death occurring in England every seven years, or a probability statistic of 2.75 million to one.[172] Critics described his remarks in court as 'irrelevant', 'biased', 'wrong' and 'totally misleading'.[173] Moreover, other medical experts waded into the debate, saying that a proven genetic abnormality could readily cause multiple cot-deaths in a given family, rendering Meadow's evidence 'scientifically illiterate'.[174]

The initial appeal failed. A further appeal in January 2002 had more success, however, when it was revealed that the prosecution's pathologist, Dr Alan Williams, had 'deliberately withheld crucial evidence' during Sally Clark's trial, which would have completely exonerated her of any wrong-doing in the death of Harry. If it had been clearly proven that Harry's death occurred by natural causes in the original trial, then Meadow's statistical evidence about the suspicious nature of multiple unexplained deaths in one family would have been inadmissible and wholly irrelevant to the proceedings.[175] Sally Clark was released in January 2003 after the second appeal successfully rendered her original conviction unsafe.[176] She was said to be the victim of 'inexcusable incompetence' and had experienced a 'double disaster', where not only had she suffered the deaths of two of her children, but she had also endured years of wrongful imprisonment. As *The Times* newspaper explained at the time:

> Mothers of cot death children complain that the normal principle of British justice – the presumption of innocence until proved guilty – is reversed in their case. They talk of an emotional bias against mothers accused of this crime, which leaves the accused in the almost impossible position of having to prove their innocence in cases where hard evidence either way is often in short supply.[177]

In the aftermath of the Sally Clark case, a lot of criticism and press attention was directed towards the imprecise and inadequate nature of expert testimony in relation to trials for new-born child murder, especially in the wake of similar miscarriages of justice, such as those involving Trupti Patel and Angela Canning in the early years of the twenty-first century.[178] Calls were made for a public inquiry, and substantial case reviews were carried out.[179] The General Medical Council investigated both Dr Alan Williams and Professor Roy Meadow in relation to the nature of their conduct and the credibility of their testimony in a range of criminal cases.[180] In 2005, Williams was suspended from doing pathology work for the Home Office and for coroner's cases for three years.[181] In the same year, Meadow was found guilty of serious professional misconduct and was struck off the medical register. He successfully campaigned against this ruling in the Court of Appeal, after it was alleged that the decision would dissuade experts from providing evidence in criminal trials. However, the General Medical Council's right to criticise Meadow (and other medical professionals more generally) was reinforced in a 2006 High Court judgement.[182] Guidance for experts giving testimony at criminal trials was subsequently produced, to help them to 'stay within the limits of their professional competence'.[183]

Sally Clark herself never fully recovered from her ordeal. The persistent reporting of her case, long after her release, owing to the criticisms levelled at Williams and Meadow must have perpetuated her agony. A year after she attained her freedom, a family friend of Mrs Clark told a reporter 'Sally still isn't well, and she never will be well again', and, according to her psychiatrist, Sally was suffering from an 'enduring personality change' brought on by a 'catastrophic experience'. Sally's husband, Steve, best summed up his wife's prevailing mood in the aftermath of her experiences, by explaining that 'she is not the happy, confident person she was before this happened to her. She is vulnerable, she has panic attacks [and] she gets flustered by things that most of us just deal with. She constantly feels like people are judging her and it is a vicious circle.'[184] Although Sally and Steve went on to have another son, Sally believed her conduct as a mother was constantly under scrutiny and suspicion, and she found that pressure too much to bear. Sally Clark was found dead in her bed on 16 March 2007. It was ruled that she died accidentally from acute alcohol intoxication. She was 42.[185]

Cases like that of Sally Clark reflect the fickle nature of attitudes towards new-born child murder and infanticide in twentieth-century Great Britain; not just in the judicial context but in the wider public arena too. The dominant ideology of motherhood has persisted through the modern era and we can expect that women who do not conform to the idealised image of a good mother will be condemned at every opportunity.[186] Yet, overall, it is probably fair to say that the media's reaction to crimes of this type in the twentieth century has been much more tempered and understated than we might expect, especially in instances where the accused was a woman.

Perfunctory headlines, such as 'Baby's Mother Arrested', 'Infanticide Trial For Mother', 'Mother "Could Not Feel Love"', 'Psychiatric Inquiry in Killer Mother Case' and 'Mother Who Could Not Cope Jailed for Infanticide', suggest that more sensational headlines are typically absent from modern press reports of cases of infanticide and new-born child murder.[187] Instead, the media's portrayal of women accused or convicted of these crimes typically mirrors the judicial approach, where a significant degree of sympathy, alongside measured curiosity regarding the causes of infanticidal behaviour, prevails.

Conclusion – past, present and future?

As this book has shown, some elements of infanticide have persisted and others have altered. In the first three chapters, we noted the ubiquity of infanticide in many societies. We considered the incidence, nature and characteristics of early modern infanticide and concluded that, although the unmarried female domestic servant was more likely to be indicted for this offence, other individuals – both male and female – were involved in the perpetration of the crime, as well as its discovery and investigation. Certainly, new-born child murder was not a crime solely restricted to the female sphere, as has often been assumed. However, it is also clear from the evidence that legal constraints and evidential problems rendered successful prosecutions for infanticide increasingly difficult to achieve.

We noted in Chapter 4 that there were a variety of methods of infant disposal open to British women in the pre-modern period. Despite this, British women continued to commit new-born child murder between 1600 and 1900. They did this when the other means available to them were considered too dangerous, too expensive or too inconvenient. The nineteenth-century history of infanticide exhibited continuities, but also some important changes. Prosecuting individuals for infanticide remained problematic, despite new legislation governing concealment and regardless of growing public concern that the offence was on the rise. Although the characteristics of defendants and the methods they employed had not significantly altered from the early modern period, more married women and accomplices were prosecuted during the Victorian era than ever before. The numerous motives associated with new-born child murder and its allied offences were examined in Chapter 6. Aside from the advent of medical explanations for infanticidal behaviour, which came to the fore in the nineteenth century, shame, poverty, isolation and pragmatism were shown to be the key causal factors for infanticide persisting throughout British history. It is important to note that, although recorded (and conceivably actual) incidences of infanticide diminished after the 1830s, such instances remained conspicuous and still excited individual and media interest.

The final chapter examined the nature and incidence of infanticide and new-born murder in Britain since 1900. The twentieth century was a period when interest in the conduct of mothers and the quality of motherhood reached its zenith as attempts were made to stabilise population figures and improve infant welfare and maternal health. It was also a time when the historic struggle between medical men and lawyers for professional authority in recorded instances of new-born child murder intensified. It was within this context that England and Wales changed the legal provision for the crime of infanticide in 1922 and again in 1938, to emphasise the association between the death of new-born infants and mental aberrations brought on by the effects of parturition and lactation. This association has now largely been disputed. The different approaches to infanticide and child murder in the legal context of Britain and further afield in the modern era illustrate both the complex nature of this offence and a continuing lack of consensus over its causes and appropriate management.

Despite ongoing difficulties of obtaining conclusive evidence of separate existence, live birth and cause of death, infanticide (and concealment of pregnancy) prosecutions persisted in the twentieth century, though they diminished significantly in the decades after 1950. Women still dominated indictments for this kind of offence, although in comparison with previous centuries more men were involved, especially in relation to the killing of older infants. The longevity of new-born child murder in modern British history can probably be explained by the limited use of contraceptives until the last third of the twentieth century, alongside the few and limited alternatives open to women facing an unwanted pregnancy.

Explanations for child murder have certainly become more nuanced since the 1970s, when categories of the offence were established and refined by academic scholars and medical professionals. Although psychiatric abnormalities account for some instances of infant homicide, they are typically pertinent in relation to the killing of older children, rather than neonates. Traditional explanations for infanticide, such as seeking to avoid the shame of an illegitimate pregnancy, isolation and desperation, now sit alongside more modern socio-economic triggers, such as revenge, jealousy and most notably poverty, as the key causal factors for the murder of young children.

One consequence of the increase in scholarship and research on the causes of infanticide in Britain in the twentieth century is a more measured response to individuals accused and/or convicted of the offence. This has led some commentators to argue that women killers are regularly overlooked in relation to tough legal sanctions. Whilst evidence from this chapter has shown that sentences and punishments for new-born child murder have usually been relatively minor in nature, this is in line with the wider treatment of female offenders in the modern period. Moreover, the data suggests that accusations of infanticide are regularly followed by formal charges, and that conviction patterns closely mirror the number of indictments laid. Thus, any notion of the lenient treatment of female offenders needs to be qualified and moderated.

The tragic case of Sally Clark illustrates the continued complexity of cases of new-born child murder in the present day, as well as the inconsistent nature of the attitudes exhibited towards those individuals suspected of the offence. Indeed, as Mrs Clark's trial showed, even by modern standards, judicial, professional and public opinion regarding individuals accused of child-killing can be dangerously flawed and at times overzealous and inappropriate. It seems that, on occasion, the pendulum of opinion relating to child murder has the potential to swing right back to the kind of hard, unsympathetic and reproachful attitude that we saw in the early chapters of this book, and again in the treatment of the young Welsh convict Mary Morgan in Chapter 5. We must not let this kind of retaliatory justice prevail anew, unless we have incontrovertible evidence that a serious, deliberate and wicked act was perpetrated against a defenceless new-born baby in the absence of mitigating factors which could explain the circumstances within which the 'crime' was committed.

The persistence of infanticide into the twenty-first century compellingly invites the historian to ponder possible solutions to this starkly enduring issue. Greater knowledge and advancement in medicine, science and education may help us to better understand, minimise or even prevent instances of new-born child murder in the future. Whether parents should be subjected to more rigorous standards of expected behaviour than other criminals is rather a moot point.[188] Rather, infanticide needs to be seen in the context of everyday life and not as a freak occurrence.[189] For one thing, the laws on abortion, child destruction, infanticide and concealment of pregnancy, along with their commensurate sentencing policies, ought to be reviewed to see if they are still appropriate, relevant and desirable in British society today.[190] Investigative procedures should likewise be modernised, in order to enable them to invoke multidisciplinary and multiagency expertise.[191] Alternatively, we might want to take the example of some states in North America and introduce 'safe haven laws', which have been specifically designed to curb infanticide and neonaticide by providing new mothers with an opportunity to voluntarily abandon their babies without legal repercussions of any kind and via a process which retains their anonymity.[192]

Teenagers (and their parents) need to be more openly and systematically educated about the potential pitfalls of unprotected sexual activity, and should be given appropriate guidance about the availability of contraceptives and how they can be employed effectively. Expectant couples could be better informed on the physical and psychological effects of pregnancy and parturition and be provided with guidelines which successfully outline recommended nurturing techniques to facilitate parental bonding and enhance the welfare of new-born infants in a more general sense. Likewise, parents should be advised on how best to identify the circumstances, characteristics and/or behaviours which are now recognised as being associated with an increased likelihood of child murder occurring. Devising a programme of interventionist therapy and preventative measures when the risk of attack seems significant would be a vital step forward.[193] Pregnant women, more particularly, should be given information on the types of support available for mothers who run into difficulties during pregnancy, parturition and maternity – be they personal, medical or financial issues.

Perhaps most importantly of all, however, is the need for us to learn from the unfortunate women who have resorted to new-born child murder in Britain and beyond, for whatever reason, since the earliest times. We now have much more accurate information about the individuals who have committed this crime, especially in relation to the twentieth century, where the testimonies of women like Sally Clark remain an important educative legacy and a constant reminder of our shortcomings in dealing with women who kill their children. We must learn from their experiences in order to better understand the complex range of circumstances within which this crime takes place. Only then might we be in a position to confine infanticide and new-born child murder to the realms of historical study, where it most definitely belongs.

Notes

1 Investigating infanticide – an enduring phenomenon

1. The thoughts of Medea upon preparing to kill her twin sons reproduced from E. Hamilton (1940) *Mythology* (Boston: Little, Brown and Co.), pp. 129–30.

2. For instance, in May of 2012 alone, the body of a new-born baby was found amongst a pile of waste at a recycling plant in Scunthorpe, England; the corpse of a new-born child was found in a stream at Dev Nagar in Delhi, India; and a dead neonate was discovered in a strawberry field in Camarillo, California in the United States of America. See respectively the *Daily Mail*, 4 May 2012; *The Times of India*, 12 May 2012; and the *Ventura County Star*, 22 May 2012.

3. P.C. Hoffer and N.E.C. Hull (1984) *Murdering Mothers: Infanticide in England and New England 1558–1803* (New York: New York University Press), p. 3. See also C.L. Meyer and M. Oberman (2001) *Mothers Who Kill their Children: Understanding the Acts of Moms from Susan Smith to the 'Prom Mom'* (New York and London: New York University Press), p. 1.

4. See for instance S.E. Pitt and E.M. Bale (1995) 'Neonaticide, Infanticide, and Filicide: A Review of the Literature', *Bulletin of the American Academy of Psychiatry and the Law*, 23, p. 3; Hoffer and Hull (1984) *Murdering Mothers*, p. 3; and J.A. Osborne (1987) 'The Crime of Infanticide: Throwing Out the Baby with the Bathwater', *Canadian Journal of Family Law*, 6, p. 49.

5. For further discussion see Meyer and Oberman (2001) *Mothers Who Kill their Children*, p. 1; C. Alder and K. Polk (2001) *Child Victims of Homicide* (Cambridge: Cambridge University Press), pp. 32–3; K.D. Moseley (1986) 'The History of Infanticide in Western Society', *Issues in Law and Medicine*, 1, pp. 346–51; R.J. Kellett (1992) 'Infanticide and Child Destruction – The Historical, Legal and Pathological Aspects', *Forensic Science International*, 53, p. 2; B.R. Sharma (2006) 'Historical and Medico-Legal Aspects of Infanticide: An Overview', *Medicine, Science and the Law*, 46, p. 152; M. Oberman (2003) 'A Brief History of Infanticide and the Law', in M.G. Spinelli (ed.) *Infanticide: Psychological and Legal Perspectives on Mothers Who Kill* (Washington, DC and London: American Psychiatric Publishing Inc.), pp. 4–5; and B.A. Montag and T.W. Montag (1979) 'Infanticide: A Historical Survey', *Minnesota Medicine*, May edition, pp. 368–72.

6. See for instance Pitt and Bale (1995) 'Neonaticide, Infanticide, and Filicide', p. 376; A. Giladi (1990) 'Observations on Infanticide in Medieval Muslim Society', *International Journal of Middle East Studies*, 22, p. 194; Alder and Polk (2001) *Child Victims of Homicide*, pp. 31–2; M. Dickemann (1984) 'Concepts and Classification in the Study of Human Infanticide: Sectional Introduction and Some Cautionary Notes', pp. 427–38; S.C.M. Scrimshaw (1984) 'Infanticide in Human Populations: Societal and Individual Concerns', pp. 439–62; S.R. Johansson (1984) 'Deferred Infanticide: excess Female Mortality during Childhood)', pp. 463–86; M. Daly and M. Wilson (1984) 'A Sociobiological Analysis of Human Infanticide', pp. 487–502; and P.E. Bugos, Jr. and L.M. McCarthy (1984) 'Ayoreo Infanticide: A Case Study', pp. 503–20, all in G. Hausfater and S.B. Hardy (eds.) *Infanticide: Comparative and Evolutionary Perspectives* (New York: Aldine).

7. L. Williamson (1978) 'Infanticide: An Anthropological Analysis', in M. Kohl (ed.) *Infanticide and the Value of Life* (New York: Prometheus), p. 61.
8. For further discussion see ibid., p. 62 and pp. 68–9; Osborne (1987) 'The Crime of Infanticide', p. 49; S.B. Pomeroy (1983) 'Infanticide in Hellenistic Greece', in A. Cameron and A. Kuhrt (eds.) *Images of Women in Antiquity* (London: Croom Helm), p. 208; W.B. Ober (1986) 'Infanticide in Eighteenth-Century England: William Hunter's Contribution to the Forensic Problem', *Pathology Annual*, 21, p. 311; E. Coleman (1976) 'Infanticide in the Early Middle Ages', in M. Mosher Stuard (ed.) *Women in Medieval Society* (Philadelphia: University of Pennsylvania Press), p. 57; and Z.E. Rokeah (1990) 'Unnatural Child Death among Christians and Jews in Medieval England', *The Journal of Psychohistory*, 18, pp. 181–226.
9. See for instance Oberman (2003) 'A Brief History of Infanticide', pp. 4–5; I. Brockington (1996, 2003 edition) *Motherhood and Mental Health* (Oxford: Oxford University Press), p. 431; and Moseley (1986) 'The History of Infanticide in Western Society', p. 349. For similar authority in other cultures see also Giladi (1990) 'Observations on Infanticide', p. 189.
10. Oberman (2003) 'A Brief History of Infanticide', pp. 4–5.
11. For further discussion see I. Lambie (2001) 'Mothers Who Kill: The Crime of Infanticide', *International Journal of Law and Psychiatry*, 24, p. 72; and Moseley (1986) 'The History of Infanticide in Western Society', p. 345.
12. For further discussion in relation to Greco-Roman cultures and others see J.E. Boswell (1984) 'Expositio and Oblation: The Abandonment of Children and the Ancient and Medieval Family', *American Historical Review*, 89, pp. 10–33; W.V. Harris (1994) 'Child-Exposure in the Roman Empire', *The Journal of Roman Studies*, 84, pp. 1–22; M. Radin (1925) 'The Exposure of Infants in Roman Law and Practice', *The Classical Journal*, 20, pp. 337–43; Moseley (1986) 'The History of Infanticide in Western Society', p. 350; Brockington (1996, 2003 edition) *Motherhood and Mental Health*, pp. 430–1; Pitt and Bale (1995) 'Neonaticide, Infanticide, and Filicide', p. 376; Sharma (2006) 'Historical and Medico-Legal Aspects of Infanticide', p. 152; Kellett (1992) 'Infanticide and Child Destruction', p. 2; Meyer and Oberman (2001) *Mothers Who Kill their Children*, p. 3; and S.X. Radbill (1968) 'A History of Child Abuse and Infanticide', in R.E. Helfer and C.H. Kempe (eds.) *The Battered Child* (Chicago: University of Chicago Press), p. 8.
13. For further discussion see Osborne (1987) 'The Crime of Infanticide', p. 49; Moseley (1986) 'The History of Infanticide in Western Society', pp. 346 and 351; Meyer and Oberman (2001) *Mothers Who Kill their Children*, pp. 1 and 3; Williamson (1978) 'Infanticide', p. 73; R. Leboutte (1991) 'Offense against Family Order: Infanticide in Belgium from the Fifteenth through the Early Twentieth Centuries', *Journal of the History of Sexuality*, 2, p. 160; Radbill (1968) 'A History of Child Abuse and Infanticide', p. 6; Giladi (1990) 'Observations on Infanticide', pp. 185, 187 and 189–90; Lambie (2001) 'Mothers Who Kill', p. 72; and Brockington (1996, 2003 edition) *Motherhood and Mental Health*, p. 430.
14. For further discussion see Pitt and Bale (1995) 'Neonaticide, Infanticide, and Filicide', p. 376; Osborne (1987) 'The Crime of Infanticide', p. 49; Meyer and Oberman (2001) *Mothers Who Kill their Children*, pp. 4–6; Williamson (1978) 'Infanticide', p. 63; Oberman (2003) 'A Brief History of Infanticide', pp. 4–5; Lambie (2001) 'Mothers Who Kill', pp. 72–3; Brockington (1996, 2003 edition) *Motherhood and Mental Health*, p. 431; B.A. Kellum (1974) 'Infanticide in England in the Later Middle Ages', *History of Childhood Quarterly*, 1, pp. 368–9; Giladi (1990) 'Observations on Infanticide', pp. 186–7; D.E. Mungello (2008) *Drowning Girls in*

China Since 1650 (Lanham, MD: Rowman and Littlefield); J. Lee, C. Campbell and G. Tan (1992) 'Infanticide and Family Planning in Late Imperial China: The Price and Population History of Rural Liaoning, 1774–1873', in T.G. Rawski and L.M. Li (eds.) *Chinese History in Economic Perspective* (Berkeley: University of California Press), pp. 145–76; and B.J. Lee (1981) 'Female Infanticide in China', *Historical Reflections/Réflexions Historiques*, 8, pp. 163–77.

15. See, for instance, Meyer and Oberman (2001) *Mothers Who Kill their Children*, p. 5; Oberman (2003) 'A Brief History of Infanticide', pp. 4–5; Brockington (1996, 2003 edition) *Motherhood and Mental Health*, p. 431; Pomeroy (1983) 'Infanticide in Hellenistic Greece', p. 216; Moseley (1986) 'The History of Infanticide in Western Society', p. 346; W. Ingalls (2002) 'Demography and Dowries: Perspectives on Female Infanticide in Classical Greece', *Phoenix*, 56, pp. 246–54; B.D. Miller (1997) *The Endangered Sex: Neglect of Female Children in Rural North India* (Delhi: Oxford University Press); and R.D. Bhatnagar, R. Dube and R. Dube (2005) *Female Infanticide in India: A Feminist Cultural History* (Albany: State University of New York Press).

16. See respectively Exodus 1:15–22 and Matthew 2:1–18. See also Sharma (2006) 'Historical and Medico-Legal Aspects of Infanticide', p. 152 and Kellett (1992) 'Infanticide and Child Destruction', p. 2.

17. For further discussion see Lambie (2001) 'Mothers Who Kill', p. 72; Brockington (1996, 2003 edition) *Motherhood and Mental Health*, p. 432; and Radbill (1968) 'A History of Child Abuse and Infanticide', pp. 8–9.

18. For further discussion see, for instance, K. Wrightson (1982) 'Infanticide in European History', *Criminal Justice History*, III, pp. 1–20; W.L. Langer (1974) 'Infanticide: A Historical Survey', *History of Childhood Quarterly*, I, pp. 353–66; Leboutte (1991) 'Offense against Family Order', p. 160; Rokeah (1990) 'Unnatural Child Death', pp. 181–226; and Giladi (1990) 'Observations on Infanticide', pp. 185–200.

19. See Wrightson (1982) 'Infanticide in European History', p. 1. For an example of the history of how this policing and disciplinary imperative was applied to blasphemy in particular from the late medieval period onwards see D.S. Nash (2007) *Blasphemy in the Christian World* (Oxford: Oxford University Press), pp. 42–71.

20. For further discussion of early punishments for infanticide see ibid., pp. 1–2; Brockington (1996, 2003 edition) *Motherhood and Mental Health*, p. 448; Langer (1974) 'Infanticide: A Historical Survey', p. 356; Kamler, M. (1988) 'Infanticide in the Towns of the Kingdom of Poland in the Second Half of the 16th and the First Half of the 17th Century', *Acta Poloniae Historica*, 58, pp. 47–8; M.W. Piers (1978) *Infanticide* (New York: Norton), p. 69; A. Rowlands (1997) '"In Great Secrecy": The Crime of Infanticide in Rothenburg ob der Tauber, 1501–1618', *German History*, 15, p. 180; and K. Johnson Kramar (2005) *Unwilling Mothers, Unwanted Babies: Infanticide in Canada* (Vancouver, BC: University of British Columbia Press), p. 23.

21. For a similar contention see Lambie (2001) 'Mothers Who Kill', p. 71 and for further discussion of the unique respect afforded infanticide in judicial proceedings across Europe in the early modern period see J.H. Langbein (1974) *Prosecuting Crime in the Renaissance: England, Germany, France* (Cambridge, MA: Harvard University Press), *passim*.

22. Radbill (1968) 'A History of Child Abuse and Infanticide', pp. 3–17.

23. Piers (1978) *Infanticide*, *passim*.

24. See, for instance, Langer (1974) 'Infanticide', pp. 353–66; Kellum (1974) 'Infanticide', pp. 367–88; and R.H. Helmholz (1975) 'Infanticide in the Province

of Canterbury during the Fifteenth Century', *History of Childhood Quarterly*, 2, pp. 379–90. For further discussion of the historiography of infanticide from this point onwards see B.H. Bechtold and D. Cooper Graves (2006) 'Towards and Understanding of Infanticide Scholarship', in B.H. Bechtold and D. Cooper Graves (eds.) *Killing Infants: Studies in the Worldwide Practice of Infanticide* (New York: Edwin Mellen), pp. 1–15 and A-M Kilday and K.D. Watson (2008) 'Infanticide, Religion and Community in the British Isles, 1720–1920: Introduction', *Family and Community History*, 11, 2, pp. 88–91.

25. See C. Damme (1978) 'Infanticide: The Worth of an Infant under Law', *Medical History*, 22, pp. 1–24 and Moseley (1986) 'The History of Infanticide in Western Society', pp. 345–61 in particular.

26. Rokeah (1990) 'Unnatural Child Death', pp. 181–226.

27. S.M. Butler (2007) 'A Case of Indifference? Child Murder in Later Medieval England', *Journal of Women's History*, 19, pp. 59–82.

28. See P.E.H. Hair (1972) 'Homicide, Infanticide and Child Assault in Late Tudor Middlesex', *Local Population Studies (Notes and Queries)*, 9, pp. 43–6; K. Wrightson (1975) 'Infanticide in Earlier Seventeenth Century England', *Local Population Studies*, XV, pp. 10–22; R.W. Malcolmson (1977) 'Infanticide in the Eighteenth Century', in J.S. Cockburn (ed.) *Crime in England 1550–1800* (London: Methuen), pp. 187–209; R. Sauer (1978) 'Infanticide and Abortion in Nineteenth Century Britain', *Population Studies: A Journal of Demography*, XXXII, pp. 81–93; Wrightson (1982) 'Infanticide in European History', pp. 1–20; Hoffer and Hull (1984) *Murdering Mothers*, *passim*; J.M. Beattie (1986) *Crime and the Courts in England 1660–1800* (Oxford: Clarendon Press), *passim*; and A.R. Higginbotham (1989) '"Sin of the Age": Infanticide and Illegitimacy in Victorian London', *Victorian Studies*, 32, pp. 319–37.

29. M. Jackson (1996) *New-Born Child Murder: Women, Illegitimacy and the Courts in Eighteenth-Century England* (Manchester: Manchester University Press).

30. See C.B. Backhouse (1984) 'Desperate Women and Compassionate Courts: Infanticide in Nineteenth-Century Canada', *The University of Toronto Law Journal*, 34, pp. 447–78; S. Wilson (1988) 'Child Abandonment and Female Honour in Nineteenth-Century Corsica', *Comparative Studies in Society and History*, 30, pp. 762–83; O. Ulbricht (1988) 'Infanticide in Eighteenth-Century Germany', in R.J. Evans (ed.) *The German Underworld: Deviants and Outcasts in German History* (London: Routledge), pp. 108–40; M. Kamler (1988) 'Infanticide in the Towns of the Kingdom of Poland in the Second Half of the 16th and the First Half of the 17th Century', *Acta Poloniae Historica*, 58, pp. 33–49; G.S. Rowe (1991) 'Infanticide, Its Judicial Resolution, and Criminal Code Revision in Early Pennsylvania', *Proceedings of the American Philosophical Society*, CXXXV, pp. 200–32; Leboutte (1991) 'Offense against Family Order', pp. 159–85; J. Kelly (1992) 'Infanticide in Eighteenth-Century Ireland', *Irish Economic and Social History*, XIX, pp. 5–26; K. Ruggiero (1992) 'Honor, Maternity and the Disciplining of Women: Infanticide in Late Nineteenth-Century Buenos Aires', *The Hispanic American Historical Review*, 72, pp. 353–73; R. Schulte (1994) *The Village in Court: Arson, Infanticide, and Poaching in the Court Records of Upper Bavaria, 1848–1910* (Cambridge: Cambridge University Press), *passim*; J. Dalby (1995) 'Women and Infanticide in Nineteenth-Century Rural France', in V. Shepherd, B. Brereton and B. Bailey (eds.) *Engendering History: Caribbean Women in Historical Perspective* (London and Kingston, Jamaica: James Currey Publishers and Ian Randle Publishers), pp. 337–68; L. Gowing (1997) 'Secret Births and Infanticide in Seventeenth-Century England', *Past and Present*,

CLVI, pp. 87–115; K.H. Wheeler (1997) 'Infanticide in Nineteenth-Century Ohio', *Journal of Social History*, XXXI, pp. 407–18; Rowlands (1997) '"In Great Secrecy"', pp. 179–99; E.C. Green (1999) 'Infanticide and Infant Abandonment in the New South: Richmond, Virginia, 1865–1915', *Journal of Family History*, 24, pp. 187–211; and many others referred to throughout this volume.

31. For further discussion see L. Rose (1986) *The Massacre of the Innocents: Infanticide in Britain 1800–1939* (London: Routledge and Kegan Paul), *passim*; Higginbotham (1989) '"Sin of the Age"', pp. 319–37; M.L. Arnot (1994) 'Infant Death, Child Care and the State: The Baby-Farming Scandal and the First Infant Life Protection Legislation of 1872', *Continuity and Change*, 9, pp. 271–311; A.N. May (1995) '"She at first Denied It": Infanticide Trials at the Old Bailey', in V. Frith (ed.) *Women and History: Voices of Early Modern England* (Toronto: Coach House), pp. 19–49; Jackson (1996) *New-Born Child Murder, passim*; M. Francus (1997) 'Monstrous Mothers, Monstrous Societies: Infanticide and the Rule of Law in Restoration and Eighteenth-Century England', *Eighteenth Century Life*, XXI, pp. 133–156; Gowing (1997) 'Secret Births', pp. 87–115; M.L. Arnot (2000) 'Understanding Women Committing Newborn Child Murder in Victorian England', in S. D'Cruze (ed.) *Everyday Violence in Britain, 1850–1950: Gender and Class* (Harlow: Pearson), pp. 55–69; and A.-M. Kilday (2002) 'Maternal Monsters: Murdering Mothers in South-West Scotland, 1750–1815' and L. Abrams (2002) 'From Demon to Victim: The Infanticidal Mother in Shetland, 1699–1802', both in Y.G. Brown and R. Ferguson (eds.) *Twisted Sisters: Women, Crime and Deviance in Scotland since 1400* (East Linton: Tuckwell), pp. 156–79 and 180–203 respectively.

32. See for instance G.K. Behlmer (1979) 'Deadly Motherhood: Infanticide and Medical Opinion in Mid-Victorian England', *Journal of the History of Medicine and Allied Sciences*, XXXIV, pp. 403–27; Arnot (1994) 'Infant Death, Child Care and the State', pp. 271–311; and K.D. Watson (2011) *Forensic Medicine in Western Society – A History* (Abingdon: Routledge), *passim*.

33. For further discussion see R. Smith (1983) 'Defining Murder and Madness: An Introduction to Medicolegal Belief in the case of Mary Ann Brough, 1854', *Knowledge and Society: Studies in the Sociology of Culture Past and Present*, 4, pp. 173–225; K. O'Donovan (1984) 'The Medicalisation of Infanticide', *Criminal Law Review*, 259, pp. 259–64; A. Payne (1995) 'Infanticide and Child Abuse', *The Journal of Forensic Psychiatry*, 6, pp. 472–6; T. Ward (1999) 'The Sad Subject of Infanticide: Law, Medicine and Child Murder', *Social and Legal Studies*, VIII, pp. 163–80; H. Marland (2004) *Dangerous Motherhood: Insanity and Childbirth in Victorian Britain* (Basingstoke: Palgrave Macmillan), *passim*; and D. Rabin (2002) 'Bodies of Evidence, States of Mind: Infanticide, Emotion and Sensibility in Eighteenth-Century England', H. Marland (2002) 'Getting Away With Murder? Puerperal Insanity, Infanticide and the Defence Plea' and C. Quinn (2002) 'Images and Impulses: Representations of Puerperal Insanity and Infanticide in Late Victorian England', all in M. Jackson (ed.) *Infanticide: Historical Perspectives on Child Murder and Concealment, 1550–2000* (Aldershot: Ashgate), pp. 73–92, 168–92 and 193–215 respectively.

34. See T.R. Forbes (1985) *Surgeons at the Bailey: English Forensic Medicine to 1878* (New Haven and London: Yale University Press) and M. Jackson (1994) 'Suspicious Infant Deaths: The Statute of 1624 and Medical Evidence at Coroners' Inquests', in M. Clark and C. Crawford (eds.) *Legal Medicine in History* (Cambridge: Cambridge University Press), pp. 64–86.

35. For examples see A. O'Connor (1991) 'Women in Irish Folklore: The Testimony Regarding Illegitimacy, Abortion and Infanticide', in M. MacCurtain and M. O'Dowd (eds.) *Women in Early Modern Ireland* (Edinburgh: Edinburgh University Press), pp. 304–17; C.L. Krueger (1997) 'Literary Defenses and Medical Prosecutions: Representing Infanticide in Nineteenth-Century Britain', *Victorian Studies*, XL, pp. 271–94; D.A. Symonds (1997) *Weep Not for Me: Women, Ballads and Infanticide in Early Modern Scotland* (University Park: Pennsylvania State University Press), *passim*; M. Jones (1999) '"Too Common and Most Unnatural": Rewriting the Infanticidal Woman in Britain, 1764–1859' (Unpublished PhD Thesis, University of York), *passim*; J. McDonagh (2003) *Child Murder and British Culture 1720–1900* (Cambridge: Cambridge University Press), *passim*; J. Thorn (2003) (ed.) *Writing British Infanticide: Child-Murder, Gender, and Print, 1722–1859* (Newark, NJ: University of Delaware Press), *passim*; and A. Hunt (2006) 'Calculations and Concealments: Infanticide in Mid-Nineteenth Century Britain', *Victorian Literature and Culture*, 34, pp. 71–94.
36. See the publications by McDonagh and Thorn in note 35 above. See also J. Galley (2007) 'Infanticide in the American Imagination, 1860–1920' (Unpublished PhD Thesis, Temple University).
37. For recent historiography on infanticide in England see for instance J.R. Dickinson and J.A. Sharpe (2002) 'Infanticide in Early Modern England: The Court of Great Sessions at Chester, 1650–1800', in M. Jackson (ed.) *Infanticide: Historical Perspectives on Child Murder and Concealment, 1550–2000* (Aldershot: Ashgate), pp. 35–51; K.D. Watson (2008) 'Religion, Community and the Infanticidal Mother: Evidence from 1840s Rural Wiltshire', *Family and Community History*, 11, pp. 116–133; D. Grey (2009) '"More Ignorant and Stupid than Wilfully Cruel": Homicide Trials and "Baby-Farming" in England and Wales in the Wake of The Children Act 1908', *Crimes and Misdemeanours: Deviance and the Law in Historical Perspective*, 3, pp. 60–77; and D. Grey (2010) 'Women's Policy Networks and the Infanticide Act 1922', *Twentieth Century British History*, 21, pp. 441–63. For Ireland see, for example, Kelly (1992) 'Infanticide in Eighteenth-Century Ireland', pp. 5–26; C.A. Conley (1995) 'No Pedestals: Women and Violence in Late Nineteenth-Century Ireland', *Social History*, 28, pp. 801–18; L. Ryan (2004) 'The Press, Police and Prosecution: Perspectives on Infanticide in the 1920s', in A. Hayes and D. Urquhart (eds.) *Irish Women's History* (Dublin and Portland, OR: Irish Academic), pp. 137–51; C. Rattigan (2008) '"I Thought from her Appearance she was in the Family Way": Detecting Infanticide Cases in Ireland, 1900–1921', *Journal of Family and Community History*, 11, pp. 134–51; and C. Rattigan (2011) *"What Else Could I Do?" Single Mothers and Infanticide, Ireland 1900–1950* (Dublin: Irish Academic Press), *passim*. For Scotland see, for instance, Symonds (1997) *Weep Not for Me*, *passim*; Abrams (2002) 'From Demon to Victim', pp. 180–203; Kilday (2002) 'Maternal Monsters', pp. 156–79; A.-M. Kilday (2007) *Women and Violent Crime in Enlightenment Scotland* (Woodbridge: Boydell), Chapter Four; A.-M. Kilday (2008) '"Monsters of the Vilest Kind": Infanticidal Women and Attitudes towards their Criminality in Eighteenth-Century Scotland', *Family and Community History*, 11, pp. 100–115; Kilday, A.-M. (2010) 'Desperate Measures or Cruel Intentions: Infanticide in Britain since 1600', in A.-M. Kilday and D.S. Nash (eds.) *Crimes in Context: Britain 1600–2000* (Basingstoke: Palgrave Macmillan), pp. 60–79. For Wales see, for example, R.W. Ireland (1997) '"Perhaps my Mother Murdered Me": Child Death and the Law in Victorian Carmarthenshire', in C. Brooks and M. Lobban (eds.) *Communities and Courts in Britain 1150–1900* (London and Rio

Grande, OH: Hambledon), pp. 229–44; and N. Woodward (2007) 'Infanticide in Wales, 1730–1830', *Welsh Historical Review*, 23, pp. 94–125.

38. See, for instance, J.S. Adler (2001) '"Halting the Slaughter of the Innocents": The Civilizing Process and the Surge in Violence in Turn-of-the-Century Chicago', *Social Science History*, 25, pp. 29–52; R. Roth (2001) 'Child Murder in New England', *Social Science History*, XXV, pp. 101–47; N. Lonza (2002) '"Two Souls Lost": Infanticide in the Republic of Dubrovnik (1667–1808)', *Dubrovnik Annals*, 6, pp. 67–102; T. Rizzo (2004) 'Between Dishonour and Death: Infanticide in the Causes Célèbres of Eighteenth-Century France', *Women's History Review*, 13, pp. 5–21; Johnson Kramar (2005) *Unwilling Mothers*, *passim*; S.A. Kowalsky (2006) 'Making Sense of the Murdering Mother: Soviet Criminologists and Infanticide in Revolutionary Russia', in B.H. Bechtold and D. Cooper Graves (eds.) *Killing Infants: Studies in the Worldwide Practice of Infanticide* (Lewiston, NY: Edwin Mellen), pp. 167–94; and S. Caron (2010) '"Killed by its Mother": Infanticide in Providence County, Rhode Island, 1870 to 1938', *Journal of Social History*, 44, pp. 213–28.

39. For further discussion see, for example, M. Oberman (2002) 'Understanding Infanticide in Context: Mothers Who Kill, 1870–1930 and Today', *The Journal of Criminal Law and Criminology*, 92, pp. 707–38; M.G. Spinelli (2003) (ed.) *Infanticide: Psychological and Legal Perspectives on Mothers Who Kill* (Washington, DC and London: American Psychiatric); M.G. Spinelli (2004) 'Maternal Infanticide Associated with Mental Illness: Prevention and the Promise of Saved Lives', *American Journal of Psychiatry*, 161, pp. 1548–57; D. Cooper Graves (2006) '"…In a Frenzy while Raving Mad": Physicians and Parliamentarians Define Infanticide in Victorian England', in B.H. Bechtold and D. Cooper Graves (eds.) *Killing Infants: Studies in the Worldwide Practice of Infanticide* (Lewiston, NY: Edwin Mellen), pp. 111–35; G.R. McKee (2006) *Why Mothers Kill: A Forensic Psychologist's Casebook* (Oxford: Oxford University Press); B.R. Sharma (2006) 'Historical and Medico-Legal Aspects of Infanticide: An Overview', *Medicine, Science and the Law*, 46, pp. 152–56; K. Johnson Kramar and W.D. Watson (2006) 'The Insanities of Reproduction: Medico-Legal Knowledge and the Development of Infanticide Law', *Social and Legal Studies*, 15, pp. 237–55; P.M. Prior (2008) *Madness and Murder: Gender, Crime and Mental Disorder in Nineteenth-Century Ireland* (Dublin: Irish Academic Press); and E. Cunliffe (2011) *Murder, Medicine and Motherhood* (Oxford and Portland, OR: Hart).

40. Damme (1978) 'Infanticide', p. 2.

41. In the entirety of this volume, the phrase 'early modern' is taken to mean the period in history between 1550 and 1800.

42. See for instance the evidence presented in B. Hanawalt (1974) 'The Female Felon in Fourteenth-Century England', *Viator – Medieval and Renaissance Studies*, 5, pp. 251–73; M. Feeley (1994) 'The Decline of Women in the Criminal Process: A Comparative History', *Criminal Justice History: An International Annual*, XV, pp. 235–74; M. Feeley and D. Little (1991) 'The Vanishing Female: The Decline of Women in the Criminal Process, 1687–1912', *Law and Society Review*, 25, pp. 719–57; J.M. Beattie (1975) 'The Criminality of Women in Eighteenth-Century England', *Journal of Social History*, 8, pp. 80–1; J.A. Sharpe (1999) *Crime in Early Modern England 1550–1750* (Harlow: Longman), p. 154; C. Emsley (1996) *Crime and Society in England, 1750–1900* (London: Longman), p. 152; and D.J.V. Jones (1992) *Crime in Nineteenth-Century Wales* (Cardiff: University of Wales Press), p. 171.

43. In the entirety of this volume, the phrase 'pre-modern' is taken to mean the period in history between 1550 and 1900.

44. For further discussion see, for instance, P. Lawson (1998) 'Patriarchy, Crime and the Courts: The Criminality of Women in Late Tudor and Early Stuart England', in G.T. Smith, A.N. May and S. Devereaux (eds.) *Criminal Justice in the Old World and the New: Essays in Honour of J.M. Beattie* (Toronto: University of Toronto Press), pp. 18 and 45–6; G. Walker and J. Kermode (1994) 'Introduction', in J. Kermode and G. Walker (eds.) *Women, Crime and the Courts in Early Modern England* (London: Routledge), p. 16; and especially S. Clark (2003) *Women and Crime in the Street Literature of Early Modern England* (Basingstoke: Palgrave Macmillan), pp. ix and 52–3 as well as L. Zedner (1991) *Women, Crime and Custody in Victorian England* (Oxford: Oxford University Press), p. 2 and Chapter One.
45. D. Taylor (1998) *Crime, Policing and Punishment in England, 1750–1914* (Basingstoke: Palgrave Macmillan), p. 59.
46. See, for instance, Sharpe, *Crime in Early Modern England*, pp. 157–59 and respectively J.A. Sharpe (1997) *Instruments of Darkness: Witchcraft in England 1550–1750* (London: Penguin); M. Ingram (1994) '"Scolding Women Cucked or Washed": A Crisis in Gender Relations in Early Modern England?', in J. Kermode and G. Walker (eds.) *Women, Crime and the Courts in Early Modern England* (London: Routledge), pp. 48–80; T. Henderson (1999) *Disorderly Women in Eighteenth-Century London: Prostitution and Control in the Metropolis 1730–1830* (London: Longman); and Jackson (1996) *New-Born Child Murder, passim*.
47. For further discussion see Clark, *Women and Crime, passim* and J. Wiltenburg (1992) *Disorderly Women and Female Power in the Street Literature of Early Modern England and Germany* (Charlottesville, VA and London: University of Virginia Press), *passim*.
48. See Wiltenburg (1992) *Disorderly Women*, pp. 8 and 253–55.
49. See Clark, *Women and Crime*, pp. 41 and 52; M.L. Arnot and C. Usborne (1999) 'Why Gender and Crime? Aspects of an International Debate', in M.L. Arnot and C. Usborne (eds.) *Gender and Crime in Modern Europe* (London: UCL Press), p. 27; and G. Walker (2003) *Crime, Gender and Social Order in Early Modern England* (Cambridge: Cambridge University Press), p. 83.
50. See, for instance, Walker and Kermode, 'Introduction', p. 6 and C. Wiener (1975) 'Sex Roles and Crime in Late-Elizabethan Hertfordshire', *Journal of Social History*, 8, pp. 38–60.
51. M. Wiener (2004) *Men of Blood: Violence, Manliness and Criminal Justice in Victorian England* (Cambridge: Cambridge University Press), p. 1.
52. See, for instance, G. Morgan and P. Rushton (1998) *Rogues, Thieves and the Rule of Law: The Problem of Law Enforcement in North-East England, 1718–1800* (London: UCL Press), p. 97; P. King (2000) *Crime, Justice and Discretion in England 1740–1820* (Oxford: Oxford University Press), pp. 196–7; F. McLynn (1989) *Crime and Punishment in Eighteenth-Century England* (London: Routledge), p. 128; Beattie, 'The Criminality of Women', p. 82; N. Castan (1993) 'Criminals', in N.Z. Davis and A. Farge (eds.) *A History of Women in the West – Volume III: Renaissance and Enlightenment Paradoxes* (Cambridge, MA: Belknap Press of Harvard University Press), pp. 482 and 486; Lawson, 'Patriarchy, Crime and the Courts', pp. 23–4; and Wiener, 'Sex Roles and Crime', pp. 42 and 49.
53. See V. McMahon (2004) *Murder in Shakespeare's England* (London and New York: Hambledon Continuum) especially Chapters Five, Eight and Nine; J. Hurl-Eamon (2005) *Gender and Petty Violence in London, 1680–1720* (Columbus: Ohio State University Press), *passim*; Walker (2003) *Crime, Gender and Social Order*, especially Chapters Three and Four; S. D'Cruze (ed.) *Everyday Violence in Britain, 1850–1950: Gender and Class* (Harlow: Pearson), *passim*; S. D'Cruze and L. Jackson

(2009) *Women, Crime and Justice in England since 1660* (Basingstoke: Palgrave Macmillan), *passim*; A.-M. Kilday (2007) *Women and Violent Crime in Enlightenment Scotland* (Woodbridge: Boydell), *passim*; and R. Martin (2007) *Women, Murder and Equity in Early Modern England* (London: Routledge), *passim*.

54. For further discussion of this, see the references in note 33 above and in particular, Kilday (2007) *Women and Violent Crime*, Chapter One and the references therein.

55. For further discussion of the interpretative problems for historians surrounding instances of infanticide see G. Walker (2003) 'Just Stories: Telling Tales of Infant Death in Early Modern England', in M. Mikesell and Adele Seef (eds.) *Culture and Change: Attending to Early Modern Women* (London and Newark: Associated University Press and University of Delaware press), pp. 98–115 and P.M. Crawford (2010) *Parents of Poor Children in England, 1580–1800* (Oxford: Oxford University Press), p. 48.

56. For concurrence with this view see Wrightson (1982) 'Infanticide in European History', p. 9; Leboutte (1991) 'Offense against Family Order', p. 164; R.H. Helmholz (1987) 'Infanticide in the Province of Canterbury during the Fifteenth Century', in R.H. Helmholz (ed.) *Canon Law and the Law of England* (London: Hambledon), pp. 162 and 165; Damme (1978) 'Infanticide', p. 3; Lonza (2002) '"Two Souls Lost"', pp. 69 and 105; Malcolmson (1977) 'Infanticide', p. 191; and Coleman (1976) 'Infanticide in the Early Middle Ages', p. 59.

57. For further discussion see Malcolmson (1977) 'Infanticide', p. 191; Hoffer and Hull (1984) *Murdering Mothers*, pp. 5–6; and Dickinson and Sharpe (2002) 'Infanticide in Early Modern England', p. 54.

58. J.A. Simpson and E.S.C. Wiener (eds.) (1989, Second Edition) *The Oxford English Dictionary – Volume VII* (Oxford: Clarendon Press), p. 918.

59. For agreement that this is the most appropriate definition to use see Kellett (1992) 'Infanticide and Child Destruction', p. 1; Sharma (2006) 'Historical and Medico-Legal Aspects of Infanticide', p. 152; Oberman (2003) 'A Brief History of Infanticide', p. 4 and Jackson (1996) *New-born Child Murder*, Introduction.

60. See for instance Wrightson (1975) 'Infanticide in Earlier Seventeenth-Century England', p. 10.

61. For further discussion see Hair (1972) 'Homicide, Infanticide and Child Assault', pp. 44–5; Ober (1986) 'Infanticide in Eighteenth-Century England', p. 311; U. Rublack (1999) *The Crimes of Women in Early Modern Germany* (Oxford: Clarendon Press), p. 165; and Kellum (1974) 'Infanticide', p. 371.

62. See Kellum (1974) 'Infanticide', pp. 375 and 382 and Helmholz (1987) 'Infanticide in the Province of Canterbury', pp. 164–5.

63. See R.W. Malcolmson (1977) 'Infanticide in the Eighteenth Century', in J.S. Cockburn (ed.) *Crime in England 1550–1800* (London: Methuen), p. 208.

64. For further discussion see C. Heywood (2001) *A History of Childhood: Children and Childhood in the West from Medieval to Modern Times* (Cambridge: Polity Press), pp. 19–40 and 43–103; H. Cunningham (1995) *Children and Childhood in Western Society Since 1500* (London: Longman), especially Chapters 3–6; A. Levene (2007) *Childcare, Health and Mortality at the London Foundling Hospital, 1741–1800: 'Left to the Mercy of the World'* (Manchester: Manchester University Press); and T. Evans (2005) *Unfortunate Objects: Lone Mothers in Eighteenth-Century London* (Basingstoke: Palgrave Macmillan).

65. See Malcolmson (1977) 'Infanticide', pp. 189–90.

66. See Hoffer and Hull (1984) *Murdering Mothers: Infanticide in England and New England 1558–1803*, p. 12.

67. For further discussion see J. Delumeau (1990) *Sin and Fear: The Emergence of a Western Guilt Culture 13th–18th Centuries* (New York: St Martin's Press).
68. For further discussion see Hoffer and Hull (1984) *Murdering Mothers*, pp. 11–18; Damme (1978) 'Infanticide', p. 11; Ober (1986) 'Infanticide in Eighteenth-Century England', pp. 311–12; and Johnson Kramar (2005) *Unwilling Mothers*, p. 25. For the experience of this change in attitude across Europe more widely see Rowlands (1997) '"In Great Secrecy"', pp. 183 and 192–3 and Oberman (2003) 'A Brief History of Infanticide', pp. 6–7.
69. For further discussion see Kilday (2007) *Women and Violent Crime*, pp. 60–2; Rublack (1999) *The Crimes of Women*, p. 165; Rowe (1991) 'Infanticide', p. 207; and Hoffer and Hull (1984) *Murdering Mothers*, pp. 6–8.
70. For further discussion see Malcolmson (1977) 'Infanticide', p. 189–90 and Francus (1997) 'Monstrous Mothers', pp. 113–56.
71. Rublack (1999) *The Crimes of Women*, pp. 165 and 170.
72. For further discussion see Jackson (1996) *New-born Child Murder*, p. 30.
73. Ibid., p. 31 and see also pp. 30–2 for further discussion.
74. Ibid., p. 31.
75. Ibid., pp. 31–2.
76. Parliamentary Papers, 21 Jac 1 c.27 (1624).
77. Jackson (1996) *New-born Child Murder*, pp. 33–4. See also Malcolmson (1977) 'Infanticide', p. 196 and Johnson Kramar (2005) *Unwilling Mothers*, pp. 24–25.
78. The Acts of the Parliaments of Scotland – Volume IX: A.D. M.DC.LXXXIX – A.D. M.DC.XCV (1822) (London: HMSO), p. 195 [Bodleian Library K5.354/9].
79. See for instance C. Larner (1981) *Enemies of God: The Witch-Hunt in Scotland* (Baltimore: John Hopkins University Press).
80. For further discussion see Jackson (1996) *New-born Child Murder*, pp. 45–7 and 51 and Johnson Kramar (2005) *Unwilling Mothers*, pp. 25–6.
81. See, for instance, Jackson (1996) *New-Born Child Murder*, p. 36 and Hoffer and Hull (1984) *Murdering Mothers*, pp. 23 and 27.
82. For further evidence see Martin (2007) *Women, Murder and Equity*, Chapter Five; Francus (1997) 'Monstrous Mothers', pp. 113–56; Gowing (1997) 'Secret Births', p. 114; and Rublack (1999) *The Crimes of Women*, p. 172.
83. See Malcolmson (1977) 'Infanticide', p. 197; Gowing (1997) 'Secret Births', p. 114; Lambie (2001) 'Mothers Who Kill', p. 73; and A. McLaren (1984) *Reproductive Rituals: The Perception of Fertility in England from the Sixteenth Century to the Nineteenth Century (London and New* York: Methuen), pp. 131–4.
84. For further discussion see especially M. Clayton (2009) 'Changes in Old Bailey Trials for the Murder of Newborn Babies, 1674–1803', *Continuity and Change*, 24, pp. 337–59 and Osborne (1987) 'The Crime of Infanticide', pp. 50–3. See also Oberman (2003) 'A Brief History of Infanticide', pp. 7–8 and Ober (1986) 'Infanticide in Eighteenth-Century England', p. 312.
85. For further discussion see Johnson Kramar (2005) *Unwilling Mothers*, pp. 26–8.
86. For further discussion see Jackson (1996) *New-born Child Murder*, Chapter Seven; McLaren (1984) *Reproductive Rituals*, pp. 132–4; and Malcolmson (1977) 'Infanticide', pp. 197–8.
87. (1813) The Parliamentary History of England from the Earliest Period to the Year 1803, Volume XVII – A.D. 1771–1774 (London: Hansard), pp. 452–3. [Accessed from http://www.books.google.co.uk].
88. For further elaboration see Jackson (1996) *New-Born Child Murder*, pp. 163–8.
89. See Wrightson (1982) 'Infanticide in European History', p. 15.

2   The archetype of infanticide in the early modern period

1. B. Mandeville (1723, 1772 edition) *The Fable of the Bees: Or, Private Vices, Public Benefits – Volume I* (Edinburgh: J. Wood) [Bodleian Library, ESTCT77574], p. 45.
2. *The Proceedings of the Old Bailey*, 13th April 1681 [t16810413-1], p. 1 of transcript. [Accessed from www.oldbaileyonline.org].
3. *The Protestant (Domestick) Intelligence*, 5th April 1681, No. 111.
4. *The Proceedings of the Old Bailey*, 13th April 1681, p. 1 of transcript.
5. Ibid.
6. *The Protestant (Domestick) Intelligence*, 5th April 1681, No. 111.
7. Ibid.
8. *The Proceedings of the Old Bailey*, 13th April 1681, p. 1 of transcript.
9. *The Proceedings of the Old Bailey*, 13th April 1681, p. 2 of transcript.
10. *The Protestant (Domestick) Intelligence*, 5th April, 1681, No. 111.
11. Ibid.
12. *The Proceedings of the Old Bailey*, 13th April 1681, p. 2 of transcript. My additions in parenthesis.
13. Ibid. My additions in parenthesis.
14. See for instance A.-M. Kilday (2007) *Women and Violent Crime in Enlightenment Scotland* (Woodbridge: Boydell), p. 59.
15. See for instance J.A. Sharpe (1983) *Crime in Seventeenth-Century England: A County Study* (Cambridge: Cambridge University Press), p. 136.
16. See for instance P.C. Hoffer and N.E.C. Hull (1984) *Murdering Mothers: Infanticide in England and New England 1558–1803* (New York: New York University Press), p. 12.
17. For further discussion see R.W. Malcolmson (1977) 'Infanticide in the Eighteenth Century', in J.S. Cockburn (ed.) *Crime in England 1550–1800* (London: Methuen), pp. 189–90.
18. See for instance J.M. Beattie (1975) 'The Criminality of Women in Eighteenth-Century England', *Journal of Social History*, VIII, p. 84.
19. See for instance N. Lonza (2002) '"Two Souls Lost": Infanticide in the Republic of Dubrovnik (1667–1808)', *Dubrovnik Annals*, 6, p. 73.
20. See for instance M. Francus (1997) 'Monstrous Mothers, Monstrous Societies: Infanticide and the Rule of Law in Restoration and Eighteenth-Century England', *Eighteenth Century Life*, XXI, pp. 133–56.
21. See Kilday (2007) *Women and Violent Crime*, p. 66.
22. D. Defoe (1728) *Augusta Triumphans: Or, The Way to Make London the Most Flourishing City in the Universe* (London: J. Wood), p. 9 [Bodleian Library, Gough Lond. 272 (8)]. For further contemporary comments along similar lines see Malcolmson (1977) 'Infanticide', p. 190.
23. In this chapter, the data used for eighteenth-century England relates only to London and to indictments for infanticide brought before the Old Bailey between 1700 and 1799 collated from data available at www.oldbaileyonline.org. The Welsh data covers the period 1730–1799 and is made up of infanticide and concealment of pregnancy cases brought before the Courts of Great Session. This data was collated from the National Library of Wales, Crime and Punishment Database at http://www.llgc.org.uk/sesiwn_fawr/index_s.htm. The Scottish data relates to indictments for infanticide heard at the Justiciary Courts between 1700 and 1799 and found in the National Records of Scotland (Edinburgh). It is recognised that attempting to draw comparisons between these data is flawed and problematic

due to the different and varying geographical, time series and legal contexts involved as well as the unknown figure of unreported offences. The comparative analyses presented here are included for illustrative purposes nonetheless and provide an interesting snapshot of attitudes to new-born child murder and its associated offences during the early modern period.

24. J. Kelly (1992) 'Infanticide in Eighteenth-Century Ireland', *Irish Economic and Social History*, XIX, p. 11. See also O. Hufton (1990) 'Women and Violence in Early Modern Europe', in F. Dieteren and E. Kloek (eds.) *Writing Women into History* (Amsterdam: Historisch Seminarium van de Universiteit Van Amsterdam), p. 77; M. Jackson (1996) *New-Born Child Murder: Women, Illegitimacy and the Courts in Eighteenth-Century England* (Manchester: Manchester University Press), p. 29; Kilday (2007) *Women and Violent Crime*, p. 70; and Hoffer and Hull (1984) *Murdering Mothers*, p. 108.

25. The involvement of married women, accomplices and male protagonists in the crime of new-born child murder will be dealt with more fully in Chapter 3.

26. See the references in Chapter 1, note 56.

27. See Kelly (1992) 'Infanticide', p. 5.

28. For more on the significance of the 'dark figure' in early modern infanticide see S. Faber (1990) 'Infanticide and Criminal Justice in the Netherlands, especially in Amsterdam', in International Commission of Historical Demography (ed.) *The Role of the State and Public Opinion in Sexual Attitudes and Demographic Behaviour* (CIDH: Madrid), p. 261; G.S. Rowe (1991) 'Infanticide, Its Judicial Resolution, and Criminal Code Revision in Early Pennsylvania', *Proceedings of the American Philosophical Society*, CXXXV, p. 203; and Malcolmson (1977) 'Infanticide', p. 191.

29. Hoffer and Hull (1984) *Murdering Mothers*, p. 6.

30. The problematic nature of the evidence relating to early modern infanticide means that analyses of this type are rarely attempted. Exceptions to this include N. Woodward (2007) 'Infanticide in Wales, 1730–1830', *Welsh Historical Review*, 23, pp. 94–125; Rowe (1991) 'Infanticide', pp. 200–32; and R. Roth (2001) 'Child Murder in New England', *Social Science History*, XXV, pp. 101–47. In the case of Woodward's study, many of the calculations are fundamentally flawed due to fundamental problems with accuracy of demographic data prior to official census records which started in 1801.

31. See Malcolmson (1977) 'Infanticide', p. 8 and Hufton (1990) 'Women and Violence', p. 77.

32. Hoffer and Hull (1984) *Murdering Mothers*, p. 108 and Rowe (1991) 'Infanticide', p. 207.

33. M. Kamler (1988) 'Infanticide in the Towns of the Kingdom of Poland in the Second Half of the 16th and the First Half of the 17th Century', *Acta Poloniae Historica*, 58, p. 33.

34. Faber (1990) 'Infanticide', p. 255 and R. Leboutte (1991) 'Offense against Family Order: Infanticide in Belgium from the Fifteenth through the Early Twentieth Centuries', *Journal of the History of Sexuality*, 2, p. 161.

35. Hufton (1990) 'Women and Violence', p. 77. See also J.R. Ruff (1984) *Crime, Justice and Public Order: The Sénéchaussées of Libourne and Bazas, 1696–1789* (London and Dover, NH: Croom Helm), p. 170.

36. O. Ulbricht (1988) 'Infanticide in Eighteenth-Century Germany', in R.J. Evans (ed.) *The German Underworld: Deviants and Outcasts in German History* (London: Routledge), p. 110.

37. For similar conclusions with regard to the persistent nature of infanticide prosecutions in early modern Europe see Leboutte (1991) 'Offense against Family Order', p. 160 and M. Jackson (1994) 'Suspicious Infant Deaths: The Statute of 1624 and Medical Evidence at Coroners' Inquests', in M. Clark and C. Crawford (eds.) *Legal Medicine in History* (Cambridge: Cambridge University Press), p. 70.

38. For similar conclusions with regard to low indictment levels for infanticide and concealment of pregnancy in early modern Europe see Wrightson (1975) 'Infanticide in Earlier Seventeenth Century England', p. 12; Faber (1976) 'Infanticide', p. 255; and Kelly (1992) 'Infanticide', p. 18.

39. For further discussion see Woodward (2007) 'Infanticide', p. 100 and Wrightson (1975) 'Infanticide in Earlier Seventeenth-Century England', p. 12.

40. Sharpe (1983) *Crime in Seventeenth-Century England*, p. 135. See also K. Wrightson (1975) 'Infanticide in Earlier Seventeenth-Century England', p. 11.

41. See respectively L. Gowing (1997) 'Secret Births and Infanticide in Seventeenth-Century England', *Past and Present*, p. 89 and J.R. Dickinson and J.A. Sharpe (2002) 'Infanticide in Early Modern England: The Court of Great Sessions at Chester, 1650–1800', in M. Jackson (ed.) *Infanticide: Historical Perspectives on Child Murder and Concealment 1550–2000* (Aldershot: Ashgate), p. 38.

42. See respectively Malcolmson (1977) 'Infanticide', p. 191 and J.M. Beattie (1986) *Crime and the Courts in England 1660–1800* (Oxford: Clarendon Press), pp. 114–15.

43. This relates to a British Academy funded project undertaken by the author. The jurisdictions of the specific Scottish Justiciary Court circuits and the caveats involved in their usage are outlined in Chapter 1. It should be noted that an investigation of the more populous Western Circuit area has not yet been conducted, and once concluded, may revise the general figures and trends proposed in this analysis.

44. See respectively Woodward (2007) 'Infanticide', p. 100 and Kelly (1992) 'Infanticide', p. 5.

45. See Ulbricht (1988) 'Infanticide', p. 114.

46. Wrightson (1982) 'Infanticide in European History', p. 5. For the widespread predominance of unmarried mothers in infanticide indictments see also P.E.H. Hair (1972) 'Homicide, Infanticide and Child Assault in Late Tudor Middlesex', *Local Population Studies (Notes and Queries)*, 9, p. 44; A. Rowlands (1997) '"In Great Secrecy": The Crime of Infanticide in Rothenburg ob der Tauber, 1501–1618', *German History*, 15, p. 179; Kamler (1988) 'Infanticide', p. 36; Hoffer and Hull (1984) *Murdering Mothers*, pp. 97 and 108; M.D. Smith (1999) '"Unnatural Mothers": Infanticide, Motherhood and Class in the Mid-Atlantic, 1730–1830', in C. Daniels and M.V. Kennedy (eds.) *Over the Threshold: Intimate Violence in Early America* (New York: Routledge), p. 173; Kelly (1992) 'Infanticide', p. 7; Jackson (1996) *New-Born Child Murder*, p. 3; Woodward (2007) 'Infanticide', p. 108; and Kilday (2007) *Women and Violent Crime*, p. 70.

47. R.H. Helmholz (1987) 'Infanticide in the Province of Canterbury during the Fifteenth Century', in R.H. Helmholz (ed.) *Canon Law and the Law of England* (London: Hambledon), p. 165.

48. See R. Adair (1996) *Courtship, Illegitimacy and Marriage in Early Modern England* (Manchester: Manchester University Press), p. 49 and P. Laslett (1980) 'Introduction: Comparing Illegitimacy Over Time and Between Cultures', in P. Laslett, K. Oosterveen and R.M. Smith (eds.) *Bastardy and its Comparative History: Studies in the History of Illegitimacy and Marital Nonconformism in Britain, France, Germany, Sweden, North America, Jamaica and Japan* (London: Edward Arnold),

p. 14. See also A. Levene, T. Nutt and S. Williams (2005) 'Introduction', in A. Levene, T. Nutt and S. Williams (eds.) *Illegitimacy in Britain, 1700–1920* (Basingstoke: Macmillan), pp. 5–6 and M. Anderson (1980) *Approaches to the History of the Western Family, 1500–1914* (Cambridge: Cambridge University Press), p. 8.

49. See L. Lenman and R. Mitchison (1987) 'Scottish Illegitimacy Ratios in the Early Modern Period', *Economic History Review*, 2nd ser., XL, p. 53 and R. Mitchison and L. Lenman (1998) *Girls in Trouble: Sexuality and Social Control in Rural Scotland 1660–1780* (Edinburgh: Scottish Cultural), p. 75.

50. See for instance Hoffer and Hull (1984) *Murdering Mothers*, p. 100.

51. See for instance Adair (1996) *Courtship, Illegitimacy and Marriage*, pp. 52 and 222 and A. Blaikie (1993) *Illegitimacy, Sex and Society: Northeast Scotland, 1750–1900* (Oxford: Clarendon), p. 12.

52. Anderson (1980) *Approaches to the History of the Western Family*, p. 6.

53. Lenman and Mitchison (1987) 'Scottish Illegitimacy Ratios', pp. 50 and 53.

54. For further discussion of the methodological problems involved in calculating illegitimacy ratios see N. Rogers (1989) 'Carnal Knowledge: Illegitimacy in Eighteenth-Century Westminster', *Journal of Social History*, 23, p. 360; A. Levene *et al.* (2005) 'Introduction', p. 7; and Laslett (1980) 'Introduction', p. 15.

55. This hypothesis and the historiography which underpins it is neatly summarised by Anderson (1980) *Approaches to the History of the Western Family*, pp. 33–4.

56. D. Levine and K. Wrightson (1980) 'The Social Context of Illegitimacy in Early Modern England', in P. Laslett, K. Oosterveen and R.M. Smith (eds.) *Bastardy and its Comparative History: Studies in the History of Illegitimacy and Marital Nonconformism in Britain, France, Germany, Sweden, North America, Jamaica and Japan* (London: Edward Arnold), p. 169. My addition in parenthesis.

57. Rogers (1989) 'Carnal Knowledge', p. 362. See also Blaikie (1993) *Illegitimacy, Sex and Society*, p. 99 who reminds us that such unions could occur in adulterous liaisons too.

58. See Anderson (1980) *Approaches to the History of the Western Family*, p. 9.

59. See evidence of this type of exploitation contributing to illegitimacy figures in Mitchison and Lenman (1998) *Girls in Trouble*, p. 100 and L. Lenman and R. Mitchison (1998) *Sin in the City: Sexuality and Social Control in Urban Scotland 1660–1780* (Edinburgh: Scottish Cultural Press), p. 61.

60. For discussion of this type of exploitation and its positive relationship with illegitimacy figures see B. Meteyard (1980) 'Illegitimacy and Marriage in Eighteenth-Century England', *Journal of Interdisciplinary History*, 10, p. 481.

61. Adair (1996) *Courtship, Illegitimacy and Marriage*, p. 87. See also Laslett (1980) 'Introduction', p. 56.

62. See, for instance, Rogers (1989) 'Carnal Knowledge', p. 367; Anderson (1980) *Approaches to the History of the Western Family*, p. 41; Lonza (2002) '"Two Souls Lost"', p. 82; and K. Wrightson (1980) 'The Nadir of English Illegitimacy in the Seventeenth Century', in P. Laslett, K. Oosterveen and R.M. Smith (eds.) *Bastardy and its Comparative History: Studies in the History of Illegitimacy and Marital Nonconformism in Britain, France, Germany, Sweden, North America, Jamaica and Japan* (London: Edward Arnold), p. 188.

63. A. Levene *et al.* (2005) 'Introduction', p. 9. See also P.M. Crawford (2010) *Parents of Poor Children in England, 1580–1800* (Oxford: Oxford University Press), p. 48.

64. Laslett (1980) 'Introduction', pp. 23–4. In Scotland, a somewhat different picture emerges, where there is a relatively low rate of pre-marital pregnancy. There, it

seems, the more mobile nature of the population may have contributed to higher levels of desertion. Scottish women who became pregnant out of wedlock were less likely to eventually marry the fathers of their illegitimate offspring than their English counterparts. See Mitchison and Lenman (1998) *Girls in Trouble*, pp. 82 and 94.

65. See A. Levene *et al.* (2005) 'Introduction', pp. 8–9.
66. See Wrightson (1980) 'The Nadir of English Illegitimacy', p. 191 and Lenman and Mitchison (1987) 'Scottish Illegitimacy Ratios', p. 59.
67. Adair (1996) *Courtship, Illegitimacy and Marriage*, p. 225.
68. Laslett (1980) 'Introduction', p. 48.
69. Ibid., p. 9.
70. See Meteyard (1980) 'Illegitimacy and Marriage', p. 482 and Jackson (1996) *New-Born Child Murder*, p. 44. Hardwicke's Marriage Act was never introduced in Scotland, although similar definitional problems related to 'regular' and 'irregular' marriage were in evidence nonetheless – see Lenman and Mitchison (1987) 'Scottish Illegitimacy Ratios', p. 56.
71. For further discussion of these problems see Laslett (1980) 'Introduction', pp. 48–53.
72. Levine and Wrightson (1980) 'The Social Context of Illegitimacy', p. 169. See also Blaikie (1993) *Illegitimacy, Sex and Society*, p. 177.
73. Laslett (1980) 'Introduction', pp. 1–2.
74. Malcolmson (1977) 'Infanticide', p. 187. See also Lonza (2002) '"Two Souls Lost"', p. 80 and Wrightson (1980) 'The Nadir of English Illegitimacy', p. 71.
75. See Rowe (1991) 'Infanticide', p. 225 and Woodward (2007) 'Infanticide', p. 112.
76. See for instance Adair (1996) *Courtship, Illegitimacy and Marriage*, p. 89; A. Levene *et al.* (2005) 'Introduction', p. 11; Blaikie (1993) *Illegitimacy, Sex and Society*, p. 63; and Smith (1999) '"Unnatural Mothers"', p. 174.
77. Crawford (2010) *Parents of Poor Children*, p. 37.
78. For more on this kind of surveillance in the early modern period see Lonza (2002) '"Two Souls Lost"', p. 93.
79. Kilday (2007) *Women and Violent Crime*, p. 61.
80. Rowlands (1997) '"In Great Secrecy"', p. 192.
81. Ibid.
82. U. Rublack (1999) *The Crimes of Women in Early Modern* Germany (Oxford: Clarendon), p. 167.
83. Jackson (1996) *New-Born Child Murder* , p. 15. My addition in parenthesis.
84. See Jackson (1996) *New-Born Child Murder*, p. 48; Lonza (2002) '"Two Souls Lost"', p. 84; and Malcolmson (1977) 'Infanticide', p. 193.
85. See for instance Blaikie (1993) *Illegitimacy, Sex and Society*, p. 63.
86. See Crawford (2010) *Parents of Poor Children*, pp. 33–39 and 66.
87. For further discussion see R. Mitchison and L. Lenman (1989) *Sexuality and Social Control: Scotland 1660–1780* (Oxford: Basil Blackwell).
88. Mitchison and Lenman (1989) *Sexuality and Social Control*, p. 9.
89. See, for instance, Mitchison and Lenman (1998) *Girls in Trouble*, pp. 1–2 and 72 and also Lenman and Mitchison (1998) *Sin in the City*, pp. 1 and 20.
90. See Lenman and Mitchison (1987) 'Scottish Illegitimacy Ratios', p. 54.
91. For evidence to support this contention see T.C. Smout (1976) 'Aspects of Sexual Behaviour in Nineteenth-Century Scotland', in A.A. MacLaren (ed.) *Social Class in Scotland: Past and Present* (Edinburgh: John Donald), p. 80.
92. Jackson (1996) *New-Born Child Murder*, p. 15. See also Francus (1997) 'Monstrous Mothers', p. 134.

93. Rowlands (1997) '"In Great Secrecy"', p. 183.
94. Laslett (1980) 'Introduction', p. 5.
95. See Crawford (2010) *Parents of Poor Children*, pp. 63–4. For more on the financial difficulties associated with illegitimacy at the parish level see T. Nutt (2005) 'The Paradox and Problems of Illegitimate Paternity in Old Poor Law Essex', in A. Levene, T. Nutt and S. Williams (eds.) *Illegitimacy in Britain, 1700–1920* (Basingstoke: Palgrave Macmillan), pp. 102–21.
96. Parliamentary Papers, 7 James c.4 (1610).
97. Jackson (1996) *New-Born Child Murder*, p. 30.
98. See, for instance, Blaikie (1993) *Illegitimacy, Sex and Society*, p. 222; Mitchison and Lenman (1998) *Girls in Trouble*, pp. 28 and 80; and Smith (1999) '"Unnatural Mothers"', p. 178.
99. Sharpe (1983) *Crime in Seventeenth-Century England*, p. 137. See also Gowing (1997) 'Secret Births', p. 89.
100. See, for instance, Crawford (2010) *Parents of Poor Children*, p. 39; Wrightson (1980) 'The Nadir of English Illegitimacy', p. 187; T. Evans (2005) '"Unfortunate Objects": London's Unmarried Mothers in the Eighteenth Century', *Gender and History*, XVII, p. 189; and Rogers (1989) 'Carnal Knowledge', p. 358.
101. See respectively Hoffer and Hull (1984) *Murdering Mothers*, pp. 108–9; Kamler (1988) 'Infanticide', p. 36; Ulbricht (1988) 'Infanticide', p. 111; Leboutte (1991) 'Offense against Family Order', p. 164; O. Hufton (1975) *The Poor of Eighteenth-Century France 1750–1789* (Oxford: Oxford University Press), p. 324; Faber (1990) 'Infanticide', p. 255; Malcolmson (1977) 'Infanticide', p. 192; Woodward (2007) 'Infanticide', p. 108; and Lonza (2002) '"Two Souls Lost"', p. 81.
102. For further discussion see J.J. Hecht (1955) *The Domestic Servant Class in the Eighteenth Century* (London: Routledge and Kegan Paul); B. Hill (1996) *Servants: English Domestics in the Eighteenth Century* (Oxford: Oxford University Press); and C. Steedman (2009) *Labours Lost: Domestic Service and the Making of Modern England* (Cambridge: Cambridge University Press).
103. P. Humfrey (1998) 'Female Servants and Women's Criminality in Early Eighteenth-Century London', in G.T. Smith *et al.* (eds.) *Criminal Justice in the Old World and the New* (Toronto: University of Toronto Press), p. 62. For further evidence of the predominance of servitude amongst female occupations in the late seventeenth and early eighteenth centuries see P. Earle (1998) 'The Female Labour Market in London in the Late Seventeenth and Eighteenth Centuries', in P. Sharpe (ed.) *Women's Work: The English Experience, 1650–1914* (London: Hodder Arnold), p. 132.
104. See D.A. Kent (1989) 'Ubiquitous but Invisible: Female Domestic Servants in Mid-Eighteenth-Century London', *History Workshop Journal*, 28, p. 112.
105. See Humfrey (1998) 'Female Servants', p. 62.
106. Kent (1989) 'Ubiquitous but Invisible', pp. 118–9 and 123.
107. Ibid., p. 122.
108. Ibid., pp. 114–5.
109. Ibid., p. 115.
110. Ibid., p. 117.
111. Ibid., pp. 115 and 117.
112. For further discussion of these arguments see ibid., p. 118.
113. See B. Hill (1989) *Women, Work and Sexual Politics in Eighteenth-Century England* (Oxford: Basil Blackwell), Chapter 8; Kelly (1992) 'Infanticide', p. 9; Malcolmson (1977) 'Infanticide', pp. 202–3; and Beattie (1986) *Crime and the Courts*, pp. 114–7. For evidence that this preoccupation continued through to

the late nineteenth and early twentieth century see M. Fahrni (1997) '"Ruffled" Mistresses and "Discontented" Maids: Respectability and the Case of Domestic Servants, 1880–1914', *Labour/Le Travail*, 39, pp. 74–5.

114. For further discussion see Crawford (2010) *Parents of Poor Children*, p. 38; Malcolmson (1977) 'Infanticide', p. 192; Wrightson (1982) 'Infanticide in European History', p. 7; T. Meldrum (1997) 'London Domestic Servants from Depositional Evidence, 1660–1750: Servant-Employer Sexuality in the Patriarchal Household', in T. Hitchcock, P. King and P. Sharpe (eds.) *Chronicling Poverty: The Voices and Strategies of the English Poor, 1640–1840* (Basingstoke: Palgrave Macmillan), p. 48; and Fahrni (1997) '"Ruffled" Mistresses', p. 89.

115. For further discussion see Hill (1996) *Servants*, p. 44 and Kelly (1992) 'Infanticide', p. 9.

116. See Kamler (1988) 'Infanticide', pp. 37–41.

117. See Hill (1996) *Servants*, Chapter 3; C. Fairchilds (1978) 'Female Sexual Attitudes and the Rise of Illegitimacy', *Journal of Interdisciplinary History*, 8, pp. 627–67; Lonza (2002) '"Two Souls Lost"', pp. 81–2; Fahrni (1997) '"Ruffled" Mistresses', p. 85; and Meldrum (1997) 'London Domestic Servants', pp. 49–51, 53 and 55–7.

118. See Jackson (1996) *New-Born Child Murder*, p. 47 and Humfrey (1998) 'Female Servants', p. 61.

119. See Humfrey (1998) 'Female Servants', pp. 69–70.

120. For further discussion of the lack of privacy that domestic servants faced see T. Meldrum (1999) 'Domestic Service, Privacy, and the Eighteenth-Century Metropolitan Household', *Urban History*, 26, pp. 27–39; Hill (1996) *Servants*, p. 45; Evans (2005) '"Unfortunate Objects"', p. 139; and Meldrum (1997) 'London Domestic Servants', p. 60.

121. Mandeville (1723, 1772 edition) *The Fable of the Bees*, p. 45.

122. For more on the typical age of domestic servants in the early modern period see Sharpe (1983) *Crime in Seventeenth-Century England*, p. 135.

123. For more on the fear of poverty associated with illegitimate pregnancy among domestic servants see Rublack (1999) *The Crimes of Women*, pp. 188–91. The potential explanations for the actions of women involved in new-born child murder will be examined in Chapter 6 of this volume.

124. This pattern in the standard of evidence was clear from both the Scottish and the Welsh datasets used in this study. It is also recognised in Francus (1997) 'Monstrous Mothers', p. 133.

125. See, for instance, Rowlands (1997) 'In Great Secrecy', pp. 192–4; Wrightson (1975) 'Infanticide in Earlier Seventeenth-Century England', p. 11; Rowe (1991) 'Infanticide', pp. 203 and 206; Francus (1997) 'Monstrous Mothers', p. 133; Kelly (1992) 'Infanticide', p. 19; L. Abrams (2002) 'From Demon to Victim: The Infanticidal Mother in Shetland, 1699–1802', in Y.G. Brown and R. Ferguson (eds.) *Twisted Sisters: Women, Crime and Deviance in Scotland since 1400* (East Linton: Tuckwell), p. 180; and M. Jackson (1995) 'Developing Medical Expertise: Medical Practitioners and the Suspected Murders of New-Born Children', in R. Porter (ed.) *Medicine in the Enlightenment* (Amsterdam: Rodopi), p. 155.

126. National Records of Scotland [Edinburgh] (NRS), Justiciary Court Records (JC), JC3/24.

127. For further evidence of the widespread nature of this trend see Jackson (1994) 'Suspicious Infant Deaths', pp. 70 and 74; Jackson (1995) 'Developing Medical Expertise', p. 158; Woodward (2007) 'Infanticide', pp. 96–7 and 122; Kelly (1992) 'Infanticide', pp. 18 and 21; Francus (1997) 'Monstrous Mothers',

p. 133; Rowe (1991) 'Infanticide', p. 207; and T. Rizzo (2004) 'Between Dishonour and Death: Infanticide in the Causes Célèbres of Eighteenth-Century France', *Women's History Review*, 13, p. 10.

128. For further discussion see Wrightson (1975) 'Infanticide in Earlier Seventeenth-Century England', p. 13; Kelly (1992) 'Infanticide', p. 5; and Roth (2001) 'Child Murder in New England', p. 113.

129. For further discussion of perceptions regarding the severity of the law and its implications on infanticide prosecutions see Woodward (2007) 'Infanticide', pp. 104 and 106; Gowing (1997) 'Secret', p. 114; and Jackson (1994) 'Suspicious Infant Deaths', p. 66.

130. For further discussion of absconding in infanticide cases in the early modern period see for instance N. Lonza (2002) '"Two Souls Lost"', p. 102 and Kelly (1992) 'Infanticide', pp. 18–19.

131. See, for instance, M. Clayton (2009) 'Changes in Old Bailey Trials for the Murder of Newborn Babies, 1674–1803', *Continuity and Change*, 24, p. 341; Rowe (1991) 'Infanticide', p. 206; and Rizzo (2004) 'Between Dishonour and Death', p. 8.

132. For further discussion see Kelly (1992) 'Infanticide', p. 19; Clayton (2009) 'Changes in Old Bailey Trials', p. 340; Rizzo (2004) 'Between Dishonour and Death', p. 10; Woodward (2007) 'Infanticide', p. 100; and Jackson (1994) 'Suspicious Infant Deaths', pp. 70 and 72–3.

133. For further discussion see Leboutte (1991) 'Offense against Family Order', p. 170; Francus (1997) 'Monstrous Mothers', p. 142; Clayton (2009) 'Changes in Old Bailey Trials', pp. 340–11; Woodward (2007) 'Infanticide', p. 121; and S. Sommers (2009) 'Remapping Maternity in the Courtroom: Female Defenses and Medical Witnesses in Eighteenth-Century Infanticide Proceedings', in E. Klaver (ed.) *The Body in Medical Culture* (Albany: State University of New York Press), pp. 37–59.

134. See respectively *The Proceedings of the Old Bailey*, 12th October 1743 [t17431012-29]; 21st April 1762 [t17620421-26]; 30th May 1781 [t17810530-42]; and 27th October 1790 [t17901027-78].

135. For further evidence on the use of this defence see Clayton (2009) 'Changes in Old Bailey Trials', p. 339.

136. See respectively NRS, High Court of Justiciary, Books of Adjournal, JC3/1 and *The Proceedings of the Old Bailey*, 17th January 1728 [t17280117-43]; 16th January 1751 [t17510116-52] and 17th September 1794 [t17940917-46].

137. For further evidence of the use of this kind of mitigation see Clayton (2009) 'Changes in Old Bailey Trials', p. 341.

138. See respectively NRS, Justiciary Court North Circuit Records, JC11/2; *The Proceedings of the Old Bailey*, 10th January 1718 [t17180110-62] and 30th August 1721 [t17210830-17]; NRS, Justiciary Court North Circuit Records, JC11/11; and *The Proceedings of the Old Bailey*, 24th October 1770 [t17701024-51].

139. For further evidence of this see Francus (1997) 'Monstrous Mothers', pp. 134–5 and Rowe (1991) 'Infanticide', p. 209.

140. For further discussion of these types of mitigation see Kamler (1988) 'Infanticide', p. 47; Clayton (2009) 'Changes in Old Bailey Trials', p. 342; Rublack (1999) *The Crimes of Women*, p. 191; and Rowe (1991) 'Infanticide', p. 214.

141. See respectively NRS, High Court of Justiciary, Books of Adjournal, JC3/6; *The Proceedings of the Old Bailey*, 5th December 1733 [t17331205-20]; and NRS, Justiciary Court North Circuit Records, JC11/39.

142. For further discussion see Malcolmson (1977) 'Infanticide', pp. 199–200; Francus (1997) 'Monstrous Mothers', pp. 142–3; Kilday (2007) *Women and Violent Crime*, p. 64; Jackson (1996) *New-Born Child Murder*, p. 134; and Beattie (1986) *Crime and the Courts*, p. 119.

143. See Beattie (1986) *Crime and the Courts*, p. 119. For further discussion of medical evidence in English infanticide trials in the early modern period see Sommers (2009) 'Remapping Maternity in the Courtroom', pp. 37–59.

144. Ibid., pp. 119–20 and Woodward (2007) 'Infanticide', p. 120.

145. See, for instance, Jackson (1996) *New-Born Child Murder*, p. 144; Wrightson (1982) 'Infanticide in European History', p. 11; Francus (1997) 'Monstrous Mothers', pp. 144–5; and Kilday (2007) *Women and Violent Crime*, p. 62.

146. The judge's summation in the case of Ann Brean at the Old Bailey in 1788 captures the importance of both evidence types in relation to convictions for infanticide, see *The Proceedings of the Old Bailey*, 10th September 1788 [t17880910-83].

147. For further discussion see Lonza (2002) '"Two Souls Lost"', p. 104; Rizzo (2004) 'Between Dishonour and Death', p. 11; Kelly (1992) 'Infanticide', p. 22; and especially Francus (1997) 'Monstrous Mothers', p. 141.

148. For further discussion see Roth (2001) 'Child Murder in New England', p. 101 and see respectively NRS, Justiciary Court North Circuit Records, JC11/1 and *The Proceedings of the Old Bailey*, 20th April 1737 [t17370420-18] and 11th July 1781 [t17810711-64].

149. See *The Proceedings of the Old Bailey*, 15th September 1784 [t17840915-149].

150. For further discussion of the problems of establishing live birth see Kamler (1988) 'Infanticide', p. 46; Clayton (2009) 'Changes in Old Bailey Trials', p. 340; and Jackson (1994) 'Suspicious Infant Deaths', p. 75.

151. For further discussion see Rowe (1991) 'Infanticide', p. 203 and Clayton (2009) 'Changes in Old Bailey Trials', p. 339.

152. For further discussion see Lonza (2002) '"Two Souls Lost"', p. 69; Rowe (1991) 'Infanticide', p. 205; and Woodward (2007) 'Infanticide', p. 109.

153. See respectively NRS, High Court of Justiciary, Books of Adjournal, JC3/19 and *The Proceedings of the Old Bailey*, 3rd July 1782 [t17820703-47] and 20th February 1793 [t17930220-38].

154. *The Proceedings of the Old Bailey*, 18th April 1798 [t17980418-11] and 20th February 1793 [t17930220-38].

155. See Woodward (2007) 'Infanticide', p. 120.

156. See respectively NRS, Justiciary Court West Circuit Records, JC13/7; *The Proceedings of the Old Bailey*, 9th September 1747 [t1717470909-11]; and NRS, Justiciary Court South Circuit Records, JC12/7.

157. See Jackson (1996) *New-Born Child Murder*, pp. 143–4.

158. See Beattie (1986) *Crime and the Courts*, pp. 123–4; Woodward (2007) 'Infanticide', p. 120; and Wrightson (1982) 'Infanticide in European History', p. 11.

159. NRS, High Court of Justiciary, Books of Adjournal, JC3/6.

160. NRS, Justiciary Court West Circuit Records, JC13/11.

161. For further discussion see A.-M. Kilday (2008) '"Monsters of the Vilest Kind": Infanticidal Women and Attitudes towards their Criminality in Eighteenth-Century Scotland', *Family and Community History*, 11, pp. 100–115.

162. See, for instance, Jackson (1994) 'Suspicious Infant Deaths', p. 69; Rublack (1999) *The Crimes of Women*, p. 170; and Kelly (1992) 'Infanticide', pp. 21 and 23.

163. For further discussion see Leboutte (1991) 'Offense against Family Order', p. 170; Rublack (1999) *The Crimes of Women*, p. 194; and Rowe (1991) 'Infanticide', p. 207.
164. For further discussion see J.C. Oldham (1985) 'On Pleading the Belly: A History of the Jury of Matrons', *Criminal Justice History*, VI, pp. 1–64.
165. For further discussion see V.A.C. Gatrell (1994) *The Hanging Tree: Execution and the English People 1770–1868* (Oxford: Oxford University Press), pp. 8, 65 and 337 and P. King (2000) *Crime, Justice and Discretion in England 1740–1820* (Oxford: Oxford University Press), pp. 286–8.
166. For further discussion see Gowing (1997) 'Secret Births', p. 114; Lonza (2002) '"Two Souls Lost"', pp. 103–4; Rizzo (2004) 'Between Dishonour and Death', p. 8; Rublack (1999) *The Crimes of Women*, p. 192; Jackson (1995) 'Developing Medical Expertise', pp. 155–6; and Abrams (2002) 'From Demon to Victim', p. 180.
167. See respectively *The Proceedings of the Old Bailey*, 28th June 1769 [t17690628-27], 10th April 1771 [t17710410-35] and 9th December 1778 [t17781209-45].
168. For further discussion see Clayton (2009) 'Changes in Old Bailey Trials', pp. 351–2.
169. Woodward (2007) 'Infanticide', p. 120.

3 Murderous mothers and the extended network of shame

1. F. Mauriceau (1697, 1863 edition, 1972 reprint) *Observations in Midwifery* [Edited from the original manuscript by H. Blenkinsop] (Wakefield: S.R. Publishers) [Bodleian Library, RSL 15083e.30].
2. For further discussion see G.B. Carruthers and L.A. Carruthers (2005) (eds.) *A History of Britain's Hospitals and the Background to the Medical, Nursing and Allied Professions* (Lewes: Book Guild), especially pp. 227–50.
3. Most works on the history of childbirth tend to concentrate on the 'typical' or 'traditional' experience of pregnancy and delivery – that of the married mother. See, for instance, A. Eccles (1982) *Obstetrics and Gynaecology in Tudor and Stuart England* (London and Canberra: Croom Helm); T. Cassidy (2007) *Birth: A History* (London: Chatto and Windus); M.J. O'Dowd (1994) *The History of Obstetrics and Gynaecology* (New York and London: Parthenon); D. Cressy (1999) *Birth, Marriage and Death: Ritual, Religion and the Life-Cycle in Tudor and Stuart England* (Oxford: Oxford University Press); and J. Gélis (1991) *History of Childbirth: Fertility, Pregnancy and Birth in Early Modern Europe* (Cambridge: Polity).
4. L. Gowing (2003) *Common Bodies: Women, Touch and Power in Seventeenth-Century England* (New Haven, CT and London: Yale University Press), p. 10.
5. Gélis, *History of Childbirth*, p. 66.
6. For further discussion see M. Jackson (1996) '"Something More Than Blood": Conflicting Accounts of Pregnancy Loss in Eighteenth-Century England', in R. Cecil (ed.) *The Anthropology of Pregnancy Loss: Comparative Studies in Miscarriage, Stillbirth and Neonatal Death* (Berg: Oxford), p. 199; R. Leboutte (1991) 'Offense against Family Order: Infanticide in Belgium from the Fifteenth through the Early Twentieth Centuries', *Journal of the History of Sexuality*, 2, p. 175; and K.H. Wheeler (1997) 'Infanticide in Nineteenth-Century Ohio', *Journal of Social History*, XXXI, p. 412. For discussion of the fact that unmarried, young domestic servants were regularly the target of this kind of accusation see L. Gowing (1997) 'Secret Births and Infanticide in Seventeenth-Century England', *Past and Present*, CLVI, p. 92.

7. L. Abrams (2002) 'From Demon to Victim: The Infanticidal Mother in Shetland, 1699–1802', in Y.G. Brown and R. Ferguson (eds.) *Twisted Sisters: Women, Crime and Deviance in Scotland since 1400* (East Linton: Tuckwell), p. 192.

8. R. Schulte (1984) 'Infanticide in Rural Bavaria in the Nineteenth Century', in H. Medick and D.W. Sabean (eds.) *Interest and Emotion: Essays on the Study of Family and Kinship* (Cambridge: Cambridge University Press), p. 97. For further discussion see also Gowing (2003) *Common Bodies*, p. 118 and A. Rowlands (1997) '"In Great Secrecy": The Crime of Infanticide in Rothenburg ob der Tauber, 1501–1618', *German History*, 15, pp. 180 and 183.

9. See U. Rublack (1999) *The Crimes of Women in Early Modern Germany* (Oxford: Clarendon), p. 182.

10. For further discussion see Gowing (1997) 'Secret Births', p. 95; G. Morgan and P. Rushton (1998) *Rogues, Thieves and the Rule of Law: The Problem of Law Enforcement in North-East England, 1718–1800* (London: UCL Press), p. 111; U. Rublack (1986) 'Pregnancy, Childbirth and the Female Body in Early Modern Germany', *Past and Present*, 150, p. 85; and K. Wrightson (1975) 'Infanticide in Earlier Seventeenth-Century England', *Local Population Studies*, XV, p. 13.

11. J.R. Dickinson and J.A. Sharpe (2002) 'Infanticide in Early Modern England: The Court of Great Sessions at Chester, 1650–1800', in M. Jackson (ed.) *Infanticide: Historical Perspectives on Child Murder and Concealment 1550–2000* (Aldershot: Ashgate), p. 46. See also P.M. Crawford (2010) *Parents of Poor Children in England, 1580–1800* (Oxford: Oxford University Press), pp. 67–9.

12. See, for instance, A.-M. Kilday (2008) '"Monsters of the Vilest Kind": Infanticidal Women and Attitudes towards their Criminality in Eighteenth-Century Scotland', *Family and Community History*, 11, p. 104 and Abrams (2002) 'From Demon to Victim', p. 190.

13. See, for instance, Gowing (1997) 'Secret Births', p. 87 and Gowing (2003) *Common Bodies*, p. 45.

14. For further discussion see ibid. and p. 93; Abrams (2002) 'From Demon to Victim', p. 190; and L.A. Pollock (1997) 'Childbearing and Female Bonding in Early Modern England', *Social History*, 22, p. 300.

15. For further discussion see Gowing (2003) *Common Bodies*, p. 65.

16. For further discussion see Gowing (1997) 'Secret Births', p. 89.

17. M. Jackson (1996) *New-Born Child Murder: Women, Illegitimacy and the Courts in Eighteenth-Century England* (Manchester: Manchester University Press), p. 60.

18. Ibid.

19. See Gowing (2003) *Common Bodies*, p. 140.

20. *The Proceedings of the Old Bailey*, 8th March 1704 [t17040308-35] [Accessed from www.oldbaileyonline.org].

21. *The Proceedings of the Old Bailey*, 11th September 1717 [t17170911-50].

22. National Records of Scotland [Edinburgh] (hereafter NRS), High Court of Justiciary, Books of Adjournal, JC3/10.

23. See Rublack (1999) *The Crimes of Women*, p. 182.

24. For further discussion see Rowlands (1997) '"In Great Secrecy"', pp. 184–5.

25. Leboutte (1991) 'Offense against Family Order', p. 177.

26. See, for instance, Gowing (2003) *Common Bodies*, pp. 45–6; P. Crawford (1981) 'Attitudes to Menstruation in Seventeenth-Century England', *Past and Present*, 91, p. 17; Abrams (2002) 'From Demon to Victim', pp. 186–7; Jackson (1996) *New-Born Child Murder*, pp. 61–2; and especially C. McClive (2002) 'The Hidden Truths of the Belly: The Uncertainty of Pregnancy in Early Modern Europe' *Social History of Medicine*, 15, pp. 209–27.

27. Gélis (1991) *History of Childbirth*, p. 46.
28. Gowing (2003) *Common Bodies*, pp. 112 and 141.
29. For further discussion of these tests see Gélis (1991) *History of Childbirth*, pp. 47–8 and Eccles (1982) *Obstetrics and Gynaecology*, p. 60.
30. Gélis (1991) *History of Childbirth*, p. 47.
31. Ibid., p. 46.
32. Ibid.
33. See Rowlands (1997) '"In Great Secrecy"', p. 181; Gowing (2003) *Common Bodies*, p. 144; Rublack (1999) *The Crimes of Women*, p. 176; and K. Ruggiero (1992) 'Honor, Maternity and the Disciplining of Women: Infanticide in Late Nineteenth-Century Buenos Aires', *The Hispanic American Historical Review*, 72, p. 358.
34. NRS, Justiciary Court North Circuit Records, JC11/6.
35. *The Proceedings of the Old Bailey*, 19th April 1732 [t17320419-8].
36. NRS, High Court of Justiciary, Books of Adjournal, JC3/32.
37. See, for instance, Gowing (1997) 'Secret Births', p. 91; Abrams (2002) 'From Demon to Victim', p. 186; and Ruggiero (1992) 'Honor, Maternity and the Disciplining of Women', p. 358.
38. Gélis (1991) *History of Childbirth*, p. 46. See also Eccles (1982) *Obstetrics and Gynaecology*, p. 61.
39. Gowing (1997) 'Secret Births', p. 96; Gowing (2003) *Common Bodies*, p. 120; Jackson (1996) *New-Born Child Murder*, p. 64; Ruggiero (1992) 'Honor, Maternity and the Disciplining of Women', p. 358; and N. Lonza (2002) '"Two Souls Lost": Infanticide in the Republic of Dubrovnik (1667–1808)', *Dubrovnik Annals*, 6, p. 88.
40. For further discussion see M.E. Wiesner (2000) *Women and Gender in Early Modern Europe* [Second Edition] (Cambridge: Cambridge University Press), pp. 54–6; Crawford (2010) *Parents of Poor Children*, p. 24; and Eccles (1982) *Obstetrics and Gynaecology*, pp. 49 and 51.
41. For further discussion see Crawford (2010) *Parents of Poor Children*, p. 24.
42. See, for instance, Rublack (1999) *The Crimes of Women*, pp. 164 and 178 and Wiesner (2000) *Women and Gender*, pp. 60–3.
43. For further discussion see Rublack (1999) *The Crimes of Women*, p. 174; Eccles (1982) *Obstetrics and Gynaecology*, p. 59; Abrams (2002) 'From Demon to Victim', p. 188; and Rowlands (1997) '"In Great Secrecy"', p. 190.
44. For further discussion see Jackson (1996) *New-Born Child Murder*, pp. 62–3; Gowing (1997) 'Secret Births', p. 91; Ruggiero (1992) 'Honor, Maternity and the Disciplining of Women', p. 360; Abrams (2002) 'From Demon to Victim', pp. 186–7; Schulte (1984) 'Infanticide in Rural Bavaria', p. 459; and K. Wrightson (1982) 'Infanticide in European History', *Criminal Justice History*, III, p. 6.
45. See, for instance, Abrams (2002) 'From Demon to Victim', p. 189 and Lonza (2002) '"Two Souls Lost"', p. 83.
46. For further discussion on the issue of the peripatetic nature of many pregnant single women see Wheeler (1997) 'Infanticide in Nineteenth-Century Ohio', p. 411 and M. Kamler (1988) 'Infanticide in the Towns of the Kingdom of Poland in the Second Half of the 16th and the First Half of the 17th Century', *Acta Poloniae Historica*, 58, p. 39. For more on the determination of these women to control the outcome of their circumstances see C.B. Backhouse (1984) 'Desperate Women and Compassionate Courts: Infanticide in Nineteenth-Century Canada', *The University of Toronto Law Journal*, 34, pp. 448 and 458.
47. See, for instance, F. Mauriceau (1697) *The Diseases of Women with Child and in Child-Bed: As Also the Best Means of Helping them in Natural and Unnatural Labours. With Fit remedies for the Several indispositions of New-born Babes. To which is*

Prefix'd an Anatomical treatise. [Translated by H. Chamberlen] (London: A. Bell). [Bodleian Library, Vet. A3 e.69]; H. King (2007) *Midwifery, Obstetrics and the Rise of Gynaecology: The Uses of a Sixteenth-Century Compendium* (Aldershot: Ashgate); J. Donnison (1988) *Midwives and Medical Men: A History of the Struggle for the Control of Childbirth* (New Barnet: Historical Publications), especially pp. 20–33; P. Rhodes (1995) *A Short History of Clinical Midwifery: The Development of Ideas in the Professional Management of Childbirth* (Hale, Cheshire: Books for Midwives); E. Shorter (1985) 'The Management of Normal Deliveries and the Generation of William Hunter' and L.J. Jordanova (1985) 'Gender, Generation and Science: William Hunter's Obstetrical Atlas', both in W.F. Bynum and R. Porter (eds.) *William Hunter and the Eighteenth-Century Medical World* (Cambridge: Cambridge University Press), pp. 372–83 and 371–412 respectively; J. Drife (2002) 'The Start of Life: A History of Obstetrics', *Postgraduate Medical Journal*, 78, p. 311; and Wiesner (2000) *Women and Gender*, pp. 79 and 82.

48. See, for instance, Gélis (1991) *History of Childbirth*, p. 97 and Eccles (1982) *Obstetrics and Gynaecology*, pp. 87–95.

49. See, for instance, Rublack (1986) 'Pregnancy, Childbirth and the Female Body', pp. 101 and 103 and Gowing (1997) 'Secret Births', p. 87.

50. Crawford (1981) 'Attitudes to Menstruation', p. 21.

51. For further discussion see A. Wilson (1985) 'Participant or Patient? Seventeenth-Century Childbirth from the Mother's Point of View', in R. Porter (ed.) *Patients and Practitioners: Lay Perceptions of Medicine in Pre-Industrial Society* (Cambridge: Cambridge University Press), p. 134; Morgan and Rushton (1998) *Rogues, Thieves and the Rule of Law*, p. 111; R. Porter (1995) *Disease, Medicine and Society in England, 1550–1860* [Third Edition] (Cambridge: Cambridge University Press), p. 26; and Abrams (2002) 'From Demon to Victim', p. 190.

52. Wilson (1985) 'Participant or Patient?', p. 137. See also Pollock (1997) 'Childbearing and Female Bonding', p. 298; Eccles (1982) *Obstetrics and Gynaecology*, pp. 109–18; Wiesner (2000) *Women and Gender*, pp. 79–81; and A. Wilson (1995) *The Making of Man-Midwifery: Childbirth in England, 1660–1770* (Cambridge, MA: Harvard University Press), p. 22.

53. For further discussion of the role of midwife in the pre-modern period see Gélis (1991) *History of Childbirth*, pp. 103–11; Cressy (1999) *Birth, Marriage and Death*, especially Chapter 3; D.A. Evenden (2000) *The Midwives of Seventeenth-Century London* (Cambridge: Cambridge University Press); A. Wilson (1985) 'William Hunter and the Varieties of Man-Midwifery', in W.F. Bynum and R. Porter (eds) *William Hunter and the Eighteenth-Century Medical World* (Cambridge: Cambridge University Press), pp. 344–69; J. Donnison (1988) *Midwives and Medical Men: A History of the Struggle for the Control of Childbirth* (New Barnet: Historical Publications); Wilson (1985) 'Participant or Patient?', pp. 135–41; and especially H. Marland (1993) (ed.) *The Art of Midwifery: Early Modern Midwives in Europe* (London: Routledge).

54. See Gélis (1991) *History of Childbirth*, p. 107.

55. For further discussion of this transformation see in particular A. Wilson (1995) *The Making of Man-Midwifery: Childbirth in England, 1660–1770* (Cambridge, MA: Harvard University Press).

56. Gowing (1997) 'Secret Births', p. 99.

57. See J.W. Leavitt (1986) *Brought to Bed: Childbearing in America, 1750–1950* (New York and Oxford: Oxford University Press), p. 14.

58. For further discussion see Eccles (1982) *Obstetrics and Gynaecology*, pp. 61–5; Gélis (1991) *History of Childbirth*, pp. 150û6; Crawford (2010) *Parents of Poor Children*, p. 145; and Crawford (1981) 'Attitudes to Menstruation', p. 22.

59. For further discussion see Gélis (1991) *History of Childbirth*, pp. 112–5 and Eccles (1982) *Obstetrics and Gynaecology*, pp. 101–8. For the introduction of 'lying-in' facilities see M.C. Versluysen (1981) 'Midwives, Medical Men and "Poor Women Labouring of Child": Lying-in Hospitals in Eighteenth-Century London', in H. Roberts (ed.) *Women, Health and Reproduction* (London: Routledge and Kegan Paul), pp. 18–49.

60. For further discussion see Wilson (1995) *The Making of Man-Midwifery*, p. 19; Crawford (1981) 'Attitudes to Menstruation', p. 22; and Rublack (1986) 'Pregnancy, Childbirth and the Female Body', p. 97.

61. My calculations based on the evidence presented in Eccles (1982) *Obstetrics and Gynaecology*, p. 125 and supported by Crawford (1981) 'Attitudes to Menstruation', p. 22.

62. Drife (2002) 'The Start of Life', p. 314.

63. See, for instance, K.D. Watson (2008) 'Religion, Community and the Infanticidal Mother: Evidence from 1840s Rural Wiltshire', *Family and Community History*, 11, p. 116; Porter (1995) *Disease, Medicine and Society*, p. 7; Crawford (1981) 'Attitudes to Menstruation', p. 23; and G. Rosen (1976) 'A Slaughter of Innocents: Aspects of Child Health in the Eighteenth-Century City', *Studies in Eighteenth Century Culture*, V, pp. 296–7.

64. For further discussion see Ruggiero (1992) 'Honor, Maternity and the Disciplining of Women', p. 360.

65. For further discussion see Gélis (1991) *History of Childbirth*, pp. 150–83.

66. See, for instance, Eccles (1982) *Obstetrics and Gynaecology*, pp. 94–100.

67. Leavitt (1986) *Brought to Bed*, pp. 73–4.

68. T. Cassidy (2007) *Birth: A History* (London: Chatto and Windus), p. 11.

69. See Donnison (1988) *Midwives and Medical Men*, p. 25 and especially P. Willughby (1672, 1863 edition, 1972 reprint) *Observations in Midwifery* [Edited from the original Manuscript by H. Blenkinsop] (Wakefield: S.R. Publishers). [Bodleian Library, RSL 15083e.30].

70. See Gowing (1997) 'Secret Births', p. 100 and Donnison (1988) *Midwives and Medical Men*, pp. 14–15.

71. See, for instance, Gowing (1997) 'Secret Births', p. 102; Wheeler (1997) 'Infanticide in Nineteenth-Century Ohio', p. 412; and Kamler (1988) 'Infanticide, p. 41.

72. Jackson (1996) *New-Born Child Murder*, p. 65.

73. For further discussion see Jackson (1996) *New-Born Child Murder*, p. 66.

74. NRS, High Court of Justiciary, Books of Adjournal, JC3/14.

75. NRS, High Court of Justiciary, Books of Adjournal, JC3/24.

76. *The Proceedings of the Old Bailey*, 4th December 1755 [t17551204-27].

77. See, for instance, respectively Abrams (2002) 'From Demon to Victim', p. 194; Schulte (1984) 'Infanticide in Rural Bavaria', p. 86; Lonza (2002) '"Two Souls Lost"', pp. 71–2; Ruggiero (1992) 'Honor, Maternity and the Disciplining of Women', p. 367; Rublack (1999) *The Crimes of Women*, p. 164; and N. Woodward (2007) 'Infanticide in Wales, 1730–1830', *Welsh Historical Review*, 23, p. 118.

78. Eccles (1982) *Obstetrics and Gynaecology*, p. 86.

79. See, for instance, Gélis (1991) *History of Childbirth*, p. 98 and Gowing (1997) 'Secret Births', p. 99.

80. For further discussion see Lonza (2002) '"Two Souls Lost"', pp. 87–8 and Gélis (1991) *History of Childbirth*, pp. 160–2.

81. Wilson (1995) *The Making of Man-Midwifery*, p. 15.

82. Ibid., p. 18.

83. Gowing (1997) 'Secret Births', p. 108.

84. For further discussion see A.R. Higginbotham (1989) '"Sin of the Age":
    Infanticide and Illegitimacy in Victorian London', *Victorian Studies*, 32,
    pp. 319–37 and Lonza (2002) '"Two Souls Lost"', pp. 89–90.
85. See, for instance, Kamler (1988) 'Infanticide', p. 42; Wheeler (1997) 'Infanticide
    in Nineteenth-Century Ohio', p. 409; Dickinson and Sharpe (2002) 'Infanticide',
    p. 45; Backhouse (1984) 'Desperate Women', pp. 459–60, 467 and 469; and
    Rublack (1999) *The Crimes of Women*, pp. 170–1.
86. NRS, High Court of Justiciary, Books of Adjournal, JC3/39. See also Gowing
    (1997) 'Secret Births', p. 110.
87. See respectively *The Proceedings of the Old Bailey*, 28th January 1702 [t170201147-
    28] and National Library of Wales (hereafter NLW), Records of the Court of
    Great Sessions, 4/616/1.
88. See Ruggiero (1992) 'Honor, Maternity and the Disciplining of Women',
    p. 358. For the common use of privies as a site of disposal in instances of new-
    born child murder in the pre-modern period see Schulte (1984) 'Infanticide in
    Rural Bavaria', p. 87; Wrightson (1982) 'Infanticide in European History', p. 1;
    Rowlands (1997) '"In Great Secrecy"', p. 179; Woodward (2007) 'Infanticide',
    p. 119; and Leboutte (1991) 'Offense against Family Order', p. 173.
89. For further discussion see Gowing (1997) 'Secret Births', p. 107 and Abrams
    (2002) 'From Demon to Victim', p. 195.
90. NLW, Records of the Court of Great Sessions, 4/827/3.
91. See Abrams (2002) 'From Demon to Victim', p. 198.
92. Lonza (2002) '"Two Souls Lost"', p. 90.
93. For further discussion see Higginbotham (1989) '"Sin of the Age"', p. 325;
    Schulte (1984) 'Infanticide in Rural Bavaria', p. 86; and Rowlands (1997) '"In
    Great Secrecy"', p. 195.
94. For further discussion see Jackson (1996) *New-Born Child Murder*, p. 66.
95. The issue of cause of death in episodes of new-born child murder and claims of
    early miscarriage will be addressed more fully in Chapter 4 of this volume. For
    further discussion of claims of early miscarriage as a defence in the pre-modern
    period see S. Sommers (2002) 'Bodies, Knowledge and Authority in Eighteenth-
    Century Infanticide Prosecutions' (Unpublished Master of Arts Dissertation,
    University of Victoria), p. 37 and Wiesner (2000) *Women and Gender*, p. 78.
96. For further discussion see Gowing (2003) *Common Bodies*, p. 114; D. Rabin
    (2002) 'Bodies of Evidence, States of Mind: Infanticide, Emotion and Sensibility
    in Eighteenth-Century England', in M. Jackson (ed.) *Infanticide: Historical
    Perspectives on Child Murder and Concealment, 1550–2000* (Aldershot: Ashgate),
    pp. 74–5; and Lonza (2002) '"Two Souls Lost"', p. 81.
97. See Woodward (2007) 'Infanticide', p. 113 and the results of a British Academy
    funded project into infanticide in early modern Scotland.
98. For further discussion see Lonza (2002) '"Two Souls Lost"', p. 81.
99. Watson (2008) 'Religion, Community and the Infanticidal Mother', p. 117.
    For further discussion see Woodward (2007) 'Infanticide', p. 98 and Backhouse
    (1984) 'Desperate Women', p. 457.
100. Rabin (2002) 'Bodies of Evidence', p. 76.
101. For further discussion see for instance G. Hanlon (2003) 'Infanticide by Married
    Couples in Early Modern Tuscany', *Quaderni Storici*, XXXVIII, pp. 453–98.
102. For further discussion see Watson (2008) 'Religion, Community and the
    Infanticidal Mother', p. 125 and P.M. Crawford (2010) *Parents of Poor Children in
    England, 1580–1800* (Oxford: Oxford University Press).

103. See, for instance, Backhouse (1984) 'Desperate Women', p. 457 and Woodward (2007) 'Infanticide', p. 113. The Scottish evidence supports this contention: in all except one of the indictments for infanticide alleged to have been carried out by married women, the accused had been supported by an accomplice.

104. For further discussion see Backhouse (1984) 'Desperate Women', p. 455.

105. For examples, see respectively Gowing (2003) *Common Bodies*, p. 156; Donnison (1988) *Midwives and Medical Men*, p. 14; Morgan and Rushton (1998) *Rogues, Thieves and the Rule of Law*, p. 113; and various cases for the Scottish Justiciary Court, such as that brought against Marion Stewart at the North Circuit Court in 1726 and the case against Katherine Dick brought before the High Court of Justiciary in Edinburgh in 1743: see NRS, Justiciary Court North Circuit Records, JC11/6 and High Court of Justiciary, Books of Adjournal, JC3/24 respectively.

106. For further discussion of the lack of formal accusations against accomplices in pre-modern Europe see Woodward (2007) 'Infanticide', pp. 100–1 and 113; Kamler (1988) 'Infanticide, p. 41; and Higginbotham (1989) '"Sin of the Age"', p. 326. An accomplice was indicted in fewer than 4 per cent of the 480 infanticide cases brought before the Scottish Justiciary Court between 1700 and 1820.

107. See, for instance, Abrams (2002) 'From Demon to Victim', p. 180; T. Evans (2005) '"Blooming Virgins all Beware": Love, Courtship and Illegitimacy in Eighteenth-Century British Popular Literature', in A. Levene, T. Nutt and S. Williams (eds.) *Illegitimacy in Britain, 1700–1920* (Basingstoke: Palgrave Macmillan), p. 33; T. Evans (2005) '"Unfortunate Objects": London's Unmarried Mothers in the Eighteenth Century', *Gender and History*, XVII, p. 137; and Morgan and Rushton (1998) *Rogues, Thieves and the Rule of Law*, p. 113.

108. See respectively NLW, Records of the Court of Great Sessions, 4/611/6; *The Proceedings of the Old Bailey*, 14th September 1752 [t17520914-65]; and NRS, High Court of Justiciary, Books of Adjournal, JC4/2.

109. See, for instance, Dickinson and Sharpe (2002) 'Infanticide', p. 41 and Morgan and Rushton (1998) *Rogues, Thieves and the Rule of Law*, p. 113.

110. T. Brewer (1610) *The Bloudy Mother, or The Most Inhumane Murthers, Committed by Iane Hattersley vpon diuers infants, the Issue of her Owne Bodie: & The Priuate Burying of Them in an Orchard with her Arraignment and Execution* (London: J. Busbie), reference number ESTC 3717.3. [Accessed from Early English Books On-Line: http://eebo.chadwyck.com/home].

111. NLW, Records of the Court of Great Sessions, 4/1013/9.

112. For further discussion see Gowing (1997) 'Secret Births', pp. 87–8; Gowing (2003) *Common Bodies*, p. 140; Rublack (1999) *The Crimes of Women*, pp. 186 and 188; Dickinson and Sharpe (2002) 'Infanticide', p. 43; and Leboutte (1991) 'Offense against Family Order', p. 177.

113. See respectively *The Proceedings of the Old Bailey*, 4th December 1754 [t17541204-33], NRS, Justiciary Court North Circuit Records, JC11/34 and *The Proceedings of the Old Bailey*, 21st May 1817 [t18170521-54].

114. See, for instance, Donnison (1988) *Midwives and Medical Men*, pp. 14–5 and Gowing (1997) 'Secret Births', pp. 87–8.

115. For further discussion see Ruggiero (1992) 'Honor, Maternity and the Disciplining of Women', p. 367; Gowing (2003) *Common Bodies*, p. 164; and Abrams (2002) 'From Demon to Victim', p. 193.

116. For further discussion see Pollock (1997) 'Childbearing and Female Bonding', p. 303.

117. For further discussion see Woodward (2007) 'Infanticide', pp. 111 and 115; Dickinson and Sharpe (2002) 'Infanticide', p. 44; and Morgan and Rushton (1998) *Rogues, Thieves and the Rule of Law*, p. 113.
118. See respectively the results of a British Academy funded project into infanticide in early modern Scotland and Woodward (2007) 'Infanticide', pp. 114–5.
119. For further discussion see Leboutte (1991) 'Offense against Family Order', p. 162 and Wheeler (1997) 'Infanticide in Nineteenth-Century Ohio', p. 408.
120. For further discussion see Gowing (1997) 'Secret Births', pp. 103–4 and 109; Woodward (2007) 'Infanticide', pp. 111 and 114; Crawford (2010) *Parents of Poor Children*, p. 74; Crawford (1981) 'Attitudes to Menstruation', p. 129; and Wheeler (1997) 'Infanticide in Nineteenth-Century Ohio', p. 408.
121. For further discussion see Woodward (2007) 'Infanticide', pp. 111 and 115; Gowing (2003) *Common Bodies*, pp. 182–4; and Crawford (2010) *Parents of Poor Children*, pp. 79–111.
122. For the full details of this case see *A Short and Impartial Account of the Proceedings against George Dewing, Keeper of the House of Correction at Halstead in Essex, For the Murder of a Bastard Child there Begotten by Him Upon the Body of one of his Prisoners: For Which he was Try'd and Condemn'd at the Assizes of Chelmsford, March the 20th, 1727–8* (London: J. Roberts), reference number ESTC 36428, pp. 1–36. [Accessed from Eighteenth Century Collections On-Line via: http://www.jischistoricbooks.ac.uk/Search.aspx].
123. Ibid., p. 27.
124. Ibid.
125. Ibid.
126. Ibid., p. 28.
127. Ibid.
128. Ibid., p. 29.
129. Ibid., p. 32.
130. Ibid., p. 35.
131. Ibid.
132. For further discussion see Woodward (2007) 'Infanticide', pp. 111 and 115 and Gowing (2003) *Common Bodies*, pp. 182–4.
133. Ibid. For further discussion see also Crawford (2010) *Parents of Poor Children*, pp. 79–111.
134. For instance, only two of the 23 men accused of new-born child murder in Scotland between 1700 and 1820 were found guilty of the charges against them. A more detailed discussion of conviction rates and sentencing for this crime can be found in Chapters 2 and 5 of this volume.
135. *A Short and Impartial Account of the Proceedings against George Dewing*, pp. 2 and 4. The 'Wild' referred to here is Jonathan Wild, a famous criminal turned thief-taker from the eighteenth century. The 'Coke' is the controversial sixteenth-century English barrister, Sir Edward Coke.
136. Ibid., pp. 18–19.
137. Ibid., pp. 21–23.
138. See, for instance, the reports of the verdict and sentence in the *London Evening Post* on 1 October 1728, No. 128. The story was not concluded at this juncture, however, as Dewing was pardoned of this crime only to be convicted of another viscous murder. Then, on his death bed, Thomas Diss proceeded to retract the accusations he made and Dewing sought a further pardon from the King in order to achieve full exoneration and the restoration of his good name. See the

coverage provided in *Daily Post (London)* 4 October 1728, No. 2820 and No. 2415; *Daily Journal (London)* 4 October 1728, No. 2415; *Mist's Weekly Journal (London)*, 7 September 1728, No. 177 and 178; the *Country Journal or The Craftsman (London)*, 5 October 1728, No. 118; the *Flying Post or The Weekly Medley (London)*, 5 October, 1728, No. 1; the *London Journal*, 5 October 1728, No. 479, 17 January 1730, No. 546, 24 January 1730, No. 547, 7 February 1730, No. 549 and 14 February 1730, No. 550. Prior to Thomas Diss's confession, George Dewing had already appealed to the King for a full pardon of *all* the accusations laid against him. See National Archives [Kew, Surrey] (hereafter NA), State Papers – Secretaries of State: Entry Book SP44/254, May–June 1728. The outcome of this pardon is not disclosed in the State Papers.

139. Indeed, George Dewing was accused of this behaviour at a later date, as is evident from a range of newspaper reports, including the *British Journal or The Censor (London)*, 15 March 1729, No. 63; *Weekly Journal or British Gazetteer* (London), 5 October 1728, No. 176; the *Country Journal or The Craftsman (London)*, 15 March 1729, No. 141; the *London Journal*, 15 March 1729, No. 502; and the *Gloucester Journal*, 18 March 1729, No. 363.

140. Higginbotham (1989) '"Sin of the Age"', p. 325.

141. Gowing (1997) 'Secret Births', p. 111.

142. See Wrightson (1982) 'Infanticide in European History', p. 10 and Higginbotham (1989) '"Sin of the Age"', p. 319. See also Rowlands (1997) '"In Great Secrecy"', p. 195 for a similar argument.

143. S. Faber (1990) 'Infanticide and Criminal Justice in the Netherlands, especially in Amsterdam', in International Commission of Historical Demography (ed.) *The Role of the State and Public Opinion in Sexual Attitudes and Demographic Behaviour* (CIDH: Madrid), p. 260 and R.W. Malcolmson (1977) 'Infanticide in the Eighteenth Century', in J.S. Cockburn (ed.) *Crime in England 1550–1800* (London: Methuen), p. 196.

144. See Lonza (2002) '"Two Souls Lost"', p. 86 and the results of a British Academy funded project into infanticide in early modern Scotland where rural locations made up 56 per cent of the indictments and urban locations 44 per cent.

145. For further discussion see Lonza (2002) '"Two Souls Lost"', p. 80.

146. For further discussion see Jackson (1996) *New-Born Child Murder*, p. 69; Schulte (1984) 'Infanticide in Rural Bavaria', pp. 93–4; Dickinson and Sharpe (2002) 'Infanticide', p. 46; and Lonza (2002) '"Two Souls Lost"', p. 94.

147. For further and more detailed discussion of the involvement of the Church in Scottish infanticide investigations during the pre-modern period see Kilday (2008) '"Monsters of the Vilest Kind"', pp. 100–115.

148. Gowing (1997) 'Secret Births', p. 111 – my addition in parenthesis.

149. See, for instance, Lonza (2002) '"Two Souls Lost"', p. 99 and Pollock (1997) 'Childbearing and Female Bonding', p. 304. The tactic of testing a suspect's reaction by introducing the dead body of a new-born child to the proceedings was commonly adopted in Scotland during the pre-modern period and typically resulted in a full confession from the individual accused.

150. NRS, High Court of Justiciary, Books of Adjournal, JC3/10.

151. See Abrams (2002) 'From Demon to Victim', p. 193. In Scotland, sometimes ministers of a particular parish undertook these examinations themselves, which must have only added to the horrific, brutal and depersonalising nature of the investigative process for the young female suspects involved. See Kilday (2008) '"Monsters of the Vilest Kind"', p. 100–115.

152. Gowing (1997) 'Secret Births', p. 96.
153. See, for instance, Rowlands (1997) '"In Great Secrecy"', pp. 186 and 189 and Gowing (2003) *Common Bodies*, p. 45.
154. For further discussion see Lonza (2002) '"Two Souls Lost"', pp. 101–2 and Jackson (1996) *New-Born Child Murder*, pp. 70–7.
155. For further discussion see Jackson (1996) *New-Born Child Murder*, pp. 72–3 and Jackson (1996) '"Something More Than Blood"', p. 206.
156. For further discussion see Lonza, p. 90; Ruggiero (1992) 'Honor, Maternity and the Disciplining of Women', p. 368; and Wilson (1985) 'Participant or Patient?', p. 136.
157. Wiesner (2000) *Women and Gender*, p. 64.
158. See, for instance, Morgan and Rushton (1998) *Rogues, Thieves and the Rule of Law*, p. 114 and Ruggiero (1992) 'Honor, Maternity and the Disciplining of Women', pp. 368–9.
159. For further discussion see Jackson (1996) '"Something More Than Blood"', p. 207.

4   Monsters of inhumanity? Methods of infant disposal

1. The *Gentleman's Magazine* August 1732: Vol. II, No. XX with reference to an indictment brought against an English abortionist in the early eighteenth century.
2. For further discussion of the recorded incidence of the crime of new-born child murder over time, see Chapters 1 and 5 of this volume.
3. R.P. Petchesky (1984, 1985 edition) *Abortion and Women's Choice* (London: Verso), p. 28.
4. For further discussion of the early history of abortion see ibid., p. 29; E. Shorter (1982) *A History of Women's Bodies* (London: Allen Lane), p. 177; A. McLaren (1977) 'Women's Work and the Regulation of Family Size: The Question of Abortion in the Nineteenth Century', *History Workshop Journal*, 4, p. 73; A. McLaren (1990, 1992 edition) *A History of Contraception – From Antiquity to the Present Day* (Oxford: Blackwell), pp. 4–5; J.M. Riddle (1991) 'Oral Contraceptives and Early-Term Abortifacients During Classical Antiquity and the Middle Ages', *Past and Present*, 132, pp. 3–32; and J.M. Riddle (1994) *Contraception and Abortion from the Ancient World to the Renaissance* (Cambridge, MA and London: Harvard University Press).
5. See N. Lonza (2002) '"Two Souls Lost": Infanticide in the Republic of Dubrovnik (1667–1808)', *Dubrovnik Annals*, 6, p. 74.
6. See D. Cressy (1999) *Birth, Marriage, and Death: Ritual, Religion, and the Life-Cycle in Tudor and Stuart England* (Oxford: Oxford University Press), p. 47; McLaren (1977) 'Women's Work', p. 74; and J.L. Harrington (2009) *The Unwanted Child: The Fate of Foundlings, Orphans and Juvenile Criminals in Early Modern Germany* (Chicago and London: University of Chicago Press), p. 47.
7. For further discussion see L. Gordon (1977) *Woman's Body: Woman's Right: A Social History of Birth Control in America* (Harmondsworth and New York: Penguin), p. 50; K. Ruggiero (2000) 'Not Guilty: Abortion and Infanticide in Nineteenth-Century Argentina', in C. Agiurre and R. Buffington (eds.) *Reconstructing Criminality in Latin America* (Wilmington, DE: Jaguar), p. 151; G.S. Rowe (1991) 'Infanticide, Its Judicial Resolution, and Criminal Code Revision in Early Pennsylvania', *Proceedings of the American Philosophical Society*, CXXXV, p. 203; and M.E. Wiesner-Hanks (2000) *Christianity and Sexuality in the Early Modern World: Regulating Desire, Reforming Practice* (London and New York: Routledge), p. 83.

8. See L. Stone (1977) *The Family, Sex and Marriage in England 1500–1800* (London: Weidenfeld and Nicolson), pp. 415–24.
9. See respectively C. Wilson (1984) 'Natural Fertility in Pre-industrial England, 1600–1799', *Population Studies*, 38, pp. 225–40 and N. Woodward (2007) 'Infanticide in Wales, 1730–1830', *Welsh Historical Review*, 23, p. 109.
10. See respectively J. Keown (1988) *Abortion, Doctors and the Law: Some Aspects of the Legal Regulation of Abortion in England from 1803 to 1982* (Cambridge: Cambridge University Press), p. 11 and Gordon (1977) *Woman's Body*, p. 51.
11. See respectively P. Knight (1977) 'Women and Abortion in Victorian and Edwardian England', *History Workshop Journal*, 4, pp. 57 and 59; McLaren (1977) 'Women's Work', p. 78; and F.B. Smith (1979) *The People's Health: 1830–1910* (London: Croom Helm), p. 74. For further discussion of the American and French experience of abortion at this time, see respectively Gordon (1977) *Woman's Body*, p. 53 and A. McLaren (1978) 'Abortion in France: Women and the Regulation of Family Size 1800–1914', *French Historical Studies*, 10, pp. 461–85.
12. R. Sauer (1978) 'Infanticide and Abortion in Nineteenth-Century Britain', *Population Studies: A Journal of Demography*, XXXII, p. 81.
13. C.C. Means Jr (1971) 'The Phoenix of Abortional Freedom: Is a Penumbral or Ninth-Amendment Right about to Arise from the Nineteenth-Century Legislative Ashes of a Fourteenth-Century Common-Law Liberty?', *New York Law Forum*, 17, pp. 335 and 373, cited in Keown (1988) *Abortion*, p. 3.
14. Sauer (1978) 'Infanticide and Abortion', p. 83.
15. For further discussion of the prevalence of this attitude in the pre-modern period see P. Crawford (1994) 'Sexual Knowledge in England, 1500–1700', in R. Porter and M. Teich (eds.) *Sexual Knowledge, Sexual Science: The History of Attitudes to Sexuality* (Cambridge: Cambridge University Press), p. 99; A. McLaren (1984) *Reproductive Rituals: The Perception of Fertility in England from the Sixteenth Century to the Nineteenth Century* (London and New York: Methuen), p. 107; McLaren (1990, 1992 edition) *A History of Contraception*, p. 161; Gordon (1977) *Woman's Body*, p. 52; and Petchesky (1984, 1985 edition) *Abortion*, pp. 29–30.
16. For further discussion see Wiesner-Hanks (2000) *Christianity and Sexuality*, pp. 43–4, 83 and 109.
17. Cressy (1999) *Birth, Marriage, and Death*, p. 47.
18. Ibid., p. 48.
19. For further discussion see A. Eccles (1982) *Obstetrics and Gynaecology in Tudor and Stuart England* (London and Canberra: Croom Helm), p. 67 and McLaren (1990, 1992 edition) *A History of Contraception*, p. 31.
20. For further discussion see G. Davis and R. Davidson (2006) '"A Fifth Freedom" or "Hideous Atheistic Expediency"? The Medical Community and Abortion Law Reform in Scotland, c. 1960–1975', *Medical History*, 50, pp. 31–2. I am grateful to Dr Clifford Williamson for alerting me to this reference.
21. See McLaren (1977) 'Women's Work', pp. 73 and 75 and Sauer (1978) 'Infanticide and Abortion', p. 84.
22. Parliamentary Papers, 43 Geo. 3 c.58 (1803).
23. See Keown (1988) *Abortion*, pp. 12–21.
24. Ibid., pp. 21–22.
25. Ibid., pp. 22–24.
26. Parliamentary Papers, 9 Geo 4 c.31 (1828). For further discussion on the revisions made see Keown (1988) *Abortion*, pp. 28–29.
27. For further discussion see Keown (1988) *Abortion*, pp. 29–33.
28. Parliamentary Papers, 7 Will. IV and Vict c.85 (1837).

29. Parliamentary Papers, 24 and 25 Vict c.100 (1861). For further discussion see Keown (1988) *Abortion*, pp. 33–35.
30. For further discussion see C.H. Dayton (1991) 'Taking the Trade: Abortion and Gender Relations in an Eighteenth-Century New England Village', *The William and Mary Quarterly*, Third Series, 48, pp. 21–21; Knight (1977) 'Women and Abortion', p. 57; and Smith (1979) *The People's Health*, p. 76.
31. For further discussion see McLaren (1984) *Reproductive Rituals*, pp. 113–44; Keown (1988) *Abortion*, pp. 39–47; J.A. Banks and O. Banks (1965) *Feminism and Family Planning in Victorian England* (Liverpool: Liverpool University Press), pp. 86–87; Petchesky (1984, 1985 edition) *Abortion*, pp. 30–31; Gordon (1977) *Woman's Body*, pp. 59–60; and M. Thomson (1998) *Reproducing Narrative: Gender, Reproduction and the Law* (Aldershot: Ashgate), Chapter 1.
32. See respectively the *Gentleman's Magazine*, August 1732: Vol. II, No. XX and the *British Medical Journal*, 26 January 1861, 8 February 1868 and 27 May 1871.
33. See R.W. Malcolmson (1977) 'Infanticide in the Eighteenth Century', in J.S. Cockburn (ed.) *Crime in England 1550–1800* (London: Methuen), pp. 187–88. For further discussion of the physical dangers of abortion in the pre-modern period see A. McLaren (1994) '"Not a Stranger: A Doctor": Medical Men and Sexual Matters in the Late Nineteenth Century', in R. Porter and M. Teich (eds.) *Sexual Knowledge, Sexual Science: The History of Attitudes to Sexuality* (Cambridge: Cambridge University Press), p. 274; J. Ermers (1990) 'Medeas or Fallen Angels? The Prosecution of Infanticide and Stereotypes of "Child Murderesses" in the Netherlands in the Nineteenth Century', in International Commission of Historical Demography (ed.) *The Role of the State and Public Opinion in Sexual Attitudes and Demographic Behaviour* (CIDH: Madrid), p. 487; Knight (1977) 'Women and Abortion', p. 60; and Sauer (1978) 'Infanticide and Abortion', pp. 83 and 88.
34. McLaren (1990, 1992 edition) *A History of Contraception*, pp. 54 and 128.
35. G.R. Quaife (1979) *Wanton Wenches and Wayward Wives: Peasant and Illicit Sex in Early Seventeenth-Century England* (London: Croom Helm), pp. 117–18.
36. For further discussion of the use of abortion within the context of illicit relationships see S. Wilson (1988) 'Child Abandonment and Female Honour in Nineteenth Century Corsica', *Comparative Studies in Society and History*, 30, p. 773; L. Pollock, (1990) 'Embarking on a Rough Passage: The Experience of Pregnancy in Early-Modern Society' in V. Fildes (ed.) *Women as Mothers in Pre-Industrial England: Essays in Memory of Dorothy McLaren* (London and New York: Routledge), p. 56 and McLaren (1984) *Reproductive Rituals*, p. 94.
37. McLaren (1977) 'Women's Work', p. 77. See also McLaren (1984) *Reproductive Rituals*, p. 90 and Sauer (1978) 'Infanticide and Abortion', p. 91.
38. For further discussion see Pollock, (1990) 'Embarking on a Rough Passage', p. 57; McLaren (1984) *Reproductive Rituals*, p. 89; Banks and Banks (1965) *Feminism and Family Planning*, p. 69; Smith (1979) *The People's Health*, p. 78; and McLaren (1990, 1992 edition) *A History of Contraception*, p. 189.
39. For further discussion see Knight (1977) 'Women and Abortion', p. 58 and McLaren (1984) *Reproductive Rituals*, pp. 89–90.
40. For further discussion see Shorter (1982) *A History of Women's Bodies*, p. 177; Knight (1977) 'Women and Abortion', p. 58; A. McLaren (1978) *Birth Control in Nineteenth-Century England* (London: Croom Helm), p. 32; McLaren (1977) 'Women's Work', p. 73; and McLaren (1990, 1992 edition) *A History of Contraception*, p. 189.

41. See, for instance, Cressy (1999) *Birth, Marriage, and Death*, p. 48; McLaren (1977) 'Women's Work', p. 72; and McLaren (1984) *Reproductive Rituals*, p. 98.
42. See, for instance, Dayton (1991) 'Taking the Trade', p. 25 and Harrington (2009) *The Unwanted Child*, p. 48.
43. O. Davies (1999) 'Cunning-Folk in the Medical Market Place during the Nineteenth Century', *Medical History*, 43, p. 72; McLaren (1984) *Reproductive Rituals*, p. 101; R.V. Schnucker (1975) 'Elizabethan Birth Control and Puritan attitudes', *Journal of Interdisciplinary History*, 4, p. 658; Lonza (2002) '"Two Souls Lost"', p. 74; Harrington (2009) *The Unwanted Child*, p. 49; Wiesner-Hanks (2000) *Christianity and Sexuality*, p. 83; and Quaife (1979) *Wanton Wenches*, p. 26.
44. See, for instance, McLaren (1984) *Reproductive Rituals*, pp. 101–106 and Schnucker (1975) 'Elizabethan Birth Control', p. 659.
45. For further discussion see J.M. Riddle (1998) *Eve's Herbs: A History of Contraception and Abortion in the West* (London and Cambridge, MA: Harvard University Press); Riddle (1991) 'Oral Contraceptives', pp. 3–32; Cressy (1999) *Birth, Marriage, and Death*, p. 50; Quaife (1979) *Wanton Wenches*, p. 119; Wiesner-Hanks (2000) *Christianity and Sexuality*, p. 83; and Shorter (1982) *A History of Women's Bodies*, pp. 179–88.
46. For further discussion see McLaren (1984) *Reproductive Rituals*, p. 104 and also Cressy (1999) *Birth, Marriage, and Death*, p. 48.
47. Schnucker (1975) 'Elizabethan Birth Control', p. 659. See also Shorter (1982) *A History of Women's Bodies*, p. 181; McLaren (1978) *Birth Control*, p. 31; and Pollock (1990) 'Embarking on a Rough Passage', p. 59.
48. For further discussion see McLaren (1984) *Reproductive Rituals*, p. 106 and Smith (1979) *The People's Health*, p. 75.
49. For further discussion see Harrington (2009) *The Unwanted Child*, p. 50; Dayton (1991) 'Taking the Trade', p. 23; Shorter (1982) *A History of Women's Bodies*, pp. 188–91; Knight (1977) 'Women and Abortion', p. 60; McLaren (1977) 'Women's Work', p. 77; and Gordon (1977) *Woman's Body*, p. 53. For more on modern techniques of instrumental abortion see Shorter (1982) *A History of Women's Bodies*, pp. 197–208 and for more on the modern drugs associated with abortion see ibid., pp. 208–24.
50. See Knight (1977) 'Women and Abortion', p. 60 and McLaren (1977) 'Women's Work', p. 71.
51. For further discussion of the unreliable nature of abortions in the pre-modern period see Cressy (1999) *Birth, Marriage, and Death*, p. 49 and Malcolmson (1977) 'Infanticide', p. 187.
52. See Pollock (1990) 'Embarking on a Rough Passage', p. 55; Harrington (2009) *The Unwanted Child*, p. 48; and Gordon (1977) *Woman's Body*, p. 52.
53. For further discussion see Knight (1977) 'Women and Abortion', p. 61 and McLaren (1978) *Birth Control*, p. 34.
54. See Quaife (1979) *Wanton Wenches*, p. 119.
55. For further discussion see Knight (1977) 'Women and Abortion', pp. 62–3; Dayton (1991) 'Taking the Trade', p. 23; and M.D. Smith (1999) '"Unnatural Mothers": Infanticide, Motherhood and Class in the Mid-Atlantic, 1730–1830', in C. Daniels and M.V. Kennedy (eds.) *Over the Threshold: Intimate Violence in Early America* (New York: Routledge), p. 178.
56. For further discussion see McLaren (1984) *Reproductive Rituals*, p. 115 and Sauer (1978) 'Infanticide and Abortion', p. 84.
57. Sauer (1978) 'Infanticide and Abortion', pp. 88 and 91.

58. McLaren (1978) *Birth Control*, p. 34.
59. For further discussion see J. Boswell (1988) *The Kindness of Strangers: The Abandonment of Children in Western Europe from Late Antiquity to the Renaissance* (London: Allen Lane); J.E. Boswell (1984) 'Expositio and Oblation: The Abandonment of Children and the Ancient and Medieval Family', *American Historical Review*, 89, pp. 10–33; and P.A. Gilje (1983) 'Infant Abandonment in Early Nineteenth-Century New York City: Three Cases', *Signs*, 8, p. 580.
60. For further discussion see Boswell (1984) 'Expositio and Oblation', pp. 19–21 and Malcolmson (1977) 'Infanticide', pp. 2–3.
61. Malcolmson (1977) 'Infanticide', p. 188. For further discussion of abandonment being used as an alternative to infanticide see also K. Wrightson (1982) 'Infanticide in European History', *Criminal Justice History*, III, p. 13; J. Kelly (1992) 'Infanticide in Eighteenth-Century Ireland', *Irish Economic and Social History*, XIX, p. 9; and R.G. Fuchs (1987) 'Legislation, Poverty and Child-Abandonment in Nineteenth-Century Paris', *Journal of Interdisciplinary History*, 18, p. 55. For further discussion on the typical age of abandoned infants in the centuries before 1900, see V. Fildes (1990) 'Maternal Feelings Re-assessed: Child Abandonment and Neglect in London and Westminster, 1550–1800', in V. Fildes (ed.) *Women as Mothers in Pre-industrial England: Essays in Memory of Dorothy McLaren* (London and New York: Routledge), pp. 148–9 and A. Levene (2007) *Childcare, Health and Mortality at the London Foundling Hospital, 1741–1800: 'Left to the Mercy of the World'* (Manchester: Manchester University Press), p. 22.
62. Fuchs (1987) 'Legislation, Poverty and Child-Abandonment', pp. 56 and 55 respectively. For further discussion of the global nature of infant abandonment in the pre-modern period see the various chapters in C. Panter-Brick and M.T. Smith (2000) (eds.) *Abandoned Children* (Cambridge: Cambridge University Press).
63. See Malcolmson (1977) 'Infanticide', p. 205 and Fildes (1990) 'Maternal Feelings Re-assessed', p. 144.
64. For further discussion see L. Leneman and R. Mitchison (1987) 'Scottish Illegitimacy Ratios in the Early Modern Period', *Economic History Review*, 2nd ser., XL, p. 57 and Woodward (2007) 'Infanticide', pp. 110 and 116.
65. For further discussion see R. Leboutte (1991) 'Offense against Family Order: Infanticide in Belgium from the Fifteenth through the Early Twentieth Centuries', *Journal of the History of Sexuality*, 2, p. 168; Rowe (1991) 'Infanticide', pp. 220–21; and Gilje (1983) 'Infant Abandonment', p. 582.
66. William Gouge (1622, 1976 edition) *Of Domesticall Duties – Eight Treatises* (Amsterdam: W.J. Johnson) [Bodleian Library, 1778 e.478], p. 507.
67. See Fildes (1990) 'Maternal Feelings Re-assessed', p. 158.
68. D.I. Kertzer (1991) 'Gender, Ideology and Infant Abandonment in Nineteenth-Century Italy', *The Journal of Interdisciplinary History*, 22, p. 1. See also Boswell (1988) *The Kindness of Strangers*, passim.
69. For further discussion see M. Kamler (1988) 'Infanticide in the Towns of the Kingdom of Poland in the Second Half of the 16th and the First Half of the 17th Century', *Acta Poloniae Historica*, 58, p. 46; Rowe (1991) 'Infanticide', p. 225 and Ermers (1990) 'Medeas or Fallen Angels?', p. 487.
70. Kelly (1992) 'Infanticide', p. 10. See also Fuchs (1987) 'Legislation, Poverty and Child-Abandonment', p. 55.
71. See, for instance, S.X. Radbill (1968) 'A History of Child Abuse and Infanticide', in R.E. Helfer and C.H. Kempe (eds.) *The Battered Child* (Chicago: University of Chicago Press), p. 10.

72. Parliamentary Papers, 24 and 25 Vict c.100 (1861).
73. For further discussion see B.S. Pullan (1988) *Orphans and Foundlings in Early Modern Europe* (Reading: University of Reading Press), p. 22 and R.B. Litchfield and D. Gordon (1980) 'Closing the Tour: A Close Look at the Marriage Market, Unwed Mothers and Abandoned Children in Mid-Nineteenth Century Amiens', *Journal of Social History*, 14, p. 458.
74. See, for instance, C.B. Backhouse (1984) 'Desperate Women and Compassionate Courts: Infanticide in Nineteenth-Century Canada', *The University of Toronto Law Journal*, 34, p. 471; Lonza (2002) '"Two Souls Lost"', p. 77; Fildes (1990) 'Maternal Feelings Re-assessed', p. 151; Fuchs (1987) 'Legislation, Poverty and Child-Abandonment', p. 57; and Malcolmson (1977) 'Infanticide', p. 188.
75. Leboutte (1991) 'Offense against Family Order', p. 163.
76. For further discussion see Boswell (1984) 'Expositio and Oblation', p. 14; Wilson (1988) 'Child Abandonment', p. 767; Lonza (2002) '"Two Souls Lost"', p. 7; Kelly (1992) 'Infanticide', p. 10; and Malcolmson (1977) 'Infanticide', p. 188.
77. For further discussion see Ermers (1990) 'Medeas or Fallen Angels?', p. 488 and Lonza (2002) '"Two Souls Lost"', p. 76.
78. Malcolmson (1977) 'Infanticide', p. 205.
79. See, for instance, Pullan (1988) *Orphans and Foundlings*, p. 12.
80. See, for instance, Radbill (1968) 'A History of Child Abuse and Infanticide', p. 10; Lonza (2002) '"Two Souls Lost"', p. 76; Wrightson (1982) 'Infanticide in European History', p. 5; and Levene (2007) *Childcare*, p. 2.
81. See Pullan (1988) *Orphans and Foundlings*, p. 9.
82. See O. Ulbricht (1985) 'The Debate about Foundling Hospitals in Enlightenment Germany: Infanticide, Illegitimacy and Infant Mortality Rates', *Central European History*, 18, p. 212 and for the history of French foundling hospitals more generally see Fuchs (1984) *Abandoned Children: Foundlings and Child Welfare in Nineteenth-Century France* (Albany, NY: State University of New York Press).
83. See Malcolmson (1977) 'Infanticide', p. 190; Kelly (1992) 'Infanticide', p. 10; D.L. Ransel (1988) *Mothers of Misery: Child Abandonment in Russia* (Princeton, NJ: Princeton University Press); and Ulbricht (1985) 'The Debate about Foundling Hospitals', p. 213 respectively. There is no evidence that this kind of provision was set up in either Scotland or Wales during the pre-modern period.
84. Leboutte (1991) 'Offense against Family Order', p. 172.
85. See Kelly (1992) 'Infanticide', p. 10.
86. See R. McClure (1981) *Coram's Children: The London Foundling Hospital in the Eighteenth Century* (New Haven: Yale University Press), p. 76 and T. Evans (2005) '"Unfortunate Objects": London's Unmarried Mothers in the Eighteenth Century', *Gender and History*, XVII, p. 129.
87. Levene (2007) *Childcare*, p. 2. See also G. Pugh (2007) *London's Forgotten Children: Thomas Coram and the Foundling Hospital* (Stroud: Tempus), p. 92; Kertzer (1991) 'Gender, Ideology and Infant Abandonment', pp. 5 and 11; and E.C. Green (1999) 'Infanticide and Infant Abandonment in the New South: Richmond, Virginia, 1865–1915', *Journal of Family History*, 24, p. 188 for evidence of a nineteenth century increase in abandonments to foundling institutions across Europe and beyond.
88. *The Guardian*, 11 July 1713, No. 105.
89. Thomas Bernard (1799) *An Account of the Foundling Hospital in London for the Maintenance and Education of Exposed and Deserted Young Children* (London: T. Jones), p. 3 [Bodleian Library, GK17741 – 8 vols.].

90. For further discussion of the origins of the London Foundling Hospital see Pugh (2007) *London's Forgotten Children*, *passim*; Levene (2007) *Childcare*, *passim*; and McClure (1981) *Coram's Children*, *passim*.

91. For further discussion see Pugh (2007) *London's Forgotten Children*, p. 44 and Levene (2007) *Childcare*, p. 7.

92. See the references in the third section of note 61 above.

93. See, for instance, Fuchs (1987) 'Legislation, Poverty and Child-Abandonment', p. 65 and Kertzer (1991) 'Gender, Ideology and Infant Abandonment', p. 10.

94. See, for instance, Boswell (1984) 'Expositio and Oblation', pp. 18–19.

95. See Levene (2007) *Childcare*, p. 30. For further evidence of this see also Pugh (2007) *London's Forgotten Children*, p. 10; Fildes (1990) 'Maternal Feelings Re-assessed', p. 157; and Evans (2005) '"Unfortunate Objects"', p. 130.

96. For further discussion see Ulbricht (1985) 'The Debate about Foundling Hospitals', pp. 240–42; Pugh (2007) *London's Forgotten Children*, p. 95; Pullan (1988) *Orphans and Foundlings*, p. 22; and Evans (2005) '"Unfortunate Objects"', p. 129.

97. For further discussion see Ulbricht (1985) 'The Debate about Foundling Hospitals', pp. 254–56; Litchfield and Gordon (1980) 'Closing the Tour', p. 458; and Fuchs (1987) 'Legislation, Poverty and Child-Abandonment', p. 61.

98. See Ulbricht (1985) 'The Debate about Foundling Hospitals', pp. 246–53; Pullan (1988) *Orphans and Foundlings*, p. 12; and Pugh (2007) *London's Forgotten Children*, p. 95.

99. See Ulbricht (1985) 'The Debate about Foundling Hospitals', pp. 235–40 and Kertzer (1991) 'Gender, Ideology and Infant Abandonment', p. 8.

100. See Pugh (2007) *London's Forgotten Children*, pp. 46–7 and 50.

101. Levene (2007) *Childcare*, p. 18.

102. Pugh (2007) *London's Forgotten Children*, p. 50 and Levene (2007) *Childcare*, pp. 60–1. For evidence of a higher infant mortality rate amongst foundling hospitals in Europe and North America see Lonza (2002) '"Two Souls Lost"', p. 72; Green (1999) 'Infanticide and Infant Abandonment', p. 198; G. Rosen (1976) 'A Slaughter of Innocents: Aspects of Child Health in the Eighteenth-Century City', *Studies in Eighteenth Century Culture*, V, p. 303; and P.P. Viazzo, M. Bortolotto and A. Zanotto (1997) 'A Special Case of Decline: Levels and Trends of Infant Mortality in Florence's Foundling Hospital 1750–1950', in C.A. Corsini and P.P. Viazzo (eds.) *The Decline of Infant and Child Mortality: The European Experience – 1750–1990* (The Hague: Kluwer), pp. 227–46.

103. Kertzer (1991) 'Gender, Ideology and Infant Abandonment', p. 9.

104. Wrightson (1982) 'Infanticide in European History', p. 14.

105. Ibid.

106. See, for instance, Kelly (1992) 'Infanticide', p. 10.

107. Leneman and Mitchison (1987) 'Scottish Illegitimacy Ratios', p. 57 and Rosen (1976) 'A Slaughter of Innocents', p. 302.

108. See Evans (2005) '"Unfortunate Objects"', pp. 127–53. For further discussion of poverty as the principle causal factor of infant abandonment in the pre-modern period see Fildes (1990) 'Maternal Feelings Re-assessed', p. 153; and Smith (1999) '"Unnatural Mothers"', p. 178; and especially Fuchs (1987) 'Legislation, Poverty and Child-Abandonment', pp. 55–80.

109. See Wrightson (1982) 'Infanticide in European History', p. 13 and Wilson (1988) 'Child Abandonment', p. 775.

110. Pullan (1988) *Orphans and Foundlings*, p. 12.

111. See, for instance, Boswell (1984) 'Expositio and Oblation', p. 13; Levene (2007) *Childcare*, p. 42; and Sauer (1978) 'Infanticide and Abortion', p. 86.

112. For further discussion of the likely good intentions of the majority of mothers who abandoned their infants to institutional or charitable care or in a public place see Boswell (1984) 'Expositio and Oblation', p. 13; Gilje (1983) 'Infant Abandonment', p. 580; Green (1999) 'Infanticide and Infant Abandonment', p. 197; Evans (2005) '"Unfortunate Objects"', p. 140; Fildes (1990) 'Maternal Feelings Re-assessed', p. 139; Smith (1999) '"Unnatural Mothers"', p. 178; and Fuchs (1984) *Abandoned Children*, especially pp. 13 and 175.

113. For further discussion see Boswell (1984) 'Expositio and Oblation', p. 15; Wrightson (1982) 'Infanticide in European History', p. 13; and Evans (2005) '"Unfortunate Objects"', p. 140.

114. V. Fildes (1988) *Wet Nursing: A History from Antiquity to the Present* (Oxford: Basil Blackwell), p. 1.

115. For further discussion see ibid., particularly Chapters 1 and 2 and R.K. Marshall (1984) 'Wet-Nursing in Scotland: 1500–1800', *Review of Scottish Culture*, I, p. 43.

116. See, for instance, Fildes (1988) *Wet Nursing: A History*, p. 34; V. Fildes (1988) 'The English Wet-Nurse and Her Role in Infant care 1538–1800', *Medical History*, 32, p. 164; L. Campbell (1989) 'Wet-Nurses in Early Modern England: Some Evidence from the Townshend Archive', *Medical History*, 33, p. 368; Rosen (1976) 'A Slaughter of Innocents', p. 300; and Marshall (1984) 'Wet-Nursing in Scotland', p. 46.

117. For further discussion see D. McLaren (1978) 'Fertility, Infant Mortality and Breast Feeding in the Seventeenth Century', *Medical History*, 22, pp. 378–96; D. McLaren (1979) 'Nature's Contraceptive, Wet-Nursing and Prolonged Lactation: The Case of Chesham, Buckinghamshire, 1578–1601', *Medical History*, 23, p. 426; F. Newall (1990) 'Wet Nursing and Child Care in Aldenham, Hertfordshire, 1595–1726: Some Evidence on the Circumstances and Effects of Seventeenth-Century Child Rearing Practices', in V. Fildes (ed.) *Women as Mothers in Pre-Industrial England: Essays in Memory of Dorothy McLaren* (London and New York: Routledge), p. 123; and Marshall (1984) 'Wet-Nursing in Scotland', p. 45.

118. For further discussion see Marshall (1984) 'Wet-Nursing in Scotland', p. 45 and R. Perry (1991) 'Colonizing the Breast: Sexuality and Maternity in Eighteenth-Century England', *Journal of the History of Sexuality*, 2, p. 337.

119. For further discussion of the use of wet-nurses by foundling hospitals see Perry (1991) 'Colonizing the Breast', p. 208; Ulbricht (1985) 'The Debate about Foundling Hospitals', p. 218; and D.I. Kertzer (1999) 'Syphilis, Foundlings, and Wetnurses in Nineteenth-Century Italy', *Journal of Social History*, 32, p. 589

120. See Fildes (1988) *Wet Nursing: A History*, p. 158.

121. See M. Lindemann (1981) 'Love for Hire: The Regulation of the Wet-Nursing Business in Eighteenth-Century Hamburg', *Journal of Family History*, 6, p. 390 and Kertzer (1991) 'Gender, Ideology and Infant Abandonment', p. 21.

122. For more detailed discussions on the nature and prevalence of wet-nursing in the pre-modern era see Fildes (1988) *Wet Nursing: A History*; J. Golden (1996) *A Social History of Wet Nursing in America: From Breast to Bottle* (Cambridge: Cambridge University Press); V. Fildes (1986) *Breasts, Bottles and Babies: A History of Infant Feeding* (Edinburgh: Edinburgh University Press); G.D. Sussman (1982) *Selling Mothers' Milk: The Wet-Nursing Business in France 1715–1914* (Chicago and London: University of Illinois Press); and L. Rose (1986) *The Massacre of the*

Innocents: Infanticide in Britain 1800–1939 (London: Routledge and Kegan Paul), Chapters 9 and 10.

123. See, for instance, Marshall (1984) 'Wet-Nursing in Scotland', p. 48; Campbell (1989) 'Wet-Nurses in Early Modern England', p. 364; Fildes (1988) *Wet Nursing: A History*, p. 196; and Fildes (1988) 'The English Wet-Nurse', p. 153.
124. For further discussion see Kertzer (1999) 'Syphilis, Foundlings, and Wetnurses', p. 590.
125. Fildes (1988) *Wet Nursing: A History*, p. 158.
126. Lindemann (1981) 'Love for Hire', p. 382. For more on the care taken to employ private live-in nurses see Campbell (1989) 'Wet-Nurses in Early Modern England', p. 369.
127. For further discussion see Lindemann (1981) 'Love for Hire', pp. 382–83.
128. For further discussion see Kertzer (1999) 'Syphilis, Foundlings, and Wetnurses', p. 590.
129. For further discussion see Fildes (1988) *Wet Nursing: A History*, pp. 49–50; Lindemann (1981) 'Love for Hire', p. 384; and McLaren (1979) 'Nature's Contraceptive', p. 431. For the widespread and popular nature of wet-nursing across pre-modern Europe and North America see also Marshall (1984) 'Wet-Nursing in Scotland', pp. 47–8; Rosen (1976) 'A Slaughter of Innocents', p. 300; Fildes (1988) 'The English Wet-Nurse', p. 143; Perry (1991) 'Colonizing the Breast', p. 220; Newall (1990) 'Wet Nursing and Child Care', p. 134; Sussman (1982) *Selling Mothers' Milk*; Golden (1996) *A Social History of Wet Nursing in America*; Kertzer (1999) 'Syphilis, Foundlings, and Wetnurses', pp. 589–602; Wrightson (1982) 'Infanticide in European History', p. 12 and Ulbricht (1985) 'The Debate about Foundling Hospitals', pp. 217–219.
130. Fildes (1988) 'The English Wet-Nurse', p. 169. See also Fildes (1988) *Wet Nursing: A History*, p. 194.
131. See, for instance, Newall (1990) 'Wet Nursing and Child Care', p. 134; Perry (1991) 'Colonizing the Breast', p. 208; Ulbricht (1985) 'The Debate about Foundling Hospitals', pp. 301–2; and McLaren (1979) 'Nature's Contraceptive', p. 431.
132. See, for instance, Perry (1991) 'Colonizing the Breast', p. 218; Fildes (1988) *Wet Nursing: A History*, p. 194; and McLaren (1979) 'Nature's Contraceptive', p. 435.
133. See, for instance, Lindemann (1981) 'Love for Hire', p. 391.
134. For further discussion regarding the spread of disease via breastfeeding see Kertzer (1999) 'Syphilis, Foundlings, and Wetnurses', pp. 590–99; Rosen (1976) 'A Slaughter of Innocents', p. 301; and Fildes (1988) *Wet Nursing: A History*, pp. 71–2. For more on the believed transfer of physical and character traits via breastfeeding see Marshall (1984) 'Wet-Nursing in Scotland', p. 45; Lindemann (1981) 'Love for Hire', p. 381; and Perry (1991) 'Colonizing the Breast', p. 222.
135. For more on changing attitudes to the use of wet-nurses and the encouragement of maternal breast-feeding see Ladies National Association for the Diffusion of Sanitary Knowledge (LNADSK) (1855) *The Evils of Wet-Nursing: A Warning to Mothers* (London: Groombridge and Sons) [Bodleian Library, G. Pamph. 2541], pp. 6–7; Sussman (1982) *Selling Mothers' Milk*, p. 27; Lindemann (1981) 'Love for Hire', p. 381; Wrightson (1982) 'Infanticide in European History', p. 11; Fildes (1988) *Wet Nursing: A History*, p. 111; Newall (1990) 'Wet Nursing and Child Care', p. 125; and Perry (1991) 'Colonizing the Breast', pp. 216, 220 and 234.
136. See, for instance, Kertzer (1991) 'Gender, Ideology and Infant Abandonment', p. 21.

137. LNADSK (1855) *The Evils of Wet-Nursing*, pp. 3 and 13. See also Fildes (1990) 'Maternal Feelings Re-assessed', p. 162.
138. LNADSK (1855) The Evils of Wet-Nursing, p. 4.
139. An argument put forward particularly by Campbell (1989) 'Wet-Nurses in Early Modern England', pp. 360 and 365.
140. See, for instance, Levene (2007) *Childcare*, p. 94 and Fildes (1988) *Wet Nursing: A History*, p. 100.
141. Levene (2007) *Childcare*, p. 204. See also Sussman (1982) *Selling Mothers' Milk*, pp. 31–2; Marshall (1984) 'Wet-Nursing in Scotland', p. 50; and Fildes (1988) *Wet Nursing: A History*, pp. 94 and 96–7.
142. For further discussion see Fildes (1988) 'The English Wet-Nurse', p. 167.
143. See, for instance, M.L. Arnot (1994) 'Infant Death, Child Care and the State: The Baby-Farming Scandal and the First Infant Life Protection Legislation of 1872', *Continuity and Change*, 9, p. 271; R.E. Homrighaus (2001) 'Wolves in Women's Clothing: Baby-Farming and the *British Medical Journal*, 1860–1872', *Journal of Family History*, 26, p. 350; and Fildes (1990) 'Maternal Feelings Re-assessed', p. 163.
144. Wrightson (1982) 'Infanticide in European History', p. 12.
145. See, for instance, G.K. Behlmer (1982) *Child Abuse and Moral Reform in England, 1870–1908* (Stanford, CA: Stanford University Press), p. 36; Homrighaus (2001) 'Wolves in Women's Clothing', p. 357; and D. Bentley (2005) 'She-Butchers: Baby-Droppers, Baby-Sweaters, and Baby-Framers', in J. Rowbotham and K. Stevenson (eds.) *Criminal Conversations: Victorian Crimes, Social Panic and Moral Outrage* (Columbus: Ohio State University Press), pp. 201 and 206.
146. For further discussion see Bentley (2005) 'She-Butchers', pp. 200 and 212.
147. For further discussion see Arnot (1994) 'Infant Death', p. 281.
148. For further discussion see Sauer (1978) 'Infanticide and Abortion', p. 87 and Wrightson (1982) 'Infanticide in European History', p. 12.
149. See for instance *The Times*, 4 July 1870, No. 26793 and Benjamin Waugh (1890) *Baby-Farming* (London: Kegan Paul) [Bodleian Library, pHV 741 (42). 1. A2 N], p. 3.
150. See Homrighaus (2001) 'Wolves in Women's Clothing', p. 356. For more on the cash nexus associated with baby-farming and the fees that could be earned see Waugh (1890) *Baby-Farming*, p. 9 and Homrighaus (2001) 'Wolves in Women's Clothing', p. 351.
151. For further discussion of mid-Victorian concerns relating to child care, motherhood and the need for infant protection in England see especially Arnot (1994) 'Infant Death', pp. 271–311; Behlmer (1982) *Child Abuse*, Chapter 2;Two and Homrighaus (2001) 'Wolves in Women's Clothing', pp. 350–72.
152. For further discussion see Rose (1986) *The Massacre of the Innocents*, especially Chapters 9 and 11 and Bentley (2005) 'She-Butchers', p. 199.
153. For further discussion of these cases and the related moral panic see Arnot (1994) 'Infant Death', pp. 277–80; Bentley (2005) 'She-Butchers', pp. 198–214; Rose (1986) *The Massacre of the Innocents*, Chapter 11; and Homrighaus (2001) 'Wolves in Women's Clothing', pp. 350–72.
154. See, for instance, the *British Medical Journal*, 28 January 1861, 8 February 1868 and 27 May 1871 as well as Waugh (1890) *Baby-Farming*. For further discussion of these investigations see Behlmer (1982) *Child Abuse*, pp. 26–38; Arnot (1994) 'Infant Death', pp. 283–87; Homrighaus (2001) 'Wolves in Women's Clothing', p. 357; and Bentley (2005) 'She-Butchers', p. 201.

155. For further discussion of the bias shown against baby-famers and nursing practices in publications in the mid- to late-Victorian era in Britain and beyond, see Arnot (1994) 'Infant Death', pp. 271 and 283–85 and J. Kociumbas (2001) 'Azaria's Antecedents: Stereotyping Infanticide in Late Nineteenth-Century Australia', *Gender and History*, 13, pp. 138–60.
156. Waugh (1890) *Baby-Farming*, pp. 4–5.
157. Parliamentary Papers, 35 and 36 Vict c.38 (1872). For further discussion see Homrighaus (2001) 'Wolves in Women's Clothing', pp. 363–65; Bentley (2005) 'She-Butchers', pp. 206–7; and Behlmer (1982) *Child Abuse*, pp. 31–43.
158. Waugh (1890) *Baby-Farming*, p. 15.
159. For further discussion see Bentley (2005) 'She-Butchers', pp. 207–9.
160. For further discussion see Behlmer (1982) *Child Abuse*, pp. 33–6 and Arnot (1994) 'Infant Death', pp. 292–6 and 299–300.
161. Waugh (1890) *Baby-Farming*, p. 15.
162. See, for instance, Woodward (2007) 'Infanticide', p. 116 and Kelly (1992) 'Infanticide', p. 11. From a British Academy funded project into the nature and incidence of infanticide in Scotland between 1700 and 1820, the gender of the victim was only provided in 11 per cent of the cases discovered. Of these instances, 55 per cent related to male new-borns and 45 per cent to female.
163. For the various sides of this historiographical debate see Francus (1997) 'Monstrous Mothers', p. 134; A.R. Higginbotham (1989) '"Sin of the Age": Infanticide and Illegitimacy in Victorian London', *Victorian Studies*, 32, p. 336; and A.-M. Kilday (2008) '"Monsters of the Vilest Kind": Infanticidal Women and Attitudes towards their Criminality in Eighteenth-Century Scotland', *Family and Community History*, 11, pp. 101–5.
164. L. Gowing (1997) 'Secret Births and Infanticide in Seventeenth-Century England', *Past and Present*, p. 106.
165. For further elaboration see R.H. Helmholz (1987) 'Infanticide in the Province of Canterbury during the Fifteenth Century', in R.H. Helmholz (ed.) *Canon Law and the Law of England* (London: Hambledon), p. 160; Radbill (1968) 'A History of Child Abuse and Infanticide', p. 9; Wrightson (1982) 'Infanticide in European History', p. 15; Malcolmson (1977) 'Infanticide', p. 195; Kelly (1992) 'Infanticide', p. 6; and K. Wrightson (1975) 'Infanticide in Earlier Seventeenth-Century England', *Local Population Studies*, XV, p. 15.
166. For further discussion see Kelly (1992) 'Infanticide', p. 25.
167. See, for instance, J. Hurl-Eamon (2005) *Gender and Petty Violence in London, 1680–1720* (Columbus: Ohio State University Press) and A.-M. Kilday (2007) *Women and Violent Crime in Enlightenment Scotland* (Woodbridge: Boydell).
168. For similar findings of mixed methodologies relating to infanticide in the early modern period see Kamler (1988) 'Infanticide', p. 42.
169. For instance, no detail of this nature is provided in works such as T.R. Forbes (1986) 'Deadly Parents: Child Homicide in Eighteenth- and Nineteenth-Century England', *Journal of the History of Medicine*, XLI, pp. 178–83; Woodward (2007) 'Infanticide', p. 116; and Wrightson (1975) 'Infanticide in Earlier Seventeenth-Century England', p. 15.
170. *The Proceedings of the Old Bailey*, 17 January 1750 [t17500117-53]. [Accessed from www.oldbaileyonline.org].
171. For more evidence of deliberate suffocation as a methodology in pre-modern infanticide see Gowing (1997) 'Secret Births', p. 106; Harrington (2009) *The Unwanted Child*, p. 57; Ruggiero (2000) 'Not Guilty', pp. 158–9; Backhouse

(1984) 'Desperate Women', p. 464; T.R. Forbes (1985) *Surgeons at the Bailey: English Forensic Medicine to 1878* (New Haven and London: Yale University Press), p. 107; and K.H. Wheeler (1997) 'Infanticide in Nineteenth-Century Ohio', *Journal of Social History*, XXXI, p. 409.

172. For further discussion of a belief in the prevalence of more passive forms of infanticide across Europe and beyond in the pre-modern period see L. Abrams (2002) 'From Demon to Victim: The Infanticidal Mother in Shetland, 1699–1802', in Y.G. Brown and R. Ferguson (eds.) *Twisted Sisters: Women, Crime and Deviance in Scotland since 1400* (East Linton: Tuckwell), pp. 196–7; Harrington (2009) *The Unwanted Child*, pp. 57–8; Kelly (1992) 'Infanticide', p. 18; Ulbricht (1985) 'The Debate about Foundling Hospitals', p. 110; S. Faber (1990) 'Infanticide and Criminal Justice in the Netherlands, especially in Amsterdam', in International Commission of Historical Demography (ed.) *The Role of the State and Public Opinion in Sexual Attitudes and Demographic Behaviour* (CIDH: Madrid), p. 499; K. Ruggiero (1992) 'Honor, Maternity and the Disciplining of Women: Infanticide in Late Nineteenth-Century Buenos Aires', *The Hispanic American Historical Review*, 72, p. 360; Backhouse (1984) 'Desperate Women', p. 464; Smith (1979) *The People's Health*, p. 81; and Sauer (1978) 'Infanticide and Abortion', p. 81. An act of poisoning could be regarded as both an 'active' and a 'passive' form of infanticide and was similarly difficult to detect in this era, see K.D. Watson (2008) 'Religion, Community and the Infanticidal Mother: Evidence from 1840s Rural Wiltshire', *Family and Community History*, 11, p. 123 and Sauer (1978) 'Infanticide and Abortion', p. 82.

173. C. Smart (1976) *Women, Crime and Criminology: A Feminist Critique* (London and Boston: Routledge and Kegan Paul), p. 16. For further discussion of the stereotypes surrounding women's violence, particularly in the Scottish context, see Kilday (2007) *Women and Violent Crime*, especially Chapters 3–7 and the Conclusion and in relation to the committal of infanticide more specifically see Kilday (2008) '"Monsters of the Vilest Kind"', pp. 102–3 and A.-M. Kilday (2002) 'Maternal Monsters: Murdering Mothers in South-West Scotland, 1750–1815', in Y.G. Brown and R. Ferguson (eds.) *Twisted Sisters: Women, Crime and Deviance in Scotland since 1400* (East Linton: Tuckwell), pp. 168–70.

174. For more evidence of drowning and burning as a methodology in pre-modern infanticide see Wrightson (1975) 'Infanticide in Earlier Seventeenth-Century England', p. 15; Kelly (1992) 'Infanticide', p. 18; Woodward (2007) 'Infanticide', p. 116; Forbes (1986) 'Deadly Parents', pp. 178–83; Ruggiero (2000) 'Not Guilty, p. 159; Wheeler (1997) 'Infanticide in Nineteenth-Century Ohio', p. 409; and Smith (1979) *The People's Health*, p. 79. For evidence of battery and blood-shed in instances of infanticide since 1600 see Wrightson (1975) 'Infanticide in Earlier Seventeenth-Century England', p. 15; Kilday (2002) 'Maternal Monsters', p. 169; Woodward (2007) 'Infanticide', p. 116; Kelly (1992) 'Infanticide', p. 18; Wheeler (1997) 'Infanticide in Nineteenth-Century Ohio', p. 409; and Ruggiero (2000) 'Not Guilty', p. 158.

175. For more on the weapons associated with violent methodologies of new-born child murder in the pre-modern era see the references in note 172 above.

176. See respectively National Records of Scotland [Edinburgh] (hereafter NRS), High Court of Justiciary, Books of Adjournal, JC3/1 and JC3/26, as well as Justiciary Court North Circuit Records, JC11/24 and JC11/59.

177. See respectively *The Proceedings of the Old Bailey*, 4 December 1719 [t17191204-7], 16 February 1737 [t17370216-21], 18 May 1774 [t17740518-23] and 12 April 1809 [t18090412-33].

178. See respectively National Library of Wales (hereafter NLW), Records of the Court of Great Sessions, 4/817/4, 4/195/3, 4/754/1 and 4/395/2.
179. For further discussion see Lonza (2002) '"Two Souls Lost"', pp. 88–9 and Harrington (2009) *The Unwanted Child*, p. 57.
180. In Scotland the proportion of women doing this from all known cases was 34 per cent. In Wales, the figure was 16 per cent and in relation to the English data the figure was 28 per cent.
181. NRS, High Court of Justiciary, Books of Adjournal, JC3/31.
182. NLW, Records of Court of Great Sessions, 4/533/6.
183. For further tentative discussion of the reasons for extreme violence in certain instances of new-born child murder see Kilday (2007) *Women and Violent Crime*, pp. 77–8; R. Roth (2001) 'Child Murder in New England', *Social Science History*, XXV, p. 123; and Lonza (2002) '"Two Souls Lost"', pp. 88–90. More detailed discussion of the motives associated with this crime in the pre-modern period will be dealt with in Chapter 5 of this volume.
184. NRS, High Court of Justiciary, Books of Adjournal, JC3/31.
185. See *The Caledonian Mercury*, 16 January 1759 and 18 January 1759 [National Library of Scotland, Mf. N. 776] and *The Scots Magazine*, March 1759: Vol. XXI [Central Library, Edinburgh AP4 S42.].
186. National Library of Scotland [Edinburgh], *The Last Speech, Confession and Dying Words of Ann Morrison* [APS.4.201.06].
187. See, for instance, P.J. Martin (1826) 'Observations on Some of the Accidents of Infanticide', *Edinburgh Medical and Surgical Journal*, 26, p. 37 and Sauer (1978) 'Infanticide and Abortion', p. 81. For further discussion of the use of medical testimony in early modern English infanticide trials see S. Sommers (2009) 'Remapping Maternity in the Courtroom: Female Defenses and Medical Witnesses in Eighteenth-Century Infanticide Proceedings', in E. Klaver (ed.) *The Body in Medical Culture* (Albany: State University of New York Press), pp. 37–59.
188. See, for instance, Rosen (1976) 'A Slaughter of Innocents', pp. 296–98; Rose (1986) *The Massacre of the Innocents*, p. 8; J. Vallin (1991) 'Mortality in Europe from 1720 to 1914: Long-Term Trends and Changes in Patterns by Age and Sex', in R. Schofield, D. Reher and A. Bideau (eds.) *The Decline of Mortality in Europe* (Oxford: Clarendon), p. 49; J. Kok, F. Van Poppel and E. Kruse (1997) 'Mortality among Illegitimate Children in Mid-Nineteenth Century The Hague', in C.A. Corsini and P.P. Viazzo (eds.) *The Decline of Infant and Child Mortality: The European Experience – 1750–1990* (The Hague: Kluwer) pp. 193 and 200; and M.N. Wessling (1994) 'Infanticide Trials and Forensic Medicine: Württembergs 1757–93', in M. Clark and C. Crawford (eds.) *Legal Medicine in History* (Cambridge: Cambridge University Press), p. 132.
189. Higginbotham (1989) '"Sin of the Age"', p. 324.
190. For further discussion see R. Millward and F. Bell (2001) 'Infant Mortality in Victorian Britain: The Mother as Medium', *Economic History Review*, LIV, pp. 706–7; Vallin (1991) 'Mortality in Europe', p. 51; and M. Flinn (1977) (ed.) *Scottish Population History from the Seventeenth Century to the 1930s* (Cambridge: Cambridge University Press), pp. 378–9 and 385.
191. Rose (1986) *The Massacre of the Innocents*, p. 7. For further discussion of the causes of infant mortality in the pre-modern period see Millward and Bell (2001) 'Infant Mortality in Victorian Britain', pp. 706–8 and 710–11; M.-F. Morel (1991) 'The Care of Children: The Influence of Medical Innovation and Medical Institutions on Infant Mortality 1750–1914', in R. Schofield, D. Reher

and A. Bideau (eds.) *The Decline of Mortality in Europe* (Oxford: Clarendon), p. 197; Flinn (1977) (ed.) *Scottish Population History*, pp. 404–5; and R. Woods, N. Williams and C. Galley (1997) 'Differential Mortality Patterns amongst Infants and Other Young Children: The Experience of England and Wales in the Nineteenth Century', in C.A. Corsini and P.P. Viazzo (eds.) *The Decline of Infant and Child Mortality: The European Experience – 1750–1990* (The Hague: Kluwer), p. 67.

192. For further discussion see K.D. Watson (2011) *Forensic Medicine in Western Society – A History* (Abingdon: Routledge), p. 23; M. Jackson (1995) 'Developing Medical Expertise: Medical Practitioners and the Suspected Murders of New-Born Children', in R. Porter (ed.) *Medicine in the Enlightenment* (Amsterdam: Rodopi), p. 145; and Coroners' Inquests, M. Jackson (1994) 'Suspicious Infant Deaths: The Statute of 1624 and Medical Evidence', in M. Clark and C. Crawford (eds.) *Legal Medicine in History* (Cambridge: Cambridge University Press), pp. 64–5.

193. For further discussion of the importance of inquests see Watson (2011) *Forensic Medicine*, pp. 39–40 and 58; M. Jackson (1996) *New-Born Child Murder: Women, Illegitimacy and the Courts in Eighteenth-Century England* (Manchester: Manchester University Press), pp. 88–90; and S. Sommers (2002) 'Bodies, Knowledge and Authority in Eighteenth-Century Infanticide Prosecutions' (Unpublished Master of Arts Dissertation, University of Victoria), pp. 81–2.

194. See, for instance, Wessling (1994) 'Infanticide Trials', p. 127; Higginbotham (1989) '"Sin of the Age"', pp. 323–4; M. Jackson (1996) '"Something more than Blood": Conflicting Accounts of Pregnancy Loss in Eighteenth-Century England', in R. Cecil (ed.) *The Anthropology of Pregnancy Loss: Comparative Studies in Miscarriage, Stillbirth and Neonatal Death* (Oxford: Berg), p. 209; and Lonza (2002) '"Two Souls Lost"', p. 87.

195. Ruggiero (2000) 'Not Guilty', p. 158.

196. W. Hunter (1783) 'On the Uncertainty of the Signs of Murder in the Case of Bastard Children', A Paper Read to the Members of the Medical Society, pp. 13–14. The essay was published a year later in *Medical Observations and Inquiries*, 6, pp. 266–90 [University of Glasgow, Sp Coll Hunterian Add. 279].

197. C. Johnson (1814) 'An Essay on the Signs of Murder in New-Born Children', *Edinburgh Medical and Surgical Journal*, 10, p. 394.

198. Jackson (1995) 'Developing Medical Expertise', p. 151.

199. *The Proceedings of the Old Bailey*, 2 April 1800 [t18000402-36].

200. For further discussion see B.R. Sharma (2006) 'Historical and Medico-Legal Aspects of Infanticide: An Overview', *Medicine, Science and the Law*, 46, pp. 155–6 and R.W. Byard (2004) *Sudden Death in Infancy, Childhood and Adolescence* (Cambridge: Cambridge University Press), p. 135.

201. See, for instance, Watson (2011) *Forensic Medicine*, p. 44; Sommers (2002) 'Bodies, Knowledge and Authority', p. 86; and Wessling (1994) 'Infanticide Trials', p. 125.

202. Jackson (1996) '"Something more than Blood"', p. 209.

203. See Jackson (1996) *New-Born Child Murder*, p. 84 and Sommers (2002) 'Bodies, Knowledge and Authority', pp. 101–2.

204. Watson (2011) *Forensic Medicine*, pp. 30–1. See also Harrington (2009) *The Unwanted Child*, p. 64.

205. For further discussion see Ruggiero (2000) 'Not Guilty', p. 158 and O. Ulbricht (1988) 'Infanticide in Eighteenth-Century Germany', in R.J. Evans (ed.) *The German Underworld: Deviants and Outcasts in German History* (London: Routledge), p. 121.

206. *The Proceedings of the Old Bailey*, 8 December 1762 [t17621208-26].
207. For further discussion of these defences and the reasons they were employed see Malcolmson (1977) 'Infanticide', pp. 198–200 and Kilday (2002) 'Maternal Monsters', pp. 159–60.
208. R. Woods (2009) *Death before Birth: Fetal Health and Mortality in Historical Perspective* (Oxford: Oxford University Press), p. 57.
209. My calculations are based on the evidence presented in Woods (2009) *Death Before Birth*, p. 92, although it should be remembered that this data largely relates to neonate mortality within institutions. The likelihood of still-births being perceived to be higher than they were in reality in the pre-modern era is a point also made by Malcolmson (1977) 'Infanticide', pp. 198–9.
210. For further discussion see Jackson (1996) *New-Born Child Murder*, p. 93 and Jackson (1994) 'Suspicious Infant Deaths', p. 75.
211. *The Proceedings of the Old Bailey*, 27 February 1718 [t17180227-25]. For further discussion of this test see the references in note 210 above as well as Sommers (2002) 'Bodies, Knowledge and Authority', pp. 102–3.
212. For further discussion see R.P. Brittain (1963) 'The Hydrostatic and Similar Tests of Live Birth: A Historical Review', *Medico-Legal Journal*, 31, pp. 189–90; Jackson (1994) 'Suspicious Infant Deaths', p. 78; Jackson (1996) *New-Born Child Murder*, pp. 93–4; and Radbill (1968) 'A History of Child Abuse and Infanticide', p. 15.
213. Jackson (1996) '"Something more than Blood"', pp. 27–8. See also Jackson (1996) *New-Born Child Murder*, p. 93; Malcolmson (1977) 'Infanticide', p. 200; Kilday (2002) 'Maternal Monsters', p. 160; and Watson (2011) *Forensic Medicine*, p. 107.
214. Rose (1986) *The Massacre of the Innocents*, p. 72.
215. For further discussion see Hunter (1783) 'On the Uncertainty of the Signs of Murder', pp. 16–19; Jackson (1996) *New-Born Child Murder*, pp. 94–5 and 99; Jackson (1994) 'Suspicious Infant Deaths', pp. 75–81; Brittain (1963) 'The Hydrostatic and Similar Tests of Live Birth', pp. 190–2; Forbes (1985) *Surgeons at the Bailey*, p. 103; Kilday (2002) 'Maternal Monsters', p. 160; Wessling (1994) 'Infanticide Trials', p. 134; Malcolmson (1977) 'Infanticide', p. 200; and Sommers (2002) 'Bodies, Knowledge and Authority', p. 107.
216. The *Gentleman's Magazine*, October 1774, p. 463.
217. *The Proceedings of the Old Bailey*, 3 July 1782 [t17820703-47] and 18 September 1802 [t18020918-134].
218. For further discussion see Watson (2011) *Forensic Medicine*, p. 107; Forbes (1985) *Surgeons at the Bailey*, pp. 105–6; Sharma (2006) 'Historical and Medico-Legal Aspects of Infanticide', pp. 154–5; and Higginbotham (1989) '"Sin of the Age"', p. 330.
219. See Byard (2004) *Sudden Death*, pp. 128–9.
220. See, for instance, Jackson (1994) 'Suspicious Infant Deaths', p. 78 and Baron D. Hume (1797) *Commentaries on the Law of Scotland, Respecting the Description and Punishment of Crimes* (Edinburgh: Bell and Bradfute), Volume I, Chapter VI, pp. 274–5 [National Library of Scotland, BCL.B1220-1221].
221. For further discussion see G.K. Behlmer (1979) 'Deadly Motherhood: Infanticide and Medical Opinion in Mid-Victorian England', *Journal of the History of Medicine and Allied Sciences*, XXXIV, p. 411 and Jackson (1996) *New-Born Child Murder*, pp. 96–7.
222. See, for instance, Jackson (1996) '"Something more than Blood"', pp. 202–5 and Sommers (2002) 'Bodies, Knowledge and Authority', pp. 91–3.

223. For further discussion see Jackson (1996) *New-Born Child Murder*, p. 91; Watson (2011) *Forensic Medicine*, p. 107; Sommers (2002) 'Bodies, Knowledge and Authority', p. 103; Jackson (1996) '"Something more than Blood"', pp. 206–7; and Jackson (1995) 'Developing Medical Expertise', p. 152.

224. See, for instance, Higginbotham (1989) '"Sin of the Age"', p. 329; Ruggiero (2000) 'Not Guilty', p. 153; Malcolmson (1977) 'Infanticide', pp. 199–200; and Sharma (2006) 'Historical and Medico-Legal Aspects of Infanticide', p. 156.

225. See Martin (1826) 'Observations', p. 35.

226. *The Proceedings of the Old Bailey*, 29 April 1767 [t17670429-52].

227. For further discussion see Sommers (2002) 'Bodies, Knowledge and Authority', p. 106; Behlmer (1979) 'Deadly Motherhood', p. 412; Ruggiero (1992) 'Honor, Maternity and the Disciplining of Women', pp. 360 and 363; and especially Jackson (1996) *New-Born Child Murder*, p. 102.

228. See, for instance, Watson (2011) *Forensic Medicine*, p. 107; Jackson (1996) *New-Born Child Murder*, p. 92; Jackson (1994) 'Suspicious Infant Deaths', p. 69; and Jackson (1995) 'Developing Medical Expertise', p. 153.

229. Wessling (1994) 'Infanticide Trials', p. 132.

230. *The Proceedings of the Old Bailey*, 15 January 1800 [t18000115-20].

231. For further discussion see ibid., pp. 129 and 132; Ruggiero (1992) 'Honor, Maternity and the Disciplining of Women', p. 369; Ruggiero (2000) 'Not Guilty', pp. 158–9; Sommers (2002) 'Bodies, Knowledge and Authority', p. 94; Behlmer (1979) 'Deadly Motherhood', p. 411; and Forbes (1985) *Surgeons at the Bailey*, pp. 101–2.

5   The pendulum of opinion: Changing attitudes to infanticide

1. *Reynolds' Newspaper*, 6 August 1865, No. 782.

2. *The Era*, 29 March 1863, No. 1279.

3. M. Jackson (1996) *New-Born Child Murder: Women, Illegitimacy and the Courts in Eighteenth-Century England* (Manchester: Manchester University Press), p. 158.

4. For further discussion see ibid., pp. 158–60.

5. For further discussion see ibid., p. 161; D. Seaborne Davies (1937) 'Child Killing in English Law', *Modern Law Review*, 1, p. 203; and M. Jackson (1994) 'Suspicious Infant Deaths: The Statute of 1624 and Medical Evidence at Coroners' Inquests', in M. Clark and C. Crawford (eds.) *Legal Medicine in History* (Cambridge: Cambridge University Press), p. 66.

6. For further discussion see ibid., p. 163.

7. For further discussion see Seaborne Davies (1937) 'Child Killing in English Law', pp. 206–7.

8. See Jackson (1996) *New-Born Child Murder*, p. 158.

9. For further discussion see ibid., pp. 164–8.

10. For further discussion see ibid., p. 162.

11. For further discussion see ibid., pp. 167–8.

12. For further discussion see G.K. Behlmer (1979) 'Deadly Motherhood: Infanticide and Medical Opinion in Mid-Victorian England', *Journal of the History of Medicine and Allied Sciences*, XXXIV, p. 412 and D. Cooper Graves (2006) '"...In a Frenzy While Raving Mad": Physicians and Parliamentarians Define Infanticide in Victorian England', in B.H. Bechtold and D. Cooper Graves (eds.) *Killing Infants: Studies in the Worldwide Practice of Infanticide* (Lewiston, NY: Edwin Mellen), p. 117.

13. For further discussion see Jackson (1996) *New-Born Child Murder*, pp. 168–72; C.B. Backhouse (1984) 'Desperate Women and Compassionate Courts: Infanticide in Nineteenth-Century Canada', *The University of Toronto Law Journal*, 34, p. 453; W.B. Ober (1986) 'Infanticide in Eighteenth-Century England: William Hunter's Contribution to the Forensic Problem', *Pathology Annual*, 21, p. 317; Seaborne Davies (1937) 'Child Killing in English Law', p. 214; and Jackson (1994) 'Suspicious Infant Deaths', pp. 72 and 81.
14. See Jackson (1996) *New-Born Child Murder*, pp. 169–70.
15. Parliamentary Papers, 43 Geo. III c. 58 (1803).
16. Ibid.
17. For further discussion see Seaborne Davies (1937) 'Child Killing in English Law', p. 214; Ober (1986) 'Infanticide in Eighteenth-Century England', p. 317; R.W. Ireland (1997) '"Perhaps my Mother Murdered Me": Child Death and the Law in Victorian Carmarthenshire', in C. Brooks and M. Lobban (eds.) *Communities and Courts in Britain 1150–1900* (London and Rio Grande, OH: Hambledon), p. 230; R. Smith (1981) *Trial by Medicine: Insanity and Responsibility in Victorian Trials* (Edinburgh: Edinburgh University Press), p. 145; Behlmer (1979) 'Deadly Motherhood', p. 412; and C. Damme (1978) 'Infanticide: The Worth of an Infant Under Law', *Medical History*, XXII, p. 13.
18. For further discussion see L. Rose (1986) *The Massacre of the Innocents: Infanticide in Britain 1800–1939* (London: Routledge and Kegan Paul), p. 70; Smith (1981) *Trial by Medicine*, p. 145; Cooper Graves (2006) '"...In a Frenzy"', p. 123; and Jackson (1994) 'Suspicious Infant Deaths', p. 82.
19. For further discussion see S. Edwards (1984) *Women on Trial: A Study of the Female Suspect, Defendant and Offender in the Criminal Law and Criminal Justice System* (Manchester: Manchester University Press), p. 92; Seaborne Davies (1937) 'Child Killing in English Law', p. 214; Smith (1981) *Trial by Medicine*, p. 145; and Behlmer (1979) 'Deadly Motherhood', p. 412.
20. Ibid.
21. For further discussion see Ober (1986) 'Infanticide in Eighteenth-Century England', p. 317; Ireland (1997) '"Perhaps my Mother Murdered Me"', p. 236; Backhouse (1984) 'Desperate Women', p. 453; Smith (1981) *Trial by Medicine*, p. 145; Cooper Graves (2006) '"...In a Frenzy"', p. 117; Damme (1978) 'Infanticide', p. 13; Seaborne Davies (1937) 'Child Killing in English Law', p. 214; and Behlmer (1979) 'Deadly Motherhood', p. 412.
22. Seaborne Davies (1937) 'Child Killing in English Law', p. 231.
23. For further discussion see Ireland (1997) '"Perhaps my Mother Murdered Me"', p. 236; Backhouse (1984) 'Desperate Women', p. 453; Smith (1981) *Trial by Medicine*, p. 145; and Damme (1978) 'Infanticide', p. 13.
24. For further discussion see Jackson (1996) *New-Born Child Murder*, pp. 172–3.
25. For further discussion see ibid., pp. 173–6.
26. Parliamentary Papers, 49 Geo. III, c. 14 (1809).
27. John Dove Wilson (1877) 'Can Any Better Measures Be Devised for the Prevention and Punishment of Infanticide?', *Transactions of the National Association for the Promotion of Social Science*, p. 291.
28. For further discussion see L. Abrams (2002) 'From Demon to Victim: The Infanticidal Mother in Shetland, 1699–1802', in Y.G. Brown and R. Ferguson (eds.) *Twisted Sisters: Women, Crime and Deviance in Scotland since 1400* (East Linton: Tuckwell), p. 180.
29. Parliamentary Papers, 9 Geo. IV, c. 31 (1828).

30. For further discussion see especially Seaborne Davies (1937) 'Child Killing in English Law', pp. 214–5 and Smith (1981) *Trial by Medicine*, p. 145; Ireland (1997) '"Perhaps my Mother Murdered Me"', p. 236; and N. Woodward (2007) 'Infanticide in Wales, 1730–1830', *Welsh Historical Review*, 23, p. 97, n. 16.

31. For further discussion see Rose (1986) *The Massacre of the Innocents*, p. 70; Seaborne Davies (1937) 'Child Killing in English Law', pp. 214–5; Damme (1978) 'Infanticide', p. 13.

32. For further discussion see Seaborne Davies (1937) 'Child Killing in English Law', p. 214; Damme (1978) 'Infanticide', p. 13; Behlmer (1979) 'Deadly Motherhood', p. 412; and Woodward (2007) 'Infanticide', p. 97, n. 16.

33. Parliamentary Papers, 24 and 25 Vict., c. 100 (1861).

34. For further discussion see Woodward (2007) 'Infanticide', p. 97 n. 16.

35. For further discussion see Seaborne Davies (1937) 'Child Killing in English Law', p. 216 and Smith (1981) *Trial by Medicine*, p. 145.

36. For further discussion see T. Ward (2002) 'Legislating for Human Nature: Legal Responses to Infanticide, 1860–1938', in M. Jackson (ed.) *Infanticide: Historical Perspectives on Child Murder and Concealment, 1550–2000* (Aldershot: Ashgate), p. 253; A.R. Higginbotham (1989) '"Sin of the Age": Infanticide and Illegitimacy in Victorian London', *Victorian Studies*, 32, pp. 319–21; Rose (1986) *The Massacre of the Innocents*, pp. 36–43; C.S. Monholland (1989) 'Infanticide in Victorian England, 1856–1878: Thirty Legal Cases' (Unpublished Master of Arts Dissertation, Rice University), pp. 8 and 21; M.L. Arnot (2000) 'Understanding Women Committing Newborn Child Murder in Victorian England', in S. D'Cruze (ed.) *Everyday Violence in Britain, 1850–1950* (Harlow: Pearson), p. 56; R. Sauer (1978) 'Infanticide and Abortion in Nineteenth-Century Britain', *Population Studies: A Journal of Demography*, XXXII, pp. 81, 85 and 90; F.B. Smith (1979) *The People's Health 1830–1910* (London: Croom Helm), p. 80; Cooper Graves (2006) '"...In a Frenzy While Raving Mad"', pp. 111–12; and A. Hunt (2006) 'Calculations and Concealments: Infanticide in Mid-Nineteenth-Century Britain', *Victorian Literature and Culture*, 34, p. 74. For evidence that a similar moral panic existed in other countries and cultures at that time, see S. Barringer Gordon (2002) 'Law and Everyday Death: Infanticide and the Backlash against Women's Rights after the Civil War', in A. Sarat, L. Douglas and M.M. Umphrey (eds.) *Lives in the Law* (Ann Arbor: University of Michigan Press), pp. 55 and 64–6; S. Swain (2006) 'Infanticide, Savagery and Civilization: The Australian Experience', in B.H. Bechtold and D. Cooper Graves (eds.) *Killing Infants: Studies in the Worldwide Practice of Infanticide* (New York: Edwin Mellen), p. 93; J. Kociumbas (2001) 'Azaria's Antecedents: Stereotyping Infanticide in Late Nineteenth-Century Australia', *Gender and History*, 13, p. 151; I.C. Pilarczyk (2012) '"So Foul A Deed": Infanticide in Montreal, 1825–1850', *Law and History Review*, 30, p. 633; K. Ruggiero (1992) 'Honor, Maternity and the Disciplining of Women: Infanticide in Late Nineteenth-Century Buenos Aires', *The Hispanic American Historical Review*, 72, p. 365; J. Dalby (1995) 'Women and Infanticide in Nineteenth-Century Rural France', in V. Shepherd, B. Brereton and B. Bailey (eds.) *Engendering History: Caribbean Women in Historical Perspective* (London and Kingston, Jamaica: James Currey and Ian Randle), pp. 343–4; and H. Altink (2007) '"I Did Not Want to Face the Shame of Exposure": Gender Ideologies and Child Murder in Post-Emancipation Jamaica', *Journal of Social History, Society and Cultures*, 41, p. 361.

37. *The Era*, 17 May 1857, No. 973.

38. *The Morning Post*, 18 September 1863, No. 28004.

39. *British Medical Journal*, 30 March 1867. See also *The Lancet*, 17 January 1863 and *British Medical Journal*, 28 April 1866.
40. *British Medical Journal*, 20 September 1862.
41. W. Burke Ryan (1862) *Infanticide: Its Law, Prevalence, Prevention, and History* (London) [Bodleian Library, (OC) 151 c/345], pp. 45–6.
42. See Behlmer (1979) 'Deadly Motherhood', pp. 404–5.
43. *Hansard Parliamentary Debates* (Third Series), 76, 5 July 1844, pp. 430–1.
44. See also M.L. Arnot (1994) 'Infant Death, Child Care and the State: The Baby-Farming Scandal and the First Infant Life Protection Legislation of 1872', *Continuity and Change*, 9, p. 272.
45. For further discussion see Burke Ryan (1862) *Infanticide*, p. 1; Hunt (2006) 'Calculations and Concealments', p. 75; Monholland (1989) 'Infanticide in Victorian England', p. 25; and J. Ermers (1990) 'Medeas or Fallen Angels? The Prosecution of Infanticide and Stereotypes of "Child Murderesses" in the Netherlands in the Nineteenth Century', in International Commission of Historical Demography (ed.) *The Role of the State and Public opinion in Sexual Attitudes and Demographic Behaviour* (CIDH: Madrid), p. 489.
46. For further discussion see Hunt (2006) 'Calculations and Concealments', pp. 78–9; Kociumbas (2001) 'Azaria's Antecedents', p. 140; and Arnot (1994) 'Infant Death', p. 283.
47. For further discussion see, for instance, the 'Address on Infanticide and Excessive Infant Mortality' presented by W. Tyler Smith and reproduced in the *British Medical Journal*, 12 January 1867; *Hansard Parliamentary Debates* (Third Series), 76, 5 July 1844, pp. 430–1; Rose (1986) *The Massacre of the Innocents*, pp. 26 and 46; Arnot (2000) 'Understanding Women Committing Newborn Child Murder', p. 57; Sauer (1978) 'Infanticide and Abortion', p. 89, Hunt (2006) 'Calculations and Concealments', p. 76; and Behlmer (1979) 'Deadly Motherhood', p. 418.
48. For discussion of this contention see S. Sen (2002) 'The Savage Family: Colonialism and Female Infanticide in Nineteenth-Century India', *Journal of Women's History*, 14, pp. 53–79; Ward (2002) 'Legislating for Human Nature', p. 253; and E.deG.R. Hansen (1979) '"Overlaying" in Nineteenth-Century England: Infant Mortality or Infanticide?', *Human Ecology*, 7, p. 347.
49. For further discussion see Ober (1986) 'Infanticide in Eighteenth-Century England', pp. 317–8; Behlmer (1979) 'Deadly Motherhood', pp. 407–10 and 423–6; Higginbotham (1989) '"Sin of the Age"', p. 324; Ward (2002) 'Legislating for Human Nature', pp. 253–4; and J. McShane Galley (1998) '"I Did it to Hide My Shame": Community Responses to Suspicious Infant Deaths in Middlesex County, Ontario, 1850–1900' (Unpublished Master of Arts Dissertation, University of Western Ontario), *passim*.
50. For evidence of similar trends elsewhere at this time see Backhouse (1984) 'Desperate Women', pp. 456 and 468; Pilarczyk (2012) '"So Foul A Deed"', p. 575; Swain (2006) 'Infanticide, Savagery and Civilization', p. 94; Altink (2007) '"I Did Not Want to Face the Shame of Exposure"', p. 355; Dalby (1995) 'Women and Infanticide in Nineteenth-Century Rural France', p. 344; Ermers (1990) 'Medeas or Fallen Angels?', pp. 484–6; and S. Wilson (1988) 'Child Abandonment and Female Honour in Nineteenth-Century Corsica', *Comparative Studies in Society and History*, 30, p. 764.
51. All of the data in this chapter was collated from the judicial statistics found in the House of Commons Parliamentary Papers (1800–1899) and accessed at http://parlipapers.chadwyck.co.uk/home.do. It should be noted that in all the

statistical information presented in relation to nineteenth-century England and Wales in this chapter, linear extrapolation was used to establish missing data for 1819 and 1852. For Scotland, there was a gap in the available data between 1819 and 1852. For further discussion of the methodological issues related to nineteenth-century criminal statistics see J. Wallis (2012) 'Lies, Damned Lies and Statistics? Nineteenth-Century Crime Statistics for England and Wales as a Historical Source', *History Compass*, 10, pp. 574–83 and V.A.C. Gatrell and T.B. Hadden (1972) 'Criminal Statistics and their Interpretation', in E.A. Wrigley (ed.) *Nineteenth-Century Society: Essays in the Use of Quantitative Methods for the Study of Social Data* (Cambridge: Cambridge University Press), pp. 336–96.

52. See, for instance, Behlmer (1979) 'Deadly Motherhood', pp. 422 and 427; I. Brockington (1996, 2003 edition) *Motherhood and Mental Health* (Oxford: Oxford University Press), p. 433; Roth (2001) 'Child Murder in New England', pp. 119–20; B.H. Bechtold (1999) 'Infanticide in Nineteenth-Century France: A Quantitative Interpretation', *Review of Radical Political Economics*, 33, p. 167; J.M. Donovan (1991) 'Infanticide and the Juries in France, 1825–1913', *Journal of Family History*, 16, p. 159; and J.S. Richter (1998) 'Child Abandonment and Abortion in Imperial Germany', *Journal of Interdisciplinary History*, 28, p. 549.

53. See Smith (1979) *The People's Health*, p. 118.

54. For further discussion regarding the implications of this for any statistical analysis of Victorian infanticide, see Monholland (1989) 'Infanticide in Victorian England', p. 19 and N. Darby (2008) 'Suffer the Little Ones: Infanticide – Social History', *Ancestors*, 75, p. 52.

55. Ermers (1990) 'Medeas or Fallen Angels?', p. 485. See also K.H. Wheeler (1997) 'Infanticide in Nineteenth-Century Ohio', *Journal of Social History*, XXXI, p. 407; Bechtold (1999) 'Infanticide in Nineteenth-Century France', p. 172; M. Oberman (2002) 'Understanding Infanticide in Context: Mothers Who Kill, 1870–1930 and Today', *The Journal of Criminal Law and Criminology*, 92, p. 716; Pilarczyk (2012) '"So Foul A Deed"', p. 590; Leboutte (1991) 'Offense against Family Order', p. 164; Ruggiero (1992) 'Honor, Maternity and the Disciplining of Women', p. 355; Donovan (1991) 'Infanticide and the Juries in France', p. 159; and Ireland (1997) '"Perhaps my Mother Murdered Me"', p. 232.

56. Wheeler (1997) 'Infanticide in Nineteenth-Century Ohio', p. 407 (my addition in parenthesis). See also Sauer (1978) 'Infanticide and Abortion', pp. 81 and 86; Smith (1979) *The People's Health*, p. 67; Ireland (1997) '"Perhaps my Mother Murdered Me"', p. 233; Donovan (1991) 'Infanticide and the Juries in France', p. 159; and K. Clarke (1980) 'Infanticide, Illegitimacy and the Medical Profession in Nineteenth-Century England', *Society for the Social History of Medicine Bulletin*, 6, pp. 11–14.

57. For further discussion see respectively Roth (2001) 'Child Murder in New England', p. 120 and Wheeler (1997) 'Infanticide in Nineteenth-Century Ohio', p. 412 as well as Brockington (1996, 2003 edition) *Motherhood and Mental Health*, p. 434.

58. *Nottinghamshire Guardian*, 23 October 1863, No. 927.

59. *Western Mail*, 18 January 1875, No. 1784.

60. *The York Herald*, 16 October 1877, No. 6454.

61. *The Dundee Courier and Argus*, 27 May 1890, No. 11509.

62. These trends are mirrored in other findings which relate to infanticide and its allied offences in the nineteenth century. See, for instance, M.L. Arnot (2002) 'The Murder of Thomas Sandles: Meanings of a Mid-Nineteenth-Century

Infanticide', in M. Jackson (ed.) *Infanticide: Historical Perspectives on Child Murder and Concealment, 1550–2000* (Aldershot: Ashgate), p. 149; Sauer (1978) 'Infanticide and Abortion', p. 86; Behlmer (1979) 'Deadly Motherhood', p. 412; Oberman (2002) 'Understanding Infanticide in Context', p. 726; Smith (1981) *Trial by Medicine*, p. 147; Richter (1998) 'Child Abandonment and Abortion', p. 513; Dalby (1995) 'Women and Infanticide in Nineteenth-Century Rural France', p. 346; Swain (2006) 'Infanticide, Savagery and Civilization', p. 95; Pilarczyk (2012) '"So Foul A Deed"', pp. 575, 584 n. 41 and 611; Backhouse (1984) 'Desperate Women', pp. 461–2; Donovan (1991) 'Infanticide and the Juries in France', p. 158; T. Ward (1999) 'The Sad Subject of Infanticide: Law, Medicine and Child Murder', *Social and Legal Studies*, VIII, p. 164; Ward (2002) 'Legislating for Human Nature', p. 255; Higginbotham (1989) '"Sin of the Age"', pp. 329 and 331; Smith (1979) *The People's Health*, p. 79; Rose (1986) *The Massacre of the Innocents*, p. 71; and Wheeler (1997) 'Infanticide in Nineteenth-Century Ohio', p. 407.

63. A. Payne (1995) 'Infanticide and Child Abuse', *The Journal of Forensic Psychiatry*, 6, p. 472. See also Backhouse (1984) 'Desperate Women', p. 448.

64. For further discussion see Behlmer (1979) 'Deadly Motherhood', p. 413; Monholland (1989) 'Infanticide in Victorian England', p. 212; Smith (1981) *Trial by Medicine*, p. 147; Arnot (2002) 'The Murder of Thomas Sandles', pp. 160 and 163; Arnot (1994) 'Infant Death', p. 291; Higginbotham (1989) '"Sin of the Age"', p. 323; and Rose (1986) *The Massacre of the Innocents*, p. 73. For similar mitigation attempts elsewhere in the Victorian era see Donovan (1991) 'Infanticide and the Juries in France', pp. 166–8; Ermers (1990) 'Medeas or Fallen Angels?', p. 489; Swain (2006) 'Infanticide, Savagery and Civilization', pp. 95–6; and Backhouse (1984) 'Desperate Women', p. 462.

65. Powys County Archive, Llowes Parish Register, R/EP/42/R/A/2. Radnorshire is a historic and former administrative county of Wales. In 1974, the area of Radnorshire was transferred and subsumed into the newly created county of Powys.

66. In total, Mary Morgan was imprisoned prior to her trial for 102 days. This is evident from a list of prisoner bills for bread found in the Quarter Session records see Powys County Archive, Radnorshire Quarter Sessions, Session Rolls 1804–1805, R/QS/R152. For more on the background to Mary Morgan's early life see J. Green (1987) *The Morning of Her Day* (London: Darf), pp. 50, 60–1 and 63–5; W. Gregg (1996) 'The Hanging of Mary Morgan', *New Law Journal*, 146, No. 6735 (Postscript), p. 390; and L. Fanthorpe and P. Fanthorpe (2003) *The World's Most Mysterious Murders* (Toronto and Oxford: Hounslow), p. 78.

67. Powys County Archive, 'Pitiful Welsh Tragedy Re-told' (Unidentified Newspaper Article), 4 June 1898, R/X/11/144.

68. National Archives [Kew, Surrey] (NA), Criminal Registers England and Wales, HO 27/1, pp. 397–8.

69. National Library of Wales (NLW), Records of the Court of Great Sessions, 4/533/3/ Document 8.

70. NLW, Records of the Court of Great Sessions, 4/533/3/Document 9. For confirmation that the inquest took place see Powys County Archive, Radnorshire Quarter Sessions, Session Rolls 1804–1805, R/QS/R151.

71. For the testimony of Margaret Haverd see NLW, Records of the Court of Great Sessions, 4/533/3/Document 13; for the testimony of Elizabeth Eveylyn see NLW, Records of the Court of Great Sessions, 4/533/3/Document 14; and for the testimony of Mary Meredith see NLW, Records of the Court of Great Sessions,

4/533/3/Document 15. For further discussion of the trial see Green (1987) *The Morning of Her Day*, pp. 64 and 67–102.

72. NLW, Records of the Court of Great Sessions, Minute Book for the Radnorshire Sessions 14/44, p. 15 and Fanthorpe and Fanthorpe (2003) *The World's Most Mysterious Murders*, p. 79. The verdict was also reported in the national media see *The Observer*, 28 April 1805.

73. Modern newspapers, retelling the Mary Morgan story, have reported that attempts were made to attain a pardon for Mary Morgan, see, for instance, Powys County Archive, 'Pitiful Welsh Tragedy Re-told' (Unidentified Newspaper Article) 4 June 1898, R/X/11/144 and Powys County Archive, *County Times and Express and Gazette*, 28 November 1981, R/X/11/145. However, there is no record of a pardon being registered for Mary Morgan in any pertinent archival sources: NA, Criminal Entry Book, HO 13/16; NA, Private and Secret Documents, HO 79/10 or NA, Judges Reports, HO 47/35. Moreover, the judge's order that the capital punishment should be carried out within forty-eight hours after sentencing would largely negate the feasibility of a pardon being organised, given that it had to be obtained from London.

74. For confirmation that the hanging was carried out see NLW, Records of the Court of Great Sessions, Black Book 28/35; NA, Criminal Registers England and Wales, HO 27/1, pp. 397–8 and *The Hull Packet*, 7 May 1805, No. 956. For confirmation of the burial of Mary Morgan see Hereford Record Office, Parish Registers (Presteigne), AN28/3 and P. Parris (1983) 'Mary Morgan: Contemporary Sources', *The Radnorshire Society Transactions*, LIII, Plate IV and Plate V, p. 52.

75. For further discussion see King (2000) *Crime, Justice and Discretion*, pp. 286–96.

76. See respectively, NLW, Records of the Court of Great Sessions, 4/178/2 and 4/736/5.

77. This conclusion was reached after a detailed analysis of the infanticide cases found in the National Library of Wales's Crime and Punishment database: http:// www.llgc.org.uk/sesiwn_fawr/index_s.htm

78. *The Hull Packet*, 7 May 1805, No. 956.

79. J. Nichols (1818) (ed.) *The Miscellaneous Works in Prose and Verse, of George Hardinge, Esq. Senior Justice of the Counties of Brecon, Glamorgan, and Radnor, Volume I* (London: J. Nichols, Son and Bentley), p. 68. [Bodleian Library 8M96BS(V1)].

80. J. Nichols (1818) (ed.) *Illustrations of the Literary History of the Eighteenth Century: Consisting of Authentic Memoirs and Original Letters of Eminent Persons, Volume III* (London: Nichols, Son and Bentley), p. 127. [Bodleian Library 13 Theta 92v3] My addition in parenthesis. See also Green (1987) *The Morning of Her Day*, pp. 68–9.

81. See *The Hull Packet*, 7 May 1805, No. 956; Nichols (1818) (ed.) *Illustrations of the Literary History of the Eighteenth Century*, pp. 126–7; Green (1987) *The Morning of Her Day*, p. 61; and Gregg (1996) 'The Hanging of Mary Morgan', p. 390.

82. For evidence of this theory see Fanthorpe and Fanthorpe (2003) *The World's Most Mysterious Murders*, p. 80 and Green (1987) *The Morning of Her Day*, p. 127.

83. See Nichols (1818) (ed.) *Illustrations of the Literary History of the Eighteenth Century*, p. 126 and Gregg (1996) 'The Hanging of Mary Morgan', p. 390.

84. For further details see J. Williams (1905) *A General History of the County of Radnor* (Brecknock: Davies and Co), pp. 86–7. [NLW, XDA1362 W72 (4to)].

85. NLW, Records of the Court of Great Sessions, Radnorshire Spring Sessions 1805 – Names of the Grand Jury, 4/533/3/Document 11. For further discussion of the significance of this see also Powys County Archive, 'Pitiful Welsh Tragedy

Re-told' (Unidentified Newspaper Article) 4 June 1898, R/X/11/144; Green (1987) *The Morning of Her Day*, p. 129; and Fanthorpe and Fanthorpe (2003) *The World's Most Mysterious Murders*, p. 82.

86. See, for instance, Nichols (1818) (ed.) *Illustrations of the Literary History of the Eighteenth Century*, p. 126. For further discussion see also Green (1987) *The Morning of Her Day*, p. 62 and Gregg (1996) 'The Hanging of Mary Morgan', p. 390.

87. *The Shrewsbury Chronicle*, 1 May 1805, Volume XXXIV, No. 1732.

88. Nichols (1818) (ed.) *The Miscellaneous Works in Prose and Verse, of George Harding*, p. 5. Hardinge's address was also reproduced in full in the popular press at the time of the trial. See, for instance, *The Cambrian*, 27 April 1805, No. 66 and *The Salopian Journal*, 1 May 1805, Vol. XIII, No. 558.

89. NLW, Records of the Court of Great Sessions, 4/391/7/Document 1.

90. This conclusion was reached after a detailed analysis of the pertinent infanticide cases Hardinge presided over found in the National Library of Wales's Crime and Punishment database: http://www.llgc.org.uk/sesiwn_fawr/index_s.htm.

91. See Nichols (1818) (ed.) *The Miscellaneous Works in Prose and Verse, of George Harding*, p. 53. See also the hymn he wrote for the new-born victims of infanticide found at ibid., p. 183.

92. Ibid., pp. 56–7.

93. See Nichols (1818) (ed.) *The Miscellaneous Works in Prose and Verse, of George Harding*, pp. 51–73 and 176–82 and Nichols (1818) (ed.) *Illustrations of the Literary History of the Eighteenth Century*, pp. 36–7 and 126–31. For further discussion of the impact of the case on Judge Hardinge see Green (1987) *The Morning of Her Day*, p. 50 and Fanthorpe and Fanthorpe (2003) *The World's Most Mysterious Murders*, p. 81.

94. Mary Morgan's grave is marked by two separate tombstones, one of which is particularly elaborate and ornate. See G. Brookes (2008) *Stories in Welsh Stone – The Secrets within Fifteen Welsh Graves* (Ceredigion: Welsh Country Magazine), pp. 12 and 17.

95. Nichols (1818) (ed.) *The Miscellaneous Works in Prose and Verse, of George Harding*, p. 59. See also another lyrical work he penned about Mary Morgan reproduced at ibid., p. 58. This piece is translated from Latin into English in Green (1987) *The Morning of Her Day*, p. 111.

96. Powys County Archive, T. Horton (1818) *An Elegy Written in the Churchyard of Presteigne, Radnorshire with Admonitory Reflections on the Grave of Mary Morgan Who was Interred there after Suffering the Awful Sentence of the Law, for the Murder of her Illegitimate Child* (Presteigne: E.J. Jones, County Printing Office), pp. 10–13, R/X/11/141.

97. In relation to the data on sentencing in England and Wales it should be noted that there were gaps in the available data between 1818 and 1833. The category listed as 'other' in Figure 5.3 refers to a handful of capital sentences meted out but never enforced, along with a few cases where probation was prescribed (typically when a defendant was very evidently suffering from some sort of mental disorder).

98. In relation to the data on sentencing in Scotland it should be noted that data was only available from 1830 onwards. The category listed as 'other' in Figure 5.4 refers to a few cases where probation was prescribed (typically when a defendant was very evidently suffering from some sort of mental disorder).

99. For further discussion see Ward (2002) 'Legislating for Human Nature', p. 256; Higginbotham (1989) '"Sin of the Age"', p. 332; P. Van der Spey (2002) 'Infanticide, Slavery and the Politics of Reproduction at Cape Colony, South Africa, in the 1820s', in M. Jackson (ed.) *Infanticide: Historical Perspectives on Child Murder and Concealment, 1550–2000* (Aldershot: Ashgate), p. 131; and Monholland (1989) 'Infanticide in Victorian England', pp. 241–2.

100. For further discussion see J. McShane Galley (2006) 'For Shame: Accusations of Infanticide and Coroner's Inquests into the Deaths of Legitimate Infants in Victorian Ontario', in B.H. Bechtold and D. Cooper Graves (eds.) *Killing Infants: Studies in the Worldwide Practice of Infanticide* (New York: Edwin Mellen), pp. 282–5.

101. See, for instance, correspondence reproduced in the *British Medical Journal*, 13 July 1878.

102. Burke Ryan (1862) *Infanticide*, p. 4.

103. Ibid., p. 26.

104. For further discussion see Donovan (1991) 'Infanticide and the Juries in France', p. 158; Darby (2008) 'Suffer the Little Ones', p. 50; C.L. Krueger (1997) 'Literary Defences and Medical Prosecutions: Representing Infanticide in Nineteenth-Century Britain', *Victorian Studies*, XL, pp. 271 and 290; Smith (1981) *Trial by Medicine*, p. 146; and Hunt (2006) 'Calculations and Concealments', p. 73.

105. *The Sheffield and Rotherham Independent*, 30 July 1842: No. 1175. See also the case against Hannah Cadel from 1829, recounted in G. Brindley (2006) *Oxford: Crime, Death and Debauchery* (Sutton: Stroud), pp. 110–13.

106. For further discussion of poverty being perceived as a key motive in instances of new-born child murder by the nineteenth century see respectively Arnot (2000) 'Understanding Women Committing Newborn Child Murder', pp. 57–8; Sauer (1978) 'Infanticide and Abortion', p. 92; and Arnot (2002) 'The Murder of Thomas Sandles', p. 160 on. For insanity in this context see Ward (2002) 'Legislating for Human Nature', p. 251; Leboutte (1991) 'Offense against Family Order', p. 161; Donovan (1991) 'Infanticide and the Juries in France', p. 169; McShane Galley (2006) 'For Shame: Accusations of Infanticide', p. 294; Ruggiero (1992) 'Honor, Maternity and the Disciplining of Women', p. 361; K. Ruggiero (2000) 'Not Guilty: Abortion and Infanticide in Nineteenth-Century Argentina', in C. Agiurre and R. Buffington (eds.) *Reconstructing Criminality in Latin America* (Wilmington, DE: Jaguar), p. 160; and T.A. Crist (2005) 'Babies in the Privy: Prostitution, Infanticide, and Abortion in New York City's Five Points District', *Historical Archaeology*, 39, p. 26.

107. For further discussion see Seaborne Davies (1937) 'Child Killing in English Law', pp. 206–11; Behlmer (1979) 'Deadly Motherhood', pp. 410–11; E.C. Green (1999) 'Infanticide and Infant Abandonment in the New South: Richmond, Virginia, 1865–1915', *Journal of Family History*, 24, pp. 200–1; Higginbotham (1989) '"Sin of the Age"', p. 330; Dalby (1995) 'Women and Infanticide in Nineteenth-Century Rural France', p. 345; Barringer Gordon (2002) 'Law and Everyday Death', p. 63; Smith (1979) *The People's Health*, p. 79; Monholland (1989) 'Infanticide in Victorian England', p. 28; and Ruggiero (2000) 'Not Guilty', pp. 158–9.

108. *British Medical Journal*, 3 March 1866.

109. See, for instance, William Cummin (1836) *The Proofs of Infanticide Considered: Including Dr Hunter's Tract on Child Murder, With Illustrative Notes and A Summary of the Present State of Medico-Legal Knowledge* (London: Longman) [Accessed from http://archive.org/details/proofsofinfantic00cumm], pp. 50–94; J.B. Beck (1817) *An Inaugural Dissertation on Infanticide* (New York: J. Seymour) [Accessed from http://archive.org/details/inauguraldissert01beck], pp. 44–82; and the *British Medical Journal*, 9 February 1848.

110. *The York Herald*, 25 November 1871, No. 5163. See also the case against Eliza Braine from 1833, recounted in Brindley (2006) *Oxford: Crime, Death and Debauchery*, pp. 51–2.

111. For a contemporary articulation of this contradiction see Burke Ryan (1862) *Infanticide*, pp. 131–76.
112. Smith (1981) *Trial by Medicine*, p. 147. See also Seaborne Davies (1937) 'Child Killing in English Law', pp. 216–23.
113. See, for instance, the comments made by Thomas Percival (1849) *Medical Ethics: Or a Code of Institutes and Precepts Adapted to the Professional Conduct of Physicians and Surgeons* (Oxford: J.H. Parker) [Bodleian Library, RB 49.1412], p. 96 and especially Beck (1817) *An Inaugural Dissertation on Infanticide*, pp. 85–92. For further discussion see also Cooper Graves (2006) '"...In a Frenzy While Raving Mad"', pp. 125–6 and Ward (2002) 'Legislating for Human Nature', p. 257.
114. *Report of the Capital Punishment Commission* (1866) (London: HMSO), pp. 44, 49 and 57.
115. See *Parliamentary Papers*, A Bill to Consolidate and Amend the Law relating to Homicide (1872); *Parliamentary Papers*, A Bill to Consolidate and Amend the Law relating to Homicide (1874); *Parliamentary Papers*, A Bill to Establish a Code of Indictable Offences, and the Procedure Relating Thereto (1878) and *Parliamentary Papers*, Report of the Royal Commission Appointed to Consider the Law Relating to Indictable Offences (1879).
116. For further discussion see Damme (1978) 'Infanticide', p. 15 and Edwards (1984) *Women on Trial*, p. 92.
117. For further discussion see Ward (1999) 'The Sad Subject of Infanticide', p. 169 and G.K. Behlmer (1982) *Child Abuse and Moral Reform in England, 1870–1908* (Stanford, CA: Stanford University Press).
118. See, for instance, Dalby (1995) 'Women and Infanticide in Nineteenth-Century Rural France', p. 338; Richter (1998) 'Child Abandonment and Abortion', p. 513; and Pilarczyk (2012) '"So Foul A Deed"', p. 610.
119. For further discussion see Chapters 4 and 6 of this volume as well as Monholland (1989) 'Infanticide in Victorian England', p. 68 and Oberman (2002) 'Understanding Infanticide in Context', p. 725.
120. For further worldwide evidence that most nineteenth-century infanticide suspects were unmarried see Dalby (1995) 'Women and Infanticide in Nineteenth-Century Rural France', p. 338; Donovan (1991) 'Infanticide and the Juries in France', p. 169; Richter (1998) 'Child Abandonment and Abortion', p. 513; Ermers (1990) 'Medeas or Fallen Angels?', p. 487; Wilson (1988) 'Child Abandonment', p. 766; Altink (2007) '"I Did Not Want to Face the Shame of Exposure"', p. 360; Ruggiero (2000) 'Not Guilty', p. 156; Backhouse (1984) 'Desperate Women', pp. 448 and 457; Crist (2005) 'Babies in the Privy', p. 26; and Oberman (2002) 'Understanding Infanticide in Context', p. 717. For further evidence that many of these suspects were young (under the age of 25) see Wilson (1988) 'Child Abandonment', p. 766; Backhouse (1984) 'Desperate Women', p. 457; Cooper Graves (2006) '"...In a Frenzy"', p. 132; Ermers (1990) 'Medeas or Fallen Angels?', p. 487; and Ruggiero (1992) 'Honor, Maternity and the Disciplining of Women', p. 356.
121. *Berrow's Worcester Journal*, 27 March 1845, No. 7426.
122. For further discussion see Chapter 3 of this volume as well as Wheeler (1997) 'Infanticide in Nineteenth-Century Ohio', p. 413.
123. H. Rebel (1993) 'Peasants against the State in the Body of Anna Maria Wagner: An Infanticide in Rural Austria in 1832', *Journal of Historical Sociology*, 6, p. 16.
124. For further discussion see Chapter 3 of this volume as well as Monholland (1989) 'Infanticide in Victorian England', p. 29 and Wilson (1988) 'Child Abandonment', p. 767.

125. *The Morning Post*, 7 October 1824, No. 16786.
126. *The Newcastle Courant*, 30 June 1848, No. 9056.
127. For evidence of the dominance of domestic servants as defendants in infanticide trials in nineteenth-century Britain see Monholland (1989) 'Infanticide in Victorian England', p. 67; Cooper Graves (2006) '"...In a Frenzy"', pp. 113 and 132; and Ermers (1990) 'Medeas or Fallen Angels?', p. 484. For similar evidence further afield at that time see Leboutte (1991) 'Offense against Family Order', p. 164; Donovan (1991) 'Infanticide and the Juries in France', p. 169; Richter (1998) 'Child Abandonment and Abortion', p. 513; Backhouse (1984) 'Desperate Women', p. 457; Crist (2005) 'Babies in the Privy', p. 26; Roth (2001) 'Child Murder in New England', p. 114; Ruggiero (2000) 'Not Guilty', p. 156; and especially S. Swain (2005) 'Maids and Mothers: Domestic Servants and Illegitimacy in 19th-century Australia', *History of the Family*, 10, pp. 461–71.
128. (1890) *Encyclopaedia Britannica* (9th edition) Vol. 13 (Chicago: R.S. Peal), p. 3.
129. *British Medical Journal*, 28 April 1866.
130. For further discussion see Behlmer (1979) 'Deadly Motherhood', p. 420 and Rose (1986) *The Massacre of the Innocents*, p. 15.
131. See, for instance, Dalby (1995) 'Women and Infanticide in Nineteenth-Century Rural France', p. 351; Ermers (1990) 'Medeas or Fallen Angels?', p. 487; and Kociumbas (2001) 'Azaria's Antecedents', p. 141.
132. *The Times*, 5 August 1865, No. 25256.
133. *The Northern Star and Leed's General Advertiser*, 24 June 1843, No. 293. The appearance of an infanticide case in this Chartist newspaper is a reminder that infanticide was sometimes seen by radicals throughout the nineteenth century as a class issue. In the 1860s, republicans would regularly suggest that servant women were the habitual sexual prey of aristocratic men, so that such an iniquitous relationship was responsible for the high level of infanticide during this period.
134. For further discussion see Rose (1986) *The Massacre of the Innocents*, p. 15 and Monholland (1989) 'Infanticide in Victorian England', pp. 58–9.
135. For further discussion see Rose (1986) *The Massacre of the Innocents*, p. 19; Cooper Graves (2006) '"...In a Frenzy"', p. 113; and Altink (2007) '"I Did Not Want to Face the Shame of Exposure"', p. 365.
136. See for further discussion Arnot (2000) 'Understanding Women Committing Newborn Child Murder', pp. 58–9; Behlmer (1979) 'Deadly Motherhood', p. 420; and R. Schulte (1984) 'Infanticide in Rural Bavaria in the Nineteenth Century', in H. Medick and D.W. Sabean (eds.) *Interest and Emotion: Essays on the Study of Family and Kinship* (Cambridge: Cambridge University Press), p. 86.
137. The lack of clarity in relation to the typicality of some defendant characteristics in British infanticide cases is typically due to an absence of sufficient pertinent detail in the published judicial statistics from the nineteenth century and the scattered nature of other types of sources. This makes data analysis and trend derivation difficult to achieve.
138. See, for instance, the predominance of rural infanticides in studies by Leboutte (1991) 'Offense against Family Order', p. 164; Donovan (1991) 'Infanticide and the Juries in France', p. 169; Ermers (1990) 'Medeas or Fallen Angels?', p. 488; and Richter (1998) 'Child Abandonment and Abortion', p. 547.
139. Regina Schulte makes a similar conclusion for nineteenth-century Bavaria, see Schulte (1984) 'Infanticide in Rural Bavaria', p. 79.

140. For confirmation of an equal gender ratio in nineteenth-century infanticide victims elsewhere in Europe see Bechtold (1999) 'Infanticide in Nineteenth-Century France', p. 171.
141. For further discussion of concerns over recidivist infanticidal mothers in the nineteenth century see D. Grey (2012) '"Almost Unknown Amongst the Jews": Jewish Women and Infanticide in London 1890–1918', *The London Journal*, 37, p. 127 and Wilson (1988) 'Child Abandonment', p. 766.
142. For contemporary fears regarding these issues see the *British Medical Journal*, 1 December 1866 and Ward (1999) 'The Sad Subject of Infanticide', p. 169. For further discussion see Chapter 4 of this volume as well as Smith (1979) *The People's Health*, p. 113; N. Williams and G. Mooney (1994) 'Infant Mortality in an "Age of Great Cities": London and the English Provincial Cities Compared, c. 1840–1910', *Continuity and Change*, 9, pp. 185–212; Rose (1986) *The Massacre of the Innocents*, pp. 79–107, 136–58 and 170–86; V. Fildes (1988) *Wet Nursing: A History from Antiquity to the Present* (Oxford: Basil Blackwell), Chapter 12; and Hunt (2006) 'Calculations and Concealments', p. 77.
143. See sections 58 and 59 of Parliamentary Papers, 24 and 25 Vict., c. 100 (1861). For further discussion see Chapter 4 of this volume as well as A. McLaren (1984) *Reproductive Rituals: The Perception of Fertility in England from the Sixteenth Century to the Nineteenth Century* (London and New York: Methuen); A. McLaren (1990, 1992 edition) *A History of Contraception – From Antiquity to the Present Day* (Oxford: Blackwell); M.E. Wright (1987) 'Unnatural Mothers: Infanticide in Halifax, 1850–1875', *Nova Scotia Historical Review*, 7, pp. 13–29; and C. Joffe (2009) 'Abortion and Medicine: A Sociopolitical History', in M. Paul, E.S. Lichtenberg, L. Borgatta, D.A. Grimes, P.G. Stubblefield and M.D. Creinin (eds.) *Management of Unintended and Abnormal Pregnancy* (1st ed.) (Oxford: John Wiley & Sons), pp. 1–9.
144. See Beck (1817) *An Inaugural Dissertation on Infanticide*, pp. 70–83.
145. For the use of these alternative terms see Dr Edwin Lankester's comments reproduced in the *British Medical Journal*, 20 September 1862.
146. See Beck (1817) *An Inaugural Dissertation on Infanticide*, pp. 70–2. See also Smith (1979) *The People's Health*, p. 81; Wilson (1988) 'Child Abandonment', p. 767; and Behlmer (1979) 'Deadly Motherhood', p. 412.
147. See Brockington (1996, 2003 edition) *Motherhood and Mental Health*, p. 442 for the belief that neglect was a common method used in infanticides. For more on the difficulty of proving intent in these kinds of cases see Beck (1817) *An Inaugural Dissertation on Infanticide*, p. 73; Crist (2005) 'Babies in the Privy', p. 30; and Higginbotham (1989) '"Sin of the Age"', p. 329.
148. See, for instance, the *British Medical Journal*, 20 September 1862 and Oberman (2002) 'Understanding Infanticide in Context', p. 734.
149. For further discussion of instances of infant abandonment and exposure in the nineteenth century see Sauer (1978) 'Infanticide and Abortion', p. 86; Ermers (1990) 'Medeas or Fallen Angels?', p. 485; Wilson (1988) 'Child Abandonment', p. 775; Oberman (2002) 'Understanding Infanticide in Context', p. 717; Backhouse (1984) 'Desperate Women', p. 471; and Green (1999) 'Infanticide and Infant Abandonment', p. 199.For more on the practice of overlaying in the Victorian era see Donovan (1991) 'Infanticide and the Juries in France', p. 164; Ermers (1990) 'Medeas or Fallen Angels?', p. 485; and especially Hansen (1979) '"Overlaying" in Nineteenth-Century England', pp. 333–52.
150. *Western Mail*, 8 March 1895, No. 8049. My emphasis added.

151. Beck (1817) *An Inaugural Dissertation on Infanticide*, pp. 73–81.
152. Ibid., p. 84.
153. For further discussion see Smith (1979) *The People's Health*, p. 79; Brockington (1996, 2003 edition) *Motherhood and Mental Health*, p. 439; Wilson (1988) 'Child Abandonment', p. 767; Crist (2005) 'Babies in the Privy', p. 30; Oberman (2002) 'Understanding Infanticide in Context', p. 717; Ruggiero (1992) 'Honor, Maternity and the Disciplining of Women', p. 356; and Swain (2006) 'Infanticide, Savagery and Civilization', p. 88.
154. *Reynolds' Newspaper*, 20 November 1859, No. 484.
155. For further discussion suggesting that violent infanticides using weapons were not as common in the Victorian era as the available evidence suggests see Brockington (1996, 2003 edition) *Motherhood and Mental Health*, p. 441 and Crist (2005) 'Babies in the Privy', p. 30.
156. A similar conclusion is evident in Swain (2006) 'Infanticide, Savagery and Civilization', p. 88.
157. Roth (2001) 'Child Murder in New England', p. 124.
158. *The Morning Chronicle*, 30 March 1829, No. 18576.
159. *The Times*, 30 April 1842, No. 17971.
160. *The York Herald*, 4 April 1863, No. 4718. My addition in parenthesis.
161. For further discussion see Dalby (1995) 'Women and Infanticide in Nineteenth-Century Rural France', p. 347 and Oberman (2002) 'Understanding Infanticide in Context', p. 727.
162. For further discussion see Rose (1986) *The Massacre of the Innocents*, p. 23; Cooper Graves (2006) '"...In a Frenzy"', p. 113; and Arnot (2000) 'Understanding Women Committing Newborn Child Murder', p. 57.
163. For further discussion of poverty as a motive for infanticide in nineteenth-century Britain see Rose (1986) *The Massacre of the Innocents*, p. 17; Hunt (2006) 'Calculations and Concealments', p. 71, Sauer (1978) 'Infanticide and Abortion', p. 85; Cooper Graves (2006) '"...In a Frenzy"', p. 114; and Smith (1981) *Trial by Medicine*, p. 149. For elsewhere, see Roth (2001) 'Child Murder in New England', p. 114; Oberman (2002) 'Understanding Infanticide in Context', p. 725; and Wilson (1988) 'Child Abandonment', p. 783.
164. *North Wales Chronicle*, 17 April 1828, No. 29.
165. *The Bury and Norwich Post and Suffolk Herald*, 22 October 1851, No. 3617.
166. For further discussion see Monholland (1989) 'Infanticide in Victorian England', pp. 17–18 and 53; Rose (1986) *The Massacre of the Innocents*, pp. 26 and 28–9; Hunt (2006) 'Calculations and Concealments', p. 76; and Arnot (2000) 'Understanding Women Committing Newborn Child Murder', p. 57.
167. For further discussion of women's wages in the nineteenth century and the extent of their link with infanticide see Arnot (2000) 'Understanding Women Committing Newborn Child Murder', p. 58; Altink (2007) '"I Did Not Want to Face the Shame of Exposure"', p. 365; Crist (2005) 'Babies in the Privy', p. 30; Green (1999) 'Infanticide and Infant Abandonment', p. 190; and Backhouse (1984) 'Desperate Women', p. 448. For more on the lack of employment opportunities for unmarried mothers at this time see Sauer (1978) 'Infanticide and Abortion', p. 89 and Green (1999) 'Infanticide and Infant Abandonment', p. 188.
168. See, for instance, Oberman (2002) 'Understanding Infanticide in Context', p. 734 and Roth (2001) 'Child Murder in New England', p. 120.
169. For further discussion see Wheeler (1997) 'Infanticide in Nineteenth-Century Ohio', p. 413; Oberman (2002) 'Understanding Infanticide in Context',

pp. 723 and 725; Backhouse (1984) 'Desperate Women', pp. 448 and 458; Richter (1998) 'Child Abandonment and Abortion', pp. 542 and 544; Altink (2007) '"I Did Not Want to Face the Shame of Exposure"', pp. 363–4; Ermers (1990) 'Medeas or Fallen Angels?', pp. 487–8; Wilson (1988) 'Child Abandonment', p. 774; P. Scully (1996) 'Narratives of Infanticide in the Aftermath of Slave Emancipation in the Nineteenth-Century Cape Colony, South Africa', *Canadian Journal of African Studies*, 30, p. 96; Van der Spey (2002) 'Infanticide, Slavery and the Politics of Reproduction', p. 147; and Schulte (1984) 'Infanticide in Rural Bavaria', pp. 84 and 90.

170. *The Yorkshire Herald* and *The York Herald*, 23 May 1891, No. 12470.
171. See, for instance, Sauer (1978) 'Infanticide and Abortion', p. 85; Monholland (1989) 'Infanticide in Victorian England', p. 34; and Brockington (1996, 2003 edition) *Motherhood and Mental Health*, p. 447.
172. For further discussion of the potential flaws of this explanation see Scully (1996) 'Narratives of Infanticide', p. 96.
173. For further discussion of this contention see Monholland (1989) 'Infanticide in Victorian England', p. 72; Smith (1979) *The People's Health*, p. 70; Brockington (1996, 2003 edition) *Motherhood and Mental Health*, p. 447; Roth (2001) 'Child Murder in New England', p. 114; Leboutte (1991) 'Offense against Family Order', p. 172; Schulte (1984) 'Infanticide in Rural Bavaria', p. 86; Donovan (1991) 'Infanticide and the Juries in France', p. 169; and Dalby (1995) 'Women and Infanticide in Nineteenth-Century Rural France', pp. 338 and 348.
174. For further discussion see Brockington (1996, 2003 edition) *Motherhood and Mental Health*, p. 443; Hunt (2006) 'Calculations and Concealments', p. 71; Smith (1981) *Trial by Medicine*, pp. 148–50; Ward (1999) 'The Sad Subject of Infanticide', pp. 164 and 166; and Schulte (1984) 'Infanticide in Rural Bavaria', p. 88.
175. *The Morning Post*, 14 March 1823, No. 16223.
176. *The Standard*, 17 August 1857, No. 10299. My addition in parenthesis.
177. For further discussion see Hunt (2006) 'Calculations and Concealments', p. 73; Cooper Graves (2006) '"...In a Frenzy"', p. 134; and Rebel (1993) 'Peasants against the State', p. 15.
178. For further discussion see Sauer (1978) 'Infanticide and Abortion', pp. 88 and 91; Behlmer (1979) 'Deadly Motherhood', p. 415; Monholland (1989) 'Infanticide in Victorian England', p. 34; Altink (2007) '"I Did Not Want to Face the Shame of Exposure"', p. 372; Schulte (1984) 'Infanticide in Rural Bavaria', p. 91; Pilarczyk (2012) '"So Foul A Deed"', p. 588; Roth (2001) 'Child Murder in New England', p. 114; McLaren (1990, 1992 edition) *A History of Contraception*, pp. 178–214; and McLaren (1984) *Reproductive Rituals*, pp. 113–44.
179. For further discussion see, for instance, *The Morning Post*, 23 September 1863, No. 28008; Arnot (1994) 'Infant Death', p. 281; and Cooper Graves (2006) '"...In a Frenzy"', p. 126.
180. Beck (1817) *An Inaugural Dissertation on Infanticide*, p. 85. For similar contentions see also *The Times*, 5 of August 1865, No. 25256 and the *Aberdeen Weekly Journal*, 29 September 1877, No. 7055. For further discussion see Cooper Graves (2006) '"...In a Frenzy"', p. 127.
181. See, for instance, W. Tyler Smith writing in the *British Medical Journal*, 12 January 1867. See also *The Times*, 5 August 1865, No. 25256 and the *British Medical Journal*, 30 March 1867. For further discussion see also Higginbotham (1989) '"Sin of the Age"', p. 320 and Arnot (1994) 'Infant Death', p. 294.

182. *British Medical Journal*, 12 January 1867. For similar contentions see *The Morning Post*, 3 February 1863, No. 27809 and the *British Medical Journal*, 28 April 1866.
183. *The Morning Post*, 18 September 1863, No. 28004. For further discussion see also Higginbotham (1989) '"Sin of the Age"', p. 320; Cooper Graves (2006) '"...In a Frenzy"', pp. 126–7; Arnot (1994) 'Infant Death', p. 294; and Smith (1979) *The People's Health*, p. 80.
184. See, for instance, *The Morning Post*, 18 September 1863 and the *British Medical Journal*, 28 April 1866, 12 January 1867 and 30 March 1867. For further discussion see Higginbotham (1989) '"Sin of the Age"', p. 320; Cooper Graves (2006) '"...In a Frenzy"', pp. 126–7; and especially Arnot (1994) 'Infant Death', pp. 271–311.
185. *Aberdeen Weekly Journal*, 29 September 1877, No. 7055.
186. *The Morning Post*, 23 September 1863, No. 28008.
187. See, for instance, the *British Medical Journal*, 28 April 1866.
188. Beck (1817) *An Inaugural Dissertation on Infanticide*, p. 85.
189. See, for instance, *The Morning Post*, 18 September 1863 and *Aberdeen Weekly Journal*, 29 September 1877, No. 7055.
190. For this contention see Beck (1817) *An Inaugural Dissertation on Infanticide*, pp. 85 and 92–4; Burke Ryan (1862) *Infanticide*, pp. 31 and 83–131; *The Morning Post*, 3 February 1863, No. 27809; *The Morning Post*, 18 September 1863, No. 28004; and the *British Medical Journal*, 28 April 1866. The proposed use of Foundling Hospitals in this context was also criticised by some contemporaries see *The Morning Post*, 18 September 1863, No. 28004 and the *British Medical Journal*, 12 January 1867.
191. *The Times*, 5 August 1865, No. 25256.
192. *The Morning Post*, 3 February 1863, No. 27809.
193. *The Morning Post*, 23 September 1863, No. 28008.

6   Explaining infanticide: Motives for murder?

1. W. Hunter (1783) 'On the Uncertainty of the Signs of Murder in the Case of Bastard Children' – A Paper Read to the Members of the Medical Society, p. 5. The essay was published a year later in the journal *Medical Observations and Inquiries*, 6, pp. 266–90 [University of Glasgow, Sp Coll. Hunterian Add. 279].
2. For further discussion see J.L. Harrington (2009) *The Unwanted Child: The Fate of Foundlings, Orphans and Juvenile Criminals in Early Modern Germany* (Chicago and London: University of Chicago Press), pp. 51–3 and C.B. Backhouse (1984) 'Desperate Women and Compassionate Courts: Infanticide in Nineteenth-Century Canada', *The University of Toronto Law Journal*, 34, p. 47.
3. This is a point reinforced by O. Ulbricht (1988) 'Infanticide in Eighteenth-Century Germany', in R.J. Evans (ed.) *The German Underworld: Deviants and Outcasts in German History* (London: Routledge), p. 114 and R. Schulte (1984) 'Infanticide in Rural Bavaria in the Nineteenth Century', in H. Medick and D.W. Sabean (eds.) *Interest and Emotion: Essays on the Study of Family and Kinship* (Cambridge: Cambridge University Press), p. 89.
4. See K. Wrightson (1982) 'Infanticide in European History', *Criminal Justice History*, III, p. 14, as well as K. Wrightson (1975) 'Infanticide in Earlier Seventeenth-Century England', *Local Population Studies*, XV, p. 19 and A.-M. Kilday (2002) 'Maternal Monsters: Murdering Mothers in South-West Scotland, 1750–1815', in

Y.G. Brown and R. Ferguson (eds.) *Twisted Sisters: Women, Crime and Deviance in Scotland since 1400* (East Linton: Tuckwell), p. 193.

5. For further discussion see M. Kamler (1988) 'Infanticide in the Towns of the Kingdom of Poland in the Second Half of the 16th and the First Half of the 17th Century', *Acta Poloniae Historica*, 58, pp. 44, 46 and 49; S. Wilson (1988) 'Child Abandonment and Female Honour in Nineteenth-Century Corsica', *Comparative Studies in Society and History*, 30, p. 762; and J. Dalby (1995) 'Women and Infanticide in Nineteenth-Century Rural France', in V. Shepherd, B. Brereton and B. Bailey (eds.) *Engendering History: Caribbean Women in Historical Perspective* (London and Kingston, Jamaica: James Currey and Ian Randle), p. 338.

6. For further acknowledgement of this problem see G.K. Behlmer (1979) 'Deadly Motherhood: Infanticide and Medical Opinion in Mid-Victorian England', *Journal of the History of Medicine and Allied Sciences*, XXXIV, p. 415.

7. For further discussion see Kilday (2002) 'Maternal Monsters', p. 170; P.C. Hoffer and N.E.C. Hull (1984) *Murdering Mothers: Infanticide in England and New England 1558–1803* (New York: New York University Press), p. 145; and Dalby (1995) 'Women and Infanticide', p. 346.

8. P.A. Gilje (1983) 'Infant Abandonment in Early Nineteenth-Century New York City: Three Cases', *Signs*, 8, p. 583.

9. See Wrightson (1982) 'Infanticide in European History', p. 6 and Wrightson (1975) 'Infanticide in Earlier Seventeenth-Century England', p. 11.

10. Parliamentary Papers, 21 Jac 1 c. 27 (1624).

11. B. Mandeville (1723, 1772 edition) *The Fable of the Bees: Or, Private Vices, Public Benefits – Volume I* (Edinburgh: J. Wood) [Bodleian Library, ESTCT77574], pp. 45–6. For further discussion see M. Jackson (1996) *New-Born Child Murder: Women, Illegitimacy and the Courts in Eighteenth-Century England* (Manchester: Manchester University Press), p. 113.

12. E. Darwin 'Letter to Unknown Man, 7th February 1767', in D. King-Hele (2007) (ed.) *The Collected Letters of Erasmus Darwin* (Cambridge: Cambridge University Press), p. 76. For further discussion see Jackson (1996) *New-Born Child Murder*, p. 114.

13. Hunter (1783) 'On the Uncertainty of the Signs of Murder', p. 7. For further discussion see Jackson (1996) *New-Born Child Murder*, p. 116.

14. For further discussion see T. Laquer (1989) 'Bodies, Details and the Humanitarian Narrative', in L. Hunt (ed.) *The New Cultural History* (Berkley: University of California Press), pp. 176–205 and Jackson (1996) *New-Born Child Murder*, Chapter 5.

15. Mandeville (1723, 1772 edition) *The Fable of the Bees*, p. 46 and Hunter (1783) 'On the Uncertainty of the Signs of Murder', p. 6. For further discussion of the social stratification of the validity of shame with regard to infanticide trials see R.W. Malcolmson (1977) 'Infanticide in the Eighteenth Century', in J.S. Cockburn (ed.) *Crime in England 1550–1800* (London: Methuen), p. 205; Jackson (1996) *New-Born Child Murder*, p. 114; and T. Rizzo (2004) 'Between Dishonour and Death: Infanticide in the Causes Célèbres of Eighteenth-Century France', *Women's History Review*, p. 13.

16. For further discussion see Jackson (1996) *New-Born Child Murder*, p. 125.

17. C. Hodgson (1800) *A Letter from a Magistrate in the Country, to his Medical Friend at Peterborough* (Peterborough), p. 2, cited in Jackson (1996) *New-Born Child Murder*, p. 127.

18. For further discussion see Jackson (1996) *New-Born Child Murder*, p. 117; Kilday (2002) 'Maternal Monsters', p. 167; Ulbricht (1988) 'Infanticide', p. 127; and

P.M. Prior (2008) *Madness and Murder: Gender, Crime and Mental Disorder in Nineteenth-Century Ireland* (Dublin: Irish Academic), p. 139.

19. A. Rowlands (1997) '"In Great Secrecy": The Crime of Infanticide in Rothenburg ob der Tauber, 1501–1618', *German History*, 15, p. 191.
20. For further discussion see L. Abrams (2002) 'From Demon to Victim: The Infanticidal Mother in Shetland, 1699–1802', in Y.G. Brown and R. Ferguson (eds.) *Twisted Sisters: Women, Crime and Deviance in Scotland since 1400* (East Linton: Tuckwell), p. 182 and U. Rublack (1999) *The Crimes of Women in Early Modern Germany* (Oxford: Clarendon), p. 184.
21. Schulte (1984) 'Infanticide in Rural Bavaria', p. 84.
22. *The Proceedings of the Old Bailey*, 11 of September 1717 [t17170911-50]. [Accessed from www.oldbaileyonline.org].
23. National Records of Scotland [Edinburgh] (NRS), Justiciary Court North Circuit Records, JC11/8.
24. *The Proceedings of the Old Bailey*, 4 July 1804 [t18040704-16].
25. In certain regions and communities across pre-modern Europe, illegitimacy was not seen as problematic and rather it was regularly welcomed by society. For further discussion see Schulte (1984) 'Infanticide in Rural Bavaria', p. 84; R. Sauer (1978) 'Infanticide and Abortion in Nineteenth-Century Britain', *Population Studies: A Journal of Demography*, XXXII, pp. 84–5; P.M. Crawford (2010) *Parents of Poor Children in England, 1580–1800* (Oxford: Oxford University Press), p. 40; R. Mitchison and L. Leneman (1998) *Girls in Trouble: Sexuality and Social Control in Rural Scotland 1660–1780* (Edinburgh: Scottish Cultural Press); and L. Leneman and R. Mitchison (1998) *Sin in the City: Sexuality and Social Control in Urban Scotland 1660–1780* (Edinburgh: Scottish Cultural Press).
26. For further discussion see Rowlands (1997) '"In Great Secrecy"', p. 192; Harrington (2009) *The Unwanted Child*, pp. 43–4; Kilday (2002) 'Maternal Monsters', p. 172; A.-M. Kilday (2008) '"Monsters of the Vilest Kind": Infanticidal Women and Attitudes towards their Criminality in Eighteenth-Century Scotland', *Family and Community History*, 11, pp. 103–4; and Wrightson (1982) 'Infanticide in European History', p. 6.
27. NRS, High Court of Justiciary, Books of Adjournal, JC3/4. My additions in parenthesis.
28. NRS, Justiciary Court North Circuit Records, JC11/14. My addition in parenthesis.
29. NRS, Justiciary Court South Circuit Records, JC12/11. My addition in parenthesis.
30. For further discussion see Crawford (2010) *Parents of Poor Children*, p. 49; Ulbricht (1988) 'Infanticide', p. 128; R. Roth (2001) 'Child Murder in New England', *Social Science History*, XXV, p. 113; and Dalby (1995) 'Women and Infanticide', p. 356.
31. NRS, High Court of Justiciary, Books of Adjournal, JC3/26.
32. National Library of Wales (hereafter NLW), Records of the Court of Great Sessions, 4/526/3.
33. For further discussion see Ulbricht (1988) 'Infanticide', p. 128 and Rublack (1999) *The Crimes of Women*, p. 184.
34. NRS, Justiciary Court West Circuit Records, JC13/1.
35. NLW, Records of the Court of Great Sessions, 4/745/1.
36. For further discussion see Rizzo (2004) 'Between Dishonour and Death', p. 13.
37. Anonymous (1861) 'The Prevalence of Infanticide', *Magdalen's Friend*, 2, p. 34 [British Library, P.P. 1098b].
38. For further discussion see N. Lonza (2002) '"Two Souls Lost": Infanticide in the Republic of Dubrovnik (1667–1808)', *Dubrovnik Annals*, 6, p. 87; Harrington

(2009) *The Unwanted Child*, p. 42; Ulbricht (1988) 'Infanticide', p. 130; Wilson (1988) 'Child Abandonment', p. 774; and Abrams (2002) 'From Demon to Victim', p. 186.

39. For further discussion see Lonza (2002) '"Two Souls Lost"', pp. 79 and 84; Malcolmson (1977) 'Infanticide', p. 193; Kamler (1988) 'Infanticide', pp. 43–4; and Harrington (2009) *The Unwanted Child*, p. 41.

40. NLW, Records of the Court of Great Sessions, 4/388/7.

41. For further discussion see Malcolmson (1977) 'Infanticide', pp. 193 and 203; D. Cooper Graves (2006) '"...In a Frenzy While Raving Mad": Physicians and Parliamentarians Define Infanticide in Victorian England', in B.H. Bechtold and D. Cooper Graves (eds.) *Killing Infants: Studies in the Worldwide Practice of Infanticide* (Lewiston, NY: Edwin Mellen), p. 113; Harrington (2009) *The Unwanted Child*, p. 44; Crawford (2010) *Parents of Poor Children*, p. 43; Wrightson (1982) 'Infanticide in European History', p. 7; Rublack (1999) *The Crimes of Women*, p. 165; M. Oberman (2002) 'Understanding Infanticide in Context: Mothers Who Kill, 1870–1930 and Today', *The Journal of Criminal Law and Criminology*, 92, pp. 722–3; and Backhouse (1984) 'Desperate Women', p. 458.

42. For further discussion see Wilson (1988) 'Child Abandonment', p. 766. See also, for , the case against Jane Evan, heard at the Court of Great Sessions in Wales and mentioned below.

43. For further discussion see Malcolmson (1977) 'Infanticide', p. 187; Backhouse (1984) 'Desperate Women', pp. 448 and 458; Crawford (2010) *Parents of Poor Children*, p. 73; and K.D. Watson (2008) 'Religion, Community and the Infanticidal Mother: Evidence from 1840s Rural Wiltshire', *Family and Community History*, 11, p. 117.

44. For further discussion see Crawford (2010) *Parents of Poor Children*, pp. 35 and 41–2; Roth (2001) 'Child Murder in New England', p. 120; Malcolmson (1977) 'Infanticide', p. 193; Rublack (1999) *The Crimes of Women*, p. 164; and Ulbricht (1988) 'Infanticide', p. 120.

45. *The Proceedings of the Old Bailey*, 10 May 1744 [t17440510-8].

46. *The Proceedings of the Old Bailey*, 6 December 1775 [t17751206-82].

47. For further discussion see M.L. Arnot (2000) 'Understanding Women Committing Newborn Child Murder in Victorian England', in S. D'Cruze (ed.) *Everyday Violence in Britain, 1850–1950* (Harlow: Pearson), p. 59; Dalby (1995) 'Women and Infanticide', p. 338; Roth (2001) 'Child Murder in New England', p. 114; Oberman (2002) 'Understanding Infanticide in Context', p. 724; Cooper Graves (2006) '"...In a Frenzy"', p. 132; and A.R. Higginbotham (1989) '"Sin of the Age": Infanticide and Illegitimacy in Victorian London', *Victorian Studies*, 32, p. 326.

48. R. Bellamy (1995) (ed.) *Cesare Beccaria – On Crimes and Punishments and Other Writings* (Cambridge: Cambridge University Press), p. 81.

49. For further discussion see Hunter (1783) 'On the Uncertainty of the Signs of Murder', pp. 8–9; Harrington (2009) *The Unwanted Child*, p. 70; J.R. Dickinson and J.A. Sharpe (2002) 'Infanticide in Early Modern England: The Court of Great Sessions at Chester, 1650–1800', in M. Jackson (ed.) *Infanticide: Historical Perspectives on Child Murder and Concealment 1550–2000* (Aldershot: Ashgate), p. 49; Wrightson (1982) 'Infanticide in European History', p. 7; Kilday (2002) 'Maternal Monsters', p. 171; Rowlands (1997) '"In Great Secrecy"', pp. 198–99; Ulbricht (1988) 'Infanticide', p. 120; and Oberman (2002) 'Understanding Infanticide in Context', p. 737.

50. For further discussion see Dalby (1995) 'Women and Infanticide', p. 359; Rowlands (1997) '"In Great Secrecy"', p. 197; Ulbricht (1988) 'Infanticide', p. 132; and Backhouse (1984) 'Desperate Women', p. 448.
51. Harrington (2009) *The Unwanted Child*, p. 44.
52. Kamler (1988) 'Infanticide', pp. 43 and 49. See also Wilson (1988) 'Child Abandonment', p. 767, who agrees that poverty was rarely used as an excuse in infanticide trials.
53. Ulbricht (1988) 'Infanticide', pp. 129–30.
54. See, for instance, Ulbricht (1988) 'Infanticide', pp. 113–14; Schulte (1984) 'Infanticide in Rural Bavaria', p. 90; Rublack (1999) *The Crimes of Women*, p. 188; Cooper Graves (2006) '"…In a Frenzy"', p. 114; Roth (2001) 'Child Murder in New England', p. 114; M.N. Wessling (1994) 'Infanticide Trials and Forensic Medicine: Württembergs 1757–93', in M. Clark and C. Crawford (eds.) *Legal Medicine in History* (Cambridge: Cambridge University Press), p. 124; and Kilday (2008) '"Monsters of the Vilest Kind"', p. 101.
55. See, for instance, Crawford (2010) *Parents of Poor Children*, p. 35 as well as Arnot (2000) 'Understanding Women Committing Newborn Child Murder', pp. 57–8; R. Smith (1983) 'Defining Murder and Madness: An Introduction to Medicolegal Belief in the case of Mary Ann Brough, 1854', *Knowledge and Society: Studies in the Sociology of Culture Past and Present*, 4, p. 182; Prior (2008) *Madness and Murder*, pp. 119 and 139; Higginbotham (1989) '"Sin of the Age"', p. 321; and Sauer (1978) 'Infanticide and Abortion', p. 85.
56. For further discussion see Crawford (2010) *Parents of Poor Children*, p. 39; Schulte (1984) 'Infanticide in Rural Bavaria', p. 85; Ulbricht (1988) 'Infanticide', pp. 116–17; Higginbotham (1989) '"Sin of the Age"', p. 327; K. O'Donovan (1984) 'The Medicalisation of Infanticide', *Criminal Law Review*, 259, p. 260; and Dalby (1995) 'Women and Infanticide', p. 353.
57. M. Daly and M. Wilson (1988) *Homicide* (New York: Aldine de Gruyter), p. 69. For more on poverty being a key motivation for infanticide in the pre-modern period see Rowlands (1997) '"In Great Secrecy"', p. 192 and Harrington (2009) *The Unwanted Child*, p. 44.
58. Oberman (2002) 'Understanding Infanticide in Context', p. 723.
59. Ibid. See also Kilday (2002) 'Maternal Monsters', p. 172; Higginbotham (1989) '"Sin of the Age"', p. 321; and Daly and Wilson (1988) *Homicide*, p. 66. For more detailed discussion see Crawford (2010) *Parents of Poor Children*, pp. 57–8.
60. For further discussion of the precarious nature of women's employment in the pre-modern period, with particular reference to single women, see especially Crawford (2010) *Parents of Poor Children*, pp. 58–9; Harrington (2009) *The Unwanted Child*, pp. 45–6; Hoffer and Hull (1984) *Murdering Mothers*, p. 115; Backhouse (1984) 'Desperate Women', p. 448; and Watson (2008) 'Religion, Community and the Infanticidal Mother', p. 125.
61. NRS, Justiciary Court South Circuit Records, JC12/3.
62. NLW, Records of the Court of Great Sessions, 4/739/1.
63. *The Proceedings of the Old Bailey*, 5 April 1841 [t18410405-1120].
64. See, for instance, A.-M. Kilday (2007) *Women and Violent Crime in Enlightenment Scotland* (Woodbridge: Boydell) and especially R.A. Cage (1981) *The Scottish Poor Law, 1745–1845* (Edinburgh: Scottish Academic Press), especially the maps on pp. 35–6 and 38–9.
65. Crawford (2010) *Parents of Poor Children*, p. 37. For further discussion see L. Hollen Lees (1998) *The Solidarities of Strangers: The English Poor Laws and the*

People, 1700–1948 (Cambridge: Cambridge University Press) and various chapters in P. King, P. Sharpe and T. Hitchcock (eds.) *Chronicling Poverty: The Voices and Strategies of the English Poor, 1640–1840* (Basingstoke: Palgrave Macmillan).

66. Crawford (2010) *Parents of Poor Children*, pp. 37–8. For some evidence that fathers rarely paid maintenance of this kind see Schulte (1984) 'Infanticide in Rural Bavaria', p. 89 and Harrington (2009) *The Unwanted Child*, p. 45.

67. For further discussion see Arnot (2000) 'Understanding Women Committing Newborn Child Murder', p. 57; C.L. Krueger (1997) 'Literary Defences and Medical Prosecutions: Representing Infanticide in Nineteenth-Century Britain', *Victorian Studies*, XL, p. 274; A. Hunt (2006) 'Calculations and Concealments: Infanticide in Mid-Nineteenth-Century Britain', *Victorian Literature and Culture*, 34, p. 72; Higginbotham (1989) '"Sin of the Age"', p. 320; and Cooper Graves (2006) '"...In a Frenzy"', p. 114.

68. Anonymous (1871) *Infant Mortality: Its Causes and Remedies* (Manchester: Ireland and Co), pp. 14–15 [Accessed from the University of Illinois Urbana-Champaign Library at http://archive.org/details/infantmortalityi00manc from the Talbot Collection of British Pamphlets, Ref. 5526548].

69. See Parliamentary Papers, 4 and 5 Will 4 c.76 (1834).

70. See Parliamentary Papers, 7 and 8 Vict c.101 (1844).

71. Parliamentary Papers, 5 Geo 4 c.83 (1824).

72. For further discussion of contemporary concerns about a perceived increase in infanticidal activity as a result of the legislative changes in the first half of the nineteenth century see Behlmer (1979) 'Deadly Motherhood', pp. 417–9.

73. *Poor Law Commissioners Report of 1834* (London: HMSO), Part II, Section 4.

74. NRS, Justiciary Court North Circuit Records, JC11/16.

75. *The Proceedings of the Old Bailey*, 27 October 1856 [t18561027-1005].

76. For further discussion see Malcolmson (1977) 'Infanticide', p. 187; Oberman (2002) 'Understanding Infanticide in Context', p. 725; O'Donovan (1984) 'The Medicalisation of Infanticide', p. 260; Behlmer (1979) 'Deadly Motherhood', p. 415; and Roth (2001) 'Child Murder in New England', p. 120.

77. See L. Rose (1986) *The Massacre of the Innocents: Infanticide in Britain 1800–1939* (London: Routledge and Kegan Paul), Chapters 15 and 16 and also Cooper Graves (2006) '"...In a Frenzy"', p. 114 and Kilday (2007) *Women and Violent Crime*, p. 76.

78. Rose (1986) *The Massacre of the Innocents*, pp. 136–7.

79. Hunt (2006) 'Calculations and Concealments', p. 80.

80. Sauer (1978) 'Infanticide and Abortion', p. 88 and Hunt (2006) 'Calculations and Concealments', p. 77.

81. For further evidence of this across Europe and North America in the pre-modern period see Rublack (1999) *The Crimes of Women*, p. 163; Watson (2008) 'Religion, Community and the Infanticidal Mother', p. 129; Hoffer and Hull (1984) *Murdering Mothers*, p. 115; Hunt (2006) 'Calculations and Concealments', p. 71; and Behlmer (1979) 'Deadly Motherhood', p. 416.

82. For further discussion of altruism as a motive for new-born child murder see Watson (2008) 'Religion, Community and the Infanticidal Mother', p. 128; Oberman (2002) 'Understanding Infanticide in Context', p. 734; Arnot (2000) 'Understanding Women Committing Newborn Child Murder', p. 54; Gilje (1983) 'Infant Abandonment', p. 583; and P.J. Resnick (1969) 'Child Murder by Parents: A Psychiatric Review of Filicide', *American Journal of Psychiatry*, 126, p. 329.

83. Hunter (1783) 'On the Uncertainty of the Signs of Murder', p. 7.

84. See, for instance, V. McMahon (2004) *Murder in Shakespeare's England* (London and New York: Hambledon and London); G. Walker (2003) *Crime, Gender and*

Social Order in Early Modern England (Cambridge: Cambridge University Press); J. Kermode and G. Walker (1994) (eds.) *Women, Crime and the Courts in Early Modern England* (London: Routledge); J. Hurl-Eamon (2005) *Gender and Petty Violence in London, 1680–1720* (Columbus: Ohio State University Press); L. Zedner (1992) *Women, Crime and Custody in Victorian England* (Oxford: Oxford University Press); Kilday (2007) *Women and Violent Crime* and A.-M. Kilday (2005) 'Women and Crime', in H. Barker and E. Chalus (eds.) *Women's History: Britain 1750–1800 – An Introduction* (Abingdon: Routledge), pp. 174–93.

85. See also Rowlands (1997) '"In Great Secrecy"', pp. 179 and 196 for further evidence of this.
86. Cooper Graves (2006) '"...In a Frenzy"', p. 134.
87. See, for, instance Abrams (2002) 'From Demon to Victim', p. 196; Dalby (1995) 'Women and Infanticide', p. 359; Wilson (1988) 'Child Abandonment', p. 774; Resnick (1969) 'Child Murder by Parents', p. 330; Rublack (1999) *The Crimes of Women*, p. 195; and Wrightson (1982) 'Infanticide in European History', p. 7.
88. For further discussion see R. Leboutte (1991) 'Offense against Family Order: Infanticide in Belgium from the Fifteenth Through the Early Twentieth Centuries', *Journal of the History of Sexuality*, 2, p. 183; Hoffer and Hull (1984) *Murdering Mothers*, p. 154; Behlmer (1979) 'Deadly Motherhood', p. 415; and Roth (2001) 'Child Murder in New England', p. 124.
89. As the hand recovered had nails on its fingers, the Justiciary Court held that evidence of maturity was proven.
90. NRS, Justiciary Court North Circuit Records, JC11/23.
91. For further discussion see Kilday (2002) 'Maternal Monsters', pp. 172–3; Schulte (1984) 'Infanticide in Rural Bavaria', p. 91; Rowlands (1997) '"In Great Secrecy"', p. 197; and Resnick (1969) 'Child Murder by Parents', p. 330.
92. NRS, High Court of Justiciary, Books of Adjournal, JC3/45. My addition in parenthesis.
93. See, for instance, M. Jackson (1995) 'Developing Medical Expertise: Medical Practitioners and the Suspected Murders of New-Born Children', in R. Porter (ed.) *Medicine in the Enlightenment* (Amsterdam: Rodopi), p. 157 and R. Smith (1981) *Trial by Medicine: Insanity and Responsibility in Victorian Trials* (Edinburgh: Edinburgh University Press), p. 144.
94. For further discussion see Wessling (1994) 'Infanticide Trials', pp. 137–8.
95. For further discussion see Jackson (1995) 'Developing Medical Expertise', p. 155 and D. Rabin (2002) 'Bodies of Evidence, States of Mind: Infanticide, Emotion and Sensibility in Eighteenth-Century England', in M. Jackson (ed.) *Infanticide: Historical Perspectives on Child Murder and Concealment, 1550–2000* (Aldershot: Ashgate), p. 74.
96. Jackson (1996) *New-Born Child Murder*, p. 119.
97. For further discussion see, for instance, Jackson (1995) 'Developing Medical Expertise', pp. 155–6; Daly and Wilson (1988) *Homicide*, p. 67; Jackson (1996) *New-Born Child Murder*, p. 128; and Krueger (1997) 'Literary Defences and Medical Prosecutions', p. 217.
98. For further discussion see H. Marland (2004) *Dangerous Motherhood: Insanity and Childbirth in Victorian Britain* (Basingstoke: Palgrave Macmillan), pp. 182–3; H. Marland (2002) 'Getting Away With Murder? Puerperal Insanity, Infanticide and the Defence Plea', in M. Jackson (ed.) *Infanticide: Historical Perspectives on Child Murder and Concealment, 1550–2000* (Aldershot: Ashgate), pp. 182–3; Crawford (2010) *Parents of Poor Children*, p. 41; Dalby (1995) 'Women and Infanticide', p. 358; Prior (2008) *Madness and Murder*, p. 124; and Ulbricht (1988) 'Infanticide', p. 112.

99. NLW, Records of the Court of Great Sessions, 4/395/2.
100. Rabin (2002) 'Bodies of Evidence', pp. 86–7. See also D.Y. Rabin (2004) *Identity, Crime, and Legal Responsibility in Eighteenth-Century England* (Basingstoke: Palgrave Macmillan).
101. J.P. Eigen (2003) *Unconscious Crime: Mental Absence and Criminal Responsibility in Victorian London* (Baltimore and London: The John Hopkins University Press), p. 71.
102. Hunter (1783) 'On the Uncertainty of the Signs of Murder', pp. 7–8. For further discussion of the association between childbirth and mental incapacity see Marland (2004) *Dangerous Motherhood*, pp. 9–27; Marland (2002) 'Getting Away With Murder?', p. 173; Jackson (1995) 'Developing Medical Expertise', p. 157; Prior (2008) *Madness and Murder*, p. 126; R. Smith (1981) *Trial by Medicine: Insanity and Responsibility in Victorian Trials* (Edinburgh: Edinburgh University Press), p. 150; L. Gowing (1997) 'Secret Births and Infanticide in Seventeenth-Century England', *Past and Present*, p. 88; Jackson (1996) *New-Born Child Murder*, pp. 120 and 123; and J.P. Eigen (1995) *Witnessing Insanity: Madness and Mad-Doctors in the English Court* (New Haven and London: Yale University Press), p. 148.
103. NRS, Justiciary Court North Circuit Records, JC11/62. See also Crawford (2010) *Parents of Poor Children*, p. 70.
104. For further discussion see Rabin (2002) 'Bodies of Evidence', p. 77.
105. Rabin (2002) 'Bodies of Evidence', p. 88.
106. For further discussion see Rabin (2002) 'Bodies of Evidence', p. 74; Wrightson (1982) 'Infanticide in European History', p. 11; and A. Loughnan (2012) 'The "Strange" Case of the Infanticide Doctrine', *Oxford Journal of Legal Studies*, 32, pp. 1–27.
107. A. Alison (1832) *Principles of the Criminal Law of Scotland* (Edinburgh: Blackwood), p. 159 [Bodleian Library, Cw UK Scotl 510 A413].
108. For further discussion see Smith (1981) *Trial by Medicine*, p. 148; Eigen (2003) *Unconscious Crime*, p. 71; Prior (2008) *Madness and Murder*, p. 119; and Anonymous (1871) *Infant Mortality*, p. 38.
109. For further discussion see Eigen (2003) *Unconscious Crime*, p. 79; C. Quinn (2002) 'Images and Impulses: Representations of Puerperal Insanity and Infanticide in Late Victorian England', in M. Jackson (ed.) *Infanticide: Historical Perspectives on Child Murder and Concealment, 1550–2000* (Aldershot: Ashgate), pp. 193–4; K.D. Watson (2011) *Forensic Medicine in Western Society – A History* (Abingdon: Routledge), p. 108; and Marland (2002) 'Getting Away With Murder?', p. 171.
110. L. Zedner (1991) *Women, Crime and Custody in Victorian England* (Oxford: Oxford University Press), p. 90.
111. H. Marland (1999) 'At Home with Puerperal Mania: The Domestic Treatment of the Insanity of Childbirth in the Nineteenth Century', in P. Bartlett and D. Wright (eds.) *Outside the Walls of the Asylum: The History of Care in the Community 1750–2000* (London and New Brunswick, NJ: Athlone), p. 45.
112. See, for instance, Gowing (1997) 'Secret Births', pp. 107–8; Leboutte (1991) 'Offense against Family Order', p. 173; Schulte (1984) 'Infanticide in Rural Bavaria', p. 89; Wilczynski (1991) 'Images of Women Who Kill their Infants', p. 80; N. Theriot (1990) 'Nineteenth-Century Physicians and "Puerperal Insanity"', *American Studies*, 26, p. 81; and Abrams (2002) 'From Demon to Victim', pp. 186, 194 and 198–9.
113. For further discussion of the history of puerperal insanity see C.L. Meyer and M.G. Spinelli (2003) 'Medical and Legal Dilemmas of Postpartum Psychiatric

Disorders', in M.G. Spinelli (ed.) *Infanticide: Psychological and Legal Perspectives on Mothers Who Kill* (Washington, DC and London: American Psychiatric Publishing), p. 168; Marland (2004) *Dangerous Motherhood*, passim; various articles in J.A. Hamilton and P.N. Harberger (1992) (eds.) *Postpartum Psychiatric Illness: A Picture Puzzle* (Philadelphia: University of Pennsylvania Press); Eigen (1995) *Witnessing Insanity*, p. 142; Eigen (2003) *Unconscious Crime*, p. 72; and T.M. Twomey and S. Bennett (2009) *Understanding Postpartum Psychosis: A Temporary Madness* (London and Westport, CT: Praeger), p. 24.

114. See Twomey and Bennett (2009) *Understanding Postpartum Psychosis*, p. 32. For the purposes of this volume, I will use the term puerperal insanity to describe this condition and all its variants. Lactational insanity has never been associated with instances of infanticide as it was considered to be an illness linked to over-exhaustion and malnutrition rather than direct action. See Marland (2004) *Dangerous Motherhood*, p. 150; Twomey and Bennett (2009) *Understanding Postpartum Psychosis*, p. 32; and Quinn (2002) 'Images and Impulses', p. 198.

115. See K. Johnson Kramar and W.D. Watson (2006) 'The Insanities of Reproduction: Medico-Legal Knowledge and the Development of Infanticide Law', *Social and Legal Studies*, 15, p. 242 and M.G. Spinelli (2004) 'Maternal Infanticide Associated with Mental Illness: Prevention and the Promise of Saved Lives', *American Journal of Psychiatry*, 161, p. 1550.

116. See, for instance, Marland (2004) *Dangerous Motherhood*, p. 6.

117. For further discussion see Quinn (2002) 'Images and Impulses', pp. 196–7; Watson (2011) *Forensic Medicine*, p. 108; and Marland (2002) 'Getting Away With Murder?', p. 176.

118. For further discussion see Marland (2002) 'Getting Away With Murder?', pp. 172 and 179; Twomey and Bennett (2009) *Understanding Postpartum Psychosis*, pp. 36 and 38; Quinn (2002) 'Images and Impulses', p. 195; Marland (1999) 'At Home with Puerperal Mania', p. 50; Theriot (1990) 'Nineteenth-Century Physicians', p. 73; and I. Lambie (2001) 'Mothers Who Kill: The Crime of Infanticide', International *Journal of Law and Psychiatry*, 24, p. 75.

119. Marland (1999) 'At Home with Puerperal Mania', p. 48. See also Marland (2004) *Dangerous Motherhood*, p. 38; Theriot (1990) 'Nineteenth-Century Physicians', p. 73; and N. Walker (1968) *Crime and Insanity in England – Volume One: The Historical Perspective* (Edinburgh: Edinburgh University Press), p. 125.

120. See, for instance, Marland (2004) *Dangerous Motherhood*, pp. 3 and 28–64 and Quinn (2002) 'Images and Impulses', p. 197.

121. With regard to the sudden but serious nature of puerperal insanity see, for instance, Marland (2004) *Dangerous Motherhood*, p. 2; Walker (1968) *Crime and Insanity in England – Volume One*, p. 127; Rabin (2002) 'Bodies of Evidence', p. 77; Eigen (1995) *Witnessing Insanity*, p. 38; Prior (2008) *Madness and Murder*, p. 122; and Eigen (2003) *Unconscious Crime*, p. 75. For further discussion of the treatment of this condition see Marland (2004) *Dangerous Motherhood*, pp. 44 and 50–63; Marland (1999) 'At Home with Puerperal Mania', pp. 45–65; Twomey and Bennett (2009) *Understanding Postpartum Psychosis*, p. 26; Theriot (1990) 'Nineteenth-Century Physicians', p. 74; Quinn (2002) 'Images and Impulses', p. 200; and J. Andrews (2002) 'The Boundaries of Her Majesty's Pleasure: Discharging Child-Murderers from Broadmoor and Perth Lunatic Department, c.1860–1920', in M. Jackson (ed.) *Infanticide: Historical Perspectives on Child Murder and Concealment, 1550–2000* (Aldershot: Ashgate), pp. 216–48.

122. See, for instance, Marland (2004) *Dangerous Motherhood*, pp. 35–7; Marland (1999) 'At Home with Puerperal Mania', pp. 51–2; Theriot (1990) 'Nineteenth-Century Physicians', p. 70; Smith (1981) *Trial by Medicine*, p. 151; and A.-U. Rehman, D. St. Clair and C. Platz (1990) 'Puerperal Insanity in the 19th and 20th Centuries', *British Journal of Psychiatry*, 156, pp. 861–5.
123. See, for instance, Marland (2004) *Dangerous Motherhood*, pp. 5 and 175; Marland (2002) 'Getting Away With Murder?', p. 191; and Rabin (2002) 'Bodies of Evidence', p. 79.
124. For further discussion see Hoffer and Hull (1984) *Murdering Mothers*, p. 146; Watson (2008) 'Religion, Community and the Infanticidal Mother', p. 117; Eigen (2003) *Unconscious Crime*, p. 83; and O'Donovan (1984) 'The Medicalisation of Infanticide', p. 264.
125. See, for instance, W. Burke Ryan (1862) *Infanticide: Its Law, Prevalence, Prevention, and History* (London) [Bodleian Library, (OC) 151 c/345] and for further discussion see Johnson Kramar and Watson (2006) 'The Insanities of Reproduction', pp. 241–2.
126. See Wrightson (1982) 'Infanticide in European History', p. 16; Eigen (2003) *Unconscious Crime*, p. 71; and Marland (2002) 'Getting Away With Murder?', p. 168.
127. The M'Naghten Rules (pronounced, and sometimes spelled, McNaughton) were a reaction to the acquittal of Daniel M'Naghten. They arise from the attempted assassination of the British Prime Minister, Robert Peel, in 1843, by Scottish woodcutter Daniel M'Naghten. In actuality, M'Naghten fired a pistol at the back of Peel's secretary, Edward Drummond, who died five days later. The House of Lords asked a panel of judges a series of hypothetical questions about the defence of insanity. The principles pronounced by this panel have come to be known as the M'Naghten Rules, even though they have only gained status through usage in the common law and M'Naghten himself would have been found guilty if they had been applied to his own trial. The rules formulated from M'Naghten's Case (1843 10 C and F 200) have been a standard test for criminal liability in relation to mentally disordered defendants in various common law jurisdictions ever since, albeit with some minor adjustments. After deliberation, the House Of Lords declared that: 'the jurors ought to be told in all cases that every man is presumed to be sane, and to possess a sufficient degree of reason to be responsible for his crimes, until the contrary be proved to their satisfaction; and that to establish a defence on the ground of insanity, it must be clearly proved that, at the time of the committing of the act, the party accused was labouring under such a defect of reason, from disease of the mind, as not to know the nature and quality of the act he was doing; or, if he did know it, that he did not know he was doing what was wrong'. When the tests set out by the rules are satisfied, the accused may be adjudged 'not guilty by reason of insanity' or 'guilty but insane' and the sentence may be a mandatory or discretionary (but usually indeterminate) period of treatment in a secure facility, or otherwise at the discretion of the court (depending on the country and the offence charged), instead of a more punitive disposal. For further discussion see *House of Lords Decisions*, 10 C and F. 200 and 8 Eng. Rep. 718 (1843) and also Twomey and Bennett (2009) *Understanding Postpartum Psychosis*, pp. 54–7; Eigen (2003) *Unconscious Crime*, p. 78; J. Macfarlane (2003) 'Criminal Defense in Cases of Infanticide and Neonaticide', in M.G. Spinelli (ed.) *Infanticide: Psychological and Legal Perspectives on Mothers Who Kill* (Washington, DC and London: American Psychiatric), p. 145; and Rabin (2002) 'Bodies of Evidence', p. 76.

128. Eigen (1995) *Witnessing Insanity*, p. 144. See also Marland (2002) 'Getting Away With Murder?', p. 178 and T. Ward (1999) 'The Sad Subject of Infanticide: Law, Medicine and Child Murder', *Social and Legal Studies*, VIII, p. 167.

129. For further discussion see Cooper Graves (2006) '"...In a Frenzy"', p. 131; Quinn (2002) 'Images and Impulses', pp. 196 and 200; Eigen (1995) *Witnessing Insanity*, p. 148; S. Day (1985) 'Puerperal Insanity: The Historical Sociology of a Disease' (Unpublished D.Phil. thesis, University of Cambridge), *passim*; Marland (2002) 'Getting Away With Murder?', p. 182; and Eigen (2003) *Unconscious Crime*, p. 72.

130. *Report of the Capital Punishment Commission* (1866) (London: HMSO), pp. 290–1.

131. For further discussion see Watson (2011) *Forensic Medicine*, pp. 108–9; Marland (2004) *Dangerous Motherhood*, pp. 172–3; and Marland (2002) 'Getting Away With Murder?', p. 172. This argument, and the evidence from the case studies presented below, is somewhat at odds with that contended by Tony Ward, who claims that puerperal insanity only applied to married women and older children – see Ward (1999) 'The Sad Subject of Infanticide', p. 167.

132. For further discussion see Smith (1981) *Trial by Medicine*, p. 150.

133. For further discussion see Marland (1999) 'At Home with Puerperal Mania', p. 48 and Quinn (2002) 'Images and Impulses', p. 200.

134. For further discussion see Wessling, 'Infanticide Trials', pp. 137–8; Rizzo, 'Between Dishonour and Death', pp. 6 and 11; A. Wilczynski (1991) 'Images of Women Who Kill their Infants: The Mad and the Bad', *Women and Criminal Justice*, 2, pp. 72 and 77; Marland (2004) *Dangerous Motherhood*, p. 171; Quinn (2002) 'Images and Impulses', p. 200; Smith (1981) *Trial by Medicine*, p. 160; Prior (2008) *Madness and Murder*, p. 131; and Theriot (1990) 'Nineteenth-Century Physicians', pp. 74 and 81.

135. See Theriot (1990) 'Nineteenth-Century Physicians', p. 71.

136. For further discussion see Smith (1981) *Trial by Medicine*, pp. 144 and 150; Lambie (2001) 'Mothers Who Kill', p. 72; and Cooper Graves (2006) '"...In a Frenzy"', p. 135.

137. *The Morning Chronicle*, 4 January 1838, No. 21261. A copper was a large container used for boiling laundry.

138. *The Morning Post*, 4 January 1838, No. 20916.

139. Ibid.

140. *The Proceedings of the Old Bailey*, 29 January 1838 [t18380129-499].

141. Ibid.

142. *The Pall Mall Gazette*, 14 October 1869, No. 1458 and *The Standard*, 28 October 1869, No. 14114.

143. *The Dundee Courier and Angus*, 15 October 1869, No. 5056 and *The Bristol Mercury*, 16 October 1869, No. 4149.

144. *The Pall Mall Gazette*, 27 October 1869, No. 1469; *The Dundee Courier and Angus*, 29 October 1869, No. 5068; *The Glasgow Herald*, 30 October 1869, No. 9306; and *Reynolds' Newspaper*, 31 October 1869, No. 1003.

145. *The Bristol Mercury*, 30 October 1869, No. 4151.

146. *The Proceedings of the Old Bailey*, 22 November 1869 [t18691122-36].

147. Ibid. See also *Lloyds Weekly Newspaper*, 31 October 1869, No. 1406.

148. *The Proceedings of the Old Bailey*, 22 November 1869 [t18691122-36].

149. Ibid.

150. *Reynolds' Newspaper*, 24 June 1894, No. 2289; *Aberdeen Weekly Journal*, 25 June 1894, No. 12293; and *The Morning Post*, 7 July 1894, No. 38088.

151. *The Proceedings of the Old Bailey*, 22 October 1894 [t18941022-849]. See also *The Times*, 26 October 1894, No. 34405 and *The Standard*, 26 October 1894, No. 21939.
152. *The Proceedings of the Old Bailey*, 22 October 1894 [t18941022-849].
153. Ibid.
154. Ibid.
155. Ibid.
156. Ibid.
157. *The Bristol Mercury and Daily Post*, 26 October 1894, No. 14496 and *The Morning Post*, 26 October 1894, No. 38183.
158. See *Western Mail*, 29 October 1894, No. 7660; *The Times*, 2 November 1894, No. 34411; *The Leeds Mercury*, 2 November 1894, No. 17653; *The Royal Cornwall Gazette, Falmouth Packet, Cornish Weekly News and General Advertiser*, 8 November 1894, No. 4763; and *The Illustrated Police News*, 10 November 1894, No. 1604.
159. Marland (2002) 'Getting Away With Murder?', p. 177. See also Twomey and Bennett (2009) *Understanding Postpartum Psychosis*, p. 26 and C.L. Meyer and M.G. Spinelli (2003) 'Medical and Legal Dilemmas of Postpartum Psychiatric Disorders', in M.G. Spinelli (ed.) *Infanticide: Psychological and Legal Perspectives on Mothers Who Kill* (Washington, DC and London: American Psychiatric Publishing), p. 169.
160. For further discussion see Quinn (2002) 'Images and Impulses', p. 197; Marland (2004) *Dangerous Motherhood*, pp. 201–9; Wilczynski (1991) 'Images of Women Who Kill their Infants', p. 75; Lambie (2001) 'Mothers Who Kill', p. 72; and Watson (2011) *Forensic Medicine*, p. 110.
161. For further discussion see Ward (1999) 'The Sad Subject of Infanticide', p. 169; Marland (2002) 'Getting Away With Murder?', p. 170; and Watson (2011) *Forensic Medicine*, p. 111.
162. See, for instance, Marland (2004) *Dangerous Motherhood*, pp. 142–50; Watson (2008) 'Religion, Community and the Infanticidal Mother', p. 129; and Marland (2002) 'Getting Away With Murder?', p. 183.
163. See Daly and Wilson (1988) *Homicide*, p. 68; Smith (1981) *Trial by Medicine*, p. 148; and Theriot (1990) 'Nineteenth-Century Physicians', p. 77.
164. *Baner ac Amserau Cymru* (or *Banner and Times Wales*), 31 October 1894, No. 1966. I am very grateful to Mrs Rhian Perridge for providing a translation of this article.
165. For a fuller description of motive categorisation in relation to infanticide see Hoffer and Hull (1984) *Murdering Mothers*, p. 145.
166. Hoffer and Hull (1984) *Murdering Mothers*, pp. 157–8. See also Kilday (2007) *Women and Violent Crime*, pp. 73–9.

7   The modern debate: Getting away with murder?

1. F.G. Frayling (1908) 'Infanticide: Its Law and Punishment, With Suggested Alternations or Amendments of the Law', *Transactions of the Medico-Legal Society*, 81, pp. 87–9.
2. See, for instance, I. Lambie (2001) 'Mothers Who Kill: The Crime of Infanticide', *International Journal of Law and Psychiatry*, 24, p. 73 and J. McDonagh (1997) 'Infanticide and the Nation: The Case of Caroline Beale', *New Formations – A Journal of Culture/Theory/Politics*, 32, p. 21.

3. For discussion of these issues see respectively P.J. Resnick (1970) 'Murder of the Newborn: A Psychiatric Review of Neonaticide', *American Journal of Psychiatry*, 126, p. 1417; McDonagh (1997) 'Infanticide and the Nation', p. 11; G.R. McKee (2006) *Why Mothers Kill: A Forensic Psychologist's Casebook* (Oxford: Oxford University Press), pp. 11–12; and K. Johnson Kramar (2005) *Unwilling Mothers, Unwanted Babies: Infanticide in Canada* (Vancouver, BC: University of British Columbia Press), pp. 1 and 9.

4. See P.J. Resnick (1969) 'Child Murder by Parents: A Psychiatric Review of Filicide', *American Journal of Psychiatry*, 126, p. 325 and Resnick (1970) 'Murder of the Newborn', p. 1414. For further discussion see McKee (2006) *Why Mothers Kill*, p. 5 and P.T. D'Orbán (1979) 'Women who Kill their Children', *British Journal of Psychiatry*, 134, p. 570.

5. For further discussion see G.R. Searle (1971) *The Quest for National Efficiency: A Study in British Politics and Political Thought, 1899–1914* (Berkeley and Los Angeles: University of California Press).

6. See L. Rose (1986) *The Massacre of the Innocents: Infanticide in Britain 1800–1939* (London: Routledge and Kegan Paul), p. 175 and A. McLaren (1990, 1992 edition) *A History of Contraception – From Antiquity to the Present Day* (Oxford: Blackwell), pp. 218 and 221–2.

7. For further discussion see J. Lewis (1980) *The Politics of Motherhood: Child and Maternal Welfare in England, 1900–1939* (London and Montreal: Croom Helm and McGill-Queen's University Press), pp. 13–34. For further discussion of the early twentieth-century preoccupation with maternal and infant welfare see L. Mahood (1995) *Policing Gender, Class and Family: Britain, 1850–1940* (London: UCL Press); L.V. Marks (1996) *Metropolitan Maternity: Maternal and Infant Welfare Services in Early Twentieth-Century London* (Amsterdam and Atlanta, GA: Rodopi); and V. Fildes, L. Marks and H. Marland (1992) *Women and Children First: International Maternal and Infant Welfare 1870–1945* (London and New York: Routledge).

8. For further discussion see Lewis (1980) *The Politics of Motherhood*, pp. 19–61 and *passim* thereafter.

9. See Rose (1986) *The Massacre of the Innocents*, p. 167. For further discussion see D. Grey (2009) '"More Ignorant and Stupid than Wilfully Cruel": Homicide Trials and "Baby-Farming" in England and Wales in the Wake of The Children Act 1908', *Crimes and Misdemeanours: Deviance and the Law in Historical Perspective*, 3, pp. 60–77.

10. For further discussion see A. Ballinger (2000) *Dead Woman Walking: Executed Women in England and Wales 1900–1955* (Aldershot: Ashgate), pp. 65–128.

11. For further discussion see E. Cunliffe (2011) *Murder, Medicine and Motherhood* (Oxford and Portland, OR: Hart), pp. 3 and 38–71; R.J. Kellett (1992) 'Infanticide and Child Destruction – The Historical, Legal and Pathological Aspects', *Forensic Science International*, 53, pp. 9–16; D. Seaborne Davies (1937) 'Child Killing in English Law', *Modern Law Review*, 1, p. 206; B. Barton (1998) 'When Murdering Hands Rock the Cradle: An Overview of America's Incoherent Treatment of Infanticidal Mothers', *Southern Methodist University Law Review*, 51, p. 606; J.S. Adler (2001) '"Halting the Slaughter of the Innocents": The Civilizing Process and the Surge in Violence in Turn-of-the-Century Chicago', *Social Science History*, 25, p. 42; Resnick (1970) 'Murder of the Newborn', p. 1418; and N. Walker (1968) *Crime and Insanity in England – Volume One: The Historical Perspective* (Edinburgh: Edinburgh University Press), p. 126.

12. See D. Grey (2010) 'Women's Policy Networks and the Infanticide Act 1922', *Twentieth Century British History*, 21, p. 446 and the contemporary writings of Professor Harvey Littlejohn seen in H. Littlejohn (1922) 'Respiration and the Proof of Live-Birth', *Transactions of the Medico-Legal Society*, 86, pp. 86–7.
13. See F. Brookman and J. Nolan (2006) 'The Dark Figure of Infanticide in England and Wales', *Journal of Interpersonal Violence*, 21, pp. 876–9 and Kellett (1992) 'Infanticide and Child Destruction', pp. 16–25.
14. See, for instance, K. O'Donovan (1984) 'The Medicalisation of Infanticide', *Criminal Law Review*, 259, p. 261; Kellett (1992) 'Infanticide and Child Destruction', p. 7; and C. Damme (1978) 'Infanticide: The Worth of an Infant Under Law', *Medical History*, XXII, pp. 1–24.
15. Seaborne Davies (1937) 'Child Killing in English Law', p. 203.
16. See Hansard: House of Lords Debates, 195, 4 November 1908: 1178. For further discussion see T. Ward (2002) 'Legislating for Human Nature: Legal Responses to Infanticide, 1860–1938', in M. Jackson (ed.) *Infanticide: Historical Perspectives on Child Murder and Concealment, 1550–2000* (Aldershot: Ashgate), p. 261; T. Ward (1999) 'The Sad Subject of Infanticide: Law, Medicine and Child Murder', *Social and Legal Studies*, VIII, p. 172; Grey (2010) 'Women's Policy Networks', p. 460; and Walker (1968) *Crime and Insanity*, p. 129.
17. See F.G. Frayling (1908) 'Infanticide: Its Law and Punishment, With Suggested Alternations or Amendments of the Law', *Transactions of the Medico-Legal Society*, 81, p. 89. Frayling's comments and the debate which ensued after the delivery of his paper were subsequently published in the *British Medical Journal* – see 16 May 1908.
18. For further discussion see Hansard: House of Lords Debates, 195, 4 November 1908: 1178 and Ward (2002) 'Legislating for Human Nature', p. 258.
19. For further discussion see Hansard: House of Lords Debates, 196, 12 November 1908: 485 and 486; Ward (2002) 'Legislating for Human Nature', pp. 258–9; Ward (1999) 'The Sad Subject of Infanticide', p. 169; and Grey (2010) 'Women's Policy Networks', p. 444.
20. For further discussion see Hansard: House of Lords Debates, 1, 4 May 1909: 722–3 and 725–7 and also Ward (2002) 'Legislating for Human Nature', pp. 259–61 and S. Edwards (1984) *Women on Trial: A Study of the Female Suspect, Defendant and Offender in the Criminal Law and Criminal Justice System* (Manchester: Manchester University Press), p. 93.
21. See National Archives [Kew, Surrey] (NA), ASSI 11/43, ASSI12/115, ASSI 13/51 and HO 144/1749/419784. See also Ward (2002) 'Legislating for Human Nature', pp. 261–3; Ward (1999) 'The Sad Subject of Infanticide', p. 170; and Grey (2010) 'Women's Policy Networks', pp. 445–6.
22. See ibid. Female jurors were first permitted in 1919, as a result of the Sex Disqualification (Removal) Act. An initial appeal against this commuted sentence failed (see *The Times*, 26 July 1921, No. 42782 and *The Manchester Guardian*, 28 July 1921), but a subsequent campaign for Roberts' release by various feminist groups was successful and Edith Roberts was released from His Majesty's Prison Liverpool on 6 June 1922 – see Grey (2010) 'Women's Policy Networks', pp. 441–63.
23. For further discussion of the attempts to reform legislation in the run up to 1922 see Ward (2002) 'Legislating for Human Nature', pp. 263–5 and Walker (1968) *Crime and Insanity*, pp. 130–2.
24. Parliamentary Papers, 12 and 13 Geo. 5, Chp. 18 (1922).

25. For further discussion see O'Donovan (1984) 'The Medicalisation of Infanticide', p. 261; Resnick (1970) 'Murder of the Newborn', p. 1418; and Kellett (1992) 'Infanticide and Child Destruction', p. 7.
26. See, for instance, the comments made in the *British Medical Journal*, 25 February 1928 as well as J.H. Morton (1934) 'Female Homicides', *The Journal of Mental Science*, LXXX, pp. 65–8.
27. See, for instance, Rose (1986) *The Massacre of the Innocents*, p. 182 and Morton (1934) 'Female Homicides', pp. 65–8.
28. See NA, CRIM 1/414; R. v. O'Donoghue (1927) 28 Cox CC 461 and R. v. O'Donoghue (1927) 20 Cr. App. R. 132 [accessed at http://www.lexisnexis.com] and *The Manchester Guardian*, 14 October 1927. See also Kellett (1992) 'Infanticide and Child Destruction', pp. 7–8; Edwards (1984) *Women on Trial*, p. 93; Ward (2002) 'Legislating for Human Nature', pp. 265–8; Grey (2010) 'Women's Policy Networks', p. 462; and Walker (1968) *Crime and Insanity*, pp. 131–2.
29. See NA, CRIM 1/850 and *The Times*, 22 July 1936, No. 47433. See also Grey (2010) 'Women's Policy Networks', p. 462; Ward (2002) 'Legislating for Human Nature', pp. 267–8; and Edwards (1984) *Women on Trial*, p. 93.
30. For further discussion of the attempts to reform legislation in the run up to 1938 see Seaborne Davies (1937) 'Child Killing in English Law', p. 205 and Walker (1968) *Crime and Insanity*, p. 132.
31. Parliamentary Papers, 1 and 2 Geo. 6, Chp. 36 (1938).
32. Parliamentary Papers, 24 and 25 Vict. C. 100 (1861).
33. For further discussion see D.R.S.D. (1938) 'The Infanticide Act, 1938', *The Modern Law Review*, 2, p. 229; O'Donovan (1984) 'The Medicalisation of Infanticide', p. 261; Kellett (1992) 'Infanticide and Child Destruction', pp. 8–9; and Walker (1968) *Crime and Insanity*, p. 132.
34. A. Norrie (1993) *Crime, Reason and History* (London: Weidenfeld and Nicholson), p. 31 cited in Ward (2002) 'Legislating for Human Nature', p. 250.
35. Parliamentary Papers, 5 and 6 Eliz.2 c.11 (1957).
36. For further discussion see Lambie (2001) 'Mothers Who Kill', p. 72 and K. Johnson Kramar (2006) 'Unwilling Mothers and Unwanted Babies: The Vicissitudes of Infanticide law in Canada', in B.H. Bechtold and D. Cooper Graves (eds.) *Killing Infants: Studies in the Worldwide Practice of Infanticide* (New York: Edwin Mellen), p. 164.
37. For further discussion see Brookman and Nolan (2006) 'The Dark Figure of Infanticide', p. 870; Barton (1998) 'When Murdering Hands Rock the Cradle', p. 617; and Ward (1999) 'The Sad Subject of Infanticide', p. 176.
38. For further discussion see O'Donovan (1984) 'The Medicalisation of Infanticide', p. 262 and Walker (1968) *Crime and Insanity*, p. 135.
39. For further discussion see Barton (1998) 'When Murdering Hands Rock the Cradle', p. 617.
40. See J. Gunn (1993) (ed.) 'The Law, Adult Mental Disorder, and the Psychiatrist in England and Wales (With Comments from the rest of the United Kingdom and Ireland)', in J. Gunn and P.J. Taylor (eds.), *Forensic Psychiatry: Clinical, Legal and Ethical Issues* (London: Butterworth and Heinemann), p. 50.
41. Ward (1999) 'The Sad Subject of Infanticide', p. 164, p. 170 and p. 174.
42. Parliamentary Papers, Home Office, Department of Health and Social Security, Report of the Committee on Mentally Abnormal Offenders, Cmnd. 6244 (1975), p. 251.
43. Ibid., pp. 249–51. My addition in parenthesis.

44. Ibid., p. 251.
45. Ibid., p. 249. For further discussion see Edwards (1984) *Women on Trial*, p. 94; E. Parker and F. Good (1981) 'Infanticide', *Law and Human Behaviour*, 5, p. 241; and O'Donovan (1984) 'The Medicalisation of Infanticide', p. 262.
46. A detailed write-up of The Royal College of Psychiatrists' Working Party Report was provided by Dr Robert Bluglass, Consultant Psychiatrist, in the second volume of the medical journal *The Psychiatrist*, published in the year of the report, 1978.
47. See R. Bluglass (1978) 'Infanticide', *The Psychiatrist*, 2, p. 140 and Parliamentary Papers, Criminal Law Revision Committee, Fourteenth report Offences against the Person, Cmnd. 7844 (1980), p. 46.
48. See respectively Bluglass (1978) 'Infanticide', pp. 139–40 and the Criminal Law Revision Committee Report, pp. 46–7. For further discussion see Parker and Good (1981) 'Infanticide', pp. 241–2 and Edwards (1984) *Women on Trial*, p. 94.
49. Criminal Law Revision Committee Report, p. 47.
50. Ibid., pp. 49 and 52.
51. Bluglass (1978) 'Infanticide', p. 141.
52. See the suggestion made at ibid. and in the Criminal Law Revision Committee Report, p. 51. For the Criminal Attempts Act see Parliamentary Papers, Criminal Attempts Act, ch. 47 (1981). For further discussion see A.J. Wilkins (1985) 'Attempted Infanticide', *The British Journal of Psychiatry*, 146, pp. 206–8; J. Gunn (1993) (ed.) 'The Law, Adult Mental Disorder, and the Psychiatrist', p. 50; and Edwards (1984) *Women on Trial*, p. 96.
53. The Law Commission (2005) 'A New Homicide Act for England and Wales? A Consultation Paper', No. 177, Part 9, pp. 224–6.
54. Ibid., p. 224.
55. Ibid.
56. Ibid., p. 240.
57. Ibid., p. 242.
58. For further discussion see England and Wales Court of Appeal (EWCA), Criminal Division, Decisions, Crim 1092 (2005) 2 Cr App R 31. See also *The Guardian*, 3 of May 2005 and *The Telegraph*, 4 May 2005.
59. The Law Commission (2005) 'A New Homicide Act', p. 243.
60. The Law Commission (2006) 'Murder, Manslaughter and Infanticide – Project Six of the Ninth Programme of Law Reform: Homicide', No. 304, Part 8, pp. 156–72.
61. Ibid., p. 156.
62. Ibid., p. 156.
63. EWCA, Crim 2789 (2007).
64. See Home Office (2008) 'Murder, Manslaughter and Infanticide: Proposals for Reform of the Law – Consultation Paper', 19/08, p. 31 and Home Office (2009) 'Murder, Manslaughter and Infanticide: Proposals for Reform of the Law – Summary of Responses and Government Position', 19/08, pp. 25–7. There was one minor point of legal clarification made as a result of this ruling and from recommendations in both the consultation paper and report from the Law Commission. This related to the potential for a woman to be charged with a homicide or an infanticide (via negligence), when a man or other adult indicted under the same circumstances would only be charged with child cruelty, which carried a much lighter sentence. Consequently, the Coroners and Justice Act 2009 made it impossible to charge infanticide in circumstances which would not

lead to a homicide charge – see Parliamentary Papers, Coroners and Justice Act, ch. 25, s.57 (2009).

65. P.T. D'Orbán (1993) 'Female Offenders', in J. Gunn and P.J. Taylor (eds.), *Forensic Psychiatry: Clinical, Legal and Ethical Issues* (London: Butterworth and Heinemann), pp. 611–12.

66. McDonagh (1997) 'Infanticide and the Nation', p. 16.

67. Edwards (1984) *Women on Trial*, p. 96.

68. O'Donovan (1984) 'The Medicalisation of Infanticide', p. 264. For a similar argument see Ward (2002) 'Legislating for Human Nature', p. 251.

69. C.L. Meyer and M. Oberman (2001) *Mothers Who Kill their Children: Understanding the Acts of Moms from Susan Smith to the 'Prom Mom'* (New York and London: New York University Press), p. 11.

70. For further discussion see Walker (1968) *Crime and Insanity*, pp. 142–4.

71. For further discussion see M.N. Marks and R. Kumar (1996) 'Infanticide in Scotland', *Medicine, Science and the Law*, 36, pp. 299–300.

72. For further discussion see M. Oberman (2003) 'A Brief History of Infanticide and the Law', in M.G. Spinelli (ed.) *Infanticide: Psychological and Legal Perspectives on Mothers Who Kill* (Washington, DC and London: American Psychiatric), pp. 9 and 14; S. Caron (2010) '"Killed by its Mother": Infanticide in Providence County, Rhode Island, 1870 to 1938', *Journal of Social History*, 44, p. 214; Johnson Kramar (2005) *Unwilling Mothers*, p. 5; Meyer and Oberman (2001) *Mothers Who Kill their Children*, p. 11; and Barton (1998) 'When Murdering Hands Rock the Cradle', pp. 593, 597, 605–11 and 615.

73. See McDonagh (1997) 'Infanticide and the Nation', pp. 11–21. See also *The Times*, 13 June 1995, 2 March 1996 and 9 March 1996.

74. *The Independent*, 8 March 1996 and the *British Medical Journal*, 16 March 1996.

75. *The Times*, 19 March 1996.

76. One minor amendment to concealment legislation in England and Wales, in 1967, extended its provision as an alternative verdict to charges of infanticide and manslaughter – see Parliamentary Papers, Criminal Law Act, ch. 58, s. 3 (1967).

77. See McDonagh (1997) 'Infanticide and the Nation', p. 21; Lambie (2001) 'Mothers Who Kill', p. 73; L. Ryan (2004) 'The Press, Police and Prosecution: Perspectives on Infanticide in the 1920s', in A. Hayes and D. Urquhart (eds.) *Irish Women's History* (Dublin and Portland, OR: Irish Academic), p. 139; and Barton (1998) 'When Murdering Hands Rock the Cradle', p. 619.

78. M.N. Marks (1996) 'Characteristics and Causes of Infanticide in Britain', *International Review of Psychiatry*, 8, p. 99.

79. For further discussion see ibid.; McKee (2006) *Why Mothers Kill*, pp. 11–12; Kellett (1992) 'Infanticide and Child Destruction', pp. 9–25; and Brookman and Nolan (2006) 'The Dark Figure of Infanticide', pp. 870 and 875–81.

80. See the *British Medical Journal*, 9 November 1940.

81. See in particular *The Guardian*, 4 January 1992 and Cunliffe (2011) *Murder, Medicine and Motherhood*, pp. 34–5.

82. R. Meadow (1989) 'ABC of Child Abuse: Suffocation', *British Medical Journal*, 10 June 1989, 298, p. 1572.

83. For further discussion see Cunliffe (2011) *Murder, Medicine and Motherhood*, pp. 54–5.

84. Maureen Marks and Ramesh Kumar conducted an analysis of infanticide in Scotland between 1978 and 1993, but their problematic definition of the offence to encompass infants up to the age of five means that the results of their statistical

analysis cannot be included in this present study as it would offer a misleading comparison with evidence relating to victims under one year of age. See Marks and Kumar (1996) 'Infanticide in Scotland', pp. 299–305.

85. The data for all of the graphs in this chapter was collected through a detailed analysis of the judicial statistics recorded in the Parliamentary Papers for Scotland, England and Wales for every year between 1900 and 1999. In the main, these were accessed via http://parlipapers.chadwyck.co.uk/marketing/index.jspbut. Where additional data was required hard copies of reports were consulted in the Bodleian Library Official Papers Room. I am very grateful to Hannah Chandler of the Bodleian Library for assisting me with this endeavour. There are several factors which significantly affected the collection of data in relation to the statistical evidence provided in this chapter. The impact of legislative change, the problems associated with the detection of criminality in wartime, altering definitions and opinions of certain types of offences and offenders, as well as methodological changes to data capture, have all impacted on how crime was recorded over the twentieth century and may result in inaccuracies in official statistics.

86. For further discussion of the use of concealment as an alternative charge/verdict in instances of new-born child murder see Seaborne Davies (1937) 'Child Killing in English Law', p. 231; K. Johnson Kramar and W.D. Watson (2006) 'The Insanities of Reproduction: Medico-Legal Knowledge and the Development of Infanticide Law', *Social and Legal Studies*, 15, p. 248; Ward (1999) 'The Sad Subject of Infanticide', p. 164; and Frayling (1908) 'Infanticide: Its Law and Punishment', p. 87.

87. Littlejohn (1922) 'Respiration and the Proof of Live-Birth', p. 101.

88. For further discussion of the perceived diminution of infanticide and concealment over time, which is borne out by the present analysis, see Rose (1986) *The Massacre of the Innocents*, p. 174.

89. For further discussion of the decreasing conviction rate for new-born child murder in the aftermath of the Infanticide Acts see A. Payne (1995) 'Infanticide and Child Abuse', *The Journal of Forensic Psychiatry*, 6, p. 243.

90. For further discussion see A. Morris (1987) *Women, Crime and Criminal Justice* (Oxford: Basil Blackwell), p. 33; Parker and Good (1981) 'Infanticide', pp. 238 and 35–6; and D'Orbán (1993) 'Female Offenders', pp. 600 and 603.

91. For further discussion of contraceptive practices and women's lives prior to World War Two see McLaren (1990, 1992 edition) *A History of Contraception*, Chapter 7; S. Bruley (1999) *Women in Britain since 1900* (Basingstoke: Macmillan), p. 11; K. Fisher (2006) *Birth Control, Sex and Marriage in Britain 1918–1960* (Oxford: Oxford University Press), pp. 1 and 5; and H. Cook (2004) *The Long Sexual Revolution: English Women, Sex and Contraception 1800–1975* (Oxford: Oxford University Press), pp. 115; 122–42 and 167–79.

92. Cook (2004) *The Long Sexual Revolution*, p. 112.

93. For further discussion of contraceptive practices and women's lives after World War Two see L.V. Marks (2001, 2010 edition) *Sexual Chemistry: A History of the Contraceptive Pill* (New Haven and London: Yale University Press); S. Szreter and K. Fisher (2010) *Sex before the Sexual Revolution: Intimate Life in England 1918–1963* (Cambridge: Cambridge University Press); Bruley (1999) *Women in Britain*, pp. 71, 135, 137–8 and 175; Fisher (2006) *Birth Control*, pp. 5, 9–12 and 189–237; J. Pilcher (1999) *Women in Contemporary Britain* (London and New York: Routledge), p. 78; and Cook (2004) *The Long Sexual Revolution*, pp. 288, 290, 295, 318 and 320.

94. Cook (2004) *The Long Sexual Revolution*, p. 326.
95. Ibid., p. 15.
96. For further discussion see Parker and Good (1981) 'Infanticide', pp. 238–40 and Rose (1986) *The Massacre of the Innocents*, p. 183.
97. For further discussion see Ryan (2004) 'The Press, Police and Prosecution', p. 150 and Johnson Kramar (2006) 'Unwilling Mothers and Unwanted Babies', p. 153.
98. For further discussion of the reasons for the increase in reported child murders at this time see Bruley (1999) *Women in Britain*, p. 115.
99. The use of infanticide as a late form of contraception was not confined to Britain at this time see S.A. Kowalsky (2006) 'Making Sense of the Murdering Mother: Soviet Criminologists and Infanticide in Revolutionary Russia', in B.H. Bechtold and D. Cooper Graves (eds.) *Killing Infants: Studies in the Worldwide Practice of Infanticide* (Lewiston, NY: Edwin Mellen), p. 174.
100. For further discussion of the history of abortion in twentieth century Britain see B. Brookes (1988) *Abortion in England 1900–1967* (London, New York and Sydney: Croom Helm); E.L. Jones (2007) 'Abortion in England, 1861–1967' (Unpublished PhD Thesis, Royal Holloway, University of London); S. Brooke (2001) '"A New World for Women"? Abortion Law Reform in Britain during the 1930s', *American Historical Review*, 106, pp. 431–59; T. McIntosh (2000) '"An Abortionist City": Maternal Mortality, Abortion, and Birth Control in Sheffield, 1920–1940', *Medical History*, 44, pp. 75–96; and McLaren (1990, 1992 edition) *A History of Contraception*, pp. 227–31.
101. Brookes (1988) *Abortion in England*, pp. 1 and 5.
102. See, for instance, Lewis (1980) *The Politics of Motherhood*, pp. 209–11 and Adler (2001) '"Halting the Slaughter of the Innocents"', pp. 39–41.
103. Parliamentary Papers, Abortion Act, ch. 87 (1967). For further discussion J. Keown (1988) *Abortion, Doctors and the Law: Some Aspects of the Legal Regulation of Abortion in England from 1803 to 1982* (Cambridge: Cambridge University Press).
104. L.L. Schwartz and N.K. Isser (2007) *Child Homicide: Parents Who Kill* (Boca Raton, FL: Taylor and Francis), pp. 75–7.
105. For further discussion see Rose (1986) *The Massacre of the Innocents*, p. 184 and Grey (2009) '"More Ignorant and Stupid"', pp. 63 and 70–3.
106. For further discussion see Cook (2004) *The Long Sexual Revolution*, pp. 122–3 and 282 and Bruley (1999) *Women in Britain*, p. 77.
107. Bruley (1999) *Women in Britain*, p. 173.
108. C. Alder and K. Polk (2001) *Child Victims of Homicide* (Cambridge: Cambridge University Press), p. 41.
109. See, for instance, Resnick (1970) 'Murder of the Newborn', p. 1415; D'Orbán (1979) 'Women who Kill their Children', p. 561; I. Brockington (1996, 2003 edition) *Motherhood and Mental Health* (Oxford: Oxford University Press), p. 447; M. Oberman (2002) 'Understanding Infanticide in Context: Mothers Who Kill, 1870–1930 and Today', *The Journal of Criminal Law and Criminology*, 92, p. 709; J. Macfarlane (2003) 'Criminal Defense in Cases of Infanticide and Neonaticide', in M.G. Spinelli (ed.) *Infanticide: Psychological and Legal Perspectives on Mothers Who Kill* (Washington, DC and London: American Psychiatric), p. 135; and Schwartz and Isser (2007) *Child Homicide*, p. 42.
110. For further discussion see Meyer and Oberman (2001) *Mothers Who Kill their Children*, p. 19 and Barton (1998) 'When Murdering Hands Rock the Cradle', p. 594.

111. See, for instance, Schwartz and Isser (2007) *Child Homicide*, pp. 131–73; McKee (2006) *Why Mothers Kill*, pp. 13–16; and D'Orbán (1979) 'Women who Kill their Children', pp. 561–2.

112. For further discussion see Bruley (1999) *Women in Britain*, pp. 38, 93–105 and 172.

113. See, for instance, Grey (2009) '"More Ignorant and Stupid"', pp. 68 and 75 and S.H. Friedman and P.J. Resnick (2007) 'Child Murder by Mothers: Patterns and Prevention', *World Psychiatry*, 6, p. 137.

114. Other studies have also identified the dominance of female perpetrators in the modern era – see Marks (1996) 'Characteristics and Causes of Infanticide', p. 100.

115. For further discussion of men's increased involvement in child murder in the modern era see Brookman and Nolan (2006) 'The Dark Figure of Infanticide', p. 871 and Johnson Kramar (2006) 'Unwilling Mothers and Unwanted Babies, p. 152.

116. For further discussion see Marks (1996) 'Characteristics and Causes of Infanticide', p. 101; Schwartz and Isser (2007) *Child Homicide*, p. 42 and Resnick (1970) 'Murder of the Newborn', p. 1417.

117. For further discussion see Brockington (1996, 2003 edition) *Motherhood and Mental Health*, pp. 530–1 and Alder and Polk (2001) *Child Victims of Homicide*, p. 73.

118. For further discussion see Marks and Kumar (1996) 'Infanticide in Scotland', p. 301; Payne (1995) 'Infanticide and Child Abuse', p. 474; Brookman and Nolan (2006) 'The Dark Figure of Infanticide', pp. 869–70 and 873; D'Orbán (1979) 'Women Who Kill their Children', p. 560; and Friedman and Resnick (2007) 'Child Murder by Mothers', p. 137.

119. M.N. Marks and R. Kumar (1993) 'Infanticide in England and Wales', *Medicine, Science and the Law*, 33, p. 332.

120. Ibid., p. 333.

121. See Marks (1996) 'Characteristics and Causes of Infanticide', p. 99.

122. For further discussion see Brookman and Nolan (2006) 'The Dark Figure of Infanticide', p. 873.

123. See Lewis (1980) *The Politics of Motherhood*, p. 120 and Johnson Kramar (2006) 'Unwilling Mothers and Unwanted Babies', p. 162.

124. See H. Winnik and M. Horovitz (1962) 'The Problem of Infanticide', *British Journal of Criminology*, 40, p. 45.

125. Data on method was not recorded in the official judicial statistics relating to child murder, infanticide or concealment in Britain between 1900 and 1999, so the conclusions here are based on newspaper evidence and secondary sources. For further discussion of the varied nature of infanticidal methods in the twentieth century see Marks and Kumar (1993) 'Infanticide in England and Wales', pp. 34–5; Resnick (1970) 'Murder of the Newborn', p. 1415; Resnick (1969) 'Child Murder by Parents', p. 328; and Morton (1934) 'Female Homicides', p. 69.

126. See, for instance, Brockington (1996, 2003 edition) *Motherhood and Mental Health*, pp. 439–42; Marks (1996) 'Characteristics and Causes of Infanticide', p. 99; and McKee (2006) *Why Mothers Kill*, p. 19.

127. For further discussion see Brockington (1996, 2003 edition) *Motherhood and Mental Health*, p. 438 and Morton (1934) 'Female Homicides', p. 71.

128. *The Manchester Guardian*, 26 February 1955 and 23 March 1955.

129. Ibid., 24 March 1955.
130. Ibid., 2 August, 1952.
131. *The Times*, 17 September 1952, No. 52419.
132. For further discussion of the classification of child murder since 1970 see, for instance, Meyer and Oberman (2001) *Mothers Who Kill their Children*, pp. 24–31 and 36–94; McKee (2006) *Why Mothers Kill*, pp. 6 and 23–33; D'Orbán (1979) 'Women who Kill their Children', p. 561; Friedman and Resnick (2007) 'Child Murder by Mothers', p. 137; and Lambie (2001) 'Mothers Who Kill', pp. 76–7.
133. Resnick (1970) 'Murder of the Newborn', p. 1415.
134. For further discussion of the continued influence of shame on episodes of new-born child murder see, for instance, Resnick (1970) 'Murder of the Newborn', pp. 1415–6; Caron (2010) '"Killed by its Mother"', p. 213; Schwartz and Isser (2007) *Child Homicide*, pp. 48–50; Johnson Kramar (2006) 'Unwilling Mothers and Unwanted Babies', p. 139; Brockington (1996, 2003 edition) *Motherhood and Mental Health*, p. 447; and Kowalsky (2006) 'Making Sense of the Murdering Mother', p. 182.
135. *The Times*, 14 March 1986, No. 62404.
136. For further discussion of the isolation associated with infanticide see Brockington (1996, 2003 edition) *Motherhood and Mental Health*, p. 447 and Oberman (2002) 'Understanding Infanticide in Context', p. 709.
137. For further discussion of denial as a common characteristic of new-born child murder and the desperation typically associated with the offence see, for instance, L.J. Miller (2003) 'Denial of Pregnancy', in M.G. Spinelli (ed.) *Infanticide: Psychological and Legal Perspectives on Mothers Who Kill* (Washington, DC and London: American Psychiatric), pp. 81–104; J. Wheelwright (2002) '"Nothing in Between": Modern Cases of Infanticide', in M. Jackson (ed.) *Infanticide: Historical Perspectives on Child Murder and Concealment, 1550–2000* (Aldershot: Ashgate), p. 272; Meyer and Oberman (2001) *Mothers Who Kill their Children*, pp. 39–67; Schwartz and Isser (2007) *Child Homicide*, p. 46; Oberman (2002) 'Understanding Infanticide in Context', p. 710; Alder and Polk (2001) *Child Victims of Homicide*, pp. 38 and 34; Brockington (1996, 2003 edition) *Motherhood and Mental Health*, pp. 14–15 and 115; S.S.M. Edwards (1986) 'Neither Bad Nor Mad: The Female Violent Offender Reassessed', *Women's Studies International Forum*, 9, p. 86; Winnik and Horovitz (1962) 'The Problem of Infanticide', p. 40; Caron (2010) '"Killed by its Mother"', p. 227; and H. Altink (2007) '"I Did Not Want to Face the Shame of Exposure: Gender Ideologies and Child Murder in Post-Emancipation Jamaica', *Journal of Social History, Society and Cultures*, 41, pp. 373–4.
138. *The Times*, 14 March 1986, No. 62404.
139. For further discussion see, for instance, Parliamentary Papers, Report of the Committee on Mentally Abnormal Offenders (1975), p. 249; P.T. D'Orbán (1971) 'Social and Psychiatric Aspects of Female Crime', *Medicine, Science and the Law*, 11, pp. 114–5; Johnson Kramar and Watson (2006) 'The Insanities of Reproduction', p. 247; D'Orbán (1993) 'Female Offenders', p. 611; and Morton (1934) 'Female Homicides', p. 70.
140. For further discussion see, for instance, the *British Medical Journal*, 15 March 1902; R.E. Hemphill (1967) 'Infanticide and Puerperal Mental Illness', *Nursing Times*, 63, pp. 1473–5; Winnik and Horovitz (1962) 'The Problem of Infanticide', pp. 48–50; Oberman (2002) 'Understanding Infanticide in Context', p. 713; Caron (2010) '"Killed by its Mother"', p. 216; and M.G. Spinelli (2009)

'Postpartum Psychosis: Detection of Risk and Management', *American Journal of Psychiatry*, 166, pp. 405–8.

141. *British Medical Journal*, 17 December, 1960.
142. See Marks and Kumar (1996) 'Infanticide in Scotland', p. 304.
143. This supposition was first put forward in an early twentieth-century issue of the *British Medical Journal* by Dr Alan Rigden – see 10 November 1906. For further discussion of the advancement of that argument see, for instance, J.A. Hamilton (1989) 'Postpartum Psychiatric Syndromes', *Psychiatric Clinics of North America*, 12, p. 97; Brockington (1996, 2003 edition) *Motherhood and Mental Health*, p. 454, Lambie (2001) 'Mothers Who Kill', p. 75; and Schwartz and Isser (2007) *Child Homicide*, pp. 55 and 117–30.
144. Brockington (1996, 2003 edition) *Motherhood and Mental Health*, pp. 205–9; Caron (2010) '"Killed by its Mother"', p. 214; and Lambie (2001) 'Mothers Who Kill', p. 78.
145. Brockington (1996, 2003 edition) *Motherhood and Mental Health*, p. 138.
146. For further discussion see the *British Medical Journal*, 22 February 1969; Spinelli (2009) 'Postpartum Psychosis', pp. 405–8; Hemphill (1967) 'Infanticide and Puerperal Mental Illness', pp. 1473–5; Hamilton (1989) 'Postpartum Psychiatric Syndromes', pp. 89–103; and K.L. Wisner et al. (2003) 'Postpartum Disorders' and D. Sichel (2003) 'Neurohormonal Aspects of Postpartum Depression and Psychosis', both in M.G. Spinelli (ed.) *Infanticide: Psychological and Legal Perspectives on Mothers Who Kill* (Washington, DC and London: American Psychiatric), pp. 35–60 and 61–79 respectively.
147. *The Times*, 10 January 1986, No. 62341 and *The Guardian*, 10 January 1986.
148. Payne (1995) 'Infanticide and Child Abuse', p. 475.
149. See for instance Lambie (2001) 'Mothers Who Kill', pp. 78-9 and Alder and Polk (2001) *Child Victims of Homicide*, p. 58.
150. See, for instance, Barton (1998) 'When Murdering Hands Rock the Cradle', p. 611; Johnson Kramar and Watson (2006) 'The Insanities of Reproduction', p. 250; and Alder and Polk (2001) *Child Victims of Homicide*, pp. 3–4.
151. For further discussion of economic factors in instances of infanticide see Morton (1934) 'Female Homicides', pp. 70 and 74; Johnson Kramar and Watson (2006) 'The Insanities of Reproduction', p. 249; Resnick (1969) 'Child Murder by Parents', p. 329; Alder and Polk (2001) *Child Victims of Homicide*, p. 50; D'Orbán (1979) 'Women who Kill their Children', p. 563; Oberman (2002) 'Understanding Infanticide in Context', pp. 710, 713 and 733–4; and Caron (2010) '"Killed by its Mother"', pp. 213 and 227.
152. For further discussion of social factors in instances of infanticide see Resnick (1969) 'Child Murder by Parents', p. 330; Alder and Polk (2001) *Child Victims of Homicide*, p. 50; Friedman and Resnick (2007) 'Child Murder by Mothers', p. 138; and Schwartz and Isser (2007) *Child Homicide*, p. 57.
153. *The Times*, 14 March 1986, No. 62404.
154. Wheelwright (2002) '"Nothing in Between"', p. 275. See also Oberman (2002) 'Understanding Infanticide in Context', pp. 708, 715 and 737.
155. Frayling (1908) 'Infanticide: Its Law and Punishment', pp. 100–1. For further discussion of the contention that leniency prevails in relation to indictments for new-born child murder see Johnson Kramar (2006) 'Unwilling Mothers and Unwanted Babies', p. 139 and Resnick (1970) 'Murder of the Newborn', p. 1418.
156. Marks and Kumar (1993) 'Infanticide in England and Wales', p. 334.

157. See, for instance, Brookman and Nolan (2006) 'The Dark Figure of Infanticide', pp. 873–4 and Resnick (1970) 'Murder of the Newborn', p. 1418. Evidence to substantiate the high and consistent conviction rate for infanticide and new-born child murder in twentieth-century Britain indicated by the statistical evidence offered in this chapter can be found in D'Orbán (1979) 'Women who Kill their Children', p. 566 and Wheelwright, J. (2002) '"Nothing in Between": Modern Cases of Infanticide', in M. Jackson (ed.) *Infanticide: Historical Perspectives on Child Murder and Concealment, 1550–2000* (Aldershot: Ashgate), p. 274.
158. The last woman to be hung for infanticide in Britain was Rebecca Smith from Wiltshire in 1849. See K.D. Watson (2008) 'Religion, Community and the Infanticidal Mother: Evidence from 1840s Rural Wiltshire', *Family and Community History*, 11, pp. 116–33.
159. For further discussion see the *British Medical Journal*, 10 July 1965; Walker (1968) *Crime and Insanity*, p. 133; Payne (1995) 'Infanticide and Child Abuse', p. 473; Ward (1999) 'The Sad Subject of Infanticide', p. 171; and Edwards (1986) 'Neither Bad Nor Mad', p. 82.
160. For further discussion of these arguments see Morris (1987) *Women, Crime and Criminal Justice*, pp. 34–9; A. Wilczynski (1997) 'Mad or Bad? Child Killers, Gender and the Courts', *British Journal of Criminology*, 37, pp. 419–36; Edwards (1986) 'Neither Bad Nor Mad', pp. 79–87; Ryan (2004) 'The Press, Police and Prosecution', p. 149; and D'Orbán (1971) 'Social and Psychiatric Aspects of Female Crime', p. 104.
161. Ryan (2004) 'The Press, Police and Prosecution', p. 149.
162. For further discussion see Cunliffe (2011) *Murder, Medicine and Motherhood*, p. 12 and Brookman and Nolan (2006) 'The Dark Figure of Infanticide', p. 875.
163. For further discussion see Marks and Kumar (1993) 'Infanticide in England and Wales', p. 336 and Ward (1999) 'The Sad Subject of Infanticide', p. 164.
164. For a personalised account of this case see J. Batt (2004, 2005 edition) *Stolen Innocence* (London: Ebury), *passim*.
165. *The Times*, 13 October 1999.
166. Ibid.
167. *The Times*, 10 November 1999 and BBC Evening News, 9 November 1999 [Accessed at http://news.bbc.co.uk/1/hi/uk/512099.stm].
168. R. Meadow (1989, 1997 edition) (ed.) *ABC of Child Abuse* (London: BMJ), pp. 27–9. For the prevalence of this belief see Cunliffe (2011) *Murder, Medicine and Motherhood*, p. 193.
169. Batt (2004, 2005 edition) *Stolen Innocence*, pp. 191–3.
170. *The Times*, 27 November 1999.
171. *The Times*, 18 July 2000.
172. *British Medical Journal*, 1 January 2000.
173. H. Joyce (2002) 'Beyond Reasonable Doubt', + *Plus Magazine: Living Mathematics*, 21 [accessed at http://plus.maths.org/content/beyond-reasonable-doubt].
174. *The Observer*, 15 July 2001.
175. *The Times*, 29 January 2003 and the *British Medical Journal*, 8 February 2003.
176. *The Times*, 30 January 2003 and the *British Medical Journal*, 8 February 2003.
177. See *The Times*, 30 January 2003, 31 of January 2003 and 4 February 2003.
178. See, for instance, *The Guardian*, 24 June 2003.
179. See *The Guardian*, 1 July 2003; *The Times*, 20 January 2004 and the *British Medical Journal*, 24 January 2004.

180. See *The Guardian*, 19 December 2003; *The Times*, 5 December 2003 and 19 December 2003; and the *British Medical Journal*, 3 January 2004, 27 January 2005, 5 February 2005 and 25 June 2005.
181. *British Medical Journal*, 11 June 2005.
182. See *British Medical Journal*, 23 July 2005, 26 January 2006 and 25 February 2006.
183. See the *British Medical Journal*, 18 February 2006 and 10 February 2007 as well as J.R. Vaughan and P.M. Kautt (2009) 'Infant Death Investigations Following High-Profile Unsafe Rulings: Throwing Out the Baby With the Bath Water?', *Policing: A Journal of Policy and Practice*, 3, pp. 89–99. For the guidance see the information at http://www.gmc-uk.org/guidance/ethical_guidance/expert_witness_guidance.asp. For further discussion of the role of medical experts in criminal trials in modern British history see T. Ward (2004) 'Experts, Juries, and Witch-Hunts: From Fitzjames Stephen to Angela Canning', *Journal of Law and Society*, 31, pp. 369–86 and S. Devaney (2007) 'Commentary – The Loneliness of the Expert Witness', *Medical Law Review*, 15, pp. 116–25.
184. *The Times*, 7 June 2004. My addition in parenthesis.
185. *Daily Mail*, 17 March 2007 and 21 March 2007; *British Medical Journal*, 24 March 2007; and *The Times*, 8 November 2007.
186. For further discussion of this expectation see Cunliffe (2011) *Murder, Medicine and Motherhood*, p. 96.
187. See respectively the case against Doreen Jeffs reported in *The Times*, 28 November 1960, No. 54940; the case against Ann Osborne reported in *The Times*, 25 February 1971, No. 58108; the case against Brenda Peck reported in *The Times*, 23 July 1975, No. 59455; the case against Sandra Riley reported in *The Guardian*, 19 February 1986; and the case against Tina Jamadar reported in *The Guardian*, 17 June 1998.
188. For further discussion of this argument see Cunliffe (2011) *Murder, Medicine and Motherhood*, pp. 203–4 and Alder and Polk (2001) *Child Victims of Homicide*, p. 2.
189. For a similar argument see Meyer and Oberman (2001) *Mothers Who Kill their Children*, pp. 168–9.
190. See also Resnick (1970) 'Murder of the Newborn', p. 1419 and Kellett (1992) 'Infanticide and Child Destruction', p. 27 for a similar suggestion.
191. For further discussion see Brookman and Nolan (2006) 'The Dark Figure of Infanticide', pp. 883–4.
192. For further discussion see McKee (2006) *Why Mothers Kill*, pp. 258–9.
193. The need for this kind of instructive information seems pertinent in the modern era when mothers are discharged from hospital very soon after birth. For further discussion see McKee (2006) *Why Mothers Kill*, pp. 34–60; Friedman and Resnick (2007) 'Child Murder by Mothers', p. 139; Schwartz and Isser (2007) *Child Homicide*, pp. 197–220; Barton (1998) 'When Murdering Hands Rock the Cradle', p. 618; and M.G. Spinelli (2003) 'The Promise of Saved Lives: Recognition, Prevention and Rehabilitation', in M.G. Spinelli (ed.) *Infanticide: Psychological and Legal Perspectives on Mothers Who Kill* (Washington, DC and London: American Psychiatric), pp. 235–55. For intervention and preventative measures more generally see Brockington (1996, 2003 edition) *Motherhood and Mental Health*, pp. 555–93 and Resnick (1969) 'Child Murder by Parents', p. 332.

Bibliography

Primary sources

Unpublished primary sources
Hereford Record Office
Parish Registers (Presteigne), AN28/3

National Archives (Kew, Surrey)
Assize Records (ASSI)
Crown Minute Books, Midland Circuit ASSI11/43, 1921–1924
Indictment Filed, Midland Circuit, ASSI12/115, 1921
Criminal Depositions and Case Papers, Midland Circuit, ASSI13/51, Roberts Case, 1921

Central Criminal Court Records (CRIM)
Depositions, CRIM 1/414, October 1927
Depositions, CRIM 1/850, July 1936

Home Office Papers (HO)
Criminal Entry Book, HO 13/16
Criminal Registers England and Wales, HO 27/1
Judges Reports, HO 47/35
Private and Secret Documents, HO 79/10
Registered Papers, Supplementary, Criminal Cases: Roberts HO 144/1749/419784, 1921

State Papers (SP)
Secretaries of State: Entry Book SP44/254, May–June 1728

National Records of Scotland (Edinburgh)
Justiciary Court Records (JC)
High Court of Justiciary, Books of Adjournal JC3/1–JC3/49 and JC4/1–JC4/11
North Circuit Records, JC11/1–JC11/62
Process Papers, JC26/–JC26/ (to find)
South Circuit Records, JC12/3–JC12/33
West Circuit Records, JC13/1–JC13/17 (to date)

National Library of Scotland (Edinburgh)
The Last Speech, Confession and Dying Words of Ann Morrison [APS.4.201.06]

National Library of Wales (Aberystwth)
Black Book, 28/35
Minute Book for the Radnorshire Sessions, 14/44

Records of the Court of Great Sessions
4/178/2, 4/195/3, 4/388/7, 4/391/7 (Document 1), 4/395/2, 4/526/3, 4/533/6, 4/533/3 (Documents 8–9, 11 and 13–15), 4/736/5, 4/745/1, 4/754/1, 4/739/1 and 4/817/4

Powys County Archive
Llowes Parish Register, R/EP/42/R/A/2

Records and photocopies donated by Mr RCB Oliver, Llandrindod Wells (December 1979) [Acc 17]
County Times and Express and Gazette, 28 November 1981, R/X/11/145
Horton, T. (1818) *An Elegy Written in the Churchyard of Presteigne, Radnorshire with Admonitory Reflections on the Grave of Mary Morgan Who was Interred there after Suffering the Awful Sentence of the Law, for the Murder of her Illegitimate Child* (Presteigne: E.J. Jones, County Printing Office), R/X/11/141
'Pitiful Welsh Tragedy Re-told' (Unidentified Newspaper Article), 4 June 1898, R/X/11/144

Radnorshire Quarter Sessions
Session Rolls 1804–1805, R/QS/R151 and R/QS/R152

University of Glasgow Library
William Hunter, *On the Uncertainty of the Signs of Murder in the Case of Bastard Children,* Read to the Members of the Medical Society, 14 July 1783 [Sp Coll Hunterian Add. 279]

Published Primary Sources

Official documents and publications (in chronological order)
Hansard: House of Lords Debates, 195, 4 November 1908: 1178
Hansard: House of Lords Debates, 196, 12 November 1908: 485–6
Hansard: House of Lords Debates, 1, 4 May 1909: 722–3 and 725–7
Hansard Parliamentary Debates (Third Series), 76, 5 July 1844: 430–1
Home Office 'Murder, Manslaughter and Infanticide: Proposals for Reform of the Law – Consultation Paper', 19/08 (2008)
Home Office, 'Murder, Manslaughter and Infanticide: Proposals for Reform of the Law – Summary of Responses and Government Position', 19/08 (2009)
House of Lords Decisions, 10 C and F. 200 and 8 Eng. Rep. 718 (1843)
Parliamentary Papers, 21 Jac 1 c.27 (1624)
Parliamentary Papers, 43 Geo 3 c.58 (1803)
Parliamentary Papers, 49 Geo. III, c.14 (1809)
Parliamentary Papers, 5 Geo 4 c.83 (1824)
Parliamentary Papers, 9 Geo 4 c.31 (1828)
Parliamentary Papers, 4 and 5 Will 4 c.76 (1834)
Parliamentary Papers, 7 Will 4 and Vict c.85 (1837)
Parliamentary Papers, 7 and 8 Vict c.101 (1844)
Parliamentary Papers, 24 and 25 Vict c.100 (1861)
Parliamentary Papers, 35 and 36 Vict c.38 (1872)
Parliamentary Papers, 9 and 10 Geo. 5, c.71 (1919)
Parliamentary Papers, 12 and 13 Geo. 5, Chp. 18 (1922)
Parliamentary Papers, 1 and 2 Geo. 6, Chp. 36 (1938)
Parliamentary Papers, 5 and 6 Eliz.2 c.11 (1957)

Parliamentary Papers, A Bill to Consolidate and Amend the Law relating to Homicide (1872)

Parliamentary Papers, A Bill to Consolidate and Amend the Law Relating to Homicide (1874)

Parliamentary Papers, A Bill to Establish a Code of Indictable Offences, and the Procedure Relating Thereto (1878)

Parliamentary Papers, Report of the Royal Commission Appointed to Consider the Law Relating to Indictable Offences (1879)

Parliamentary Papers, Abortion Act, ch, 87 (1967)

Parliamentary Papers, Criminal Law Act, ch. 58, s. 3 (1967)

Parliamentary Papers, Home Office, Department of Health and Social Security, Report of the Committee on Mentally Abnormal Offenders, Cmnd. 6244 (1975)

Parliamentary Papers, Criminal Law Revision Committee, Fourteenth Report Offences Against the Person, Cmnd. 7844 (1980)

Parliamentary Papers, Criminal Attempts Act, ch. 47 (1981)

Parliamentary Papers, Coroners and Justice Act, ch. 25, s.57 (2009)

Poor Law Commissioners Report of 1834 (London: HMSO)

Report of the Capital Punishment Commission (1866) (London: HMSO)

The Acts of the Parliaments of Scotland – Volume IX: A.D. M.DC.LXXXIX – A.D. M.DC. XCV (1822) (London: HMSO) [Bodleian Library K5.354/9]

The Law Commission, 'A New Homicide Act for England and Wales? A Consultation Paper', No. 177, Part 9 (2005)

The Law Commission, 'Murder, Manslaughter and Infanticide – Project Six of the Ninth Programme of Law Reform: Homicide', No. 304, Part 8 (2006)

Newspapers and periodicals

Aberdeen Weekly Journal, 29 September 1877, No. 7055 and 25 June 1894, No. 12293

Baner ac Amserau Cymru, 31 October 1894, No. 1966

Berrow's Worcester Journal, 27 March 1845, No. 7426

The Bristol Mercury and Daily Post, 26 October 1894, No. 14496

The Bristol Mercury, 16 October 1869, No. 4149 and 30 October 1869, No. 4151

British Journal or The Censor (London), 15 March 1729, No. 63

British Medical Journal, 9 February 1848, 26 January 1861, 20 September 1862, 3 March 1866, 28 April 1866, 1 December 1866, 12 January 1867, 30 March 1867, 8 February 1868, 27 May 1871, 13 July 1878, 15 March 1902, 10 November 1906, 16 May 1908, 25 February 1928, 9 November 1940, 17 December 1960, 10 July 1965, 22 February 1969, 16 March 1996, 10 June 1989, 1 January 2000, 8 February 2003, 24 January 2004, 3 January 2004, 27 January 2005, 5 February 2005, 11 June 2005, 25 June 2005, 23 July 2005, 26 January 2006, 18 February 2006, 25 February 2006, 10 February 2007 and 24 March 2007

The Bury and Norwich Post and Suffolk Herald, 22 October 1851, No. 3617

Caledonian Mercury, 16 January 1759 and 18 January 1759

The Cambrian, 27 April 1805, No. 66

Country Journal or The Craftsman (London), 5 October 1728, No. 118 and 15 March 1729, No. 141

Daily Journal (London), 4 October 1728, No. 2415

Daily Mail, 17 March 2007, 21 March 2007 and 4 May 2012

Daily Post (London), 4 October 1728, No. 2820

The Dundee Courier and Angus, 15 October 1869, No. 5056, 29 October 1869, No. 5068 and 27 May 1890, No. 11509

Edinburgh Medical and Surgical Journal, July 1814, No. 10 and July 1826, No. 26

The Era, 17 May 1857, No. 973 and 29 March 1863, No. 1279

Flying Post or The Weekly Medley (London), 5 October 1728, No. 1

Gentleman's Magazine, August 1732, Vol. II, No. XX, October 1774 and November 1774

The Glasgow Herald, 30 October 1869, No. 9306

Gloucester Journal, 18 March 1729, No. 363

The Guardian, 11 July 1713, No. 105, 10 January 1986, 19 February 1986, 4 January 1992, 17 June 1998, 24 June 2003, 1 July 2003, 19 December 2003 and 3 May 2005

The Hull Packet, 7 May 1805, No. 956

The Illustrated Police News, 10 November 1894, No. 1604

The Independent, 8 March 1996

The Lancet, 17 January 1863

The Leeds Mercury, 2 November 1894, No. 17653

Lloyds Weekly Newspaper, 31 October 1869, No. 1406

London Evening Post, 1 October 1728, No. 128

London Journal, 5 October 1728, No. 479, 15 March 1729, No. 502, 17 January 1730, No. 546, 24 January 1730, No. 547, 7 February 1730, No. 549 and 14 February 1730, No. 550

Magdalen's Friend and Female Holmes' Intelligencer, 1860–1864, 5 Volumes.

The Manchester Guardian, 28 July 1921, 14 October 1927, 2 August, 1952, 26 February 1955, 23 March 1955 and 24 March 1955

Mist's Weekly Journal (London), 7 September 1728, No. 177–8

The Morning Chronicle, 30 March 1829, No. 18576 and 4 January 1838, No. 21261

The Morning Post, 14 March 1823, No. 16223, 7 October 1824, No. 16786, 4 January 1838, No. 20916, 3 February 1863, No. 27809, 18 September 1863, No. 28004, 23 September 1863, No. 28008, 7 July 1894, No. 38088 and 26 October 1894, No. 38183

The Newcastle Courant, 30 June 1848, No. 9056

North Wales Chronicle, 17 April 1828, No. 29

The Northern Star and Leed's General Advertiser, 24 June 1843, No. 293

Nottinghamshire Guardian, 23 October 1863, No. 927

The Observer, 28 April 1805 and 15 July 2001

The Pall Mall Gazette, 14 October 1869, No. 145 and 27 October 1869, No. 1469

The Penny Illustrated Paper and Illustrated Times, 3 November 1894, No. 1745

The Protestant (Domestick) Intelligence, 5 April 1681, No. 111

Reynolds' Newspaper, 20 November 1859, No. 484, 6 August 1865, No. 782, 31 October 1869, No. 1003 and 24 June 1894, No. 2289

The Royal Cornwall Gazette, Falmouth Packet, Cornish Weekly News and General Advertiser, 8 November 1894, No. 4763

The Salopian Journal, 1 May 1805, Vol. XIII, No. 558

The Scots Magazine, March 1759, Vol. XXI

The Sheffield and Rotherham Independent, 30 July 1842, No. 1175

Shrewsbury Chronicle, 1 May 1805, Volume XXXIV, No. 1732

The Standard, 17 August 1857, No. 10299, 28 October 1869, No. 14114 and 26 October 1894, No. 21939

The Telegraph, 4 May 2005

The Times of India, 12 May 2012

The Times, 30 April 1842, No. 17971, 5 August 1865, No. 25256, 4 July 1870, No. 26793, 26 October 1894, No. 34405, 2 November 1894, No. 34411, 26 July 1921,

No. 42782, 17 September 1952, No. 52419, 28 November 1960, No. 54940, 25 February 1971, No. 58108, 23 July 1975, No. 59455, 10 January 1986, No. 62341, 14 March 1986, No. 62404, 13 June 1995, 2 March 1996, 9 March 1996, 19 March 1996, 13 October 1999, 10 November 1999, 27 November 1999, 18 July 2000, 29 January 2003, 30 January 2003, 31 January 2003, 4 February 2003, 5 December 2003, 19 December 2003, 20 January 2004, 7 June 2004 and 8 November 2007
Ventura County Star, 22 May 2012
Weekly Journal or British Gazetteer (London), 5 October 1728, No. 176
Western Mail, 18 January 1875, No. 1784, 29 October 1894, No. 7660 and 8 March 1895, No. 8049
The York Herald, 4 April 1863, No. 4718, 25 November 1871, No. 51 and 16 October 1877, No. 6454
The Yorkshire Herald and York Herald, 23 May 1891, No. 12470

On-Line Sources

Anonymous (1871) *Infant Mortality: Its Causes and Remedies* (Manchester: Ireland & Co), pp. 14–15 [Accessed from the University of Illinois Urbana-Champaign Library at http://archive.org/details/infantmortalityi00manc from the Talbot Collection of British Pamphlets, Ref. 5526548]
A Pittilesse Mother That most Vnnaturally at one time, Murthered two of her owne Children at Acton within six miles from London vppon Holy Thursday last 1616. The ninth of May. Being a Gentlewoman named Margret Vincent, wife of Mr. Iaruis Vincent, of the same towne. With her Examination, Confession and True Discouery of all the Proceedings in the said Bloody Accident. Whereunto is added Andersons repentance, who was Executed at Tiburne the 18. of May being Whitson Eue 1[161] Written in the time of his Prisonment in Newgate (London: J. Trundle), reference number STC 24757 [Accessed from Early English Books On-line via: http://www.jischistoricbooks.ac.uk/Search.aspx]
A Short and Impartial Account of the Proceedings against George Dewing, Keeper of the House of Correction at Halstead in Essex, For the Murder of a Bastard Child there Begotten by Him Upon the Body of one of his Prisoners: For Which he was Try'd and Condemn'd at the Assizes of Chelmsford, March the 20th, 1727–8 (London: J. Roberts), reference number ESTC 36428 [Accessed from Eighteenth Century Collections On-Line via: http://www.jischistoricbooks.ac.uk/Search.aspx]
BBC Evening News, 9 November 1999 [Accessed at http://news.bbc.co.uk/1/hi/uk/512099.stm]
Beck, J.B. (1817) *An Inaugural Dissertation on Infanticide* (New York: J. Seymour) [Accessed from http://archive.org/details/inauguraldissert01beck]
Bloody Newes from Dover. Being a True Relation of the Great and Bloudy Murder, Committed by Mary Champion (an Anabaptist) who Cut off her Childs Head, being 7. weekes old, and Held it to her Husband to Baptize. Also, another Great Murder Committed in the North, by a Scottish Commander, for which fact he was Executed Printed in the Yeare of Discovery, Feb. 13. 1647 (London: S.N.), reference number Thomason E.375[80] [Accessed from Early English Books On-line via: http://www.jischistoricbooks.ac.uk/Search.aspx]
Brewer, Thomas (1610) *The Bloudy Mother, or The Most Inhumane Murthers, Committed by Iane Hattersley vpon diuers infants, the Issue of her Owne Bodie: and The Priuate Burying of Them in an Orchard with her Arraignment and Execution* (London: J. Busbie), reference number ESTC 3717.3 [Accessed from Early English Books On-Line: http://eebo.chadwyck.com/home]
Criminal Legal Cases (England and Wales), R. v. O'Donoghue (1927) 28 Cox CC 461 and R. v O'Donoghue (1927) 20 Cr. App. R. 132 [Accessed from http://www.lexisnexis.com]

Cummin, William (1836) *The Proofs of Infanticide Considered: Including Dr Hunter's Tract on Child Murder, With Illustrative Notes and A Summary of the Present State of Medico-Legal Knowledge* (London: Longman) [Accessed from http://archive.org/details/proofsofinfantic00cumm]

House of Commons Parliamentary Papers, Judicial and Criminal Statistics (multiple volumes relating to 1800–1999) [Accessed from http://parlipapers.chadwyck.co.uk/home.do]

England and Wales Court of Appeal – Criminal Division, Decisions, Crim 1092 (2005), 2 Cr App R 31 (2005) and Crim 2789 (2007) [Accessed from http://www.netk.net.au]

National Library of Wales, Crime and Punishment Database [Accessed from http://www.llgc.org.uk/sesiwn_fawr/index_s.htm]

(1813) *The Parliamentary History of England from the Earliest Period to the Year 1803, Volume XVII – A.D. 1771–1774* (London: Hansard) [Accessed from http://www.books.google.co.uk]

The Proceedings of the Old Bailey, 13 April 1681 [t16810413-1], 11 September 1717 [t17170911-50], 27 February 1718 [t17180227-25], 4 December 1719 [t17191204-7], 16 February 1737 [t17370216-21], 10 May 1744 [t17440510-8], 17 January 1750 [t17500117-53], 8 December 1762 [t17621208-26], 18 May 1774 [t17740518-23], 6 December 1775 [t17751206-82], 3 July 1782 [t17820703-47], 15 January 1800 [t18000115-20], 18 September 1802 [t17670429-52], 4 July 1804 [t18040704-16], 12 April 1809 [t18090412-33], 29 January 1838 [t18380129-499], 5 April 1841 [t18410405-1120], 27 October 1856 [t18561027-1005], 22 November 1869 [t18691122-36] and 22 October 1894 [t18941022-849] [All accessed from www.oldbaileyonline.org]

Sharp, Jane (1697) *The Midwives Book or The Whole Art of Midwifery Discovered* (London: S. Miller), reference number S2969B [Accessed from Early English Books On-Line: http://eebo.chadwyck.com/home]

Other Works

(1890) *Encyclopaedia Britannica* (9th edition) Vol. 13 (Chicago: R.S. Peal)

(1952) *The Holy Bible – The Old Testament: Revised Standard Version* (New York and Glasgow: Collins)

(1971) *The Holy Bible – The New Testament: Revised Standard Version* (New York and Glasgow: Collins)

Alison, A. (1832) *Principles of the Criminal Law of Scotland* (Edinburgh: Blackwood), p. 159 [Bodleian Library, Cw UK Scotl 510 A413]

Bernard, Thomas (1799) *An Account of the Foundling Hospital in London for the Maintenance and Education of Exposed and Deserted Young Children* (London: T. Jones) [Bodleian Library, GK 17741]

Burke Ryan, W. (1862) *Infanticide: Its Law, Prevalence, Prevention, and History* (London) [Bodleian Library, (OC) 151 c/345]

Defoe, Daniel (1728) *Augusta Triumphans: Or, The Way to Make London the Most Flourishing City in the Universe* (London: J. Wood) [Bodleian Library, ESTC70330]

Gouge, William (1622, 1976 edition) *Of Domesticall Duties – Eight Treatises* (Amsterdam: W.J. Johnson) [Bodleian Library, 1778 e.478]

Hume, Baron D. (1797) *Commentaries on the Law of Scotland, Respecting the Description and Punishment of Crimes* (Edinburgh: Bell and Bradfute) Volumes I and II [National Library of Scotland, BCL.B1220-1221]

Ladies National Association for the Diffusion of Sanitary Knowledge (1855) *The Evils of Wet-Nursing: A Warning to Mothers* (London: Groombridge and Sons) [Bodleian Library, G. Pamph. 2541]

Ladies National Association for the Diffusion of Sanitary Knowledge (1855) *The Health of Mothers* (London: Groombridge and Sons) [Bodleian Library, G. Pamph. 2541]

Mandeville, Bernard (1723, 1772 edition) *The Fable of the Bees: Or, Private Vices, Public Benefits – Volume I* (Edinburgh: J. Wood) [Bodleian Library, ESTCT77574]

Marcus (1839) *Suppressed Work! On the Possibility of Limiting Populousness. To Which is Added The Theory of Painless Extinction.* Third Edition (London: W. Dugdale) [Bodleian Library, Johnson D. 2644]

Mauriceau, François (1697) *The Diseases of Women with Child and in Child-Bed: As Also the Best Means of Helping them in Natural and Unnatural Labours. With Fit remedies for the Several indispositions of New-born Babes. To which is Prefix'd an Anatomical treatise.* Translated by H. Chamberlen (London: A. Bell) [Bodleian Library, Vet. A3 e.69]

Nichols, J. (1818) (ed.) *Illustrations of the Literary History of the Eighteenth Century: Consisting of Authentic Memoirs and Original Letters of Eminent Persons, Volume III* (London: Nichols, Son and Bentley) [Bodleian Library 13 Theta 92v3]

Nichols, J. (1818) (ed.) *The Miscellaneous Works in Prose and Verse, of George Hardinge, Esq. Senior Justice of the Counties of Brecon, Glamorgan, and Radnor, Volume I* (London: J. Nichols, Son and Bentley) [Bodleian Library 8 M96BS(V1)]

Percival, Thomas (1849) *Medical Ethics: Or a Code of Institutes and Precepts Adapted to the Professional Conduct of Physicians and Surgeons* (Oxford: J.H. Parker) [Bodleian Library, RB 49.1412]

Scott, Sir Walter (1818) *The Heart of Mid-Lothian* (London: Macmillan)

Simpson, J.A. and E.S.C. Wiener (1989, Second Edition) (eds.) *The Oxford English Dictionary – Volume VII* (Oxford: Clarendon)

Waugh, Benjamin (1890) *Baby-Farming* (London: Kegan Paul) [Bodleian Library pHV 741 (42). 1. A2. N]

Williams, J. (1905) *A General History of the County of Radnor* (Brecknock: Davies and Co.) [National Library of Wales XDA1362 W72 (4to)]

Willughby, Percivall (1672, 1863 edition, 1972 reprint) *Observations in Midwifery* [Edited from the original Manuscript by H. Blenkinsop] (Wakefield: S.R. Publishers) [Bodleian Library, RSL 15083e.30]

Secondary sources

Monographs and key edited collections

Adair, R. (1996) *Courtship, Illegitimacy and Marriage in Early Modern England* (Manchester: Manchester University Press)

Alder, C. and K. Polk (2001) *Child Victims of Homicide* (Cambridge: Cambridge University Press)

Anderson, M. (1980) *Approaches to the History of the Western Family, 1500–1914* (Cambridge: Cambridge University Press)

Arnot, M.L. and C. Usborne (1999) (eds.) *Gender and Crime in Modern Europe* (London: UCL Press)

Ballinger, A. (2000) *Dead Woman Walking: Executed Women in England and Wales 1900–1955* (Aldershot: Ashgate)

Banks, J.A. and O. Banks (1965) *Feminism and Family Planning in Victorian England* (Liverpool: Liverpool University Press)

Batt, J. (2004, 2005 edition) *Stolen Innocence* (London: Ebury)

Beattie, J.M. (1986) *Crime and the Courts in England 1660–1800* (Oxford: Clarendon)

Bechtold, B.H. and D. Cooper Graves (2006) (eds.) *Killing Infants: Studies in the Worldwide Practice of Infanticide* (New York: Edwin Mellen)

Behlmer, G.K. (1982) *Child Abuse and Moral Reform in England, 1870–1908* (Stanford, CA: Stanford University Press)

Bellamy, R. (1995) (ed.) *Cesare Beccaria – On Crimes and Punishments and Other Writings* (Cambridge: Cambridge University Press)

Bhatnagar, R.D., R. Dube and R. Dube (2005) *Female Infanticide in India: A Feminist Cultural History* (Albany: State University of New York Press)

Boyd, K.M. (1980) *Scottish Church Attitudes to Sex, Marriage and the Family, 1850–1914* (Edinburgh: John Donald)

Boswell, J. (1988) *The Kindness of Strangers: The Abandonment of Children in Western Europe from Late Antiquity to the Renaissance* (London: Allen Lane)

Brindley, G. (2006) *Oxford: Crime, Death and Debauchery* (Sutton: Stroud)

Brockington, I. (1996, 2003 edition) *Motherhood and Mental Health* (Oxford: Oxford University Press)

Brookes, B. (1988) *Abortion in England 1900–1967* (London, New York and Sydney: Croom Helm)

Brookes, G. (2008) *Stories in Welsh Stone – The Secrets within Fifteen Welsh Graves* (Ceredigion: Welsh Country Magazine)

Brown, Y.G. and R. Ferguson (2002) (eds.) *Twisted Sisters: Women, Crime and Deviance in Scotland since 1400* (East Linton: Tuckwell)

Bruley, S. (1999) *Women in Britain since 1900* (Basingstoke: Macmillan)

Byard, R.W. (2004) *Sudden Death in Infancy, Childhood and Adolescence* (Cambridge: Cambridge University Press)

Cage, R.A. (1981) *The Scottish Poor Law, 1745–1845* (Edinburgh: Scottish Academic)

Carruthers, G.B. and L.A. Carruthers (2005) (eds.) *A History of Britain's Hospitals and the Background to the Medical, Nursing and Allied Professions* (Lewes: Book Guild)

Cassidy, T. (2007) *Birth: A History* (London: Chatto and Windus)

Cecil, R. (1996) (ed.) *The Anthropology of Pregnancy Loss: Comparative Studies in Miscarriage, Stillbirth and Neonatal Death* (Oxford: Berg)

Clark, M. and C. Crawford (1995) (eds.) *Legal Medicine in History* (Cambridge: Cambridge University Press)

Clark, S. (2003) *Women and Crime in the Street Literature of Early Modern England* (Basingstoke: Palgrave Macmillan)

Cockburn, J.S. (1977) (ed.) *Crime in England 1550–1800* (London: Methuen)

Cook, H. (2004) *The Long Sexual Revolution: English Women, Sex and Contraception 1800–1975* (Oxford: Oxford University Press)

Conley, C.A. (1991) *The Unwritten Law: Criminal Justice in Victorian Kent* (Oxford: Oxford University Press)

Crawford, P. (2004) *Blood, Bodies and Families in Early Modern England* (Harlow: Pearson Education)

Crawford, P.M. (2010) *Parents of Poor Children in England, 1580–1800* (Oxford: Oxford University Press)

Cressy, D. (1999) *Birth, Marriage, and Death: Ritual, Religion, and the Life-Cycle in Tudor and Stuart England* (Oxford: Oxford University Press)

Crist, T.A. (2005) 'Babies in the Privy: Prostitution, Infanticide, and Abortion in New York City's Five Points District', *Historical Archaeology*, 39, pp. 19–46 [CHP5]

Cunliffe, E. (2011) *Murder, Medicine and Motherhood* (Oxford and Portland, OR: Hart).

Cunningham, H. (1995) *Children and Childhood in Western Society Since 1500* (London: Longman)

Daly, M. and M. Wilson (1988) *Homicide* (New York: Aldine de Gruyter)

Daniels, C. and M.V. Kennedy (1999) (eds.) *Over the Threshold: Intimate Violence in Early America* (New York: Routledge)

D'Cruze, S. (2000) (ed.) *Everyday Violence in Britain, 1850–1950: Gender and Class* (Harlow: Pearson)

D'Cruze, S. and L. Jackson (2009) *Women, Crime and Justice in England since 1660* (Basingstoke: Palgrave Macmillan)

Delumeau, J. (1990) *Sin and Fear: The Emergence of a Western Guilt Culture 13th–18th Centuries* (New York: St Martin's)

Donnison, J. (1988) *Midwives and Medical Men: A History of the Struggle for the Control of Childbirth* (New Barnet: Historical Publications)

Eccles A. (1982) *Obstetrics and Gynaecology in Tudor and Stuart England* (London and Canberra: Croom Helm)

Edwards, S. (1984) *Women on Trial: A Study of the Female Suspect, Defendant and Offender in the Criminal Law and Criminal Justice System* (Manchester: Manchester University Press)

Eigen, J.P. (2003) *Unconscious Crime: Mental Absence and Criminal Responsibility in Victorian London* (Baltimore and London: The John Hopkins University Press)

Eigen, J.P. (1995) *Witnessing Insanity: Madness and Mad-Doctors in the English Court* (New Haven and London: Yale University Press)

Emsley, C. (1996) *Crime and Society in England, 1750–1900* (London: Longman)

Evenden, D.A. (2000) *The Midwives of Seventeenth-Century London* (Cambridge: Cambridge University Press)

Fanthorpe, L. and P. Fanthorpe (2003) *The World's Most Mysterious Murders* (Toronto and Oxford: Hounslow)

Fildes, V. (1986) *Breasts, Bottles and Babies: A History of Infant Feeding* (Edinburgh: Edinburgh University Press)

Fildes, V. (1990) (ed.) *Women as Mothers in Pre-Industrial England: Essays in Memory of Dorothy McLaren* (London and New York: Routledge)

Fildes, V. (1988) *Wet Nursing: A History from Antiquity to the Present* (Oxford: Basil Blackwell)

Fildes, V., L. Marks and H. Marland (1992) *Women and Children First: International Maternal and Infant Welfare 1870–1945* (London and New York: Routledge)

Fisher, K. (2006) *Birth Control, Sex and Marriage in Britain 1918–1960* (Oxford: Oxford University Press)

Flinn, M. (1977) (ed.) *Scottish Population History from the Seventeenth Century to the 1930s* (Cambridge: Cambridge University Press)

Forbes, T.R. (1985) *Surgeons at the Bailey: English Forensic Medicine to 1878* (New Haven and London: Yale University Press)

Fuchs, R.G. (1984) *Abandoned Children: Foundlings and Child Welfare in Nineteenth-Century France* (Albany, NY: State University of New York Press)

Gatrell, V.A.C. (1994) *The Hanging Tree: Execution and the English People 1770–1868* (Oxford: Oxford University Press)

Gélis, J. (1991) *History of Childbirth: Fertility, Pregnancy and Birth in Early Modern Europe* (Cambridge: Polity)

Golden, J. (1996) *A Social History of Wet Nursing in America: From Breast to Bottle* (Cambridge: Cambridge University Press)

Gordon, L. (1977) *Woman's Body, Woman's Right: A Social History of Birth Control in America* (Harmondsworth and New York: Penguin)

Gowing, L. (2003) *Common Bodies: Women, Touch and Power in Seventeenth-Century England* (New Haven and London: Yale University Press)

Green, J. (1987) *The Morning of Her Day* (London: Darf)

Gunn, J. and P.J. Taylor (1993) (eds.) *Forensic Psychiatry: Clinical, Legal and Ethical Issues* (London: Butterworth and Heinemann)

Hamilton, E. (1940) *Mythology* (Boston: Little, Brown and Co.)

Hamilton, J.A. and P.N. Harberger (1992) (eds.) *Postpartum Psychiatric Illness: A Picture Puzzle* (Philadelphia: University of Pennsylvania Press)

Harrington, J.L. (2009) *The Unwanted Child: The Fate of Foundlings, Orphans, and Juvenile Criminals in Early Modern Germany* (Chicago and London: University of Chicago Press)

Hay, D., P. Linebaugh, J.G. Rule, E.P. Thompson and C. Winslow (1976) *Albion's Fatal Tree: Crime and Society in Eighteenth-Century England* (London: Allen Lane)

Hausfater, G. and S.B. Hardy (1984) (eds.) *Infanticide: Comparative and Evolutionary Perspectives* (New York: Aldine)

Hecht, J.J. (1955) *The Domestic Servant Class in the Eighteenth Century* (London: Routledge and Kegan Paul)

Helfer, R.E. and C.H. Kempe (1968) (eds.) *The Battered Child* (Chicago: University of Chicago Press)

Henderson, T. (1999) *Disorderly Women in Eighteenth-Century London: Prostitution and Control in the Metropolis 1730–1830* (London: Longman)

Henry, B. (1994) *Dublin Hanged: Crime, Law Enforcement and Punishment in Late Eighteenth Century Dublin* (Dublin: Irish Academic Press)

Heywood, C. (2001) *A History of Childhood: Children and Childhood in the West from Medieval to Modern Times* (Cambridge: Polity)

Hill, B. (1996) *Servants: English Domestics in the Eighteenth Century* (Oxford: Oxford University Press)

Hill, B. (1989) *Women, Work and Sexual Politics in Eighteenth-Century England* (Oxford: Basil Blackwell)

Hoffer, P.C. and N.E.C. Hull (1984) *Murdering Mothers: Infanticide in England and New England 1558–1803* (New York: New York University Press)

Hollen Lees, L. (1998) *The Solidarities of Strangers: The English Poor Laws and the People, 1700–1948* (Cambridge: Cambridge University Press)

Hufton, O. (1974) *The Poor of Eighteenth-Century France 1750–1789* (Oxford: Oxford University Press)

Hurl-Eamon, J. (2005) *Gender and Petty Violence in London, 1680–1720* (Columbus: Ohio State University Press)

Jackson, M. (1996) *New-Born Child Murder: Women, Illegitimacy and the Courts in Eighteenth-Century England* (Manchester: Manchester University Press)

Jackson, M. (2002) (ed.) *Infanticide: Historical Perspectives on Child Murder and Concealment, 1550–2000* (Aldershot: Ashgate)

Johnson Kramar, K. (2005) *Unwilling Mothers, Unwanted Babies: Infanticide in Canada* (Vancouver: University of British Columbia Press)

Jones, D.J.V. (1992) *Crime in Nineteenth-Century Wales* (Cardiff: University of Wales Press)

Keown, J. (1988) *Abortion, Doctors and the Law: Some Aspects of the Legal Regulation of Abortion in England from 1803 to 1982* (Cambridge: Cambridge University Press)

Kermode, J. and G. Walker (1994) (eds.) *Women, Crime and the Courts in Early Modern England* (London: Routledge)

Kohl, M. (1977) (ed.) *Infanticide and the Value of Life* (New York: Prometheus)

Kilday, A.-M. (2007) *Women and Violent Crime in Enlightenment Scotland* (Woodbridge: Boydell)

King, P. (2000) *Crime, Justice and Discretion in England 1740–1820* (Oxford: Oxford University Press)

King, H. (2007) *Midwifery, Obstetrics and the Rise of Gynaecology: The Uses of a Sixteenth-Century Compendium* (Aldershot: Ashgate)

King, P. (2000) *Crime, Justice and Discretion in England 1740–1820* (Oxford: Oxford University Press)

King, P., P. Sharpe and T. Hitchcock (1997) (eds.) *Chronicling Poverty: The Voices and Strategies of the English Poor, 1640–1840* (Basingstoke: Palgrave Macmillan)

King-Hele, D. (2007) (ed.) *The Collected Letters of Erasmus Darwin* (Cambridge: Cambridge University Press)

Langbein, J.H. (1974) *Prosecuting Crime in the Renaissance: England, Germany, France* (Cambridge, MA: Harvard University Press)

Larner, C. (1981) *Enemies of God: The Witch-Hunt in Scotland* (Baltimore: John Hopkins University Press)

Laslett, P., K. Oosterveen and R.M. Smith (1980) (eds.) *Bastardy and its Comparative History: Studies in the History of Illegitimacy and Marital Nonconformism in Britain, France, Germany, Sweden, North America, Jamaica and Japan* (London: Edward Arnold)

Leavitt, J.W. (1986) *Brought to Bed: Childbearing in America, 1750–1950* (New York and Oxford: Oxford University Press)

Leneman, L. and R. Mitchison (1998) *Sin in the City: Sexuality and Social Control in Urban Scotland 1660–1780* (Edinburgh: Scottish Cultural)

Levene, A. (2007) *Childcare, Health and Mortality at the London Foundling Hospital, 1741–1800: 'Left to the Mercy of the World'* (Manchester: Manchester University Press)

Levene, A., T. Nutt and S. Williams (2005) (eds.) *Illegitimacy in Britain, 1700–1920* (Basingstoke: Palgrave Macmillan)

Lewis, J. (1980) *The Politics of Motherhood: Child and Maternal Welfare in England, 1900–1939* (London and Montreal: Croom Helm and McGill-Queen's University Press)

Mahood, L. (1995) *Policing Gender, Class and Family: Britain, 1850–1940* (London: UCL Press)

Marks, L.V. (1996) *Metropolitan Maternity: Maternal and Infant Welfare Services in Early Twentieth-Century London* (Amsterdam and Atlanta, GA: Rodopi)

Marks (2001, 2010 edition) *Sexual Chemistry: A History of the Contraceptive Pill* (New Haven and London: Yale University Press)

Marland, H. (2004) *Dangerous Motherhood: Insanity and Childbirth in Victorian Britain* (Basingstoke: Palgrave Macmillan)

Marland, H. (1993) (ed.) *The Art of Midwifery: Early Modern Midwives in Europe* (London: Routledge)

Martin, R. (2008) *Women, Murder and Equity in Early Modern England* (New York and London: Routledge)

McClure, R. (1981) *Coram's Children: The London Foundling Hospital in the Eighteenth Century* (New Haven: Yale University Press)

McDonagh, J. (2003) *Child Murder and British Culture 1720–1900* (Cambridge: Cambridge University Press)

McKee, G.R. (2006) *Why Mothers Kill: A Forensic Psychologist's Casebook* (Oxford: Oxford University Press)

McLaren, A. (1990, 1992 edition) *A History of Contraception – From Antiquity to the Present Day* (Oxford: Blackwell)

McLaren, A. (1978) *Birth Control in Nineteenth-Century England* (London: Croom Helm)

McLaren, A. (1984) *Reproductive Rituals: The Perception of Fertility in England from the Sixteenth Century to the Nineteenth Century* (London and New York: Methuen)

McLynn, F. (1991) *Crime and Punishment in Eighteenth-Century England* (Oxford: Oxford University Press)

McMahon, V. (2004) *Murder in Shakespeare's England* (London and New York: Hambledon and London)

Meadow, R. (1989, 1997 edition) (ed.) *ABC of Child Abuse* (London: BMJ Publishing)

Medick, H. and D.W. Sabean (1984) (eds.) *Interest and Emotion: Essays on the Study of Family and Kinship* (Cambridge: Cambridge University Press)

Meyer, C.L. and M. Oberman (2001) *Mothers Who Kill their Children: Understanding the Acts of Moms from Susan Smith to the 'Prom Mom'* (New York and London: New York University Press)

Miller, B.D. (1997) *The Endangered Sex: Neglect of Female Children in Rural North India* (Delhi: Oxford University Press)

Mitchison, R. and L. Leneman (1989) *Sexuality and Social Control: Scotland 1660–1780* (Oxford: Basil Blackwell)

Mitchison, R. and L. Leneman (1998) *Girls in Trouble Sexuality and Social Control in Rural Scotland 1660–1780* (Edinburgh: Scottish Cultural Press)

Morgan, G. and P. Rushton (1998) *Rogues, Thieves and the Rule of Law: The Problem of Law Enforcement in North-East England, 1718–1800* (London: UCL Press) [6]

Morris, A. (1987) *Women, Crime and Criminal Justice* (Oxford: Basil Blackwell)

Moscucci, O. (1990) *The Science of Woman: Gynaecology and Gender in England, 1800–1929* (Cambridge: Cambridge University Press)

Mungello, D.E. (2008) *Drowning Girls in China Since 1650* (Lanham, MD: Rowman and Littlefield)

Nash, D.S. (2007) *Blasphemy in the Christian World* (Oxford: Oxford University Press)

O'Dowd, M.J. (1994) *The History of Obstetrics and Gynaecology* (New York and London: Parthenon)

Panter-Brick, C. and M.T. Smith (2000) (eds.) *Abandoned Children* (Cambridge: Cambridge University Press)

Petchesky, R.P. (1984, 1985 edition) *Abortion and Women's Choice* (London: Verso)

Piers, M.W. (1978) *Infanticide* (New York: Norton)

Pilcher, J. (1999) *Women in Contemporary Britain* (London and New York: Routledge)

Pollock, L. (1983) *Forgotten Children: Parent-Child Relations from 1500 to 1900* (Cambridge: Cambridge University Press)

Pollak, O. (1950) *The Criminality of Women* (Philadelphia: University of Pennsylvania)

Porter, R. (1995) *Disease, Medicine and Society in England, 1550–1860* [Third Edition] (Cambridge: Cambridge University Press)

Prior, P.M. (2008) *Madness and Murder: Gender, Crime and Mental Disorder in Nineteenth-Century Ireland* (Dublin: Irish Academic Press)

Pugh, G. (2007) *London's Forgotten Children: Thomas Coram and the Foundling Hospital* (Stroud: Tempus)

Pullan, B.S. (1988) *Orphans and Foundlings in Early Modern Europe* (Reading: University of Reading Press)

Quaife, G.R. (1979) *Wanton Wenches and Wayward Wives: Peasant and Illicit Sex in Early Seventeenth-Century England* (London: Croom Helm)

Rabin, D.Y. (2004) *Identity, Crime, and Legal Responsibility in Eighteenth-Century England* (Basingstoke: Palgrave Macmillan)

Ransel, D.L. (1988) *Mothers of Misery: Child Abandonment in Russia* (Princeton, NJ: Princeton University Press)

Rattigan, C. (2011) *'What Else Could I Do?' Single Mothers and Infanticide, Ireland 1900–1950* (Dublin: Irish Academic Press)

Rhodes, P. (1995) *A Short History of Clinical Midwifery: The Development of Ideas in the Professional Management of Childbirth* (Hale: Books for Midwives)

Riddle, J.M. (1992, 1994 edition) *Contraception and Abortion from the Ancient World to the Renaissance* (London and Cambridge, MA: Harvard University Press)

Riddle, J.M. (1998) *Eve's Herbs: A History of Contraception and Abortion in the West* (London and Cambridge, MA: Harvard University Press)

Rose, L. (1986) *The Massacre of the Innocents: Infanticide in Britain 1800–1939* (London: Routledge and Kegan Paul)

Rowbotham, J. and K. Stevenson (2005) (eds.) *Criminal Conversations: Victorian Crimes, Social Panic and Moral Outrage* (Columbus: Ohio State University Press)

Rublack, U. (1999) *The Crimes of Women in Early Modern Germany* (Oxford: Clarendon) [6]

Ruff, J.R. (1984) *Crime, Justice and Public Order: The Sénéchaussées of Libourne and Bazas, 1696–1789* (London and Dover, NH: Croom Helm)

Ruff, J.R. (2001) *Violence in Early Modern Europe 1500–1800* (Cambridge: Cambridge University Press)

Schulte, R (1994) *The Village in Court: Arson, Infanticide, and Poaching in the Court Records of Upper Bavaria, 1848–1910* (Cambridge: Cambridge University Press)

Schwartz, L.L. and N.K. Isser (2007) *Child Homicide: Parents Who Kill* (Boca Raton, FL: Taylor and Francis)

Searle, G.R. (1971) *The Quest for National Efficiency: A Study in British Politics and Political Thought, 1899–1914* (Berkeley and Los Angeles: University of California Press)

Sharpe, J.A. (1983) *Crime in Seventeenth-Century England: A County Study* (Cambridge: Cambridge University Press)

Sharpe, J.A. (1984) *Crime in Early Modern England, 1550–1750* (London: Longman)

Sharpe, J.A. (1997) *Instruments of Darkness: Witchcraft in England 1550–1750* (London: Penguin)

Shorter, E. (1982) *A History of Women's Bodies* (London: Allen Lane)

Smart, C. (1976) *Women, Crime and Criminology: A Feminist Critique* (London and Boston: Routledge and Kegan Paul)

Smith, F.B. (1979) *The People's Health 1830–1910* (London: Croom Helm)

Smith, G.T., A.N. May and S. Devereaux (1998) (eds.) *Criminal Justice in the Old World and the New: Essays in Honour of J.M. Beattie* (Toronto: University of Toronto Press)

Smith, R. (1981) *Trial by Medicine: Insanity and Responsibility in Victorian Trials* (Edinburgh: Edinburgh University Press)

Spinelli, M.G. (2003) (ed.) *Infanticide: Psychological and Legal Perspectives on Mothers Who Kill* (Washington, DC and London: American Psychiatric)

Steedman, C. (2009) *Labours Lost: Domestic Service and the Making of Modern England* (Cambridge: Cambridge University Press)

Stone, L. (1977) *The Family, Sex and Marriage in England 1500–1800* (London: Weidenfeld and Nicolson)

Sussman, G.D. (1982) *Selling Mothers' Milk: The Wet-Nursing Business in France 1715–1914* (Chicago and London: University of Illinois Press)

Symonds, D.A. (1997) *Weep Not for Me: Women, Ballads and Infanticide in Early Modern Scotland* (Pennsylvania: Pennsylvania State University Press)

Szreter, S. and K. Fisher (2010) *Sex before the Sexual Revolution: Intimate Life in England 1918–1963* (Cambridge: Cambridge University Press)

Taylor, D. (1998) *Crime, Policing and Punishment in England, 1750–1914* (Basingstoke: Palgrave Macmillan)

Thomson, M. (1998) *Reproducing Narrative: Gender, Reproduction and Law* (Aldershot: Ashgate)

Thorn, J. (2003) (ed.) *Writing British Infanticide: Child-Murder, Gender, and Print, 1722–1859* (Newark: University of Delaware Press)

Tooley, M. (1983, 1985 edition) *Abortion and Infanticide* (Oxford: Clarendon)

Twomey, T.M. and S. Bennett (2009) *Understanding Postpartum Psychosis: A Temporary Madness* (London and Westport, CT: Praeger)

Walker, G. (2003) *Crime, Gender and Social Order in Early Modern England* (Cambridge: Cambridge University Press)

Walker, N. (1968) *Crime and Insanity in England – Volume One: The Historical Perspective* (Edinburgh: Edinburgh University Press)

Watson, K.D. (2011) *Forensic Medicine in Western Society – A History* (Abingdon: Routledge)

Wiener, M. (2004) *Men of Blood: Violence, Manliness and Criminal Justice in Victorian England* (Cambridge: Cambridge University Press)

Wiesner, M.E. (2000) *Women and Gender in Early Modern Europe* [Second Edition] (Cambridge: Cambridge University Press)

Wiesner-Hanks, M.E. (2000) *Christianity and Sexuality in the Early Modern World: Regulating Desire, Reforming Practice* (New York and London: Routledge)

Wilson, A. (1995) *The Making of Man-Midwifery: Childbirth in England, 1660–1770* (Cambridge, MA: Harvard University Press)

Wiltenburg, J. (1992) *Disorderly Women and Female Power in the Street Literature of Early Modern England and Germany* (Charlottesville, VA and London: University Press of Virginia)

Woods, R. (2009) *Death before Birth: Fetal Health and Mortality in Historical Perspective* (Oxford: Oxford University Press)

Zedner, L. (1991) *Women, Crime and Custody in Victorian England* (Oxford: Oxford University Press)

Journal articles

Adler, J.S. (2001) '"Halting the Slaughter of the Innocents": The Civilizing Process and the Surge in Violence in Turn-of-the-Century Chicago', *Social Science History*, 25, pp. 29–52

Altink, H. (2007) '"I Did Not Want to Face the Shame of Exposure: Gender Ideologies and Child Murder in Post-Emancipation Jamaica', *Journal of Social History, Society and Cultures*, 41, pp. 373–4

Arnot, M.L. (1994) 'Infant Death, Child Care and the State: The Baby-Farming Scandal and the First Infant Life Protection Legislation of 1872', *Continuity and Change*, 9, pp. 271–311

Backhouse, C.B. (1984) 'Desperate Women and Compassionate Courts: Infanticide in Nineteenth-Century Canada', *The University of Toronto Law Journal*, 34, pp. 447–78

Barton, B. (1998) 'When Murdering Hands Rock the Cradle: An Overview of America's Incoherent Treatment of Infanticidal Mothers', *Southern Methodist University Law Review*, 51, pp. 591–619

Beattie, J.M. (1975) 'The Criminality of Women in Eighteenth-Century England', *Journal of Social History*, VIII, pp. 80–116

Bechtold, B.H. (1999) 'Infanticide in Nineteenth-Century France: A Quantitative Interpretation', *Review of Radical Political Economics*, 33, pp. 165–87

Behlmer, G.K. (1979) 'Deadly Motherhood: Infanticide and Medical Opinion in Mid-Victorian England', *Journal of the History of Medicine and Allied Sciences*, XXXIV, pp. 403–27

Bennet, H. (1923) 'The Exposure of Infants in Ancient Rome', *The Classical Journal*, 18, pp. 341–51

Boswell, J.E. (1984) 'Exposition and Oblation: The Abandonment of Children and the Ancient and Medieval Family', *American Historical Review*, 89, pp. 10–33

Brittain, R.P. (1963) 'The Hydrostatic and Similar Tests of Live Birth: A Historical Review', *Medico-Legal Journal*, 31, pp. 189–94

Brooke, S. (2001) '"A New World for Women"? Abortion Law Reform in Britain During the 1930s', *American Historical Review*, 106, pp. 431–59

Brookman, F. and J. Nolan (2006) 'The Dark Figure of Infanticide in England and Wales', *Journal of Interpersonal Violence*, 21, pp. 869–89

Butler, S.M. (2007) 'A Case of Indifference? Child Murder in Later Medieval England', *Journal of Women's History*, 19, pp. 59–82

Campbell, L. (1989) 'Wet-Nurses in Early Modern England: Some Evidence from the Townshend Archive', *Medical History*, 33, pp. 360–70

Caron, S. (2010) '"Killed by its Mother": Infanticide in Providence County, Rhode Island, 1870 to 1938', *Journal of Social History*, 44, pp. 213–28

Clark, G. (1987) 'A Study of Nurse Children, 1550–1750', *Local Population Studies*, 39, pp. 8–23

Clarke, K. (1980) 'Infanticide, Illegitimacy and the Medical Profession in Nineteenth-Century England', *Society for the Social History of Medicine Bulletin*, 6, pp. 11–14

Clayton, M. (2009) 'Changes in Old Bailey Trials for the Murder of Newborn Babies, 1674–1803', *Continuity and Change*, 24, pp. 337–59

Conley, C.A. (1995) 'No Pedestals: Women and Violence in Late Nineteenth-Century Ireland', *Social History*, 28, pp. 801–18

Coutts, W. (1986) 'Women, Children and Domestic Servants in Dumfries in the 17th Century', *Transactions of Dumfriesshire and Galloway Natural History and Antiquarian Society*, LXI, pp. 73–83

Crawford, P. (1981) 'Attitudes to Menstruation in Seventeenth-Century England', *Past and Present*, 91, pp. 47–73

Damme, C. (1978) 'Infanticide: The Worth of an Infant Under Law', *Medical History*, XXII, pp. 1–24

Darby, N. (2008) 'Suffer the Little Ones: Infanticide – Social History', *Ancestors*, 75, pp. 48–52

Davies, O. (1999) 'Cunning-Folk in the Medical Market Place During the Nineteenth Century', *Medical History*, 43, pp. 55–73

Davis, G. and R. Davidson (2006) '"A Fifth Freedom" or "Hideous Atheistic Expediency"? The Medical Community and Abortion Law Reform in Scotland, c. 1960–1975', *Medical History*, 50, pp. 29–48

Dayton, C.H. (1991) 'Taking the Trade: Abortion and Gender Relations in an Eighteenth-Century New England Village', *The William and Mary Quarterly*, Third Series, 48, pp. 19–49

Devaney, S. (2007) 'Commentary – The Loneliness of the Expert Witness', *Medical Law Review*, 15, pp. 116–25

Donovan, J.M. (1991) 'Infanticide and the Juries in France, 1825–1913', *Journal of Family History*, 16, pp. 157–76

D'Orbán, P.T. (1971) 'Social and Psychiatric Aspects of Female Crime', *Medicine, Science and the Law*, 11, pp. 104–16

D'Orbán, P.T. (1979) 'Women who Kill their Children', *British Journal of Psychiatry*, 134, pp. 560–71

Dove Wilson, John (1877) 'Can Any Better Measures Be Devised for the Prevention and Punishment of Infanticide?', *Transactions of the National Association for the Promotion of Social Science*, pp. 284–94

Drife, J. (2002) 'The Start of Life: A History of Obstetrics', *Postgraduate Medical Journal*, 78, pp. 311–15

D.R.S.D. (1938) 'The Infanticide Act, 1938', *The Modern Law Review*, 2, p. 229

Edwards, S.S.M. (1986) 'Neither Bad Nor Mad: The Female Violent Offender Reassessed', *Women's Studies International Forum*, 9, pp. 79–87

Engles, D. (1908) 'The Problem of Female Infanticide in the Greco-Roman World', *Classical Philology*, 75, pp. 112–20

Ermers, J. (1990) 'Medeas or Fallen Angels? The Prosecution of Infanticide and Stereotypes of "Child Murderesses" in the Netherlands in the Nineteenth Century', in International Commission of Historical Demography (ed.) *The Role of the State and Public Opinion in Sexual Attitudes and Demographic Behaviour* (CIDH: Madrid), pp. 483–92

Evans, T. (2005) '"Unfortunate Objects": London's Unmarried Mothers in the Eighteenth Century', *Gender and History*, XVII, pp. 127–53

Faber, S. (1976) 'Infanticide, Especially in Eighteenth-Century Amsterdam; With Some References to Van Der Keessel', *Acta Juridica*, 253, pp. 253–67

Fairchilds, C. (1978) 'Female Sexual Attitudes and the Rise of Illegitimacy', *Journal of Interdisciplinary History*, 8, pp. 627–67

Fahrni, M. (1997) '"Ruffled" Mistresses and "Discontented" Maids: Respectability and the Case of Domestic Servants, 1880–1914', *Labour/Le Travail*, 39, pp. 69–97

Feeley, M. (1994) 'The Decline of Women in the Criminal Process: A Comparative History', *Criminal Justice History: An International Annual*, XV, pp. 235–74

Feeley, M. and D. Little (1991) 'The Vanishing Female: The Decline of Women in the Criminal Process, 1687–1912', *Law and Society Review*, 25, pp. 719–57

Fildes, V. (1988) 'The English Wet-Nurse and Her Role in Infant Care 1538–1800', *Medical History*, 32, pp. 142–73

Forbes, T.R. (1986) 'Deadly Parents: Child Homicide in Eighteenth- and Nineteenth-Century England', *Journal of the History of Medicine*, XLI, pp. 175–99

Francus, M. (1997) 'Monstrous Mothers, Monstrous Societies: Infanticide and the Rule of Law in Restoration and Eighteenth-Century England', *Eighteenth Century Life*, XXI, pp. 133–56

Frayling, F.G. (1908) 'Infanticide: Its Law and Punishment, With Suggested Alternations or Amendments of the Law', *Transactions of the Medico-Legal Society*, 81, pp. 87–9

Friedman, S.H. and P.J. Resnick (2007) 'Child Murder by Mothers: Patterns and Prevention', *World Psychiatry*, 6, pp. 137–41

Fuchs, R.G. (1987) 'Legislation, Poverty and Child-Abandonment in Nineteenth-Century Paris', *Journal of Interdisciplinary History*, 18, pp. 55–80

Garrett, E. and A. Wear (1994) 'Suffer the Little Children: Mortality, Mothers and the State', *Continuity and Change*, 9, pp. 179–84

Giladi, A. (1990) 'Observations on Infanticide in Medieval Muslim Society', *International Journal of Middle East Studies*, 22, pp. 185–200

Gilje, P.A. (1983) 'Infant Abandonment in Early Nineteenth-Century New York City: Three Cases', *Signs*, 8, pp. 580–90

Gowing, L. (1997) 'Secret Births and Infanticide in Seventeenth-Century England', *Past and Present*, CLVI, pp. 87–115

Graham, D. (1994) 'Female Employment and Infant Mortality: Some Evidence from British Towns, 1911, 1931 and 1951', *Continuity and Change*, 9, pp. 313–46

Green, E.C. (1999) 'Infanticide and Infant Abandonment in the New South: Richmond, Virginia, 1865–1915', *Journal of Family History*, 24, pp. 187–211

Gregg, W. (1996) 'The Hanging of Mary Morgan', *New Law Journal*, 146, No. 6735 (Postscript), p. 390

Grey, D. (2009) '"More Ignorant and Stupid than Wilfully Cruel": Homicide Trials and "Baby-Farming" in England and Wales in the Wake of The Children Act 1908', *Crimes and Misdemeanours: Deviance and the Law in Historical Perspective*, 3, pp. 60–77

Grey, D. (2010) 'Women's Policy Networks and the Infanticide Act 1922', *Twentieth Century British History*, 21, pp. 441–63

Grey, D. (2012) '"Almost Unknown Amongst the Jews": Jewish Women and Infanticide in London 1890–1918', *The London Journal*, 37, pp. 122–35

Hair, P.E.H. (1966) 'Bridal Pregnancy in Rural England in Earlier Centuries', *Population Studies*, 20, pp. 233–43

Hair, P.E.H. (1972) 'Homicide Infanticide and Child Assault in Late Tudor Middlesex', *Local Population Studies (Notes and Queries)*, 9, pp. 43–6

Hamilton, J.A. (1989) 'Postpartum Psychiatric Syndromes', *Psychiatric Clinics of North America*, 12, pp. 89–103

Hanawalt, B. (1974) 'The Female Felon in Fourteenth-Century England', *Viator – Medieval and Renaissance Studies*, 5, pp. 251–73

Hanlon, G. (2003) 'Infanticide by Married Couples in Early Modern Tuscany', *Quaderni Storici*, XXXVIII, pp. 453–98

Hansen, E. de G.R. (1979) '"Overlaying" in Nineteenth-Century England: Infant Mortality or Infanticide?', *Human Ecology*, 7, pp. 333–52

Harris, W.V. (1994) 'Child-Exposure in the Roman Empire', *The Journal of Roman Studies*, 84, pp. 1–22

Helmholz, R.H. (1975) 'Infanticide in the Province of Canterbury During the Fifteenth Century', *History of Childhood Quarterly*, 2, pp. 379–90

Hemphill, R.E. (1967) 'Infanticide and Puerperal Mental Illness', *Nursing Times*, 63, pp. 1473–5

Higginbotham, A.R. (1989) '"Sin of the Age": Infanticide and Illegitimacy in Victorian London', *Victorian Studies*, 32, pp. 319–37

Hindus, M.S. Schwart(1977) 'The Contours of Crime and Justice in Massachusetts and South Carolina, 1767–1878', *The American Journal of Legal History*, 21, pp. 212–37

Homrighaus, R.E. (2001) 'Wolves in Women's Clothing: Baby-Farming and The *British Medical Journal*, 1860–1872', *Journal of Family History*, 26, pp. 350–72

Hunt, A. (2006) 'Calculations and Concealments: Infanticide in Mid-Nineteenth-Century Britain', *Victorian Literature and Culture*, 34, pp. 71–94

Ingalls, W. (2002) 'Demography and Dowries: Perspectives on Female Infanticide in Classical Greece', *Phoenix*, 56, pp. 246–54

Jackson, M. (1994) 'A Little Rumour in the Family', *New Law Journal* (18 November 1994), p. 1606

Jackson, M. (1996) 'Infanticide: Historical Perspectives', *New Law Journal* (22 March 1996), pp. 416–20

Johnson, C. (1814) 'An Essay on the Signs of Murder in New Born Children', *Edinburgh Medical and Surgical Journal*, X, p. 394

Johnson Kramar, K. and W.D. Watson (2006) 'The Insanities of Reproduction: Medico-Legal Knowledge and the Development of Infanticide Law', *Social and Legal Studies*, 15, pp. 237–55

Joyce, H. (2002) 'Beyond Reasonable Doubt', + *Plus Magazine: Living Mathematics*, 21 [accessed at http://plus.maths.org/content/beyond-reasonable-doubt]

Kamler, M. (1988) 'Infanticide in the Towns of the Kingdom of Poland in the Second Half of the 16th and the First Half of the 17th Century', *Acta Poloniae Historica*, 58, pp. 33–49

Kellett, R.J. (1992) 'Infanticide and Child Destruction – The Historical, Legal and Pathological Aspects', *Forensic Science International*, 53, pp. 1–28

Kellum, B.A. (1974) 'Infanticide in England in the Later Middle Ages', *History of Childhood Quarterly*, 1, pp. 367–88

Kelly, J. (1992) 'Infanticide in Eighteenth-Century Ireland', *Irish Economic and Social History*, XIX, pp. 5–26

Kent, D.A. (1989) 'Ubiquitous but Invisible: Female Domestic Servants in Mid-Eighteenth-Century London', *History Workshop Journal*, 28, pp. 111–28

Kertzer, D.I. (1991) 'Gender, Ideology and Infant Abandonment in Nineteenth-Century Italy', *The Journal of Interdisciplinary History*, 22, pp. 1–25

Kertzer, D.I. (1999) 'Syphilis, Foundlings, and Wetnurses in Nineteenth-Century Italy', *Journal of Social History*, 32, pp. 589–602

Kilday, A.-M. (2008) '"Monsters of the Vilest Kind": Infanticidal Women and Attitudes Towards Their Criminality in Eighteenth-Century Scotland', *Family and Community History*, 11, pp. 100–15

Kilday, A.-M. and K.D. Watson (2008) 'Infanticide, Religion and Community in the British Isles, 1720–1920: Introduction', *Family and Community History*, 11, 2, pp. 88–91

Knight, P. (1977) 'Women and Abortion in Victorian and Edwardian England', *History Workshop Journal*, 4, pp. 57–68

Kociumbas, J. (2001) 'Azaria's Antecedents: Stereotyping Infanticide in Late Nineteenth-Century Australia', *Gender and History*, 13, pp. 138–60

Kord, S. (1993) 'Women as Children, Women as Childkillers: Poetic Images of Infanticide in Eighteenth-Century Germany', *Eighteenth-Century Studies*, XXVI, pp. 449–66

Krueger, C.L. (1997) 'Literary Defenses and Medical Prosecutions: Representing Infanticide in Nineteenth-Century Britain', *Victorian Studies*, XL, pp. 271–94

Lambie, I. (2001) 'Mothers Who Kill: The Crime of Infanticide', *International Journal of Law and Psychiatry*, 24, pp. 71–80

Landsman, S. (1998) 'One Hundred Years of Rectitude: Medical Witnesses at the Old Bailey, 1717–1817', *Law and History Review*, 16, pp. 445–94

Langer, W.L. (1974) 'Infanticide: A Historical Survey', *History of Childhood Quarterly*, I, pp. 353–66

Leboutte, R. (1991) 'Offense against Family Order: Infanticide in Belgium from the Fifteenth through the Early Twentieth Centuries', *Journal of the History of Sexuality*, 2, pp. 159–85

Lee, B.J. (1981) 'Female Infanticide in China', *Historical Reflections/Réflexions Historiques*, 8, pp. 163–77

Lenman, L. and R. Mitchison (1987) 'Scottish Illegitimacy Ratios in the Early Modern Period', *Economic History Review*, 2nd ser., XL, pp. 41–63

Lindemann, M. (1981) 'Love for Hire: The Regulation of the Wet-Nursing Business in Eighteenth-Century Hamburg', *Journal of Family History*, 6, pp. 379–95

Litchfield, R.B. and D. Gordon (1980) 'Closing the "Tour": A Close Look at the Marriage Market, Unwed Mothers and Abandoned Children in Mid-Nineteenth-Century Amiens', *Journal of Social History*, 14, pp. 458–72

Littlejohn, H. (1922) 'Respiration and the Proof of Live-Birth', *Transactions of the Medico-Legal Society*, 86, pp. 86–113

Lonza, N. (2002) '"Two Souls Lost": Infanticide in the Republic of Dubrovnik (1667–1808)', *Dubrovnik Annals*, 6, pp. 67–102

Loughnan, A. (2012) 'The "Strange" Case of the Infanticide Doctrine', *Oxford Journal of Legal Studies*, 32, pp. 1–27

Marks, M.N. (1996) 'Characteristics and Causes of Infanticide in Britain', *International Review of Psychiatry*, 8, pp. 99–106

Marks, M.N. and R. Kumar (1993) 'Infanticide in England and Wales', *Medicine, Science and the Law*, 33, pp. 329–39

Marks, M.N. and R. Kumar (1996) 'Infanticide in Scotland', *Medicine, Science and the Law*, 36, pp. 299–305

Marshall, R.K. (1984) 'Wet-Nursing in Scotland: 1500–1800', *Review of Scottish Culture*, I, pp. 43–51

Martin, P.J. (1826) 'Observations on Some of the Accidents of Infanticide', *Edinburgh Medical and Surgical Journal*, XXVI, pp. 34–7

McClive, C. (2002) 'The Hidden Truths of the Belly: The Uncertainty of Pregnancy in Early Modern Europe', *Social History of Medicine*, 15, pp. 209–27

McDonagh, J. (1997) 'Infanticide and the Nation: The Case of Caroline Beale', *New Formations – A Journal of Culture/Theory/Politics*, 32, pp. 11–21

McIntosh, T. (2000) '"An Abortionist City": Maternal Mortality, Abortion, and Birth Control in Sheffield, 1920–1940', *Medical History*, 44, pp. 75–96

McLaren, A. (1978) 'Abortion in France: Women and the Regulation of Family Size 1800–1914', *French Historical Studies*, 10, pp. 461–85

McLaren, A. (1977) 'Women's Work and Regulation of Family Size: The Question of Abortion in the Nineteenth Century', *History Workshop Journal*, 4, pp. 69–81

McLaren, D. (1978) 'Fertility, Infant Mortality and Breast Feeding in the Seventeenth Century', *Medical History*, 22, pp. 378–96

McLaren, D. (1979) 'Nature's Contraceptive, Wet-Nursing and Prolonged Lactation: The Case of Chesham, Buckinghamshire, 1578–1601', *Medical History*, 23, pp. 426–41

Meldrum, T. (1999) 'Domestic Service, Privacy, and the Eighteenth-Century Metropolitan Household', *Urban History*, 26, pp. 27–39

Meteyard, B. (1980) 'Illegitimacy and Marriage in Eighteenth-Century England', *Journal of Interdisciplinary History*, 10, pp. 479–89

Millward, R. and F. Bell (2001) 'Infant Mortality in Victorian Britain: The Mother as Medium', *Economic History Review*, LIV, pp. 699–733

Montag, B.A. and T.W. Montag (1979) 'Infanticide: A Historical Survey', *Minnesota Medicine*, May Edition, pp. 368–72

Morton (1934) 'Female Homicides', *The Journal of Mental Science*, LXXX, pp. 64–74

Moseley, K.D. (1986) 'The History of Infanticide in Western Society', *Issues in Law and Medicine*, 1, pp. 345–61

Ober, W.B. (1986) 'Infanticide in Eighteenth-Century England: William Hunter's Contribution to the Forensic Problem', *Pathology Annual*, 21, pp. 311–19

Oberman, M. (2002) 'Understanding Infanticide in Context: Mothers Who Kill, 1870–1930 and Today', *The Journal of Criminal Law and Criminology*, 92, pp. 707–38

O'Donovan, K. (1984) 'The Medicalisation of Infanticide', *Criminal Law Review*, 259, pp. 259–64

Oldham, J.C. (1985) 'On Pleading the Belly: A History of the Jury of Matrons', *Criminal Justice History*, VI, pp. 1–64

Osborne, J.A. (1987) 'The Crime of Infanticide: Throwing Out the Baby with the Bathwater', *Canadian Journal of Family Law*, 6, p. 49

Parker, E. and F. Good (1981) 'Infanticide', *Law and Human Behaviour*, 5, pp. 237–43

Parris, P. (1983) 'Mary Morgan: Contemporary Sources', *The Radnorshire Society Transactions*, LIII, pp. 57–64

Patterson, C. (1985) 'Not Worth the Rearing: The Causes of Infant Exposure in Ancient Greece', *Transactions of the American Philological Association*, 115, pp. 103–23

Payne, A. (1995) 'Infanticide and Child Abuse', *The Journal of Forensic Psychiatry*, 6, pp. 472–6

Perry, R. (1991) 'Colonizing the Breast: Sexuality and Maternity in Eighteenth-Century England', *Journal of the History of Sexuality*, 2, pp. 204–34

Pilarczyk, I.C. (2012) '"So Foul A Deed": Infanticide in Montreal, 1825–1850', *Law and History Review*, 30, pp. 575–634

Pitt, S.E. and E.M. Bale (1995) 'Neonaticide, Infanticide, and Filicide: A Review of the Literature', *The Bulletin of the American Academy of Psychiatry and the Law*, 23, pp. 375–86

Pollock, L.A. (1997) 'Childbearing and Female Bonding in Early Modern England', *Social History*, 22, pp. 286–306

Radin, M. (1925) 'The Exposure of Infants in Roman Law and Practice', *The Classical Journal*, 20, pp. 337–43

Rattigan, C. (2008) '"I Thought from her Appearance she was in the Family Way": Detecting Infanticide Cases in Ireland, 1900–1921', *Journal of Family and Community History*, 11, pp. 134–51

Rebel, H. (1993) 'Peasants against the State in the Body of Anna Maria Wagner: An Infanticide in Rural Austria in 1832', *Journal of Historical Sociology*, 6, pp. 15–27

Rehman, A.-U., D. St. Clair and C. Platz (1990) 'Puerperal Insanity in the 19th and 20th Centuries', *British Journal of Psychiatry*, 156, pp. 861–5

Resnick, P.J. (1969) 'Child Murder by Parents: A Psychiatric Review of Filicide', *American Journal of Psychiatry*, 126, pp. 325–34

Resnick, P.J. (1970) 'Murder of the Newborn: A Psychiatric Review of Neonaticide', *American Journal of Psychiatry*, 126, pp. 1414–20

Richter, J.S. (1998) 'Child Abandonment and Abortion in Imperial Germany', *Journal of Interdisciplinary History*, 28, pp. 511–51

Riddle, J.M. (1991) 'Oral Contraceptives and Early-Term Abortifacients During Classical Antiquity and the Middle Ages', *Past and Present*, 132, pp. 3–32

Rizzo, T. (2004) 'Between Dishonour and Death: Infanticide in the Causes Célèbres of Eighteenth-Century France', *Women's History Review*, 13, pp. 5–21

Rogers, N. (1989) 'Carnal Knowledge: Illegitimacy in Eighteenth-Century Westminster', *Journal of Social History*, 23, pp. 355–75

Rokeah, Z.E. (1990) 'Unnatural Child Death among Christians and Jews in Medieval England', *The Journal of Psychohistory*, 18, pp. 181–226

Rosen, G. (1976) 'A Slaughter of Innocents: Aspects of Child Health in the Eighteenth-Century City', *Studies in Eighteenth Century Culture*, V, pp. 293–316

Roth, R. (2001) 'Child Murder in New England', *Social Science History*, XXV, pp. 101–47

Rowe, G.S. (1991) 'Infanticide, Its Judicial Resolution, and Criminal Code Revision in Early Pennsylvania', *Proceedings of the American Philosophical Society*, CXXXV, pp. 200–32

Rowlands, A. (1997) '"In Great Secrecy": The Crime of Infanticide in Rothenburg ob der Tauber, 1501–1618', *German History*, 15, pp. 179–99

Rublack, U. (1986) 'Pregnancy, Childbirth and the Female Body in Early Modern Germany', *Past and Present*, 150, pp. 84–110

Rudolph, J. (2008) 'Gender and the Development of Forensic Science: A Case Study', *English Historical Review*, CXXIII, pp. 924–46

Ruggiero, K. (1992) 'Honor, Maternity and the Disciplining of Women: Infanticide in Late Nineteenth-Century Buenos Aires', *The Hispanic American Historical Review*, 72, pp. 353–73

Sauer, R. (1978) 'Infanticide and Abortion in Nineteenth-Century Britain', *Population Studies: A Journal of Demography*, XXXII, pp. 81–93

Schnucker, R.V. (1975) 'Elizabethan Birth Control and Puritan Attitudes', *Journal of Interdisciplinary History*, 4, pp. 655–67

Scott Smith, D. and M.S. Hindus (1975) 'Premarital Pregnancy in America 1640–1971: An Overview and Interpretation', *Journal of Interdisciplinary History*, 4, pp. 537–70

Scully, P. (1996) 'Narratives of Infanticide in the Aftermath of Slave Emancipation in the Nineteenth-Century Cape Colony, South Africa', *Canadian Journal of African Studies*, 30, pp. 88–105

Seaborne Davies, D. (1937) 'Child Killing in English Law', *Modern Law Review*, 1, pp. 203–23

Sen, S. (2002) 'The Savage Family: Colonialism and Female Infanticide in Nineteenth-Century India', *Journal of Women's History*, 14, pp. 53–79

Sharma, B.R. (2006) 'Historical and Medico-Legal Aspects of Infanticide: An Overview', *Medicine, Science and the Law*, 46, pp. 152–6

Smith, R. (1983) 'Defining Murder and Madness: An Introduction to Medicolegal Belief in the Case of Mary Ann Brough, 1854', *Knowledge and Society: Studies in the Sociology of Culture Past and Present*, 4, pp. 173–225

Spierenburg, P. (1997) 'How Violent Were Women? Court Cases in Amsterdam, 1650–1810', *Crime, History and Societies*, 1, pp. 9–28

Spinelli, M.G. (2004) 'Maternal Infanticide Associated with Mental Illness: Prevention and the Promise of Saved Lives', *American Journal of Psychiatry*, 161, pp. 1548–57

Spinelli, M.G. (2009) 'Postpartum Psychosis: Detection of Risk and Management', *American Journal of Psychiatry*, 166, pp. 405–8

Stannard, D.E. (1991) 'Recounting the Fables of Savagery: Native Infanticide and the Functions of Political Myth', *Journal of American Studies*, 25, pp. 381–417

Sussex, L. (1995) 'Portrait of a Murderer in Mixed Media: Cultural Attitudes, Infanticide and the Representation of Frances Knorr', *Australian Feminist Law Journal*, 4, pp. 39–54

Swain, S. (2005) 'Maids and Mothers: Domestic Servants and Illegitimacy in 19th-Century Australia', *History of the Family*, 10, pp. 461–71

Swain, S. (2005) 'Towards a Social Geography of Baby Farming', *The History of the Family*, 10, pp. 151–9

Theriot, N. (1990) 'Nineteenth-Century Physicians and "Puerperal Insanity"', *American Studies*, 26, pp. 69–88

Trexler, R.C. (1973) 'Infanticide in Florence: New Sources and First Results', *History of Childhood Quarterly*, I, 98–116

Ulbricht, O. (1985) 'The Debate about Foundling Hospitals in Enlightenment Germany: Infanticide, Illegitimacy and Infant Mortality Rates', *Central European History*, 18, pp. 211–56

Vaughan, J.R. and P.M. Kautt (2009) 'Infant Death Investigations Following High-Profile Unsafe Rulings: Throwing Out the Baby with the Bath Water?', *Policing: A Journal of Policy and Practice*, 3, pp. 89–99

Wallis, J. (2012) 'Lies, Damned Lies and Statistics? Nineteenth-Century Crime Statistics for England and Wales as a Historical Source', *History Compass*, 10, pp. 574–83

Ward, T. (1999) 'The Sad Subject of Infanticide: Law, Medicine and Child Murder', *Social and Legal Studies*, VIII, pp. 163–80

Ward, T. (2004) 'Experts, Juries, and Witch-Hunts: From Fitzjames Stephen to Angela Canning', *Journal of Law and Society*, 31, pp. 369–86

Watson, K.D. (2008) 'Religion, Community and the Infanticidal Mother: Evidence from 1840s Rural Wiltshire', *Family and Community History*, 11, pp. 116–33

Wheeler, K.H. (1997) 'Infanticide in Nineteenth-Century Ohio', *Journal of Social History*, XXXI, pp. 407–18

Wiener, C. (1975) 'Sex Roles and Crime in Late Elizabethan Hertfordshire', *Journal of Social History*, 8, pp. 38–60

Wiener, C.Z. (1976) 'Is a Spinster an Unmarried Woman?', *American Journal of Legal History*, 20, pp. 27–31

Wilczynski, A. (1991) 'Images of Women Who Kill their Infants: The Mad and the Bad', *Women and Criminal Justice*, 2, pp. 71–88

Wilczynski, A. (1997) 'Mad or Bad? Child Killers, Gender and the Courts', *British Journal of Criminology*, 37, pp. 419–36

Wilkins, A.J. (1985) 'Attempted Infanticide', *The British Journal of Psychiatry*, 146, pp. 206–8

Williams, N. and G. Mooney (1994) 'Infant Mortality in an "Age of Great Cities": London and the English Provincial Cities Compared, c. 1840–1910', *Continuity and Change*, 9, pp. 185–212

Wilson, C. (1984) 'Natural Fertility in Pre-Industrial England, 1660–1799', *Population Studies*, 38, pp. 225–40

Wilson, S. (1984) 'The Myth of Motherhood a Myth: The Historical View of European Child-Rearing', *Social History*, IX, pp. 181–98

Wilson, S. (1988) 'Child Abandonment and Female Honour in Nineteenth-Century Corsica', *Comparative Studies in Society and History*, 30, pp. 762–83

Winnik, H. and M. Horovitz (1962) 'The Problem of Infanticide', *British Journal of Criminology*, 40, pp. 40–52

Woodward, N. (2007) 'Infanticide in Wales, 1730–1830', *Welsh Historical Review*, 23, pp. 94–125

Wright, M.E. (1987) 'Unnatural Mothers: Infanticide in Halifax, 1850–1875', *Nova Scotia Historical Review*, 7, pp. 13–29

Wrightson, K. (1975) 'Infanticide in Earlier Seventeenth-Century England', *Local Population Studies*, XV, pp. 10–22

Wrightson, K. (1982) 'Infanticide in European History', *Criminal Justice History*, III, pp. 1–20

Chapters from edited collections

Abrams, L. (2002) 'From Demon to Victim: The Infanticidal Mother in Shetland, 1699–1802', in Y.G. Brown and R. Ferguson (eds.) *Twisted Sisters: Women, Crime and Deviance in Scotland since 1400* (East Linton: Tuckwell), pp. 180–203

Allen, J. (1982) 'Octavius Beale Re-Considered: Infanticide, Babyfarming and Abortion in NSW 1880–1939', in Sydney Labour History Group (ed.) *What Rough Beast? The State and Social Order in Australian History* (Sydney and London: George Allen & Unwin), pp. 111–29

Andrews, J. (2002) 'The Boundaries of Her Majesty's Pleasure: Discharging Child-Murderers from Broadmoor and Perth Lunatic Department, c.1860–1920', in M. Jackson (ed.) *Infanticide: Historical Perspectives on Child Murder and Concealment, 1550–2000* (Aldershot: Ashgate), pp. 216–48

Arnot, M.L. (2000) 'Understanding Women Committing Newborn Child Murder in Victorian England', in S. D'Cruze (ed.) *Everyday Violence in Britain, 1850–1950: Gender and Class* (Harlow: Pearson), pp. 55–69

Arnot, M.L. (2002) 'The Murder of Thomas Sandles: Meanings of a Mid-Nineteenth-Century Infanticide', in M. Jackson (ed.) *Infanticide: Historical Perspectives on Child Murder and Concealment, 1550–2000* (Aldershot: Ashgate), pp. 149–67

Arnot, M.L. and C. Usborne (1999) 'Why Gender and Crime? Aspects of an International Debate', in M.L. Arnot and C. Usborne (eds.) *Gender and Crime in Modern Europe* (London: UCL Press), pp. 1–43

Barringer Gordon, S. (2002) 'Law and Everyday Death: Infanticide and the Backlash against Women's Rights after the Civil War', in A. Sarat, L. Douglas and M.M. Umphrey (eds.) *Lives in the Law* (Ann Arbor: University of Michigan Press), pp. 55–81

Bechtold, B.H. and D. Cooper Graves (2006) 'Towards an Understanding of Infanticide Scholarship', in B.H. Bechtold and D. Cooper Graves (eds.) *Killing Infants: Studies in the Worldwide Practice of Infanticide* (New York: Edwin Mellen), pp. 1–20

Bentley, D. (2005) 'She-Butchers: Baby-Droppers, Baby-Sweaters, and Baby-Farmers', in J. Rowbotham and K. Stevenson (eds.) *Criminal Conversations: Victorian Crimes, Social Panic and Moral Outrage* (Columbus: Ohio State University Press), pp. 198–214

Black, J. (2005) 'Who Were the Putative Fathers of Illegitimate Children in London, 1740–1810', in A. Levene, T. Nutt and S. Williams (eds.) *Illegitimacy in Britain, 1700–1920* (Basingstoke: Palgrave Macmillan), pp. 50–65

Bugos Jr., P.E. and L.M. McCarthy (1984) 'Ayoreo Infanticide: A Case Study', in G. Hausfater and S.B. Hardy (eds.) *Infanticide: Comparative and Evolutionary Perspectives* (New York: Aldine), pp. 503–20

Callaway, H. (1978) '"The Most Essentially Female Function of All": Giving Birth', in S. Ardener (ed.) *Defining Females: The Nature of Women in Society* (London: Croom Helm), pp. 163–85

Campbell Orr, C. (2011) 'Aunts, Wives, Courtiers: The Ladies of Bowood', in N. Aston and C. Campbell Orr (eds.) *An Enlightenment Statesman in Whig Britain: Lord Shelburne in Context, 1737–1805* (Woodbridge: Boydell), pp. 51–78

Castan, N. (1993) 'Criminals', in N.Z. Davis and A. Farge (eds.), *A History of Women in the West – Volume III: Renaissance and Enlightenment Paradoxes* (Cambridge, MA: Belknap Press of Harvard University Press), pp. 475–88

Coleman, E. (1976) 'Infanticide in the Early Middle Ages', in M. Mosher Stuard (ed.) *Women in Medieval Society* (Philadelphia: University of Pennsylvania Press), pp. 47–70

Cooper Graves, D. (2006) '"…In a Frenzy while Raving Mad": Physicians and Parliamentarians Define Infanticide in Victorian England', in B.H. Bechtold and D. Cooper Graves (eds.) *Killing Infants: Studies in the Worldwide Practice of Infanticide* (Lewiston, NY: Edwin Mellen), pp. 111–35

Crawford, P. (1990) 'The Construction and Experience of Maternity in Seventeenth-Century England', in V. Fildes (ed.) *Women as Mothers in Pre-Industrial England: Essays in Memory of Dorothy McLaren* (London and New York: Routledge), pp. 3–38

Crawford, P. (1994) 'Sexual Knowledge in England, 1500–1750', in R. Porter and M. Teich (eds.) *Sexual Knowledge, Sexual Science: The History of Attitudes to Sexuality* (Cambridge: Cambridge University Press), pp. 82–106

Dalby, J. (1995) 'Women and Infanticide in Nineteenth-Century Rural France', in V. Shepherd, B. Brereton and B. Bailey (eds.) *Engendering History: Caribbean Women in Historical Perspective* (London and Kingston, Jamaica: James Currey and Ian Randle), pp. 337–68

Daly, M. and M. Wilson (1984) 'A Sociobiological Analysis of Human Infanticide', in G. Hausfater and S.B. Hardy (eds.) *Infanticide: Comparative and Evolutionary Perspectives* (New York: Aldine), pp. 487–502

Dickemann, M. (1984) 'Concepts and Classification in the Study of Human Infanticide: Sectional Introduction and Some Cautionary Notes', in G. Hausfater and S.B. Hardy (eds.) *Infanticide: Comparative and Evolutionary Perspectives* (New York: Aldine), pp. 427–38

Dickinson, J.R. and J.A. Sharpe (2002) 'Infanticide in Early Modern England: The Court of Great Sessions at Chester, 1650–1800', in M. Jackson (ed.) *Infanticide: Historical Perspectives on Child Murder and Concealment, 1550–2000* (Aldershot: Ashgate), pp. 35–51

D'Orbán, P.T. (1993) 'Female Offenders', in J. Gunn and P.J. Taylor (eds.), *Forensic Psychiatry: Clinical, Legal and Ethical Issues* (London: Butterworth and Heinemann), pp. 599–623

Earle, P. (1998) 'The Female Labour Market in London in the Late Seventeenth and Eighteenth Centuries', in P. Sharpe (ed.) *Women's Work: The English Experience, 1650–1914* (London: Hodder Arnold), pp. 121–43

Ermers, J. (1990) 'Medeas or Fallen Angels? The Prosecution of Infanticide and Stereotypes of "Child Murderesses" in the Netherlands in the Nineteenth Century', in International Commission of Historical Demography (ed.) *The Role of the State and Public opinion in Sexual Attitudes and Demographic Behaviour* (CIDH: Madrid), pp. 483–92

Evans, T. (2005) '"Blooming Virgins all Beware": Love, Courtship and Illegitimacy in Eighteenth-Century British Popular Literature', in A. Levene, T. Nutt and S. Williams (eds.) *Illegitimacy in Britain, 1700–1920* (Basingstoke: Palgrave Macmillan), pp. 18–33

Evenden, D. (1993) 'Mothers and their Midwives in Seventeenth-Century London', in H. Marland (ed.) *The Art of Midwifery: Early Modern Midwives in Europe* (London: Routledge), pp. 9–26

Faber, S. (1990) 'Infanticide and Criminal Justice in the Netherlands, especially in Amsterdam', in International Commission of Historical Demography (ed.) *The Role of the State and Public Opinion in Sexual Attitudes and Demographic Behaviour* (CIDH: Madrid), pp. 497–501

Fildes, V. (1990) 'Maternal Feelings Re-Assessed: Child Abandonment and Neglect in London and Westminster, 1550–1800', in V. Fildes (ed.) *Women as Mothers in Pre-Industrial England: Essays in Memory of Dorothy McLaren* (London and New York: Routledge), pp. 139–78

Gatrell, V.A.C. and T.B. Hadden (1972) 'Criminal Statistics and their Interpretation', in E.A. Wrigley (ed.) *Nineteenth-Century Society: Essays in the Use of Quantitative Methods for the Study of Social Data* (Cambridge: Cambridge University Press), pp. 336–96

Geyer-Kordesch, J. (1993) 'Infanticide and Medico-Legal Ethics in Eighteenth-Century Prussia', in A. Wear, J. Geyer-Kordesch and R. French (eds.) *Doctors and Ethics: The Earlier Historical Setting of Professional Ethics* (Rodopi: Amsterdam), pp. 181–202

Gunn, J. (1993) (ed.) 'The Law, Adult Mental Disorder, and the Psychiatrist in England and Wales (With Comments from the rest of the United Kingdom and Ireland)', in

J. Gunn and P.J. Taylor (eds.), *Forensic Psychiatry: Clinical, Legal and Ethical Issues* (London: Butterworth and Heinemann), pp. 21–115

Harley, D. (1993) 'Provincial Midwives in England: Lancashire and Cheshire, 1660–1760', in H. Marland (ed.) *The Art of Midwifery: Early Modern Midwives in Europe* (London: Routledge), pp. 27–48

Hay, D. (1975) 'Property, Authority and the Criminal Law', in D. Hay, P. Linebaugh, J.G. Rule, E.P. Thompson and C. Winslow, *Albion's Fatal Tree: Crime and Society in Eighteenth-Century England* (London: Allen Lane), pp. 17–63

Helmholz, R.H. (1987) 'Infanticide in the Province of Canterbury during the Fifteenth Century', in R.H. Helmholz (ed.) *Canon Law and the Law of England* (London: Hambledon), pp. 157–68

Hess, A.G. (1993) 'Midwifery Practice among the Quakers in Southern Rural England in the Late Seventeenth Century', in H. Marland (ed.) *The Art of Midwifery: Early Modern Midwives in Europe* (London: Routledge), pp. 49–76

Hufton, O. (1990) 'Women and Violence in Early Modern Europe', in F. Dieteren and E. Kloek (eds.) *Writing Women into History* (Amsterdam: Historisch Seminarium van de Universiteit Van Amsterdam), pp. 75–95

Humfrey, P. (1998) 'Female Servants and Women's Criminality in Early Eighteenth-Century London', in G.T. Smith, A.N. May and S. Devereaux (eds.) *Criminal Justice in the Old World and the New: Essays in Honour of J.M. Beattie* (Toronto: University of Toronto Press), pp. 58–84

Ingram, M. (1994) '"Scolding Women Cucked or Washed": A Crisis in Gender Relations in Early Modern England?', in J. Kermode and G. Walker (eds.) *Women, Crime and the Courts in Early Modern England* (London: Routledge), pp. 48–80

Ireland, R.W. (1997) '"Perhaps my Mother Murdered Me": Child Death and the Law in Victorian Carmarthenshire', in C. Brooks and M. Lobban (eds.) *Communities and Courts in Britain 1150–1900* (London and Rio Grande, OH: Hambledon), pp. 229–44

Jackson, M. (1994) 'Suspicious Infant Deaths: The Statute of 1624 and Medical Evidence at Coroners' Inquests', in M. Clark and C. Crawford (eds.) *Legal Medicine in History* (Cambridge: Cambridge University Press), pp. 64–86

Jackson, M. (1995) 'Developing Medical Expertise: Medical Practitioners and the Suspected Murders of New-Born Children', in R. Porter (ed.) *Medicine in the Enlightenment* (Amsterdam: Rodopi), pp. 145–65

Jackson, M. (1996) '"Something more than Blood": Conflicting Accounts of Pregnancy Loss in Eighteenth-Century England', in R. Cecil (ed.) *The Anthropology of Pregnancy Loss: Comparative Studies in Miscarriage, Stillbirth and Neonatal Death* (Oxford: Berg), pp. 197–214

Joffe, C. (2009) 'Abortion and Medicine: A Sociopolitical History', in M. Paul, E.S. Lichtenberg, L. Borgatta, D.A. Grimes, P.G. Stubblefield and M.D. Creinin (eds.) *Management of Unintended and Abnormal Pregnancy* (First edition) (Oxford: John Wiley & Sons), pp. 1–9

Johansson, S.R. (1984) 'Deferred Infanticide: Excess Female Mortality during Childhood', in G. Hausfater and S.B. Hardy (eds.) *Infanticide: Comparative and Evolutionary Perspectives* (New York: Aldine), pp. 463–86

Johnson Kramar, K. (2006) 'Unwilling Mothers and Unwanted Babies: The Vicissitudes of Infanticide Law in Canada', in B.H. Bechtold and D. Cooper Graves (eds.) *Killing Infants: Studies in the Worldwide Practice of Infanticide* (New York: Edwin Mellen), pp. 138–66

Jordanova, L.J. (1985) 'Gender, Generation and Science: William Hunter's Obstetrical Atlas', in W.F. Bynum and R. Porter (eds.) *William Hunter and the Eighteenth-Century Medical World* (Cambridge: Cambridge University Press), pp. 385–412

Kilday, A.-M. (2002) 'Maternal Monsters: Murdering Mothers in South-West Scotland, 1750–1815', in Y.G. Brown and R. Ferguson (eds.) *Twisted Sisters: Women, Crime and Deviance in Scotland since 1400* (East Linton: Tuckwell), pp. 156–79

Kilday, A.-M. (2005) 'Women and Crime', in H. Barker and E. Chalus (eds.) *Women's History: Britain 1750–1800 – An Introduction* (Abingdon: Routledge), pp. 174–93

Kilday, A.-M. (2010) 'Desperate Measures or Cruel Intentions: Infanticide in Britain Since 1600', in A.-M. Kilday and D.S. Nash (eds.) *Crimes in Context: Britain 1600–2000* (Basingstoke: Palgrave Macmillan), pp. 60–79

Kok, J., F. Van Poppel and E. Kruse (1997) 'Mortality among Illegitimate Children in Mid-Nineteenth Century The Hague', in C.A. Corsini and P.P. Viazzo (eds.) *The Decline of Infant and Child Mortality: The European Experience – 1750–1990* (The Hague: Kluwer Law International), pp. 193–212

Kowalsky, S.A. (2006) 'Making Sense of the Murdering Mother: Soviet Criminologists and Infanticide in Revolutionary Russia', in B.H. Bechtold and D. Cooper Graves (eds.) *Killing Infants: Studies in the Worldwide Practice of Infanticide* (Lewiston, NY: Edwin Mellen), pp. 167–94

Laqueur, T.W. (1989) 'Bodies, Details and the Humanitarian Narrative', in L. Hunt (ed.) *The New Cultural History* (Berkeley: University of California Press), pp. 176–204

Laslett, P. (1980) 'Introduction: Comparing Illegitimacy Over Time and Between Cultures', in P. Laslett, K. Oosterveen and R.M. Smith (eds.) *Bastardy and its Comparative History: Studies in the History of Illegitimacy and Marital Nonconformism in Britain, France, Germany, Sweden, North America, Jamaica and Japan* (London: Edward Arnold), pp. 1–65

Lawson, P. (1998) 'Patriarchy, Crime and the Courts: The Criminality of Women in Late Tudor and Early Stuart England', in G.T. Smith, A.N. May and S. Devereaux (eds.) *Criminal Justice in the Old World and the New: Essays in Honour of J.M. Beattie* (Toronto: University of Toronto Press), pp. 16–57

Lee, J., C. Campbell and G. Tan (1992) 'Infanticide and Family Planning in Late Imperial China: The Price and Population History of Rural Liaoning, 1774–1873', in T.G. Rawski and L.M. Li (eds.) *Chinese History in Economic Perspective* (Berkeley: University of California Press), pp. 145–76

Levene, A., T. Nutt and S. Williams (2005) 'Introduction', in A. Levene, T. Nutt and S. Williams (eds.) *Illegitimacy in Britain, 1700–1920* (Basingstoke: Macmillan), pp. 1–17

Levine, D. and K. Wrightson (1980) 'The Social Context of Illegitimacy in Early Modern England', in P. Laslett, K. Oosterveen and R.M. Smith (eds.) *Bastardy and its Comparative History: Studies in the History of Illegitimacy and Marital Nonconformism in Britain, France, Germany, Sweden, North America, Jamaica and Japan* (London: Edward Arnold), pp. 158–75

Macfarlane, A. (1980) 'Illegitimacy and Illegitimates in English Society', in P. Laslett, K. Oosterveen and R.M. Smith (eds.) *Bastardy and its Comparative History: Studies in the History of Illegitimacy and Marital Nonconformism in Britain, France, Germany, Sweden, North America, Jamaica and Japan* (London: Edward Arnold), pp. 71–85

Macfarlane, J. (2003) 'Criminal Defense in Cases of Infanticide and Neonaticide', in M.G. Spinelli (ed.) *Infanticide: Psychological and Legal Perspectives on Mothers Who Kill* (Washington, DC and London: American Psychiatric), pp. 133–65

Malcolmson, R.W. (1977) 'Infanticide in the Eighteenth Century', in J.S. Cockburn (ed.) *Crime in England 1550–1800* (London: Methuen), pp. 187–209

Marland, H. (1993) 'Introduction', in H. Marland (ed.) *The Art of Midwifery: Early Modern Midwives in Europe* (London: Routledge), pp. 1–8

Marland, H. (1999) 'At Home with Puerperal Mania: The Domestic Treatment of the Insanity of Childbirth in the Nineteenth Century', in P. Bartlett and D. Wright (eds.) *Outside the Walls of the Asylum: The History of Care in the Community 1750–2000* (London and New Brunswick, NJ: Athlone), pp. 45–65

Marland, H. (2002) 'Getting Away With Murder? Puerperal Insanity, Infanticide and the Defence Plea', in M. Jackson (ed.) *Infanticide: Historical Perspectives on Child Murder and Concealment, 1550–2000* (Aldershot: Ashgate), pp. 168–92

May, A.N. (1995) '"She at First Denied It": Infanticide Trials at the Old Bailey', in V. Frith (ed.) *Women and History: Voices of Early Modern England* (Toronto: Coach House), pp. 19–49

McLaren, A. (1994) '"Not a Stranger: A Doctor": Medical Men and Sexual Matters in the Late Nineteenth Century', in R. Porter and M. Teich (eds.) *Sexual Knowledge, Sexual Science: The History of Attitudes to Sexuality* (Cambridge: Cambridge University Press), pp. 267–83

McShane Galley, J. (2006) 'For Shame: Accusations of Infanticide and Coroner's Inquests into the Deaths of Legitimate Infants in Victorian Ontario', in B.H. Bechtold and D. Cooper Graves (eds.) *Killing Infants: Studies in the Worldwide Practice of Infanticide* (New York: Edwin Mellen), pp. 280–309

Meldrum, T. (1997) 'London Domestic Servants from Depositional Evidence, 1660–1750: Servant-Employer Sexuality in the Patriarchal Household', in T. Hitchcock, P. King and P. Sharpe (eds.) *Chronicling Poverty: The Voices and Strategies of the English Poor, 1640–1840* (Basingstoke: Palgrave Macmillan), pp. 47–69

Michaltk, K. (2006) 'The Development of the Discourse on Infanticide in the Late Eighteenth Century and the New Legal Standardization of the Offense in the Nineteenth Century', in U. Gleixner and M.W. Gray (eds.) *Gender in Transition: Discourse and Practice in German-Speaking Europe, 1750–1830* (Ann Arbor: University of Michigan Press), pp. 51–71

Miller, L.J. (2003) 'Denial of Pregnancy', in M.G. Spinelli (ed.) *Infanticide: Psychological and Legal Perspectives on Mothers Who Kill* (Washington, DC and London: American Psychiatric), pp. 81–104

Morel, M.-F. (1991) 'The Care of Children: The Influence of Medical Innovation and Medical Institutions on Infant Mortality 1750–1914', in R. Schofield, D. Reher and A. Bideau (eds.) *The Decline of Mortality in Europe* (Oxford: Clarendon), pp. 196–219.

Newall, F. (1990) 'Wet Nursing and Child Care in Aldenham, Hertfordshire, 1595–1726: Some Evidence on the Circumstances and Effects of Seventeenth-Century Child Rearing Practices', in V. Fildes (ed.) *Women as Mothers in Pre-Industrial England: Essays in Memory of Dorothy McLaren* (London and New York: Routledge), pp. 122–38

Nutt, T. (2005) 'The Paradox and Problems of Illegitimate Paternity in Old Poor Law Essex', in A. Levene, T. Nutt and S. Williams (eds.) *Illegitimacy in Britain, 1700–1920* (Basingstoke: Palgrave Macmillan), pp. 102–21

Oberman, M. (2003) 'A Brief History of Infanticide and the Law', in M.G. Spinelli (ed.) *Infanticide: Psychological and Legal Perspectives on Mothers Who Kill* (Washington, DC and London: American Psychiatric), pp. 3–18

O'Connor, A. (1991) 'Women in Irish Folklore: The Testimony Regarding Illegitimacy, Abortion and Infanticide', in M. MacCurtain and M. O'Dowd (eds.) *Women in Early Modern Ireland* (Edinburgh: Edinburgh University Press), pp. 304–17

Ogier, D. (2005) 'New-Born Child Murder in Reformation Guernsey', in G. Dawes (ed.) *Commise 1204: Studies in the History and Law of Continental and Insular Normandy* (St Peter Port, Guernsey: The Guernsey Bar), pp. 133–51

326 *Bibliography*

Pollock, L. (1990) 'Embarking on a Rough Passage: The Experience of Pregnancy in Early-Modern Society', in V. Fildes (ed.) *Women as Mothers in Pre-Industrial England: Essays in Memory of Dorothy McLaren* (London and New York: Routledge), pp. 39–67

Pomeroy, S.B. (1983) 'Infanticide in Hellenistic Greece', in A. Cameron and A. Kuhrt (eds.) *Images of Women in Antiquity* (London: Croom Helm), pp. 207–19

Purkiss, D. (2003) 'Losing Babies, Losing Stories: Attending to Women's Confessions in Scottish Witch-Trials', in M. Mikesell and A. Seeff (eds.) *Culture and Change: Attending to Early Modern Woman* (Newark: University of Delaware Press), pp. 143–58

Quinn, C. (2002) 'Images and Impulses: Representations of Puerperal Insanity and Infanticide in Late Victorian England', in M. Jackson (ed.) *Infanticide: Historical Perspectives on Child Murder and Concealment, 1550–2000* (Aldershot: Ashgate), pp. 193–215

Rabin, D. (2002) 'Bodies of Evidence, States of Mind: Infanticide, Emotion and Sensibility in Eighteenth-Century England', in M. Jackson (ed.) *Infanticide: Historical Perspectives on Child Murder and Concealment, 1550–2000* (Aldershot: Ashgate), pp. 73–92

Radbill, S.X. (1968) 'A History of Child Abuse and Infanticide', in R.E. Helfer and C.H. Kempe (eds.) *The Battered Child* (Chicago: University of Chicago Press), pp. 3–17

Ruggiero, K. (2000) 'Not Guilty: Abortion and Infanticide in Nineteenth-Century Argentina', in C. Agiurre and R. Buffington (eds.) *Reconstructing Criminality in Latin America* (Wilmington, DE: Jaguar), pp. 149–66

Ryan, L. (2004) 'The Press, Police and Prosecution: Perspectives on Infanticide in the 1920s', in A. Hayes and D. Urquhart (eds.) *Irish Women's History* (Dublin and Portland, OR: Irish Academic)

Schulte, R. (1984) 'Infanticide in Rural Bavaria in the Nineteenth Century', in H. Medick and D.W. Sabean (eds.) *Interest and Emotion: Essays on the Study of Family and Kinship* (Cambridge: Cambridge University Press), pp. 77–102

Scrimshaw, S.C.M. (1984) 'Infanticide in Human Populations: Societal and Individual Concerns', in G. Hausfater and S.B. Hardy (eds.) *Infanticide: Comparative and Evolutionary Perspectives* (New York: Aldine), pp. 439–62

Shorter, E. (1985) 'The Management of Normal Deliveries and the Generation of William Hunter', in W.F. Bynum and R. Porter (eds.) *William Hunter and the Eighteenth-Century Medical World* (Cambridge: Cambridge University Press), pp. 372–83

Sichel, D. (2003) 'Neurohormonal Aspects of Postpartum Depression and Psychosis', in M.G. Spinelli (ed.) *Infanticide: Psychological and Legal Perspectives on Mothers Who Kill* (Washington, DC and London: American Psychiatric), pp. 61–79

Smith, M.D. (1999) '"Unnatural Mothers": Infanticide, Motherhood and Class in the Mid-Atlantic, 1730–1830', in C. Daniels and M.V. Kennedy (eds.) *Over the Threshold: Intimate Violence in Early America* (New York: Routledge), pp. 173–84

Smout, T.C. (1976) 'Aspects of Sexual Behaviour in Nineteenth-Century Scotland', in A.A. MacLaren (ed.) *Social Class in Scotland: Past and Present* (Edinburgh: John Donald), pp. 55–85

Sommers, S. (2009) 'Remapping Maternity in the Courtroom: Female Defenses and Medical Witnesses in Eighteenth-Century Infanticide Proceedings', in E. Klaver (ed.) *The Body in Medical Culture* (Albany: State University of New York Press), pp. 37–59

Spinelli, M.G. (2003) 'The Promise of Saved Lives: Recognition, Prevention and Rehabilitation', in M.G. Spinelli (ed.) *Infanticide: Psychological and Legal Perspectives on Mothers Who Kill* (Washington, DC and London: American Psychiatric), pp. 235–55

Swain, S. (2006) 'Infanticide, Savagery and Civilization: The Australian Experience', in B.H. Bechtold and D. Cooper Graves (eds.) *Killing Infants: Studies in the Worldwide Practice of Infanticide* (New York: Edwin Mellen), pp. 86–105

Tausiet, M. (2001) 'Witchcraft as Metaphor: Infanticide and its Translations in Aragón in the Sixteenth and Seventeenth Centuries', in S. Clark (ed.) *Languages of Witchcraft: Narrative, Ideology and Meaning in Early Modern Culture* (Basingstoke: Macmillan), pp. 179–96

Ulbricht, O. (1988) 'Infanticide in Eighteenth-Century Germany', in R.J. Evans (ed.) *The German Underworld: Deviants and Outcasts in German History* (London: Routledge), pp. 108–40

Vallin, J. (1991) 'Mortality in Europe from 1720 to 1914: Long-Term Trends and Changes in Patterns by Age and Sex', in R. Schofield, D. Reher and A. Bideau (eds.) *The Decline of Mortality in Europe* (Oxford: Clarendon), pp. 38–67

Van der Spey, P. (2002) 'Infanticide, Slavery and the Politics of Reproduction at Cape Colony, South Africa, in the 1820s', in M. Jackson (ed.) *Infanticide: Historical Perspectives on Child Murder and Concealment, 1550–2000* (Aldershot: Ashgate), pp. 128–48

Versluysen, M.C. (1981) 'Midwives, Medical Men and "Poor Women Labouring of Child": Lying-in Hospitals in Eighteenth-Century London', in H. Roberts (ed.) *Women, Health and Reproduction* (London: Routledge and Kegan Paul), pp. 18–49

Viazzo, P.P., M. Bortolotto and A. Zanotto (1997) 'A Special Case of Decline: Levels and Trends of Infant Mortality at Florence's Foundling Hospital 1750–1950', in C.A. Corsini and P.P. Viazzo (eds.) *The Decline of Infant and Child Mortality: The European Experience – 1750–1990* (The Hague: Kluwer Law International), pp. 227–46

Walker, G. (2003) 'Just Stories: Telling Tales of Infant Death in Early Modern England', in M. Mikesell and A. Seeff (eds.) *Culture and Change: Attending to Early Modern Woman* (Newark: University of Delaware Press), pp. 98–115

Ward, T. (2002) 'Legislating for Human Nature: Legal Responses to Infanticide, 1860–1938', in M. Jackson (ed.) *Infanticide: Historical Perspectives on Child Murder and Concealment, 1550–2000* (Aldershot: Ashgate), pp. 249–69

Wessling, M.N. (1994) 'Infanticide Trials and Forensic Medicine: Württembergs 1757–93', in M. Clark and C. Crawford (eds.) *Legal Medicine in History* (Cambridge: Cambridge University Press), pp. 117–44

Wheelwright, J. (2002) '"Nothing in Between": Modern Cases of Infanticide', in M. Jackson (ed.) *Infanticide: Historical Perspectives on Child Murder and Concealment, 1550–2000* (Aldershot: Ashgate), pp. 270–85

Williamson, L. (1978) 'Infanticide: An Anthropological Analysis', in M. Kohl (ed.) *Infanticide and the Value of Life* (New York: Prometheus), pp. 61–75

Wilson, A. (1985) 'Participant or Patient? Seventeenth-Century Childbirth from the Mother's Point of View', in R. Porter (ed.) *Patients and Practitioners: Lay Perceptions of Medicine in Pre-Industrial Society* (Cambridge: Cambridge University Press), pp. 129–44

Wilson, A. (1985) 'William Hunter and the Varieties of Man-Midwifery', in W.F. Bynum and R. Porter (eds.) *William Hunter and the Eighteenth-Century Medical World* (Cambridge: Cambridge University Press), pp. 344–69

Wisner, K.L. et al. (2003) 'Postpartum Disorders', in M.G. Spinelli (ed.) *Infanticide: Psychological and Legal Perspectives on Mothers Who Kill* (Washington, DC and London: American Psychiatric), pp. 35–60

Woods, R., N. Williams and C. Galley (1997) 'Differential Mortality Patterns among Infants and Other Young Children: The Experience of England and Wales in the Nineteenth Century', in C.A. Corsini and P.P. Viazzo (eds.) *The Decline of Infant and Child Mortality: The European Experience – 1750–1990* (The Hague: Kluwer Law International), pp. 57–72

Wrightson, K. (1980) 'The Nadir of English Illegitimacy in the Seventeenth Century', in P. Laslett, K. Oosterveen and R.M. Smith (eds.) *Bastardy and its Comparative History: Studies in the History of Illegitimacy and Marital Nonconformism in Britain, France, Germany, Sweden, North America, Jamaica and Japan* (London: Edward Arnold), pp. 176–91

Unpublished theses and dissertations

Day, S. (1985) 'Puerperal Insanity: The Historical Sociology of a Disease', (Unpublished D.Phil Thesis, University of Cambridge)

Galley, J. (2007) 'Infanticide in the American Imagination, 1860–1920' (Unpublished PhD Thesis, Temple University)

Jones, E.L. (2007) 'Abortion in England, 1861–1967' (Unpublished PhD Thesis, Royal Holloway, University of London)

Jones, M. (1999) '"Too Common and Most Unnatural": Rewriting the Infanticidal Woman in Britain, 1764–1859' (Unpublished PhD Thesis, University of York)

Kilday, A.-M. (1998) 'Women and Crime in South-West Scotland: A Study of the Justiciary Records, 1750–1815' (Unpublished PhD Thesis, University of Strathclyde)

McShane Galley, J. (1998) '"I Did it to Hide My Shame": Community Responses to Suspicious Infant Deaths in Middlesex County, Ontario, 1850–1900' (Unpublished Master of Arts Dissertation, University of Western Ontario)

Monholland, C.S. (1989) 'Infanticide in Victorian England, 1856–1878: Thirty Legal Cases' (Unpublished Master of Arts Dissertation, Rice University)

Sommers, S. (2002) 'Bodies, Knowledge and Authority in Eighteenth-Century Infanticide Prosecutions' (Unpublished Master of Arts Dissertation, University of Victoria)

Key websites

National Library of Wales, Crime and Punishment Database, 1730–1830: http://www.llgc.org.uk/sesiwn_fawr/index_s.htm

Parliamentary Papers Online: http://parlipapers.chadwyck.co.uk/marketing/index.jsp

The Proceedings of the Old Bailey Online, 1674–1913: http://www.oldbailey online.org/

Legal Research Library for England and Wales: http://www.lexisnexis.com

Index

abandonment of infants, 12, 14, 77, 84–90, 109, 118, 141, 151, 200, 216, 250–1, 272
and married women, 90
and single women, 90
gender of victims, 88
trends in, 85
abdication crisis (1936), 188
abortifacients, 82–3
abortion, 3, 12, 14, 64, 66, 77–84, 90, 108–9, 118, 137, 140, 143, 151, 157, 165, 199, 216, 246–8, 293
Abrams, Lynn, 53
accidental incidents of infanticide, 164, 185, 195
accomplices, 65–75, 243
acquittals, 25, 71, 125, 152, 171
pardons (or remissions) associated with, 25, 71, 125,
Adamson, Adam, 67–8
adoption, 176
Adoption Act (1926), 200
afterbirth, 57, 62
alcohol, and involvement in instances of infanticide, 167
Alder, Christine, 200
Alison, Archibald (Sir), 169
altruism as motive for infanticide, 144, 164, 203, 280
Alven, Mr, 139
American War of Independence, 113
An Act Anent the Destroying and Murthering of Bastard Children (1624), 16, 24, 26, 41, 153
criticisms and attempted repeal of, 113–8
Act Anent Murdering of Children (1690), 18, 41
criticisms and attempted repeal of, 113–18
ancient civilisations, 2–5, 84; Ancient Egypt, 3; Sparta, 3
Angus, Mary, 45
Annesley, Christine, 207

'anti-motherhood', 19, 120
Aristotle, 3
Armor, Ann, 99
arson, 4
Arthur, Elizabeth, 155
Ashtol, Mary, 54
Asquith, Herbert (Home Secretary), 178
assault, 10

baby-farming, 12, 14, 77, 93, 94–6, 109, 120, 137, 140, 147, 150–1, 185, 200, 256
and media sensationalism, 95
banishment, 46–9
Barclay, John (Dr), 135
Barrett, Miss, 143
bastardy, 16, 21, 25, 31, 34, 37, 50, 68–9, 125, 154–5, 159, 166
Bastardy Act (1610), 37
Beale, Caroline, 194
Beare, Eleanor, 81
Beattie, John, 30, 43
Beccaria, Cesare, 159
Belgium, 28, 38
Bible, 4
Black, Jean, 99
blasphemy, 4
Beck, John, 141–2, 146
Bloudy Mother, 67–8
Boag, Janet, 168
Boer War, 184
Bowman, Magdalen, 158
Bradford, Hannah, 56
breastfeeding, 90–1
Bristow, Mary, 43
British Medical Journal, 81, 95, 119, 135, 139, 204
Brockington, Ian, 205
Brookman, Fiona, 185, 207
Brown, Anna, 54
Buckham, Isabella, 62
Bunbury, Charles (Sir), 113
burial clubs, 140, 163–4
Burke, Edmund, 19

Burke Ryan, William, 119–20, 133, 147, 171–2
Butler, Edith, 203
Butler Report on Mentally Abnormal Defenders (1975), 190–1

Canada, 26, 37, 41, 47, 50, 193–4
Canning, Angela, 212
Cassidy, Tina, 60
causal factors for infanticide, 7, 14, 100, 150–82, 184, 203–7, 215
cause of death in newborns, 14, 44, 78, 104, 135–6, 185, 202, 215
Champion, Mary, 20
child abuse, 5, 185, 202, 211
childbirth (or parturition), 7, 51–2, 58–64, 134, 140–1, 145, 161, 167, 169, 180–1, 185, 187, 190, 202, 205, 237
and increasing safety of, 59–60
and labour, 52, 62, 76
and unexpected delivery, 62, 107, 204
carried out in secret, 23–4, 118, 137, 164
complications associated with, 60, 62–3, 68, 106–7, 141, 217
concealment of, 61, 64, 169, 180, 196–8
fatalities related to, 23, 27, 44, 76–7, 106–7, 141
'green woman', symptoms of recent delivery, 74
lactation test, 74
mental illness associated with: see mental illness
registration of, 95, 123, 147, 150
self-delivery, 44, 64, 73, 76, 145, 164, 180, 204
childcare, 94, 110, 147–8, 150, 184–5, 206, 214
Children's Act (1908), 186
China, 3
Christianity, 2
Church, 32, 33, 37, 59, 73–4, 84, 156
in Scotland, 36, 45–6, 53, 73, 156–7
and investigative role in infanticide cases, 156–7, 245
Church, Sarah, 42
clandestine marriage, 34
Clandestine Marriage Act (1754), 34
Clark, Sally, 210–14, 217
Concealment of Birth (Scotland) Act (1809), 116–17

concealment of pregnancy, 7, 18–19, 21, 23, 27, 45, 51, 53–4, 58, 64, 66, 73, 76, 101, 105, 115–17, 122–5, 129, 133–4, 136–7, 143, 147, 149, 161, 165, 172, 187, 194, 196–8, 201–2, 204–5, 207–10, 214–16
conception, symptoms and signs of, 55–8, 165
confessions, 23, 73–4, 152
contraception, 65, 78, 140, 198–200, 206, 215–16, 292–3
convictions for infanticide, trends in, 28–31, 41–9, 66, 71, 75, 115–25, 129, 149, 152, 167, 187, 197–203, 207–14, 264–5, 268
Cooper Graves, Donna, 165
Coram, Thomas, 87–8
Cornforth, Jane, 99
Cornwall, Eliza, 68
coroners, 6, 102, 121, 124, 141, 173
corporal punishment, 49, 72
cot death, 211–12
Coupar, Elizabeth, 162
Court of Appeal, 213
Courts of the Great Sessions (Wales), 63, 66, 68, 101, 125–31, 158, 167, 228–9
Cowan, Jean, 44
Cowley, Rebecca, 42
Crawford, Patricia, 58
Criminal Attempts Act (1981), 191
Criminal Law Revision Committee (1980), 191
cruelty against children, 136
Curgenven, J. Brendon, 119
Curtis, Elizabeth, 44

Dalgleish, Marion, 99
Daly, Martin, 160–1
Dancer, Lucy, 145
'dark figure', 13, 27, 42, 85, 123–4, 185, 195, 229, 297
Darwin, Erasmus, 153
David, Wenllian, 63
defences offered, 135, 137, 152, 166, 176, 242
definitions of infanticide, 6, 15–22, 183, 188–9, 191–2, 200, 203, 215
Defoe, Daniel, 25, 27, 31
deviance, 9, 19, 76, 181

Dewing, George, 69–72, 76
Dickenson, Sarah, 42
diminished responsibility, 189–90, 193
discipline, 7
disposal of infant body, 63–4, 66–7, 72, 117, 124, 141
Doe, Mary, 43
domestic servants, 38–40
    and infanticide, 7, 12–3, 23, 25, 37–40, 50, 54, 61, 127, 138–41, 149, 160, 165, 201, 214, 271
    sexual harassment of, 40
domestic abuse, 207
domesticity, 172, 210
Drake, Lucy, 98
Dubrovnik (Republic of), 72
Dyer, Amelia, 95

ecclesiastical courts, 32
Edinburgh, 56, 61, 96, 99, 100–1
Edwards, Susan, 193
Eigen, Joel, 168
Ellis, Sarah, 95
Emerson, Joseph, 68
English places
    Birmingham, 192, 207
    Cambridge, 195
    Cheshire, 206, 210–14
    Dorset, 138
    Essex, 30, 69
    Hartlepool, 143
    Hertfordshire, 105, 188
    Leicester, 187
    Lincoln, 146
    London, 23, 28–9, 38, 41, 44, 47, 56, 87–90, 93, 142–3, 150, 159, 161, 163, 173–5, 177, 188, 203
    Manchester, 203
    Middlesex, 156
    Midlands, 124
    North Yorkshire, 136, 144
    Nottingham, 134
    Plymouth, 204
    Scunthorpe, 218
    Somerset, 139, 204
    South Yorkshire, 143
    Suffolk, 144
    Surrey, 30
    Worcestershire, 137, 145
English Assize Courts, 30, 31, 195, 204

Ermers, Jolie, 123
eugenics, 184
Europe, 7, 16, 25–6, 28–9, 35, 37, 41, 47, 50, 53, 55, 59, 63, 65–6, 68, 74–6, 78, 84–7, 89, 91, 92, 97, 139, 140, 156, 159, 160, 163
Evan, Jane, 161
Evans, Margaret, 99
Evans, Sharon, 204
evidential difficulties and infanticide, 14, 25, 40–9, 75, 113–14, 118, 123–4, 135–6, 141–2, 185–6, 195, 202, 210–15, 229, 281–2; determining maturity, 75, 107; determining viability, 107
execution, 4, 24, 47–9, 71, 101, 113, 126, 136, 171, 178, 187–8, 207
Exodus, Book of, 4
exposure of infants, 3, 12, 14, 77, 84–90, 118, 141, 272
    and married women, 90
    and single women, 90
    gender of victims, 88

Faber, Sjoerd, 28, 72
family limitation, 14
family planning (or fertility control), 79, 80, 163, 180, 198–200, 215–16
Featherstone, Doreen, 203
female criminality, 3, 6, 8–11, 19, 164–6, 181, 210
    with violence, 10–11, 98–9, 164–5
female perpetrators, 6, 25–7, 50, 135, 137, 180, 201–2, 210, 214–15
Fildes, Valerie, 91
filicide, 183
Fletcher, Elizabeth, 45
flogging, 4
forensic medicine, 6
Foster, Ann, 44
foundling hospitals, 86–9, 91, 109, 148, 251–2
Fox, Charles James, 19–20
France, 31, 38, 87
    Paris, 28
    Rouen, 89
    Toulouse, 28
Francus, Marilyn, 96
Frayling, F.G., 186, 207
Freedman, Adelaide, 174–5

Gates, Grace, 66
Gauls, 2
Gèlis, Jacques, 56
gendered criminality, 3–4, 7, 24, 26–7,
    50, 69–72, 135, 138, 157, 180,
    201–2, 210, 215, 294
General Medical Council, 210–13
Gentleman's Magazine, 81, 106
Germany, 28, 31, 38
Gooch, Robert, 170
Gordon, Linda, 79
Gore, Lisa, 192–3
Gouge, William, 85
Gowing, Laura, 30, 52, 55, 59, 63,
    72–3, 96
Greece, 2
Grounds, Adrian, 193

Hadley, Elinor, 126
Hale, Brenda, 188
Hardinge, George (Judge), 127
Harrington, Joel, 160
Harveian Society, 136, 146
Harvey, William, 60
Hattersley, Jane, 67
Haywood, Ann, 105
Heatly, Jannet, 57
heresy, 4
Herod, King, 4, 111
Higginbotham, Ann, 72, 102
historiography, 5–7, 164–5, 223–4
Hodges, Elizabeth, 173
Hodgson, Christopher, 154
Hoffer, Peter, 19, 27, 181
Holt, William, 44
Home Office, 213
homicide (or murder), 4, 10, 114, 115,
    133, 172, 186–7, 189–90, 193, 196,
    198, 202, 207, 210
Homicide Act (1957), 189–90
    and diminished responsibility, 189–90,
    193
Hopkins, Sarah, 107
hospitals (including asylums), 62, 171,
    174–5, 192–4, 202, 206, 208
    and facilities for lying in, 60, 95, 105,
    202
    and maternal care, 51, 90, 148, 150,
    179, 184–5, 202, 206, 214, 287,
    298

    and neonatal care, 51, 60, 150, 179,
    184–5, 202–3, 206, 214, 287
    provision for foundlings, 86–9, 91,
    109, 251–2
House of Commons, 186
House of Lords, 12, 113, 186
Howard, Florence Mabel, 195
Hull, Nathalie, 19, 27, 181
humanitarianism, 113–14, 149, 154, 181
Humphries, Jane, 126
Hunter, Sarah, 49
Hunter, William, 103, 153–4, 168
hydrostatic test, 44, 105–6

illegitimacy, 3, 5–7, 13, 16, 19, 21, 24,
    26, 29, 31–7, 50–1, 53, 61, 70, 85,
    89, 115, 117, 139, 143–4, 154–8,
    180, 200, 215, 231–4, 277
    and economic misfortune, 37, 53, 69,
    138, 155, 159, 165
    and shame, 35–6, 70, 76, 89, 140,
    153–60, 165, 178, 180, 200, 204,
    207
    rates of, 122
imprisonment, 12, 37, 47, 49, 69, 72,
    80–1, 85, 115–18, 122–3, 125, 131–2,
    144, 146, 148–9, 175, 177–8, 186–8,
    191–2, 194, 203, 205, 207–10, 212
incest, 4, 157
India, 3, 121, 127, 218
indictments (or prosecutions) for
    infanticide
    trends in, 28–31, 41–9, 75, 119–25,
    184, 194–203, 207, 215, 264–5, 280
Infant Life Protection Act (1872), 95, 148
Infanticide Act (1922), 118, 187–8, 215
    criticisms of, 188
Infanticide Act (1938), 118, 188–94, 208,
    215
    criticisms of, 189–94
Infant Life Protection Society, 136, 146
infant mortality, 92–6, 140, 258–9
    causes of, 102, 185
    rate of, 102, 123
insanity, 7
intent (wilful), 44, 145–6, 151, 153–4,
    164–6, 192–3, 202
investigation, 73–5, 123–4
Ireland, 7, 87, 116–17
    Dublin, 31, 87

isolation (or desperation), as motive for
   infanticide, 52, 64, 76, 140, 144–5,
   150, 153–60, 161, 164, 168, 204,
   214–5, 295
Italy, 87
   Milan, 86
   Rome, 2

Jackson, Mark, 6, 19, 21, 35–6, 54, 61,
   74, 104, 106, 113
Jarvis, Elizabeth, 108
Jenkins, Sarah, 68
Johnson, Christopher, 103
Johnstoun, Elizabeth, 43
Jones, Ann, 99, 167
Jones, Catherine, 141
Jones, Elizabeth, 141
Jones, Rees, 157
Judeo-Christian–Islamic tradition, 4
judicial attitudes, 7, 24–5, 45–50, 101,
   111–50, 166–79, 182–4, 207–16,
   268, 294; leniency, 114, 124, 126,
   129, 133, 135–6, 145, 149, 166–79,
   186, 207–10, 215
Justices of the Peace, 37

Kai-Whitewind, Chaha'Oh-Niyol, 192
Kamler, Marcin, 28, 39, 160
Kelly, James, 26
Kempe, Henry, 5
Kempt, Elizabeth, 43
Keown, John, 79, 80
King, Jessie, 95
Kings, Jane, 137
Kirk Session, 36, 156–7
Knight, Patricia, 79
Kumar, Ramesh, 202, 205, 207

Leavitt, Judith, 60
lactational insanity, 170, 173, 187–92,
   203, 215
Lancet, The, 119
Lankester, Edwin J. (Dr), 119, 139, 171
Law Commission, 191–2
Leboutte, René, 28, 55
legal context, 7, 13, 15–22, 24, 26, 41,
   46–9, 60–1, 80–1, 85, 101, 112–18,
   122–3, 125, 129, 131–7, 147,
   166–79, 182–94, 207–16, 288–91; in
   Scotland, 18, 41, 116–17, 193

legal professionals
   and infanticide, 5, 12, 42, 112–18,
      129, 131–7, 147, 154, 166–79, 182,
      185–6, 191–2, 207–14
   leniency, 114, 124, 126, 129, 133,
      135–6, 145, 149, 166–79, 186,
      207–10, 215
Leneman, Leah, 85
Levene, Alysa, 87, 93
Lewis, Mary, 44
live birth, determination of, 44, 78, 115,
   185, 195, 215
Lloyd, Catherine, 63
Lloyd, Mary, 157
Lockhart, Thomas, 113
Longley, Harriet, 161
Lonza, Nella, 63
Lyall, Jane, 103
Lyne, Jane, 54

Mabe, Ann, 105
Mackie, Anne, 63
Maddox, Elizabeth, 68
Malcomson, Robert, 30, 72, 86
*Malicious Shooting or Stabbing Act (or Lord
   Ellenborough's Act) (1803)*, 80–1,
   114–17, 129
   criticisms of, 116
man-midwives (or *accouchers*), 59, 169,
   185
Mandeville, Bernard, 40, 153–4
manslaughter in cases of infanticide,
   187, 189–90, 193–4
Marcé, Louis Victor, 170
Marks, Maureen, 202, 205, 207
Marland, Hilary, 170, 178
marriage, 33, 34
married women
   and infant abandonment, 90
   and infanticide 11, 14, 50, 52, 65,
      137, 146, 163, 172–4, 198, 203–6
   and motives for infanticide, 137, 163,
      199
maternity, 15
M'Carthy, Joanna, 106
McCandy, Marjory, 156
McDonagh, Josephine, 193
McDonald, Margaret, 68
McGuffock, Agnes, 45
McIntyre, Florence, 68

McLaren, Angus, 79, 82–4
McLaren, Margaret, 99
McLean, Margaret, 43
Meadow, Roy (Professor), 195, 211–13
Medea, 1, 218
media sensationalism, 95, 119–25, 211, 213–14
medical professionals, 94, 100, 185–6
　and abortion, 81–4
　and infanticide, 5–6, 12, 22, 74–5, 79, 101–8, 121, 124, 153–4, 169, 173–9, 181, 191–2, 195, 199, 203, 210–14, 259–60, 281–2
medicine, development of, 51, 78
Medico-Legal Society, 186
men:
　and accusations of infanticide, 24, 26–7
　as perpetrators of infanticide, 50, 69–72, 135, 138, 157, 180, 201–2, 210, 214–15, 294
menstruation, cessation as sign of pregnancy, 57
mental illness
　and childbirth (or parturition), 169, 173–9, 181, 187–92, 203–7, 210, 215–17; lactational insanity, 170, 173, 187–92, 203–7, 210, 215; puerperal insanity, 169–79, 181, 187–92, 203–7, 210, 215
　and infanticide, 6–7, 14, 21, 134–5, 137, 145–6, 150, 152–3, 160, 166–79, 181, 187–92, 203–7, 210, 215, 282–5, 295; evidence of diminished responsibility, 189, 193
Meredith, William (Sir), 113
Mesopotamia, 2
methods, 7, 12, 70, 77–110, 124–6, 138, 140–3, 145–6, 149–50, 155–7, 159, 161–3, 165–7, 173, 176, 181, 184, 188, 192, 194–5, 202–7, 214, 257–8; overlaying, 15, 141
midwives, 58–9, 60, 74, 169, 185
　and link to infanticide, 23, 68, 240
Miller, Martha, 42
Milnes, Mary (1842) [Nottingham], 134
Milnes, Mary (1842) [South Yorkshire], 143
Minna, Margaret, 45
miscarriage, 64, 78, 80, 107, 118, 242

Mitchell, Thomas, 138
Mitchison, Rosalind, 85
M'Naghten Rules, 171, 284
modern era, and infanticide, 14, 183–217
Monholland, Cathy, 140
morality, 7
moral panics, 31, 95, 111, 119–25, 136, 146, 149, 150, 185, 263
Morgan, Mary, 125–31, 137, 149, 216
Morrieson, Anne, 100
Morris, Mary, 129
motherhood, 54, 120, 184–6, 210, 213–14
motives for infanticide, 3, 5–7, 14, 52, 134–5, 143–6, 150–82, 199, 203–7, 214–15, 269, 280
　altruism, 144, 164, 280
　family limitation, 14
　isolation (or desperation), 52, 76, 140, 144–5, 150, 153–60, 161, 164, 168, 204, 214–15, 295
　mental illness, 14, 134–5, 137, 145–6, 150, 152–3, 160, 166–79, 181, 188, 203–7, 215–17, 295
　poverty, 3, 5, 14, 134, 138, 144, 150, 153, 159, 160–4, 178, 180–1, 188, 206, 214–15, 273
　pragmatism, 144, 146, 150, 153, 164–6, 180, 214
　shame, 3, 5, 14, 134, 144–5, 150, 152–60, 178, 180–1, 199, 204, 207, 214, 295
Munro, Christian, 165
Munro, Helen, 99

Nairn, Anna, 43
National Society (and Asylum) for the Prevention of Infanticide, 147–8
neonaticide, 123, 183, 200, 202, 204–5, 216
Netherlands, 31
　Amsterdam, 27, 38
Nolan, Jane, 185, 207
Nun, William, 66

Oberman, Michelle, 161
obstetrics, 170, 178
O'Donoghue, Mary, 188
O'Donovan, Katherine, 193
Offences against the Person Act (or Lord Lansdowne's Act) (1828), 81, 117–18

Offences against the Person Act (1837), 81
Offences against the Person Act (1861), 81, 85, 117–18, 140, 189
criticisms of, 136–7, 146–7
offenders (including suspected individuals):
Adamson, Adam, 67–8; Alven, Mr, 139; Angus, Mary, 45; Annesley, Christine, 207; Armor, Ann, 99; Arthur, Elizabeth, 155; Ashtol, Mary, 54; Barrett, Miss, 143; Beale, Caroline, 194; Black, Jean, 99; Boag, Janet, 168; Bowman, Magdalen, 158; Bradford, Hannah, 56; Bristow, Mary, 43; Brown, Anna, 54; Buckham, Isabella, 62; Butler, Edith, 203; Canning, Angela, 212; Champion, Mary, 20; Church, Sarah, 42; Clark, Sally, 210–14, 217; Cornforth, Jane, 99; Cornwall, Eliza, 68; Coupar, Elizabeth, 162; Cowan, Jean, 44; Cowley, Rebecca, 42; Curtis, Elizabeth, 44; Dalgleish, Marion, 99; Dancer, Lucy, 145; David, Wenllian, 63; Dewing, George, 69–72, 76; Dickenson, Sarah, 42; Doe, Mary, 43; Drake, Lucy, 98; Dyer, Amelia, 95; Ellis, Sarah, 95; Emerson, Joseph, 68; Evan, Jane, 161; Evans, Margaret, 99; Evans, Sharon, 204; Featherstone, Doreen, 203; Fletcher, Elizabeth, 45; Foster, Ann, 44; Freedman, Adelaide, 174–5; Gates, Grace, 66; Gore, Lisa, 192; Hadley, Elinor, 126; Hattersley, Jane, 67; Haywood, Ann, 105; Heatly, Jannet, 57; Hodges, Elizabeth, 173; Hopkins, Sarah, 107; Howard, Florence Mabel, 195; Humphries, Jane, 126; Hunter, Sarah, 49; Jarvis, Elizabeth, 108; Jenkins, Sarah, 68; Johnstoun, Elizabeth, 43; Jones, Ann, 99, 167; Jones, Catherine, 141; Jones, Elizabeth, 141; Jones, Rees, 157; Kai-Whitewind, Chaha' Oh-Niyol, 192; Kempt, Elizabeth, 43; King, Jessie, 95; Kings, Jane, 137; Leavitt, Judith, 60; Lewis,

Mary, 44; Lloyd, Catherine, 63; Lloyd, Mary, 157; Longley, Harriet, 161; Lyall, Jane, 103; Lyne, Jane, 54; Mabe, Ann, 105; Mackie, Anne, 63; Maddox, Elizabeth, 68; M'Carthy, Joanna, 106; McCandy, Marjory, 156; McDonald, Margaret, 68; McGuffock, Agnes, 45; McIntyre, Florence, 68; McLaren, Margaret, 99; McLean, Margaret, 43; Miller, Martha, 42; Milnes, Mary (1842) [Nottingham], 134; Milnes, Mary (1842) [South Yorkshire], 143; Minna, Margaret, 45; Mitchell, Thomas, 138; Morgan, Mary, 125–31, 137, 149, 216; Morrieson, Anne, 100; Morris, Mary, 129; Munro, Christian, 165; Munro, Helen, 99; Nairn, Anna, 43; Nun, William, 66; O'Donoghue, Mary, 188; Oliphant, Christian, 42; Parker, Diana, 42–3; Parkins, Elizabeth, 49; Patel, Trupti, 212; Peacock, Elizabeth, 157; Philp, Janet, 45; Price, Ann (1681), 23–5, 33, 37, 40, 41, 49; Price, Ann (1809), 101; Proctor, Eliza, 136; Reynolds, Sarah, 159; Richard, Gwenllian, 99; Riley, Emma, 163; Riley, Sandra, 206; Robert, Mary, 99; Roberts, Edith, 187; Roberts, Pleasant, 43; Russell, Christian, 63; Russell, Sarah, 44, 106; Sach, Amelia, 185; Samson, Mr, 138; Scrogham, Eleanor, 42; Shrewsbury, Mary, 99; Smith, Ann, 156; Smith, Sarah Ann, 143; Spires, Hannah, 42; Spraggs, Mary, 204–5; Stewart, Margaret, 61; Stewart, Maria, 144; Stirling, Isabell, 61; Stourie, Jean, 161; Strachan, Christian, 156; Tait, Isobel, 166; Taylor, Anne, 49; Terry, Ann, 159; Thomas, John, 66; Thompson, Diana, 68; Thompson, Sarah Ellen, 144; Thomson, James, 66; Todd, Sophie, 95; Tomlin, Elizabeth, 99; Toshiak, Katherine, 56; Troup, Barbara, 44; Vincent, Margaret, 20; Walker, Agnes, 156; Warner, Elizabeth, 43; Waters, Margaret, 95; Welch, Catherine, 144;

Wells, Minnie, 175–9; Whiggham, Margaret, 66; Williams, Ada Chard, 185; Wilson, Adam, 157; Wilson, Mary, 44; Windsor, Charlotte, 95; Woolfitt, Mrs, 146; Old Bailey, 23, 28, 30, 44, 49, 54, 63, 66, 68, 98, 103, 106, 108, 155, 159, 163, 173–5, 177, 188, 228–9
Old Poor Law, 161–2
Oliphant, Christian, 42
overlaying, 15, 272

pardons (or remissions), 25, 71, 125,
parental neglect of children, 136, 141, 180, 185
parental responsibility for children, 147, 179–80
Parker, Diana, 42–3
Parkins, Elizabeth, 49
parricide, 4, 66
Patel, Trupti, 212
paternity, 61
  maintenance associated with, 162
  registration of, 147, 150
  responsibility for, 150, 161–2, 179–80
patriarchy, 172
Payne, Andrew, 124, 206
Peacock, Elizabeth, 157
'Peoples of the Book', 4
petitions for banishment, 46
Philp, Janet, 45
Phoenicians, 2
Plato, 3
'plead the belly', 47
Pliny, 3
Poland, 28, 38
policing and infanticide, 147, 161
Polk, Ken, 200
Poor Law Amendment Act (or New Poor Law) (1834), 120–1, 144, 147, 162
popular attitudes, 25, 101, 111–50, 183–4, 207–16
population control, 6
Portugal, 87
post-mortem, 101, 126
post-traumatic stress disorder, 190
poverty, 65
  and association with illegitimacy, 37, 53, 69, 138, 155, 159, 160–5, 180

  as motive for infanticide, 3, 5, 14, 134, 138, 144, 150, 153, 155, 159, 160–4, 178, 180–1, 188, 206, 215, 273
pragmatism, as motive for infanticide, 144, 146, 150, 153, 164–6, 180, 214
pregnancy, 51–2, 54–8, 63, 76, 116, 140–1, 146, 167, 169
  and concealment of, 7, 18–19, 21, 23, 27, 45, 51, 53–4, 58, 64, 66, 72–3, 75–6, 101, 105, 115–17, 122–5, 129, 133–4, 136–7, 143, 147, 149, 161, 165, 180, 187, 194, 196–8, 201–2, 204–5, 207–10, 214–15
  and difficulties associated with, 64, 78, 80, 107, 242
  ascertaining, 55–8
  'quickening' associated with, 79
  unwanted, 77, 79, 84, 169, 200
pre-menstrual syndrome, 190
pre-modern period and infanticide, 53, 61, 64–5, 68–9, 73–5, 97, 151–82
Price, Ann (1681), 23–5, 33, 37, 40–1, 49
Price, Ann (1809), 101
Proctor, Eliza, 136
promise of marriage, 33
prostitution, 9, 91, 201
psychiatry (or alienism), 169–70, 178–9, 194, 208
puerperal insanity, 169–79, 181, 187–92, 204, 215
punishment
  of infanticide, 4–5, 7, 12, 21, 37, 46–9, 69, 72, 80–1, 85, 101, 113, 115–18, 122–3, 125–6, 129, 131–7, 144, 146, 148–9, 171, 177–8, 186–9, 191–2, 194, 203, 205, 207–15; post-mortem, 101, 126; strategies associated with, 113, 189

Rabin, Dana, 65, 167, 168
rape, 33, 157, 192
recidivism, in infanticide cases, 140, 158, 272
Reid, Robert (Lord Loreburn), 186
religion, 13
religious context, and attitudes to infanticide, 12, 147–8, 156

Resnick, Phillip, 183, 203, 207
Reynolds, Sarah, 159
Richard, Gwenllian, 99
Riker's Island Penitentiary, 195
Riley, Emma, 163
Riley, Sandra, 206
Robert, Mary, 99
Roberts, Edith, 187
Roberts, Pleasant, 43
Rose, Lionel, 163
Roth, Randolph, 142
Rowlands, Alison, 155
Royal College of Psychiatrists'
    Working Party on Infanticide
    (1978), 191
Ruggiero, Kristin, 103
rural locations, 53, 72–3, 140
Russell, Christian, 63
Russell, Sarah, 44, 106
Russia, 31, 87

Sach, Amelia, 185
Samson, Mr, 138
Sanger, Margaret, 198
Schulte, Regina, 155
scolding, 9
St Matthew, 4
Scottish places:
    Aberdeen, 162, 168
    Ayrshire, 32
    Berwickshire, 156
    Dumfries, 156
    Dundee, 124
    Edinburgh, 56, 96, 99, 101, 166
    Elgin and Forres, 155
    Fife, 32, 56
    Haddington, 166
    Highlands, 99
    Inverness, 156, 165
    Jedburgh, 161
    Kinross, 157
    Lothians, 32, 63, 74
    Lowlands of, 32
    Perth, 99
    Stirling, 157
Scottish Justiciary Courts, 30–1, 56, 61,
    100, 155–6, 162, 166, 228–9
Scrogham, Eleanor, 42
Seaborne Davies, David, 116, 186
Self-delivery, 44, 145, 164, 180, 204

Seneca, 3
sentencing of infanticide, 7, 24, 46–9,
    101, 115–18, 122–3, 125–6, 129,
    131–7, 190–1, 207–16
sexual immorality, 16, 24, 31–3, 35, 45,
    50, 69, 82, 89, 93, 114, 145, 150,
    154–7, 199
sexual revolution, 198
shame:
    as motive for infanticide, 3, 5, 19,
        71, 134, 144–5, 150, 153–60, 178,
        180–1, 207, 295
    of illegitimacy, 35–6, 76, 89, 140,
        153–60, 165, 180, 200
Sharpe, James, 30, 37
Shrewsbury, Mary, 99
Silesia (Hapsburg Empire), 105
single women, 5, 12, 24, 31, 50, 52–3,
    55, 61, 64, 69, 72–3, 76, 93, 115,
    117, 137, 144, 149, 153–62, 168,
    172, 180, 198, 230, 270
Smart, Carol, 98
Smith, Ann, 156
Smith, Francis, 79
Smith, Roger, 136
Smith, Sarah Ann, 143
'social evil', 120
sodomy, 4
soldiers, 156
Spain, 87
Spires, Hannah, 42
Spraggs, Mary, 204–5
Stephen, James Fitzjames, 171
Stewart, Margaret, 61
Stewart, Maria, 144
still-birth, 27, 44, 77, 106, 135, 147
Stirling, Isabell, 61
Stone, Lawrence, 79
Stopes, Marie, 198
Stourie, Jean, 161
Strachan, Christian, 156
substance (or drug) abuse, and episodes
    of infanticide, 201, 206
Sudden Infant Death Syndrome (SIDS),
    195, 211–12
suggested solutions, 112–13, 146–50,
    184, 216–17
superstition, 4
Sweden, 31
syphilis, 92

Tait, Isobel, 166
Taylor, Anne, 49
Terry, Ann, 159
theft with violence, 10
Thomas, John, 66
Thompson, Diana, 68
Thompson, Sarah Ellen, 144
Thomson, James, 66
Todd, Sophie, 95
Tomlin, Elizabeth, 99
torture, 4, 74
Toshiak, Katherine, 56
Troup, Barbara, 44

Ulbricht, Otto, 28, 160
United States of America, 21, 26–8,
    37–8, 41, 47, 50, 113, 142, 193–4,
    203, 216, 218
unmarried mothers:
  and abandonment by suitor, 155–6,
    166
  and access to contraception, 200, 206
  and association with infanticide, 5,
    12, 24, 31, 50, 52–3, 55, 61, 64, 69,
    72–3, 76, 93, 115, 117, 137, 144,
    149, 153–62, 168, 172–3, 180, 198,
    214, 230, 270
  and infant abandonment, 90
urban locations, 72–3, 140

vagrancy, 35
Viardel, Cosme, 56
victims, 3–4, 23, 72–4, 76, 104, 117–18,
    124, 141, 202
  gender of, 3–4, 23, 140, 202
  maturity of, 78, 107
  separate existence of, 106, 185, 187,
    195, 215
  twins, 175–7
  viability of, 107, 152
Victoria, Queen, 111, 125
Victorian era, and infanticide, 53, 65,
    111–82
Vikings, 2
Vincent, Margaret, 20
violence:
  by women, 10–11
  evidence of in infanticide cases, 44,
    78, 105, 107–8, 125–6, 141–3, 165–6,
    183, 202

Wakley, Thomas (MP for Finsbury), 120,
    171
Welsh places
  Breconshire, 99, 129, 158, 167
  Carmarthenshire, 99, 157
  Denbighshire, 161
  Montgomeryshire, 99
  Pembrokeshire, 63, 99, 141
  Radnorshire, 101, 125–31, 157
  Taff Valley, 124
Walker, Agnes, 156
Warner, Elizabeth, 43
Waters, Margaret, 95
Watson, Katherine, 65, 104
Waugh, Benjamin, 96
Webster, Richard (Lord Alverstone), 186–7
Welch, Catherine, 144
Wells, Minnie, 175–9
wet-nursing, 12, 14, 77, 90–4, 109, 120,
    137, 140, 147, 150–1, 200, 253–5
Wheeler, Kenneth, 124
Wheelwright, Julie, 207
Whiggham, Margaret, 66
Williams, Ada Chard, 185
Williams, Alan (Dr), 212–13
Willis, Rhoda (alias Leslie James), 185
Willughby, Percival, 60
Wilson, Adam, 157
Wilson, Adrian, 59, 62
Wilson, Margo, 161
Wilson, Mary, 44
Windsor, Charlotte, 95
witchcraft, 4, 9, 19, 181
women:
  and accusations of infanticide, 6, 25–7,
    50, 135, 137, 180, 201–2, 210, 214–15
  and investigative role in infanticide
    cases, 54–8, 75
  and occupational status, 7, 9, 12–13,
    23, 25, 37–40, 50, 54, 61, 91, 127,
    138–40, 141, 149, 160, 165, 201, 271
  legal subordination of, 189, 191
Woodward, Nick, 69, 79, 85
Woolfitt, Mrs, 146
World War One, 184, 187, 201
Wrightson, Keith, 21, 72, 89, 94, 151

Yorke, Philip, First Earl of Hardwicke, 34

Zedner, Lucia, 169

CPSIA information can be obtained
at www.ICGtesting.com
Printed in the USA
LVOW07*2050051017
551317LV00011B/237/P